A GLOSSARY OF INDIAN RELIGIOUS TERMS AND CONCEPTS

A Glossary of Indian Religious Terms and Concepts

Narendra Nath Bhattacharyya

MANOHAR
1999

First published 1990
Reprinted 1999

ISBN 81-85054-85-1

Published by
Ajay Kumar Jain for
Manohar Publishers & Distributors
2/6 Ansari Road, Daryaganj
New Delhi 110002

Typeset by
Spantech Publishers Pvt. Ltd.
5/58 Old Rajendra Nagar, Shankar Road
New Delhi 110060

Printed at
Print Perfect
A-23 Mayapuri, Phase II
New Delhi 110064

For

My Wife

Manjula

Contents

Preface

Prof. Suniti Kumar Chatterji told us that once while he was in France he was shown a machine which could translate English into French and French into English. Out of curiosity he wanted to have the French version of the English phrase 'out of sight, out of mind' which the machine did instantly. Then, caught by a naughty idea, he wanted to have once again the English rendering of what he had received in French. This time the machine yielded 'blind and insane'. This story might have been a joke intended to amuse us. But the joke is really instructive, for it shows how difficult it is to translate the inner significance of one language into another. A particular expression of one language, when translated literally, cannot yield the same in another language. The problem becomes more complicated when the religious terms and concepts of one language are required to be translated into another. Apart from the usual difficulties with which one is generally confronted—such as the deceptive character of etymological meaning, the symbolic significance of words, the cases of *arthaviparyaya* or reversal of meaning, the archaic nature of language, the time-gap between the period of the formation of the texts and that of the composition of their commentaries, the divergences of interpretations and so forth—there are others which may be called 'internal' and are required to be discussed in some detail (See Introduction).

The Western Indologists and their Indian counterparts undoubtedly rendered commendable service by editing, translating and interpreting the ancient religious texts as a result of which new horizons have been opened in the field of religious studies. But at the same time one should admit that, notwithstanding their sincere attempts, their vision was circumscribed by the outlook they inherited from their own culture and tradition. In most cases they interpreted the Indian religio-philosophical terms in close dependence on those of the West. But it will be wrong to say that they were indifferent to such problems. They did their best by applying all the existing methods to arrive at the original and the secondary meanings of the word. Still in many cases some kind of superficial rendering could not be avoided, and it is not possible even now. The impact of Western education has made everyone so accustomed to Western terms and concepts that it has now almost become impossible to stand squarely on pure Indian tradition. Even admitting that the Western scholars had their traditional cultural preoccupations which had influenced them while rendering Indian terminology in their own languages, one cannot overlook the ambivalence inherent in the Indian tradition itself.

In order to illustrate the situation we may refer to the term Yajña, which has always been vaguely translated as 'sacrifice,' meaning 'the slaughter of animals or the surrender of a possession to a god for the purpose of pleasing him'. Behind such a rendering must have worked the impact of the Biblical legend of Abraham's sacrifice of his own son to appease God—a legend with which the Western scholars were traditionally accustomed. Although this interpretation is fallacious, the same was also held by a good number of early Indian authorities. Śabara had to make an enormous intellectual exercise to convince his contemporaries that the Yajña had nothing to do with the propitiation of gods, since they had no ownership of worldly objects and were utterly incapable of bestowing them on the performer, and that Yajña was the means of yielding *puruṣārtha*—that which was achieved through human effort. This shows that the significance of Yajña was misunderstood even in remote antiquity. So there is no need of blaming modern scholars and their interpretations. Another problem was that the meaning of certain words underwent changes from time to time. For example, the word *darśana*, which originally meant 'perception,' was used by Haribhadra, Mādhava and others in the sense of 'philosophy'; despite the warning of modern interpreters like Dasgupta or Radhakrishnan that the Indian concept of *darśana* should not be confused with the Western concept of 'philosophy'. In this case the ancients did not oblige the moderns.

The compiler of the present Glossary does not have even the slightest pretension to solve the problems outlined above, but rather has depended solely on the meanings suggested by the lexicographers and the interpretations made by modern scholars, both Western and Indian. Still, as a life-long student of Indian religious history he feels that some of these problems could have been solved if the approach be not wholly one-sided and if the vast indigenous theological and dogmatic tradition, enriched and explained by teachers of various sects and creeds, be taken into account. The question of one-sidedness in approach requires a little clarification. Scholars who had taken up various aspects of Indian religion as the subject of their study were more interested in the dissection of the constituents and in finding out the processes through which they were assembled in various shapes in different historical periods than to understand the system in its totality. They displayed wonderful knowledge in literature, epigraphy, palaeography, numismatics, art, architecture, iconography and allied disciplines required for historical researches on religion, but they did not care to know religion in itself; to understand what a particular creed along with all its intricacies really meant to its followers; or to appreciate the logic which conditioned and justified even the most strange and unintelligible beliefs and practices associated with different systems.

The purpose of the present Glossary is purely utilitarian. It is meant not for the specialists, but for the beginners. Scholars of the past wrote for scholars only. The celebrated earlier authors on Indian religious systems, whose works have now acquired the status of classics, did not bother about the indiscriminate use of terms and concepts in original which they thought their cultivated readers were competent enough to understand. But now, when that 'golden age' is no more, when the 'classics' are going beyond the reach of ordinary readers and, at the same time, when owing to some sort of democratisation in the field of education persons are increasingly attracted to the study of Indian religious systems, some sort of a guide-book is necessary to convey to them an elementary idea of Indian religious terms and concepts. So far as the entries are concerned the author of the present volume has to be selective because it is not possible to incorporate everything within a given space. But a detailed index has been provided not only for cross-references but also for many other terms which could not be included within the main body of the Glossary as separate entries, and in all such cases their meanings have also been supplied. The introductory portion deals with the sources along with a brief history of lexical and terminological studies. A detailed bibliography has also been supplied.

The author's thanks are due to Sri Ramesh Jain of Manohar Publications who has tried his best to make it a very attractive production, to his daughter Parnasabari who has so laboriously prepared the index, to his pupil Rachel Fell McDermott who has helped in many ways during the final stage of its printing and to Mrs Jasjit Mansingh who has gone through every line of this work and suggested improvements. Despite the author's best endeavour the presence of some mistakes and blemishes in this volume could not be avoided for which he craves the indulgence of the readers.

Dept. of Ancient Indian History
and Culture, Calcutta University
51/2 Hazara Road
Calcutta-700019

NARENDRA NATH BHATTACHARYYA

Introduction

In the Indian tradition of literary criticism there is a controversy in regard to the proper approach to the interpretation of words and their meanings. This has been explained in detail in the *Sāhityadarpaṇa*, but the Mīmāṃsakas were the first to start the controversy. According to Kumārila and his followers, words have different senses of their own and when they combine in a sentence, they yield a further sense. This view is known as *abhihitānvayavāda* according to which every word has its individual power or potentiality through which it reveals its meaning quite independently. When individual words are correlated on the basis of their further requirement or desirability (*ākāṅkṣā*), capability (*yogyatā*) and vicinity or sequence (*āsatti*), they constitute the inner undifferentiated meaning of a sentence. In other words, in the case of a sentence when an undifferentiated and uniform meaning is perceived or felt, it is nothing but a coherent correlation of the separate meanings of the individual words constituting the sentence. On the other hand, the school of Prabhākara holds that no word is significant in isolation but that words become significant when joined together in a sentence. This view is known as *anvitābhidhānavāda*, according to which no word within the frame of a sentence can express its meaning independently. At first they are correlated with one another and through this correlation (*anvaya*) they receive or acquire their own meanings. So the question with which one is finally confronted is whether the words in a sentence are at first characterised (*abhihita*) and then correlated (*anvita*), or at first correlated and then characterised, whether each word has a sense or meaning independent of other words in a sentence or whether its individual meaning is a bi-product of its association with others.

The question even bothered the ancient commentators. Yāksa, for example, had stated that the inner meaning of a religious term, or even that of the name of a deity, depends on the context, but this context is something more than mere correlation of the apparent suggestivity of the words. The Mīmāṃsakas hold that no part of the Veda, not even a word, is *anarthaka* or meaningless. The Mīmāṃsā rules of interpretation fall into several categories. (i) Where there is a doubt about the exact meaning of a term or a concept of a passage, it may be determined by relying on the remaining parts of a passage. (ii) Śabara categorically says that as far as possible the words are to be understood in the sense in which they are understood in popular usage and not in a secondary or technical sense. One and the same word must not be used in two senses in the same sentence. (iii) The primary sense of a word is got by its own literal suggestivity (*abhidhā*) and the secondary by its figurative characteristics (*lakṣaṇā*) and implied indications (*vyañjanā*). These are three *vṛttis* or functions of a word. (iv) Where there is a single substance connected with several attributes, all the attributes should be taken to refer to the same one substance. (v) In regard to a *vākya* or sentence, there must be a number of words, uttered or put down together. The words must have an expectancy for each other. They must serve one purpose or convey together one meaning.

A monistic philosophical approach to the words was popularised by the grammarians. This particular approach might have been due to the Upaniṣadic concept of *śabda-brahman*, the concept of the Universal Self in the form of sound. According to this doctrine the real form of *vāc* (speech) lies far beyond the range of ordinary perception. Sound and its articulation are the outer expressions of pure consciousness (*caitanya* or *brahman*) equated with *ātman* or Individual Self, which assume the forms of words and their meanings. Sound (*śabda*) is the quality (*guṇa*) or space (*ākāśa*). It has four states (*bhāva*) called Parā,

Paśyantī, Madhyamā and Vaikharī. Parā is motionless casual sound conceived of as existing in the remote unconscious. Vaikharī is the gross sound, the uttered speech by which ideas are expressed. Paśyantī and Madhyamā are in between these two, the former representing a non-particularised motion and the latter, a cognitive aspect of mental movement. The sound when unlettered is known as *dhvanyātmaka-śabda* and when lettered as *varṇātmaka-śabda*. By mental action such sounds are co-ordinated into words (*pada*) and sentences (*vākya*) from which a meaning (*artha*) transpires. The mind is thus both cogniser (*grāhaka*) and the cognised (*grāhya*), revealer (*prakāśa*) and the revealed (*prakāśya*), denoter (*vācaka*) and the denoted (*vācya*). A word in the last analysis is thus the reflection of the mind, which is at the same time in itself the cogniser and the cognised. This is the basis of monistic approach. While the purpose of Pāṇini's grammar was mostly confined to the formulation of the rules for the guidance of words, Patañjali converted grammar into a philosophy, a spiritual discipline, the aim of which was to understand the nature of the ultimate reality, to attain union with *brahman* through the study of the words. Bhartṛhari insisted on the atomic essence of sound (*sphoṭa*) as the only existent reality and held that all words and their meanings are nothing but apparently different (if not illusory) aspects of one and the same reality.

Theoretical speculations apart, for practical purposes it was, however, required that a durable and standing meaning of words be maintained, and this requirement was fulfilled by the ancient etymologists and lexicographers. The so called *Nighaṇṭus* or Glossaries were collections of rare and obscure words occurring in the Vedic hymns which contained five lists of words divided into three sections. The first section (*Naighaṇṭukakāṇḍa*) consists of three lists in which the Vedic words are collected under certain main ideas. The second section (*Naigama-kāṇḍa* or *Aikapadika*) contains a list of ambiguous and particularly difficult words of the Veda, while the third section (*Daivatakāṇḍa*) gives a classification of the deities according to the three regions—earth, sky, and heaven. The first commentary on the *Nighaṇṭus* was the celebrated *Nirukta* of Yāska which was composed between c. 800 and 500 B.C. Yāska in the explanation of difficult words relied basically on etymology and frequently gave two or more different interpretations of one and the same word. Certain it is that Yāska had many predecessors (he quoted 17 names) and also successors, but nothing is preserved to us of their works. It should be mentioned in this connection that there was a second commentary on the *Nighaṇṭus* which was known as *Nighaṇṭu-nirvacana*. It was composed by one Devarāja Yajvan of the twelfth century A.D. There are two commentaries on the *Nirukta*, one by the tenth century scholar Durgācārya and the other by Skandasvāmin and Maheśvara who might have lived between eleventh and fourteenth centuries.

Th. Zachariae had rightly described the *Nighaṇṭus* as precursors of the subsequent lexical works. Among the ancient lexicographers we have a few names like Vyāḍī, Kātya, Utpala, Dhanvantarī and others whose works have not, however, been found, but are cited in the works of later writers. The *Amarakoṣa* of Amarasiṃha, also known as *Nāmaliṅgānuśāsana* and *Trikāṇḍī*, which was compsoed about A.D. 500, was a landmark in the history of Indian lexicography. Its importance is proved by the fact that it has no less than sixty commentaries. The principal commentaries on the *Amarakoṣa* are: Kṣīrasvāmin's *Amarakoṣodghāṭana*; Subhūticandra's *Kāmadhenu*; Sarvānanda's *Ṭīkā-sarvasva*; Trilocanadāsa's *Amarakoṣaṭīkā*; Durlabhavallabha's *Amarakoṣaṭīkā*; Paramānanda's *Amarakoṣamālā*; Bṛhaspati's *Padacandrikā*; Nārāyaṇa's *Padārthakaumudī*; Bharatasena's *Mugdhabodhinī*; Bhanuji Dikṣita's *Vyākhyāsudhā*; Maheśvara's *Amarakoṣaviveka*; Mathureśa's *Sārasundarī*; Liṅgabhaṭṭa's *Amarakoṣapadavivrti*; Nārāyaṇa

Vidyāvinoda's *Sabdārthasandīpikā*; and Maheśvara Sukthankara's *Śiśubodhinī*. Śāsvata's *Anekārthasamuccaya* (sixth century), Mahākṣapaṇaka's *Anekārthadhvanimañjarī* (tenth century), Halāyudha's *Abhidhānaratnamālā* (tenth century), and Yādavaprakāśa's *Vaijayantī* (eleventh century) are also important lexical works.

The next period in the history of Sanskrit lexicography began with Hemacandra's *Abhidhānacintāmaṇi* and *Anekārthasaṃgraha*, which were followed by Maheśvara's *Viśvaprakāśa*, Dhanañjaya's *Nāmamālā*, Medinīkara's *Medinīkoṣa*, Keśava's *Nānārthārṇavasaṅkṣepa*, Maṅkha's *Maṅkhakoṣa*, Mahīpa's *Anekārthatilaka*, Irugappadaṇḍādhinātha's *Nānārtharatnamālā*, Ajayapāla's *Anekārthakoṣa*, Keśava's *Kalpadrukoṣa*, Shahji's *Sarvaratnasamanvaya*, Viśvanātha's *Koṣakalpataru*, etc. These were all composed between the twelfth and eighteenth century. There were other lexical works pertaining to different branches of science, most of them dealing with botany and medicine. Instead of alphabetical arrangement of words Sanskrit lexicographers depended on the traditional system of versification. This trend was continued even in some nineteenth century lexical works like Rāghava Āpā Khaṇḍekar's *Koṣāvataṃsá*. A modern approach based on alphabetical arrangement and careful selection of suggestive words is found at least in three works of nineteenth century Indian scholarship. These are Paravastu Venkaṭa Raṅgācārya's *Sarvārthasarvasva*, Tārānātha Tarkavācaspati's *Vācaspatya* and Radhākānta Deva's *Śabdakalpadruma*.

Without a reference to European scholarship, the present sketch of the development of Sanskrit lexicography cannot be complete. As early as in 1808, Colebrooke published a modern edition of the *Amarakoṣa* with marginal translation. The first Sanskrit-English Dictionary was prepared by Wilson which was published in 1819. Its revised edition came out in 1832. Monier-Williams compiled a bigger dictionary in 1851 which was, however, overshadowed by the publication in 1852 of the first part of the monumental *Sanskrit Wörterbuch* (also known as *St. Petersburg Dictionary*) compiled by Rudolph Roth and Otto Bohtlingk. Benfey's *Sanskrit English Dictionary* comprising selected words with greater emphasis on the contents of the works of Sanskrit authors, came out in 1866. After the publication of the first part of the *St. Petersburg Dictionary* (the seven volume project was completed in 1875) Monier-Williams felt the need of bringing out a fresh and more detailed dictionary which was eventually published in 1872 (an enlarged and improved edition of it came out in 1899). Macdonell also published a *Sanskrit-English Dictionary* in 1892 which laid more emphasis on the Vedic words. Th. Zachariae's *Die Indischen Wörterbucher* was published in 1897. Louis Renou's *Dictionarie Sanskrit Francais* was published in 1938.

Modern studies on Indian religious terminology were evidently rooted in the researches on Vedic language and literature. Franz Bopp's *Glossarium Linguae Sanskritae* (1830) was the first modern work of Sanskrit technical terms dealing with various topics pertaining to religious ideas. His *Comparative Grammar* (1833–52) opened up a new horizon in the study of comparative philology in which Vedic words served as the standard of association with those of other Indo-European languages. In 1852 Rudolf Roth published the first critical edition of Yāska's *Nirukta*. The first exhaustive glossary of the *Ṛgveda* was prepared by Hermann Guenther Grassman in two volumes under the title *Wörterbuch zum Ṛgveda* (1867–77). It was followed by Victor Henry's *Manual de Sanskrit Vedic* (1890). Macdonell's edition and translation of the *Bṛhaddevatā* which is in content a glossary though in form a compendium of Vedic religion embracing every aspect of it, was a landmark in this branch of study. Maurice Bloomfield's *Vedic Concordance* (1906) came out as a novel guide for the specification of the Vedic verses which was no less effective than a modern computer.

Another important publication was *The Vedic Index* by A.A. Macdonell and A.B. Keith which came out in 1912. Though its purpose was to deal with non-religious topics, it contained interpretations of a good number of terms with reference to their sources which had direct bearing on religious aspects. M. Winternitz's *General Index to the Names and Subjectmatters of the Sacred Books of the East Series* which was published from Oxford in 1901, as the 50th volume of the series itself, should specially be mentioned in this connection. The *Sacred Book of the East* series was planned by F. Max Müller in 1875 for the purpose of introducing the Western readers with the actual contents of the major religious texts of the Orient. Among the 49 volumes of this series, 21 were devoted to Vedic and Brahmanical, 10 to Buddhist and 2 to Jain texts. The *General Index* of Winternitz was subsequently re-issued in 1925 under the title, *A Concise Dictionary of Eastern Religion*. Among the recent works Viśvabandhu's *Vedic Word Concordance* (1955–73), published in 16 volumes, deserves special mention. S.C. Cakravarti's *Paribhāṣās in the Śrautasūtras* (1980) should also be referred to in this connection.

The modern study of Buddhism rested, since its very inception, upon corresponding studies of manuscripts in at least four languages—Pali, Sanskrit, Chinese and Tibetan. As early as in 1824 Benjamin Clough published from Colombo a book under the title, *A Compendious Pali Grammar with a Copious Vocabulary in the Same Language*. The edition in Roman characters with an English translation of the first 38 chapters of the *Mahāvaṃsa* in 1837 by George Turner marked the first important attempt to introduce the treasures of Pali literature to the scholars of the West. An important advance was marked by the publication of the well-known *Dictionary of the Pali Language* in 1875 by R.C. Childers, but with the increase in the publicatons of the Pali Text Society (founded by T.W. Rhys Davids in 1881) when this dictionary was found to be inadequate, Prof. Rhys Davids conceived the idea of compiling a Pali dictionary through international collaboration (1902). But it was not until 1916 that he set to work on this dictionary with the assistance of William Stede. Rhys Davids lived to see only the first three parts of this project. His eminent colleague Stede compiled the work till 1925. It was followed by *Critical Pali Dictionary* by Dines Anderson and Helmer Smith (1927–28). The *Pali-Tripiṭaka Concordance* prepared by scholars like Woodward and others and edited by E.M. Hare was brought out by the PTS in 1952–55. Mention must also be made in this connection to the celebrated *Dictionary of Pali Proper Names* compiled in two volumes by G.P. Malalasekera (1937–38). Buddhist Sanskrit terms have been dealt with in the Sanskrit dictionaries, but there is a hybrid-Sanskrit used by the early Buddhist writers, which has been studied by Franklin Edgarton in his *Buddhist Hybrid Sanskrit Grammar and Dictionary* (1953). Among numerous lexical works P.C. Bagchi's *Deux Lexiques Sanskrit-Chinois* (1929, 1937) is most useful insofar as the study of the Buddhist terminology is concerned. The study of Tibetan Buddhist terminology was initiated by Alexander Csoma de Koros and followed by a host of eminent scholars. In this connection we may specially refer to Sarat Chandra Das, one of the founders of modern Tibetan Studies, whose *Tibetan English Dictionary* came out in 1902. Among the Japanese scholars, K. Kasahara published, as ealry as in 1885, a work entitled *Dharmasaṃgraha* which was an ancient collection of Buddhist technical terms. C. Anakuma's *Dictionary of Proper Names in Indian Buddhism* came out in 1930. In 1926 S. Levi sponsored the project of compiling an encyclopaedic dictionary, the *Hobogirin*. His collaborators were Takakusu, Anesaki, Inoue, Suziama and others.

The first landmark in the history of Jain terminological study was the publication of the German translation of Hemacandra's *Abhidhānacintāmaṇi* in 1847 by Böhtlingk Riew.

Since 1920, researches on Jainism had taken a manifold course, though the main emphasis was on literary studies. Besides critical editions and translations of the canonical and non-canonical texts, comprehensive and analytical historical works, and specialised studies, religious and philosophical terms of Jainism were studied by Weber, Bühler, Jacobi, Hoernle, Glasenapp, Kamptz, Schübring and their successors. So far as the modern lexical works are concerned, Vīrarājendra Suri's Sanskrit encyclopaedia *Abhidhāna-rājendra* (1913–25) incorporated numerous Jain Prakrit terms taken from the canonical and scholastic literature of the Śvetāmbaras. This was followed by Muni Ratnacandra's *Ardhamāgadhī Dictionary* (1923–32) and Haragovinda Das Seth's *Prakrit-Hindi Dictionary*. A complete Digambara Jain Dictionary entitled *Bṛhad Jaina Śabdārṇava* came in two volumes between 1930 and 1934. Among subsequent works the most important is *Lexicographical Studies in Jain Sanskrit* by B.J. Sandasara and G.P. Thakur (1962).

In the case of the Vedic words, the Western scholars did their best by applying all the existing methods to arrive at the real meaning. As is known to all, it is only with the help of the commentaries that the Vedic texts can be read or even partially understood. Moreover, there was a wide time-gap between the period of the formation of the texts and the composition of the commentaries. Sāyaṇa's commentary was composed 2500 years after the compilation of the *Ṛgveda*. It is not unlikely that Sāyaṇa might have consulted some earlier commentaries which are now non-existent, but the fact cannot be ignored that the meanings he had attributed to the words of the *Ṛgveda* were partly his own invention. The religious terms and concepts of the later Saṃhitās and Brāhmaṇas are in certain cases so obscure that the earlier commentators failed to make out any sense from most of them. In extreme cases they were rather compelled to use the word *utsanna*, meaning 'gone out of vogue'. Some of the older European interpreters of the *Ṛgveda*, such as H.H. Wilson, depended solely on the commentary of Sāyaṇa, while Rudolph Roth denied that a commentator, who lived more than two thousand years after the composition of the book explained by him, could know anything which the modern scholars with their philological criticism and with the resources of linguistic science, could not fathom and understand better. Most researchers, however, took an intermediary position. The general approach was that where they had found Indo-European roots they sought to reach at the original meaning on the basis of comparative study taking into account similar words found in other Indo-European languages. Where situation did not permit they banked on indigenous commentaries.

While translating the Buddhist texts scholars tried to make literal translation as far as possible, but this did not yield tangible results. At the dawn of Buddhalogical studies, there had been a controversy between the French scholar E. Burnouf and the Russian scholar V.P. Vasilev on the question whether Buddhism could be best understood from the Indian sources alone, or whether the Chinese and Tibetan sources were necessary as well. According to the former, only Indian sources provided evidence on genuine Buddhism, while the latter held that Buddhism in the totality of its development could be understood only from Tibetan and Chinese sources in addition to the Indian ones. Vasilev's viewpoint enabled him to determine the exact meaning of the crucial term *śūnyatā* in which he had discovered under a dialectical terminology an idea similar to absolute idealism of the West. Studies in Mahāyāna philosophical treatises, according to a group of authorities especially belonging to the Russian school, had substantiated Vasilev's viewpoint. While the Pali school discovered in Mahāyāna nothing but degeneration and nihilism, Minayeff, Stcherbatsky and Rosenberg had claimed to have established the exact meaning of the basic technical terms of the system which, according to their opinion had so far been translated just anyhow, either on the basis of etymology or of comon sense. For example, they explained the term *dharma* as meaning 'elements of existence', the term *saṃskāra* as meaning 'co-operating elements of existence,' and the term *pratītyasamutpāda* as meaning 'co-operation of the elements of existence'. According to them these terms as well as others referred to one and the same system of pluralistic empiricism, and this was the core of early Buddhism. E. Conze held that the Mahayanic Buddhist terms had not adequately been interpreted and that perhaps five per cent of the Mahayanic Sutras had so far been edited and two per cent intelligibly translated. While some terminological works in the field of Buddhism and Jainism have recently been done, the Brahmanical systems (except in the field of the Vedas) and their offshoots have not sufficiently been treated. The basic reason is that, unlike the Buddhist and Jain texts, the Purāṇas and other sectarian treatises have not been favoured with critical editions. It is only in the case of the Tantras that we have a good number of terminological works, thanks to the efforts of Sir John Woodroffe and his colleagues.

Buddhism and Jainism belonged to the same intellectual-cultural complex and the religio-philosophical terminology is almost the same in both cases. Though Buddhism and Jainism had some functional differences with Brahmanism and its sectarian offshoots, which subsequently came to be known as Hinduism, from the viewpoint of religio-philosophical terms and concepts the basic similarity underlying all these systems can not be overlooked or ignored. This may be sufficiently demonstrated with reference to such concepts as *duḥkha, nirvāṇa, mokṣa, karma*, etc. The logical, epistemological and metaphysical terms and concepts, as also those pertaining to the functional aspects of réligous life, originated from one primary source and these were subsequently adapted in all the religio-philosophical systems in India with necessary modification. An in-depth study in religious terminology is therefore expected to demonstrate sufficiently that hitherto in the studies on Indian religion the so-called differences of various systems have been over-emphasized by most scholars and their basic unity has been ignored. When Mādhavācārya in his *Sarvadaśanasaṃgraha* dealt with Buddhism and Jainism he considered them merely as different schools of thought belonging to the same category as the Mīmāṃsā or the Sāṅkhya or the Vedānta. He never thought that these were different religious systems. It was not an unusual phenomenon in India that the Jain authors would write commentaries on Buddhist philosophical treatises or the Vaiṣṇava *Lakṣmītantra* would be regarded as quite authoritative by the Śāktas. A structural study of Vaiṣṇavism and Śaivism on the basis of religious terminology would reveal that both the systems were nothing but the two aspects of the same ideological phenomena. Both in their earlier stages banked upon the Sāṅkhya principles, but later they resorted to the Vedānta, particularly to its theistic interpretations. Both Viṣṇu and Śiva were equated with *brahman* and regarded as the efficient and material cause of the universe. The relation between *brahman* and the world was described in identical terms in both the systems. The same terms and concepts were used on the one hand by the Kashmirian, Tamil and Karnataka exponents of Śaivism and on the other by the southern exponents of Vaiṣṇavism. In regard to the functional aspects both the systems had the same to suggest. The starting point was suffering and the aim was its extinction (*mokṣa* or *nirvāṇa*) which was possible only through the merger of the individual self into the *brahman* or the cosmic self represented by Viṣṇu or Śiva. In order to achieve this end in both the systems (as also in others) the same methods were prescribed, such as *kriyā, caryā, jñāna, yoga, bhakti*, etc. Again in each of these specific methods the ingredients were the same.

Ritualistic terms were also common to all the systems. India maintained a unique tradition of preserving all the ritual practices flowing from the most obscure period of time by endowing them with new meaning and significance at different periods of history under diverse sets of religio-philosophical ideas. Historically, tribes of various cultural grades—even those remaining in most primitive conditions—were brought within the fold of the broader Hindu way of life through a socio-cultural-economic process known as the caste system. Notwithstanding its various defects, especially pertaining to the question of inequality, the caste system had an amazing functional success in all spheres of Indian life through the ages. This was due to the fact that on the one hand this system offered occupational security to each and every caste-society, whatever its status might have been in the hierarchy, and on the other guaranteed absolute cultural freedom to each of them. As a result of this, when tribes were inducted within the caste fold, their cults, and rituals were not discontinued or interrupted. Rather a good many of these cults and rituals were able to make their way into the higher forms of religious life for their mass adaptability. This may be illustrated with reference to the cult of the primitive Mother Goddesses which later contributed a great deal to the development of the concept of the Female Principle which characterised all the major thought-complexes of India. The popularity of these goddesses among the agricultural tribes and of the rituals by which they were worshipped—the so-called primitive Tantric undercurrent—was responsible for their penetration into Brahmanism, Buddhism and Jainism. The cults of the Puranic goddesses, which later crystallized in Śāktism, as well as the Buddhist Tārādevīs and other female divinities, the Jain Mātṛkās, Vidyādevīs, Śāsanadevatās, Yoginīs, etc., carried with them various sets of primitive rituals which could not be forsaken or stamped out. That is why rituals and ritualistic terms have found a common mode of expression in all the systems.

Indian philosophical systems were inextricably blended with religious ideas and vice-versa and hence the terms and concepts were same in both the fields. From an historical point of view, it may be said that the Pythagorean definition of philosophy which was 'contemplation, study and knowledge of nature' was foreshadowed in the religion of the Vedas But just as in Greece, after Aristotle, the term metaphysics lost its original meaning and its subject matter came to be identified with speculative philosophy as against the pre-Socratic naturalism of the Ionian physicists, so also from the age of the Upaniṣads most of the Indian systems set to themselves the task of prying into the transcendental being above and behind the physical universe, of explaining the concrete realities of existence in the light of a hypothetical Absolute. As a result of this, we find in the Indian philosophical arena the development of absolute materialism on the one hand, represented by the Cārvāka system, and that of absolute idealism on the other, represented by the Advaita Vadānta, Mādhyamika and Yogācāra schools. In between these two extremes there were a number of systems which were basically materialistic but had eventually developed idealistic tendencies under different historical conditions. Of these systems the Nyāya Vaiśeṣika, Vaibhāṣika and Sautrāntika had become overpowered by the spirit of idealism. The Sāṅkhya and Mīmāṃsā, despite their idealistic accretions, had been able to maintain their original materialistic character. The same held good also in the case of Jain philosophy. In all the systems there was a conflict between the empiric ideas of the earlier tradition and the *a priori* ideas which were grafted later. To empirical perception was added transcendental perception, and this opened the door for idealism. The earlier empirical basis of philosophy was clearly found in the expression *darśana* which literally meant the act of perception, derived from the root *dṛś*, to see. But the meaning and significance of the word *darśana* was changed, and it was argued that perception should not be physical. It must be intuitional, for the direct realization of the Self which was conducive to liberation, *mokṣa*. Accordingly the *darśana-śāstra* (science of perception) came to be defined as *mokṣa-śāstra* (science of liberation). It was at this point that religion and philosophy met and mingled with each other, because the professed ideal of the former was liberation from worldly fetters. It therefore follows that no system of Indian philosophy or religion allows any purely isolated treatment. The development of each system being largely conditioned by its inter-connections and contradictions with others, it can be properly understood only when the vast terminological resources of each system with their many-sided suggestivity are diligently worked out from a comparative point of view.

abdapūrti Same as Varṣavardhana (q.v.); it is a sacrament in which provision is made for some ceremonies for one year for each month on the day of the birth of a child and on every anniversary of the day of birth throughout life. *Gobhila Gr.* II.8.19–20, *Śāṅ.Gr.* I.25.10–11 *Baudh. Gr.* III.7, *Kāṭhaka Gr.* XXXVI.12.14; *Vaik*, III.20–21.

abhaṅga Devotional lyrical poems, composed by the saints of Maharashtra like Jñānadeva, Nāmadeva, Ekanātha, Tukārāma, Rāmadāsa and others which express exalting mystic experiences.

ābhāsavāda The theory of creation in Kashmir Śaivism which holds that the universe consists of appearances which are all real in the sense that they are aspects of the ultimate reality. Just as reflected things in the mirror are inseparable from the mirror, yet they are distinct from one another and also from the mirror so in the case of universe which though void of disinction appears distinct from the perfectly pure vision of the Supreme Being. Diverse conditions are all a part of Śiva just as the diverse products from the juice of the sugarcane belong to the sugarcane itself. The manifestation of the universe is effected through the power (*Śakti*) of Śiva which is not different from him. With the unfolding of Śakti, the universe appears and with her closing up, it disappears. Abhinavagupta's *Paramārthasāra* 12 ff.

abhāva Non-existence which is considered to be a negative category in the Nyāya-Vaiśeṣika. It is of two kinds; namely Saṃsargābhāva (absence of *something* in something else) and Anyonyābhāva (difference between one thing and another). The former is subdivided into three kinds, namely, Prāgabhāva or antecedent non-existence, i.e., non-existence of a thing before its production; Dhvaṃsābhāva or non-existence of a thing on account of its destruction after production; Atyantābhāva or absolute non-existence in the absence of a connection between two things at any time.

abhāvamātra Negation of everything which is often wrongly confused with the state of Nirvāṇa (q.v.). *AKV* II.55.

abhayagaṇa A class of *mantras* (q.v.) from the *AV* used in connection with puṣyasnāna (q.v.). *Atharvaṇa-pariśiṣṭa* XXXII.12, 29.

abhayagirivāsin A Buddhist sect of the Sthavira group which had its centre in Ceylon.

abhaya-mudrā An iconic *mudrā* depicting gesture of protection. The hand showing this *mudrā* should be slightly elevated and up-turned, the palm facing outward, the fingers outstretched and raised.

abhaya-śānti A kind of *śānti* or propitiation to avoid calamities with the use of *mantras* from *AV* I.19.1, VI.13.1. etc.

abheda Non-duality, distinctionlessness. According to Rāmānuja the condition of *abheda* belongs to the *paramārthika-daśā* or absolute state of an individual, while *bheda* or duality belongs to the *vyavahārika* or phenomenal state.

abhicāra Rites for performing black deeds and causing harm to others; for example *māraṇa* or killing, *vaśīkaraṇa* or hypnotizing, *stambhana* or arresting, *ucāṭana* or driving away, *vidveṣaṇa or* creating bad blood and so on. *Śāradātilaka* XXIII. 123–25, *Śáktisaṅgama*, Kālī, VIII. 102–105. Such acts should not be indiscriminate. *Tantrarāja*, XIII. 94–95.

abhicārika-sthānaka One of the four groups of Viṣṇu images worshipped for the purpose of inflicting defeat or death on enemies. These were set up and worshipped in forests, mountains, marshy tracts, fortresses and other such isolated places.

abhidharma One of the branches of Buddhist Tripiṭaka. The random views expressed in the earlier Pali canons later developed into a system embodied in the Abhidharmas of the sarvāstivādins, the earliest of all the groups deviating from the Sthaviravādins or Theravādins. The Vaibhāṣika system of the Sarvāstivāda accepted seven Abhidharma books as revealed scriptures and the commentaries on them—called Vibhāṣā—as the most authoritative treatises. On the other hand the Sautrāntikas, another system of the Sarvāstivādins considered the books as works of human inspiration and therefore liable to error, and maintained that the Buddha had not composed treatises dealing with Abhidharma or given indications for the composition of such books under his authority but had taught Abhidharma doctrines in certain Sūtras or Sūtrāntas. The Pali texts dealing with Abhidharma are known as *Dhammaśaṅgaṇi Vibhaṅga*, *Dhātukathā*, *Puggalapaññatti*, *Kathāvatthu*, *Yamaka* and *Paṭṭhāna*. The philosophy of Abhidharma was compiled in Sanskrit by Vasubandhu in a book of eight chapters called *Abhidharmakośa*.

ābhidharmika The followers of the doctrine of elements in Buddhism. They hold that by *dharma* is meant the idea that existence is an interplay of a plurality of subtle, ultimate and not further analyzable elements of matter/mind forces. The *ābhidharmika* system is analogous to the Sāṅkhya in a more stable sense. See under Sarvāstivāda, Sautrāntika, Vaibhāṣika.

abhihitānvayavādin Followers of Kumārila who hold that each word has a different sense of its own and that when words combine in a sentence they yield a further sense. They were theoretically opposed to the Anvitābhidhānavādins, the followers of Prabhākara who hold that no word is significant in isolation and that words become significant when joined together in a sentence.

abhijñā See under *abhiññā*.

abhijāti The Ājīvika concept of six classes of mankind which has evidently some bearing on the Jain classification of beings and the Jain concept of Lesyā (q.v.). The highest, or milk-white group, comprises the followers of Gośāla and his two predecessors. Below is the category of white containing other groups of the Ājīvikas (q.v.). The third is green to which belong the Acelakas (q.v.); this is followed by red to which belong the Nirgranthas (q.v.) wearing single garment. Then comes blue comprising of *bhikkhus* who live as thieves and are also believers of *Karma*. The lowest class is black and comprises thieves, hunters and others who live by violence.

abhijit A Vedic sacrifice which is performed as a penance for murdering a Brāhmaṇa. This sacrifice belongs to the Ekāha (q.v.) category and follows the procedure of Soma (q.v.) sacrifice. *Jaimini* VI, 7.14, VIII.1.16, *Āśv.Sr.* VIII.5.13.

abhimānī Presiding deities that make the sense-organs (*indriyas*) and their objects (*artha*) and also mind (*manas*) and the different aspects of intelligence (*buddhi*) function. The concept of *abhimānī-devatās* as intermediate functionaries between *cetana* (conscious) and *acetana* (unconscious) is found in Madhva's system.

abhimukhī A stage on the way towards Bodhisattvahood, one of the ten *bhūmis* (q.v.). In this stage the potential Bodhisattva comprehends the dependent origination of worldly beings and objects. Perfect knowledge (*prajñā*) predominates in his mind on account of his realisation of voidness (*śūnyatā*).

abhinandana Enjoyment in Mahāyāna Buddhist terminology.

abhiniveśa One of the five *kleśas* or hindrances to be minimised mentioned in *Yogasūtra* II.5–9. This is the 'will to live' or 'clinging to life' which has its own innate force. In Buddhism *abhiniveśa* means adherence which is required for progress along the path to *nirvāṇa*.

abhiññā Higher powers attained by the *arhats* (q.v.). These are six in number, namely, *iddhi* (miraculous power), *dibbasotadhātu* (heavenly ear), *paracittañāna* (thought-reading), *pubbenivasañāna* (knowledge of previous births), *dibbacakkhu* (heavenly eye) and *āsavānaṃ khayañāna* (knowledge of the extinction of one's own impurities). In Buddhism it is regarded as one of the various but not essential attainments of an *arhat*.

abhiplava A Vedic sacrifice of the Ahina (q.v.) category, belonging to the lesser group of the Soma-Yāgas (q.v.).

abhisamaya Realisation of the four truths simultaneously. This concept is popular among the Theravādins and the Mahāsaṅghikas.

abhisaṃskāra Thought construction according to Buddhism which produce thought-seed (*citta-vījam*).

abhisecanīya A principal coronation rite in the Rājasūya. It is a sprinkling ceremony which begins with an offering to Savitṛ, Agni, Soma, Bṛhaspati, Indra, Rudra, Mitra and Varuṇa. The consecration water (*abhiṣecanīya āpaḥ*) is made up of seventeen kinds of liquid including the water from the river Sarasvatī, sea-water, water from a whirlpool, a pond, a well and dew. The sprinkling is performed by a Brāhmaṇa priest, a kinsman or brother of the king-elect, a friendly Rājaṇya and a Vaiśya. The ceremony lasts for five days. The first day is meant for *dīkṣā* or anointing and the last one for pressing Soma. *Śat. Br.* V.2.3.9 ff.

abhiṣecikī A form of consecration in which the teacher worships Śiva and Śakti in a vessel and then anoints the disciple with its water. Rāghava on *Śāradātilaka* V. 127–140.

abhiṣeka Consecration of the aspirant to be performed before or after initiation (into any special aspect of human life, religious or secular). One of the earliest and simplest *abhiṣeka* ceremonies dealing with the consecration of a king is found in *Taitt.Br.* II.7.15–16. Elaborate rituals are met with in connection with Aindra-Mahābhiṣeka, Aśvamedha, Rājasūya and other royal functions. Initiation into different religious creeds had also to be started with a preliminary rite of *abhiṣeka*. For certain features of these rites see Abhisecanīya (q.v.). In Tantric tradition *abhiṣeka* is of two kinds, Śākta or general and Pūrṇa or complete. Rāghavabhaṭṭa on *Śāradātilaka* II.5. The former is done by sprinkling holy water on the aspirant with chanting *mantras* to propitiate different deities specially those effective for driving away evil spirits. *Puraścāryarṇava* V, 405 ff. The candidate for Pūrṇābhiṣeka or complete consecration has to pass through severe ordeals. This special form of consecration bestows upon the aspirant a divine nature. *Śaktisangama*, Kālī, XI. 29–37 In certain cases the preceptor gives a new name to the disciple after the consecration.

abhiṣekabhūmi The tenth *bhūmi* (plane) of Bodhisattva in which he receives omniscience. See also Dharmamegha, Parama-vihāra, Bhūmi.

abhivādana Salutation or bowing to a person. There are three kinds of salutations: *nitya* (obligatory everyday), *naimittika* (to be done on certain occasions) and *kāmya* (to be done only if a person has certain rewards in view). A Brāhmaṇa should salute stretching forward his right arm on the level with his ears. But a Kṣatriya should do it by joining both palms at the level with his chest, a Vaiśya on level with his waist and a Śūdra on level with his feet. The salutation shall be by joining both the palms. *Āp.Dh.S. I.2.5.12–17.*

abhyāsa Cultivation of detachment (*vairāgya*) or freedom from passion in a systematic way. *Yogasūtra* I.12–14.

abhyāsa-yoga Act of subjective concentration according to the *Bhagavadgītā* VI.10–18.

abhyudaya Worldly happiness and prosperity according to the *Vaiśeṣika Sūtra* I.1.2.1–2. The word has however been variously interpreted by the commentators on Kaṇāda's Sūtra. cf. Bharata's *Nāṭyaśāstra* (GOS), IV.263. Some take it to mean *svarga* or heaven in contradistinction to *niḥśreyasa* which means *mokṣa* (liberation) or *amṛtatva* (immortality). Śāntarakṣita in his *Tattvasaṃgraha* 905 has used this word in the sense of worldly happiness while dealing with the question of the validity of Tantric *mantras* and rituals.

ābhyudayika A kind of Śrāddha (q.v.) which is performed when there is a lucky event. It is to be performed in the morning, except on the birth of a son when it should be done at once regardless of the time. *Piṇḍas* (q.v.) are offered to the Pitṛs or the paternal ancestors up to the seventh grade and Mātṛs or maternal ancestors up to the third grade. Brāhmanas are invited and fed on the occasion. *Āśv. Gr.* II.5.13–15, *Sān.Gr.*IV.4. *Gobhila Gr.* IV.3.35–37, *Kauṣītaki Gr.* IV. 4, *Baudh. Gr.* III.12.2–5.

abrahmacariyāvasa Those who lead an impure life and are fond of eulogizing themselves and disparaging others. The Buddhists applied this term to the Ājivika (q.v.) monks. *Majjhima* I. 524.

acalā See under Anābhoga-ninirmitta-vihāra.

ācamana Sipping water which is one of the constituents of the Saṃdhyā prayer. The ritual is to be performed in a sitting posture facing north or east. The water should be sipped thrice from the right hand with which then the performer should touch his eyes, ears. nose, heart and head. The water is to be poured in the hollowed palm of the right hand which should be shaped in the form of a cow's ear. *Gobhila Gr.* I.2.5–6; *Āp. Dh.S.* I.5.15–16, *Gaut.* I.35–40, *Manu*, II.58–62, *Yāj*, I.18–21. In Tantric tradition, Ācamana is the symbolic purification of body by sipping water from the palm and sprinkling it on different parts of the body. It consists in the purification of the three forms of body, namely, gross, subtle and causal. *Mahānirvāṇa* V. 39.

ācāra Rites, norms and rules, observances, conduct, behaviour customs and kindred characteristics pertaining to different stages of individual, family, communal, social and religious life. These are described in detail in the Smṛtis and digests under different categories and specific terms. For individuals. there are *ācāras* belonging to Sauca category connected with cleanliness of the body. The Saṃskāras (q.v.) or sacraments connected with different stages of individual life form *ācāra* of a different category. *Vratas* or religious rites belong to another class which being effected make a particular thing or person fit for a specific purpose. Āhnika (q.v.), Tarpaṇa (q.v.), Mahāyajña (q.v.), Devayajña (q.v.), Vaiśvadeva (q.v.), Nṛyajña (q.v.), Dāna (q.v.), Pratiṣṭhā (q.v.), etc., also fall in the category of *ācāra*, a few of which are non-obligatory. Apart from the codified *ācāras*, there are the customary ones connected with the harvest, seasonal changes and so on. A few of them like Holi, Dīpāvalī, Cart-festival etc., have transcended the limits of their original significance and have assumed a national character. In Tantra *ācāra* is the means of spiritual attainment which varies from person to person according to competence. *Mahānirvāṇa* V.39. *Ācāras* are generally of seven kinds—Veda, Vaiṣṇava, Śaiva, Dakṣiṇa, Vāma, Siddhānta and Kaula, falling into two broad categories—Daksiṇa and Vāma. Interpretations vary regarding the nature and grouping of the *ācāras*. It is generally held that those who participate in the rituals of the five Ms (*pañcamakāra*, q.v.) belong to the category of Vāmācāra. *Kaulamārgarahasya* 11. According to a different tradition everyone is a follower of Dakṣiṇācāra by birth. It is only by initiation that one becomes a Vāmācārī. *Prāṇatoṣaṇī* VII.7.532. Some authorities are inclined to exclude Veda and Vaiṣṇava from the category of Tantric *ācāras*. *Mātṛkābheda*, 6. In a few works we come across a two fold division, Aghorācāra and Yogācāra.

ācāra-liṅga Principle in Vīra-Śaiva cosmology which is a modification of Ṣaṭ-sthala (q.v.). It is the symbol of *kriyāśakti* or power of action of the supreme being.

ācārya The teacher. Though the words Ācārya, Guru and Upādhyāya are very often mentioned as synonyms, there is a difference in their ranks and functions. Ācārya is supposed to be superior to an Upādhyāya. The *Nirukta* I.4. defines Ācārya as follows: 'He makes the student understand the proper course of conduct, or he collects or gathers together the meaning of words or he increases the intelligence of the student'. *Gautama* I.10–11, *Vas.Dh.S.* III.21, *Manu* II.140, *Yāj* I.34 etc. define the Ācārya as one who performs the Upanayana (q.v.) of the student and imparts the whole Veda to him. In the Tantric tradition Ācārya means the preceptor who has mastery over the scripture, who understands the real significance of rites and who is disciplined physically and mentally. *Kulārṇava* XVII.

acelaka A class of ascetics which preferred to remain naked.

acetana Non-sentient. See under *Acit*. The Madhva school uses the term in the sense of non-spirit, that which does not know. It consists of two aspects: positive and negative or *bhāva* and *abhāva*. The positive is that which is apprehended as existent at the first instance of its apprehension and the negative as non-existent. The Nyāya-Vaiśeṣikas broadly divide reality into self (*cetana*) and non-self (*acetana*), the latter being subdivided into mental and extra-mental realities. Neither of the two depends on the other for its existence but there does exist a peculiar relation between them insofar as the existence of the *cetana* element is manifested through the operation of the *acetana* aspect. *Nyāyasūtra* III.2.59, *Vaiśeṣikasūtra* VII.1.23.

acetana-kāraṇa-vāda See under Kāraṇa.

acetana-pariṇāma Transformation of matter. According to the Bhedābheda school of Bhāskara, the unconditioned one assumes a multiplicity of names and forms and becomes either Jīva—the subjects of experience or *acetana*—the object of experience. The power of *brahman* (q.v.) is thus two fold, *jīva-pariṇāma* and *acetana-pariṇāma*.

acintyabhedābheda Caitanya's conception of the relation between *brahman* and the self. It holds that the relation between the two is of an inconceivable kind of identity-in-difference which cannot be explained in terms of ordinary logic and analysis. It holds that the Upanisads are authorities by themselves, that *brahman* is the material as well as the efficient cause of the universe and that it transforms itself into the universe yet remaining unaffected by the transformation. *Caitanya-caritāmṛta* I.4, I.5, I.7.117ff. II.8.

acit Non-sentient. It is the term for matter as opposed to *cit* or consciousness. The material world is therefore viewed as *acit* in the Indian religious and philosophical tradition.

acit-śakti One of the two forms of Śakti (q.v.). the other being *cit* or consciousness. It is also known as *parigraha-śakti* and *upādāna-śakti*, i.e.. material cause, of which the universe is a manifestation.

adbhuta An ancient word which later came to denote phenomena of ill omens such as earthquakes, eclipses, comets, falling stars, cow yielding blood-red milk and so on. The Gṛhyasūtras refer to *adbhuta-śāntis* or protective measures against such happenings. The 67th *Āthravana-pariśiṣṭa*, based on the *Adbhutabrāhmaṇa* of the *Sāmaveda*, is called *adbhutaśānti* which prescribes as *śānti* (q.v.) *japa* (q.v.), making brāhmaṇas to say 'svasti', honouring and feeding brāhmaṇas.

addhariya Prakrit from of Adhvaryu (q.v.) mentioned in the Buddhist texts.

adhaḥ-āmnāya One of the six geographical regions of the Tantric cult, presided over by goddesses such as Vāgīśvarī, Vajrayogini, Paṇṇagī, Nairteśvarī, etc. of Buddhist and Jain affiliation. *Śaktisaṅgama*, Sundarī III.182–87, *Prāṇtoṣaṇī* I. 9. 64, *Puraścaryārṇava* I, 13.

ādhāra The base or container or ground denoting the individual who is ready to bear the inrush and impact of divine energy. Again the nature of the Absolute or the cosmic ground is often defined by means of the relation of *ādhāra* and *ādheya* (support and the thing supported). According to the Viśiṣṭādvaitavāda, reality has three essential attributes which are *ādhāratva*, *vidhātṛtva* and *śeṣitva* (the qualities of being the ground, the supporter and the whole). The Acintyabhedābheda (q.v.) school refers to *ādhāra-śakti* of *brahman* (q.v.) in the sense of receptive power.

adharma The principle of rest which in Jain cosmic conception creates conditions for the immobility of objects, just as the shade of a tree helps a traveller to rest. It is complementary to Dharma (q.v.) the principle of motion, both being eternal and formless, pervading the entire world-space. The Nyāya-Vaiśeṣikas view *adharma* in terms of demerit and regard it as one of the 24 constituents of *guṇa* (q.v.) or quality. *TTDS* V.1. 17–18, *Vaiś. Sūt* I.1.16.

ādhibhautika One of the three kinds of pain which, according to the Sāṅkhya, is produced by extra-organic natural causes like murder, snake-bite, the prick of thorns and so forth.

adhicca-samuppannika Fortuitous Originists mentioned in the *Brahmajāla-sutta* who were divided into two groups. They believed that the world originated owing to the transformation of objects by themselves (*svabhāva*, q.v.) or accidentally without any cause (*yadṛcchā*, q.v.). They probably belonged to a group which was later characterised by the epithets Lokāyatika, Bārhaspatya, Cārvāka, etc. The doctrine of Ajita Keśakambalī had some bearing on this school.

adhicittavihāra Also known as Prabhakarī, it is the third *bhūmi* or ground of Bodhisattvas in which they should develop the following ten *cittāśayas* or mental attainments: *śuddha* (pure), *sthira* (firm), *nirvid* (world-disgustful), *avirāga* (non-detached), *avinivṛta* (non-returning), *dṛḍha* (strong), *uttapta* (energetic), *atṛpta* (never satisfied), *udāra* (noble) and *māhātmya* (magnanimous). In this stage the Bodhisattva realises that constituted beings and things are impermanent, full of suffering, are ephemeral and decaying, are without beginning or end, and are subject to causal law.

ādhidaivata An explanation of the universe, the theory that all manifestations of energy proceed from conscious beings, whether visible or not.

ādhidaivika One of the three kinds of pain which, according to the Sāṅkhya, is caused by extra-organic supernatural conditions like pains inflicted by ghosts, demons, etc.

adhikāra Qualification and competence for Tantric worship. Only those who are free from all narrowness and are actively engaged in working for human welfare have this competence. Sarvahiṃsāvinirmuktaḥ sarvaprāṇihiterataḥ, so' asmin śāstre' adhikārī tadanyo brahmasādhaka. *Gandharvatantra* II.19. There are various types of Tantric *sādhanā* with a variety of purposes, hence the qualifications for initiation vary from person to person according to the nature of the *sādhanā* one undertakes. Those who do not believe in the Vedic way are specially entitled to have Tantric initiation. *Kaulamārgarahasya*, 91, 105. According to the *PMS* VI.1 everyone belonging to the three higher castes has right to perform the Vedic sacrifices with the exception of those who suffer from incurable defects such as blindness, etc. In the Mīmāṃsā tradition, when a Vedic text stipulates that 'one desirous of securing heaven should offer a Yāga,' heaven is made the principal factor. Yāga becomes subsidiary matter and the qualification of the performer (*adhikāra*) is laid down by the word *svargakāma*.

adhikaraṇa Also called *nyāyas* or conclusions on topics for discussion according to the Pūrva-Mīmāṃsa tradition. An *adhikaraṇa* is described as having five constituents, namely, the topic for discussion, the doubt about it, the *prima facie* view, the refutation of the *prima facie* view and the final conclusion.

adhikaraṇasamatha The seven methods of making up differences which were prescribed by Buddha. *Majjhima* II. 238 ff.

adhimokkha The process of freely choosing to attend to an object, that is, selecting the object for perception. It is a Buddhist concept.

adhimukticaryā-vihāra One of the ten *bhūmis* (q.v.) of Bodhisattva and one of the two divisions of *prākṛticaryā* i.e., the worldly virtues of a being, e.g. respectfulness to parents, Śramaṇas and Brāhmaṇas, performance of the ten Kuśala-karmapathas, worship of Buddhas, etc.

adhiprajñāvihāra: A stage in the attainment of Bodhisattvahood. In Hīnayāna Buddhism Adhipaññā is the fourth stage to attain Arhathood. *Aṅguttara* I.229. In the *Bodhisattvabhūmi* three different means are prescribed in relation to this stage; they are the practice of *prajñā* or wisdom with reference to the *bodhipakṣīya-dharmas* (q.v.), to the truths and to the law of causation.

adhiśīla-vihāra The rules of pātimokkha (q.v.) and minor disciplinary rules prescribed in the Vinaya piṭaka are known as *adhiśīla*. *Aṅguttara* I. 230f. Adhiśīla-vihāra, also known as Vimala, is the second *bhūmi* (q.v.) of Bodhisattva in which stage he develops ten *cittāśayas* or mental attainments: *ṛju* (plain), *mṛdu* (soft). *kārmaṇya* (pliable), *dama* (submissive), *śama* (tranquil), *kalyāṇa* (beneficial), *asamsṛṣṭa* (unlogged), *anapekṣa* (indifferent), *udāra* (noble) and *māhātmya* (magnanimous). *Bodhisattvabhūmi* 11.

adhiṣṭhāna The four qualities in the *Acalā* or *Anābhoga-nirnimitta* (q.v.) stage towards the attainment of Bodhisattvahood. They are *satya* (truth), *tyāga* (renunciation), *upasama* (remission) and *prajñā* (wisdom). Adhiṣṭhāna is also the term for the moulded basement of a temple, a synonym for *vedī-bandha*.

adhokṣaja A sub-vyūha (q.v.) of Viṣṇu.

adhrigupraiṣa An invocation recited by the Hotṛ priest in connection with animal sacrifice in which the limbs of the victim are identified with different deities. It is done immediately before the animal is tied to the sacrificial post. *Tai.Br.* III.6.6; *Ait.Br.* VI. 6–7. Twelve *adhikaraṇas* (q.v.) on this topic are given in *PMS*, IX. 3–4.

adhvan The Tantric concept of six paths leading to the realization of the supreme being through the six centres of the body.

adhvaryu The priest who does all the manual works in a scarifice. He is the 'performer' who executes all the sacrificial acts, muttering simultaneously the prose prayer and sacrificial formulae (*yajus*).

adhvaśodhana The process of purifying the body. It consists of six *adhvas* technically known as *varṇa, pada, mantra, kalā, tattva* and *bhuvana*. Rāghavabhaṭṭa on *Śāradātilaka* V. 77.

adhyāsa The process of the imaginary attribution of something where it does not exist. In phychological terminology it is similar to projection. From a religious viewpoint it is a form of symbol worship. The objective approach to the symbol is known as *sampad*, while the subjective is known as *adhyāsa*. The former is like the visualization of the deity or idea in a thing, may be an image or a symbol, while in the case of the latter, though the thing exists and is used as a means of concentration, the main emphasis is on the mind of the worshipper and on the deity or idea that is chiefly concerned. Āropyapradhānā sampat adhiṣṭhānapradhāno' adhyāsaḥ, *Vedāntakalpataru* I.1.4.

ādhyātmika One of the three kinds of pain which, according to the Sāṅkhya, is due to intraorganic causes like bodily disorders, diseases and mental suffering caused by fear, anger, greed, etc.

ādi A subtle body like the etheric double. The scheme of the body in the Upanisads is only a description of the manifest bodies; it is said that over and above these there are two unmanifested bodies which may be called the monadic and the divine, the *anupadaka* and the *ādi*.

ādi-mūrti Viṣṇu image in which the god is shown resting on the coils of the great serpent Ādiśeṣa.

ādi-śakti First among the five principal *śaktis* or energies of Śiva, others being *parā, icchā, jñāna* and *kriyā*.

ādityadarśana Also known as Niṣkramaṇa, Upaniṣkramaṇa or Nirṇayaṇa; it is the rite of taking the child, when it is four months old, out of the house in the open. *Pār.Gr.* I.17; *Baudh* Gr. II.2; *Mānava Gr.* XIX.1; *Viṣṇu Dh.S.* XXVII. 10; *Manu* II.34; *Yāj.* I.11.

ādityavrata A discipline to be observed by the Brahmacārins or students living in the teacher's house. Those who observe the Ādityavrata wear a single garment, do not allow anything to come between them and the sun, except trees and houses, and do not descend into water more than knee-deep. *Gobhila Gr.* III.1.26–31.

adṛṣṭa The stock of merit and demerit accruing from good or bad actions. The Nyāya-Vaiśeṣikas use this concept to explain the differences in the lot of human beings in terms of good or bad deeds. They hold that *adṛṣṭa* being an unintelligent principle requires to be guided by an intelligent agent, namely, God. It is God's creative will that has reference to the stock of merit and demerit acquired by individual souls in a previous life.

advaita, advaya Non-dualism, as opposed to dualism (*dvaita*) which is one of the main features of the idealistic philosophical systems of India. In all forms of Indian religious beliefs, Tantrism included, this philosophical concept plays a significant role. In the *Vedāntasūtra* it is stated that *brahman* (q.v.) and the world are not different and that the power of creation belongs to the pure stainless *brahman*, the material and efficient cause, which for its own sport develops itself into the world without itself undergoing the least change (I.3.1, I.4.23–27, I.33, II.1.27 etc). Gauḍapāda in his *Māṇḍukyakārikā* III.19.21 etc., holds that there cannot be any such thing as creation at all because *brahman* cannot be subject to change. According to Śaṅkara, the question of *brahman's* transformation into the world cannot arise because the world exists only for those who are under the influence of *avidyā* or ignorance. This purely illusory position of the world, as suggested by the absolute non-dualistic form of

Vedānta on the basis of the logic that the cause alone is real and its apparent transformation in the form of effect is only an illusion created much confusion among the different religious systems which had equated *brahman* with the supreme deity of their creed. The Vaiṣṇava theistic sects conceived of the relation between *brahman* and the world either in terms of difference or in that of identity-in-difference. The same position was also taken by the Śaiva and Śākta schools which sought to establish the dogma of the static (*prakāśa*) and vibrating (*vimarśa*) aspects of *śakti* in terms either of transformation (*pariṇāma*) or of transfiguration (*vivarta*) of *brahman*. In Tantric Buddhism *advaya* or non-duality stands for a psycho-physical process. The union of Prajñā (q.v.) and Upāya (q.v.) symbolising the female and male principles of creation respectively, through the principles of Yuganaddha (q.v.) for the purpose of realisation of the non-dual state, symbolised by the physical union of the adept and his female partner, brings in succession *rāga* and *mahārāga* (emotion and intense emotion, evidently transcendental, resulting from a genuine feeling of compassion), *sāmarasa* (oneness of emotion in which there is no cognition of Prajñā and Upāya) and finally the *mahāsukha* or great bliss leading to Nirvāṇa. This *mahāsukha* (q.v.) or great bliss is of the nature of the absolute unity of Prajñā and Upāya, the non-dual quintessence of all the entities without which perfect wisdom is never possible. *Advayavajrasaṃgraha* 50.

ādyāśakti Primordial energy conceived as a goddess.

āgama General term for denoting scriptures used by all religious sects of India. The term was specially used by the Śaiva and Tantra schools. The Jain texts are also known as *āgamas*. The Chinese versions of the Buddhists *nikāyas* are also mentioned as *āgamas*. In the Tantric tradition it is said that the word is formed by the first letters of *āgata* (that which comes from Śiva), *gata* (that which goes to Pārvatī), and *mata* (that which is established). The terms *tantra*, *āgama* and *saṃhitā* are very often used in the same sense.

āgamāntin Śaivas who base their tenets on the Āgamas (28 in number) and enjoin that there are three principles—the Lord (Pati or Śiva), the individual soul (Paśu) and fetters (Pāśa)—which bind the individual to his mundane existence. Like other Śaiva groups they also believe in Caryā, Kriyā, Yoga and Jñāna (qq.v.) as means of a well-regulated religious life. Women, Śūdras and Pratilomas are allowed to participate in this system.

aghamarṣaṇa The rite of driving out sin; it consists in taking water in the right hand formed in the shape of cow's ear, holding it near one's nose, breathing out from the nose on the water—with the idea of driving away sin from oneself—to the accompaniment of three verses from *Ṛgveda* (X.190.1–3) and then casting the water away to one's left on the ground. The *Prāyaścittasāra* speaks of Aghamarṣaṇa-vrata, the performer of which has to fast for three days, stand up by day, sit up by night, and donate a milch cow at the end. *Gaut.Dh.S.* XXIV.11, *Baudh.Dh.S.* IV.2.19–20, *Vas.Dh.S.* XXVI.8, *Viṣṇu Dh.S.* XLVI.1–9, LV.7, *Manu* XI.259–60, *Yāj* III.301, *Śaṅkha*, XXIII.1–2, *Mālinītantra* quoted in *Tantrasāra* 79.

aghātin-karma One of the two major groups into which eight kinds of *karma* (q.v.) from Jain viewpoint have been divided. It includes *āyu* (length of time which a *jīva* (q.v.) must spend in the form with which his *karma* had endowed him), *nāma* (the conditions by which the *jīvas* are governed), *gotra* (country, caste, etc. determining the specific conditions) and *antarāya* (condition of individual differences) types of *karma*.

aghora One of the five forms of Śiva; this is black in colour, terrible in nature, and is the presiding deity of the southern region. *Nirvāṇatantra* quoted in *Prāṇatoṣaṇī* I.9. 63–64. Name of a Śaiva sect following the Vāmācāra (q.v.) way. *Śaktisaṅgama*, Tārā, I.92–94. Name of one of the two general divisions of Tantric Ācāras (q.v.) the other being Yoga. Aghorī means 'terrible' or 'fearful'.

āgneya-kalā Aspects of a particular state of cosmic evolution. These are connected with the element of fire symbolised by ten goddesses—Dhūmrārci, Umā, Jvālinī, Visphuliṅginī, Suśrī, Surūpā, Kapilā, Havyavahā and Kavyavahā. *Prapañcasāra* III.18–19.

āgneyakṛcchra The name of a penance imposed for committing minor sin; in accordance with it the sinner should live for twelve days on sesame only. *Agni* CLXXI.14.

āgneya snāna A kind of symbolic bath in which the body is smeared with holy ashes. It may be performed when one is either ill or unable to have a regular bath or when there is no time for one. *Parāśara* XII.9–11, *Dakṣa*, II.15–16.

āgneya-varṇa Letters connected with the element

of fire according to the Tantric tradition. These are *ya*, *ra*, *la*, *ba*, *śa*, *ṣa*, *sa*, *ha*, and *kṣa*. Rāghava's com. on *Śāradātilaka* II.1–3.

agnicayana The construction of fire-altar for the Śrauta sacrifices. The altar has five layers. The second and fourth layers are arranged in a pattern which is different from the first, third and fifth. It may have several forms such as that of a trough, a chariot wheel, a hawk, a heron, an eagle, etc. It requires bricks of several shapes and a knowledge of geometry and mason craft. Every brick is placed after repeating a *mantra*. The bricks have various names to distinguish them. *Tai.Saṃ*. V.4.11; *Vāj.Saṃ*. XII. 55; *Śat.Br*. XI.8.18; *Jaimini* V.3.17–20.

agnīdh A Vedic priest who was regarded as a second *adhvaryu* (q.v.) as it were because of his duties such as kindling the fire, keeping it burning, etc.

agnihotra Kindling, maintenance and worship of fire employed to attain manifold ends. Oblations thrown into fire are supposed to reach the sun that sends rain which produces crops, the sustenance of all beings. Offering fuel to the fire has been equated with sacrifice and its importance is stressed in *Ch. Up*.V.24. The fire to be tended has two categories—Śrauta and Smārta. As to the first, there are certain rules in regard to the competence of the performers (*Āśv.Gr*.I.1.4; *Vas.Dh.S*. XI.45–48). It is of three kinds—Āhavanīya (q.v.), Gārhapatya (q.v.) and Dakṣiṇāgni (q.v.). Not only must one who has consecrated the sacred fires offer Agnihotra everyday, but each householder must do so twice everyday (*Āp.Dh.S*. I.4.13–22; *Manu* IV.25, *Yaj*. I.99). According to *Gautama* VIII.20 there are seven forms of Haviryajñas (q.v.) of which Agnihotra is the second. Jaiminī (VI.3. 1–10) holds that since Agnihotra is obligatory it may be undertaken even by those who are not able to perform every detail of it in its entirety. According to one view all the three fires should be permanently maintained by the householders, while according to the other only the Gārhapatya should be permanently kept. There are two views on the point whether Agnihotra is to be performed before sunrise or after sunrise (*Ait.Br*. XXIV.4–6; *Kauṣītaki Br*.II.9). Śabara on Jaiminī V.4.16 expressly says that there is no such particular time fixed for kindling the sacred fires. The deities to whom Agnihotra is offered in the morning and evening are Agni (Sun according to some sources) and Prajāpati. The oblations must be made of cooked food, and only such corn as is fit to be offered to fire (*Āśv.Gr*. I.2.1). The general rule is that when no particular material is specified for Homa (q.v.) in the fire, clarified butter is to be used as offering; and when no particular deity is mentioned, then the deity is to be Prajāpati (*Gobhila Gr*. I.113). The fire in which oblations are to be offered must be fed by plenty of dry wood. The daily Homa should be offered by the man himself, but in his absence it may be performed by priests, teachers and relatives on his behalf. If going out on business he should leave the fire in charge of his wife and the priest. He who makes the sacred fire go out or allows it to be extinguished is supposed to incur the sin of a killer (*Taitt.S*. I.5.2.1; *Kaṭhaka S*. IX.2).

agnimaruta-śāstra The final recital in the Agniṣṭoma (q.v.) which should be done rapidly. The Hotṛ (q.v.) recites *RV* X.9.1–3 which is a part of this Śāstra (q.v.), and while doing so he touches water—once for each verse. Other priests touch him removing the coverings from their heads. When the last verse is being recited, a Soma-offering (q.v.) is made by the Adhvaryu (q.v.).

agniṣṭoma One of the seven forms of Soma sacrifices (q.v.); it is an integral part of the Jyotiṣṭoma, so much so that the two are often considered to be identical. It is so called because in it Agni is praised, and the last chant is addressed to Agni. It is to be performed every year in spring, on the day of the New Moon or the Full Moon. Permission for the site of the sacrificial pavilion has to be taken from the king. The sacrificer and his wife first have to clean their bodies and then their purification (*pavana*) and initiation (*dīkṣā*) is done by the Adhvaryu (q.v.) with rites indicating rebirth. The initiated one and his wife have to follow certain rules. After initiation, the first rite is the *prāyanīya* or opening Iṣṭi (q.v.) in which *caru* (rice cooked in milk) is offered to Aditi (*Jaiminī*, IX.4.32–40) and four offerings of *ājya* (clarified butter) to four more deities, namely, Pathyā Svasti, Agni, Soma and Savitṛ, in the four directions. Soma is purchased and there is a rite of haggling about its price. A bundle of Soma stalks, placed on antelope skin spread on a cart, is brought to the east of the pavilion. The bundle is placed on a couch of *udumbara* wood and brought to the south of the Āhavanīya (q.v.). After this the *tanūnaptra*, a solemn covenant of the sacrificer and priests not to injure each other, takes place. The sacrificer has to undergo the Pravargya (q.v.) and Upasad (q.v.) rites; the former is supposed to endow the sacrificer with a new body while the latter is an Iṣṭi (q.v.) the chants of which refer to seiges of iron, silver and gold castles. On the second day of the Upasad a great altar (*mahāvedī*) is prepared, on which a quadrangular platform (*uttaravedī*) is raised. On this a square hole (*nābhi*) is made for the fire which is brought on the fourth day from the original Āhavanīya. It is followed by offering of an animal and clarified butter to different deities. The recitation of a long prayer called *prātarānuvāka* by the Hotṛ (q.v.) and extracting Soma juice from plants, a rite known as *mahābhiṣava* or great pressing. After the function of Soma-offering to various deities, priests move towards the north corner of the great altar where they chant the Bahispavamāna (q.v.) laud. The pressing of Soma continues the midday and evening pressing is accompanied by priestly rituals and chanting of varieties of *stotras* or hymns like Mādhyandian pavamāna, Pṛṣṭha, Ārbhava-pavamāna, etc. Daksiṇā or sacrificial fees are given to the priests. Then there are the concluding chants and offerings after which the *avabhṛtha*, or final bath, takes place. The sacrificer and his wife enter water and each rubs the other's back. Fuel-sticks are given to the fire and five offerings, called *devikā* are made to Dhātṛ, Anumati, Rākā, Sinīvālī and Kuhū. *Taitt. Saṃ.*I.2–4, III.1–3, VI.1–6, VII.1; *Taitt.Br.* I.1–1, I.4.1–6; I.5.4, II.2.8; *Śat.Br.*III–IV; *Ait.Br.* I–15; *Āp.Sr.*X–XIV; *Kāt.Sr.* VII–XI, *Baudh.Sr.* VI–X; *Āśv.Sr.* IV–VI.

agniṣṭut A Vedic sacrifice to be performed by one who has committeed murder unintentionally. It is a form of Ekāha (q.v.). Manu XI.74. prescribes Aśvamedha, Gosava or Agnistut and several other sacrifices for the removal of the grave sin of Brāhmaṇa murder. For details see *Taitt.Br.* II.7.12, *Āśv.Sr.* IX.7.22–23.

agnitanu A formula required for establishing the Āhavanīya-fire (q.v.) given in *Āp.Sr.* V.13.7.

agnyādheya Also known as Agnyādhāna; it is the first of the seven Haviryajñas (q.v.) and belongs to the nature of Iṣṭi (q.v.). It occupies two days, the first day called *upavastha* being taken up by primary matters and the second with the performance of the main rites. Agnyādheya means the placing of burning coals for the generation of Gārhapatya (q.v.) and other fires at a particular time and place by a particular person to the accompaniment of certain *mantras*. It comprises several acts. First the *araṇis* (two wooden logs) are brought as an offering for the *pūrṇāhūti* (the complete and final offering). The sacrificer and his wife wearing silken garments have to establish fire, which is brought in the afternoon by the Adhvaryu priest; grains are cooked on it; this cooked food is called *brahmaudana* and is to be eaten by the Brāhmaṇas. The sacrificer observes a vow of silence and staying awake that night. At daybreak the Adhvaryu heats two *araṇis* to make a new fire after which the old one on which *brahmaudana* was cooked is extinguished. He invokes the fire with *mantras*. Each of the new fires kindled from the older ones has a special name. The Adhvaryu makes the sacrificer repeat in the right-ear of the sacrificial horse the Agnitanu-formulae (q.v.). Fires are set up in different parts of the sacrificial area with *mantras* and rites and these are propitiated by butter and fuel-sticks after repeating certain formulae. The Sāmans (q.v.) are sung by the Brahmā priests (q.v.) in Agnyādheya. There is no Udgātṛ (q.v.) priest. After the final offering, the sacrificer gives gifts, mutters certain auspicious formulae and waits in worship upon three or five fires. If the sacrificer is a Kṣatriya dice play takes place (cf. Rājasūya). Gifts are given to the priests as specified in accordance with the sacrificer's ability. After establishing the Vedic fires the sacrificer should observe complete celibacy for twelve nights. *Taitt. Br.* I.1.2–10, 1.2.1; *Śat.Br.* II.1–2; *Āśv.Sr.*-II.1.9 ff; *Āp.Sr.* V.1–22; *Kāt.Sr.* IV.7–10; *Baudh Sr.* II.6–21.

agrahaṇa Non-apprehension; an aspect of *avidyā* (q.v.) according to Maṇḍana. *Brahmasiddhi* III.

agrahāyaṇī A domestic rite of renovation, raised to the rank of Pākayajña (q.v.), performed on the full moon day of the month of Mārgaśīrṣa or Agrahāyana (Nov-Dec). Having renovated the house with plaster and by levelling the floor, after sunset the performers offer oblations of *pāyasa* (milk-rice) to various deities with *mantras* from the *Ṛgveda.* The Brāhmaṇas are fed and their blessings are sought. *Pār.Gr.*III.2, *Gobhila Gr.* III.9, *Mānava Gr.* II.7.1–15; *Bhār.Gr.* II.2; *Āp.Gr.* XIX.3–5; *Kāṭhaka Gr.* LX.1 ff., *Hir.Gr.* II.17.1

agra-maṇḍapa Entrance porch of a temple, same as mukha-maṇḍapa.

āgrayana The rite of the offering of first corn. It is also called Navayajña in *Gobhila Smrti* III.103

and Navasasyeṣṭi in Manu IV.17. As a form of Iṣṭi (q.v.) it is prescribed in the *Āśvalāyana* II. 9 and other Śrauta sūtras or those who have consecrated the three Vedic fires. This rite is also mentioned in the Gṛhyasūtras for those who have not set up the Śrauta fires. Having prepared a mixture of cooked food with fresh corn the performer of this rite offers oblations to various deities. He then fills his mouth with grains of rice, swallows them, takes *ācamana* (q.v.) and having rolled up a lump of rice throws it up on the top of his house (*Āp.Gr.* XIX.6–7). The *Vaikhānasa* IV.2 connects it with the Pitṛs. According to the *Mānava Gr.* II. 3.9–14 Āgrayaṇa should be performed in spring with the first barley and in autumn with the first rice. *Āśv.Gr.* II.2, *Śāṅ.Gr.* III.8, *Pār.Gr.* III.1, *Gobhila Gr.* III.8.9–24; *Khadira Gr.* III.3.6–15.

ahamgrahopāsanā The form of worship which, according to Appaya Dikṣita's commentary on the *Bhavanopaniṣad*, is based upon the feeling of total identity of the worshipper and the deity.

ahaṃkāra The principle of egoity; it is the second evolute of Prakṛti (q.v.) according to the Sāṅkhya. It determines one's attitude towards the objects of the world and is of three kinds. The first called *vaikārika* or *sāttvika*, owing to its relation to the *sattva* (q.v.) element, gives rise to five Jñānendriyas (q.v.) or organs of perception, five Karmendriyas (q.v.) or organs of action and Manas (q.v.) or mind. The second kind of Ahaṃkāra called *rājasa*, owing to its relation with *rajas* (q.v.) serves as a link between the products of the first and those of the third, *tāmasa* (owing to its affiliation with the *tamas* element), which germinates the five Tanmātras (q.v.) or the subtle elements. *Śāṅ.Kārikā* 25, *Śāṅ.Pra.Bhāṣya* II.18. In Tantra, *ahaṃkāra* is brought in relation to *ājñācakra* (q.v.), one of the six nerve plexuses situated within the body. According to Tamil Śaivism *ahaṃkāra* or egoity is produced from *buddhi* or intellect and in turn produces *taijasa* (sense organs), *vaikṛta* (organs of action) and *tanmātra* (five subtle elements). *Mṛgendra Āgama* II.3–7, III.1 etc. *Pauṣkara* II.17, III.4, V.9.

āhavanīya One of the three fires for Vedic rites, collectively called Tretā, others being Gārhapatya (q.v.) and Dakṣiṇa (q.v.). The Āhavanīya fireplace is square, Gārhapatya is round and Dakṣiṇa is in the form of half the orb of the moon. Its place is to the east of the Gārhapatya at a distance of eight *prakarmas*. The procedure for establishing the Āhavanīya stipulates that the fire be established when half of the sun's disc rises above the eastern horizon.

ahiṃsā The doctrine of non-violence; Buddhism and Jainism are based on this and its ideals are also appreciated and upheld in Brahmanism. In a wide sense non-violence means that one should not harm others, avoid exploitation for furthering one's own interests, and behave with others as one would wish them to behave. One should take only what one needs, control one's desires and not be jealous of the comforts of others. Jainism regards vegetarian food, fasting, self-purification, suffering hardships and forgiveness as unavoidable for the pursuit of non-violence. In a narrow sense Ahiṃsā emphasises non-killing of animals for religious purposes. The *Ch.Up.*VIII.15.1 says that wise men who have attained correct knowledge should not cause any injury to living beings. One reason for the insistence on Ahiṃsā was the metaphysical concept that all life was one and that even the meanest insect was a manifestation of the divine essence, and hence it should not be destroyed. The other reason was probably the idea of defilement caused by eating flesh. The sentence *ahiṃsā paramo dharmaḥ* occurs, frequently in the *Mbh.*VII.192.38, XIII.115.25, etc. cf. *Vasiṣṭha* IV.4, *Manu* X.63, *Yāj.* I.122. *Vāmana Pu.* XIV.1–2, The *Brahmāṇḍa Pu.*II.31.35 says that Ahiṃsā is the door of *dharma* while the *Padma* Pu V. 43.38 holds that there is no *dāna* or *tapas* equal to Ahiṃsā.

ahīna A class of soma sacrifices (q.v.) extending over more than one day. Aśvamedha (q.v.), Dvādasāha (q.v.) etc., belong to this class.

āhitāgni One who has kindled and maintained Vedic fires. Śabara on *Jaimini* XI.3.34 says that when the person who has maintained the sacred fires dies, he is cremated with his Vedic fires and with his sacrificial vessels.

āhnika Daily duties of an individual forming one aspect of the Ācāras (q.v.). The principal matters of the Āhnika are Śauca (q.v.) or rules relating to bodily purity, Saṃdhyā (q.v.), Tarpaṇa (q.v.), the five Mahāyajñas (q.v.), attending the fire, Bhojana (q.v.) obtaining wealth, studying and teaching, gifts, going to bed, and performing sacrifices at certain stated times. The *Parāśarasmṛti* I.39 summarises the most important daily duties as bathing, performing the Saṃdhyā prayers, *japa*, *homa*, worship of gods and honouring of guests and Vaiśvadevas. Manu IV.52 also enumerates the principal daily actions which must be performed in the morning: answering the call of nature, toilet, bathing, brushing the teeth, applying collyrium to the eyes and worship of the gods. The word Āhnika is derived from *ahaḥ* which stands for the period from sunrise to sunrise including day and night.

āhuti Offering of different articles to gods through the medium of fire, the commonly used article being clarified butter. The Adhvaryu puts butter into the butter-pot which is placed on the Gārhapatya (q.v.) fire to melt. There are two spoons, one for dipping (*sruva*) and the other for offering (*juhu*). Two blades of *darbha* grass, put into the heated butter, are used as strainers. The offering is made while uttering of the formula *agnaya idam na mama*.

aikādaśina A special form of group sacrifice of eleven animals to Agni, Sarasvatī, Soma, Puṣan, Bṛhaspati, Viśvadevas, Indra, Maruts, Indra-Agni, Savitṛ and Varuṇa *Āśv.Sr.* III.7–8, *Āp.Sr.* XIV.5–7; *Jaimini* II.3.19, VIII.1.14. IX.4.56–60.

aikabhāvika The doctrine according to which if one can refrain from actions prompted by the desire of fruits of the action (*kāmya*) and those prohibited by the scriptures as well as perform the obligatory ones (*nitya*), one may achieve liberation.

aikya-sthala Vīra Śaiva concept of the state of identity (*sama-rasabhakti*) with *mahāliṅga*, the supreme entity. See under Ṣaṭ-sthala.

aiṅginī Śakti or energy of Gaṇeśa.

airiṇidāna A rite subsequent to marriage in which the mother of the bridegroom is presented with a basket of bamboo containing lighted lamps. It is mentioned in the *Saṃskāra-Kaustubha* of Anantadeva.

aiśvarya Power and almightiness that constitute the essence of godhead. The term is also used to denote divine wealth which is of six types. See under Ṣaḍaiśvarya.

ajamantra The multiplicity of individual souls (*puruṣabahutva*) as vaguely indicated in *Śvetāśvatara* IV.5

ajapā A special form of effortless meditation. Rāghavabhaṭṭa on *Śāradātilaka* XIV.91. The sounds *haṃ* and *saḥ* processed by the movements of breath themselves constitute the *mantra* and hence there is no need of muttering anything. The automatic constitution of the *haṃsa-mantra* takes place simultaneously in *mūlādhāra* (q.v.), *anāhata* (q.v.) and *ājñā* Cakras (q.v.). *Gheraṇḍa* V.85. Ajapā is two-fold—secret and expressed. The latter is again divided into two categories—sound and light. See under Haṃsa.

ajātivada The view that no world was ever produced at all. It purports to hold that the cause (*brahman*) only is real while the effect (world) is an illusion, as false as a dream, because the former cannot be the subject of transformation or transfiguration. Its best and earliest exponent is Gauḍapāda. *Māṇḍukyakārikā* IV.22,70.

ajīva Non-living entities among the Astikāya (q.v.) objects in Jain belief. They consist of the objects responding to the sense-organs and are classified into *rūpa*, i.e. those *with* form like Pudgala (q.v.) or matter and *arūpa*, i.e. those *without* form like Dharma (q.v.), Adharma (q.v.), Ākāśa (q.v.) and Kāla (q.v.). These five categories constitute the world or *loka* and beyond is the immeasurable infinite called *aloka*, *PTSMS*, 3.

ājīvika The doctrine of immutability or a predetermined fate propagated by the religious order established by Gośāla Maṅkhaliputta, a senior contemporary of the Buddha and Mahāvīra. The term is also applied to the followers of this doctrine. Gośāla had two spiritual predecessors, namely Nanda Vacca and Kisa Saṃkicca. Two other contemporaries of Gośāla, Puraṇa Kassapa and Pakudha Kaccāyana, also seem to have contributed to the growth of this doctrine. From the combined testimony of the Jain and Buddhist sources we learn that according to Gośāla, all beings are subject to a fixed and unchangeable series of existence, each of which has its own unalterable characteristics. He denies the effect of action and energy, since he holds that every being is helpless, unable either to help himself or others. This doctrine is described in the *Majjhima Nikāya* (I.409, II.121) as *ahetuka* (denying cause) and *akiriyā* (denying the effects of action). Mahāvīra was closely associated with Gośāla and was to a certain extent influenced by him. The general outcome of Ājīvīkism is the doctrine of Niyati (q.v.) or Destiny which has however nothing to do with Jainism. However, Jainism and Ajivikism have many points in common. The Ājīvīkas believed in the existence of seven elemental categories described as unmanufactured, barren and firm, neither moving, nor developing, nor affecting one another. They had their own epistemology and logic. The main sources of information on Gośāla and Ājīvīkism are *Bhagavatī* XV.I with Abhayadeva's com. *Suyagaḍa*

I.2.1–14, I.4.7–9, II.1.29, II.6 with Śīlāṅka's com. *Aupapātika* 118, 120, *Dīgha* I.53–54 with Buddhaghoṣa's com., *Saṃyutta* III.69, *Aṅguttara* I.286, etc.

ājñacakra One of the six nerve-plexuses of the Tantric tradition. It is situated between the eyebrows, and looks like a two-petalled white lotus, symbolised by the letters *ha* and *kṣa*. It is regarded as the seat of mind. *Ṣaṭcakranirūpaṇa* XXXII. Ājñā denotes command, evidently of the Guru (q.v.) who is supposed to reside symbolically within the nerve-cycle. *Saubhāgyabhāskara* on *Lalitāsahasranāma* 90. Within the pericarp of the lotus resides the six-faced and white-complexioned goddess Hākinī.

ajñāna Ignorance (also known by the terms Avidyā and Aviveka) which is the basic cause of all misery and bondage according to all schools of Indian thought. According to Buddhism, human misery and suffering, like all else, depend on certain conditions there being a chain of cause and effect which leads to suffering in this world. If the transitory, painful nature of the worldly existence was perfectly realized, there would not arise any *karma* resulting in rebirth. Ignorance or Avidyā is therefore the root cause of tendencies that cause rebirth. It is the first constituent of the twelve sources (*dvādasá-nidāna*) of the wheel of existence (*bhavacakra*). See under *Paṭiccasamuppāda*. According to the Sāṅkhya tradition, ignorance or Aviveka is the cause of suffering. This ignorance is due to the lack of *vivekajñāna* (q.v.) which is the discrimination between the experiencing subject (*draṣṭā*) and experienced object (*dṛśya*). *Sāñ. Kārikā* 62. *Sāñ. Prav. Bh.* 3.72. According to Vedānta, ignorance, i.e., Ajñāna or Avidyā, has the double function of concealment (*āvaraṇa) and* distortion (*vikṣepa*) of reality. Illusion is the product of ignorance; it prevents one from seeing the real nature of the thing and makes one see something else in its place. In the Tantric tradition it is divided into two kinds, *pauruṣa* which concerns human nature, and *bauddha* which concerns intellect. The former is known as *ānava-mala* which is the root of worldly existence. *Tantrāloka* I.55. Vṛtti on *Paraśurāmakalpasūtra* I.3.

ajñānavāda Scepticism and Agnosticism. Mahāvīra's term Aṇṇāniya or Ajñānika evidently refers to Sañjaya Belaṭṭhiputta and his school (*Sūyagaḍa* I.6.27, I.12.1–2, II.2.79, *Uttarādhyayana* XVIII.3) corresponding to the Amarāvikkhepikas (q.v.) or evasive disputants of the Buddhists who refused to give categorical answers to the questions put to them. The Jain texts mention 67 kinds of Ajñānavāda.

ājya Clarified butter; it is used for Homa (q.v.) unless otherwise expressly specified. Oridnarily it is made from cow's milk. She-buffalo's ghee or sesame oil may also be substituted.

ājyabhāga The names of two actions with ājya (q.v.) regarded as the eyes of Yajña (q.v.). The Adhvaryu (q.v.) asks the Hotṛ (q.v.) to recite the anuvākya (invitatory verse) for Agni and offers clarified butter in the northern and most blazing part of the Āhavanīya (q.v.). The second action is also of the same nature and is rendered to Soma. The Ājyabhāgas under different conditions are known as Vārtraghna and Vṛdhanvantau *Āśv. Sr.* I.5.32ff, *Jaimini* III.1.23 *Taitt.S.*, II.5.2.1, *Śat. Br.* I.6.3.38.

ākāṅkṣā Nyāya-Vaiśeṣika law of mutual expectancy. According to this law each word in a sentence must carry some meaning which is by itself incomplete and raises some expectation.

akārakavāda The doctrine of fortuitous causation. Different groups of the Akriyāvādins (q.v.) subscribed to it.

ākāśa Space in Jain cosmic conception which falls into the Ajiva (q.v.) category. It is divided into Lokākāśa (the part occupied by the world of things) and Alokākāśa (the space beyond it which is absolutely void and empty). In the Lokākāśa this universe forms only a part. Ākāśa is that which gives space and makes room for the existence of all extended substances. If a lamp is lighted it is the space or Ākāśa that makes room for its beams to shine. Likewise a wall may be the Ākāśa for a nail to be knocked into. Ākāśa is divided into *skandha, deśa* and *pradeśa*. (Guṇaratna on *SDSC* 49). According to the Nyāya-Vaiśeṣika, Ākāśa or ether is the fifth physical substance which is the substratum of the quality of sound. It is one, eternal, an all pervading physical substance which is imperceptible. In the Sāṅkhya, Ākāśa is one of the five *mahābhūtas* or gross physical elements having the specific property of sound. The Cārvākas hold that the world is made of four elements and exclude the fifth element Ākāśa on the ground that its existence cannot be perceived. In Buddhism Ākāśa belongs to the *asaṃskṛta* or unconstituted category. It is defined as an open space without any obstructing object. It is infinite, however much it may remain covered and uncovered. The Vaibhāṣikas admit its existence as real. *AKV* I.5. The term Ākāśadhātu is also used by the Buddhists. *Bodhisattvabhūmi* 14ff.

ākāśagāmī Sādhyas and Siddhas (*qq.v.*) belonging to the class of Vyantara-devatās (q.v.)

ākhyāna Legends relating to the events of hoary antiquity which were very often recited by the Hotṛ (q.v.) in sacrifices before a select audience as part of the ritual.

akhyāti Prabhākara's theory which explains errors as the experience of a false presentation in which there is only a mental omission (*asaṃsargagraha*). In Kashmir Śaivism the term denotes non-intention.

akiriyadiṭṭhi The viewpoint of non-action which leads to the rejection of the right way according to Buddhism. *Visuddhimagga* 513.

akriyāvāda The doctrine of non-action which is virtually opposed to Kriyāvāda (q.v.). The Jain accounts elaborate Akriyāvāda into 84 varieties. The *Sūyagaḍa* I.12.4 states that the Akriyāvādins teach the annihilation of good actions by denying the potentialities of *Karma* (q.v.) in future existence. They believe that all human actions and endeavours are futile. The *Thāna* IV.4. mentions eight classes of Akriyāvādins: (1) Ekkavādins or Monists, Theists and Monotheists; (2) Anikkavādins or Pluralists; (3) Mitavādins or Extensionists; (4) Nimittavādins or Cosmogonists; (5) Sāyavadins or Sensualists; (6) Samucchedavādins or Annihilationists; (7) Niyavādins or Eternalists; and (8) Na-Santi Paralokavādins or Materialists. The *Ācaraṅga-Ṭīkā* (ed. Dhanapati 14) mentions six types of Akriyāvadins: the upholders of the doctrines of Kāla (q.v.), Īśvara (q.v.), Ātman (q.v.), Niyati (q.v.), Svabhāva (q.v.) and Yadṛcchā (q.v.) as the first principles. The doctrines of Purana Kassapa, Pakudha Kaccāyana, Gośāla Maṅkhaliputra and a few other contemporaries of the Buddha and Mahāvira are in close agreement with the views upheld by the Akriyāvādins. *Suyagada* I.12.4–10.

akṣamālā The string of beads carried by saints or religious minded persons and used in icons. It is made of various objects, the most popular of which is a kind of dried seed called *rudrākṣa*.

akṣara One of the forms of *brahman* (q.v.), the others being *kāla* (time), *karma* (action) and *svabhāva* (nature) according to the Vallabhites. Akṣara appears in the forms of Prakṛti (q.v.) and Puruṣa (q.v.), the former developing through many stages. *Tattvārthadīpa* I.94, II.86. The *puruṣa* of the cosmology in *Muṇḍaka Up.* II.1.1. ff. is identical with *akṣara* with which creation starts. Creation is thought to be as an emanatory process in *Muṇḍaka* I.1, II.1, III.2, similar to the springing forth of hair or nail from the body, sparks from a fire or the web from a spider, so that from the viewpoint of created objects the First Cause might be conceived as the *avyakta*, i.e. as their totality in an unmanifested form, while in itself it is called *akṣara* or the immutable which is identical with *puruṣa* inasmuch as the distinction between the subject and the object does not hold good prior to creation.

akṣayatṛtīyā Third lunar day of the bright half of the month of Vaiśākha (May-June); it is regarded as auspicious for performing rituals. Gifts of pitchers filled with water, together with sweets and seasonal fruits, are held to be conducive to the benefit of departed ancestors.

akula The Śiva aspect of Śakti according to the Tantras. Akulasyāsya devasya kulaprathanaśālinī, *Tantrāloka* III.67. According to Abhinavagupta that which is manifested from Kula or Śakti is *akula* and is endowed with the elements of Śiva.

akusalakarmapatha Seven evil deeds according to the Buddhist way of life; they are *prāṇātipāta* (taking life), *adattadāna* (stealing), *Kāme-mithyācāra* (misconduct), *anṛtavacana* (telling lies), *piśunavacana* (malignant speech), *paruṣavacana* (harsh speech) and *sambhinnapralāpa* (frivolous talks).

alakhnāmi A medieval liberal religious sect; the formless and incomprehensible one; it was founded by Lalgir also known as Lalbeg. The followers of this sect do not worship images, but meditate upon the invisible one; their creed is non-violence, catholicity, charity and purity. The sect has a wide distribution in the Bikaner region of Rajasthan. They greet each other with the words *alakh-kaho*.

ālambana-pratyaya The conception of the non-spirituality of the living self. The term is used by the Vijñānavādin Buddhists. The conception of *bhūtātman* of the Cārvākas is also in almost the same sense.

ālambhana A term for sacrifice.

alaukika Things transcendent and so subject to never-ending enquiry. Ordinarliy it is a term used for denoting the supernatural.

alaukika-pratyakṣa Extraordinary perception; according to the Nyāya, it is of three kinds·

sāmānyalakṣaṇa or perception of classes, *jñāna-lakṣaṇa* or perception of experience and *yogaja or* intuitive perception.

ālaya-vijñāna The Buddhist Yogācāra-Vijñāna-vāda concept of mind as the home of all latent ideas. It may be regarded as the potential-mind, which through culture and control can stop the illusion of external objects and attachment to them. It is not an unchanging substance like *ātman* (q.v.), the soul of other systems, but is a stream of continuously changing states.

ālīḍha A particular *āsana*, or attitude of legs found in seated cult images. It resembles the attitude adopted in drawing the bow charged with an arrow: the right leg is outstretched while the left is slightly bent. When the position of the legs is reversed, it is called Pratyālīḍha.

āliṅgana-mūrti One of the placid forms of Śiva images depicting the god with his consort Umā, often in an embracing posture.

alokākāśa See under Ākāśa.

āḷvār South Indian devotional poets who popularised the 'love and devotion' concept of Vaiṣṇavism between the sixth and the ninth century A.D. Twelve such Āḷvār saints are known who may be regarded as the precursors of the later Vaisnava Ācāryas. More than 4000 songs of these Āḷvārs have come to light and have been collected in an anthology called *Pravandham*.

amākalā A type of Kalā (q.v.) or the active aspect of Śakti. It is equated with *Ṣoḍaśīkalā* in *Ṣaṭcakra-vivṛti* and described as eternal and creative containing nectar flowing from the union of Śiva and Śakti. See *Tantric Texts* II, 130. It has also been brought in relation to the phases of the moon. It is said to reside within the triangle of *sahasrāra* lotus.

āmantraṇa Invitation; this is same as Nimantraṇa according to *Manu* III.187, 191. But Pāṇini III.3.161 considers there to be a difference between the meanings of the two words. According to the *Mahābhāṣya*, Āmantraṇa is an invitation which one is free to reject without incurring blame and that which if rejected without proper cause involves a fault or sin is called Nimantraṇa.

amarāvikkhepika Evasive disputants mentioned in the *Brahmajāla-sutta* who declined to give any categorical answer to the questions relating to life and universe This school corresponds to the Ājñānavāda (q.v.) of the Jain texts. Sáñjaya Belaṭṭhiputta, a contemporary of Buddha and Mahāvīra, belonged to this line of thinking. *Dīgha* I.

amāśrāddha Śrāddha (q.v.) with uncooked grains to be performed in the forenoon. It may be offered by one who is eligible to offer Pārvaṇa-śrāddha (q.v.). It is prescribed mainly for the Śūdras. It may also be performed by twice-born persons when Brāhmaṇas or sacrificial materials are not easily available or when one is on a journey or when one's wife is menstruating or in child birth. *Skanda* VII.1.206.52, *Saura* XIX.32, *Madan-apārijāta* 483.

amāvasyā New-moon night which is of two kinds, Sinīvālī and Kuhū. On the former an *āhitāgni*, one who maintains the Śrauta-fire, and on the latter the Śūdras and those who do not keep Śrauta fire should offer Śrāddha (q.v.). In the *AV* it is addressed as a deity. *Gaut. Dh.S.* XV.1–2.

ambuvācī Ritual connected with fertility and vegetation symbolising the period of the earth's menstruation commencing between the seventh and eleventh day of the month of *āṣāḍha* (June-July). During this period widows must follow certain taboos since the act of procreation is forbidden to them. During the days of *ambuvācī* ploughing, sowing and other farm work is forbidden.

āmikṣā Also known as Payasyā, it is a form of milk offered to Viśve Devaḥ or All-Gods. Milk is drawn in the morning and heated, then the sour milk from the preceding evening is added to it. The mixture divides itself into two portions, the solid one being called Āmikṣā and the liquid above it Vājina. Śabara on *Jaimini* II.2.23, IV.1.22; *Baudh.Sr.* V.1.

āmnāya Zones in Tantric culture, five or six in number. *Kulārṇava* III.7, *Śaktisaṅgama*, Sundarī, V.182–87.

amṛta Immortality; the ultimate goal of life in the form of self-realization. It is also conceived of in terms of nectar-essence which, according to the Tantric tradition, may be consumed from the body itself by Yogic processes, to revitalise the body. According to the Raseśvara school (q.v.) it may be prepared chemically.

amṛtīkaraṇa Purification of the deity according to the Tantric rites. The aspirant should recite three times the *mūla-mantra*, the *dipanī-mantra* and the *mātṛka*, then with letters and then with *dhenu-mudrā* he should sprinkle water on the head of the deity. *Puraścaryārṇava* V. 343.

aṃśa Part of the whole. It is subdivided into *kalā*—a portion of a part, and *kalāṃśa*—a part of a portion. Lesser deities are very often regarded as representing *aṃśa, kalā*, and *kalāṃśa* of a powerful deity.

anābhoga-nirnimitta-vihāra Also known as Acalā, it is the fourth stage in the ten *bhūmis* of Bodhisattvahood. This stage, also known as the immovable stage, marks a definite advance in the progress of the potential Bodhisattva who now knows where and when he will become a Buddha by usual prophecy (*vyākaraṇa*).

anadhyāya Days of cessation from Veda study. On the 1st, 8th, 14th and 15th *tithis* of the bright and dark half of the month there should be a cessation of Vedic study for the whole day. *Yāj* I. 148–51 speaks of 37 *tatkālika-anadhyāyas* when Vedic study is suspended as long as the occasion or disturbance stated lasts. Owing to natural calamities or deaths or other reasonable grounds Vedic study may be stopped. The subject of Anadhyāya is discussed in the Gṛhya and Dharma Sûtras and in almost all Smṛtis. *Taitt.Ār.* II.5, *Ait.Ār.* V.3.3, *Āp.Dh.S.* I. 3.9.4 to I.3.11, *Gaut.* XIV.5–49; *Sāṅ.Gr.* IV.7; *Manu*, IV.102–128, *Yāj* I.144–51. The *Ap.Sr.* XXIV.1. 37 says that the rules about Anadhyāya apply only to the learning of Vedic mantras, but do not apply to the performance of various rites. Jaimini XII.3.18–19 establishes the proposition that the rules about Anadhyāya being prescribed for acquisition of the Vedic *mantras* have no application in the performance of sacrifices.

anāgāmi One of the fruits of sanctification accruing to those who have advanced spiritually. An Anāgāmi gets rid of five lower fetters (*sakkāyadiṭṭhi, vicikicchā, silabbataparāmāsa, kāmacchanda* and *vyāpāda* q.v.) and destroys completely three hindrances (*rāga, doṣa* and *moha*, qq.v.). The Anāgāmis are divided in five subclasses, namely, Antarāparinibbāyi (q.v.), Upahaccaparinibbāyi (q.v.), Asaṅkhāraparinibbāyi (q.v.), Sasaṅkhāraparinibbāyi (q.v.) and Uddhaṃsola Akaniṭṭhagāmi (q.v.). *Visuddhimagga* 84ff, *Puggalapannatti* 16ff.

anāhata One of the six nerve-plexuses (*ṣaṭcakra*) situated in the heart region. It is conceived of as a twelve-petalled lotus and is the seat of the element of air. The goddess Kākinī is its presiding deity. Anāhata is also the name of a particular form of sound.

anākhya-śakti One of the five concepts of Śakti found in the *Krama* (q.v.) doctrine.

ānanda Bliss or rather pure bliss-consciousness in which the distinction of subject and object ceases. It is the state of *mukti* (q.v.), *mokṣa* (q.v.) or *nirvāṇa* (q.v.) in which the self becomes free from all fetters. In all Indian religious and philosophical traditions *ānanda* or bliss is a characteristic of *brahman*, others being *sat* (existence) and *cit* (consciousness).

ānandabhairava, bhairavī The chief male and female deities of the *bhairavī-cakra* (q.v.). Their meditation on them is necessary for the purification of wine. *Prāṇatoṣaṇi* VII.2, 511. For the *mantras* used in meditation see *Mahānirvāṇa* VIII.166–67.

ānandakanda Name of the eight-petalled lotus in the *anāhata-cakra*.

ānandanātha A name generally prefixed before the term *guru*. *Śáktisaṅgama*, Sundarī, I. 139–40.

anantacaturdaśī A vrata or observance celebrated on the 14th day of the bright half of *bhādrapada* (August-September); it consists mainly in the worship of Visnu as Ananta and in wearing, on the right hand for men and the left hand for women, a holy strap or thread made of cotton or silk and dyed with saffron.

ānantariya kamma Immoralities and offences belonging to the category of the most heinous ones according to Buddhism.

anantaśayana Iconic representation of Viṣṇu which shows him recumbent on the folds of the great snake Ādi or Ananta Nāga, with the hoods serving as a canopy over his head.

ananta-viññāna Infinite consciousness; which is often wrongly understood as the state of Nirvāṇa. *Suttanipāta* 198, *Saṃyutta* I. 13, *Dīgha* I. 223, *Majjhima* I. 329, *Papañcasūdanī* I. 413.

anarpita-hāra A *hāra* (q.v.) or string of miniature shrines standing free from the main wall of the *vimāna* (q.v.).

anasakti-yoga Also known as Asparśa-yoga, it is the doctrine of non-attachment which strikes the balance between *pravṛtti* (desire) and *nivṛtti* (extinction of desire). It takes away the sting or the binding taint from *karma* (q.v.) by the surrender of its fruit or by dedicating it to the supreme being and by the disinterested discharge of it as one's ordained duty. *Manu.* I.89ff.

anāsrava dharma(s) Pure elements of which the Buddhas are supposed to be made. These objects or elements are *śīla, samādhi, prajñā, vimukti* and *vimuktijñāna* and not the ordinary ones like *rūpa, vedanā, saṃjñā, saṃskāra* and *vijñāna* which are known as Sāsrava-dharmas.

anastikāya Substances which, according to Jain cosmological speculations, fall in the category of 'non-extended'. Every substance possesses extension, with the exception only of Time or Kāla (q.v.) which is devoid of extension and hence falls into the Anastikāya group. See under Samaya.

anātmā, anāttavāda The theory of the non-existence of soul. This is one of the central teachings of Buddhism. It holds that the conception of *ātman* as a permanent substance cannot explain the continuity of a person through different births or through the different states of childhood, youth and old age caused by the law of universal change and impermanence: Life is an unbroken stream of successive states which are causally connected and this stream extends backward and forward making the past, present and future lives continuous. Just as a chariot is a collection of wheels, axles, shafts, etc. so also man is constituted of body (*kāya*), mind (*manas* or *citta*), consciousness (*vijñāna*) and faculties in which there is no room for soul. Also see under Anattā.

anattā Anātman or absence of soul which is the subject matter of Buddha's second discourse. In the Pali texts it is stated that the belief in the existence of soul, or in other words, the heresy of individuality (*sakkāya-diṭṭhi*) is due to the misapprehension of one of the five constituents (*khandakas*) as the soul. In *Mādhyamikavṛtti* 432 and *Paṭisambidāmagga* I. 146–50 is explained how this misapprehension takes place—when the object of meditation is converted into a concept identical with one's self like the flame of a burning lamp with its colour; when the *khandakas* (constituents of a being) are conceived of as belonging to the self like a tree and its shadow; when they are conceived as existing in the self like smell and flower; or when they are conceived of as the container of the self just as a casket is of a jewel. According to the Buddhists *attā* (*ātman*) or soul does not exist. It is only a word of common usage. *Dīgha* I. 202. If there is soul, it should either be identical to—one or more than—all the *khandakas* (constituents of a being) or be wholly different from them. Both the above propositions, according to the Buddhists, are wrong (*micchā-diṭṭhi*) *Dīgha* II. 338. *Mādhyamikavṛtti* 432 ff, *Mādhyamakāvatāra* Tib. ed. 435, *Milinda* 55, 86.

anavalobhana A rite to ensure the safety of a pregnancy. It is also known as Garbharakṣaṇa, and apparently a part of Puṃsavana (q.v.). This rite is so called because by virtue of its performance the foetus does not fall out, nor is it destroyed. A drug called *durvārasa* is dropped in the woman's right nostril to the accompaniment of prayers to the gods and offering a sacrifice of cooked food to Prajāpati. *Āśv.Gr.* I.13.5–7.

anāvaraṇa-vimokṣa-jñāna The unscreened knowledge of emancipation which a potential Bodhisattva attains in the third stage of his spiritual progress known as Prabhakarī (q.v.) or Adhicittavihāra (q.v.).

anavasthollāsa The last state of spiritual progress according to some Tantric schools. The preceding stages are *ārambha, taruṇa, yauvana, prauḍha, tadanta* and *unmana*. According to the *Paraśurāmakalpasūtra* X. 68, the first four stages belong to the Samayācāra and the last three, *anavasthā* included, to Svairācāra. At this stage the mind of the aspirant becomes totally absorbed in the deity.

āṇavī-dīkṣā One of the three forms of *dīkṣa* (q.v.) or initiation mentioned in the *Rudrayāmala*. The other two forms are Śakti and Śāmbhavī. It is an elaborate system of initiation in which *mantra, arcanā, āsana, nyāsa, dhyāna* and different *upacāras* or articles are required. *Prāṇatoṣaṇī* II.4.117. It is of various types like *smārtī, mānasīkī, yaugī, cākṣuṣī, spārsanī, vācikī, māntrikī, hotrī, śāstrī* and *abhiṣecakī*. Rāghava's com. on *Śāradātilaka* V.127–40.

ānavopāya A means of spiritual attainment which is also known as *kriyā-upāya* in Tantrism. Though *kriyā* means action, it is used in the sense of knowledge: According to Abhinavagupta when knowledge is derived after the control of desires it is known as *kriyā*. *Tantrāloka* I.151. The knowledge by which *ānavopāya* or *kriyā-upāya* is characterised is, however, dualistic and to some extent dependent on external objects. *Ibid.* I. 219–20.

aṇḍaka Turret-design for temples.

andhaka The Buddhist Śaila schools are collectively known by this name including also the Rājagirikas and Siddhatthikas. Their views are mostly in agreement with those of the Mahāsaṅghikas (q.v.)

anekāntavāda The doctrine of non-absolutism which characterises Jain logic. Any dogmatic claim of a particular viewpoint (*ekāntavāda*), it says, amounts to the fallacy of exclusive predication. Reality is so complex in its structure that it baffles all attempts to describe it directly, completely and finally. Hence the limitation of a particular judgement and the possibility of other alternative judgements which should be acknowledged. For example, an object may be described affirmatively by a judgement which predicates of it any of the characteristics it possesses, or it may be described negatively by denying amongst its characteristics that which is absent but which may belong to other objects. Hence the Jain logicians insist on the conditional or relative character of both the affirmative and negative judgements. See under Syādvāda and Naya.

aṅga A class of Jain canonical literature; it comprises twelve texts which are supposed to have been compiled in a special assembly summoned at Pāṭaliputra (fourth century B.C.) and finalised at the council of Valabhī (fifth-sixth century A.D.). The texts are *Āyāra* (Ācāra), *Sūyagaḍa* (Sūtrakṛta), *Ṭhāna* (Sthāna), *Samavāya*, *Viyāhapaññatti* (Vyākhyāprajñapti), *Nāyādhammakahāo* (Jñātādharma-kathā), *Uvāsagadasāo* (Upāsakadaśā), *Panhāvāgaraṇaim* (Praśnavyākaraṇāni), *Antagaḍadasāo* (Antaḥkṛddaśā), *Anuttarovavāiyadasāo* (Anuttarapapādikadaśā), *Vivāgasuya* (Vipākaśrūta) and *Diṭṭhivāya* (Dṛṣṭivāda, now non-existent). The Digambaras consider the existing versions of all the Aṅga texts to be wholly spurious. In Brahmanical tradition *aṅga* denotes parts of limbs and also applies to sacred texts. Six *aṅgas* of the Vedas are well known. The Buddhist scriptures are also supposed to be divided into twelve *aṅgas* (*dvādasāṅga*).

aṅgahāra Movements of limbs dependent on *karaṇas* or postures. See under *mudrā*.

aṅganyāsa Feeling of the deity in the different parts of the body. It is five-fold (*pañcāṅga*) or sixfold (ṣaḍaṅga). The centres are heart, head, protective symbol, eyes and intestines. See under *nyāsa*.

anicca See under Anityatā.

anikkavāda Pluralism mentioned in *Ṭhāna* IV.4. See under Akriyāvāda.

aṇimā A kind of *siddhi* or attainment of miraculous power.

anirvacanīya Inexplicable and indefinable. The term is often used to denote *māyā*. The illusion of individuality which suggests the theory of objective illusion is known as *anirvacanīyakhyātivāda*.

anityatā The doctrine of impermanence or rather evanescence of phenomenal objects. The Buddhists qualify impermanence (the Pali term is *aniccatā*) with momentariness (*kṣaṇikatva* q.v.). It means that phenomenal objects are subject to change every moment within their place of origin (*utpatti*), duration (*sthiti*) and decay (*vināśa*). The Buddha repeatedly said, 'aniccā vata saṅkhārā uppādavayadhammino', that is, impermanent are the composites which are subject to origin and decay.

añjali Name of an iconic *mudrā* or gesture, also known as *sarvarājendra-mudrā* or the *sampuṭāñjali*. In this gesture the two hands are clasped against the chest, palm to palm, and extended upwards with all fingers erect or slightly bent.

āñji Regarded as a *kalā* q.v.) or evolute of Śakti, often described as the *vyāpikā-śakti* or all-pervading energy. Kālicaraṇa's com. on *Ṣaṭcakranirūpaṇa* XL. It is often described as an alphabetical symbol.

aṅkuśa Elephant-goad found as a weapon in the iconic representation of deities. When a goad is surmounted by a *vajra*, it is called *vajrāṅkuśa*.

anna One of the three basic elements according to the Upaniṣadic speculations; the others are *ap* and *tejas*. Anna signifies whatever is solid; it only indirectly designates the earth or food.

annaprāśana Feeding a child cooked food for the first time. Most Smṛtis prescribe the sixth month from birth as the time of this *saṃskāra* (q.v.). The *Mānava Gr.* I.20.2–6 says that it may be fifth or sixth, while Śaṅkha quoted by Aparārka says that it should be performed either at the end of one year or at the end of six months. The *Kāṭhaka Gr.* XXXIX.1–2 enjoins the sixth month from birth or the time when the child first cuts teeth. *Āśv.Gr.* I.16.1–6; *Āp.Gr.* XVI.1–2, *Pār.Gr.* I.19; *Hir.Gr.* II.5.1–3; *Bhār.Gr.* I.27; *Vaik* III.22.

antaḥkaraṇa The collective name for intellect (*buddhi*), egoity (*ahaṃkāra*) and mind (*manas*). *Tantrāloka* IX. 236, *Śāradātilaka* I.36. The Advaita treats *antaḥkaraṇa* as being composed of four divisions while the Mīmaṃsā treats it as composed of only one entity, namely, *manas*.

antānantika Limitists and unlimitists mentioned in the *Brahmajāla-sutta*. The speculations of the Antānantikas, subdivided into four groups are mainly cosmological in character, according to which (1) the world is limited in extent and circular in shape, (ii) unlimited in extent and without any end, (iii) limited upwards and downwards but unlimited breadthwise and (iv) neither limited nor unlimited. *Dīgha*, I.

antarābhava Intermediate state of existence

according to certain Buddhist schools. The Sāmmityas like the Sarvāstivādins hold that every being, whether destined for *kāmaloka* or *rūpaloka* by his *karma*, remains for some time in an intermediate state of existence.

antarābhavadeha The intermediate body between the dead physical body and the future physical body described in the *Janmamaraṇavicāra* of Bhaṭṭa Vāmadeva.

antarāla Intermediate compartment between the shrine and the *maṇḍapa*.

antarāparinibbayī Sanskrit Antarāparinirvāyin, i.e., those who practice the path which leads to the destruction of the five higher (*uddhambhāgiya*) fetters. The journey is undertaken just after coming into being and before reaching the middle of their lives. It is a Buddhist concept connected with Anāgāmi (q.v.). *Puggalappaññatti* 16.

antardaśāra The inner ground of the mystic tantric diagrams. According to *Kāmakalāvilāsa* 30, it is the inner shade of the flames of the *cakras*, known as *vindu*, *trikoṇa* and *aṣṭakoṇa*, while the outer one is known as *bahirdasāra* (q.v.). According to the *Nityaṣoḍaśikārṇava* VI.15 it is the expressed ray of the *navatrikoṇa* or *navayonicakra*, i.e. the *cakra* consisting of nine triangles.

antaramātṛkānyāsa Feeling of the deity in the region around the neck where the existence of the Tantric *viśuddha-cakra* as a sixteen petalled lotus is conceived. The letter or *mātṛkā* symbolising the essence of the deity supposed to exist in each petal is to be meditated upon and felt. *Jñānārṇava* quoted in *Tantrasāra* 68. See also *Puraścaryārṇava* V. 330.

antartīrtha Tīrthas or holy places supposed to exist within the human body. *Prāṇatoṣaṇī* III.3, 178.

antarīkṣa Mid-plane, mid-region. Antarīkṣa-loka means the sphere of intermediary space where certain gods and souls reside. It is conceived as a finer aspect of the universe.

antaryāga Internal worship meant for Tantric aspirants belonging to higher grades. It is mental worship in which external formalities are redundant. *Mahānirvāṇatantra* V.143–49. According to the *Devībhāgavata* VII.39.44 pure-consciousness is the absolute form of the goddess, beyond all attributes and the complete merger of the self of the aspirant in this stream of consciousness is *antaryāga*. The *Gautamīyatantra* IX says that *antaryāga* leads to salvation within the span of one's life. Its virtues are elaborately stated in the *Gandharvatantra* XII.24–27.

antaryāmī The being who is immanent in the worlds, which according to the Hindu thought are countless, and regulates the motions and changes in them. Yājñavalkya in *Bṛhadāraṇyaka* III.7.3–23 identifies it with *ātman*. The concept of *antaryāmī* is a basic feature of the Pāñcarātra system which has been explained in the *vibhutiyoga* of the *Bhagavadgītā*.

antyeṣṭi Funeral rites regarded as one of the sixteen or more saṃskāras (q.v.) to be performed by the twice-born with Vedic *mantras* (*Manu* II.16, *Yāj.*I.10) and by women and Śūdras without Vedic *mantras* (*Aśv.Gr.* I. 15.12, I.16.6, I.17.12, *Manu* II.66, X.127). Funeral rites and rites after death vary in accordance with caste and religious position, nature of death, time and space factors, etc., connected with the deceased. The Śrauta and Gṛhyasūtras differ among themselves in many details on the same topic. Moreover the procedure became more elaborate in medieval and later times. The word Antyeṣṭi is used in a wide sense which includes, apart from the disposal of the dead (*mṛtasaṃskāra*), all sorts of postmortem rites.

aṇu Atom. See under Paramāṇu. It also denotes one of three categories of Trika (q.v.) philosophy indicating *jiva* or individual, also known as *paśu*. When Śiva owing to his own independence expresses himself in the contracted form of fettered individual he is called *aṇu*. *Tantrasāra* 6. The term *aṇu* is also used to denote a means (*upāya*) for spiritual attainment and has an element of dualism. It leads to *vikalpa* knowledge, i.e. knowledge based on an object, which is a means to an end but not the end itself. *Tantrāloka* I.150–51, I.219–21. According to Abhinavagupta that which is fettered by six false coverings in the body is called *aṇu* and as such the term is a synonym of *paśu*, *puruṣa* or *jīva*. Every being is enveloped by *kañcuka* or coating of impurity. This coating is known as *āṇavamala; ibid.* I.74, IX.113, 144, 205, 206. *Aṇu* is also a term for *mantra*. As the external form of an individual is pure, so also the material body of a *mantra* constituted by sound appears to be a fettered entity, a mere combination of words and sound, although in reality it is a conscious principle. Bhāskara's *Setubandha* Com. on *Nityaṣoḍaśikārṇava*.

anubandha Indispensable elements in every Śāstra according to the Pūrvamīmāṃsā tradition. These are *viṣaya* (the subject to be treated of), *prayojana* (the purpose or the object), *sambandha* (the relation of the Śāstra to the *prayojana*) and *adhikārin* (the person entitled or competent to study).

anubandhyā The rite of offering a barren cow after Udayanīyā or the concluding *iṣṭi*. *Āp.Sr.* XIII.22–23, *Āśv.Sr.* VI.14.3.

anubhava Experience. It is of four kinds, namely, perception, inference, analogy and testimony.

anugraha-mūrti An image in the attitude of bestowing grace and compassion.

anukalpa Substitutes, especially of the Tantric five Ms such as garlic for meat, coconut-water for wine etc. This substitution holds good also in the case of sacrifices.

anumāna Inference in Indian logical system; it is the knowledge of objects not through perception but through the apprehension of some marks (*liṅga*) and is invariably related to the inferred objects. The invariable relation between the two is called *vyāpti*. In inference there are at least three propositions and at most three terms—the *pakṣa* or minor term about which we infer something, the *sādhya* or major term which is the inferred object, the *liṅga* or *sādhana* or *hetu*, or middle term which is invariably related to the major and is present in the minor. Inference is *svārtha* and *parārtha* depending in whether it is meant for oneself or for others. Again it is *pūrvavat*, *śeṣavat* and *sāmānyatodṛṣṭa* depending on whether it passes from cause to effect or vice-versa or whether it is based on observed points of similarity.

anupadaka See under Ādi.

anupādiśesa-nibbāna The foretaste of what an *arhat* (q.v.) is going to experience permanently according to Hīnayāna Buddhism.

anupalabdhi Non-perception; according to the Bhāṭṭa-Mīmāṃsā, and the Advaita Vedānta, it is the source of cognition of the non-existence of an object. For example, the non-existence of a jar on table is known from the absence of its cognition, that is, from its non-perception

anupātaka Certain sins which are declared by Manu XI.55.58 and Yāj.III. 228–233 to be equal to or like one or other of the Mahāpātakas (q.v.) The *Viṣṇu Dh.S.* XXXVI. provides that those guilty of them should regain purity by making the Aśvamedha sacrifice or by resorting to pilgrimages. Such sins are removed by the penances which are slightly less severe than those for the Mahāpātakas themselves.

anupāya Knowledge resulting from *ānanda* (q.v.) or bliss which leads to the realisation of non-duality with Śiva. *Tantrāloka* I. 242.

anupravacanīya A sacrifice to be performed after a part of the Veda has been learnt. *Āp.Gr.* I.22.10–16, *Gobhila Gr.* III.2.46–47.

anupraveśa The theory of the creator's entrance into his creation according to certain Upaniṣads. *Bṛhadāraṇyaka* I.4.7ff, V.9, *Chāndogya* VI.2, *Maitrāyaṇī* II.6, *Taittirīya* II.6, *Śvetāśvatara* VI.II.etc.

anuprekṣā See under Bhāvanā.

anurāga Attachment to God in which the object of love, even though realised and relished always, appears to have a fresh charm and be attractive every moment. *Ujjvalanīlamaṇi*, sthāyī, 102.

anuṣaṅga A principle regarding sentences. It pertains to the extension of a word or clause from one sentence to another or other sentences provided all the sentences are of the same type or form.

anuśaya Inclination. According to Buddhism there are seven kinds of inclination: *kāmarāga* (attachment to worldly objects), *paṭigha* (enmity), *diṭṭhi* (wrong view), *vicikicchā* (doubt about the creed), *māna* (pride), *bhavarāga* (desire for existence) and *avijjhā* (ignorance) *Saṃyutta* V.64–65.

anusmṛti A new *aṅga* of Yoga (see Yogāṅga) according to the *Guhyasamāja* 163.

anussati Recollections. According to Buddhism these are ten in kinds: cognition of the merits of Buddha, Dhamma, Saṅgha, Śīla (observance of precepts), Cāge (charity), Devatā (ways and means by which one is reborn in the realm of gods), Maraṇa-sati (recollection of inevitable death), Kāyagatā-sati (of the contents of physical body), Ānāpāna-sati (of inhalation) and Upasamanussati (of final quietude).

anustaraṇī The cow that is offered as a gift in a funeral.

anutpādajñāna The cognizance of a stage of spiritual development when an individual is assured of overcoming rebith. It is a Mahāsaṅghika Buddhist concept. *Abhidharmakośa* (Poussin) VI.67, *Aṭṭhasālini* 54.

anutpattika dharmakṣānti Faith in the non-origination of all *dharmas* or elements; a dogma characteristic of Mahāyānism. *Mādhyamikavṛtti* (Poussin) 363, *Laṅkāvatāra* 81, *Aṣṭasāhasrikā Pr.* (ASB) 33˙

anuttara The manifested form of the supreme

being. The term is used in a variety of senses. *Parātriṃsikā*, 19ff. Anuttara is the name of a form of Śakti according to Kāśmīra Śaivism. *Tantrāloka* III.186.

anuvrata See under Mahāvrata (q.v.); vows for laymen. The lesser vows meant for Jain householders. They are abstinence from *hiṃsā* (violence), *asatya* (untruthfulness), *adattadāna* (stealing), *abrahmacarya* (sensualism), *parigraha* (attachment), *krodha* (anger), *māna*(egoism), *māyā* (hypocrisy), *lobha* (greed), *rāga* (personal attachment), *dveṣa* (hatred), *kleśa* (quarrelsomeness), *abhākhyāna*(scandals), *paiśunya* (gossiping), *paraparivāda* (telling ill of others), *rati-arati* (sexuality), *māyāmṛṣa* (sinful acts under the pretext of goodness) and *mithyādarśanaśalya* (ascribing reality to the unreal). Also see under Kaṣāya, Caritra.

anuvāda A text which contains something which has already been ascertained by other means.

anuvyañjana See under Lakṣaṇa.

anuvyavasāya Mental perception or introspection according to the Nyāya school.

anuyaja Offerings subsequent to the principal ones. Three such offerings are made in the *darśapūrṇamāsa* (q.v.) sacrifices. *Taitt. Br.* III.5.9. *Taitt.S.*I.6.4.1., *Āp.Sr.* IV.12.1; *Āśv.Sr.* I.8.7.

anuyoga Sacred tests of the Digambaras (q.v.) often descirbed as four Vedas. These are divided into four classes of Prathamānuyoga, Karaṇānuyoga, Dravyānuyoga and Caraṇānuyoga.

anvārambhaṇīya An *iṣṭi* (q.v.) performed in connection with *darśapūrṇamāsa* (q.v.) sacrifices. A cake cooked on eleven potsherds is offered to Agni and Viṣṇu, another cooked on twelve potsherds to Sārasvat and a third on eight potsherds to Agni-bhagin. According to *Jaimini* IX.1.34–35, it should be performed only once. *Taitt. S.*III.5.1, *Āśv.Sr.* II.8, *Āp.Sr.* V.23.4–9, *Baudh.Sr.*II.21.

anvaṣṭakā A form of Śrāddha (q.v.); the procedure for it is the same as that of Piṇḍapitṛyajña (q.v.). The most notable characteristic of this rite is that female ancestors are invoked. Liquor, the scum of boiled rice, collyrium and garlands are offered. Some say that Aṣṭakā (q.v.) is the basic model for the procedure of Śrāddhas while others hold that Aṣṭakā and Anvaṣṭakā are modelled on monthly Śrāddha. *Āśv.Gr.* II.5.2–15, *Pār.Gr.* III.3, *Kāṭhaka Gr.* LXV.7–8.

ānvīkṣikī The science of critical study; the term is often attributed to the Nyāya system. The word corresponds to a certain extent to what is understood by the European concept of philosophy. The Sāṅkhya, Yoga and the Lokāyata doctrines are also placed in the *ānvīkṣikī* category. *Kauṭilya* I.2, *Mahābhāṣya* on *Pāṇini* VII.3.45.

anvitābhidhānavādin See under Abhihitānvayavādin.

anyathāgrahaṇa Misapprehension according to the Advaita-Vedānta terminology. The Nyāya-Vaiśeṣikas hold that there cannot but be some misapprehension, or taking one thing for another, in any act of error. Error means an 'otherwise' (*anyathā*) apprehension (*khyāti*) of something, i.e., to know something to be other than what it actually is.

ap The liquid element belonging to the tripartite scheme of division in the elements found in the Upanisads which only indirectly designates water. It is regarded as one of the four or five material elements constituting the world in all the philosophical systems of India. In Tantrism it is symbolically represented as belonging to the *svādhiṣṭhāna-cakra* (q.v.) of the human body. *Ṣaṭcakranirūpaṇa* 15ff.

āpad A period of distress or catastrophy when it is not possible to live in accordance with the norms prescribed by the Śāstras. In such a condition the norms relating to food and profession can be violated for which no sin is accrued. *Manu* X.116 enumerates ten means of maintaining oneself in *āpad* or distress which pertain especially to the Brāhmaṇas and Kṣatriyas. *Yāj* III.42 enumerates seven of these.

apāna One of the five constituents of Prāṇa (q.v.). Apāna is in the penis or anus region which is a seat of vital air. Besides Prāṇa in the heart and Apāna in the lower region there are three other airy constituents, namely Samāna, Udāna and Vyāna (qq.v.) each, having different functions.

Apāṅkteya Those who are not fit to sit and eat in the same row as Brāhmaṇa diners; or those defiling a row of diners at Śrāddha on various grounds such as bodily and mental defects, and disease, belonging to certain avocations, moral lapses, being guilty of crime, being followers of unorthodox systems, or being inhabitants of certain countries.

aparā The term tor material or mundane. Aparā Vidyā is material knowledge. Likewise Apara Śakti is that aspect of Śakti which confers a variety of material attainments upon the worshipper. The same holds good in the case of Apara Brahman (q.v.). Aparā worship is meant for practical purposes.

apara brahman Brahman (q.v.) transferred to the position of Īśvara or Almighty.

aparānta-kappika Philosophical school speculating about the future goal of creation. It consists of sixteen kinds of Saññivada (q.v.), eight kinds of Asaññivāda (q.v.), eight kinds of Nevasaññināsaññivāda (q.v.), seven kinds of Ucchedavāda (q.v.) and five kinds of Ditthadhammanibbānavada (q.v.).

aparaśaila A sub-sect of the Mahāsaṅghikas (q.v.). They were also known as Caityaka and lived in the Andhra region.

aparā-vidyā Material knowledge, also known as *avidyā*. It is supposed to be a body of contingent truths, half-truths and fallacies. *Chāndogya* VII.1.

aparigraha Non-possession. One of the five great vows of the Jains. Also see under Mahāvrata. In the Brahmanical tradition too *aparigraha* means not accepting from another anything beyond what is necessary for preserving the body. It is one of the five *yamas* of the *Yogasūtra* II. 30–31.

apariyāpanna Mental state accompanying different kinds of meditation. It belongs to the sphere of the four stages of sanctification according to Buddhaghoṣa.

aparokṣānubhūti Immediate realisation of the self as *brahman*, of the microcosm as the macrocosm. It is the constant presence of a conviction of the form 'I am *brahman*'.

apasmāra-puruṣa Evil personified. It is presented as a prostrate dwarf figure being stamped upon with the right leg of the dancing Śiva in Naṭarāja type of images.

apatiṭṭhitaviññāna Supportless consciousness which arises only when attachment (*rāga*) to material elements of the body (*rūpa*) and the four other constituents is removed. According to early Buddhism it is a step towards *nirvāṇa* (q.v.). *Saṃyutta* II.65, III.53–61.

apātrikaraṇa Rendering the perpetrator unworthy of receiving a gift. Manu XI.69 holds that accepting presents from condemned men (such as those mentioned in *Manu* IV.84) trading, serving Śūdras and speaking a falsehood make a man unworthy to receive gifts

apauruṣeya 'Self revealed', a term applied to the Vedas.

apavarga Liberation which is absolute freedom from pain. It is a state in which the soul is released from all its bonds with the body and the senses. The self ceases to have any experience, painful or pleasurable, and exists as a pure substance devoid of consciousness. See under Mokṣa. The *Amarakoṣa* regards *mukti*, *kaivalya*, *nirvāṇa*, *śreyas*, *niḥśreyasa*, *amṛta*, *mokṣa* and *apavarga* as synonymous. Apavarga occurs in the *Maitri Upaniṣad* VI.30 and is the goal laid down by the very first *sūtra* of Nyāya philosophy.

appanā Literally means placing or fixing (*arpaṇa*) the mind on the object of meditation. According to the Buddhists, in this stage the adept can fix his attention on the subject of meditation for a whole day or a whole night. There are ten ways and means to reach this stage. *Visuddhimagga* 126 ff, 282–83.

apramā Non-valid presentative knowledge; according to the Nyāya it is divided into doubt (*saṃśaya*), error (*bhrama* or *viparyaya*) and hypothetical argument (*tarka*).

apratiratha Verses of *RV* X.103 are so called in the *Taitt.Sam.* IV.6.4. Kātyāyana in his Śrāddhasūtra prescribes that among the holy texts to be recited when the Brāhmaṇas are eating the *śrāddha* dinner are the Rākṣoghni verses and the Apratiratha hymn.

apratisaṃkhyā-nirodha Emancipation without knowledge according to certain Buddhist schools. The Buddhists admit two kinds of *nirodha*. One attained by means of knowledge (*pratisaṃkhyā*) and the other by complete removal of all impurities and not by knowledge. The Mahāsaṅghikas hold that the latter is *paścād abhāva* (subsequent absence) of *dharmas*. (q.v.)

āprī Ten hymns of the RV (I.13, I.142, I.188, II.3, III.4, V.4, VII.2, IX.5, X.70 and X.110) ascribed to different sages to be chanted on different sacrificial occasions. The word Āprī appears to be used in two senses. The first is 'a deity or deities' invoked by the verses of the hymn. The second is 'a verse' (*yajyā*) that gratifies a deity. *Nirukta* VIII.4–22.

āptoryāma Soma sacrifice, an amplification of Atirātra (q.v.). According to *Āśv.Sr.* IX.9.22–23, IX.11.1, he whose cattle do not live or who desires to secure cattle of good breed should perform this sacrifice. The *Tāṇḍya Br.* XX.3.4–5 states that the rite is so called because by its performance one secures whatever object one desires (from *ap*, to obtain).

apūrva The Mīmāṃsaka theory of the soul's invisible, mysterious or subtle potency for enjoyment of the fruits of rituals. In connection with the question of causation the Mīmāṃsakas formulate the theory of potential energy (*śakti*) according to which there is an imperceptible power in every cause, producing the effect. This theory of potency (i.e., power for generating the fruit of an action) seeks to explain how an action like sacrifice can bear fruit long after its performance. Literally *apūrva* means the yielding of that which did not exist before. It is proved by *arthāpatti* and not by any other *pramāṇa*.

āpyāyana Processing of the *mantras* by various means. *Tantrasāra* 54.

ārambha-villāsa The first of the seven stages of spiritual attainment according to Tantrism; the others are *taruṇa*, *yauvana*, *prauḍha*, *prauḍhānta*, *unmana* and *anavasthā*. *Paraśuramakalpasūtra* X.68.

ārambhavāda The theory of the beginning of the effect anew. See Asatkāryavāda.

āraññaka Buddhist monks living in forests. There are special rules for them in the Vinaya.

āraṇyaka One of the principal categories of Vedic texts. These texts were mostly composed by those sages who had gone into the forest after completing their lives as householders. The Āraṇyaka texts reveal a type of philosophical enquiry on the intricacies of life and the universe. The line of demarcation between the Brāhmaṇa literature and the Āraṇyakas and between the Āraṇyakas and the Upaniṣads is not clear.

āraṇya-ṣaṣṭhī A ritual of child-protection associated with the cult of the goddess Ṣaṣṭhī which is held in the month of Jaiṣṭha (May-June). On this day groups of matrons go out of the village to a banyan tree in a neighbouring jungle, and hold a sort of picnic as a part of the function.

aratisaṃkhyānirodha Emancipation by meditational practices and not necessarily with knowledge. According to the Vaibhāṣikas, it is unconstituted and is not attained by supra-mundane path. It can neither be a cause nor an effect of exertion *AKV* I.16, II.55.

ārbhava-pavamāna Verses from the ninth *maṇḍala* of the *RV* (IX.1.1–3, IX.75.1–3, IX. 101.1–3, IX.106.1–3, IX.108.1–2) to be chanted of the evening pressing of *soma* during the Agniṣṭoma (q.v.)

arcā Cult image.

arcirmārga Way or path of the gods. See Devayāna.

arciṣmati Bright or radiant stage, the fourth *bhūmi* (q.v.) of the Bodhisattvahood, in which the potential Bodhisattva becomes perfect in energy (*vīrya-pāramitā*) and applies himself to the acquisition of 37 *bodhipakṣīya-dharmas* (q.v.). This stage is also known as Bodhipakṣyapratisaṃyuktādhiprajñāvihāra.

ardhacandra-śakti Symbolical half-moon as the repository of Śakti where the aspirant becomes all-knowing according to the Tantras. It has five *kalā* or functional aspects known as Jyotsnā, Jyotsnāvatī, Kānti, Suprabhā and Vimalā.

ardhakṛcchra A method for expiation of sin. According to the *Āpastamba-Smṛti* IX.43–44 this extends over six days. The method is to take food only once in the day for the first day, only once in the evening for the next day, to eat only the food that is offered on the third and fourth day and to fast completely for the last two days.

ardha-maṇḍapa Pillared hall of one bay usually at the entrance of a temple. Same as *mukhamaṇḍapa*.

ardhaparyaṅka A particular *āsana* or posture of sitting. Both the legs are on the same pedestal but one is bent with the knee raised up while the other is bent with the knee remaining horizontal. It is also called *mahārājalīlā*.

ardhapluta One who soars only half way. On account of meditations practised by him, he is born in the Brahmakāyika heaven, from which he passes to Suddhāvāsa and thence to Akaniṣṭha to attain *nirvāṇa* there. *Abhidharmakośa* (Poussin) IV.37.

ārdrākṣatāropaṇa Mutual showering of wet unbroken rice grains by the bride and bridegroom. It is the concluding part of the marriage rites. The priest sprinkles on their head water with an *udumbara* twig together with *dūrvā* grass after reciting verses *āpo hi ṣṭhā* etc., from *RV* X.9.

arghya Respectful offering of water or water with unhusked rice-grains, flowers, etc., to gods or venerable persons.

arhat A person having to his credit sufficient merits so as to reach a particular stage of sanctification, a spiritual fulfilment according to Buddhism and Jainism. According to the Buddhists, an *arhat* gets rid of all fetters, afflictions and impurities and comprehends finally the real sense of the four truths, i.e., he obtains perfect knowledge and his mind is completely freed. He will have no more rebirth and will attain *nirvāṇa*. The *arhats* may be of two categories: Ubhatobhāgavimutta (q.v.) and Paññavimutta (q.v.). *Dīgha* II.71. There are some *arhats* who in addition to their general attainments, acquire four kinds of analytical knowledge and are distinguished as Saha-paṭisambhidā. *Milinda* 18, *Aṅguttara* II. 169. *Mahāvaṃsa* 35.

ariyamagga The path leading a man to become an Ārya or a man capable of attaining the highest knowledge. The path, according to the Hīnayāna Buddhism, is eight-fold and consists of the completion of fifteen *kṣaṇas* of the Darśanamārga (q.v.) which enable one to drift along the stream (*sota*) of sanctification.

ariyasacca The four noble truths preached by the Buddha, in Sanskrit Ārya-satya. The first is Dukkha (q.v.) or suffering, the second Dukkha-samudaya (q.v.) or origin of suffering, the third Dukkha-nirodha (q.v.) or need of ending of suffering and the fourth Magga (q.v.) or right way for the extinction of suffering. The *Abhidharmakośavyākhyā* VI.4 puts the four truths under two categories, namely, cause and effect or world (*samsāra*) and cessation (*nirvāṇa*). Dukkha and Samudaya are placed under the former and Nirodha and Magga under the latter.

arkavivāha Marriage with *arka* plant. A rite to be performed by one who has lost two wives by death before marrying a third so that the third one may not die.

arpita-hāra A *hāra* (q.v.) attached to the main wall of the *vimāna* (q.v.)

ārṣa The form of marriage in which the bride's father accepts from the bridegroom one pair of cattle (a cow and a bull) or two pairs only as a matter of fulfilling the law (and not as a sale of the girl).

ārṣajñāna Intuition. It is a form of supernormal consciousness, but different from Yogic perception.

artha Economic pursuits regarded as a goal of human life which are one of the three constituents of *trivarga*, others being Dharma and Kāma. Kauṭilya I.7. says that Artha is the principal of the three aspects of life, as Dharma and Kāma both spring from Artha. Manu II.124 after setting out several views about which of the three is primary states that if Artha or Kāma is in conflict with Dharma one should give up Artha or Kāma as the case may be. The term is also used to denote 'meaning' and 'expression'. Yāska defines it as 'fruit or flower of speech'. In certain cases it is the synonym of *puruṣārtha* meaning the ultimate aim of life.

arthakarma The giving of the staff of the Maitrā-varuṇa priest after Soma is purchased.

arthapañcaka Vaiṣṇava doctrine according to which Rāma is the God or supreme being who, after crossing *moha* (delusion) in the form of the forest and killing *rāga* (passion) and *dveṣa* (hatred) symbolised by the Rākṣasas, shines resplendently united with *śānti* (peace) in the form of Sītā. Lakṣmaṇa is the soul seeking God's grace (*śaraṇāgati*) as the means (*upāya*) and attainment (*prāpti*) of God as the goal (*phala*).

arthāpatti Postulation which, according to the Mīmāṃsakas, is the necessary supposition of an unperceived fact to explain conflicting phenomena. Knowledge so obtained is neither through perception nor inference. Knowledge by postulation arises where we have to postulate something as the only explanation of any apparent conflict. This method of knowledge is used very frequently in life. For example, one easily concludes from the absence of a man in his house that he must be somewhere outside. It is of two kinds: *dṛṣṭārthāpatti* (q.v.) and *śrutārthāpatti* (q.v.). Śabara on *Jaimini* I.1.5.

arthavāda The second great division of Vedic texts. The *arthavādas* are of three kinds; when an *arthavāda* text is in conflict with ordinary experience it is metaphorical (*guṇavāda*); when something is definitely ascertained by other means of knowledge it is *anuvāda*; and when a text is not opposed to other *pramāṇas* (q.v.) or is not definitely ascertained otherwise it is called *bhūtārthavāda* (statement of an accomplished fact or of a past event). *PMS* I.2.

aruṇā Name of the presiding Śakti of one of the eight corners of the Tantric *aṣṭakoṇa-cakra*. *Nityaṣoḍaśikārṇava* I.191–92.

aruṇmukha Name of the class of Yatis (q.v.) killed by Indra. *Taitt.S.* VI.2.7. 5, *Kāṭhaka.S.* VIII.5, *Ait.Br.* XXXV. 2, *Kauṣ.Up.* III.1.

arūpadhamma Buddhist term for non-material entities. *Kathāvatthu* XII.3–4.

arūpadhātu A region or sphere where a class of beings described as matterless in Buddhist cosmological speculations live. They are not made of material elements, but they are not wholly free from attachment (*vītarāga*). *Abhidharmakośa* (Poussin) III.3. In the Abhidharma texts it is stated that the beings of Arūpadhātu have four *khandas* and two *āyatanas* only. *Vibhaṅga* 405–07.

arūpa-liṅga Formless symbols like Śālagrāma,

Śivaliṅga, Śrīyantra, Śrīcakra, etc. associated with the deities like Viṣṇu, Śiva, Śakti and others. See Arūpa-Vigraha.

arūpāvacara A class of beings belonging to a particular level of existence according to Buddhist cosmological speculations. Their areas (*āyatana*) are known as *ākāśa*, *viññāna*, *akiñcana* and *nevasaññānasaññā*. These are also names of their mental states according to the nature of their meditation. See under Arūppa.

arūpa-vigraha Formless images as opposed to those with forms, having face, hands, etc. (*sarūpa-vigraha*).

ārūppa Higher *jhānas* or meditations, also called *samāpattis* which carry the mind of the adept to the region of *arūpaloka*, i.e., beyond the *rūpa* or material world according to the Buddhist conception. The first meditation is of unlimited space (*ākāsānañcāyatana*), the second of unlimited consciousness (*viññānanancāyatana*), the third of nothingness (*akiñcaññāyatana*) and the fourth of neither perception nor non-perception (*nevasaññināsaññāvatana*). *Visuddhimagga* 125 ff.

āryasatya See Ariya-sacca.

ārādupakāraka Acts or rites prescribed which do not have a specific objective but which are part of the principal ceremony. Rites such as *prayājas*, *āghāras*, *ājyabhāgas* etc. pertaining to *darśa-pūrṇamāsa* (q.v.) fall within this category.

asaṃkhata Sanskrit Asaṃskṛta, meaning 'unconstituted' in Buddhist terminology. That which has neither origin, nor decay nor any change belongs to this category which comprise *ākāśa* (uncovered space), *pratisaṃkhyā-nirodha* (liberation by means of knowledge) and *apratisaṃkhyā-nirodha* (emancipation by meditational practices). *Aṅguttara* I.152, *AKV* I.5ff, II.45 ff., *Dhammasaṅgaṇi* 583, 983, 1086.

asamprajñāta-samādhi Another name for *nirvikalpa-samādhi* (q.v.).

asamprajñāta-yoga Yoga par excellence. In this state there is a complete cessation of all mental modifications and, consequently, the entire absence of all knowledge including that of the contemplated object. In this state the knowing-self abides in its own essence as pure consciousness.

asaṃskṛta-dhātu See Asaṃkhata.

āsana A seat; attitude or posture of sitting found in cult images. The word Padmāsana means the seat of lotus. Similarly Siṃhāsana means the lion-throne or the seat of a lion. The word Sukhāsana means any easy attitude of sitting. When used in a technical sense Āsana is of various kinds, such as the Paryaṅkāsana, Vajraparyaṅkāsana, Lalitāsana, Ardhaparyaṅkāsana, Bhadrāsana, Āḷīḍhāsana, Pratyālīḍhāsana, Nātyāsana, etc. Āsana is the third discipline of Yoga.

āsanamūrti A Visnu-image showing the god in a seated posture.

āsana-paṭṭa A flat moulding of the *kakṣāsana* or balconied window in a temple structrue.

asaṅkhāraparinibbāyī One of the five sub-classes of the Anāgāmis (q.v.) comprising those who attain *parinibbāna* (see Nirvāṇa) by putting an end to all impurities without great effort. *Aṅguttara* II.156, *Abhidharmakośa* (Poussin) VI. 211, *Puggalapaññatti* Com. 199.

asaññivāda A belief in the existence of the unconscious soul after death. Eight such groups are mentioned in the Buddhist texts according to which the unconscious soul may be either material or non-material, both material and non-material, neither material nor non-material and so forth.

asat Non-existence, non-entity. In *RV* X.129. 1 it is stated that there was once a time when there was neither existence (*sat*) nor non-existence (*asat*). In *RV* X.72.2. *asat*, however, means unmanifested (*avyakta*) not non-existence. The *Chāndogya* VI.3. 1–3 asserts that since in the beginning there was *sat* without a second, the theory of transition from non-existence (*asat*) to existence cannot stand. However, the *Taitt.Br.* II.2.9.1ff says that the non-existent became fervent and from that fervour smoke, fire and light were generated in succession. Śaṅkara commenting on *Vedāntasūtra* I.4.15 refers to *Taitt.Up.* II.7 'asad vā idam-agra āsīt', *Chāndogya* III.19.1 'asad-evedamagra āsīt', etc., as subject to various interpretations.

asatkāryavāda The view that *kārya* or effect is *asat* or non-existent before its production. In other words it is the theory which holds that the effect does not exist in the material cause prior to its production.

āśauca Impurity on birth and death. The word Āśauca is formed from *śuci* (pure) with the negative prefix (Pāṇini V.1.131, VII.3.30). The *Mit.* on *Yāj* III.1 defines Āśauca as an emergent attribute attaching to a person, which is removed by the lapse of time or a bath and the like. It is of two kinds, viz. that arising on birth (and so called *janamāśauca* or *sutaka*) and that arising on death (and therefore called *śavāśauca* or *mṛtakāśauca* or *maraṇāsauca*). The Brāhmaṇa who has studied the Vedas and kept Vedic fires becomes free from impurity in one day, one who has only mastered the Veda in three days, and one who has neither studied the Vedas nor kept the Vedic fires in ten days. Generally the length of time of Āśauca for the four Varnas fixed at ten, twelve, fifteen and thirty days. There are rules about Āśauca on death of *bandhus* such as maternal grandfather-grandmother, maternal uncle, daughter's son, father-in-law, mother-in-law, son-in-law and wife's brother, on death of Ācārya, his wife or son of a Guru or pupil and when the knowledge of birth or death comes to a man after lapse of the periods fixed. The rules of Āśauca do not hold good in some cases such as unofficially adopted son or foster father; a mother when there is abortion, or slaves when their master dies and so on. Notwithstanding various rules, usage of the country or common practice is the most important matter that counts in the observance of such rites.

āsava A kind of wine used in Tantric rites.

āsavakhayakāraṇañāna The sixth *abhiññā* (q.v.) which the Hīnayāna Buddhist aspirant attains in striving towards salvation. It is the knowledge of the destruction of his impurities.

asmitā Sense of personality which consists in the seen (the self) being held as if identical with the instruments of seeing such as mind and sense-organs. *Yogasūtra* II.5–9.

aśoka A kind of tree which bears red flowers. From time immemorial this tree has been regarded as sacred in India. It is believed that when chaste women kick the tree they cause it to blossom.

aśokāṣṭamī A ritual performed by women in the month of Caitra (March-April) in which tiny buds of the *aśoka* plant are taken by housewives to ensure immunity from sorrow (*śoka*).

asparśa-yoga See Anāsakti-Yoga.

āsphānaka-yoga Yoga of psychic expansion said to have practised by the Buddha himself. *Lalita-vistara*, ed. Mitra, 315.

āśrama The four stages of life—Brahmacarya, Gārhastha, Vānaprastha and Sannyāsa (qq.v.)—known from the times of the most ancient Dharmasūtras (*Āp.Dh.S.* II.9.21, *Gaut. Dh.S.* III.2, *Vas.Dh.S.* VII.1–2, *Baudh.D.S.* II.6.17). As stated in *Manu* IV.1 the first part of a man's life is Brahmacarya in which he learns at his teacher's house. After he has finished his studies, in the second part of his life he marries and becomes a householder, discharges his debts to his ancestors by begetting sons and to the gods by performing *yajñas* (V.169). When he becomes sufficiently older he resorts to the forest (VI.1–2) where he spends the third part of his life. The rest of his life he lives as an ascetic (VI.33). The word Āśrama does not occur in the Saṃhitās or Brāhmaṇas. This does not, however mean that the stages of life were unknown at that period. The concept may be attributed to tribal heritage when the transition from one stage of life to another is ceremoniously adopted through the *rites de passage*. The word Āśrama is derived from *śram* 'to exert, to labour' and etymologically means 'a stage in which one exerts oneself.'

āśramadharma Such rules as 'begging', 'carrying a staff', or 'collecting fuel', 'tending cows of the teacher' etc., enjoined on a Brahmacārī (q.v.).

āśrava The influx of the *karma* particles into the soul. According to Jainism, all kinds of jīvas have to suffer the worldly experiences in the diverse spheres of life on account of the *karma* they acquire individually. Just as water flows into a boat through a hole in it, so also the *aśravas* represent the channels or modes through which the *karmas*, as transformation of subtle matter, enter the soul. Āśrava is broadly divided into *bhāvāsrava* (q.v.) and *karmāsrava* (q.v.), the former denoting thought-activities through which the *karma* particles enter the soul, and the latter, their actual entrance. *DS*, 29–30, also *vṛtti*.

aṣṭadalapadma Eight-petalled lotus, actual or imaginary, used as universal Tantric symbol in the composition of the *cakras* within and without the human body and also in the diagrams. The petals are said to contain the letters *ka, ca, ṭa, ta, pa, ya, sa*, and *la*. *Kāmakalāvilāsa* 33. The presiding goddesses are: Anaṅgakusumā, Anaṅga-mekhalā, Anaṅgamadanā, Anaṅgamadanāturā, Anaṅgarekhā, Anaṅgaveginī, Anaṅgāṅkuśā and Anaṅgamālinī. *Nityaṣoḍaśikārṇava* I.177–78. They are known as Guptatarayoginī. The attainment is known as *mahimāsiddhi*, associated *mudrā* is *akarṣīnī*. *Gandharvatantra* V.96, XVII, 42.

aṣṭakā Days fit for Aṣṭakā *homas* (q.v.). This is to be performed on the 8th day of the dark half of the moon for four months from Mārgaśīrṣa (*Āśv.Gr.* II.4.1) or for the three months of Pauṣa, Māgha and Phālguṇa. On these days Vedic studies are forbidden (Anadhyāya, q.v.). There was the custom of killing cows in Aṣṭakā-śrāddhas (q.v.) or funeral rites. *Hir.Gr.* II.15.1, *Baudh.Gr.* II.11.51 *Vaik* IV.3.

aṣṭakā-śrāddha One of the important Śrāddhas (q.v.) described in *Gaut.Dh.S.* VIII.19 as the first among the seven kinds of Pākayajñas (q.v.) and as one of the forty Samskāras (q.v.). Aṣṭakā appears to have meant the 8th *tithi* in any month after the full moon day (*Śat.Br.* VI.4.2.10), or the 8th *tithis* of the dark halves of the months of Mārgaśirṣa, Pauṣa, Māgha and Phālguna (*Āśv.Gr.* II.4.1). Most of the Gṛhyasūtras, however, exclude Phālguna. There are great variations on almost all points connected with Aṣṭakā, such as the number of days and the months in which they were to be performed, the deities to be worshipped, the offerings to be made and the procedure. The procedure for Aṣṭakā comprises three parts: *homa* (q.v.), inviting Brahmanas for dinner, and the rite called Anvaṣṭakā or Anvaṣṭakya (q.v.). According to the *Khadira Gr.* III.4.1 flesh of cow may also be offered. For details see *Āp.Gr.* VIII.21–22, *Khadira Gr.* III.5, *Gobhila Gr.* IV.2–3, *Śān:Gr.* III.13, *Āśv.Gr.* II.5.

aṣṭakoṇacakra Octogonal diagram said to be the extension of *trikoṇa-cakra* or triangular diagram. *Kāmakalāvilāsa* 29. It is regarded both as the gross and as the subtle body of goddess. *Cidvallī*. Com. on *ibid* 40ff. Each of the eight corners of this *cakra* is presided over by a goddess or Śakti, known respectively as Vaśinī, Kāmeśī, Modinī, Vimalā, Aruṇā, Jayinī, Sarveśī and Kaulinī. *Nityaṣoḍaśikārṇava* I.191–92. The attainment resulting from this *cakra* worship is known as *bhuktisiddhi*. The presiding deities collectively are known as Rahasyayoginī and they are propitiated by offerings in Khecarī-mudrā. *Gandharvatantra* XVII.74–76.

aṣṭamaithunāṅga Eight techniques required for sexual union. They are *smaraṇa* (evocative rememberance), *kīrtana* (uttering sweet words), *keli* (sport), *prekṣaṇa* (special looks), *guhyabhāṣana* (secret dialogue), *saṅkalpa* (determination), *adhyavasāya* (patience and perseverence) and *kriyāniṣpatti* (completion of sexual intercourse). *Dakṣasaṃhitā* VII. 31–32.

aṣṭamātṛka Eight *mātṛkā* goddesses—Brahmāṇī, Māheśvarī, Kaumārī, Vaiṣṇavī, Vārāhi, Aindrī, Cāmuṇḍā and Mahālakṣmī—supposed to reside in the *viṣṇurekhā* of the *bhūpura-yantra* in Tantric tradition. *Nityaṣoḍaśikārṇava* I.169–71.

aṣṭāṅga-yoga See Yogāṅga.

aṣṭanidhi Eight treasures. They are *padma, mahāpadma, makara, kacchapa, mukunda, nīla, nanda* and *śaṅkha*, according to the *Mārkaṇḍeya-purāṇa* list.

aṣṭapada The eight-terraced mountain (or its representation) where Ādinātha attained liberation.

aṣṭapāśa Eight fetters leading to human bondage: *ghṛṇā* (hatred), *lajjā* (shame), *bhaya* (fear), *śaṅkā* (misgiving), *jugupsā* (upbraiding), *kula* (pedigree), *śila* (manners) and *jāti* (birth or caste) *Parasurāmakalpasūtra* X.70.

aṣṭaprakṛti Collective name of the first eight Sāṅkhya *tattvas*: Prakṛti, Mahat, Ahaṃkāra and five Tanmātra.

aṣṭasiddhi Eight miraculous attainments.

aṣṭāvarana Eightfold shields which, according to the Vīra-Śaivas, protect the devotee from the snare of nescience. These are *guru, liṅga, jaṅgama, pādodaka, prasāda, bhasma, rudrākṣa* and *mantra*.

asteya One of the five great vows of the Jains which is abstention from stealing or misappropriation of others' property.

āstika One of the two broad streams of Indian philosophy comprising the Mīmāṃsā, Vedānta, Sāṅkhya, Yoga, Nyāya and Vaiśeṣika systems. The current meaning of *āstika* and *nāstika* is generally 'theist' and 'atheist' respectively. In Sanskrit philosophical literature *āstika* means 'one who believes in the authority of the Vedas' while the word *nāstika* means the opposite of this. For example, the Sāṅkhya school does not believe in the existence of god but it believes in the authority of the Vedas and hence it is *āstika*.

astikāya Substances which, according to Jain cosmological conception, fall in the category of the 'extended'. They exist (*asti*) like body (*kāya*) possessing extension. It literally means 'mass of all that is'. Astikāya substances are divided into two kinds; Jīva (q.v.) and Ajīva (q.v.). *Uttara* XXVIII, XXXVI, *DS*.24, *SDS*, III.33, *PTSMS* 129–32.

aṣṭottaraśata(sahasra)-liṅga A type of Śiva-phallus, so called chiefly on the basis of the different ways of modelling the *rudra-bhāga* or top section.

aśubha Ten unpleasant objects of meditation which refer to the ten states through which an uncared for corpse passes before it is completely destroyed according to the Buddhist viewpoint. *Visuddhimagga* 175ff.

aśucikara Certain sinful acts which cause impurity but no loss of caste. These are gambling, black magic, subsisting by gleaning corn fallen in the field by one who has not consecrated sacred fires, subsisting by begging on the part of one who has returned home after finishing Vedic study or staying on for more than four months at the teacher's seminary, gaining livelihood by astrology and so on. *Baudh.Dh.S.* II.1.60–61, *Āp.Dh.S.* I.7.21, 7–11.

aśuddha-māyā One of the two kinds of *māyā* (q.v.) according to the Śaiva Siddhānta. It is the material cause from which are produced *kāla* (time), *niyati* (destiny) and *kalā* (instrument). From *kalā* come *vidyā* (finite knowledge) and *prakṛti* (q.v.); from *vidyā* comes *rāga* (attachment) and from *prakṛti* come *citta* (mind) and *buddhi* (intellect) and from the latter *ahaṃkāra* (q.v.) and its evolutes. *Mṛgendra Āgama* II.3–7, III.1, VII.11, VIII.1–5, IX.2–4, *Pauṣkara Āgama* II.17, III.4, V.9, *Śivajñānabodham* II.5, XII.3.

āsura The form of marriage, when the girl is given away at the father's will after the bridegroom gives as much wealth as he can afford to pay to the relatives of the girl and to the girl herself. It is referred to even in *RV* I.109.2 and *Nirukta* VI.9.

āsurī-sampad Materialistic and hedonistic outlook.

aśvakrāntā The region extending from the Vindhya hills to the great sea. In the *Mahāsiddhasāra-tantra* the western boundary of Aśvakrāntā has been located on the Ḳaratoyā in the Dinajpur district and the eastern boundary in Yavadvīpa or Java. It is a Tantric region.

Āśvalāyana Water, named after a sage, which is offered in *tarpana* (q.v.)

aśvamedha Horse sacrifice. It was originally a fertility-cum-agricultural ritual which later became transformed into a ceremonial for royal paramountcy. From *AV*.XI.7.7–8, *Taitt.S.* V.4.12.3, *Śat.Br*.XIII.3.3.6 it appears that even in ancient times this sacrifice was rare and regarded as having gone out of vogue (*utsanna*). Details of the procedure of the Aśvamedha are given in the Śrautasūtras (*Āśv*.X, *Ap*.XX, *Kāt*.XX, *Lāṭ*.IX, *Śān*.XVI.etc.) from which at least two significant features may be derived at a glance. First, that women in general and queens in particular had a very important part to play in the function; and, second, that *mantras* are all quoted from the earlier texts: from the *RV*.I.162–63 (in connection with the killing of the horse) and from the *Taitt. S.* and especially from the *Vāj.Saṃ*. XXII–XXIII in connection with the chief queen's ceremonial union with the dead horse. The verses of the *Vāj.Saṃ*. which were exchanged between the priests and the queens, while the chief queen was lying embracing the slain horse, clearly indicate that the form of Aśvamedha which was current in the Vedic age was a relic or rather a transformation of an older ritual in which a man, evidently the king or priest, had ceremonial intercourse with the queen after which he was put to death—a role played later by the sacrificial horse. Such a sexual union was evidently a fertility rite. It was necessary for the queen to conceive so that the earth might bear fruit, her sexual life being a cycle of mimetic magic. Her partner's participation in the ritual was a part of the function which the primitive tribal chief or priest or king was expected to discharge on behalf of the community. In the sophisticated form of the Aśvamedha, which could only be performed by the paramount king, there was a recognition of the archaic notion that the institution of divine kingship was derived from the belief that the well-being of the social and natural orders depended on the vitality of the leader which was to be infused into others by the sacrifice of his body. Since the king's dedication of his physical body was out of question in the historical period, the horse was used as a substitute. The sophisticated Aśvamedha sacrifice lasted for three days. It required the presence of four queens, accompanied by princesses and a large retinue. There were rules stipulating the colour and qualities of the sacrificial horse. After it was selected it was allowed to roam over the country, for the period of one year under guard. During the horse's absence three Iṣṭis (q.v.) were to be offered every day to Savitṛ followed by chants by a Brāhmaṇa and also by a Kṣatriya lute-player. The Hotṛ recited to the king, surrounded by his sons and ministers, the narrative called Pāriplava. Also every day for a year four oblations called Dhṛti were made in the *āhavanīya* (q.v.). At the end of the year the horse was brought back for the sacrifice and the sacrificer took Dikṣā (q.v.). 21 *yupas* were erected and a large number of animals were slaughtered. The horse was annointed by the four queens on various parts of the body and a dialogue between the Hotṛ (q.v.) and the Brahmā (q.v.) took place. After the horse was killed, the queens went round it and fanned it with their garments, while the crowned queen lay embracing the horse, both covered with a mantle. Dialogues dealing with the archaic and antiquated ritual of the queen's sexual intercourse with the priest were now repeated between Hotṛ and crowned queen (Mahiṣī), between the Brahmā and the favourite wife (Vāvātā) and between the four principal priests and chamberlain on one side and the queens and their attendants on the other. The fat and blood of the horse was offered to the deities, and a theological dialogue (*brahmodaya*) of questions and riddles took place. The remnants of the sacrificial materials were sprinkled over the king. Soma was pressed all the three days. The function ended with a ceremonial bath (*avabhṛtha*).

āśvayujī One of the seven Pākayajñas (q.v.) which is to be performed on the full-moon day of Āśvina. Offerings consisting of cooked food and clarified butter are to be made to Śiva and the Aśvins. On that night calves are allowed to join their mothers and drink their full of milk. *Āśv.Gr.* II.2.1.3; *Sān.Gr.* IV.6.

atharvan Mentioned as a class of Pitṛs (q.v.) in *RV* X.14.6. The term also denotes magic rituals and their performers. The Iranian equivalent of the word is *athravan* which means priest. The Vedic text *Atharvaveda* was originally known as *Atharvāṅgirasaḥ*, that is, *atharvan* (holy magic bringing happiness) and *āṅgirasa* (hostile or black magic).

atibhaṅga Iconic pose of a deity with exaggerated flexion.

atideśa The process or method by which the details prescribed in connection with one sacrifice are transferred to another. The seventh chapter of *PMS* deals with the general question of the extension or transference of details in general to Aindrāgna and other sacrifices. It is frequently resorted to by Smṛtis and Digests. *Yāj* I. 236, 242, *Parāśara* VII.18–19.

atikṛcchra A penance lasting for twelve days which according to *Manu* XI.213 consisted of eating only one morsel of food for three days in the morning only; one morsel for three days in the evening only, for three days eating one morsel got without asking for it and observing a complete fast for the next three days. *Yāj* III.319 prescribes the eating of just as much food as would fill a cupped hand. Manu (XI.208) prescribes this penance for striking a Brāhmaṇa with a weapon. *Gautama Dh.S.*XXVI. 22 states that this penance purifies a man of all sins except the Mahāpātakas (q.v.). *Baudh.Dh.S.* IV.5.8, *Viṣṇu.Dh.S.* LIV.30, *Parāśara* XI.54–55.

atimārgī Follower of an extreme path.

atinaya An aspect of the *krama* (q.v.) doctrine.

atipātaka Great sin caused by sexual intercourse with one's mother, daughter or daughter-in-law. There is no penance for such sins except entering fire according to *Viṣṇu.Dh.S.* XXXIV.1–2. These are included in the Mahāpātaka (q.v.) list by Manu XI.58 and *Yāj*.III.233–34.

atirahasyayoginī Collective name of the three presiding goddesses of the three angles of the trikoṇa or mystic triangle. The goddess at the apex is known as Kāmeśvarī, on the right angle as Vajreśvarī and on the left angle as Bhagamalinī. *Gandharvatantra* V. 112–13.

atisāntapana The penance for the expiation of sin in which for six days one has to subsist on cow urine. *Viṣṇu Dh.S.*XLVI.21, *Agni Pu.*CLXXI.10. According to *Mit.* on Yaj III.315 this penance lasts for 12 days.

atirātra Soma sacrifice (q.v.) referred to even in *RV* VII.103.7, which is to be performed before Agniṣṭoma (q.v.) all through the night in four stages (Paryāyas). Puroḍāsa and animals, as well as cups of Soma, are offered to different deities, especially to the Aśvins. *Ait.Br.* XIV.3, *Śat.Br.* IX.7, *Āp.Sr.* XIV.3–8, XIV.4.11, *Āśv.Sr.* VI.4.10.

ātivāhika Intermediate body for the soul between the dead body and the future body.

ātma-bodha Same as *artha-pañcaka* (q.v.)

ātmaguṇa The eight cardinal virtues; they are kindness to all creatures, forbearance, freedom from envy, purity, ease, right conduct, magnanimity and contentment. *Gaut.Dh.S.* VIII.20–21.

atma-jñāna Knowledge of the self.

ātman The Self, the inner reality, which in the form of pure consciousness is manifested in every being. As infinite and conscious reality this self or Soul of a man (*jīvātmā*), according to the Upaniṣads, is identical with the self or Soul of all beings (*sarvabhūtātmā*) and therefore with *Brahman* which is the all-pervasive reality (*paramātmā*) underlying all things (*Bṛhadāraṇyaka* I.4.1, I.4.10, II.5.19, IV.6.5 *Aitareya* I.1, *Muṇḍaka* II.2.11, *Chāndogya* III.14.1, VI.2.1, VII.25.2, etc.). The body, the senses, the mind, the intellect and the like are merely sheaths (*koṣas*), the outer covers, the changing modes, not the permanent essence of the Self. According to the *Chāndogya* VIII.7.1. "The Self (*ātman*) which is free from sin, free from old age, from death and grief, from hunger and thirst, whose desires are true, whose cognitions are true, that is to be searched for, that is to be enquired; he gets all his desires and all worlds who knows that Self." The problem of the Vedic or early Brahmanical speculations was to define the relation between the *ātman* and the external world. A painful world, full of hunger and thirst, sorrow and confusion, old age and death, when contrasted with the all-perfect, all-pervading and all-beautiful *ātman*, would naturally give birth to absolute pessimism, the conception of metempsychosis, the endless cycles of births and deaths, and finally the doctrine of *karma* (q.v.) as the power predetermining the course of the migration of the soul from one state of being to another. That is why Buddhism seeks to explain these conditions in terms of an unbroken stream of successive states causally connected and extending backward and forward (making the past, present and future lives continuous) determined by the law of universal change and impermanence, and not in terms of Self or Soul. The Cārvākas also do not subscribe to the conception of *ātman* on the ground that consciousness can be no more than a quality of the body itself. In early Jainism the term Jiva (q.v.) stood for the vital principle rather than for the Soul or Self. Later on, however, the question of consciousness was emphasised (*TTDS* II.8, Guṇaratna on *SDSC* 47) and the Jīvas or living beings were theoretically arranged according to the degree of their consciousness. In accordance with the concept of *ātman*, the intrinsic nature of Jīva was conceived of as one of perfection, and it was characterised by infinite intelligence, infinite peace, infinite faith and infinite power. But owing to its association with *karma*, the forces of passions and desire, it becomes a victim of bondage. In the same way the later commentators on the Sankhya tried to interpret the anomalous concept of Puruṣa in terms of the Self which was thought to be in itself free and immortal, but under the influence of *avidyā* or ignorance it became confused with the body, the senses and the mind and thus become fettered. According to the Nyāya-Vaiśeṣikas the Self is a unique substance to which all cognitions, feelings and conations belong as its attributes. There are different selves in different bodies. They along with the Prābhākara Mīmāṃsakas maintain that the self is an unconscious substance which may acquire the attribute of consciousness under certain conditions. The Bhāṭṭa Mīmāṃsakas, on the other hand, think that the Self is a conscious entity which is partially hidden by ignorance, as appears from the imperfect and partial knowledge that men have of their own selves. The Advaita Vedānta holds that the Self is pure eternal consciousness. It is one, unchanging, and self-shining consciousness which is neither a subject nor an object. (*svaprakāśa-caitanya*). The Viśiṣṭādvaita Vedānta, however, holds that the Self is not a pure consciousness as such but a conscious subject called the ego (*jñātā ahamartha evamātmā*). See under Anātmā, Brahman.

ātmaśuddhi Purification of the self by various processes. *Kulārṇava* VI.

ātmatattva Doctrine of the Self.

ātmavali Sacrifice of the self. Complete surrender of one's mental faculties like thinking, feeling and willing to the supreme goddess according to Tantrism. *Gāyatrītantra* V.

ātma-yajña Sacrifice in the form of meditation on the Self.

aṭṭhamaka Those who have just stepped into the Buddhist Sotāpannahood (q.v.) which is the eighth or the lowest stage in the fruits of sanctification.

aṭṭhaṅgika-magga The path of eight-fold practices, the fourth truth preaced by Buddha, to be taken up by one seeking liberation; in Sanskrit Aṣṭāṅgika-mārga. It is divided into three sections; Śīla (q.v.) or moral precepts, i.e. observance of all the disciplinary rules embodied in the Vinaya Piṭaka, Citta (q.v.) or mind-control through various methods including meditations, and Pañña (q.v.) i.e. acquisition of knowledge by comprehending the nature and constitution of a being. In the category of Śīla are *sammā-vācā* (right speech), *sammā-kammanta* (right conduct) and *samma-ājiva* (right livlihood); in that of Citta *samma-saṅkappa* (right resolve), *sammā-vyāyāma* (right effort), *sammā sati* (right mindfulness) and *samma-samādhi* (right concentration; and in that of Pañña *sammā-diṭṭhi* (right perception.)

ātura-saṃnyāsa Asceticism for those who are suffering from disease and are about to die. All that is required is that they should declare in words and resolve in their minds to enter the order of Sannyāsa (q.v.).

atyagniṣṭoma One of the seven fundamental forms (*saṃsthās*) of the *sutyā* festival of the Soma sacrifice.

atyantasukha Extreme happiness, a precondition of *nirvāṇa* (q.v.). *Bodhisattvabhūmi* 9.

audakasnāna Bathing in a river. It is also known as Vāruṇasnāna.

aupaniṣada A curriculum of Vedic study meant

for the Brahmacārins (q.v.) mentioned in the *Gobhila Gr.* III.1.26–31. It comprised the study of Upaniṣad-Brāhmaṇa.

avabhṛtha Final purificatory bath in Agniṣṭoma (q.v.) and other sacrifices. A handful of *kuśa* grass is thrown into water to make it as pure as the *āhavanīya* (q.v.) for all offerings. *mahīyā-ṛk* (*RV.* VIII.48.3) is muttered by the Yajamāna (q.v.), priests and wife. Only a cake to Varuṇa is offered. The *sāman* (q.v.) chanted on this occasion is known as *avabhṛtha-sāman*. The Unnetṛ priest leads the sacrificer and others to the bath after which all sacrificial utensils are thrown into water. *Jaimini* X.7.47–50, *Āp.Sr.* XIII.19, *Taitt.S.*I.4.

avacchedavāda Vedantist theory of limitation according to which finitude is imposed on reality only by ignorance. Just as the same space is conceived to exist everywhere and yet it is conventionally divided, so also Brahman, which is one and all-pervasive reality, is supposed, through ignorance, to be limited and divided into different objects and souls. Liberation therefore consists in breaking the illusory barriers.

avadhi Form of knowledge which, according to the Jain conception, belongs to the category of *pratyakṣa* or direct knowledge of things. It is beyond the range of perception and be acquired through intuition. *TTDS*, I, 9ff.

avadhūta A class of ascetics who are beyond all restrictions. According to the *Sannyāsopaniṣad* 13 they take food from persons belonging to all Varṇas, except those who are charged with moral sins. They eat like an *ajagara*, i.e., while lying down and opening only the mouth without any effort, and are solely absorbed in contemplation. According to the Tantras, Avadhūta is the aspirant who commands universal reverence, who is free from all prejudices and who has knowledge of his own. *Kulārṇava* XVII. Avadhūtas are divided into two classes—householders and recluses. *Prāṇatoṣaṇī* VII.4. 532. Avadhūtas belonging to the highest grade are known as Kulāvadhūtas. *Mahānirvāṇa* VII.271–83. Avadhūta is also the name of a nerve.

avadhūtī Tantric name of a nerve channel. It is same as *susumnā*.

avaguṇṭhana-Mudrā A hand pose formed by clasping all the fingers of the left hand with the thumb except the index finger which remains open and pendant.

āvāhanī-mudrā A hand pose made by joining two outstretched palms while the thumbs touch the ring finger. *Tantrasāra* 567.

avakīrṇin A Brahmacārin (q.v.) who having undertaken the vow of celibacy happens to have sexual intercourse with a woman. Different types of penances are prescribed for him. Manu XI.118–21 and *Viṣṇu.Dh.S.* XXVIII. 49–50 prescribe that a person so guilty should, for one year, wear the skin of an ass and beg for food at seven houses announcing to them his lapse. Śabara says that he should sacrifice an ass to Nirṛti. Cf. *Āp.Dh.S.* I.9.26.8, *Yāj.*III.220.

avarabhāgīya Lower fetters in the way to Nirvāṇa (q.v.).

āvaraṇa The veil which keeps the soul away from freedom. According to certain Vedantic schools Jīvas or individuals are said to be constituted by the *āvaraṇa*-power of Avidyā or Māyā. In Tantric tradition *āvaraṇa* sometimes means enclosure, nine of which form the Śrīcakra. In Buddhism there are two such veils in regard to the impurities (*kleśa*) and truth (*jñeya*).

āvaraṇa-cakra Another name of *navacakra* (q.v.). *Tantrarāja* V.9–11.

āvaraṇa-devatā Tantric goddesses, also known as Yoginīs, presiding over the nine *cakras*. Their names are Prakaṭā, Guptā, Sampradāyā, Kulakaulyā, Nigarbhā, Rahasyā, Atirahasyā and Parapararahasyā. *Setubandha* Com. on *Nityaṣoḍaśikārṇava* I. 164–65. Āvaraṇa-devatā also means deities of a subsidiary character or accessory figures in the shrines of the major cult deities.

āvāsa Residence, especially for the Buddhist and Jain monks, to live collectively under rules of discipline for the purpose of spiritual self-culture. An *āvāsa* was circumscribed by metes and bounds, so that the residents therein during the period of rain retreat often formed a sectarian communion.

avatāra Incarnation. In the *Mbh* and *Rām*, the popular view is frequently expressed that God comes down to earth often to punish the wicked, to protect the good and for the establishment of *dharma*. The concept of *avatāra* influenced in some way or other all the religious system of India, but the incarnations of Viṣṇu are the most popular. The origin of this conception may be traced to *RV* VIII.17.13 in which Indra is supposed to have descended on earth in human form. The idea of spiritual generation is not also unknown in the Jain and Buddhist tradition. The succession of Tīrthaṃkaras and also the concept of the past and future Buddhas as well as that of Buddha's rebirth in different forms as found in the Jātakas must have some bearing on the incarnation theory.

avayava Constituent propositions of syllogism, being one of the sixteen philosophical topics of the Nyāya. These are *pratijña* which asserts something; *hetu* or reason for the assertion; *udāharaṇa* or showing the connection between the asserted fact and reason with known examples; *upanaya* or application of the universal proposition to a particular case and *nigamana* or the conclusion which follows. The Mīmāṃsakas and the Vedāntists hold that the first three or the last three are sufficient for inference.

āveśāvatāra An Avatāra (q.v.) or god incarnate for a little period of time.

aveṣṭi A form of Iṣṭi (q.v.) required in the Rājasūya (q.v.) in which *puroḍāsas* are offerd to Agni and others. It is also an independent Yāga which may be performed by any one of the three *varṇas*. The *Nirṇayasindhu* relies upon this difference in Aveṣṭi for its conclusions about Devīpūjā or the worship of the goddess on different dates.

avidhavānavamī A Śrāddha (q.v.) performed for one's mother or other woman of one's family who predeceases her husband. It should be performed on the 9th day in the dark half of the month of Bhādrapada. In this Śrāddha besides a Brāhmaṇa, a woman whose husband is alive is to be fed and presented with a girdle, a garland and bangles.

avidyā See under Ajñāna and Avijjā. According to the Yoga, *avidyā* is one of the five *kleśas* (q.v.) or sources of afflictions. It is wrong knowledge of the non-self as the self, of the unpleasant as the pleasant, and of the impure as pure. According to Śaṅkara the world exists only for those who are under the influence of *avidyā* or *māyā* (q.v.). Both the terms have been used by him also to denote the material cause of the world. The term is also used in the sense of material or imperfect knowledge as a synonym of *aparā-vidyā*.

avidyopādanabhedavāda The theory that *avidyā* or *māyā* is the staff of the world of diversity.

avijjā Lack of true knowledge. The usual meaning attributed to it in the Buddhist Nikāyas is 'non-comprehension of four truths' while in the Abhidhamma it is non-comprehension of the world-beginning (*pubbānta*) and world-end (*aparānta*), eternalism (*sāssata*) and annihilationism (*uccheda*) and of 'this-conditional' nature of objects (*idappaccayatā*).

avikṛtapariṇāma The Vallabhite doctrine according to which the *brahman* (q.v.) creates the world out of himself for *līlā* or sport, and is thus both the efficient and material cause of the universe. He does not undergo any change even when he transforms himself into the world. The universe is the effect of *brahman* representing his *ādhibhautika* (material) form which is non-different from it. *Tattvārthadīpa* I. 94, II.86 etc.

avinābhava sambandha Relation of non-duality or identity which holds good in the case of Śiva and Śakti in the Tantras.

avīra Tantric aspirants belonging to the probationary stages of *ārambha, taruṇa, yauvana* and *prauḍha*, Rāmeśvara's *vṛtti* on *Paraśurāmakalpasūtra* X.58. They are not sufficiently advanced in spiritual attainment to qualify as Vīra.

avirati Want of control; according to Jainism it is one of the constituents of *bhāvāsrava* (q.v.). It is of five kinds: *hiṃsā* or violence, *anṛta* or falsehood, *caurya* or stealing, *abrahma* or incontinence and *parigrahākāṅkṣā* on covetousness of the property of other persons.

aviruddhaka A class of wandering ascetics mentioned in *Aṅguttara* III.276–76.

aviveka See under Ajñāna.

aviyoga-vrata A ceremonial in which food is to be distributed to helpless people.

avyakta See Prakṛti. In the Tantric *Saubhāgyabhāskara* 99 the term *avyakta* has been used to denote *kāraṇa-vindu* or the root cause manifested in effect.

avyākṛta 'Indeterminable' in the Buddhist concept. The *avyākṛtas* also refer to those problems which Buddha left unanswered. These problems are always mentioned in a stereotyped form in all Buddhist texts, whether Hīnayāna or Mahāyāna.

avyaṅga The waist-girdle peculiar to the Sun images of the north.

ayācita A substitute method for an absolute fast on *ekādaśī* or the eleventh day after the full and new moon.

āyāgapaṭa A slab carved with sacred Jain figures and symbols.

ayaḥśūlika A class of wandering ascetics mentioned by Pāṇini who probably carried a bamboo staff, or iron spear, or trident.

āyatana The sense organs and their objects; the former being distinguished in Buddhism as internal (*ajjhattika*) and the latter as external (*bāhira*). The function of the *āyatanas* is not only to develop the perceptions (*viññāna*) but also to entangle a being in repeated existence.

āyudha Weapons serving as attributes of different deities in their conceptual and iconic representations.

āyudhapuruṣa Weapons meant to be placed in the hands of the deities when personified and represented anthropomorphically, e.g., *cakrapuruṣa* (wheel in the form of a man), *gadādevī* (club in the form of a woman) and so on. These are installed as accessory figures flanking the main deity.

āyuṣya A rite in the Jātakarma (q.v.) consisting in muttering over the navel or in the right ear of the child a *mantra* to invoke the bestowal of long life. *Āśv.Gr.* I.15.

ayutahoma A *homa* (q.v.) in which ten thousands oblations are offered. It is a kind of Navagrahaśānti or appeasement of the nine planets so that they may not do any harm. It is also performed at marriages, installation of images and on various other occasions.

bādhita The fallacy of contradicted probans according to Nyāya and other schools of Indian thought. This fallacy arises when the absence of the probandum in the subject is ascertained by means of other evidence. For example, when it is argued that fire is not-hot because it is a substance and all substances like water, etc., are known to be not-hot, it becomes a case of *bādhita* fallacy.

bahiḥpūjā See Bahiryāga.

bahirdaśāra The outer ground of mystic Tantric diagrams, meant for the representation of the five elements like space, etc., and five *tanmātras* (q.v.) like sound, etc., symbolised by the ten letters beginning with *ka*. *Nityaṣoḍaśikārṇava* VI.16. The ten triangles by which the theme is represented are presided over by ten goddesses, (*ibid.* I. 184–86). They belong to the clan of *āvaraṇa-devatā* (q.v.) and are styled Kulakaula-yoginī. *Gandharvatantra* V. 102.

bahirmatṛkānyāsa Feeling the deity in three forms—creative, sustaining and destructive—in the outer parts of the body in terms of the symbolism of prescribed letters known as mātṛkās (q.v.). It is to be done after performing the antarmātṛkānyāsa (q.v.). Tantrasāra 89.

bahiryāga External worship; counterpart of *antaryāga* (q.v.) or internal worship.

bahispavamāna First *stotra* (q.v.) in the morning pressing of Soma. It has nine verses; *RV* IX.11. 1–3, IX.64.28–30, IX.66.10–12.

bahuśrutīya A sect of the Mahāsaṅghikas (q.v.) which flourished in the north-west of India about the beginning of the Christian era. This school preferred a syncretism of Hīnayāna and Mahāyāna and adopted the *Satyasiddhiśāstra* of Harivarman as its main text. According to Vasumitra, this school held that Buddha's teaching relating to the transitoriness, suffering, non-existence of objects, absence of soul and the ultimate goal were *lokottara* (supramundane) while his teachings on topics other than these were *laukika* (mundane). According to Paramārtha, this school attributed two meanings to the teachings of Buddha, *nitārtha* (direct) and *neyārtha* (indirect).

bāhyapūjā Same as Bahiryāga.

baindava-śarīra See under Praṇava-tanu.

bākapañcaka Five days in Kārtika (Oct-Nov) beginning with the eleventh *tithi* or day according to the lunar rotation, that is the bright half of the month during which abstinence from flesh-eating is desired.

bala Five (sometimes ten) supernatural powers possessed by a Tathāgata. *Majjhima* I.69–71.

bāla-kṛcchra A form of penance also known as Śiśu-Kṛcchra and Laghu-Kṛcchra. It lasts for four days; on the first day food is eaten once only in the day time, on the second day it is eaten only once but at night, on the third day it is eaten once and that food got without asking, and a complete fast is observed on the fourth day. *Baudh. Dh.S.* II.1.92, *Yāj* III.318.

balarāmī A liberal mystic sect of medieval North India which was greatly influenced by the Sahajiyā, Nairañjanī and Nātha cults and to a certain extent by Islam.

bali Sacrifice, oblation, gift offering.

baliharaṇa A Vaiśvadeva ritual, also known as Bhūtayajña in which an offering of cooked food is made to all gods, to the waters, to the herbs and trees, to all day-walking beings, to the Rākṣasas, to the Pitṛs and so on. The offering is not made to the fire but placed on the ground. Food must also be distributed among men of the lower castes and even among crows and dogs. Whatever remains of the *bali* food is offered to the Pitṛs. *Āśv. Gr.* I.2.3–11, *Gobhila Gr.* I.4.5–15, *Pār Gr.* II.9, *Āp.Dh.S.* II.2.3.15–11, II.4.9; *Gaut. Dh.S.* V.10–15, *Mbh.* III.2.59, *Manu* III.121.

balipratipadā The day on which the lunar bright half begins in the month of Kārtika (Oct-Nov), or next day after Dīpāvalī, sacred to Bali, the demon king who was thrust into the nether region by Viṣṇu. On this day the image of Bali is worshipped. This day is also marked by Govardhanapūjā for the increase of cattle and by *annakūṭa* (food offering to all persons). In some parts of the country, people engage in gambling in memory of the fact that on this day Śiva was defeated in dice-play by Pārvatī.

bāṇaliṅga Symbolic phallus of Śiva, made of white stones found in rivers. It is believed that 14 crores of *liṅgas* were established in various spots by Bāṇa, an Asura devotee of Śiva, and these are known as Bāṇaliṅgas. It is one of the three forms of *liṅga* (phallus), the others being *itara* and *svayambhū*. In the Tantric conception it is said to reside within the triangle of the *anāhata-cakra* (q.v.). *Saṭcakranirūpaṇa* XXV.

bandha Bondage; it commonly means the process of birth and rebirth and the consequent miseries to which an individual is subject. The term is especially used in Jainism; there are two kinds of bondage: *bhāva-bandha* caused by passion or bad disposition and *dravya-bandha* caused by the influx of matter which the Jīva (q.v) takes up in accordance with its *karma* (q.v.) See *TTDS*, VIII.2 ff. The term *duḥkha* (suffering) is very often used in different systems like the Sāṅkhya to denote bondage. In Buddhism it has been explained in terms of a chain of causes and effects (see Paṭiccasamuppāda). According to the Nyāya-Vaiśeṣikas, owing to the body and sense organs the individual has to experience pain and suffering. The Sāṅkhya admits of three kinds of pain, namely, *ādhyātmika* (q.v.). *ādhibhautika* (q.v.) and *ādhidaivika* (q.v.). *Sān. Kārikā* 44–68, *Sāṅ. Sūt.* 3.65–84. According to the Yoga, the self's bondage is due to its identification with mental modifications caused by the five sources of afflictions (*kleśas*, q.v.) to which a human being is subject; *vidyā, asmitā, rāga, dveṣa* and *abhiniveśa* (qq.v.). *Yogasūtra* I.1–4, I. 12–18, I.23 etc. The Advaita Vedāntins hold that bondage is due to the soul's association with body. Out of ignorance it forgets that it is really *brahman*, and this is bondage. See also Mokṣa. Nirvāṇa.

bandha-karma The *karma* (q.v.) which is being accumulated in the present life according to Jain conception.

bandhu Friend or kin (described by the *Mit.* on *Yāj* II. 135 as *bhinnagotra-sapiṇḍa* who is involved in with funeral impurities by virtue of his relation to the departed one. Bandhus are of three kinds: *ātmabandhu, pitṛbandhu* and *matṛbandhu*. A *bandhutā* theory is found in Brahmāṇa literature which is based on the association of certain common characteristics of the gods and the rituals connected with them.

bārhaspatya A doctrine akin to the views of the Lokāyatas (q.v.) and the Cārvākas (q.v.). Named after Bṛhaspati this doctrine upholds a materialist worldview. See under Cārvāka, Lokāyata, Svabhāvadāda, Yadṛcchā, Bhūtavāda.

baṭuka-bhairava Youthful (*baṭuka*) Śiva of the *bhairava* (q.v.) category. In iconic representation he is shown nude, terrific in appearance with protruding fangs, round rolling eyes, holding a sword or other weapons, often wearing wooden sandals and accompanied by a dog.

bhadrāsana A particular *āsana* (q.v.) or posture of sitting found in cult images in which both legs are pendant.

bhadrayānika A Buddhist sect to which is attributed the doctrine of *anupubbābhisamaya* or gradual realisation of the four truths in *Kathāvatthu* II.4. On many points this school is in agreement with the views of the Sāmmitīyas (q.v.).

bhaga Term for generative organ. The word later came to mean different qualities of a human being. In a special sense it is applied to the six qualities or types of non-material wealth (*ṣaḍaiśvarya*); fulness of sway, manliness or energy, glory, auspiciousness, knowledge and indifference to worldly objects.

bhaga-liṅga-kriyā Actions involving female and male genital organs in the cult of the Female Principle.

bhagavat Derived from *bhaga* (q.v.) the word applies to God. The word may also be applied to those possessing special qualities. That person may be called *bhagavān* who knows about the creation and dissolution of the world, about the origin and final destiny of beings, and knows what is *vidyā* and *avidyā*. Knowledge, strength, power, sway, manliness, splendour—all these in their entirety are expressed by the word *bhagavat*. *Viṣṇupurāṇa* VI.5. 78–79.

bhāgavata One who worships *bhagavat* (q.v.). In a specific sense the word denotes the worshipper of Vāsudeva. In the Ghosundi stone inscription (*EI*, XVI.25–27, *IA*, LXI. 203–205) there is reference to both Saṅkarṣaṇa and Vāsudeva as *bhagavat* while in the Besnagar column inscription Heliodoros calls himself *bhāgavata* and a devotee of Vāsudeva. The *Śvetāśvatara* III.11 speaks of Śiva as *bhagavān*. Patañjali in his com. on Pāṇini V.2.76 speaks of Śivabhāgavata. It appears that the followers of devotional (*bhakti*) monotheism, in which the supreme being is conceived of in terms of a personal god, were known as *bhāgavatas*.

bhaga-yāga See under Latā-sādhanā.

bhairava A human teacher who seems to have attained complete spiritual emancipation and become almost Śiva; their views are reflected in the Tantric Yāmala literature. Eight Yāmalas are said to have been communicated by the eight Bhairavas: Svacchanda, Krodha, Unmatta, Ugra, Kapālin, Jhaṅkāra, Śekhara and Vijaya. The term Bhairava also applies to Śiva, his emanations, incarnations and attendants and also the consort-cum-priests of the Mother Goddesses of different Śakti-pīṭhas. The Tantric aspirant may consider himself as a Bhairava in any of the senses mentioned above.

bhairavaikātmya A Tantric term for *mokṣa* or *jīvanmukti* (liberation). It is the unity of *jīva* (individual) with *bhairava* (supreme being who is

Śiva). Only those who are born of parents mentally approximating Śiva and Śakti are entitled to this form of liberation *Paratrṃśikā* 234.

bhairavī Female partner of the Tantric aspirant who is supposed to impersonate Śakti or the Female Principle of Creation, the supreme being of the Śākta-Tantric cults.

bhairavī-cakra A Tantric Cakra (q.v.) ritual in which the five Ms (see *pañcatattva*) are used. The male and female aspirants sit together and perform the rites which include drinking of wine and sexual intercourse. For details see *Mahānirvāṇa* VIII 54–206, *Kulārṇava* VIII, *Kaulāvalinirṇaya* VII.

bhajana The art of surrendering one's own self to the supreme being. The word also stands for devotional songs. In the second sense it has a two-fold significance—praise of the Lord and music of a particular type.

bhakta Devotee. According to the degree of intensity of their love of God, the Bhaktas are divided into four classes. Dāsya-bhaktas—loving servants with the consciousness of the superiority of God's position as their master; Sakhya-bhaktas—friends who consider themselves equal to God in every respect; Vātsalya-bhaktas—parents like Yaśodā and Nandagopa; and Kāntā-bhaktas who consider themselves as lovers, like the Gopīs.

bhakti Loving faith in God and surrender to him. Sāṇḍilya defines *bhakti* as *sāparānuraktirīśvara*. This means either 'the highest form of *bhakti* is affection fixed on God' or '*bhakti* is the highest affection fixed on God'. It is also explained as the state of mind having the supreme being as its object. The Gītā derives the word from the root *bhaj* meaning 'to resort to'. Bhakti is divided into *laukikī* (of the common people), *vaidikī* (laid down by the Veda) and *ādhyātmikī* (philosophical), or *mānasī* (mental), *vācikī* (verbal) and *kāyikī* (done with body such as fast, *vratas*, etc.); or into *sāttvikī, rājasī* and *tāmasī*. *Padmapurāṇa* V.15.164–68, VI.126.4–11, *Bhāgavata* III. 29.7–16, *Brahmāṇḍa* III.34.38–41. The theory propounded in the *Bhagavadgītā* and other works on *bhakti* is that it leads to the *prasāda* (grace or favour) of God which enables the devotee to attain liberation.

bhāṇaka Buddhist term for reciter of the texts.

bhāṇḍabrahmāṇḍatattva The theory that the body (*bhāṇḍa*) is the microcosm of the universe (*brahmāṇḍa*).

bhāṇḍikera A Tantric sect metioned in the *Śakti-saṅgama-tantra*.

bhasma The inner intuition which reveals the self and destroys by burning illusion. As an outer symbol of this the Pāsupata, the Liṅgāyata and other forms of Śaiva religion enjoin *bhasma-dhāraṇa* or besmearing the body with ashes.

bhāṣya That which sets out the meaning of the sūtra (q.v.) or an aphorism which follows the text of the *sūtra* and makes its own contribution to the elucidation of the subject of the *sūtra*. Commonly the term is used in the sense of commentary.

bhauma-snāna Smearing the body with loose earth; also known as Pārthiva-snāna.

bhava Desire for existence. The word has two distinct meaning. One is existence according to one's past deeds, called *kammabhava* and is regulated by three kinds of *saṅkhārā* (q.v.)—merit (*puñña*), demerit (*apuñña*) and neither merit nor demerit (*āneñja*). The other is the plane of existence wherein a being is reborn called *uppatibhava*; the three planes of existence are Kāma, Rūpa and Arūpa Lokas. *Visuddhimagga* 572.

bhāva Dispositions according to which mankind is classified in Tantrism. These are *divya* or the man with a divine disposition, *vīra* or the man with a heroic disposition and *paśu* or the man with an animal disposition. In Vaiṣṇavism, bhāva is the mode of approach to devotion like *dāsya* (servant-like), *sakhya* (friend-like), *vātsalya* (filial), *kānta* or *madhura* (romantic) etc. The *Gītā* explains the term as 'tendency' and classifies it into *sattva* (q.v.), *rajas* (q.v.) and *tamas* (q.v.). In philosophical tradition it denotes existence, positiveness and so on.

bhāva-bandha One of the two major classes of the Jain concept of *bandha* (q.v.) or bondage caused by the union of the soul with *pudgala* (q.v.). The states of thought which condition the accumulation of *karma* (q.v.) are called *bhāva-bandha* on account of which the actual connection between *karma* and the *Jīva* (q.v.) takes place. *DS* (vṛtti), 30ff., *VP* XVI.44.

bhāvābhāvādvaya Identity of existence and non-existence which belongs to the ten kinds of 'sameness' to be realised by a potential Bodhisattva in its sixth *bhūmi* (q.v.), according to the Mahāyāna Buddhist conception.

bhāvādvaita A type of non-dualism which excludes the duality of positive entities, but does not exclude the existence of negatives like *avidyāh-*

vaṃsa (destruction of ignorance) and *prapañcābhāva* (disappearance of manifestations). *Brahmasiddhi* III.

bhāva-liṅga One of the three forms of *liṅga* (q.v.) according to the Vīra-Śaiva conception. It is associated with *yogāṅga* (q.v.) or the highest stage leading to perfection. Bhāva-liṅga is the infinite Divine which sees the truth in itself as the truth in its becoming as well as in its essence. It contains comprehensively and not separately all that emerges as ideas. Bhāva-liṅga and *yogāṅga* are concerned with *prajñājīva* (q.v.), the condition of deep sleep symbolic of a transformation into a new state of consciousness.

bhāvanā One of the constituents of the Jain concept of *bhāvasaṃvara* (q.v.). It is meditation or contemplation on twelve aspects of Jain dogma: *anitya* (transitoriness), *aśaraṇa* (no shelter), *saṃsāra* (cycle of rebirth), *ekatva* (loneliness), *anyatva* (reality of soul as separate from body), *aśauca* (impurity), *āsrava* (influx from outside), *saṃvara* (way to stop influx), *nirjarā* (thinking about performing austerities), *loka* (thinking about the universe), *bodhi* (belief in the probability of getting better) and *dharma* (belief in the truth of the creed). In Pūrva-mīmāṃsā *bhāvanā* means a particular operation or activity of an agent which initiates the desired result. It is of two kinds, *śābdī* (word-force) and *ārthī* (result-producing force). In Buddhism *bhāvanā* is comprehension which is regarded as one of the two ways or (*mārgas*) leading to salvation, the other being *darśana*.

bhavanapati A class of gods in the Jain pantheon belonging to the residential group.

bhāvanāsiddhi A form of devotion and attainment in which the deity is conceived in terms of one's own mental formulation of it.

bhavaṅga A form of subliminal consciousness which results from one's past actions. It becomes inactive when the organs of sense grow strong enough to function in their respective spheres. *Saṃyutta* I. 122, II.67, 103.

bhavaṅguppaccheda The boundary between being and thought which is called the threshold of mind in Buddhism.

bhava-pratyaya The class of beings who are born without organic encumbrances and possessing a natural capacity to know themselves. They are not possessed of perfect knowledge. That is why they do not have automatic salvation. They require to shake off the little ignorance which fetters them. *Yogasūtra* I.19.

bhavasaṃvara One of the two classes of Saṃvara (q.v.) or stoppage of the influx of *karma* (q.v.) according to Jain ideas. It comprises the observance of the following rules and restraints: the five vows; the *samitis* consisting of the avoidance of the killing of insects (*iryā*), undertaking gentle and holy talk (*bhāṣā*), and receiving proper alms (*iṣaṇā*), etc.; *guptis* or restraints of body, mind and speech; *dharmas* consisting of the ten virtues; *anuprekṣā* consisting or meditations of various forms; *parīsahājaya* consisting of the conquering of all kinds of external conditions and *cāritra* (q.v.) or right conduct.

bhavasantati Buddhist term for denoting the continuity of existence.

bhavāsava Impurities caused by worldly attachments. It is a Buddhist conception. *Paṭisambhidāmagga* II.96.

bhāvāsrava One of the two classes of *āsrava* (q.v.) denoting thought activities through which the *karma* (q.v.) particles enter the soul according to Jainism. It is of five kinds, namely, *mithyātva* (q.v.) or delusion, *avirati* (q.v.) or want of control, *pramāda* (q.v.) or inadvertence, *yoga* or activities of body, mind and speech and *kaṣāya* (q.v.) or passions.

bhāvatva A term for 'being'.

bhāvin A term for Devadāsī, i.e., girls dedicated to temples. This word is especially used in the southern part of the Ratnagiri district.

bheda Difference, which is generally supposed to be of three kinds; amongst the *Jīvas* (q.v.) themselves, amongst insentients themselves and that between the *jīvas* and insentients. According to another classification it is five-fold: one *jīva* and another, *jiva* and *brahman*, insentients and the *jīvas*, one insentient and another, and insentients and *brahman*.

bhedābheda Rāmānuja's conception of the relation between *brahman* and the Self. While Śaṅkara holds that it is one of complete identity (*abheda*) Rāmānuja holds it to be identity-in-difference (*bhedābheda*) by regarding the self as a part of *brahman*, since the relation between part and the whole is both of identity and difference. (Rāmānuja's com. on *Ved. Sūt.* II.1.15, II.1.22, II.3, 42 etc.). Bhāskara holds that the world of matter has real existence, though it is essentially of the same nature as *brahman* which becomes manifold by its *pariṇāmaśakti* (q.v.) or power of transformation like the spider weaving its web. The Self is naturally one with *brahman* while its difference with *brahman* is due to its *upādhis* (q.v.). (Bhāskaras com. on *Ved. Sūt.* I.4.25, II.3, IV.4). According to Yādava, *brahman* is transformed into Īśvara, *cit* and *acit*, the causal constituents of the universe. Conscious (*cit*) and material (*acit*) forms are only different states (*avasthābheda*) of one substance and not different substances themselves. *Sarvārthasiddhi* III. 27.

bhikkhu Same as *bhikṣu*.

bhikṣā Alms obtained by begging. It was the duty of householders to give alms to the Brahmacārīs (students) and Yatis (ascetics). Food might be begged from all the Varṇas except from those who are *abhiśapta* (guilty of grave sins) and *patita* (outcasted). Food obtained by begging was supposed to be pure and was to be placed before the teacher. Apart from the students, begging was allowed to the diseased and those oppressed by hunger and to such persons who did it for the teacher, for one's marriage, for a sacrifice, in anxiety to support one's parents, and to ward off the sin caused by the non-observance of the duties expected of a worthy person and so on. *Āp.Dh.S.* I.1.3.25–44, II.5.10.1–4, *Vas.Dh.S.* XII.2–3, *Baudh.Dh.S.* I.2.17, I.2.54, I.5.56, II.1.64, *Viṣṇu.Dh.S.* III.79–80, *Gaut.* Dh.S. XVIII. 28–30, *Āśv.Gr.* I.22. 7–8, *Manu.* II.182–189, *Yāj.* I.29–32, 187, III.43.

bhikṣātanamūrti The iconic form of Śiva in which the god begged for food and received it from his consort. There is a mythological background to this conception.

bhikṣu Representatives of the Sannyāsa (q.v.) order. The *Bṛhadāraṇyaka* Upaniṣad (III.5.1, IV.2.22) defines Bhikṣus as those who give up desire and practise begging in order to realise *brahman* (q.v.). In Buddhism the term received a special significance. It came to denote the monks residing in the *saṅgha* under certain definite rules and regulations. Although begging from the householders for subsistence was a part of their daily duties, they had other important functions to perform as preachers of the creed and as enlightened persons free from worldly fetters. The status of a *bhikṣu* had to be attained through a prolonged course of religious exercises and after undergoing proper initiation. The nuns were called *bhikṣuṇīs*. There are many Buddhist texts which dealing with the rules and regulations to be followed by *bhikṣus* and *bhiksuṇīs*. See also *pravrajyā* and *upasampadā*.

bhīma Name of the six-petalled lotus of the *svādhiṣṭhāna-cakra* (q.v.). *Nirvāṇatantra* V.

bhoga Trials and troubles of common life, experience, etc. *Bhogabhūmi* is the term for material world.

bhogāṅga The transformed *taijasa-jīva*(the soul in the dreaming condition) according to the Vīra Śaiva conception. The subtle body is the means through which the *taijasa-jīva* experiences pleasure and pain by means of sensuous objects. The devotee, having given up carnal objects, and taken to the realisation of self, takes delight only in what is conducive of spiritual growth. Hence he is called *bhogāṅgin*; for him Prāṇa-liṅga (q.v.) becomes the object of worship.

bhogopabhogapariṇāma A Jain vow of physical discipline consisting in strict adherence to limited food and comfort.

bhogya Things enjoyable represented by the *acit* (q.v.). The term *bhogya-kāṇḍa* denotes in Āgamic Śaivism the 24 impure principles corresponding closely to the evolutes of *prakṛti* (q.v.) of the Sāṅkhya.

bhojana Partaking of a meal; this was raised to the level of a sacred ritual. In the Vedic literature great importance was attached to the purity of food and there were elaborate rules about every aspect of eating. For example when food was to be eaten, the direction in which one had to be seated to eat, the vessels to be used, preliminaries before eating (such as *ācamana*, *prāṇāhutis*, etc.), the posture at the time of eating, how much to eat, how *paṅktis* (rows of dinner) were distinguished and who were the *paṅktipāvana* Brāhmaṇas and etiquette while eating. Occasions like eclipses were specified for abstaining from taking food, or what food should or should not be taken and various grounds on which food was forbidden. Flesh-eating was never taboo but there were elaborate rules about the flesh of beasts, birds and fishes. Exhaustive lists of persons are found from whom food may not be accepted by Brāhmanas and there are great variations in these rules. All intoxicants were forbidden to the Brāhmaṇas from the time of the Sūtras but these were allowed to the Kṣatriyas and others. *RV.*I.187.1–7, *Ch.Up.*VII.26.2, *Taitt.Br.* I.4.9, II.1.1, III.1.3, *Śat.Br.* II.4.2–6, *Āp.Dh.S.* I.11.31.1 etc. *Baudh.-Dh.S.* II.7–31–32 etc. *Manu* V.1 ff. etc.

bhoktṛ The enjoyer represented by the *jīva* (q.v.).

bhrama-saṃskāra One of the two kinds of indeterminable *avidyā* (q.v.) which is error-impression, referred to by Vācaspati in the introductory verse of *Bhāmatī*.

bhṛtyācāra It is the devotee's attitude of complete humility towards Śiva and his devotees in the Vīra Śaiva concept.

bhujaṅgama-mantra A class of defective *mantras* (q.v.). Rāghava on *Śāradātilaka* II. 111.

bhukti-mukti All-round success.

bhuktisiddhi An attainment consisting of material and spiritual success; it is to be achieved through the rituals of *aṣṭakoṇacakra*. *Gandharvatantra* XVIII.75.

bhūman The infinite principle which, according to the Upaniṣads, as a universal cannot be defined in terms of finite categories. Same as *brahman* (q.v.) or *ātman* (q.v.).

bhūmi States of spiritual progress of a potential Bodhisattva (q.v.). These are ten in number: Pramuditā (q.v.) or joyous, Vimalā (q.v.) or immaculate, Prabhākari (q.v.) or shining, Arciṣmati (q.v.) or radiant, Sudurjayā (q.v.) or hard-to-win, Abhimukhi (q.v.) or right-in-front, Duraṅgamā (q.v.) or far-going, Acalā (q.v.) or immovable, Sādhumati (q.v.) or stage of good thought and Dharmamegha (q.v.) or cloud of the law. In the Brahmanical tradition, the term denotes state or objective conditions.

bhūmikā The stages of realisation in the Yoga system. It is almost same as the Buddhist concept of *bhūmi* (q.v.). The difference is that while in the latter it is attained by meditation upon the categories of existence in the former it is attained by meditation upon ethical properties.

bhūmisparśa A mudrā or hand pose characteristic of Buddha images. The right hand exhibits this mudrā; the palm turned inward and the fingers outstretched with the tips touching the ground. Also called Bhūmisparśana or Bhūsparśa.

bhupura A Tantric quadrangle with four doors and a triangle inside, the lines of which are known as Brahmā, Viṣṇu and Śiva. On the Brahmā line are situated ten *siddhis* (q.v.) on the Viṣṇu line eight *mātrkās* (q.v.) and on the Śiva line the ten *mudrā-śaktis* (q.v.). *Gandharvatantra* V.76, *Nityaṣoḍaśikārṇava* I.166ff.

bhūr Synonym of earth.

bhūta The First Principle according to certain cosmogonical speculations as recorded in *Śvetāśvatara Up.* (I.1–2) along with Yoni and Puruṣa. In *Suśruta*, Śārīra I.11, Puruṣa has been excluded and Bhūta and Yoni have been substituted by Prakṛti (q.v.) which implies that Bhūta or Elements, the basic constituents of matter, formed the substratum of the Sāṅkhya. There are five elements: earth, water, fire, air and space. See Mahābhūtas. The *RV* refers to one element, namely, water. The Upaniṣads refer to additional elements like fire and air. The Svabhāvavādins (q.v.) believed in four elements excluding space as the fifth. Five elements are recognised in the Sāṅkhya as evolutes of Prakṛti. The doctrine of elements is also recognised by the Nyāya-Vaiśeṣikas and the Mīmāṃsakas. The first four elements have colour and sensivity while the fifth one, space, is the substratum of sound. The *Vaiś.Sūt.* II.1.6–7, V.1.17–18, V.2.13. etc., says that every element, being cause, can produce effect, but the production of effect is conditional. Water can produce vapour as well as ice under diverse conditions. Earth is hard by itself but under certain conditions it can be reduced into atoms. Earth and water have motion and gravity, but the latter quality is absent in fire and air. Matter of wider dimension can hold that of smaller dimension, and as such that which is widest, namely ākāśa or space, can contain everything.

bhūta A class of mischievous spirits or hobgoblins.

bhūtāpasāraṇa Chasing away evil spirits and disturbances with the help of *mantras*. During sacrifice, it is done by sprinkling white mustard seeds around the altar. *Tantrasāra* 616, *Puraścaryārṇava* III.154, Rāghava on *Śaradātilaka* IV.10.

bhūtārthavāda One of the three kinds of *arthavāda* (q.v.). When a text is not opposed to other *pramāṇas* (q.v.) or is not definitely ascertained otherwise it is called *bhūtārthavāda*, i.e. statement of an accomplished fact or of a past event. It is a *Mīmāṃsaka concept. Śaṅkara on Ved.Sūt.* I.3.33 calls it Vidyamānavāda. It is otherwise known as *bhūtārthanuvāda*.

bhūtarūpa Primal matter out of which things come into existence. It is constituted by the *mahābhūtas* (q.v.)

bhūtaśuddhi Purification of the five elements—earth, water, fire, air and space—of which the body is constituted. It is done with *mantras* and magical rites and also with the help of Yogic exercises. *Tantrasāra* 85–87, *Prāṇatoṣaṇi* III.5, 202, *Puraścaryārṇava* III.6, 166–68, *Tārābhaktisudhārṇava* V. 153–57.

bhūta-tathatā Perfect knowledge of reality as neither existent nor non-existent, neither both nor either, according to Mahāyāna conception.

bhūtavāda One of the five basic principles of the Cārvāka philosophy, according to which the four material elements—earth, water, fire and air—are the only real entities by the combination of which everything is formed.

bhūtayajña Same as Baliharaṇa. In the Purāṇas *bhūtayajña* means feeding living beings both visible and invisible. The ethics of *bhūtayajña* rests on the knowledge of the *ātman* as immanent in all creatures. *Viṣṇu* II.6.

bhuvana(s) The ethereal, the aerial, the igneous, the aquatic and the terrene regions. These are names of the worlds of subtle or gross planes of matter according to most of the religious systems of India. In the Tantras, these *bhuvanas* are equated with the different stages of the body and mind of the aspirant. The *Vāyavīya Saṃhitā* says that the lowest of these *bhuvanas* is *mūlādhāra* (q.v.) and the highest *unmanī* (q.v.)

bhuvas Synonym of atmosphere, conceived as a region.

bīja Seed. In Tantric belief it signifies the germ syllable which takes the form of a deity. It is also a term for semen.

bīja-bhūmi The seed of the universe which is Śakti in Tantric belief. It is described as void (*śūnya*) or great void (*mahāśūnya*) because nothing has manifested itself in this stage. That is why it is called *niṣedha-vyāpārarūpa* or the process of negating. *Paramārthasāra* 13–14.

bījākṣara Seed letters like *hrīṃ*, *krīṃ* etc. These letters or rather sounds have well-defined meanings and are rationally planned.

bīja-mantra Abbreviated letters or words, symbolic of the tenets of the creed, which are conveyed by the teacher to his disciple after initiation. These *bīja mantras* are regarded as microcosms of the actual *mantras* and the meanings suggested by them.

bījapura Citron, a characteristic symbol of the Buddhist god Jambhala.

bimba That which causes reflection. According to certain Vedāntic schools (especially of Madhva) *bimba* is the source of reality of the *pratibimba* (derived being) and as such it is *brahman* itself. Sureśvara in defining *ābhāsavāda* (q.v.) holds that God is not a reflection but *brahman* in the aspect of being the original (*bimba-caitanya*) of reflections which constitute the Jīvas. See Pratibimba, Paratantra.

bindu The seed which according to the Tantric ideas issues from the creative union of Śiva (perfect consciousness at rest) and Śakti (which becomes dynamic as creative activity). It also means the state of infinite concentration and condensation and therefore of potency. It is formed when Śakti, which is the substance or matter, approaches to *cit* or consciousness causing rise in the former the desire to create (*vickīrṣā*).

bindu-cakra The central point in the Śrīcakra (q.v.), the mystic Tantric diagram, symbolising the universe and its divine cause by two sets of triangles. This is the point (*bindu*, q.v.) in which reside Kāmeśvara (Śiva in the form of pure consciousness) and Lalitā (Śakti as dynamic creative activity) in undifferentiated union (*abheda*).

bindu-dhāraṇa The process of checking the downward flow of the semen, of holding up the breath and of stabilising the mind for the attainment of the state of neutrality which is required for the spiritual upliftment of an individual. Also known as *pavana-niścala* and *citta-nirodha*.

bisāpanthī One of the five Digambara subsects of the Jains.

bodhana Processing of a *mantra*. *Tantrasāra* 54.

bodhāṅga Same as *bodhipakṣīya-dharmas* (q.v.), the thirty seven *dharmas* or practices leading to *bodhi* or enlightenment. *Mahāvastu* III. 331–33.

bodhi Buddhist term for 'enlightenment'.

bodhicitta Enlightenment (*bodhi*) by which mind (*citta*) is characterised. According to the Mahāyāna, *śūnyatā* (q.v.) and *karuṇā* (q.v.), on being combined, develop *bodhicitta* (etymologically intellectual and mental faculties) which helps an individual to obtain *bodhi* or the highest knowledge. This *bodhicitta* is achieved through ten stages or *bhūmis*. The highest stage is known as *dharmamegha* where the striving individual becomes a Bodhisattva (q.v.). In Tantric Buddhism the concept of *bodhicitta* acquired a changed significance. Its function here is to create *mahāsukha* (q.v.) or *nirvāṇa* through the sexual union between a man and a woman. In *Hevajra* X the union of *prajñā* (q.v.) and *upāya* (q.v.) is supposed to produce *bodhicitta* as the embodiment of *śūnyatā* and *karuṇā*. This view is maintained in Vājrayāna (q.v.) and other schools of Tantric Buddhism which hold that *bodhicitta* is a state of supreme realisation transcending both *bhava* (existence) and *nirvāṇa* (extinction). It is without beginning or end, quiescent, immutable in existence and also in non-existence; it is the non-duality of *śūnyatā* and *karuṇā*. *Jñānasiddhi* 72–73.

bodhinī A form of Śakti situated on the second point above the *ājñācakra*. It is considered as a seed. Kālīcaraṇa on *Ṣaṭcakranirūpaṇa* XL. Bodhinī is also described as one of the five *kalās* or manifestations of *nirodhinī-śakti* (the *śakti* which offers resistance to the upward march of *kuṇḍalinī*).

bodhipakṣīya-dharma Thirty-seven acquisitions leading to the attainment of perfect knowledge which form the sum total of Buddha's teachings. These are divided into seven groups: (1) *smṛty-upasthāna* or alertness to what is happening in one's body (*kāya*), feeling (*vedanā*), mind (*citta*) and acquisitions (*dhamma*); (2) *samyakprahāna* or right exertions; (3) *ṛddhipāda* or attainment of supernatural powers; (4) *indriya* or cultivation of faculties; (5) *bala* or cultivation of strength; (6) *sambodhyaṅga* or acquisitions leading to full enlightenment; and (7) *mārga* (q.v.). *Mahāparinibbānasutta*. cf. *Majjhima* I, 55, *Saṃyutta V*. 141f.

bodhipraṇidhi-citta One of the two divisions of Bodhicitta (q.v.) according to the *Bodhicaryāvatāra* 23–25. It is simply an aspiration to become a Buddha in order to save worldly beings from misery without seriously undertaking the duties of making the highest gifts and acquiring other virtues.

bodhiprasthāna-citta One of the two subdivisions of Bodhicitta, the other being *bodhipraṇidhi* (q.v.). It is the resolution to observe *bodhisattvasaṃvaras* (disciplines) and to strive for the acquisition of merits. The *Bodhicaryāvatāra* 23–25 compares *bodhipraṇidhi* to a traveller thinking of going to another country and *bodhiprasthāna* to one who has actually set out on his journey.

bodhisattva A term by which the Hinayanists (q.v.) mean all the previous existences of Gautama Buddha. As a *bodhisattva* he lived the life of an average being acquiring merits and avoiding demerits as far as possible. According to the Mahāsaṅghika-Lokottaravādins, the *bodhisattva* in his last existence as Gautama Buddha was not conceived in the womb and that he was more than a mortal being (*lokottara*). The Mahāyānists contend that there are among worldly beings such individuals who cherished the intention of becoming great like a *buddha*. These beings are in a position to develop bodhicitta (q.v.), to attain *bodhi* (q.v.) and to fulfil the *pāramitās* (q.v.), and become a *buddha*. The Mahayanists added that the development of *bodhicitta* should include the condition that the adept must dedicate his life in his several existences to the service of others and should not care to attain his own salvation until and unless others have attained it. The methods of becoming a *bodhisattva* and the stages or *bhūmis* (q.v.) of his mental, moral and intellectual attainments, to the extent of realising *dharmaśūnyatā* (q.v.) were carefully outlined. In course of time from among the countless *bodhisattva* some were given concrete forms and qualities. The texts began to describe the powers and virtues of several *bodhisattvas* like Avalokiteśvara, Mañjusrī, Vajrapāni and others who were looked upon as benign gods to be adored and worshipped, each was given a definite form and insignia and elaborate rituals were prescribed for the purpose of worship.

bodhisattva-bhūmi See under *bhūmi* and the topics mentioned therein.

bodhisattva-saṃvara See under *bodhiprasthāna-citta*.

brāhma Form of marriage. It is the gift of a daughter, after decking her with valuable garments and honouring her with jewels, etc., to a man learned in the Vedas and of good conduct whom the father of the girl himself invites. *Manu* III.27–34.

brahmā A class of priests employed in the Vedic sacrifices. A priest belonging to this class is required to be most learned in Vedic lore and has to observe silence while the *mantras* are being repeated. He superintends all actions and permission is taken from him by the Adhvaryu (q.v.) at the time of doing most of the ritual acts such as leading forward the *praṇīta* water and sprinkling the bundle of fuel-sticks and *kuśa* grass. He may also be employed in all the *pākayajñas* (q.v.). He is represented by a bundle of *kuśa* in the Gṛhya rites. *Āp.Sr.*III.18.1.

brahmabandhu A Brāhmaṇa by birth or by caste and not by deeds. It is a term of contempt for one who is a Brāhmaṇa in name only. These are of six kinds; one who is hired by a Sūdra or a king as a servant; one who has a Śūdra woman as his wife; a village priest; and those who subsist by killing animals or by catching them.

brahmabhāga The square, lowest section of the Śivaliṅga.

brahmabhūta Becoming one with *brahman*, It can be experienced either by mind through meditation, or by the path of knowledge or by the path of selfless action. *Gītā*, II.72, VI.27, XIV.26, XVIII.53–54.

brahmacakra The *cakra* (q.v.) representing the equilibrium of Śakti in the form of *vindu* (q.v.). It has been equated with the *pīṭha* (holy resort of the Mother Goddess) of Uḍḍīyāna. *Gandharvatantra* V.23, *Nityaṣoḍaśikārṇava* VIII.171.

brahmacariyavāsa A Buddhist term for the formative period of religious life. According to the *Kathāvatthu* I.3. this condition does not mean merely *pravrajyā* or ordination, *muṇḍiyam* or shaven-headedness and so forth. It includes *maggabhāvanā* or the attempt to visualise the potencies of the ways leading to enlightenment and salvation.

brahmacarya Period of studenthood. Brahmacārī means an inquisitive student who after his Upanayana (q.v.) resorted to a teacher for learning and stayed with him for a period of no less than twelve years. After completing his studies he ordinarily got married and had a settled domestic life. It is the first stage of *āśrama* (q.v.), the others being *gārhasthya* (q.v.), *vānaprastha* (q.v.) and *sannyāsa* (q.v.). A longer period of *brahmacarya* was not unknown. The student who remained with his teacher till his death was known as Naiṣṭhika-Brahmacārī or perpetual student. The student had to serve the teacher by tending his cattle, had to beg for good and announce it to the teacher and to look after his sacred fires. He was expected to abstain from certain activities: he should not look at the sun and should avoid honey, flesh, perfumes, garlands, sleeping by day, rubbing oil on the body, putting collyrium in the eyes, going in a cart, wearing shoes and holding an umbrella, love-affairs, anger, covetousness, infatuation, worthless and proud discussions, playing on musical instruments, luxurious baths with hot water, making the teeth attractively clean, an ecstatic state of mind, dancing, singing, gazing at women or touching young women, gambling, serving a low person, injury to animals, obscene talk, drinking wine and so on. Not only was he expected to avoid gazing at a woman or touching her, but if he suffered from night emissions he was required to bathe, worship the sun and make penance with specific *mantras*. Further he should not assist the wives of his teacher in their toilet and bath, nor wash their feet, nor shampoo them. A student who is full 20 years old shall not honour the young wife of a teacher by clasping her feet. After finishing the entire course of study, the student should return to his own house. This was done after performing the rite called *samāvartana* (q.v.). A ceremonial bath was the main feature of the rite and that is why a student who had completed his course of study and taken the ceremonial bath was known as a *snātaka* (q.v.). *Śān.Gr.* II.11–12, IV.8, *Hir.Gr.* I.9–13, *Baudh.Dh.S.* 1.2.37, II.2.45, *Vai.Dh.S.* VI.1, VII.11, *Āp.Dh.S.* I.1.2.26–32, I.1.4.29, *Gaut.Dh.S.* I.2.37, *Manu* II.4 ff., *Yāj.*I.33

brahmādvaita Non-dualism of *brahman* (q.v.).

brahmadvāra The passage through which the *kuṇḍalinī* (q.v.) moves. Viśvanātha's com. on *Ṣaṭcakranirūpaṇa* III.

brahmagranthi One of the three knots situated in the *mūlādhāra-cakra* (q.v.). Com. on *Brahmavidyopaniṣat* 70.

brahmahatya Killing a Brāhmaṇa; an act regarded as a grave sin. *Taitt. Saṃ.* II.5.1.1; *Gaut.Dh.S.* XXI.1.

brahma-jñāna Knowledge of *brahman* (q.v.). The Madhva school holds that *brahman* is the object of knowledge (*prameya*) while Śruti (q.v.) is the source of knowledge (*pramāṇa*). So with regard to the highest truth both *prameya* and *pramāṇa* are required. To abstract from the other is to negate both. The process of finding them is *jijñāsā* (q.v.) or enquiry.

brahmakapāla The severed head of Brahmā who is credited with four faces, grey beard and a crown of matted hair. The Buddhists display their aversion towards the Hindus as well as the superiority of their gods to the gods of the alien faith by depicting the Buddhist gods triumphantly carrying the severed head of Brahmā.

brahmakṛcchra A penance lasting for 12 days on each of which one has to drink *pañcagavya* (a mixture of cowdung, cow urine, clarified butter, milk and curd) in a temple or cowpen after offering it, with *mantras*, in a fire.

brahmakūrca A penance consisting of fast for one day and taking *pañcagavya* (cowdung, cow urine, clarified butter, milk and curd combined) on the next day. *Mit.* on *Yāj* III 314. *Parāśara* XI.27–28 holds that *brahmakūrca* and *pañcagavya* are synonyms.

brahmaloka The highest world of *brahman* (obviously in the Saguṅa conception in which he is regarded as the all-powerful God) in which virtuous persons are supposed to have a place after death. The term is also used to denote the heaven of the Brāhmaṇas.

brahmamedha Procedure for the disposal of the dead body of an *ācārya* (teacher) or a *sotriya* (learned Brāhmaṇa) in which *mantras* called *caturhotaraḥ* are recited. *Śat.Br.* XXIV.3.20–22.

brahma-mīmāṃsā Madhva's system. See Dvaitavāda.

brahman See Ātman. It is the all pervasive reality in Indian religio-philosophical tradition. In the earlier Vedic texts the word *brahman* is used in various senses like prayer, priest, hymns, chants and ritual formulae, and also as the essence of cosmic phenomena which was identified with various deities including the older concept of Puruṣa (q.v.). *AV* IX.6.1–2, *Taitt.Saṃ.*VII.3.1.4, *Taitt.Br.* II.2.1.4, II.8.9.6 ff., *Śat.Br.* II.1.4.10ff, III.1.4.15, etc. In the Upaniṣads with the general enlargement and universalising of the concept of *brahman* not only everything in the universe is identified with it, but also it is correlated with the finite ego, the essence of the organic and mental functions of the human person, in other words with the individual self or soul (*ātman*). *Bṛhadāraṇyaka* I.2, *Chāndogya* III.18, *Aitareya* I, etc. In the *Vedānta Sūtra* it is held that the power of creation belongs to the pure stainless *brahman*, the material and efficient cause which for its own sport develops itself into the world without itself undergoing the least change. It is also stated that *brahman* and the world are not different (*ananya*). (I.1.2, I.1.20–24, I.3.1, I.4:23–27, II.1.14, II.1.23–27 etc.). Various theories have been put forward to explain the relation between the infinite, pure conscious, eternal and changeless *brahman* and the finite, material and impermanent world, between the universal and the individual soul and also to trace the evolution of the latter from the former in terms of cause-effect relations. Gauḍapāda in his *Māṇḍukyakārikā* III.19–21 etc. says that there can be no such thing as creation at all because the real cannot be subject to change. Some commentators try to explain this in terms of the theory of *pariṇāma* or transformation. See *brahmaparināmavāda*. According to Śaṅkara, the question of *brahman's* transformation into the world cannot arise because the world exists only for those who are under the influence of Avidyā or Māyā (q.v.). *Śārīrakabhāṣya* I.4.3, II.1.14, II.1.20, II.2.2 etc. Rāmānuja is not at all troubled regarding the question of how the world of imperfection rises from *brahman*, the absolute perfection, since he is willing to accept on the authority of the Śruti that the finite springs from the infinite. For theistic interpretations see Viśiṣṭādvaita, Bhedābhedavāda, Dvaitādvaitavāda, Śuddhadvaitavāda and Acintyabhedābhedavāda. From a purely Advaita (q.v.) or non-dualist viewpoint, the eternal and infinite *brahman* cannot consist of parts and cannot be subject to change. It therefore follows that no one can be a part or emanation of *brahman* which is one without a second. The entire world of phenomena is merely a delusion, comparable to a *fata morgana* which disappears on closer examination like a dream-image appearing real only to the sleeper but vanishing in waking hours. See also under Māyā and Īśvara.

brahmanāḍī A nerve situated within the *citriṇī* nerve, or it may be on the inner side of *citriṇī*. Some authorities equate it with *susumṅa*. *Yogaśikhopaniṣat* V.17.

brahmāṇḍa A great *dāna* or gift in which two vessels of gold, resembling the two halves of the hemisphere (to represent the *brahmāṇḍa*, i.e., the dome of heaven above and the earth below), weighing from 20 *palas* to 1000, according to the donor's ability, are offered to the preceptor and priests. *Matsya Pu.* CCLXXVI. Ordinarily *brahmāṇḍa* means the world or universe, a mythological interpretation of which has been supplied by the cosmogonic ideas of Brahmā's egg, the golden germ, etc. See Hiraṇyagarbha. The Vaiṣṇavas believe that there are an infinite number of *brahmāṇḍas* (worlds) and that Kṛṣṇa manifests his Vṛndāvana-līlā (q.v.) in each of them successively. *Caitanya-caritāmṛta* II.20, 216,316.

brahmāṇī, brāhmī One of the seven or eight Mātṛkās.

brahmānvādhāna A rite in the procedure of taking *sannyāsa* (q.v.) or asceticism. It consists of putting fuel-sticks on the fire in order to secure knowledge of *brahman*. *Baudh.Dh.S.* II.10.11–30.

brahmapadma Name of the four-petalled lotus of the *mūlādhāra* (q.v.). *Nirvāṇatantra* IV.

brahmapariṇāmavāda The theory of the transformation of *brahman* which has been postulated to explain the genesis of an imperfect effect (the world and its finite beings) from an absolutely perfect cause (*brahman*). Gauḍapādā in his *Māṇḍukyakārikā* III.19–21 etc. hold that there can be no such thing as creation at all because *brahman* cannot be subject to change. Śaṅkara holds that *brahman* is not subject to the mutations of the world and asserts that it is impossible to explain through logical categories the relation between *brahman* and the world. On the other hand, Rāmānuja believes that the entire creative process is the self-expression of *brahman* which reveals itself in creation. Bhāskara holds that at the time of creation, *brahman* which is ever-existent (*sat*) without a second, becomes manifold by its *pariṇāmaśakti* or power of transformation (see Bhedābheda). Yādava finds no contradiction in saying that *brahman* and the world are both different and non-different. According to him *brahmatva* or pure being is the causal unity of the universe constituted by the unity of *īśvara* (q.v.), *cit* (q.v.) and *acit* (q.v.). He holds that *brahman* can really be transformed into the aforesaid three constituents. Conscious (*cit*) and material (*acit*) forms are only different states of one substance and not different substances themselves. See Māyā and Īśvara.

brahmarandhra A passage in the cerebral region according to Tantric belief.

brahma-saṃhati A subsect of the school of Śaṅkaradeva in Assam. The followers of this school are distinguished by a special adherence to Brahmanical ideas. Also known as Bāmuniā.

brahmaśiraśchedaka The iconic form of Śiva in which he holds the skull of Brahmā in his hand, whom according to a legend he has killed.

brahmasthāna A sanctuary or a shrine.

brahmasvarūpiṇī An attribute of Śakti conceived as a supreme being.

brahmavarca Splendour of the Vedas, that is, the attainment of special pre-eminence in sacred knowledge which should begin when a boy is five years old. *Gaut.Dh.S.* I.5–7.

brahmavidyā Knowledge of *brahman* (q.v.). In Kashmir Tantric texts and also in Gauḍapāda's *Subhagodaya* it has been equated with Śrīvidyā (q.v.).

brahmavihāra The four states of mental purity: *metta* (*maitrī*, amity), *karuṇā* (compassion), *muditā* (sympathetic joy) and *upekkhā* (*upekṣā*, equanimity) according to early Buddhism. These are so called because they make the minds of the adepts pure like those of the Brahmakāyikā-gods and after death they are reborn in a higher plane of existence. *Visuddhimagga* 320.

brahma-yajña One's own daily study of the Veda. *Śat.Br.* XI.5.6.3–18. The *Taitt.Ār.* II. 10–13 refers to the place, position, purification and other necessary preliminaries before sitting down to study (*svādhyāya*). cf. *Āśv.Gr.* II.2.2–III.3.4. The *Śān.Gr.* I.4 prescribes several hymns and verses of the *Ṛgveda* for reciting in the *brahma-yajña*. The *Dharmasindhu*, pūrva, III.299 says that it is to be performed once either after morning *homa* or after midday *saṃdhyā* or after Vaiśvadeva (qq.v.).

brahmāyatana Shrines dedicated to Brahmā.

bṛhaspatisava A kind of one day Soma sacrifice (q.v.) performed by a Brāhmaṇa who has performed the Vājapeya (q.v.) *Āśv.Sr.* IX.9.19, *Āp.Sr.* XVIII.7.15.

buddhakārakadharma Cultivation of the ten *pāramitās* (q.v) or virtues. *Jāt.*I.14, 25, *Mahābodhivaṃsa* 9. These are *dāna* (gift), *śīla* (moral observances), *kṣānti* (forbearance), *vīrya* (energy), *dhyāna* (meditation), *prajña* (knowledge), *praṇidhāna* (aspiration), *upāya-kauśalya* (skilfulness), *bala* (strength) and *jñāna* (knowledge).

buddha-kṣetra The areas of the activities of different Buddhas.

buddhayāna Another name for Mahāyāna.

buddhi The first product of the evolution of Prakṛti, also known as Mahat in the Sāṅkhya. Its special functions are ascertainment and decision and it is the ground of all intellectual processes. Being influenced by the three constituents (*guṇas*) of Prakṛti (q.v.) it is capable of producing different attributes. *Sān.Sūt.* I.71, II.40–43, *Kārikā* 36–37. This conception also occurs in the view of Āḷāra, the teacher of Buddha in the *Buddhacarita* XII.17 ff. In the Śaiva Siddhānta it is conceived as an evolute of *aśuddha-māyā* (q.v.), *Mṛgendra Āgama*, II.3.7, III.1 etc. *Pauṣkara Āgama* II.17, III.4, *Śivajñānabodham* II.5. In Tantra it is a category of quality. *Kaṅkālamālinī* II, Rāghava on *Śāradātilaka* I.17.

buddhīndriya The five organs of perception, according to the Sāṅkhya, which are the senses of sight, hearing, smell, taste and touch. These are all evolutes of Ahaṃkāra (q.v.).

caḍaka The death and resurrection theme which finds expression in popular rituals in connection with Śiva worship performed mostly by peoples belonging to the lower ranks of society on the last day of the year. The participants observe *sannyāsa* (q.v.) or celibacy and *asauca* (state of impurity) in the same way as these are observed in the case of death in a family, and on the appointed day they display the supernatural power they claim to have thus acquired by hook-swinging, perforating the tongue, piercing different parts of the body with sharp weapons, walking on fire and other feats of physical endurance. In conclusion, the chief devotee cooks a fish by roasting it in embers. Some parboiled and husked rice is also cooked. The fish and the rice are placed in an earthen pot and rice-wine is poured on them. At midday the pot is taken to a tree standing in some lonely meadow and the food is placed on a plantain leaf land left there for the ghosts to devour. This offering is sometimes made in the meadow where the village dead are cremated. See also Gājana.

caitanya Consciousness by which *jīvas* or individuals are characterised. Absolute, all-pervading, perfect and pure consciousness is *brahman* according to most of the religious and philosophical systems of India. In Tantric internal worship (*antaryāga*) the aspirant has to think that the goddess is enshrined within his body as pure consciousness, or the Self. *Guru*, *mantra* and *devatā* are also conceived of as three forms of Caitanya. *Śaktisaṅgama*, Sundarī, III.11–13. For other conceptions see Cetana, Ātman, Brahman, Vijñānavāda.

caitya Same as Stūpa. The Buddhist sanctuary, representing the Buddhist universe, sometimes square and sometimes round, with spires or steps on the capital. Each spire or step represents a heaven, the uppermost portion being a point which is supposed to be the highest peak of Mount Sumeru, the mythical mountain of the Buddhists. On the four sides of the *caitya* the figures of the Dhyānī Buddhas appear. The corners are occupied by figures of the divine Buddhaśaktis or their symbolic representations in the form of *yantras*. The *caitya* may also show at the four cardinal points the Caturmahārājikas or the Great Rulers of the quarters namely, Vaisravaṇa, Virupākṣa, Virudhaka and Dhrtarāṣṭra. The word *caitya* is associated with *citā* or funeral pyre. See Caitya-vṛkṣa.

caityaka A branch of the Mahāsaṅghikas (q.v.), often identified with the Lokoṭtaravādins (q.v.), who give much importance to the worship of the *caitya* (q.v.). Their name is found in inscriptions from Amaravati and Nagarjunikonda. *EI*, XX.100ff. The Caityakas are often identified also with the Pūrvaśailas (q.v.).

caityaśaila A branch of the Mahāsaṅghikas (q.v.) mentioned by Vasumitra. According to Paramārtha this branch was founded by a renegade teacher named Mahādeva. The Caityaśailas hold that the *bodhisattvas* are average beings and may be born in the lower states of existence and that offerings made to a Caitya are not necessarily of great merit. The Caityaśailas therefore should be distinguished from the Caityakas (q.v.)

caitya-vṛkṣa Trees serving the purpose of a *caitya* (q.v.) or *stūpa* (q.v.) which later became the symbol of Buddhism. The word *caitya* comes from *citā* or funeral pyre. Mortal remains of the great saints used to be buried under the earth forming mounds on which trees were grown. These trees (*rukkhacetiyāni* or *vṛkṣa-caityas*) were regarded as sacred and were commonly worshipped. This was at the root of the subsequent development of *caitya* architecture. This was not a feature unique to the Buddhist religion alone.

cakra A wheel or disc. Usually the sun wheel, the characteristic symbol of Viṣṇu. It is also a Buddhist symbol suggestive of the Dharmacakrapravartana or setting the wheel of law in motion.

cakra Circle, used in a variety of senses, symbolising the endless rotation of Śakti (q.v.). In Tantric rituals there are different *cakra-sādhanās* in which male and female aspirants assemble and perform the rites of *pañcamakāra* (consisting of wine, meat, fish, cereals and sexual intercourse. See Bhairavī-cakra. According to the *Niruttaratantra* X, *cakras* are of five types—*rāja*, *mahā*, *deva*, *vīra* and *paśu*—each symbolising the grade of spiritual attainment. The term *cakra* is also used to denote Yantras (q.v.) or mystic diagrams which are variously known as *trikoṇa* (three-angled), *aṣṭakoṇa* (eight-angled) and so forth. The term is also used to denote different nerve-plexuses within the body. See Ṣaṭcakra.

cakrapuruṣa Viṣṇu's wheel (*cakra*) which is conceived and represented iconically in an anthropomorphic form. According to the *Viṣṇudharmottara* III.85.13–14 the *cakrapuruṣa* should be a male figure with round eyes and a drooping belly; it is to carry a *caurī* (fly whisk) and is to be adorned with various ornaments. It is also to be carved in such a manner as to indicate that it is showing a desire to gaze upon Viṣṇu. The left hand of the god should be made to rest upon the head of *cakrapuruṣa*.

cakravartin Ideal of universal sovereignty. The term is often applied to great religious teachers like Buddha or Mahāvīra who are regarded as sovereigns of the spiritual world.

cākṣusī-dīkṣā A form of initiation in which the *guru* or preceptor having concentrated his mind on the supreme being converts the disciple with only one glance. It is otherwise called *dṛk-dīkṣā*. *Kulārṇava* XIV, Rāghava on *Śaradātilaka* V. 127–140, *Merutantra* quoted in *Puraścaryārṇava* V. 390.

cakṣu-vijñāna The science of perception in Buddhist belief. In the *Kathāvatthu* XVIII.9 the Mahāsaṅghikas are said to have held the opinion that the organs of sense perceive directly and not by their perceptive faculty (*vijñāna*). This is also the view of the Vaibhāṣikas. The Śaila schools and the Theravādins hold the opposite view.

cāmara Caurī or the fly-whisk consisting of the tail of a Yak. It is used during the performance of any worship. Cauri-bearers usually shown on the representations of cult images.

cañcalā See under Caramālā.

caṇḍālī Female energy having the force of fire which resides in the *nirmāṇa* (q.v.) according to Tantric Buddhism. It has correspondence to the Kulakuṇḍalini-śakti of the Śākta Tantras. This *caṇḍālī*, being accelerated, kindles the *dharma* and *sambhoga-cakras* (q.v.) and ultimately reaches the *uṣṇīṣakamala*, the highest cerebral region, and then returns to its own place.

caṇḍeśānugrahamūrti One of the iconic forms of Śiva bestowing grace on Caṇḍeśa whom he made the chief of the host of his *gaṇas*. Images of this type are common in South India, mostly hailing from the Cola region. The four-armed god accompanied by his consort is generally shown as putting a garland round the head of Caṇḍeśa who is depicted as offering homage to his master.

cāndra A Vāmācārī sect mentioned in *Śakti-saṅgama-tantra*, Tārā, I, 92–94.

candrakalā The symbol of crescent moon which exists on the crown of most Tantric goddesses as the source of everflowing nectar. It is also found on the matted locks of Śiva. *Mahānirvāṇa* XIII.7.

candranāḍī Name of the nerve *iḍā* (q.v.) which is conceived as a feminine entity, white in colour and representing Śakti in the form of the moon. *Ṣaṭcakranirūpaṇa* I.

candraśekhara-mūrti An iconic form of Śiva who is called Candraśekhara because of the presence of the crescent moon on his *jaṭā* or matted locks. Gopinatha Rao describes three types of this form: Kevala, Umāsahita and Āliṅgana on the basis of *Aṃśumadbhedāgama* and other Śaiva Āgamas. In Kevala the god is shown alone, but in the Umāsahita and Āliṅgana, the god either stands with Umā by his side or he embraces her lovingly.

candratattva The introvert mind which develops with successful control of the functions of *iḍā* nerve.

cāndrāyana Penance consisting of reducing gradually the quantity of food taken everyday in accordance with the gradual waning of the moon. This penance may be undertaken by the forest hermits to acquire merit. It may also be followed to get rid of such sins as caused by eating forbidden food, having sexual intercourse with *sagotra* (of the same kin) woman, marrying maternal uncle's or paternal uncle's daughter, etc. Candrāyaṇa is of two types *yavamadhya* (like the middle of the grain of *yava*) and *pīpilikāmadhya* (like the middle of an ant). *Baudh.Dh.S.* III.8. 33, *Manu* V.21, XI.27, XI.221–225 *Yāj* III:323 ff, *Gaut.* XXVII. 2–11.

capetadāna Mudrā or hand-pose found in certain Buddhist icons which shows the right hand menacingly extended upwards, just as though it is ready to slap someone.

caraka Travelling scholars mentioned in Pāṇini's *Aṣṭādhyāyī* who after completing their education used to wander in different countries to gain experience. In the *Saddharmapuṇḍarīka* (AS) 180 *caraka* is compounded with *parivrājaka* and classed as a heretic with the Ājīvikas and Nirgranthas (q.v.). In the Pali texts *carakas* are replaced by *paribrājakas* (q.v.).

caramālā A garland made of *rudrākṣa*, conch, crystal or other objects meant for *japa* or recalling the name of the deity. *Tantrasāra* 29.

caraliṅga The dynamic *liṅga* in Viraśaiva conception. It is connected with *ādyā-śakti* or the primal energy.

caraṇa Various schools of the Veda. Caraṇa also indicates a body of people who, though pledged to the reading and study of a particular *śākhā* or branch, have a wider curriculum which may include other texts.

cāritra Certain rules of moral behaviour recorded in Hemacandra's *Yogaśāstra* in which we have an interpretation of the five Jain vows. Certain external rules of conduct are also included in this category, e.g., *īryyā* (precaution while walking to prevent oneself from treading on insects, etc.), *bhāṣā* (to talk pleasantly), *iṣaṇa* (to beg alms in proper monastic manner), *dānasamiti* (inspection of seats to avoid transgression), *utsargasamiti* (careful movement of the body), *manogupti* (to remove all false thoughts), *vāggupti* (absolute silence), *kāyagupti* (steadiness of the body), etc. *DS* (vṛtti) 35. The five categories of Cāritra are to give up evil conduct, (*sāmāyika*), to believe in repentence (*chedopasthāpana*), to practice virtues (*parihāraviśuddha*), to control passions (*sukṣmasamparyāya*) and to follow the five rules of conduct (*yathākhyāta*).

cārvāka Materialistic school of thought also known as Bārhaspatya (q.v.) and Lokāyata. The followers of the Cārvāka school were divided into various sects like Vitaṇḍāvādins (q.v.), Dhūrta (q.v.), Suśikṣita, (q.v.), etc. The Cārvāka doctrine is described in Mādhava's *Sarvadarśanasaṃgraha* I, Haribhadra's *Ṣaḍdarśanasamuccaya*, Śāntarakṣita's *Tattvasaṃgraha*, Kṛṣṇamiśra's *Prabodhacandrodaya* Act II and other works. According to the Cārvāka system, there are only four elements: earth, water, fire and air. From the combination of these elements intelligence is produced. While consciousness is not observed to inhere in the elements of matter, yet when these are arranged in a certain order they are known to have life and consciousness. Perception is the only valid source of knowledge. Indirect sources of knowledge like inference, testimony, etc., are unreliable and misleading. Consciousness ceases with the body; when a man dies nothing is left of him to enjoy or suffer the consequences of his actions hereafter. The existence of God is a myth and it is therefore foolish to perform religious rites. On the same grounds the authority of the Vedas is rejected. In short, the Cārvākas represent that system of thought which refuses to recognise any first cause of the creation of the world other and higher than the mere working out of the forces and tendencies inherent in the non-sentient matter, unsupervised by any non-material power or principle like God or any supreme being. Cārvāka philosophy is based on five principles: Bhūtavāda (q.v.), Dehātmyavāda (q.v.), Pratyaksaprāmāṇyavāda (q.v.), Paralokavilopavāda (q.v.), and Svabhāvavāda (q.v.).

caryā Means to achieve the end. The term is used especially in connection with the Śaiva and Tantric cults. In the Pāśupata system the *caryās* are divided into two categories, namely, *vratas* (vows) and *dvāra* (door). In Buddhist *Dhāraṇi* literature the *caryās* are regarded as one of the five main aspects of spiritual realisation. In all forms of Śaivism *caryā* is regarded as the first step for an individual to become free from worldly bondage. From a practical point of view *caryā* consists of prescribed rites and meditation relating to *sālokya* (q.v.) in which the devotee should feel himself as the servant of God.

caryāpadas The earliest specimens of regional religious literature of Eastern India. The Caryā poems deal with subtle philosophical questions from the viewpoint of Sahajayāna (q.v.) under the garb of the facts of real life; the pursuits, hopes and aspirations of common persons; love hatred and emotion; the beauty of nature and women; the social classes, conflicts and amalgamations; technical and manual labour; and a variety of other things.

caturdaśāra A mystic Tantric diagram supposed to represent the combined effects of various *cakras* (q.v.). It is made of fourteen triangles, each presided over by a goddess. These goddesses are collectively known as Sampradāya-yoginī. The attainment dervied from it is known as *īśitvasiddhi*. *Nityaṣodaśikārṇava* IV.149, VI. 17,XI.179–83, *Gandharvatantra* V.99, XVII.49.

cāturmāsya Seasonal celebration lasting for a period of four months observed with various austerities. It begins from the waxing eleventh day of the full-moon in *āṣāḍha* (June-July) or at the *saṃkrānti* or solar transition to *śrāvaṇa* (July-August) and concludes after four months.

caturmukha An appellation of Brahmā.

caturmūrti Iconic representation of Viṣṇu in his *vyūha* (q.v.) concept combining the aspects of Vāsudeva, Saṃkarṣaṇa, Pradyumna and Aniruddha. This idea of one-in-four is illustrated by four-faced images, each symbolising *bala* or strength, *jñaña* or knowledge, *aiśvarya* or wealth and *śakti* or energy.

caturthī-karma Ceremonial defloration of the bride by the husband on the fourth night after marriage. *Śāṅ.Gr.* I.18–19, *Pār.Gr.*I.11, *Āp.Gr.* VIII.10.11, Hir.Gr. I.7.23.11ff. It is also known as *caturthī-homa*.

caturvarga The four aspects of human life. They are morality or sacrificial duty (*dharma*), earthly prosperity including economy and statecraft (*artha*), conjugal necessity (*kāma*) and salvation (*mokṣa*).

caturviṃśati-mūrti Twenty-four forms of Vāsudeva-Viṣṇu, representing the twenty-four tenets of the *vyūha*(q.v.) doctrine, which have often found sculptural expression. All these twenty-four images are very much alike, each in standing form with no bends in the body, possessing four-arms and adorned with *kīriṭa*-crown and other usual ornaments.

caturviṃśati-tattva The twenty-four Sāṅkhya fundamentals which have become the base of different religious systems. These are five *bhūtas* (q.v.) or gross elements, five *tanmātras* (q.v.) or subtle elements, five *jñānedriyas* (q.v.) or sense-organs, the five *karmendriyas* (q.v.) or organs of action and *manas* (q.v.) or mind, *buddhi* (q.v.) or intellect, *ahaṃkāra* (q.v.) or egoity and *prakṛti* (q.v.) or primordial substances.

caturvyūha See under Vyūhavada.

caturyāma The four vows prescribed by Pārśva for the followers of his creed. These are not to take life (*ahiṃsā*), not to lie (*anṛta*), not to steel (*asteya*) and not to own property (*aparigraha*). To these Mahāvīra added a fifth—not to indulge in sensual pleasure. See Mahāvrata.

catuṣkūṭa Arrangement of letters peculiar to the cult of Śrīvidyā. *Tantrasāra* 244.

caula Same as Cuḍākaraṇa (q.v.).

cetana Consciousness; that which knows. Madhva observes three kinds of *cetana*: the disposition (*svarūpa*) of the individual, the quest (*jijñāsā*) and the understanding of the principal object of knowledge (*bimba*). See also Caitanya.

cetana-kāraṇa vāda See Kāraṇa.

cetasika Mental properties, according to Buddhism, which are of two kinds, good and bad. There are seven universal good mental properties: contact (*phassa*), feeling (*vedanā*), perception (*saññā*), volition (*cetanā*), oneness of object (*ekāggatā*), psychic life (*jivitindriya*) and attention (*manasikāra*). The specific good mental properties are six: *vitakka* (reasoning), *vicāra* (exercise of mind), *adhimokkha* (process of freely choosing to attend to an object), *viriya* (energy), *piti* (interest in the object) and *chanda* (intention to act with regard to the object). There are four universal and two specific bad properties; *moha* (delusion), *ahirika* (shamelessness) *anottappa* (remorselessness), *uddhacca* (distraction), *lobha* (greed) and *ditthi* (error) respectively.

cetopariyāyañāna The Buddhist concept of the power of knowing the thoughts of others. It is one of the *abhiññās* (q.v.) possessed by the Arhats. *Visuddhimagga* 431.

cetovimutti Purification of mind which is one of the two means for attaining perfection according to early Buddhism. It is also described as a 'supportless consciousness'. After death an Arhat on account of his Cetovimutti attains *nirvāṇa* (q.v.). *Aṅguttara* 10, 257ff, *Saṃyutta* III.124, *AKV* VI.607.

chāgavaktra Goat-headed; it was an appellation of Dakṣa-Prajāpati and later became an epithet of Skanda or his companion.

chala A kind of unfair reply; in using *chala* an attempt is made to contradict a statement by taking it in a sense other than the intended one. It is one of the sixteen philosophical topics of the Nyāya.

channagarika A Buddhist sect which has some views in common the Sāmmitīyas (q.v.), Dharmottarīyas (q.v.) and Bhadrayānīyas (q.v.). These schools differed in their views regarding the attainments of an *arhat* (q.v.) and the consequent chances of his fall from arhathood. To the Channagarikas is attributed the doctrine of *dukkhāhāroti*, i.e. the utterance of the word *dukkha* leads to knowledge.

chaṭ A folk-festival observed in Bihar and Uttar Pradesh which begins on the sixth day of the bright half of Kārtika (Oct-Nov). Women who have, or desire, a home full of happy children fast on this day. Clad in gay clothes they proceed to a sacred stream singing while carts laden with plaintains follow. The fruits are dipped in water and taken back home and on the following day the fast is broken.

cheyasutta The six texts forming part of the Jain canon. They are *Āyāradasāo, Vavahāra, Nisīha, Mahānisīha, Paṃcakappa* (now lost and replaced by *Jīyakappa*) and *Kappa* (i.e. *Kalpasūtra* attributed to Bhadrābahu). Two other texts, *Piṇḍanijjutti* and *Oghanijjutti*, are sometimes included in this group.

cīnacāra The Chinese rituals, mainly connected with the goddess Tārā, supposed to be imported by Vaśiṣtha, which form the substratum of Tantric *vāmācāra* (q.v.). The Taoist rituals which came into the fold of the Tārā cult in China as well as Yinism or Exaltation of the Female Principle in Taoism, which developed in that system as a corollary of the Chinese Buddhist cult of the Female Principle, were also able to exert a counter-influence upon the development of the Indian *vāmācāra* rites of both the Buddhist and the non-Buddhist Tantras. The qualifications for *cīnācāra*, also known as *cīna-krama* and *cīna-sādhanā* are given in *Tantrasāra* 20, *Saktiśaṅgama*, Sundrī, I.188ff., *Puraścaryārṇava* I.20.

cintāmaṇi The gem that satisfies all desires. The jewel is sometimes represented in the form of a small round object and sometimes in the shape of a flame.

cit Consciousness, the sentient principle.

cit-acit-śakti See *dharmabhūtajñāna.*

citkalā Name of *saṃvit* or pure consciousness. It is that which forms the vibration caused by the break of *prakāśa-vimarśa* (q.v.) equilibrium of the Supreme Being.

citra-śikhandin Seven sages who were the earliest and best promulgators of the Bhāgavata lore according to the Nārāyaṇīya section of the *Mahābhārata.*

citriṇī A nerve, also known as *brahma-nāḍī*, which is like the fibre of a lotus stem. It is very often equated with *susumnā* (q.v.). It is also said that the *susumnā* is constituted by three *nāḍis* (nerves)—*citriṇī* which is of *sattva* (q.v.) quality, *vajra* which is of *rajas* (q.v.) quality and *brahma* (q.v.) which is of *tamas* (q.v.) quality. *Prānatoṣaṇī* I.4, 32.

citśakti The principle of consciousness. According to the Acintya-bhedābheda school it is the *svarūpa-śakti* or auto-energy of *brahman* (q.v.) on account of its being sentient. It is very intimately connected with *brahman* and thus it also called his *antaraṅga-śakti* (internal and intimate power).

citta Mind and mental discipline. In Buddhism the culture of *citta* is to be attained by following four of the eight-fold path (*atthaṅgika-magga*): *sammā-vyāyāma* (effort to remove existing evil thoughts and to preserve and increase good thoughts), *sammā-sati* (mindfulness of all that is happening within the body and mind and at the same time suppressing covetousness), *sammā-samādhi* (four stages of meditation) and *sammā-saṅkappa* (resolution for renunciation, as also for refraining from hatred and injury to other beings).

cittabhūmi The levels of mental life according to the Yoga. These are *kṣipta* or *mūḍha* (torpid), *vikṣipta* (distracted), *ekāgra* (concentrated) and *niruddha* (restrained). The last two are conducive to Yoga. When *ekāgra* or the state of concentration is firmly established it is called *samprajñāta-yoga* (q.v.) and when the state of *niruddha* is firmly established it is called *asamprajñātayoga* (q.v.).

citta bīja Thought seeds in Buddhist ideas which are produced from some *abhisaṃskāras* or thought-constructions. These become contaminated (*sāsrava*), being full of *upādāna* (attachment to existence), and productive of birth, old age, death and rebirth.

citta-nirodha Stabilising the mind; it is the aim of Yogic practices.

citta-samprayukta The Buddhist conception that the *anuśayas* (dormant passions or latent bias) do not combine (*samprayujati*) with *citta* or mind while the *paryavasthānas* (actual appearance of passions) do. On this question there is a difference of opinion among different schools. The reverse concept is known as *citta-viprayukta*.

cittāśaya Mental attainments pertaining to the spiritual progress of the potential Bodhisattva which are required in each of the ten stages of upliftment. See *bhūmi* and the topics under this heading.

cittaśuddhi Purification of mind.

citta-vijñāna Effect produced by the *saṃskāras* (q.v.) (impressions), arising from *avidyā* (ignorance), in the form of four *upādāna-skandhas* (q.v.), that is the aggregate of existence causing the mass of sufferings according to Buddhist ideas.

cīvaramāsa Robe-month of the Buddhists during the first half of which the practice of the eight-fold path is inculcated.

cuḍācakra A type of spiritual exercise meant only for those who have attained the status of *vīra* (q.v.). This exercise consists of *laya-yoga* (q.v.). *Śaktisaṅgama*, Sundarī, I.197–200.

cuḍakaraṇa Tonsure; it is the eighth *saṃskāra* (q.v.). The purpose of this is to evoke a long life and beauty for its recipient *Āśv.Gr.*I.17.42. According to the Gṛhyasūtras, the Cuḍākaraṇa ceremony should take place at the end of the first year or before the expiry of the third year, though later authorities extend the age to the seventh year. The distinguishing feature of this sacrament is the arrangement of the hair tuft (*śikhā* or *cuḍā*) as the name of the *saṃskāra* suggests. *Suśruta*, Śārīra VI.83, Laghu-Hārīta IV, Vaśiṣtha quoted in the *Vīramitrodaya* I.296.

dadhikṛcchra Spoken of by the *Prāyascittaprakāśa* as a penance in which the sinner subsists on only curds for a month.

dagdhayoga An inauspicious conjunction.

dahara-vidyā Seven-fold perfection referred to in the *Ch.Up.* VIII.1.1.

daiṣṭika Same as the Ājīvīkas (q.v.) referred to in Pāṇini IV.4.60.

daiva A form of marriage for priests in which the father gives away his daughter, after decking her with ornaments, etc., to the priest who duly officiates at a sacrifice, during the course of its performance. *Baudh.Dh.S.* I.11.5. Medhātithi on *Manu* III.28 is against the idea of the bride being a part of the sacrificial fee. The *daiva* also means luck, fate or destiny as opposed to *puruṣakāra* or human endeavour.

daiva Fate or destiny which is believed to be the collective force of one's own actions in past lives (*pūrvajanmakṛtam-karma*). Among the conditions responsible for the success of any work the *Bhagavadgītā* XVIII.14 mentions both *ceṣṭā* (effort) and *daiva*. *Yāj.*I. 351 says that just as a chariot cannot move on one wheel, so fate (*daiva*) without personal endeavour (*puruṣakāra*) cannot lead to success.

daivika-liṅga A class of static (*sthira*) Śiva-liṅgas.

daivī-sampad Divine treasure; it is attained through the *sāttvika* purification, the opposite is *āsuri-sampad* (demoniac treasure).

ḍākinī Various types of deities, especially celebrated in Tantric Buddhism. In the *Nāradapāñcarātra* Ḍākinī is described as the companion of Pārvatī and connected with the emergence of Chinnamastā. *Prāṇatoṣaṇī* V.6. 378–79. Regarded as a special forms of Parāśakti, the existence of Ḍākinī is to be conceived in the *mūlādhāra* (q.v.). *Tantrasāra* 338. As a presiding deity of the *mūlādhāra-cakra* Ḍākini imparts spiritual knowledge to the aspirant. *Ṣaṭcakranirūpaṇa* VIII.

dākṣāyaṇa Modification of *darśa-pūrṇamāsa* (q.v.) sacrifice. *Āp.Sr.* III. 17.4 ff., *Āśv.Sr.* II.14.7ff, Com. on *Kāt.Sr.*I.2.11.

dakṣiṇā Sacrificial fee and also the fee for making a gift. It should consist mostly of gold, but if the gift itself is the gold then *dakṣiṇā* as fee of making the gift, also to be received by the donee, may be of silver. *Gautama Dh.S.*V.16–17, *Agnipurāṇa* CCXI.31. Among other articles which can be offered as a sacrificial fee the best is a cow. The sacrificer may also give goats, sheep, horses, elephants, clothes, chariots, slaves, corns, etc. *Āp.Sr.*XIII.5–7, *Śat.Br.* IV.3.4.

dakṣiṇācāra Way of spiritual attainment without the use of *pañca-makāra* (q.v.) and other extreme forms of rituals. Often Vedācāra, Vaiṣṇavācāra and Śaivācāra are included in this category. The followers of Dakṣiṇācāra worship the great goddess in the traditional way. They believe in *varṇāśrama* and in the existing Brahmanical methods.

dakṣiṇāgni Sacrificial fire, also known as *anvāhāryapācana* because boiled rice was cooked on it with which the piṇḍa-pitṛyajña (q.v.) offerings to ancestors, was performed on the day of the new moon. Śabara on *Jaimini* XII.2.3., *Taitt.Br.* I.1.10, *Manu* III.123. This fire was lighted to the south-east of the Gārhapatya (q.v.) on a semicircular mound. The fire with which *dakṣiṇāgni* is established may be brought from the house of a person belonging to any caste, provided he is prosperous. It may also be brought from the *gārhapatya* fire or it may be produced by attrition. *Āśv.Sr.* I.2.1, *Baudh.Sr.* II.17.

dakṣiṇāmūrti Iconic representation of Śiva in the aspect of *guru* or master in various arts such as dancing, playing on musical instruments, expounding the *śāstras* and practising Yoga. The Jñāna-Yoga and Vyākhyāna Dakṣiṇāmūrtis of Śiva are common in South India.

dakṣiṇāyana The time when the sun journeys towards the south.

dama Self-control. It is one of the virtues inculcated in the *Gītā* XVI.1–2.

damanakāropaṇa Worship of various deities with *damanaka* plant.

ḍāmara A class of Tantric texts traditionally six in number. They are Yoga, Śiva, Durgā, Sārasvata, Brahmā and Gandharva.

ḍamaru A small drum, such as is carried by Śiva.

dāna Making a gift. It consists in the cessation of one's ownership and the creation of the ownership of another over the thing in which acceptance may be mental or vocal or physical. Śabara on *Jaimini* IV.2.28, Mit. on Yaj II.27. There are six *aṅgas* or constituents of *dāna*: the donor, the donee, śraddhā (charitable attitude), the subject of the gift, proper time and proper place (cf. *Manu* IV.226–27). Any one including women and Śūdras, can make a gift. *Dakṣa* III.17–18 states that a gift made to one's parents, *guru*, friend, to a well educated man, to one to whom the donor is under an obligation, to the poor, the helpless and to those endowed with special excellence, leads to rewards. *Manu* IV.193–200 and *Viṣṇu Dh.S.* XVIII.7–13 contains a list of persons to whom gifts should not be made. According to Devala, that is a proper subject of gift which has been acquired by the donor himself without causing pain or loss to another or without worry and trouble to himself, whether it be small or valuable. Gifts of certain objects are called *mahādāna* (q.v.). Dānas are divided into *nitya* (whatever is given every day such as food etc.), *naimittika* (what is given at specified times) and *kāmya* (what is given motivated by the desire to secure progeny, victory, prosperity, heaven, wife, etc.). Certain things when offered voluntarily by a person with his own hand must be accepted and not spurned even by one who does not ordinarily accept gifts. *Manu* IV. 247–250, Yāj I.214–15, *Āp.Dh.S.* I.6–19. 13–14, *Viṣṇu.Dh.S.* LVII.11. Certain objects cannot be donated because one has no ownership over them or because they are not considered to be suitable as gifts (*Jaimini* VI.7.1–7) and certain things are forbidden to be accepted as gifts like spirituous liquor, weapons, poisonous substances etc. *Vas.Dh.S* XIII.55. There are proper times for making gifts; specially recommended is the time of eclipses, the end of the lunar months and on holy days. Making gifts also involves certain rites and formalities. The *Bhagavadgītā* XVII.20–22 says that when a gift is made because one feels it is one's duty, and it is made at a proper time and place and to a worthy person who will not return it, it is called *sāttvika*; when it is made with the expectation that the donee will do a good turn in return, or with a view to securing some reward therefrom and is given grudgingly, it is *rājasa*; and when a gift is made at an improper time and place and to an unworthy person and without showing honour to the recipient and with disrespect and contempt, it is *tāmasa*.

dāna-pāramitā Gift, which is one of the ten *pāramitās* (q.v.) is of an extraordinary nature according to Buddhism.

daṇḍa A staff of mace carried by the Buddhist god Hayagrīva. It cannot be translated as the magic wand, since the *khatvāṅga* serves that purpose. When the staff is surmounted by a *vajra*, it is called *vajradaṇḍa*.

daṇḍājina Such persons as want to achieve their spiritual ends by means of a staff (*daṇḍa*) and animal skin (*ajina*); mentioned in Patañjali's com. on Pāṇini V.2.75 as a class of wandering ascetics.

danta-dhāvana Brushing the teeth; it is recommended for physical purification and has to be done in the morning and after meals. The texts describe the length and breadth of the twig, trees from which the twigs and the *mantras* to be recited when using a twig as a brush. *Yāj.*I.98, *Dakṣa* II.6, *Viṣṇu Dh.S.* LXI.16, *Pār.Gr.* II.6, *Āp.Gr.*XII.6. The *Taitt.Saṃ* II.5.1.7. says that brushing of teeth is forbidden to women during their monthly periods.

darbha A kind of grass required in numerous rituals. These are said to have sprung from the hair and perspiration of Viṣṇu in the boar incarnation. *Viṣṇudharmottara* I.139.12, *Matsya Pu.* XXII.89.

darśana The vision and realisation of truth by which a man becomes free from all fetters and attains liberation. *Manu* VI.74. It also means both perception as well as a philosophic point of view.

darśana-mārga Path of insight into the four truths which has been especially treated in the *Abhidharmakośa*. It is divided into sixteen points of comprehension, each of the four truths (*ārya satya* q.v.) being multiplied by the sense of *dharma* (ingredients), *bhāvanā* (concept of truth) and *anvaya* (synthesis), and viewed in terms of *kṣānti* (faith). See Poussin's summary of *darśana-mārga* in the intro. to his trans. of *Abhidharmakośa*. V-VI.

darśa-pūrṇamāsa Yajña (q.v.) performed at the time of the new-moon and full-moon: Darśa means *amavāsyā* or new-moon and *pūrṇamāsa* means full-moon. The *Āp.Sr.* III.14.11–13 describes *darśāpūrṇamāsa* as a sacrifice which is to be performed throughout a person's life. It is regarded as the archetype of all other Iṣṭis (q.v., the *yajña* in which the performer employs four priests). It begins with *anvārambhaṇīya-iṣṭi* when the sacrificer resolves to perform it and employs the priests. It is followed by *śākhāharaṇa* (bringing of fresh branches of *palāśa* or *śamī* tree by the Adhvaryu), *barhirāharaṇa* (bringing bundles on *kuśa* grass), *idhmāharaṇa* (bringing fuel sticks), *sāyam-doha* (evening milking from the cows), *brahmāvaraṇa* (choosing the *brahmā*, q.v. or priest), *praṇītāpraṇayana* (filling up vessels with sacred water), *nirvāpa* (taking out handfuls of grains or a portion of other sacrificial material), *prokṣaṇa* (sprinkling of sacrificial material), the *haviṣkṛt* call (invocation of Mother Earth as the Corn Mother, followed by beating the grains of rice and baking) *puroḍāśa* (cake on potsherds), *patnisaṃnahana* (girding up the sacrificer's wife, cf. wife's role in Aśvamedha q.v.), *barhirāstarana* (strewing the *vedī* or altar with *kuśa* grass), recital oi *sāmidhenı* verses (*RV* verses III.27.1 ff) and *pravaramantras* (invocation of fire), making two *āghāras* (pouring of *ājya* or clarified butter in a continuous stream), *hotṛvaraṇa* (selection of the *hotṛ*, q.v. priest), five *prayāja* offerings (addressed to five sacrificial articles each symbolising a deity), offerings to Agni-sviṣṭakṛt, cutting off a portion of the cake called *prāśitra* for Brahmā, *iḍopahvānam* (invocation of the Mother Goddess Iḍā by the Hotṛ), cutting off portions of the *puroḍāśa* or sacrificial cake and eating by the sacrificer and the four priests, cooking of a mess of boiled rice called *anvāharya*, as fee for the four priests, recitation of the *sūktavāka* (formulae addressed to Agni) by the Hotṛ, throwing the *prastara* (first handful of *kuśa* grass that is cut) by Adhvaryu into fire, *śaṃyuvāka* formulae (from *Taitt.Br.* III.5.11) recited by the Hotṛ, *patnīsaṃyāja* (offering made to the wives of the gods), and concluding rituals desiring prosperity, happiness, and fulfilment of human desires. It appears that *darśa-pūrṇamāsa* was originally a simple agricultural rite which later assumed sophisticated garb. For details see *Taitt.Saṃ.*I.1.1–13, I.6–7, II.5–6, *Śat.Br.*I, *Āśv.Sr.* I.1.4–I.13.10, *Āp.Sr.* I–IV, *Kāt.Sr.*II–IV, *Baudh.Sr.*I.

dārṣṭāntika A group of the Buddhist Sarvāstivādins, probably an offshoot of the Tāmraśāṭīya branch, out of which developed the Sautrāntika school.

daśa-bhūmi The ten stages of a Bodhisattva's perfection. See *bhūmi*.

daśahārā A *vrata* or rite which takes place on the 10th of the bright half of Jeyṣṭha (May-June). The day is sacred to the Ganges. It is so called because it removes ten sins.

daśahotṛ Ten sentences occurring in *Taitt.Ār.* III.1 and *Ait.Br.* XXIV.6, used as a *mantra* in connection with Śrauta sacrifices. They deal with ten subjects connected with the human body.

dāśakūṭa Subdivision of the Brahma sect founded by Madhva. It corresponded to the Tenkalai (q.v.) group of the Śrīvaiṣṇavas (q.v.). The earliest development of this devotional movement was in Deccan. The followers of this system insisted on equality and democracy and expounded the principles of the *dvaita* (q.v.) system.

daśalakṣana-parva See Paryūṣana.

daśa-mahāvidyā Ten Tantric goddesses—Kālī, Tārā, Ṣoḍaśī, Bhuvaneśvarī, Bhairavī, Chinnamastā, Dhūmāvatī, Vagalā, Mātaṅgī and Kamalā. *Prāṇatoṣaṇi* V.6.374. The names vary in different Tantras.

dāsa mārga The term applies to the ordinary initiates of Āgamānta Śaivism who are supposed to belong to the *sālokya* (q.v.) stage of spiritual progress in which they should feel themselves as servants of God. See also *samaya-dīkṣā*.

daśa-mudrāśakti Ten Tantric goddesses, known as *mudrā-śakti*, who are supposed to reside in the *śiva-rekhā* (a special line) of the mystic triangle. *Nityaṣoḍaśikārṇava* I.199–200.

daśapeya A rite performed on the tenth day after the *abhiṣecanīya* (q.v.). *Lāṭ.Sr.* IX.2.1, *Kāt.Sr.* XV.8. This rite is so called because in it each of the ten *camasas* (cups) of *soma*-wine are partaken of by ten *brāhmaṇas*. *Āśv.Sr.* XVIII.21.3.

daśa-saṃskāra The ten sacraments. See Saṃskāra.

daśa siddhi The ten miraculous attainments. See *Siddhi*.

daśāvatāra Ten incarnations of Viṣṇu.

dāsya The attitude of servitude towards God. The emotion behind it is known as *dāsya-rati*.

dattātreya The unity of Brahmā. Viṣṇu and Śiva.

dayā Observance of a partial fast current among the Jains; also known as *saṃvara*. The word also means that type of love which exists between husband and wife. It is also a synonym of kindness.

deha sādhanā See Kāya-sādhanā.

dehātmyavāda One of the five basic principles of the Cārvāka (q.v.) philosophy; it means that the concept of soul apart from the body is baseless.

devadāsī Dancing girls attached to temples. They are also known by the terms *basabī* and *bhāvin*. The institution is referred to in the *Rājataraṅgiṇī* IV.269, in the Vaghli (Khandesh) stone inscription of Govindarāja (*EI*.II.227), in an inscription of the Cāhamana king Jojaladeva (*EI*,XI.26–27), an inscription from Ittagi (*EI*, XIII.58) and other sources.

devadhammika A religious sect which flourished at the time of Buddha. Nothing is known about it except the name. *Aṅguttara* III. 276–77.

deva-koṣṭha A niche containing a cult image.

devakṛcchra A penance for minor sins which lasts for 21 days. It is characterised by occasional fasting.

devakula A place where cult image is installed.

devakulaṅkula A stage of sanctification which

according to early Buddhism an individual acquires when he is reborn among the gods. *Abhidharmakośa*(Poussin) II.34.

devalaka A temple priest who should not be invited in *śrāddha* or rites for a dead person's spiritual welfare. *Manu* III.152.

devapūjā Worship of deity, either as an image or a symbol or in the mind. The word *devapūjā* occurs in the *vārtika* on Pāṇini I.3.25. The digests try to show that, just as Yāga (sacrifice) consists in giving up materials accompanied by a *mantra* with reference to a deity that is then principally in view, so *pūjā* is also a *yāga*, because in it also the dedication of materials to a deity.

devāram Devotional poems by the South Indian Śaiva saints known as the Nāyanārs or Samayācāryas. The first seven collections of such poems are known as *devāram*, composed by the saints Sambandar, Āppar his older contemporary, and Sundarar, all of whom flourished in the seventh century A.D.

devatā Deity. In *Nirukta* VII.6–7 it is said that deities are of three kinds; those that have anthropomorphic form, those that have no anthropomorphic form and those that may partake of both characters, that is those deities who though really non-anthropomorphic may assume various forms to carry out a specific purpose or activity. Jaimini VIII.1.32–34 says that in sacrifice, the principle of Yajña is the most important, *devatā* is secondary. Reward is conferred by the sacrifice and not by the deities.

devatāśuddhi Purification of the image of a deity through *mantras* and water. *Puraścaryārṇava* III.153.

devayajana A place of sacrifice.

devayajña Offering fuel-sticks to fire with '*svāhā*' uttered after the name of the deities in the dative case. *Āp.Dh.S* I.3.14.1, *Baudh.Dh.S.* II.6.4, *Manu* II.70. It is almost same as *homa* (q.v.).

devayāna The way of the gods literally. The followers of this line believed that by practising faith (*śraddhā*), truthfulness (*satya*) and austerities (*tapasyā*) an individual would go to the path of the gods and never return to the world. *Chāndogya* V.10.1, VI.2.16, *Bṛhadāraṇyaka* VI.2.15; cf. *Dīgha* II.239.

devayātrotsava Days on which *yātrā* (q.v.) festivals of certain gods are to be celebrated.

devī-cakra General name of nerve plexuses.

dhāma The four holy places of pilgrimage; they are Badrinatha, Jagannātha, Rāmeśvara and Dvārakā.

dhanadakṛcchra A penance for minor sins which consists in subsisting for a month on food just sufficient to fill the extended, hollowed (like the ear of a cow) palm. The food should be touched with gold.

dharādāna Also known as Haima-dharādāna, it is a form of *mahādāna* or great-gift, in which a miniature figure of the world made out from 5 to 1000 *palas* of gold, according to one's means, should be made and donated to those persons qualified to receive such gifts.

dhārāliṅga A kind of Śiva-linga having vertical fluted facets.

dhāraṇā Attention consisting in fixing the mind on the desired object; it is the sixth discipline of Yoga.

dhāraṇa yantra The *yantras* (q.v.) generally used as an amulet or talisman. These are drawn on leaves and dedicated in the name of different deities. Their use is regarded as efficacious for warding off evil spirits and in the attainment of merit. *Tantrasāra* 585, *Śaktisaṅgama*, tārā, LI.2.

dhāraṇī, dhāriṇī A conglomeration of syllables, occasionally containing one or two intelligible words, used as a charm or prayer by the followers of Tantric Buddhism. These were composed between the fourth and eighth centuries A.D. and formed part of Mahāyāna Buddhist literature. The Dhāraṇīs refer to Tantric concepts like *mantra, mudrā, kriyā, caryā*, etc.

dharma Principle of motion which according to Jain cosmic conception helps the Jīva associated with Pudgala (matter) to progress just as water helps the movement of a fish. It is eternal and formless prevading the entire world of space, and in nature passive. (Guṇaratna on *SDSC*, 49, *TTDS*, V. 17–18). The Nyāya-Vaiśeṣikas view *dharma* in terms of merit and regard it as one of the 24 constituents of *guṇa* (q.v.) or quality (*Vaiś.Sūt.* I.1.16). According to the Mīmāṃsakas *dharma* is identical with Vedic injunctions or laws which enjoins the performance of a variety of actions in different walks of life. (*codanālaksaṇo'rtho-dharmaḥ*). This interpretation was followed in the Brahmanical tradition which equated *dharma* with law and behaviour. That is why the legal treatises were known as Dharmasūtras and Dharmaśāstras. The Buddha used the term *dharma* or *dhamma* to denote the moral laws prescribed by him. Subsequently the term came to be used in the sense of nature, duty, phenomena or elements, doctrine, truth, justice, virtue, laws, quality and predicate in Buddhism. In plural it denotes element. In the Abhidhamma texts, by *dharma* is meant a fundamental principle, viz. the idea that existence is an interplay of a plurality of subtle, ultimate, and not further analysable elements of matter, mind and force. In Puranic tradition *dharma* as a moral order was in the pristine glory in Kṛta-Yuga the earliest of the traditional ages, it then had four feet but lost one foot in each succeeding Yuga (q.v.). It should be noted in this connection that three important words of the *Ṛgveda*, viz. *ṛta, vrata* and *dharma* were transformed into other meanings later on.

dharmabhāṇaka Preacher of religion. *Bodhisattva-bhūmi* 23.

dharmabhūtajñāna Term for consciousness according to the Rāmānuja school. It is regarded as an attribute in relation to Self and God.

dharmacakra Also known as Vyākhyāna-mudrā it is the gesture of hands exhibited by Lord Buddha while preaching the first sermon at Sarnath. The palms are placed near the breast in the mode of explaining something. The pose is depicted variously but the most artistic and correct representation of this *mudrā* is to be found in the celebrated Prajñāpāramitā image from Java. See Getty, *GNB*, 187. Dharmacakra is also one of the four nerve-cycles in the Tantric Buddhist conception. It is situated near the region of the heart and is connected with the *dharma-kāya* of Buddha. It is kindled by a female energy having the force of fire known as *caṇḍālī*, like the *kuṇḍalinī-śakti* (q.v.) of the Śākta Tantras.

dharmacakra-pravartana Setting of the Wheel of Law in motion, the term which is used to denote the first sermon of the Buddha at Sarnath. This happened on full moon in the month of Māgha (Jan-Feb). This day is celebrated by the Buddhists as sacred.

dharmadhātu Buddhist name of the universe.

dharmagupta A Buddhist sect which did not accept the *prātimokṣa* (q.v.) rules of the Sarvāstivādins as authoritative on the ground that the original teachings of the Buddha were lost. This sect had a Vinaya of its own and also a text called *Abhiniṣkramana-sūtra*.

dharma-kāya See Trikāya.

dharmaloka The ten spheres in the Buddhist concept. These are *sattva* (world of sentient beings), *loka* (various worlds), *dharma* (universe), *ākāśa* (space), *vijñāna* (world of consciousness), *kāma* (world of desires), *rūpa* (world of forms), *arūpa* (world of formlessness), *udārādhyā-śayādhimukti* (world of noble intention) and *māhātmyādhyā-śayādhi-mukti* (world of magnanimous aspiration). *Bodhisattva-bhūmi* 14ff.

dharmamegha The final stage of *saṃprajñāta-samādhi* (q.v.) which like cloud showers on the Yogin is the blessing of self-realisation. *Yogasūtra* IV.29. In Mahāyāna Buddhism it is the tenth *bhūmi* in the process of the attainment of Bodhisattvahood. In this stage the Bodhisattvas attain the excellence and pre-eminence of a Buddha.

dharma-nairātmya Same as Dharma-śūnyatā (q.v.) of the Buddhist Mādhyamika philosophy which denies not only the reality of substance (*pudgala*) but also that of its separate elements.

dharmānusārī Those who set themselves to practice the *bodhipakṣīya-dharma* (q.v.) through the study of the scriptures; in Pali Dhammānusārī. *Abhidharmakośa* (Poussin) VI.29. According to the *Puggalapaññatti* 15 those who have dominance of knowledge in a great measure are called Dhammānusārī.

dharmarucika Buddhist sect of Ceylon; same as the Abhayagirivasin (q.v.). *Mahāvaṃsa* V.13.

dharmaśūnyatā According to the Hinayānists, it means egolessness of constituted (*samskṛta*, *saṃkhaṭa*) things in particular and that of other things in general. Nāgārjuna has used the term as the essence of the Mādhyamika (q.v.) world-view in the sense that all things are like echo, mirage or images seen in dreams—as false as the beauty of the daughter of a barren woman. See Dharmanairātmya.

dharmatā A Buddhist term for eternal truth.

dharmāyatana Buddhist term meaning the fields of objects of ideation.

dharmuttarīya A Buddhist sect which according to Vasumitra held views in common with the Sāmmitīyas (q.v.) in many cases.

dhātu A Buddhist concept with a very wide meaning. When a *dhātu* is said to be constituted (*saṃkhata*) it means all the beings and things of the world, e.g. the three spheres of existence, *kāma, rūpa* and *arūpa* (qq.v.), the four great elements (*mahābhūtas*), the sense organs and their objects (*āyatanas*); the material and non-material constituents (*khaṇḍas*), etc. Besides these, are also included mental and physical pain and pleasure, equanimity, ignorance, desire, renunciation, hatred, as also *ākāśa* and *nibbāna* or *nirodha*. The last two, however, are called unconstituted (*asaṃkhata*) *dhātus*. Etymologically *dhātu* means those elements which uphold a being.

dhātuśakti Collective name of Ḍākinī, Rākinī, Lākinī, Kākinī, Śākinī and Hākinī, presiding goddesses of the *cakras* (q.v.).

dhauti One of the six actions of Yogic practices denoting washing, internal and external, for making the body pure. Dhauti is of four kinds—*antar, danta, hṛd*, and *mūlaśodhana*. *Gheraṇḍa* I.13.

dhavana Literally means 'sexual intercourse' but the term is employed to describe the procedure for erecting a mound over the bones of one who has performed the special rite of *agnicayana* (q.v.).

dhenu Gifts of certain articles, so called in imitation of the gift of the cows. The *Matsyapurāṇa* LXXXII.17–22 speaks of ten *dhenus*, viz. jaggery, clarified butter, sesame, water, milk, honey, sugar, curd, other liquids and the cow itself. See also *Mbh* XIII.71.39–41, *Agni Pu.* CCX.11–12 etc.

dhenumudrā A yogic pose which required to offer *naivedya* (food-offering) to God in the ritual of worship; it signifies a cow.

dhṛti An aspect of *kṣamā* or mercy.

dhruva-bera Principal types of Visnu images which are grouped under three broad heads: *sthānaka* (standing), *āsana* (seated) and *śayana* (recumbent).

dhruva-śrāddha Śrāddha (q.v.) or rites for the welfare of the departed one which should be performed on the day of death.

dhūpa Incense stick; when it burns it emits a fragrance. It is required in the worship of deities.

dhūrta-cārvākas A section of the followers of the Cārvāka system who maintained that perception was the only source of valid knowledge. They had no faith in inference since one inference required another inference leading finally to the fallacy of an *ad infinitum* retrogression.

dhūtāṅga Thirteen rigorous practices prescribed for Buddhist monks. These are to wear robes of left-over cloth; to eat food collected by begging; to beg food; to take a meal only at one sitting; to possess only one bowl; not to take food when the belly is full; to dwell in the forest; to live in a place without a shed; not to have more than three robes; to live in an open space; to live in a cemetery, to use whatever bed or seat is allotted; and to spend the night sitting. *Milinda* 357–55, *Visuddhimagga* 59–88. In the Nikayas and the Vinaya dhūtāṅgas are not mentioned. These were probably due to the influence of the Devadatta faction.

dhūtavādin Those who practise *dhūtāṅgas* (q.v.).

dhyāna Meditation. It refers generally to that portion of the Sādhanā of the Mahāyāna Buddhists in which instruction is given as to the description of the deity with whom the worshipper is to identify himself. Dhyāna is also the name of a *mudrā* and an *āsana*. (see Samādhi-mudrā and Vajraparyṅkāsana respectively). It is defined as steady contemplation of the object without break which reveals the reality of the contemplated object to the aspirant's mind. It is the seventh discipline of Yoga.

dhyānāsana See Vajraparyaṅka.

dhyānayoga Mental concentration on the process of the upward march of Kuṇḍalinī (q.v.).

dhyānī-buddha Deification of the five cosmic elements or *skandhas* (q.v.) in Vajrayāna Buddhism. The five Dhyānī Buddhas are Amitābha, Akṣobhya, Amogasiddhi, Ratnasambhava and Vairocana. Each of them is an embodiment of a particular element (*rūpa, vedanā, saṃjñā, saṃskāra* and *vijñāna* respectively), belongs to a particular *kula* or tribe has attendant bodhisattvas, emanated gods and goddesses, and *śakti* or consort.

digambara A class of *avadhutas* (q.v.) having the quality of Śiva. *Prāṇatoṣani* VII.7, 532. The term also applies to a sect following Vāmācāra (q.v.). Laksmidhara's com. on *Saundaryalaharī* 32.

digambara-śvetāmbara Two main divisions of the Jains. The Jain tradition records eight schisms, the first of which took place as early as the days of Mahāvīra under the leadership of his own son-in-law, Jamāli. The second was caused by Gośāla (actually he did not belong to the creed), the third by Āṣāḍha Ācārya, the fourth by Aśvamitra, the fifth by Gaṅga, the sixth by Rohagupta and the seventh by Goṣṭha. The last schism which was based on seven main tenets in which the Digambaras were opposed to the Śvetāmbaras resulted in a sharp division of the church, each section claiming greater authenticity than the other. It was during the patriarchy of Vajrasena that the great schism took place. The points on which emphasis is laid by the Digambaras are that the Tirthaṃkaras (q.v.) must be represented as nude and with downcast eyes, that women cannot attain Mokṣa (q.v.), that the Kevalajñānins (q.v.) require no food, that Mahāvīra was never married, that the compiled canonical works are not valid since they are man-made, that the ascetics must be entirely nude and that Ācāryas after Jambusvāmī do not represent the entire community.

dig-gaja Mythical guardians of the quarters conceived of in the form of elephants.

dikpāla Eight guardians of the quarters. Indra (east), Yama (south), Varuṇa (West), Kubera (north), Agni (southeast), Nirṛti (southwest), Īśāna (northeast) and Vāyu (northwest).

dīkṣā Consecration, initiation. It is required in various walks of life from *rites de passage* (cf. *Ait.Br.* I.3, *Śat.Br.* III.3.3.12) to the entry into a religious creed. In the case of Vedic sacrifices, the sacrificer must undergo an initiation of *dīkṣā* ceremony, the rules of which are laid down in *Āpastamba* X.10–12 and other Śrautasūtras. The word *dīkṣā* is derived from the root *dā* (to give) and *kṣi* (do destroy). According to most of the sources, *dīkṣā* is of two kinds, Vedic and Tantric. In order to lead a religious life as prescribed by the Vedas and texts of Vedic tradition a formal initiation is required but it is not as important as in the case of Tantric *sādhanā* in which it is an essential precondition. According to the *Viśvasāra-tantra* it is of four types—*kriyāvatī, kalāvatī, varṇamayī* and *vedhamayī*. *Prāṇatoṣaṇī* II.4, 1 118. According to *Kulārṇava* XIV, it is of seven kinds—*kriyā, varṇa, kalā, sparśa, vāk, dṛk* and *mānasa*. These are again subdivided into different categories. According to the *Rudrayāmala, dīkṣa* is of three types—*āṇavī, śāktī* and *śāmbhavī*. *Prāṇatoṣaṇī* II.4. There are other types of *dīkṣa* like *krama, pañcāyatana, ekamantra*, etc. The *Jayadratha-Yāmala* mentions 25 kinds of *dīkṣā*. Different forms of *dīkṣā* have been treated separately in the present volume. See the individual entries of the kinds of *dīkṣā* mentioned above.

dīkṣaṇīya-iṣṭi A form of *iṣṭi* (q.v.) required in the Agnistoma (q.v.) the rules of which are laid down in *Āp.Sr.* X.4.9, *Kāt.Sr.* VII.2.31–32, VII.3. 23, *Jaimini* V.3.29.31, VII.1.3–10, XI.4.48–49 etc. After performing this *iṣṭi*, with rites resembling those followed for the process of the brith of a new baby, person becomes *dīkṣita* or initiated as if he receives a new life.

dīkṣāpāla Agni and Viṣṇu conceived of as guardians of initiation in *Ait.Br.* I.4.

dīpa The sacred lamp fed with *ghee* or clarified butter.

dīpana Processing of *mantra*. *Tantrasāra* 54.

dīpāvalī The festival of lights and fireworks which is one of the most joyful festivals observed in India on the night of the new moon of Kārtika (Oct–Nov), also known as Diwali. Basically a ritual of death and resurrection, it is also connected with the demise of Lord Mahāvīra. Now it is celebrated with illumination and crackers; temples and homes are decorated with lamps. In Bengal this ceremony is connected with the worship of Kālī, the goddess of death and revival. The preceding night is called *bhūta-caturdaśī* and is dedicated to the ghosts and goblins associated with Śiva. The Jains on this day pay homage to the memory of Lord Mahāvīra. Exchange of Diwali greetings and sweetmeats is a regular feature of the ceremony. In some places gambling is a part of the celebration. See under Bali-pratipadā. Some people worship the goddess Lakṣmī on Diwali; the essential feature of the worship is the driving away of Alakṣmi, the goddess causing disaster.

ditthadhammanibbānavāda The doctrine of the attainment of Nibbāna (q.v.) in one life. Five schools upholding this doctrine are mentioned in the Buddhist texts. According to this doctrine the soul attains perfection when it enjoys fully the pleasures of the five senses, and hence the *summum bonum* of life is enjoyment of worldly pleasures.

diṭṭhippatta A designation for the Dharmānusāris (q.v.) because of their greater interest in philosophical studies than in higher meditation.

diṭṭhivisuddhi The true Buddhist view about the nature of reality. For attaining this one must comprehend the nature of *khaṇḍas* or constituents of a being, *āyatanas* or organs of sense and their spheres, *indriyas* or faculties and characteristics of the four *dhātus*, the true meaning of the *ariyasaccas* (*āryasatyas* q.v.) and of *paṭiccasamuppāda* (law of causation).

divya-bhāva The highest spiritual standard of the Tantric aspirant.

divyacakra A cakra (q.v.) ritual meant only for those who have attained much spiritual progress; also known as *tattvacakra*. *This cakra* also requires the use of the five Ms. *Mahānirvāṇa* VIII. 204–19.

divya-deha Rejuvenated body. See Raśeṣvaradarśana.

divya-pāna One of the three forms of drinking wine before the goddess, others being Paśu and

Vīra. *Kulārṇava* VII, *Śaktisaṅgama*, Tārā, XXXIII.6–8.

divya-sādhaka The aspirant whose spiritual exercise is of the highest level.

divya-tattva One of the three categories of *pañcatattva* (q.v.), others being *pratyakṣa* and *anukalpa*.

divyaugha One of the three lines of succession of the Tantric *gurus* (q.v.), others being *siddhaugha* and *manavaugha*. *Bhavacuḍāmaṇi* quoted in *Śyāmārahasya* III.

dola-yātrā An ancient festival celebrated on the day of the full moon in Phālguna (Feb-March). It is celebrated throughout India, with gaity and frolic marked by ribald songs and music and the exchange of coloured water or powder. Originally a ceremony of death and resurrection, probably of the year. In Bengal it is associated with the legend of Kṛṣṇa's dalliance with Rādhā. Same as Holikā or Holi (q.v.).

doṣa Faults. These are five according to *Mbh* XII. 232.4–7 namely, *kāma* (lust), *krodha* (anger), *lobha* (covetuousness), *bhaya* (fear) and *svapna* (sleep). These are disturbances in the path of Yoga. In Tantric belief *doṣa* means defects in regard to *mantras*. Defective *mantras* like *chinna*, *ruddha*, etc., do not produce any result. *Śāradātilaka* II.64–108.

drāviḍa-veda Devotional compositions of the southern Vaiṣṇava Āḷvāras (q.v.)

dravya A common term in Indian religio-philosophical tradition by which is generally understood substance, that which is capable of becoming this or that. A Dravya is possessed of some unchanging essential characters or Guṇas (q.v.) and changing modes or Paryāyas (q.v.). The different senses of the word Dravya are but different ways of conveying the same idea. The word is variously interpreted in Patañjali's *Mahābhāṣya*. One interpretation is defined as the basic character which remains unimpaired even in the midst of the emergence of newer qualities. In the *Vaiśeṣika Sūtra* I.1.15 the word stands for the substratum of qualities and actions. Thus earth, etc., are nine Dravyas according to this system. The Buddhists, however, hold that the changing qualities alone can be perceived and that there is no unchanging substance behind them. In Jainism the word Dravya is used differently (cf. *TTDS*, I.5, V.31, *Bhagavatī* III.19), but it is normally used in the sense of the basic types of entities found in the universe. For example, Jīva, Pudgala, etc., form the six Dravyas. In the Nyāya-Vaiśeṣika, there are nine Dravyas—earth (*pṛthivī*), water (*āp*), fire (*tejas*), air (*vāyu*), ether (*ākāśa*), time (*kāla*), space (*dik*), self (*ātman*) and mind (*manas*). The first five are called *bhūtas* (elements) having some special quality that can be perceived by one or other of the external senses. See Guṇa and Paryāya.

dravya-bandha One of the two major classes of the Jain concept of *bandha* (q.v.) or bondage. It denotes the real connection between *karma* (q.v.) and *jīva* (q.v.) which is like the sticking of dust on an oily cloth. If oil is spilled on a cloth, dust will easily adhere; the cloth represents *jīva*, the oil the passions, transgressions and activities and the dust, the *pudgala* (q.v.) *DS* (Vṛtti) 30 ff., *VP* XVI.44, *TTDS* VII.1.

dravyamaya-yajña Material sacrifice, i.e. sacrifice with material objects for the purpose of achieving material gains. This type of sacrifice is belittled in the *Gītā* VIII.9–11.

dravyasaṃvara One of the two main classes of *saṃvara* (q.v.) or stoppage of the influx of *karma* (q.v.) according to Jain conception. It is connected with the reactions of the external objects, which in the form of infra-atomic particles of matter, soil the soul through the five senses and four passions. *DS*, *Vṛtti* 35, *VP*, XVI.67–68.

dravyāsrava The substratum of Karmāsrava (q.v.) which is concerned with the influx of *karma*-particles into the soul through external agencies.

dravyaśuddhi Purification of cultic materials with *mantras* and *dhenumudrā*. *Puraścaryārṇava* III.153.

dṛk-dīkṣā See under Cākṣuṣī-dīkṣā.

dṛṣṭānta An example which illustrates a general rule. It is one of the sixteen philosophical topics of the Nyāya.

dṛṣṭārthāpatti One of the two kinds of *arthāpatti* (q.v.) or postulation which is employed to explain something which is perceived. For example, when a man who is growing fat, is observed to fast during the day, one has to admit that the man must eat at night. It arises out of a demand to explain logically an observed phenomenon.

dṛṣti-sṛṣṭi-vāda Vedantic solipsism which holds Jīva (q.v.) with its nescience to be the material cause and creator of the world of appearance. It holds that the *esse* of things is their *percipi*, not as modes of absolute consciousness, but as mental creation of individual percipients. See Ekajīva-vāda.

dukkha Suffering. The first of the four truths preached by the Buddha. It is due to the failure to obtain what a man wants. In Buddhist terminology the combination of five aggregates (*khandas*) ends in suffering and is always accompanied with pain on account of constant change and ultimate decay. By Dukkha is therefore meant 'existence in the world with concomitant pain and pleasure' which are without any real substance (*anattā*) and are impermanent (*anicca*). *Vinaya* I.10, *Dīgha* II.306, *Majjhima* III.249f, *Vibhaṅga* 99. The *Visuddhimagga* 498.99 refers to seven kinds of Dukkha: *dukkha, vipariṇāma, saṅkhārā, paṭicchanna, appaṭicchanna, pariyāya* and *nippariyāya*. cf. *AKV* I.18.

dukkha-nirodha Absolute ending of suffering which is the third of the four truths preached by the Buddha. It is the cessation of *dukkha-samudaya* (q.v.), complete detachment from desires, relinquishment of all worldly objects and of desire to possess them. It is unborn (*ajātam*) and unoriginated (*abhūtam*), uncreated (*akatam*) and unconstituted (*asaṃkhaṭam*). *Itivuttaka* 37, *Udāna*. 80, *AKV* I. 48.

dukkhānta One of the five categories of the Pāśupata system. It is the extermination of suffering. The Pāśupatasūtra (IV.49) states that suffering will be ended only for one who is free from all sorts of illusion by the grace of God: *apramādī gacchet duḥkhānāṃ antan īśāprasādāt*.

dukkha-samudaya The origin of suffering which is the second of the four truths preached by the Buddha. See under Paṭiccasamuppāda (q.v.) which traces the source of suffering to ignorance (*avijjā*) of the three varieties: *anattā* (q.v.), *anicca* (q.v.) and *dukkha* (q.v.)

duraṃgamā The seventh *bhumī* (q.v.) for the potential Bodhisattva. It is a "far going stage" in which the would-be Bodhisattvas acquire compassion (*karuṇā*), knowledge of the five elements of existence (*skandhas*), aspiration to *bodhi*, and have immaculate sojourn in existence and extreme energy (*vīrya-pāramitā*).

dūtī Female partner of the aspirant.

dūtīyaga Ritual union with Dūti (q.v.) is known as *dūtīyāga*. Her organ is conceived of as the sacrificial fire and the semen of the aspirant as the clarified butter which is to be offered in the fire. *Paraśurāmakalpasūtra* X.63.

dvādaśāha Soma sacrifices which are celebrated for more than one day but not exceeding twelve. It is both a *sattra* and an *ahina*. *Āśv.Sr.*X.5.2. There are several varieties of *dvādaśāha*, one being called Bharata-*dvādaśāha* (*Āśv.*Sr.X5.8, *Āp.Sr.*XXI.14.5). The 12 days of *dvādaśāha* as a *sattra* are constituted by *prāyaṇīya* (commencing rite), *pṛṣṭhya-ṣaḍāha* (6 days), *chandomas* (3 days), *atyagniṣṭoma* on the tenth day and the *udayanīya* (concluding rites). Though called *sattra*, the *dvādaśāha* has also differences from the former. The *sattra* is performed by brāhmaṇas; it may take a longer period; there is no difference between the sacrificer and the priest; it does not involve *dakṣiṇā* or sacrificial fee. In *dvādaśāha* none of these holds good.

dvaitādvaita The school of Nimbārka which seeks to explain the concept of *brahman* in theistic terms. According to this school *brahman* is both material and efficient cause of the world. It is not the impersonal Absolute but a personal god who is Krsna or Hari. Since *brahman* is the material cause it transforms itself into the world and the process of such transformation is due to its efficient character. During dissolution (*pralaya*) the entire universe returns to and remains in it in a subtle state as its natural powers, but at the beginning of creation it manifests its *cit-śakti* (power of sentience) and *acit-śakti* (power of non-sentience) in the form of souls and *prakṛti* (q.v.), and from the latter there is a gradual evolution of the material world. The cause-effect relation between the *brahman* and the world is that of identity-in-difference. *Brahman* is different from the universe because it is transcendent to it, and non-different because it is immanent in it. Creation is due not to any want on god's part, but merely for his sport (*līlā*).

dvaitavāda The school of Madhva known as that of unqualified dualism which seeks to explain the concept of *brahman* in theistic terms. According to this school, *brahman* is *alaukika* (transcendent) and so subject to never-ending enquiry. The Sruti (q.v.) establishes *brahman* as the one single principle of creation, existence and destruction. *Brahman* is independent and maker of all, the *bimba* or source, and that which it makes is *pratibimba* or derived reflection. The latter is not independent of the former, nor an illusion, for it is the work of *brahman*. The world of *cetana* (conscious) and *acetana* (material) is real, essentially *paratantra* (dependent) having derived reality from Viṣṇu, the *brahman*. If the world is unreal then there is no occasion to find out and conceive *brahman* as the ground of all that exists.

To understand the world as *pratibimba* or *paratantra* is to understand its principle which is *brahman* identified with Viṣṇu.

dvāpara See under Yuga.

dveṣa The really painful or the pleasureable, inasmuch as in anger and hatred there is a peculiar pleasure attached, though the experience is really painful. In ordinary use the word stands for hatred.

dvija, dvijāti The three higher castes supposed to have been twice-born after Upanayana (q.v.) or initiation into studenthood. The *Āp.Dh.S.*I.1.1.16–18 says: The teacher causes him (the boy who is initiated in Vedic study) to be born from *vidyā* (i.e. by imparting Vedic knowledge); that birth is superior; the parents produce only the body. cf. *Manu* II. 147–48.

dyuloka The celestial sphere, the topmost plane of existence.

ekabhakta A penance for the expiation of minor sins. It consists in taking only one meal a day for a month.

ekabījī Mentioned in the Pali texts, as one of the two sub-stages between Sotāpanna and Kolaṃkola (qq.v.) meaning an individual who will have one more existence before attaining *nirvāṇa* (q.v.); in Sanskrit Ekavīcika, *Aṅguttara* I. 233, IV. 380–81, *Saṃyutta* V.205, *Visuddhimaga* 709. The *Abhidharmakośa* (Poussin) VI.36 gives the etymology thus: *vīci* is internal separation i.e., they are separated from *nirvāṇa* by one more birth.

ekacca-sassatavāda Partial Eternalism which holds that the body and the sense organs are impermanent while the mind and consciousness are permanent. It recalls the contents of the *Maitrī Upaniṣad* II. 34 according to which the soul is pure (*śuddha*), tranquil (*śātna*) and eternal (*śāśvata*) and the body is possessed of the reverse qualities. Four groups of Partial Eternalists are mentioned in the Brahmajāla-sutta. *Dīgha* I.

ekādaśinī Recital of Rudra *mantras* from *Taitt.-Saṃ*. IV.5.1.11 eleven times.

ekādaśīvrata Observance of fast on the eleventh lunar day. There are 24 *ekādaśīs* in a year, each having a separate name. If *ekādaśī* spans two days, householders should fast on the first and Sannyāsins on the second. A person above 8 years and less than 80 years of age of whatever *varṇa* or *āśrama* is eligible to perform: *ekādaśī*. Fast on *ekādaśī* is of two kinds: adhering to the prohibition about taking food and the other is of the nature of a *vrata*. The main features of *ekādaśī* are fast, worship of Viṣṇu image, and to stay awake at night with songs, etc. The fast is concluded on the next day by *pāraṇa* which consists in feeding a brāhmaṇa and giving him *dakṣiṇā* or fees. Texts on *ekādaśī* are Ragunandana's *Ekādaśītattva* and Śūlapāṇi's *Ekādaśīviveka*. Extremely exaggerated praise of the efficacy of fasting is indulged in by many Purānas.

eka-deva One god. A term for the ultimate unitary principle which is also described as *tad-ekam* (that one).

ekāggatā The Buddhist concept of the oneness of objects connected with the seven universal good mental properties (*cetasikas*).

ekāgratā Singularity of mind, according to *Yoga-sūtra* III.11.12.

ekāha One-day sacrifice, also known as *aikāhika*, the typical example of which is Agniṣṭoma (q.v.). Some sacrifices are classified into those that are finished in one day (and so called *ekāha*), those that are celebrated for more than one but not more than twelve (and so called *ahīna*) and those that extend beyond twelve days (and are called *sattra*). *Jaimini* X.6.60–61. Among the important *ekāhas* are sacrifices like Viśvajit, Gosava, Sarvasvāra Bṛhaspatisava, Śyena, Udbhid, Vrātyaṣṭoma etc. (qq.v.).

ekajīvavāda The sigularity or oneness of Jīva (q.v.). The theory is as follows : The seeming plurality of the Jīvas is due to the plurality of bodies. The one infinite Self, which is of the nature of self-consciousness and bliss, imagines itself to be a worldly Jīva through its own ignorance. When, again, this Jīva hankers after freedom, it regains its real state of freedom by destroying its ignorance. Then, of course, no other Jīva or the world remains. The world is nothing more than its perception (*dṛṣṭireva sṛṣṭi*). Everything other than *brahman* is appearance (*prātibhāsika*), having no existence outside perception (*ajñatāsattva*). It is an extreme form of subjective idealism, also known as *dṛṣṭi-sṛṣṭi-vāda* (q.v.).

ekakṣaṇika-citta Characteristic of a Buddha's mind which, like a mirror, can comprehend everything in one moment and answer any question immediately without a pause for reflection.

ekamevādvitīyam Ultimate unity of absolute existence; 'that one without a second'.

ekamukha-liṅga One-faced *liṅga* or phallus of Śiva. It is the depiction of a human face of Śiva on the *pūjā-bhāga* or *rudra-bhāga* of the *liṅga*. According to the *Rūpamaṇḍana* in a one-faced type the face should be in front. See Mukhaliṅga.

ekāntavāda Jain term for absolutistic philosophical systems as opposed to their relativistic and many-sided (*anekānta*) worldview.

ekāntika Equivalent also to Nārāyaṇīya, Sātvata, Bhāgavata, and Pāñcarātra, it is stated at many places to be the best form of Vaiṣṇavism. The Nārāyaṇīya section of the *Mbh*, XII.334–51 is the earliest exposition of the Ekāntika dharma which preaches sole devotion to Nārāyaṇa or the supreme Lord, as the only means of seeing him. The system is said to have been originally promulgated by the seven sages, who were collectively called the Citraśikhaṇḍin (q.v.) in a hundred thousand verses. These contain rules, in harmony with the Vedas, for all affairs of men and precepts about the religious life of action and contemplation. The Śāntiparvan of the *Mbh* states that this *dharma* was revealed to Janamejeya in the *Hari-Gītā* and also that it was related to Arjuna at the beginning of the Bhārata war.

ekapāda-mūrti A form of Śiva image which represents Śiva standing on one leg, the figures of Viṣṇu and Brahmā projecting from his left and right sides respectively, with the hands of the central image held in the *añjali* pose. This type appears to be based on the Vedic Aja Ekapāda described in the epic texts both as one of the eleven Rudras and as an epithet of Śiva.

ekārṇavaśāyin Name of an *avatāra* of Viṣṇu found in the *Sātvatasaṃhitā* which enumerates as many as 39 incarnatory forms.

eka-śaranīa-dharma Religion of refuge in one Lord.

ekaśṛṅgatanu The first incarnatory form of Viṣṇu. Same as Matsya-avatāra.

ekāṣṭakā The eighth *tithi* after full moon in the month of *māgha* (Jan–Feb) which is said to be the wife of the year. *AV* III.10.8, *Jaimini* VI.5.32–37. It is the most auspicious day to undergo *dīkṣā* (q.v.) or initiation. *Āp.Gr.* VIII.21.10, cf. *Hir.Gr.* II.15.9.

ekavākyatā Rules for reconciling differences in conflicting texts. When several sentences, coveying its own sense, are brought together, one is the principal and the others auxiliary, they form one syntactical whole, called *mahāvākya*. cf. *Vedānta-sūtra* III.4.24.

eka-vyavahārika A Buddhist sect, a branch of the Mahāsaṅghikas. In Pali Ekabbohārika. Their views were in agreement with those held by the Mahāsaṅghikas (q.v.)

ekkavāda Monism, theism, monotheism etc. *Ṭhāna* IV.4. See under Akriyāvāda.

ekavrātya An epithet of Rudra.

ekoddiṣṭa A śrāddha (rite for the spiritual welfare of a departed being) which is modification of *pārvaṇa-śrāddha* (q.v.). *Sān.Gr.* IV.2. *Baudh.Gr.* III.12.6, Yaj I. 251–52. The word means 'that in which only one deceased person is intended to be invoked or benefited.' *Mit* on *Yaj* I. 217. In this *śrāddha* only one *arghya* (respectful offering of water) and one *piṇḍa* (food-lump) are offered. No brāhmaṇas are invited to represent the viśva-devas. Ekoddiṣṭa-śrāddhas are of three kinds—***nava***, ***navamiśra*** and ***purāṇa***.

gaccha Regional seats of the Jains. By the eighth century A.D. various *gacchas* originated in North India with the traditional 84 disciples of Uddyotana who, according to the *Kharataragaccha-paṭṭāvali* flourished 550 years after Devardhi (*IA*, XI.248). The Gandhani inscription of A.D. 880, though it mentions Uddyotana and his two disciples does not refer to the *gacchas* (*JLS*, III.164). But other inscriptions, speciallv of the South, refer to Addakali, Deśika-Gaṇa, Hottage, Mesapasana, Nandī, Pogala, Pogari, Pulikal, Pustaka, Sārasvata, Tagarigal, Tintrinika and Vakra *gacchas*.

gadā Mace. One of the weapons of Viṣṇu.

gadā-devī Mace or *gadā*, the weapon of Viṣṇu, conceived of as an anthropomorphic entity. Because the word *gadā* is in feminine gender, its personified form is shown as a beautiful woman.

gāi-yātrā A Nepalese festival on the first day after the full-moon in *śrāvaṇa* (July–Aug) which is observed by cow-worship. It is akin to *goṣṭhāṣṭamī*.

gajacchāya Same as *mahālayā*, the day for offering homage to the departed ancestors. It is in the latter half of the *bhādra* (Sept–Oct) when the sun comes to the virgo point of the zodiac.

gajakrāntā A geographical region of Tantric culture; same as Aśvakrāntā (q.v.).

gajalakṣmī The goddess Lakṣmī anointed by a pair of elephants.

gājana Rituals dedicated to Śiva or Dharma, performed in different parts of Bengal, mainly by persons belonging to the lower ranks of society, on the last day of the Hindu calendar. Preparations are made throughout the whole month. The participants observe a ceremonial impurity for a month, live on vegetarian diet, practice celibacy and sleep on the ground, take the vow of *sannyāsa* and impersonate Śiva and his attendants. The Śiva image or phallus is worshipped and dances of Śiva are held by the participants along with the beating of the drums. In some places *bāṇavrata* is held which is a ritual with human skull. Basically the Gājana is an expression of primitive beliefs relating to fertility, death and resurrection. The participants also give a show of feats of physical endurance. See also Caḍaka and Gambhīrā.

gajāsura-saṃhāra-mūrti Śiva images depicting the legend of the killing of Gajāsura, the elephant demon. The sculptures generally represent the irate god engaged in a vigorous dance of fierce ecstasy on the elephant demon's head.

gaja-thara Frieze of elephants found in temples.

gajendra-mokṣa An aspect of Viṣṇu image illustrating his *Kari-varada* form in which the Lord delivers Gajendra, the king of elephants, from the clutches of an aquatic monster.

gambhīrā Festival of Śiva held in the month of Caitra (March–April). Men and women, particularly the followers of the Nātha cult, which has Buddhist and Śaiva elements, celebrate the festival by accepting a temporary monastic vow and singing legends about him. It is known as *gambhīrā* in the Malda district of North Bengal and *gājana* (q.v.) elsewhere. Fairs held on such occasions draw large gathering in important centres of Śiva worship, and the marriage of Śiva and Pārvatī is enacted.

gaṇa Same as *saṃgha* (q.v.), *vrāta, puga, samūha, śākhā, kula* and *gaccha*, the term basically denoted a collective body, a tribe or an assembly. In Jainism it came to mean a community of brethren and later regional seats or sub-groups like Balagara, Balatkara, Deśīya, Deva, Dramila, Eregittur, Kalor, Kavasuri, Kranur, Nandī, Pogariya, Punnagavṛkṣamūla, Sarasvatī, Sena, Śruta, Tavula, Valahari, etc. The patriarchs of the Jain Church were known as Gaṇadharas or tribal heads. In Buddha's days the term was specially applied to a body of religieux, wandering or dwelling in a town or village. In the course of time it came to be applied to an organised body of religieux upholding a definite philosophical view, observing a particular form of discipline, wearing a special type of dress and bearing or carrying a significant symbol. From the stereotype description of the religious leaders of the time of Mahāvīra and Buddha it appear that the term Saṅgha or Gaṇa meant a religious body subscribing to particular principles and rules of discipline. cf. *Vimānavatthu-aṭṭhakathā* 233. The term Gaṇa is found in connection with the Bodhisattvas in the Mahāyāna texts. cf. *Saddharmapuṇḍarīka* (A.S.) 193, 259. In the *Milindapañha* 101, Gaṇa is used in the sense of a close body of secular or religious men. See Saṃgha.

gaṇācāra One of the *pañcācāras* or five Vīra Śaiva codes of conduct. It represents the spirit of vindication. The Vira-Śaivas should not tolerate adverse remarks against the Godhead and ill-treatment of men and animals by others. As a member of the community one has to strive for its upliftment and welfare. This attitude is known as *gaṇācāra*.

gaṇa-homa Offering sacrifice to fire by a group of

persons accompanied by verses such as *agne naya supathā*, etc.

gaṇapati-pūjana Worship of Ganapati; a preliminary act in all rites. It consists in inviting the presence of the elephant faced god Gaṇeśa on a betelnut placed in a handful of husked rice.

gāṇapatya-liṅga A class of Śiva-liṅga (q.v.) mentioned in the *Kāmikāgama* without any specification.

gandharva A class of mythical beings, semi-divine in character, who played a secondary part in religious literature and art. They are believed to be the denizens of the air or atmospheric region.

gāndharva A form of marriage. The union of a girl and her lover by their mutual consent is known as *gāndharva*.

gandharva-tattva The lore of singing named after the semi-divine Gandharvas mentioned in the epico-puranic tradition as residing in the heavenly abode beyond Mount Kailāsa.

gandhāṣṭaka Eight fragrant substances—*candana, agaru, karpura, cora, kumkuma, goracanā, jaṭāmāmsī* and *kāpi*—combined together and used as a substitute for wine. Wine is of three kinds—connected with Śakti, Śiva and Viṣṇu respectively. *Śāradātilaka* IV.79–80.

gaṇeśa-caturthī Vrata or ritual dedicated to Gaṇeśa on the fourth lunar day in the month of *māgha* (Jan–Feb). The day is also known as Śivā and the ritual as *varada caturthī*. It is basically a fertility rite.

gaṇeśvara An epithet of Śiva and also a name of Viṣṇu.

gaṅgādhara That aspect of Śiva in which he holds Gaṅgā, or the river Ganges, on his head.

gantha-dhura Path of knowledge, self-control and meditational practices prescribed for adepts with sharp faculties. It is connected with *apratisaṃkhyā-nirodha* (q.v.).

garbhādhāna The rite for causing pregnancy which requires sexual intercourse on an appointed day with *mantras* and purificatory observances; here procreation is conceived of in terms of a Yajña or sacrifice. *AV.* V.25, *Br.Up.* VI.4.13,19–22. It is identified with the rite of *niṣeka* in *Manu* II.16, 26, *Yāj.*I.10–11, *Vīṣnu Dh.S.* II.3, XXVII.1 and with *caturthīkarma* (q.v.) or *caturthīhoma* in *Sān.Gr.* I.18–19, *Pār.Gr.*I.11 and *Āp.Gr.* VIII. 10–11. According to *Vaik.*III.10, the *garbhādhāna* rite follows *niṣeka* or *ṛtu-saṅagamana* (union of married pair after menstruation) and consists in ensuring conception. See. *Baudh.Gr.* IV.6.1, *Kāṭhaka. Gr.* XXX.8, *Gaut.* VIII.14, *Yāj.*I.11.

garbhagṛha Sanctum sanctorum of a temple.

garbharakṣaṇa A rite performed to ensure that the foetus does not fall out or is not destroyed. It is performed in the fourth month of pregnancy and consists in offering six oblations of cooked food, besmearing the limbs of the wife with clarified butter, putting the juice of *durvā* grass into her nostril and so on. *Śāṅ.Gr.* I.21.1–3, *Āśv.Gr.* I.13.5–7. Same as Anavalobhana.

gārhapatya One of the three kinds of fire required in sacrifice. Also known as *prajāhita* (*Jaimini* XII.1.13) it means the domestic fire which is to be permanently maintained. *Āp.Sr.* VI.2.13. The mound on which it is kept is circular. It is set up by attrition. From the *gārhapatya* fire, other fire (*āhavanīya* and *dakṣiṇā*, qq.v.) are kindled for sacrificial purposes.

gārhasthya The householder's life; the second stage in the *āśrama* or order of life, in which the individual has to discharge numerous duties towards his fore-fathers and gods through a series of elaborate rituals as prescribed in the sacred texts.

garuḍa The mythical bird supposed to be the destroyer of serpents and regarded as the vehicle of Viṣṇu. Garuḍa emblem is found in religious art. Iconically Garuḍa is represented as a huge bird with human body, two wings and a sharp beak, generally with hands clasped against the chest.

gāthā-nārāśaṃsī Songs in praise of valiant persons. They gradually developed into lengthy ballads and various song-cycles with intricate plots. The *Mahābhārata* and the *Rāmāyaṇa* represent the finished products of this antecedent process.

gatipañcaka Five classes of beings among whom the five *skandhas* (q.v.) are distributed according to Buddhism.

gauḍa-sampradāya A sect of Vāmācārī Tantrics belonging to eastern India. This sect depends solely on the rituals of the Five Ms. and believes categorically in the unity of Devatā, Guru and Mantra as manifestation of the energy of the great goddess. *Puraścaryārṇava* IX.866, *Śakti-saṅgama*, Sundarī, III.15–18.

gauḍīya-sampradāya The Bengal school of Vaiṣṇavism founded by Caitanya on the basis of *acintya-bhedābheda* (q.v.) philosophy. According to this school *brahman* creates the universe with the help of his *māyā-śakti* (q.v.) which has two aspects *guṇa-māyā* and *jīva-māyā*, the former consisting of the three *guṇas* (q.v.) which are transformed at the time of creation into the constituents of the material world. The latter, *jiva-māyā*, with the power transmitted which is insentient or material, as opposed to *cit* or the sentient, effects the mundane creation by making individuals forget their own selves and their relation with *brahman*. Thus the universe is the *pariṇāma* (transformation) of *brahman* transfused with the *māyā-śakti* but still remaining untouched by *māyā*. *Brahman* is identified with Kṛṣṇa who has a form resembling that of a human being but who is really infinite and all-pervading.

gauṇi-bhakti A form of devotion marked by meditation, worship, muttering of names of the deity and so on.

gauracandrikā Preface to Kīrtana or devotional songs. This is the narration of certain events of the life of Caitanya (whose other name was Gaurāṅga) which is intended to serve as an introduction to the particular *līlā* (sport) of Kṛṣṇa to be sung.

gaurīpaṭṭa The pedestal on which a Śiva-liṅga is erected. It looks like the female organ which it symbolises. It is also known as *yoni* (female organ).

gautamaka A religious sect mentioned in *Aṅguttara Nikāya* III.276–77.

gavām-ayana The model for all *sattras* (q.v.) of a duration of one year or more (*sāmvatsarika*). This sacrifice is performed for various rewards, such as progeny, prosperity, plenty, high position, heaven, etc. In it the procedure for *dvādasāha* as a *sattra* is followed. *Āp.Sr.* XXI. 15.2–3, *Jaimini* VIII.1.17. There are no separate priests but the Yajamānas (q.v.) themselves are priests. *Śat.Br.* XVI.1. 21. *Jaimini* X.6.45–59. Different parts of this sacrifice are described in *Tāṇḍya* XXIV.20.1, *Āśv.Sr.* XI.1.2–6, XI.7.2–12, *Śat.Br.* XVI.5.18–40, *Āp.Sr.* XXI.15ff.

gāyadān The festival held in Bihar, Orissa and other places on *balipratipadā* (q.v.)

gāyatrī The sacred verse (*RV* III.62.10; quoted in other Vedas also) addressed to Savitṛ (the sun) and is interpreted as a prayer to the source and inspirer of everything. Literally it is. we contemplate that esteemed refulgence of the divine Savitṛ who may inspire our intellects'. It is meant only for the *dvijātis*, though according to some it is restricted only to the brāhmaṇas. It must be recited several times in *saṃdhyā* every day. The *Pañcaparameṣṭhi-mantra* is often described as the Jain *gāyatrī* which is dedicated to the 'five brilliant ones' of the creed. The *gāyatrī* of the Tantrics is in the names of their own deities, e.g. *Kālikāyāi vidmahe śmaśānavāsinyai dhīmahi, tanno ghore pracodayāt.*

ghaṇṭā Bell. When the bell is surmounted by a *vajra* it is called vajraghaṇṭā and becomes a symbol of Vajrasattva.

ghaṭa A pot full of water which used, either by itself or in addition to other forms, to represent the deity or the formless all-prevading spirit. The word *ghaṭa* or vessel is also used to designate the human body, and the space within it (*ghaṭākāśa*) designates the soul. It is held that as there is no difference between the space inside the *ghaṭa* and that outside it, so also there is no difference between the individual and universal soul. Also known as *kumbha* or *pūrṇakumbha*.

ghaṭa-pallava Design of pot-and-foliage.

ghātin-karma one of two major groups into which the eight kinds of *karma* (q.v.) from the Jain viewpoint have been divided. It includes *jñānāvaraṇīya* (that which hides all aspects of knowledge), *darśanāvaranīya* that which prevents beholding the faith), *mohanīya* that which generates worldly attachments and passions) and *vedanīya* (that which causes the experience of the pleasure of happiness and the pains of misery) types of *karma*.

ghoṣa-śānti Propitiatory ceremonies with loud (*ghoṣa*) recitation of Vedic *mantras*.

giripradakṣiṇa Going round a sacred hill by devotees while singing devotional songs. It is a common practice among the South Indian Śaivas and Vaiṣṇavas.

godāna A sacrament which consists in shaving the head and also the hair on the other parts of the body; also called *keśānta*. It is observed during initiation and at other turning points of life. *Śat.Br.* III.1.2.4, *Śān.Gr.* I.28.20, *Baudh.Dh.S.*I.2.7, *Manu* II.65, *Yāj* I.36, etc.

gokula The abode of Kṛṣṇa. In Vaiṣṇavite Tantras this place has been equated with the *sahasrāra* (q.v.) region. *Brahmasaṃhitā* 2–4.

gokulika A branch of the Mahasanghikas (q.v.) mentioned in the *Kathāvatthu*. Vasumitra describes them as Kukkuṭika. They believe that *kleśas* (corruptions) and *mārgas* (paths) exist side by side, so also *karma* and *vipāka* (fruit).

gomatī-vidyā Laudation of cows so that abundant benefits may be obtained from them.

gomukaprasava-śānti A rite of child welfare. On a new winnowing basket a red piece of cloth is spread. The new-born child is placed thereon and brought near a cow's mouth in a make-belief mime that the infant is born from the cow's mouth. The child is then bathed with cow's milk to the accompaniment of verses from *RV* X.181.1, *AV*.V.25.5 and *Br.Up*. VI.4.21.

gomutra-kṛcchra A kind of penance for the expiation of sins. It enjoins that the individual should make a cow to eat satiety grains of wheat mixed with barley and then collect the whole grains found in its dung. These are required to be eaten by the individual along with the cow's urine.

gopī Female partners in Kṛṣṇa's sport. The relation between Kṛṣṇa and the *gopīs* is conceived of in Vaiṣṇava tradition as the very ideal of a relation of unrestricted love between a lover and his beloved, which is contracted only for love and subsists on it alone. In the *gopīs*, the divine love is developed in its fullest degree to the state technically known as *mahābhāva* or supreme love. The *gopīs* are believed to be the wives of other persons but their eternal relationship is with Kṛṣṇa.

gopicandana Clay used to mark the forehead after a bath.

gopura Main gateway; the structure over the entrance of a temple.

gorakṣa-panthā The system propagated by Gorakṣanātha, one of the Ādi-Siddhas of the Nātha cult. It is a strictly celibate and rigidly austere Yogic system. Gorakh-panth in Hindi-Rajasthani.

gosahasra One of the sixteen *mahādānas* (q.v.) or great gifts. *Matsya Pu*. CCLXXVIII, *Liṅga Pu*. II.38. It is a gift of one bull and ten cows selected out of a thousand. They should be covered with clothes, have their horns gold-tipped and the hooves tipped with silver.

gosava A one-day soma sacrifice consisted of strange practices. The *Taitt.Br*. II.7.6 briefly describes it. One who desires *svārājya* (sovereignty) may perform it. The *Āp.Sr*. XXII.12.12–20, XXII. 13.1–3 says that for a year thereafter the sacrificer should follow *pasuvrata* (act like cattle).

goṣṭhāṣṭamī A festival held in the month of Kārtika (Oct-Nov) at which cows are worshipped and fed sumptuously.

goṣṭhī-śrāddha Rite for the spiritual welfare of the departed ones performed collectively by a number of persons when it is difficult for them to perform it individually owing to the scarcity of materials.

gotrabhū The stage prior to *sotāpanna* (q.v.) according to the Theravāda Buddhist tradition. It refers to a class of persons who are on the way to *arhat*-hood (q.v.) and may be in possession of one of the eight fruits of sanctification (*maggaphala*). *Paṭisambhidāmagga* I.66–68.

gotrabhūmi A Mahāsaṅghika (q.v.) conception in regard to the status of Srota-āpannaka (q.v.). It is a preparatory stage leading to the comprehension of the four truths. This stage marks the crossing of the state of a common man (*pṛthagjana*, *puthujjana*). The concept is elaborated in Mahāyāna *gotrabhūmiraṣṭamaka*.

gotravihāra Mahāyanic concept of a stage of spiritual progress which corresponds to the *gotrabhu* (q.v.) of Hīnayāna.

govardhana-pūjā The feeding, decorating and worship of cows during *balipratipadā* (q.v.). The assembled persons are also fed generously with cooked rice (*annakūṭa*).

go-vrata A form of penance for the expiation of sin. The sinner is required to spend a month among cows and imitate their behaviour in regard to standing, sitting, sleeping, eating, etc.

grāma-devatā Village deities.

grahamukha A rite for propitiating the planets. It is performed before Upanayana (q.v.) and in Vāstu-śānti (q.v.) and also on other occasions.

grahaṇālambana The attitude of devotion similar to the feeling of a baby below two years who knows none but its mother.

grahaśānti A rite for propitiating the planets in order to have prosperity, end of calamities, good rains, long life etc. Metallic images of the nine planets should be made or images may be painted in circles on the ground with colours. Offerings are made in the fire in their names. Rice mixed with jaggery, rice cooked in milk, rice with curds or clarified butter, etc., are given to the Brāhmaṇas as food. *Yāj*. I.295–308.

graha-devatā The planets worshipped as deities, being conceived in anthropomorphic form.

granthi The three 'Gordian knots' which bind the soul to the *prākṛta* or natural order, according to the Tantric tradition.

gṛha-devatā Household deities, especially worshipped for averting calamities.

gṛhapraveśanīya-homa A sacrifice which is required in marriage on entering the bridegroom's house. *Śān.Gr*. I. 16.1–2, *Gobhila Gr*. II.3. 8–12, *Āp.Gr*. VI. 6–10.

grahītrālambanā Attitude of devotion marked by non-difference from the deity, just as a baby in the womb is inseparable from its mother.

grāhyālambanā Attitude of devotion marked by the feeling of a baby between three and five years of age who demands everything of its mother.

gṛhāvadhūta A Tantric *sādhaka* who is a householder. He who is with clothes and with wife, who is a thinker, an aspirant and a pure entity, who is devoted to his teacher, wise, internally and externally faithful, accustomed to Yogic practices, free from passions and is pure in soul is known as *gṛhāvadhūta*. *Prāṇatoṣaṇī* VII.7, 532.

gṛhya Domestic fire which is to be maintained for manifold purposes. Besides the three Śrauta fires (Āhavanīya, Dakṣiṇā and Gārhapatya), there are two more fires, *gṛhya* (or *aupāsanīya*) and *laukika* (or *pacana*) fires. If the *gṛhya* fire goes out, either the husband or the wife has to observe a fast that day as a penance. *Āp.Gr.* V.19.

Guhyaka A class of semi-divine beings associated with the Yakṣas (q.v.).

guhya-liṅga Secret Liṅgas (q.v.) of Śiva known as Hariścandra, Āmrātakeśvara, Jaleśvara, Śrīparvateśvara, Mahālaya, Kṛmicaṇḍeśvara, Kedāra and Mahābhairava.

guhya-sādhanā Observance of secret rituals, meant for aspirants at the *vīra* stage. The symbolic features are to be understood from the teacher. These rituals are performed in secret *cakra* assembly. Uninitiated persons are not entitled to participate. *Niruttaratantra* X.

guhyasamāja Secret societies in the Buddhist Saṅgha, the members of which believed in Tantrism. They composed their own scriptures and had them sanctioned by the words of Buddha. A Buddhist Tantric text also bears this name as its title.

gumanapanthī One of the five Digambara subsects of the Jains.

guṇa A common term in Indian religio-philosophical tradition which is generally understood to mean some unchanging essential characters of a substance, although the word is variously interpreted. In the sense of qualities (existence, enjoyability, substantiveness, knowability, specific characters and the capability of possessing forms, etc.) the Guṇas adhere to specific substances and cannot exist by themselves. In all changes some collection of qualities appears to remain unchanged (*dhrūva*), some new qualities are generated (*utpāda*) and some old qualities are destroyed (*vyaya*). In the Nyāya-Vaiśeṣika Guṇas are conceived as inherent in the substance and dependent upon it. At the same time they are also conceived as distinct from substance, because they can by themselves be known and are thus independent realities. In the Sāṅkhya, Prakṛti (q.v.) has been characterised by the equilibrium of three Guṇas—*sattva*, *rajas* and *tamas*. These Gunas are not qualities in our sense of the word, but constituents of primordial matter. In Jain texts both the words Guṇa and Paryāya (q.v.) are used sometimes in identical and sometimes in different meanings. According to the Nyāya-Vaiśeṣikas, there are 24 kinds of qualities *rūpa* (colour), *rasa* (taste), *gandha* (smell), *sparśa* (touch), *śabda* (sound), *śaṅkhyā* (number), *pariṇāma* (magnitude), *pṛthakatva* (distinctness), *saṃyoga* (conjunction), *vibhāga* (disjunction), *paratva* (remoteness), *aparatva* (nearness), *buddhi* (cognition), *sukha* (pleasure), *duḥkha* (pain), *icchā* (desire), *dveṣa* (aversion), *prayatna* (effort), *gurutva* (heaviness), *dravatā* (fluidity), *sneha* (viscidity), *saṃskāra* (tendency), *dharma* (merit), and *adharma* (demerit), *Vaiś.Sūt.* I.1.16.

guṇadharma Certain duties, such as the protection of subjects in the case of a crowned king.

guṇa-karma Quality and action; the nature of the work one performs; the basis of the *varṇa* system according to the *Bhagavadgītā*. The term also denotes subsidiary actions in the Mīmāṃsa tradition.

guṇa-māyā One of the two aspects of *māyā* (q.v.). the other being *jīva-māyā* (q.v.). The *guṇa-māyā*, with the help of the power transmitted by the *brahman*, transforms itself into the constituents of infinite varieties of the things in the universe and thus becomes the constituent cause of the world. *Paramātma-sandharva* 73.

guṇasthāna Fourteen steps to liberation from *karma* (q.v.) according to the Jain conception. These steps are: *mithyātva* (when the Jīva is completely under the influence of *karma*); *svāśvāsadana* (when a Jiva begins to distinguish a little between what is real and what is false); *miśra* (when he is still uncertain); *aviratisamyagdṛṣṭi* (when he feels the urge to control his instincts); *deśavirati* (when he realises the great importance of conduct); *pramatta* (when slight passions are controlled but negligences remain); *apramatta* (when anger is controlled); *apurvakaraṇa* (when pride is controlled); *aniyatibādra* (when deceit disappears); *sukṣmasamparyāya* (when annihilation of greed begins); *upaśāntamoha* and *kṣīṇamoha* (when all *kaṣāyas* (q.v.) are removed), *sayogikevalī* and *ayogikevalī* (when all *karma* is purged away).

guṇatraya The three constituents of Prakṛti (q.v.)—*sattva* (q.v.), *rajas* (q.v.) and *tamas* (q.v.)—held in a state of equilibrium (*sāmyāvasthā*). Guṇa (q.v.) here means a constituent element of component, and not an attribute or quality. This Sāṅkhya concept of Guṇa is basically different from that of the Jain or Nyāya-Vaiśeṣika. The Guṇas are in a state of both conflict and co-operation with one another and are subject to change and transformation. See also Sāmyāvasthā.

guṇa-vāda One of the three kinds of *arthavāda* (q.v.) which denotes a conflict between the subject of a text and ordinary experience.

guṇavrata Additional vows for Jain laymen. See also Mahāvrata, Anuvrata, Kaṣāya and Cāritra.

guptatarayogini Collective name of the goddesses serving as *āvaraṇa-devatā* (q.v.) of the mystic diagram known as *aṣṭadalapadma*. *Gandharvatantra* V.96.

gupti Term for keeping the *mantra* to be uttered in secret. *Tantrasāra* 54.

guru Teacher. Though the words *ācārya* (q.v.), *upādhyāya* (q.v.) and *guru* (q.v.) are often used as synonyms, ancient writers made a distinction between them. According to *Manu* II.141–42 and *Yaj* I.34–35, Guru is one who performs the *saṃskāras* (q.v.) and imparts the Veda. The word *guru* is often used in the sense of any elderly person, male or female, who is entitled to respect. The father, mother and the *ācārya* are often regarded as the three highest *gurus*. *Manu* II.227–37, *Viṣṇu Dh.s* XXXII. 1–2. Guru is the pivot of Tantric *sādhanā*, the one who dispells darkness. The characteristics of guru, woman-guru and false-guru are recorded in *kulārṇava* XIII, XVI, *Rudrayāmala*, uttara II. *Prāṇatoṣaṇī* II.2, VI.4, *Tantrasāra*, 2, *Gandharvatantra* II, *Tantrarāja* I, *Śāradātilaka* II. Methods for securing a *guru*, the testing of his competence, his divinity and the duties of the disciples towards him are described in *Mahānirvāṇa* XV. 139, Rāghava on *Śāradātilaka* II.143–44, *Kulārṇava* XI.XIV, *Prāṇatoṣaṇī* II.2, III.1. Complete self surrender to the *guru* is necessary. If he commands the performance of any low work it should be done. Rāmeśvara on *Paraśurāmakalpasūtra* X. *Saktānandataraṅgiṇī* II. His mere command leads to liberation. *Kaulāvalīnirṇaya* X. Hymns for worshipping *guru*. *Gandharvatantra* VI.19–25. Gifts are to be offered to him. *Śāradātilaka* II. The best form of *guru* is Kaula *guru*. *Mahānirvāna* X.200–201.

guru-catuṣṭaya Four classes of teachers—*guru, paramaguru, parāparā-guru* and *parameṣṭhi-guru*—conceived of as identical with Śiva. *Nirvāṇatantra* III.

guru-dakṣiṇā Proper fees given to the preceptor by students.

gurudhyāna Meditation on the *guru* who is to be conceived of as a god of white complexion with two hands held in *varada* and *abhaya* postures and with Śakti on his left side. *Tantrasāra* 78.

guru-pātra Pot of wine required in Tantric rites. *Kaulāvalinirṇaya* III.

gurutva Gravity; it is a characteristic of matter. *Vaiśeṣika Sūtra* V.1.18, *Padārthadharmasaṃgraha* 133, *Kiraṇāvalī* 37.

gurvāyatana A class of shrines erected by various sectarian clericals.

hādimata, hādividyā A Tantric school which was influential in Kerala and Kashmir. The followers of this school held that their *vidyā* (knowledge, *mantra* and deity) came from a source which was known as Kāmarājavīja. *Ha* is the symbol of Śiva after which the school was designated. Hakārat Śivarūpatvaṃ tad-hādimatamirtīam, *Śakti-saṅgama*, Tārā, LVIII.81.

haimavata A branch of the Sthaviravādins (q.v.). According to Vasumitra, the Haimavata school was so named owing to its association with the Himalayan region. This school, like the Sarvāstivādins (q.v.) denied any special eminence to the *bodhisattvas* (q.v.) who were considered by them to be no more than common men (*pṛthag-janas*), but unlike the Sarvāstivādins, they would not admit that the heretics can get supernatural powers or that gods can lead the holy life (brahmacarya).

hākinī The presiding goddess (Śakti) of the Tantric *ājñā-cakra* (q.v.). She is six faced and white in complexion according to the *Ṣaṭcakranirūpaṇa*.

haṃsa A symbolic *mantra* in the form of inhaling (*haṃ*) and exhaling (*saḥ*) of breath. Haṃ is the symbol of Vindu (Puruṣa, the male principle of creation) and Saḥ of Visarga (Prakṛti, the female principle of creation). Kālīcaraṇa on *Ṣaṭcakra-nirūpaṇa* XLIII.

haṃṣamantra Name of the *mantra* based on *haṃ* and *saḥ* symbolic for the awakening of *kuṇḍalinī* (q.v.).

haṃsanyāsa One of the several kinds of *nyāsas* (mentally invoking gods or *mantras* or holy texts to come and occupy certain parts of the body in order to make the body pure and a fit receptacle for worship and meditation) mentioned in Rāghava's com. on *Śāradātilaka* IV.19–41. Here *haṃ* is identified with the essence of Puruṣa (q.v.) and *saḥ* with that of Prakṛti (q.v.) and thus *haṃsa* is an invocation of both on the body of the aspirant.

haṃsapāda See Hārdhakalā.

haṃsapīṭha The region of *haṃsa* supposed to exist within the pericarp of the lotus of *sahasrāra* (the highest cerebral region). It is indicated by the *a-ka-tha* triangle and is marked by the letters *ha-la-kṣa*. In this region the aspirant should meditate on the *guru* as the form of Śiva. Kālīcaraṇa on *Pādukāpañcaka* I.

hāra A string of miniature shrines comprising *kūtas, śālas* and *pañjaras* (qq.v.) decorating each story of the south Indian *vimāna* (q.v.).

haragaurisṛṣṭi Chemical processing of mercury and mica to make the elixir of immortality.

hārdhakalā The sex organ drawn on mystic diagrams. It is also known as *haṃsapāda* or *yoni*. Hārdhakalā is also the name of the wave of bliss arising out of the union of Śiva-Śakti.

haridrā One of the six aspects of Gaṇapati. Turmeric. This plant forms part of *navapatrikā* or nine plant symbols of the goddess Durgā.

haritilaka-vrata A *vrata* or ritual performed by women of the Maharashtra region. It is observed either on the third or on the fourth day of *bhādra* (Sept-Oct) in the bright half of the month.

harmya Attic storey. The attic portion of a south Indian *vimāna* (q.v.)..

haṭhayoga A form of physical exercise for making the body so disciplined as to serve all spiritual purposes. In the *Yogaśikhopaniṣat* I. 133 it is described as the unity of the sun (*ha*) and the moon (*ṭha*). In the *Haṭhayogapradīpikā* I.10 it is regarded as the source of all forms of Yoga.

haviryajña A sacrifice in which there is burnt offering but no Soma. There are seven such sacrifices: Agnyādheya, Agnihotra, Darśapūraṇamāsa, Āgrayana, Cāturmāsyas, Nirudhapaśubandha and Sautrāmaṇī.

havis An oblation of clarified butter or milk or *soma* or grain offered in *yajña* or rituals.

haviṣkṛt Literally it means 'one who separates the grains from the husks'. According to *Taitt.Br.* II.2.4. it indicates the formula for calling a person. In the case of a brāhmaṇa it is *ehi* (come hither), for a kṣatriya *āgahi* (approach), for a vaiśya *ādrava* (hasten hither) and for a śūdra *ādhāva* (run hither). cf. *Śat.Br.*I.1.4.12, *Āp.Sr.* I.19.9–10. According to some Haviṣkṛt is Parjanya. The com. on *Āp.Sr.* says that the term means the person who prepares the *havis* and also the formula used to call him. Jaimini III.2.59 holds that in certain Vedic passages Haviṣkṛt indicates an injunction to summon thrice the wife or any other person who separates grains.

haviṣya Oblations made in the morning and evening of cooked food but only such corn as is fit to be offered to the fire as *havis* should be used. *Āśv.Gr.* I.2.1. Boiled rice or barley is preferred most. *Āp.Gr.* VII.19, *Gobhila Smṛti* I. 131, III.114. According to a verse quoted by Nārāyaṇa on *Āśv.Gr.* I. 9.6 ten materials can be offered as *havis* into fire: milk, curd, *yavagu*, clarified butter, boiled rice, husked rice, *soma*, flesh, sesame oil and water. Manu III.257 specifies some articles as naturally fit for being employed as *havis*. cf. *Āp.Dh.S.* II.6.15, 12–14. Though flesh is allowed as offering in some sacrifices, it cannot be employed in the morning and evening *homa* (q.v.). *Āśv.Gr.* I.9.6.

hemahastiratha A *mahādana* or great gift. It should be a golden chariot resembling a toy-cart in its entirety and contain small images of certain deities. *Matsya* CCLXXXII.

hema-śrāddha Śrāddha (q.v.) with gold, i.e., money. When a person is unable, for certain reasons, to perform even *amāśrāddha* (q.v.), it is performed by offering the price of the materials required.

heramba A form of Gaṇapati.

hetu Also known as *liṅga* (q.v.) and *sādhana* (q.v.). It is the middle term, the 'reason' of connecting the *sādhya* (q.v.) and the *pakṣa* (q.v.) in the Indian system of logic.

hetuvādin Vetulyakas or Vaipulyakas, a Buddhist sect, also known as Mahāśūnyatāvādins. The Sarvāstivādins (q.v.) were also known by the name Hetuvādins. They were credited with the view that insight is not meant for the man of the world, and that happiness may be passed on to others.

hetvābhāsa Fallacies of inference which are one of the sixteen philosophical topics of the Nyāya. These are *savyabhicāra* (the irregular middle), *viruddha* (contradictory middle), *satpratipakṣa* (inferentially contradicted middle), *asiddha* (unproved middle) and *bādhita* (non-inferentially contradicted middle).

hiṃsā Violence. It is of four kinds according to the Jains; the householder is enjoined to abstain from *saṃkalpī-hiṃsā* or intentional violence, but not from accidental (*gṛhārambhī*), occupational (*udyamī*) and protective (*virodhī*) violence. However, one who has renounced the life of a householder must avoid all the four kinds of Hiṃsās. In the Vedic texts, though violence as a principle is condemned, the killing of animals is prescribed for sacrificial purposes.

hīnayāna One of the two major forms of Buddhism. To the early Buddhists the term Hīnayāna was unknown. It was a term coined by the Mahāyānists on the grounds that Mahāyāna is meant for those superior beings who achieve their own salvation without anybody's help and who help others to attain it by giving them the necessary aid and guidance while persons of average intellect, who are somehow capable of attaining perfection only by listening to and practising the *dharma* that was promulgated by Buddha are known as the followers of Hīnayāna or lower vehicle. Hināyāna is also known as Śrāvakayāna and Pratyekabuddhayāna. Asaṅga says that the Hīnayānists start practising the Buddhist codes of physical and mental discipline from the day of their initiation, and it is only after they have attained the state of an *arhat* (q.v.) that they go forth to explain the teachings which had benefited them. Asaṅga considers such a course to be selfish and justifies thereby the use of the prefix *hīna* or low for the Śrāvakayānists. Secondly, according to the Mahāyanists, the Hīnayānists concern themselves only about the removal of the *kleśāvaraṇas* (the cover of impurities) and not with the *jñeyāvaraṇas* (the cover of false knowledge). See Mahāyāna. The Hīnayānists differ from Mahāyāna on points relating to the deification of Buddha (they consider him as a mortal being), on the concept of *bodhisattva*-hood as opposed to *arhat*-hood, and on the question of *śūnyatā* (q.v.).

hiraṇyagarbha The cosmic principle, it is supposed to be the Golden Germ, produced from primeval waters or chaos and eventually identified with *brahman*. *RV* X. 121. *Sat.Br.* XI.1.6.1. The Ṛgvedic conception of this Golden Germ afterwards developed into that of the World Egg of *brahman*. The various processes of growth and change constantly visible in nature might have suggested the notion of the world having gradually arisen out of nothing (*asat*, q.v.) or out of a pre-existing undeveloped substance. Such an idea of the spontaneous evolution (of an entity like the Golden Germ) from a primeval principle or out of the primordial substance, which subsequently came to be known as *prakṛti*, (q.v.) formed the substratum of the Sāṅkhya philosophy.

hiraṇyagarbha A great gift (mahādāna) connected with the primitive concept of death and resurrection. The donor should bring golden vessel, shaped like a *muraja* (tabor), enter it and sit holding his head between the knees as if to simulate the position of the foetus in the mother's womb which is symbolised by the vessel. The priest then repeats on the golden vessel the *mantras* of *garbhādhāna* (q.v.), *puṃsavana* (q.v.) and *sīmantonnayana* (q.v.), i.e. rites relating to conception. He then makes the donor emerge from the vessel and performs the twelve *saṃskāras* (q.v.). The donor thus gets a new body and is considered to be reborn. This *rite de passage* marking the transition from one stage of life to another, was used for different purposes. There are instances of certain kings belonging to lower castes who performed this rite and thus disowned their former bodies, posed to have a new existence, and claimed to be Kṣatriyas.

hiraṇyāśva A *mahādāna* or great gift in which small golden horse is donated to the *guru. Matsya* CCLXXX.

hiraṇyaśvāratha A *mahādāna* or great gift in which miniature golden chariot with seven or four horses along with chowries, umbrella, silken garments and cows according to one's means is donated. *Matsya* CCLXXXI.

hlādinī The blissful Śakti of the Supreme Being. In later Vaiṣṇavism as well as in the Vaiṣṇavite Tantras it is symbolised by Rādhā. *Caitanyacaritāmṛta* I.1.5.

holi, holikā Also known as Hutāśanī and Phālgunika. A festival on the full moon in *phālguna* (March). It is celebrated with gaiety and fun throughout India though all parts do not observe it in the same way. The word may be derived from *homa* (q.v.). A bonfire is kindled everywhere as a part of *holi* festival. In some places the ashes from the bonfire are sprinkled on the fields to aid cultivation. The origin of this festival may be traced to primitive agricultural and fertility rites and also to ancient beliefs about death and resurrection. In Bengal it is *dolayātrā* (q.v.) where swinging of Kṛṣṇa image is done. Ribald songs and music, sprinkling of coloured water or powder characterise its essential aspects; obscene sex references may also be observed in this festival.

homa Offering made to fire in the name of different deities. It is necessary in numerous ceremonies and rites. To perform *homa* a raised square platform known as *sthaṇḍila*, is built. In the middle of this a line is drawn from north to south, and five straight lines from east to west are drawn from the middle one. The area covered by these six lines is where the fire should be made. To the north of the platform are kept *havis*, *idhma* (fuel) and *barhis* (*kuśa). The brahmā* (q.v.) sits on the south facing the north and sacrificer sits on the west facing the east, that is to the priest's left. Offerings are thrown into the fire with *mantras*. If there is no specific directive as to the deities to whom the offerings are to be made, the deities should be Agni, Indra, Prajāpati and Viśva-devas. At the end there is an offering to Agni Sviṣṭakṛt. *Āśv.Gr.*I.3, *Śāṅ.Gr* I.7. Elaborate rules about *homa*, the competence of the performer, time place and other related aspects are given in the Dharmaśāstras. In the Tantric tradition, there are several kinds of *homa*: *sthūla* (gross), *sukṣma* (subtle), *parā* (transcendental), *bāhya* (external), *antara* (internal), *nigraha* (for the purpose of black acts), *saumya* (for the purpose of beneficial acts) and so on. *Mātṛkābheda* XI.8, *Puraścaryārṇava* VI.515, *Tantrarāja* XXIX-XXXII, *Tantrasāra* IV, *Śāradātilaka* XVII-XVIII, *Tārābhaktisudhārṇava* 247ff.

hotṛ One of the four major kinds of priests required to perform a sacrifice. He is the 'invoker' who must praise the gods and invoke them to the sacrifice and whose duty it is to select the canon for each particular rite of the Soma sacrifice (q.v.) by selecting the verses applicable to it from the hymns of the *Ṛgveda* and to recite them.

hotrī-dikṣā A form of Tantric initiation in which the *guru* (q.v.) offers *homa* for purifying the six quarters. Rāghava on *Śaradātilaka* V. 127–40.

hṛdaya Heart. Also another name of God, for its derivative meaning is *hṛdi-ayam* (He is in the heart). *Chāndogya* VIII.3.3.

icchā Desire; in particular of the Supreme Being, which is also regarded as one of its aspects, the others are *ānanda* (bliss), *cit* (consciousness), *jñāna* (knowledge) and *kriyā*; and is also regarded as *śakti* or energy.

icchā-śakti Power of will, conceived as the inherent energy (*śakti*) of the Supreme Being.

iḍā One of the fourteen principal nerves. It is a symbol of the moon and is situated on the left side of the spinal cord, on the right is situated *piṅgalā*—the symbol of sun. *Saṭcakranirūpaṇa* I. It is conceived of as white in colour and represents *amṛta*, the life-giving power aspect of Śakti.

idam The known; the enjoyed; the object; the 'itness' and so on. The opposite concept is *aham*, the knower or the enjoyer.

idantā Objecthood, as opposed to *ahantā* or subjecthood. *Pratyabhijñā-hṛdaya* 10.

iḍāpātra Sacrificial pot made of *aśvattha* wood which has a bowl of four *aṅgulas* wide and is as long as the foot of the sacrificer. The word *iḍā* is the appellation of a *devatā*. It also applies to sacrificial materials and to a rite. Com. on *Śat.Br.* II.3, *Āp.Sr.* III.1.1ff, *Baudh.Sr.*I.18.

idappaccayatā The 'this-conditioned' nature of an object. It is a fallacious approach based on non-comprehension according to early Buddhism. *Majjhima* I. 191, *Dhammasaṅgaṇi* 162.

iddhi The attainment of miraculous power; in Sanskrit *ṛddhi*. Ten *iddhis* are mentioned in Buddhist texts like the *Brahmajāla-sutta* I.26, *Mahāvagga* VI.24, *Cullavagga* V.8. etc.

iddhipāda Four ways mentioned by Buddha as conducive to the attainment of supernatural powers. These are *chando* (will), *viriyam* (effort), *cittam* (thought) and *vīmaṃsa* (investigation).

indradhvaja Votive column erected in the honour of Indra.

indrayajña A rite observed on the day of the full moon in *bhādrapada* (Aug-Sept) in which *pāyasa* (rice cooked in milk) and cakes are offered to Indra, Aja Ekapāda, Ahirbudhnya and others. *Pār.Gr.* II.15.

indra-yātrā A four day festival in honour of Indra held in Nepal before and after the full moon in *bhādra* (Aug-Sept).

indrayoni A nerve plexus situated between the *viśuddha* and *ājñā* (qq.v.) *cakras*.

indriya Sense organs. According to the Nyāya-Vaiśeṣikas and the Mīmāṃsakas *manas* or mind is also an *indriya*. The five external ones are of sound, sight, touch, taste and smell. In Buddhism the word also means dominant factors or forces which are connected with *śraddhā* (faculty of faith), *vīrya* (faculty of energy), *smṛti* (faculty of memory), *samādhi* (faculty of concentration) and *prajñā* (faculty of intellect).

indriya-nigraha Control of the ill-functioning of the sense organs. In a restricted sense the term applies to absolute control of the sexual instinct.

iriyāpatha A vision of the supramundane (*lokottara*) Buddha either standing, walking, sitting or supine according to *Mahāvastu* I.167–68.

īśāna An aspect of Śiva. It is also the name of a *dikpāla*.

īśānabali An offering of the flesh of an ox to Śiva, a rite which had to be performed in autumn (*śārad*) or spring (*vasanta*) on the day of the full moon or under the constellation of *ādrā*. Also known as Śūlagava. *Āśv.Gr.* IV.9.2, *Baudh Gr.* II.7.1-3, *Kāṭhaka* Gr. LII.2-3, *Bhār-Gr.* II.8, *Hir.Gr.*II.8.

iśitva-siddhi The spiritual attainment from the rituals of Caturdasāra (q.v.) *Nityaṣodaśikārṇava* VIII.149.

iṣṭadevatā The personal god; the chosen deity of a person through whose adoration and worship he tries to attain the highest goal of life.

iṣṭa-liṅga The distinctive mark of Vīra-Śaivism which advocates the wearing of a *liṅga* (phallic symbol) upon the body of each person, so that the body shall be a temple fit for god to dwell in. Iṣṭaliṅga is also conceived of as one of the three aspects of the Divine, the others being Prāṇa and Bhava.

iṣṭa-mantra The secret *mantra* (q.v.) imparted to the aspirant by the *guru* (q.v.).

iṣṭāpūrta Cumulative spiritual result of, or merit due to a man's performance of sacrifices and charitable acts. *RV* X.14.8, *AV* II.12.4, III.29. 1, *Taitt.Saṃ.* V.7.7.1-3, *Taitt.Br.* II.5.5, III.9.14 *Vāj.Saṃ.* XV. 54, *Kaṭha Up.* I.1.8, *Muṇḍaka. Up* I.2.10, *Manu* IV. 226-27.

iṣṭi A sacrifice performed by a sacrificer and his wife with the help of four priests: *adhvaryu, āgnīdhra, hotṛ and brahmā*. The *darśapūrnamāsa* (q.v.) sacrifice is the pattern or archetype (prakṛti) of all other *iṣṭis*.

iṣṭiśrāddha Ninth among the twelve classes of *śrāddhas* (q.v.). It is also known as Karmāṅga-śrāddha.

iṣu-yāga A magic rite referred to in *PMS* VII.1.13–16 in whch the details are the same as in *śyena-yāga* (q.v.).

Īśvara First Principle according to certain cosmogonical speculations as recorded in *Śvetāśvatara Upaniṣad* I.1–2. It is the most popular concept of a Supreme Being creating, maintaining and destroying the world and the only principle of the comprehension and attainment of grace (*prasāda*) through *bhakti* or devotion according to all theistic systems of India.

In the early Vedic literature there are numerous gods representing different aspects of natural phenomena—some transparent, some transluscent, some opaque, according to the degree of anthropomorphism—but the idea of an all-powerful and all-pervading supreme being is absent although there are some attempts to establish the oneness of God as the reality behind all appearance. In the Brāhmaṇa literature, and subsequently in the Pūrva-mīmāṃsā tradition, Yajña (q.v.) or sacrifice is the chief principle and gods are subordinate even to men. In fact the idea of an almighty God is in fact ridiculed.

With the development of the Upaniṣadic concept of *brahman*, the infrastructure of the concept of an absolute, all pervading, omniscient and omnipotent god was established. However, the relation between the infinite, pure conscious, eternal and changeless *brahman* (q.v.) and the finite, material, impermanent and imperfect world was not settled. In the Advaita Vedānta of Śaṅkara, which claims to interpret the Upaniṣadic concept of *brahman* in its real perspective, the inexplicity of the relation between *brahman* and the world is sometimes expressed by the term *māyā* (q.v.). This māyā is not independent of *brahman*; the latter being associated with the former becomes Saguṇa-brahman or Īśvara. *Māyā* is thus the energy of the creator which becomes transformed into Upādhi (q.v.) or limitation, the unmanifested matter from which all existence issues. *Śārīrakabhāṣya* I.4.3, II.1.4, II.2.2. Since the world cannot be due to *brahman* (because the latter is not subject to change), nor could it be traced to *prakṛti* or *māyā* (which is unintelligent), it became necessary to posit the former alongside the latter. As a result, the *saguṇa* or changing *brahman* was conceived, who as Īśvara, combined within himself the natures of both the unattached *brahman* and the unconscious *prakṛti* or *māyā*. But this Īśvara also cannot be real, like the world, because of his finite existence.

The theistic interpreters of Vedānta, the celebrated Vaiṣṇava Ācāryas, the exponents of different schools of Śaivism and Śāktism were not at all troubled regarding the question of how the world of imperfection can transpire from *brahman*, the absolute perfection, since they were willing to accept on the authority of the Śruti that *brahman* or Īśvara, equated with the supreme being of their respective creeds, was itself the material and efficient cause of the world. The Nyāya-Vaiśeṣika school tried to justify the concept of Īśvara on the following grounds. All things of the world such as mountains and seas, the sun and the moon, are effects because they are made up of parts. Therefore, they must have a maker (*kartā*). The individual selves or souls cannot be the maker or creator of the world, because they are limited in power and knowledge. The creator of the world must be an intelligent spirit with unlimited power and wisdom without whose guidance the material factors of the composite substances, namely the atoms, cannot have just that order and coordination which enable them to produce the composite objects, the definite effects. And this intelligent agent or cause can be no other than God. Just as a potter, as an efficient cause, makes a pot out of the unintelligent cause, namely clay, so also God as a macrocosmic potter (*brahmāṇḍa-kaulāla*) fashions the world by handling the unintelligent material cause, the atoms. The atoms cannot move or act by themselves. The ultimate source of their actions is to be found in the will of God who directs their operations according to the law of *karma* (q.v.). The atoms are made to compose a world that befits the unseen moral deserts (*adṛṣta*, q.v.) of individual souls and serve the purpose of moral dispensation. *Nyāyabhāṣya* II.2, IV.1, IV.2, *Kusumāñjali* I.19, II.1, III.1–23.

The Nyāya-Vaiśeṣika concept of God has been refuted by the Mīmāṃsakas, Sāṅkhyas, Buddhists and the Jains on the following grounds. If the world is created by God, like the potter making a pot out of clay, then God must be an agent under bondage and not a free agent. He has to work with a given material, namely the atoms, and with a given body, like the potter, both of which are not created by him. When atoms are said to perform the work of creation guided by the will of God, it is illogical because the atoms are devoid of intelligence and it is impossible on their part to follow, or even to understand, the will of God. *Ślokavārtika*, Jha's tr. 355–68.

The Mīmāṃsakas and the Jains hold that since no interference of any divine being is found in the production of men and animals, which owe their existence to the parents, it cannot therefore be said that the atoms act under the will of God. The universe as a whole has neither beginning nor end. God cannot create out of pity, since there was no being to whom compassion could be shown. If creation is said to be for the amusement of God, then it contradicts the theory that he is perfect. If the will of God is responsible for the world, then there is no room for the doctrine of *karma* (q.v.).

The Buddhist Vaibhāṣikas (q.v.) and Sautrāntikas (q.v.) hold that if God was the sole cause, the world would have been created in its totality at one and at the same time. But it is seen that creatures come into existence not simultaneously but successively, some from wombs, some from buds and so on. The other two Buddhist schools have totally nihilistic approach (see Mādhyamika and Yogācara). According to the Sāṅkhya, the existence of God cannot be proved by perception or inference or testimony, the valid sources of knowledge. God is said to be an eternal and immutable self, but what is unchanging can not be the cause of anything. *Sāṅ.Kārikā* 67–68, *Sāṅ.Prav. Bhāṣya* III.76–84, V. 116, *Sāṅ.Sūt.* I.92–95, III.56–57.V.2–12.

Yoga system follows the Sāṅkhya scheme of the evolution of Prakṛti, but places Īśvara or God on the top of this scheme and gives the following arguments in favour of God's existence. Firstly, the testimony of the scriptures speaks of the existence of God. Secondly, the law of continuity as applied to degrees of knowledge and power points to the existence of God. And thirdly, the association and dissociation of *puruṣa* (q.v.) and *prakṛti* (q.v.) can be possible only by the intervention of God. *Yogasūtra*, *bhāṣya* and *vṛtti*, I.23–29, II.1ff, III.45.

Thus it appears that the concept of an all-powerful, all-pervading and all-merciful God, to be approached by reverence and devotion, could not have been very popular among the elitists and intellectuals belonging to most of the Brahmanical philosophical schools and also to Buddhism and Jainism. The sole insistence of Brahmanism, Buddhism and Jainism on the doctrine of *karma*, transmigration and rebirth, the process on which God can have no control theoretically, did not really contribute to the development of absolute theism. The concept of an all-powerful supreme being, and its relation with the individual at a personal level, arose mainly from the masses: the God who would bestow grace and forgive human weaknesses and limitations, a God to be propitiated only through love and devotion. This popular sentiment underlay the theistic interpretation of Vedānta which formed the basis of the *bhakit*, or devotion-oriented, schools of Vaiṣṇavism, Śaivism, Śāktism and other religious systems.

īśvarakāraṇavādin The theists, according to the Buddhist texts, who held that everything in the universe originated from Īśvara or the Supreme Being, the first cause.

īśvarapraṇidhāna A stage of spiritual development mentioned in the *Yogasūtra* I.23–29 which has been explained in *Vyāsabhāṣya* in two ways—special devotion and the offering up of all actions to God or, in other words, the renunciation of the fruits of all action. Īśvarapraṇidhāna does not lead to union with Īśvara, but it enables the bonded soul to become what Īśvara always is.

itarajana An appellation of the Yakṣas.

itara-liṅga One of the three forms of *linga* or phallus. The symbol of Śiva, the others are *bāṇa* and *svayambhū*. In Tantrism it is connected with *ājñā-cakra* (q.v.). *Śāradātilaka* IV.

itihāsa-saṃvāda Poetry of the great epics, composed by the great ascetic sages, which teaches universal morality, love of all human beings and renunciation of the world, It comes under the category of *nīti*, or the science of human norms, values and behaviour.

itikartavyatā The procedure for sacrifices. *PMS* III.3.11.

jaḍa Matter; the non-conscious which is by itself inert, devoid of sentiency and is mutable. See Avidyā, Māyā, Prakṛti.

jaḍaśakti The material cause of creation.

jāḍya-kumbha The lowest moulding of the *piṭha* (socle) of a medieval temple.

jagadambā Mother of the world; an epithet for the Female Principle of creation conceived as the Supreme Being in the Śākta scheme of cosmic evolution. Also called Jaganmātā; the concept is well developed in the Durgāstutis of the Purāṇas.

jagamohinī A medieval religious community of Bengal which insisted on love and devotion to a personal god, mystic experience and based its social relations on liberal principles.

jāgara The vow of remaining sleepless throughout the night.

jāgrata The waking state.

jalādhāra Sacred aquatic animals often considered as *vyantara-devatās* (q.v.).

jala-kṛcchra See Toyakṛcchra.

jālandharavadha-mūrti A form of Śiva image showing him killing the demon Jālandhara. It belongs to the category of the Saṃhāra-mūrtis of Śiva.

jalaśāyin An aspect of Viṣṇu which has iconic representations. It depicts the god recumbent on the folds of Ādi or Ananta Nāga, the hoods of the latter serving as a canopy over his head. Also known as Śeṣaśayana or Anantaśayana.

jalpa Wrangling or arguing by which the parties aim to achieve victory by proving their points. It is one of the philosophical topics of the Nyāya. Such wranglings are common in ordinary life in which invalid reasons and arguments predominate.

jalpi A maze of speculation. *RV* VIII.48.14.

janana Procreation. The term is also used in the sense of processing a *mantra*, its gradual recovery from the *mātṛkā-yantra*. Tantrasāra 54.

janārdana An aspect of Viṣṇu.

jaṅgama A Śaiva sect mentioned in Ānandagiri's *Śaṅkaravijaya*. It is also a synonym for *guru*.

jaṅghā The middle portion of a temple which is above the basement and below the *śikhara*.

janmāṣṭamī See Kṛṣṇajanmāṣṭamī.

japa To internalise and mutter the syllables relating to the identity of *guru* (q.v.), *mantra* (q.v.) and *devatā*—the personal, or sectarian god—by the worshipper. It is conceived as the easiest process of spiritual attainment. There are three kinds: *vyakta* (manifested), *avyakta* (unmanifested) and *sukṣma* (subtle), also called *vācika*, *upāṃsu* and *mānasa* respectively. The first is loud utterance heard by everyone, the second is whispered and to be heard only by the practitioner himself, and the third is mental and is heard by none. There are other three categories of *japa: nitya* (to be done everyday), *naimittika* (to be done occasionally) and *kāmya* (to be done for some special purpose). *Puraścaryārṇava* VI.541, *Yogasūtra* I.28, *Kulārṇava* XV, XVII, *Rudrayāmala*, Uttara XXVI, *Śaktisaṅgama*, Tārā XLVI.2–3, *Gandharvatantra* XXIX.9, Rāghava on *Śāradātilaka* IV.55–56. The Smṛtis prescribe *japa* as part of *saṃdhyā* adoration. *Yāj.*I.99, *Manu* II.85, etc. *Japa* is supposed to remove sin. It should be performed while seated on *Kuśa* grass either in the house or on a river bank or some other selected place. The repetition of the *mantra* should be counted on one's fingers, or by drawing lines, or by telling the beads of a rosary. cf. *Raghuvaṃśa* XI.66, *Kādambarī* 37, *Japa* is regarded as the best way of prayer for Śūdras and women.

japamālā A necklace made of *rudrākṣa* and other articles to count the number of recitations used in *japa* (q.v.)

japasamarpaṇa The last feature of *japa* (q.v.) ritual. After the *japa* is complete its result is to be surrendered to the deity. *Śyāmārahasya* III.

japayoga Mental concentration with the help of *japa* (q.v.).

jarā A demoness conceived of as the protectress of children. A painting of her likeness on the wall is supposed to ensure the welfare of the children of the household. Her Buddhist parallel is Hārītī and the Jain Ambikā.

jaṭā One of the various modes of repeating the Veda. The term is also used to denote matted hair.

jātakarma A ritual performed after the birth of a child. Early references to this rite are found in *Taitt.Saṃ* II.2.5.3–4, *Br. Up.* VI.4.24–28, *Jaimini* VI.3.38, etc. According to certain Gṛhyasūtras it should be performed before the umbilical cord is cut. *Pāraskara* I.16, *Gobhila* II.7.17, *Khādira* II.2.32. It consists of a *homa* (q.v.), uttering a *mantra* in the child's right ear, giving the child a lick of some curds or honey, addressing the child with a secret name, putting the child to the mother's breast and addressing the mother with *mantras*. *Āśv.Gr.* I.15.1–4, *Śān.Gr* I.24.1–12.

jaṭāmukuta The crown of matted hair. The hair is tied up above the head in such a way as to resemble a crown or a tiara.

jātasutaka The born child. Since *mantra* (q.v.) is a living entity it is conceived of as a new-born child during initiation. *Śaktisaṅgama*, Tārā, XLV.7.

jāti An unfair reply based on false analogy; for example 'sound must be eternal because it is incorporeal like the sky'. It is one of the sixteen philosophical topics of the Nyāya. In Buddhism the term means birth for worldly existence. The term is also equated with *varṇa* or caste. *Manu* III.15, VIII.177, IX.86. The expression jātidharma (rules of castes) occurs in *Gautama* XXI.20, *Vasiṣṭha* I.17, XIX.7, *Manu* I.118, VIII.41 and the word *jāti* meaning caste occurs also in *Āp.Dh.S.* II.3. 6.1, II.1.2.3 and in the *vārtika* on Pāṇini IV.1.137. *Varṇa* and *jāti* are sometimes clearly distinguished as in *Yāj* II.69, II.206.

jātibhraṃśakara A class of sins effecting loss of caste. Such sins are incurred by committing minor offences. Expiation is possible by the performance of *sāntapana* and *prājāpatya*.

jaṭilaka A religious sect mentioned in *Aṅguttara* III.276.

jātyapakarṣa A fall in caste status which is caused due to a disadvantageous marriage or by following a lower ranking occupation. *Yāj.*I.96.

jātyutkarṣa A rise in caste status which is caused by an advantageous marriage or by following a higher ranking occupation through successive generations.

javana The power of extending the inner faculties of the individual which is caused by the intensive mental exercise according to early Buddhism. *Atthasālini* 270.

jaya A class of *mantras* (q.v.), 13 in all, which consists of verses from the *Taitt.Saṃ.* III.4.4.1.

jayantī The eight lunar day of the dark half of the moon in Śrāvaṇa (July-August) when the Rohiṇī star enters the zodiac.

jetavanīya A Buddhist sect of Ceylon. The Jetavanīyas were a sub-sect of the Dhammarucikas. They occupied the Jetavana-vihāra built by king Mahāsena in the compound of the Mahāvihāra. They adopted some of the Mahāyānic views.

jhāna Dhyāna or meditation. According to Buddhism four *jhāna* stages are to be gone through on the four levels of consciousness or the four planes of experience called *avacaras*. These are *kāma*, *rūpa*, *arūpa* or *lokattara*.

jhulana-yātrā A Vaiṣṇava festival held in the month of Śrāvaṇa (Aug-Sept) in remembrance of Kṛṣṇa's sport with the Gopīs.

jihmaga A class of sacred reptiles which is supposed to belong to the category of Vyāntara-devatās (q.v.).

jijñāsā The intensive exercise of mind, an investigation, according to the *Vārttika* on Pāṇini III.1.6. In the Brāhmaṇas it implies a discussion about some ritual practice and in the Upanisads it is used in reference to a spiritual concept. In Indian philosophical terminology *jijñāsā* is the process of finding both *pramāṇa* (source of knowledge) and *prameya* (the object of knowledge).

jina The conqueror of worldly bondage according to the Jain concept. The Siddha-parameṣthin (see Parameṣṭhī) endowed with the qualities of infinite perception, knowledge, bliss and power, may attan this *jina*-hood and serve as the ideal for all pêrsons who desire to escape the cycle of birth and death characteristic of worldly existence.

jina-pāda Foot-marks of the Jinas engraved on stones.

jīva The individual. The earliest mention of jiva is found in *RV* I.164.30. The term is also used to denote 'self' or 'individual soul' and as such is synonymous with *jīvātman*. According to the Cārvākas it is the living body with the attribute of consciousness. The Buddhists reduce it to a stream of thought or a series of cognitions. The Nyāya-Vaiśeṣikas hold it as a unique substance, to which all congnitions, feelings and conations belong as attributes. According to the Mīmāṃsakas it is a substance which has the capability of consciousness. The illusory character of the Jīva is denied by the theistic commentators of the *Brahmasūtra*. In the different religious systems we find two kinds of Jīvas: those who are eternally free and those who are under the bondage of *māyā*. This bondage is due to a person's assumptions about the *guṇas* (attributes) of *māyā* (q.v.), and in practice liberation consists in its removal.

jīva Living entities among the Astikāya (q.v.) objects in Jain belief. It is of two kinds; *mukta* (emancipated like the Tīrthaṃkaras) and *baddha* (fettered like ordinary persons). The latter is further divided into two kinds, Trasa (q.v.) or moving and Sthāvara or non-moving, e.g. those living in the bodies of earth, etc. Although there is a tendency among scholars to explain Jīva in terms of Ātman (q.v.) and Puruṣa (q.v.) of other schools of Indian thought, the concept really stands for 'what lives or is animate'. Thus the term in the original sense stands for the vital principle rather than for the soul. Later, however, the question of consciousness was emphasised and the Jīvas were theoretically arranged in a continuous series according to their degree of consciousness. It has been conceived of as existing permanently, acting and being acted upon, as an experient (*bhoktā*) and agent (*kartā*). The intrinsic nature of Jīva is thus conceived of as being perfect. It has also been thought that Jīva is capable of expansion and contraction according to the dimensions of the physical body and that it acquires the size of the body wherein it lives just as a lamp which while remaining the same illumines all the space in a room regardless of whether the room is small or big. *TTDS*, II,8,22–23, Guṇaratna on *SDSC*, 47–49, NVT, 31, *SVDM*, 8. See Trasa.

jivanmukti Liberation within the span of life. It is possible, according to the Sāṅkhya, by the complete destruction of the three-fold misery (*duḥkhatrayābhighāta*)—*ādhyātmika* (q.v.), *ādhibhautika* (q.v.) and *ādhidaivika* (q.v.). In Tantric tradition, he who has complete grasp of the knowledge of the Self, has dispelled from within the darkness of false knowledge by constant practice and meditation and is reaping the fruits of his *karma* may be called a *jīvanmukta*. The term is also used in the sense of immortality (see *amṛta*) which is possible by transforming the material body through certain chemical processes into a divine one. *Sarvadarśanasaṃgraha* IX.

jīvantasvāmin The standing image of Mahāvīra wearing crown and ornaments.

jīvaśakti Name of the Kuṇḍalinī (q.v.) which works as the energising force within the human body. *Tantrarājatantra* XXX.34. In other theistic systems, all the Jīvas or living beings, human or otherwise, are in essence the *jīva-śakti* or marginal power of God. It is also known as *taṭastha-śakti*.

jīvaśrāddha Śrāddha, or rituals for the spiritual welfare of the departed, when performed by a man for himself while alive for the benefit of his soul after death. Details of the procedure are given in the *Baudhāyana Gṛhyaśeṣasūtra* III.19 and *Liṅga Purāṇa* II.45.8–90.

jīvātman Individual soul. See under Jīva.

jīvatattva Jīva or individual fettered by *niyati* (destiny), *kāla* (time), *rāga* (dissatisfaction), *kalā* (conceit) and *avidyā* (ignorance). Also known as Puruṣatattva. Rāmeśvara on *Paraśurāmakalpasūtra* I.4.

jīvitendriya The organ of vitality sustaining the Rupakkhanda or the world of elements, as water is to the lotus according to early Buddhism.

jñāna Knowledge or congnition. It is divided into *anubhava* or presentive and *smṛti* or representative. According to the Nyāya-system, each of the two may be valid (*yathārtha*) or non-valid (*ayathārtha*). From the religious point of view it is that which eliminates suffering which arises from *avidyā* or false notions. It is basically of two kinds—*bauddha* (intellectual) and *pauruṣa* (intuitive). By meritorious practices the latter is developed within the human being and is conducive to *mokṣa* or liberation. It should, however, be supplemented by some sort of intellectual attainment; this is possible through the study of the scriptures, deep meditation and so on. *Tantrāloka* I.41ff.

jñānabhūmika Seven stages of knowledge, often identified with the seven Tantric *ācāras*.

jñānacatuṣka The four means of Tantric knowledge: *anupāya* (q.v.), *sāmbhavopāya* (q.v.), *śaktopāya* (q.v.) and *ānavopāya* (q.v.).

jñāna-dakṣiṇāmūrti A form of Śiva image; it shows the god as the expounder of Śāstras.

jñāna-homa The *homa* (q.v.) offered during internal worship or *antarpūjā* (q.v.). *Nityatantra* quoted in *Prāṇatoṣaṇī* VIII.4.535.

jñāna-kāṇḍa That portion of the Vedic texts which deals with the supreme knowledge.

jñāna-lakṣaṇa A form of perception; it takes place through and extraordinary contact of two cognitions.

jñānamārga 'Way of knowledge'. It leads one to enlightenment or the realisation of the Absolute.

jñānamiśra-bhakti An auspicious combination of devotion and knowledge.

jñāna-pañcamī The fifth day of the bright half of the moon in Kārtika (Oct-Nov) which is a sacred day for the Jains. On this day all books are dusted and preserved from insects by sprinkling them with sandal-wood powder.

jñāna-pāramitā The faculty of knowledge which a potential Bodhisattva develops at the *bhūmi* or stage known as *dharmamegha* (q.v.) or *paramavihāra*. This attainment establishes in him the *samādhi* of omniscience (*sarvajñānaviśeṣābhiṣeka*).

jñāna-śakti The 'Power of knowledge' which according to the Vīra-Śaivas is associated with *guru-liṅga* symbolising the preceptive modification of the supreme being.

jñāna-saṃnyāsin The being who has renounced

the world and whose mind is always rooted in the knowledge of *ātman* (q.v.). *Padmapurāṇa* I.59.3–10.

jñāna-svarūpa An epithet for *ātman* (q.v.) which is in itself the substratum and substance of pure knowledge. This substantive knowledge has a distinguishable adjunct which inheres in it as an inseparable concomitance just as does the glow in a flame.

jñāna-tanu The spiritual body; according to the Siddha tradition, it is the transfiguration of the material body for those who aspire to *jīvanmukti* (q.v.) or liberation within the span of life.

jñānayoga The form of Yoga which yields knowledge of the *tattvas* or basic principles. It consists of three stages: *śravaṇa* (study of the texts under a competent guide), *manana* (reflection on what the texts teach), and *nididhyāsana* (continued meditation on their purport).

jñānendriya Organs of knowledge. There are five external organs and one internal. The former correspond to the five external senses and are the organs of smell (*ghrāṇa*), taste (*rasanā*), sight (*cakṣu*), touch (*tvak*) and hearing (*śrotra*). They are physical in nature and each of them is constituted by that very same physical element whose qualities are sensed by it. Mind (*manas*) is the internal organ which perceives such qualities of the soul as desire (*icchā*), aversion (*dveṣa*), striving (*prayatna*), pleasure (*sukha*), pain (*duḥkha*) and cognition.

jñānopāya The means through which *nirvikalpa* (complete) knowledge is reached from *vikalpa* (lesser degree) knowledge. It is also known as *śaktopāya*.

jñeyāvaraṇa The cover of ignorance that hides the truth, according to Buddhism. The Mahāyanists hold that by removing this cover one realises both *pudgalaśūnyatā* (absence of individuality) and *dharmaśūnyatā* (non-existence of all worldly objects).

juhū Ladle to be employed in all offerings.

jyeṣṭasāmāni A class of *sāmans* (hymns) to be chanted in different sacrifices.

jyeṣṭhasāmika A *vrata* (vow) which is a prerequisite for the higher study of the Vedas. The student who undertakes this has to observe certain rules throughout his life. For example, he cannot marry or have sexual intercourse with a Śūdra woman, cannot eat bird's flesh, cannot restrict himself to one kind of corn or one country, and should always wear two garments.

jyotirdhyāna Meditation of the self supposed to reside on the Kuṇḍalinī coil in the *mūlādhāra* (q.v.) in the form of light. It is also known as *tejodhyāna*. *Gheraṇḍa* VI.17.

jyotirliṅga Twelve *liṅga* or phallus of Śiva which are located at Somanātha, Saurāṣṭra; Mallikārjuna on Śriśaila hill (Karnul district); Mahākāla in Ujjayinī; Parameśvara in Oṃkāra-kṣetra (an island on the Narmadā); Kedāra in the Himalayas, Bhīmaśaṅkara in Dākinī (north-west of Pune); Visveśvara in Varanasī; Tryambakeśvara on Godāvarī near Nasik; Vaidyanātha in Citābhūmi; Nāgeśa in Dārukavana, Rāmeśvara in Setubandha and Ghṛṣneśa in Śivālaya (Daulatabad). *Śivapurāṇa* XIV-XXXIII.

jyotiṣka A class of gods in the Jain pantheon belonging to the stellar group.

jyotiṣṭoma Soma sacrifice (q.v.) which occupies generally five days. The chief rites performed on each of these days are: (i) choosing of priests and performance of *madhuparka*, *dīkṣānīyeṣṭi* and *dīkṣā* (qq.v.); (ii) *prāyaṇīyāiṣṭi* i.e. opening *iṣṭi*, purchase of Soma, *ātitheyeṣṭi* (*iṣṭi* offering hospitality to Soma), *pravargya* (q.v.), *upasad* (q.v.) or homage twice a day on the second day, (iii) *pravargya* and *upasad* on the third day, (iv) *pravargya*, *upasad*, *agnipraṇayana*, *agnisomapraṇayana*, *havirdhāna-praṇayana* and animal sacrifice on the fourth day; and (v) pressing of Soma, offering it and drinking it, *udayanīya* (concluding *iṣṭi*) and *avabhṛtha* (final purificatory bath) on the fifth day.

kabandha A class of superhuman beings conceived as belonging to the group of *vyantara-devatās*. Their iconographical representations portray them as chimera-like creatures of the imagination. In the art of Amarāvati and Gandhāra, the Kabandhas are shown as having one head on their belly (*Kabandhā udare mukhāḥ*). For the legends about them see *Rāmāyaṇa* III.69.27ff.

kādimata One of the three principal Tantric schools mentioned in the *Śaktisaṅgama*, Tārā, LVIII.81–82. Its theoretical doctrines make the letter *ka* as their symbol. This school is also known as Vīrādanuttara and Kālīmata. It was popular in the Gauḍa region. *Ibid.* Kālī V.24–26.

kādividyā Special knowledge in Tantrism which derives its name from the first letter of the Vāgbhava-vīja (*ka, e, i, la, hrāṅ*). Com. on *Śāradātilaka* I.1.

kahādimata One of the three principal Tantric schools mentioned in the *Śaktisaṅgama-tantra*, Tārā, LVIII.81–882. It is also known as Tāriṇīmata. *Ibid.* Kali, VI.125.

kaivalya Splendid 'isolation' or 'aloofness', the final state of a released soul, complete freedom from material contact. *Yogasūtra* III.50, III.55, IV.26, IV.34, *Sān.Kārikā* 17ff. In Vedānta the term *kaivalya* denotes final emancipation which is immediate oneness with *brahman*. The Buddhists and the Jains also use the term in the sense of liberation. The word Kaivalya does not occur in the early Vedas or older Upanisads. The word Kevala (q.v.) occurs in the *Śvetāśvatara* IV.18, VI.11.

kākinī The presiding goddess of the *anāhata-cakra* (q.v.). She is three-eyed, yellow in colour, and has her abode within the pericarp of a twelve petalled red lotus. *Ṣaṭcakranirūpaṇa* XXIV.

kāla Time conceived of as the First Principle in the *AV* XIX.54, *Śvet.Up.* I.2, VI.6 and *Suśruta*, Śārīra I.11. Nīlakaṇṭha commenting in *Mbh.*XII. 232.21 says *Kāla iti dravyajñānam*. The question of time has some importance in the Buddhist theory of momentariness. It is also one of the nine substances of the Nyāya-Vaiśeṣikas and, eleven substances of the Mīmāṃsakas. It is described as an evolute of *aśuddha-māyā* in the Śaiva Āgamas. In Jain cosmology Kāla falls in the category of *anastikāya* (q.v.) (unextended substance). The successive movements of the world are strung on Kāla or time. *TTDS* V.22 says that it makes possible the continuity, modification, movement, newness and oldness of substances. Gunaratna on *SDSC* 49 says that it is an indivisible substance present everywhere at the same time. According to *DS* 21 empirical or conventional time (*vyavahārika-kāla* or *samaya*) may be divided, but real time or *paramārthika-kāla* is eternal. Like space, time is also inferred, though not perceived. By inference, it may be said that modification or change of states cannot be conceived without time. According to Rāmeśvara's com. on *Paraśurāmakalpasūtra* I.4 it is said that the eternalism of Śiva, owing to the influence of six *bhavavikāras* or conditions, becomes contracted and is known as Kāla. When the goddess Kālī is described as *kālagatā-śakti* it is in the sense of time. cf. *Mahānirvāṇa-tantra* IV.30–32.

kalā Evolutes of Varṇa (q.v.). In Tantra every letter or *varṇa* symbolically reflects an aspect of the Great Mother. From the three groups of letter—Saumya, Saura and Āgneya—thirty-eight Kalās are emanated: sixteen from Saumya, twelve from Saura and ten from Āgneya. This theory holds good also for the different branches of Śaivism. *Prapañcasāra* III.11–12. A Kalā is identical with the *varṇa* from which it evolves. Rāghava on *Śāradātilaka* III.111. According to another tradition there are fifty Kalās which emanate from the five parts of *praṇava*—A, Va, Ma, Vindu and Nāda. *Ibid.* II.17. In the Tantras and other Śaiva-Śākta texts the term Kalā has also been used in other senses. It denotes Prakṛti, Śakti and Māyā. *Ibid.* I.6, I.15; *Prapañcasāra* I.26. In the com. on *Haṭhayogapradīpikā* V.1 Kalā is described as *nādaikadeśaḥ*, i.e. a portion of *nāda*. The term is also used to denote 'parts' or 'portions' of greater gods and goddesses and the various arts.

kāla-cakra A minor nerve-cycle; it is situated above the *viśuddha* and below the *ājñā*. It is also known as *lalanā-cakra*. Kālacakra denoting the wheel of time is the principal god of the Tantric Buddhist Kālacakrayāna (q.v.).

kālacakryāna An offshoot of Vajrayāna (q.v.) Buddhism based on the cult of Kāla Cakra (wheel of time) which came into vogue in the 10th century and became popular in Tibet and China. On the basis of the *Kālacakratantra*, *Sekoddeśaṭikā* and *Vimalaprabhā* it may be said that by *kāla* is denoted the ultimate immutable and unchanging reality of all the elements; by *cakra* is meant the unity of the three kinds of existence. As such Kālacakra is the same as the unity of *prajñā* (q.v.)

and *upāya* (q.v.). In principle there is therefore no difference between Vajrayāna and Kālacakrayāna.

kālāgni The Nātha concept of the Sun as the principle of destruction through the process of decay and death.

kālāmukha An extremist Śaiva sect, akin to the Kāpālikas (q.v.) mentioned by Rāmānuja, Keśava Kāśmīri, Haribhadra and others. Epigraphical evidence establishes the existence of this sect at Kanchi, Tiruvariyur, Melpadi, Kodumbalur and other places.

kalāmūrti Complete or fragmentary forms of the figure of the *śakti* of the deity. In Tantra, the *śakti* of any deity is divided in sixteen Kalās. When the figure is complete in sixteen Kalās it is known as *pūrṇa-kalā-mūrti* and the parts are known as *kalā-mūrti*. Futher subdivisions are known as *aṃśa-mūrti* and *aṃśāṃśa-mūrti*.

kalānyāsa Feeling the existence of the deity in different parts of the body of the Śakti or female partner of the Tantric aspirant. *Tantrasāra* 628.

kālāri-mūrti A form of the *saṃhāra-mūrtis* (a fierce image showing the chastiser of the offender) of Śiva which depicts the theme of Śiva's saving his devotee and punishing Kāla or Yama.

kalasa, kamaṇḍalu, kuṇḍikā Water vessel of metal or earth. Kalasa is different from Kamaṇḍalu or Kuṇḍikā, which is smaller in size and is provided with a projecting pipe for discharging water. Kalasa or jar is used on auspicious occasions like marriage, coronation, etc.

kalā-tattva The contracted manifestation of Śiva in individuals. *Tantrāloka* IX.155.

kalāvati-dīkṣā A form of initiation in which the *ācārya* (q.v.) locates the existence of five *kalās* known as *nivṛtti*, *pratiṣthā*, *vidyā*, *śānti* and *śāntyātīta* in different parts of the body of his disciple, and having meditated on them, anoints him. *Śāradātilaka* V.121–26.

kali The last of the traditional division of ages in which certain aspects of the social and religious life of the earlier ages are forbidden. See Yuga.

kālī-kula A Tantric school which lays supreme importance on the cult of Kālī. The scriptures of this school are *Kālajñāna*, *Kālottara*, *Mahākālasaṃhitā*, *Vyomakeśasaṃhitā*, *Jayadrathayāmala*, *Uttaratantra* and *Śaktisaṅgamatantra*.

kālī-mata See Kadī-mata.

kāli-naya Another name for the Karma (q.v.) doctrine.

kalivarjya Acts which are forbidden in the *Kali* age.

kalkin A future *avatāra* or incarnation of Viṣṇu.

kalpa A very vast period of time, containing numerous *manvantaras* (q.v.) and *yugas* (q.v.) at the end of which the universe dissolves. The Vedic texts have no elaborate theory of *kalpa*. The term is mentioned in an inscription of Aśoka. The *Vāyupurāṇa* names thirty-three *kalpas*. In the Vedic tradition *kalpa* reffers to ritual texts which is subdivided into Śrauta-Sūtras, Gṛhya-Sūtras and Dharma-Sūtras, dealing respectively with sacrificial rites, domestic rituals and social rules.

kalpapādapa Certain trees, the worship of which is said to attain any desire or wish. They are: *mandāra, parijātaka, santāna, kalpavṛkṣa* and *haricandana*.

kalpataru Wish-fulfilling tree; same as Kalpapādapa (q.v.). In the Tantras the term is used to denote the *anāhatacakra* (q.v.). Kalpataru gives more than is desired. *Ṣaṭcakranurūpaṇa* XXII.

kalpavṛkṣa A *mahādāna* or great gift ceremony mentioned in the Hathigumpha inscription of Khāravela. It consists of a small golden tree laden with fruits. The amount of gold used may be from three *palas* to a thousand according to one's means. It should be placed on a heap of jaggery along with the images of certain deities, especially that of Kāmadeva. Five branches of the other four trees (see under Kalpapādapa) made in gold are also to be planted. These are to be donated to the *guru* and the four priests along with other articles after performing some propitiatory rites. *Matsya*, CCLXXVII, *Liṅga* II.33.

kalyāṇasundara-mūrti A class of Śiva images illustrating the theme of his marriage with Umā. Also known as Vaivāhika.

kāma Desire. In *RV* X.129.4 it is said to have been the first movement that arose in the One. It is mentioned as a great cosmogonic force in *AV* IX.2. The conception of sexual dualism as a cosmogonic principle of the creative process in terms of procreative process has given much importance to the Kāma doctrine, and in this connection we frequently come across such terms as *jan, sṛj* (procreation), *garbha* (womb), *retas* (semen) etc. In subsequent Indian tradition Kāma came to be looked upon as one of the three principal ways of life (*trivarga*), the others being *dharma* and *artha*. In the *Kāmaṣūtra* of Vātsyāyana it is categorically stated that without *kāma* or desire (and the sexual urge in a narrow sense) *artha* or material prosperity is not possible, and without *artha* it is impossible to follow the way of *dharma*.

kāmacchanda The Buddhist concept of fetters caused by Kāma or passion.

kāmadahana-mūrti Also known as Kāmāntaka it is a form of the *saṃhāramūrtis* (q.v.) of Śiva illustrating the theme of his burning Kāma or Madana, the god of love.

kāmadhātu One of the three cosmic spheres in the Buddhist conception, the others being Rūpa and Arūpa. In the Kāmadhātu live all hellish beings, spirits, human beings, animals, birds, insects, etc. They possess all the five constituents, or *khandas* (q.v.) and depend for their origin on gross material food and sexual propensities both of which produce the desire (*kāma*) for worldly pleasures *AKV* III.6, *Atthasālinī* 62, *Mahāvyutpatti* 156.

kāmadhenu A *mahādāna* (great gift) ceremony in which the figures of a cow and a calf are made from pure gold and donated to the *guru* with other articles and propitiatory rites. *Matsya* CCLXXIX, *Linga* II.35.

kāmakalā The sexual art. In sophisticated Tantric belief Kāma is the equilibrium of the Prakāśa (static) and Vimarśa (dynamic) Śakti of Śiva. *Setubandha* com. on *Nityaṣoḍaśikārṇava* VI.10–11. Technically Kāmakalā is conceived of as the combination of the three Vindus (q.v.) of Ravi, Agni and Soma. Conceived as Mahātripurasundarī it is of the nature of consciousness (*cit*), bliss (*ānanda*), will (*icchā*), knowledge (*jñāna*) and action (*kriyā*). Cidvallī com. on *Kāmakalāvilāsa* VII. In the human body Kāmakalā is said to reside in the form of a triangle within the *candramaṇḍala* (lunar orb) of the pericarp of the inverted white lotus known as *sahasrārapadma* (q.v.) situated in the cerebral region. Kālīcaraṇa on *Ṣaṭcakranirūpaṇa* XI.

kāmākhyāyonī The soft and bright Tantric triangle on the *mūlādhāra* (q.v.) lotus. Viśvanātha on *Ṣaṭcakranirūpaṇa* VIII.

kāmarājakūṭa Totality of Tantric Kāmarāja-vīja (q.v.). Kūṭa means total and hence it is the complete recitation of the letters belonging to the said category.

kāmarāja-vīja Name given to the Tantric letters Ha, Sa, Ka, Hā, La, Hrāñ, each symbolising an aspect of Śakti or Vidyā. *Siddheśvarīmata* quoted in the com. on *Śāradātilaka* I.1.

kāmastuti Verses which are repeated in many ceremonies such as marriage, adoption, or when gifts made on the approach of death, and so on *AV*, III.29.7, *Taitt.Br.* II.2.5.9, *Taitt.Ār.* III.10, *Āśv.Sr.* V. 13.15.

kāmatattva Theoretical interpretation of sex symbolism. According to *Tantrāloka* III.150 the effect of sexual intercourse brings a mental detachment which is conducive to obtaining pure knowledge.

kāmāvacara A class of supramundane beings according to early Buddhist conception. This class is subdivided into two groups; (1) beings of Niraya, Tiracchānayoni, Petaloka, Asurabhavana and Manussaloka and (2) the gods of Cātummahārājika, Tāvatiṃsa, Nimmānarati and Paranimmitavasavatti.

kāmeśvara, kāmeśvarī The Being and the Power-to-Become, symbolised by the Male and Female Principles in the concrete form of the deities. The first represents the *prakāśa* or static aspect and the second *vimarśa* or dynamic aspect in Tantric cults.

kāmikā The seat used when reciting Kāmya-japa, the *mantra* meant to attain a certain purpose. It is either made of the skin of deer, tiger and ram or of cane. *Puraścaryārṇava* VI.420.

kamma See Karma. According to Buddhist belief, in the formula of causal sequence, the *saṃskāras* or mental dispositions, which arise owing to non-realisation of truth (*avidyā*) represent the accumulated karmic effects left in a being before its rebirth. The results of acts done in the previous life are transmitted to that consciousness which brings about re-existence (*pratisandhivijñāna*) and this transmission takes place ceaselessly and uninterruptedly (*sanātana*) like water flowing in a stream. Kammas are divided into three categories: those which yield fruit in this life (*diṭṭhadhammavedanīya*); in the next life (*uppajjavedanīya*); and in a future life (*aparāpariyavedanīya*). *Aṅguttara* I.134, 223, *Mahāvastu* III.63, *Suttanipāta* 653–54, etc.

kammaṭṭhāna The Buddhist concept of the projects of meditation which are forty in number. These are classified according to six types of mental attitudes: *rāga, doṣa, moha, vitarka, śraddhā* and *buddhi*. *Visuddhimagga* 114, *Abhidhammattha-saṅgaha* 41–42, *Udāna* IV.1.

kāmya Literally 'desirable', an act meant to achieve a specific end. It is one of the three categories of the nature of performance of any act or rite, others being *nitya* (permanent) and *naimittika* (occasional). Kāmya rites should be undertaken only when one is able to perform all the constituent parts. *Jaimini* VI.3.8–10.

kāmyapūjā Worship for the attainment of certain purpose. *Gandharvatantra* XXII.12.

kāmyeṣṭi Sacrifice for securing certain desires. It is a form of *iṣṭi* mentioned in *Āsv.Sr.* II.10–14, *Āp.Sr.* XIX.18–27, etc.

kañcuka Contracting and restricting factors. There are five: *niyati* (determining or binding factor), *kāla* (the 'tense' factor), *rāga* (desire or appetite factor), *kalā* (developing factor) and *avidyā* (veiling factor).

kanda The root of the *nāḍis* or nerves. According to the *Śivasaṃhitā* V.79–80 it is situated near the Yoni or the female sex organ. It looks like the egg of a bird. Kālīcaraṇa on *Ṣaṭcakranirūpaṇa* I.

kāṇḍānusamaya A method of preference used in performing rituals. It is described in the *PMS* V.2.7–9

kaṅkāla-mūrti A terrific type of Siva image. It depicts Siva carrying on the prongs of the trident the skeleton of Viṣvakasena, the gate-keeper of Viṣṇu who was killed by Śiva for refusing to admit him into the presence of Viṣṇu.

kaṅkaṇabandhana The part of marriage ritual in which the couple garland each other and tie a thread with a turmeric piece on each other's hand. Also known as Kaṭuka-bandhana.

kanphaṭ-yogī A sect of ascetics who believe in the theories and practices of Haṭhayoga and the Nāthasiddha tradition.

kanyādāna The gift of the bride. In this rite the father of the girl asks the bridegroom not to prove false to the bride in *dharma, artha* and *kāma* and he responds with the words 'I shall not do so' (*nāticarāmi*). This is done even now. *Pār.Gr.* I.4, *Mānava Gr.* I.8.6–9.

kapāla Either the severed head of a man, or a cup made of a skull or a bowl. The skull-up is of two kinds: when it is filled with blood it is called Asṛkkapāla and when with human flesh it is called Māṃsakapāla. The deities are supposed to partake of the blood or the flesh carried in these cups. Potsherds for baking sacrificial cakes are also known as Kapāla. It also denotes a type of Bhairava (q.v.).

kapālabhāti One of the *ṣaṭkarmas* or six acts required for Yogic exercise. The others are *dhauti, vasti, neti, laukiki* and *trāṭaka*. Kapālabhāti is of three kinds—*vāmakrama, vyutkrama* and *sitkrama*. These practices prevent various diseases. *Gheraṇḍa* I.13–60, *Haṭhayogapradīpikā* II.24–35.

kāpāli Ramya-Śakti; it is the personification of that aspect of Śakti which becomes sexually passionate on seeing the performance of her rites *Niruttaratantra* XV. In the *Uttaratantra* such aspects of Śakti are mentioned as Kulanāyikā. *Tantrasāra* 627.

kāpālika An extremist Śaiva sect committed to the Tantric cult of Śakti, mentioned in Mahendravarman's *Mattavilāsa*, Bhavabhūti's *Mālatimādhava*, Ānandagiri's *Śaṅkaravijaya* and other works. According to the *Śaṅkaravijaya*, they did not believe in the Vedas. They used to drink wine in human skulls which they considered as the elixir of life resulting from the union of Śiva and Śakti. The *Gorakṣasiddhāntasaṃgraha* 16ff connects Kāpālikism with Nāthism. Reference to a Kāpālika text known as *Kapāla-āgama* is found in *Sūtasaṃhitā* I.1.12. The Śākta conception of Kāpālika is recorded in the *Śaktisaṅgama-tantra*, Kālī, VIII.9–10.

kāraṇa Cause and causal relation in Indian philosophical tradition. When the cause of the world is conceived in terms of a conscious principle it is known as *cetana-kāraṇa-vāda* and when it is conceived in terms of an unconscious principle it is known as *acetana-kāraṇa-vāda*. The doctrine of *brahman* is illustrative of the former while that of the Cārvākas or Lokāyatas is of latter. The Vedāntic doctrine that the cause alone is real and that its apparent transformation in the form of effect is only an illusion is known as Sat-Kāraṇavāda. In the Pāśupata system Kāraṇa is one of the five categories denoting the supreme being who creates. The evolution of Kārya and its production from Kāraṇa in the Pāśupata system follow the Sāṅkhya pattern. While the Buddhists trace the cause of suffering to *avidyā* or false knowledge, the Pāśupatas ascribe it to the failure to recognise Śiva as the creator, preserver and destroyer at one and the same time.

karaṇa A *mudrā* or hand pose; it shows the hand held palm facing outward with the index and little fingers erect, while the two middle fingers are pressed towards the palm of the hand by the thumb.

kāraṇa Tantric term for wine. In the *Kaivalyatantra* it is said that since wine is the cause (*kāraṇa*) of all knowledge of *dharma, artha, kāma* and *mokṣa* it is known as Kāraṇa *Prāṇatoṣaṇī* VII.2, 510.

kāraṇa-brahman The causal state of brahman; in

this state it is with pure matter and soul in an unmanifested form according to the interpretation of Rāmānuja. *Śrībhāṣya* I.1.1.ff.

kāraṇa-citta Potential mind which is essentially ubiquitous and may be recovered by Yogic practices, according to the Yoga system. The absolute ubiquity of the Kāraṇa-citta is, however, denied in the Sāṅkhya which admits only its relative expansiveness in different types of bodies.

kāraṇa-deha, śarīra A form of subtle body capable of containing the doctrines of Śiva.

kāraṇavidyā Primal nescience which produces series of delusions. Also called *mūlavidyā*.

kāraṇa-yoga A type of Yogic-exercise.

karanyāsa Feeling the deity in the palms. The fingers and the back of the hand are used to invoke deities in the forms of letters. *Tantrasāra* 88 ff.

kārīriṣṭi A sacrifice, a kind of *iṣṭi*, employed for securing rains. *Āśv. Sr.* II.13.1–13, *Āp.Sr.* XIX.25.16ff.

karivarada An aspect of Viṣṇu.

karma Physical movement. According to the Vaiśeṣika system it is one of the seven categories of reality. There are five kinds: *utkṣepana* or throwing upward, *avakṣepana* or throwing downward, *akuñcana* or contraction, *prasāraṇa* or expansion and *gamana* or locomotion.

karma The doctrine according to which all actions, good or bad, produce their proper consequences in the life of the individual who acts. In the early Vedic ideas *karma* denotes sacrifice. In the later Vedic texts and in the Upanisads *karma* is presented in two forms—simple and sophisticated. The simple form of this doctrine is that just as good seeds bring a good harvest and bad seeds bad, so also a man becomes good by good deeds and bad by bad deeds. At the sophisticated level, however, *karma* is regarded as a blind unconscious principle governing the whole universe. It is not subject to the control even of God. It is inextricably blended with the doctrines of transmigration of the soul and rebirth (*Īśā* II, *Chāndogya* III.1.10, III.14.1, V.10, VII.1.6, etc. *Maitrāyaṇī* III.2 etc., *Bṛhadāraṇyaka* III.2.13, IV.4 etc., *Muṇḍaka*, III.2 etc.). In Jainism, unlike other systems, *karma* is conceived as being material and permeating the Jīvas (q.v.) and weighing them down to the mundane level. Through the actions of body, speech and mind *karma* is formed as a subtle matter. The passions of a man act like a viscous substance that attracts the *karma* matter, which thus pours into the soul and sticks to it; gradually it ripens and exhausts itself in accordance with the suffering and enjoyment of the individual. If through proper self-discipline the stored *karma* can be purged and the influx of *karma* can be arrested, the Jīva becomes liberated. In certain other systems like Buddhism, Sāṅkhya and Mīmāṃsā, the law of *karma* is autonomous and works independently of the will of God. The Buddhist law of *karma* is only a special form of the more general law of causation. Since life is thought of as an unbroken stream of successive states which are causally connected, the present existence of an individual is in accordance with that of *karma*, the effect of the past. Rebirth is, therefore, not transmigration but a continuity in life-series in which process *karma* serves as a causal connection. The Mīmāṃsakas hold that the world is always there, neither created nor destroyed, but regulated by *karma*. The law of *karma* is thought to guide the formation of objects. The world is composed of living bodies wherein the souls reap the consequences of their past deeds (*bhogāyatana*), the Indriyas or organs which are instruments for suffering or enjoying of those consequences (*bhogasādhana*) and the objects which constitute the fruits to be suffered or enjoyed (*bhogaviṣaya*). Those Mīmāṃsakas believing in atomism hold that the autonomous law of *karma* independently regulates the atoms. According to the Vedāntins *karmas* accumulated in past lives admit of a two-fold division, those that have borne their effects (*prārabdha-karma*) and those still lying accumulated (*sañcita-karma*). There is another class—the *karmas* which are being stored in the present life (*sañciyamāna*). The bondage of the soul to the body is due to its *karma*. As the effect of its *karma*, the soul is associated with the particular kind of body it deserves; its consciousness becomes limited by the condition of the organs of knowledge; and it identifies itself with the body which results in egoism or *ahaṃkāra* which is the source of all false knowledge (*avidyā*). The followers of the Nyāya-Vaiśeṣika school believe that the law of *karma* is under the guidance and control of God who creates the world in accordance with the law. *Adṛṣṭa* (q.v.) or the stock of merits and demerits of *karmas* of the individual souls, cannot by itself lead to their proper effects, because it is an unintelligent and unconscious principle. It is therefore God who controls the *adṛṣṭa* and dispenses all the joys and sorrows of human life.

But most of the Indian schools of philosophical thought hold that the origin and order of the world can be explained by the law of *karma* without the supposition of god. The ethics of the law of *karma* is that every deed must produce its natural effect in the world and as such also leaves an impression on the mind. It is this impression or *saṃskāra* that inclines one to repeat the deed that has been once done. A man cannot escape the deeds but he can control them; by self-discipline he can strengthen the good impulses and weaken the bad ones.

karmakāṇḍa A theoretical division of the Vedic texts; it pertains to those portions which apply to some ritual or sacrifice. The Mīmāṃsakas hold that the main purpose of the Vedas is to denote some *karma* or rite, and therefore all those portions which do not exclusively speak of rituals should be considered redundant or figurative.

karma-mārga The so-called external means for achieving the highest object of life; the performance of rites and ceremonies. The Mīmāṃsakas hold that the ways involving certain actions, especially rituals, lead to the highest goal of life.

karma-mīmāṃsā Authoritative dissertations on ritual practice, like the Brāhmaṇa literature, which have been highly acclaimed in the Mīmāṃsā tradition.

kārmaṇa-śarīra The Jain conception of the *karma* doctrine. It is held that subtle matter ready to be transformed into *karma* pours into the Jīva (q.v.) which is called *āsrava* (q.v.) or influx. In the usual state a soul harbours *kaṣāya* (q.v.) or passion which acts like a viscous substance and retains the subtle matter coming into contact with the soul. The subtle matter thus caught by the soul enters, as it were, into a chemical combination with it. This is called *bandha* (q.v.) or binding of *karma* matter. The subtle matter 'bound' or amalgamated by the soul is transformed into eight kinds of *karma*, and forms a kind of subtle body or Kārmaṇa-śarīra which clings to the soul in all its migration and future births and determines the individual state and the lot of that particular soul.

karmāśaya The storehouse of all the latent forces that burst into activity when the occasion arises. It is a Sāṅkhya and Yoga concept which corresponds to the *ālaya* or *ālayavijñāna* of the Buddhists.

karmāṅga-śrāddha That kind of Śrāddha (q.v.) performed at the time of the *garbhādhāna* (q.v.) rite, or at a *soma* (q.v.) sacrifice or at *sīmantonnayana* (q.v.), *puṃsavana* (q.v.) etc.

karma-saṃnyāsa Renunciation of works for worldly gains. This doctrine presupposes a belief that ultimately finite beings are tools for the implementation of divine plans.

karmāsrava One of the two classes in the Jain concept of *āsravas* (q.v.) (the process of the actual entrance of *karma* particles into the soul). The effect on the soul of the actual influx of *karma* is of eight kinds: *jñānāvaraṇīya, darśanāvaraṇīya, vedanīya, mohanīya, āyu, nāma, gotra* and *antarāya*.

karmavipāka The fruition of evil deeds The Smṛtis hold that if a sinner does not undergo proper penance he has to suffer torments in hell. Thereafter he becomes born as an insect or lower animal or a tree on account of some remnants of his sins. Or he may be born as a human being afflicted with certain diseases or with defects. The Buddhist *kamma-vipāka* also means the consequence of one's own action.

karmayoga Action without any desire of the fruit thereof. The nature of *karma* or action is that it binds the soul by bringing a reward. Each act is prompted by a particular motive and it is the motive that governs its nature. Because an act is undertaken for the definite purpose of enjoying its result, the result affects the soul. But if action could be performed without a desire for the personal enjoyment of the result, then it would be devoid of its sting. *Karma* thus becomes karmayoga in which the soul remain unaffected. This doctrine is set forth in the *Bhagavadgītā* in great detail.

karmendriya The five organs of action, according to the Sāṅkhya. They are located in the mouth, hands, feet, anus and the sex organ performing the function of speech, prehension, movement, excretion and reproduction respectively. The imperceptible power through which the functions of these organs are executed is known by inference, *Sān.Sūt.* II. 23, *Kārikā*, 26, 28.

karṇavedha Piercing the lobes of the ears of the child. This rite is omitted in almost all ancient Smṛtis. It is mentioned in *Vedavyāsa-smṛti* I.19, *Baudh.Gr. Śeṣa-sūtra* I.12–1 and in the *Kātyāyana-sūtra* which is a supplement of *Pār.Gr.*

karppara Same as Kapāla (q.v.).

kartābhajā A medieval religious community of

Bengal which banked on liberal social views and absolute surrender to God impersonated by the Guru.

kartari, karttari A small knife which serves as a weapon of god. Sometimes the edge is serrated like the edge of a saw. It is called Vajrakartari when surmounted with a Vajra (q.v.). Kartari is also a form of *mantra* containing two letters. *Tantrarāja* XXXV. 28–29.

karuṇā A term used basically to denote compassion (of Buddha). Karuṇā gradually came to be counted as one of the four *brahmavihāras*, others being *maitri, muditā* and *upekṣā*. In Mahāyāna Śūnyatā and Karuṇā become two basic principles and their combined work is supposed to generate bodhicitta (q.v.). In Vajrayāna Śūnyatā has been identified with Prajñā or knowledge and Karuṇā, the principle of compassion, with Upāya or means to attain perfect knowledge. The *bodhicitta* can become ultimate reality through the principle of Karuṇā. This Karuṇā is symbolised in the form of Avalokiteśvara, the great compassionate Bodhisattva (q.v.).

kārunikasiddhānti A Śaiva-Tantric sect which was theoretically akin to the Kāpālikas (q.v.).

kārya Effect. The question whether the effect originally exists in the material cause prior to its production has been a matter of debate in Indian philosophical tradition. The Buddhists and the Nyāya-Vaiśeṣikas hold that the effect cannot be said to exist before it is produced by some cause. This is known as *asat-kārya-vāda* (q.v.). The Sāṅkhya repudiates this theory and establishes *satkārya-vāda* (q.v.) which holds that the effect exists in the material cause even before it is produced. This theory has two different forms. *Pariṇāmavāda* (q.v.) i.e. when an effect is produced there is a real transformation of the cause into the effect; and *vivartavāda* (q.v.) i.e. when there is transfiguration. Kārya is one of the five tenets of the Pāśupata system; in this context it means all the problems and conditions of worldly existence.

kārya-brahman The manifested form of *brahman* (q.v.) which may be called its effect state according to the interpretation of Rāmānuja. *Śrībhāṣya* I.1.1ff, II.1.15.

kārya-brahmaloka Heavenly abodes for those who worship different deities and symbols according to the Vallabha school. However, they can never attain *brahman* which is limited only to those who worship Kāraṇa-brahman through *samādhi* and meditation.

kāryavidyā Term for derivative nescience described by Vācaspati in the introductory verse of *Bhāmatī*.

kārya-vimukti Release of insight from effects; it is a stage of sanctification according to the *Yoga-sūtra*.

kāryavindu Vindu (q.v.) in effect. Of the various connotations of *vindu* one is that which is the contracted form of the conscious Śakti when it desires to create. *Prapañcasāra* I.41. This is causal or *kāranavindu* and when it manifests itself into effect it is known as *kāryavindu*.

kaṣāya The Jain term for passions which act as viscous substances in retaining *karma* matter. They consist of four sins: anger (*krodha*), conceit (*māna*), intrigue (*māyā*) and greed (*lobha*). Each of these four sins is taken into account from four viewpoints—*anantānubandhī* (when the sin is cherished throughout the whole life), *apratyākhyāna* (when it is cherished for a year), *pratyākhyāna* (when it is cherished only for four months) and *sañjvalana* (when it is cherished for short while). Besides these sixteen categories of Kaṣāya there are nine others making a total of twenty-five. These are laughter, pleasure, disgust, fear, grief and four other minor faults. The Kaṣāyas result in tying men to the cycle of rebirth. The effects of the Kaṣāyas are given in details in *Dasav*. VIII. 37–39; cf. *Suya* I.1.4.11ff, I.2.2.29, I.9.11.

kasiṇa A Prakrit form of the Sanskrit *kṛtsna* meaning 'entire' or *karṣaṇa* meaning 'cultivation' (of mind). The term is applied in Buddhism to those subjects of meditation which occupy the entire mind. *Kasiṇas* are associated with meditations on earth (*pathavī*), water (*āpa*), fire (*tejo*), air (*vāyo*), blue (*nīla*), yellow (*pīta*), red (*lohita*), white (*odāta*), light (*āloka*) and circumscribed space (*paricchinnākāśa*). *Visuddhimagga* 125, 170, 174–75.

kāśmīra sampradāya Tantrics of Kāśmīra region whose theories and practices are described in the *Śaktisaṅgama-tantra*, Sundarī, III.11ff. and *Puraścaryārṇava* IX.866. They depend also on the texts of Kāśmīra Śaivism.

kāśyapīya A branch of the Sarvāstivādins (q.v.). Also known by three other names: Sthāvīrīya, Saddharmavarṣaka and Suvarṣaka. They had a cannon similar to that of the Dharmagupta (q.v.). According to the Kāśyapīyas Arhats have both *kṣaya-jñāna* and *anutpāda-jñāna* and are not subject to passions; Saṃskāras perish every moment;

and the past which has not produced its fruit exists, the present exists, and some of the future exists.

kaṭaṅkaṭa A class of evil spirits.

kathakatā Traditional method of popular religious instruction through the recital and interpretation of the scriptures and devotional texts by competent speakers capable of influencing masses. Sometimes learned scholars took to this profession and it was always ennobling to listen to their impressive discourses, based upon an extensive knowledge of the Śāstras, on life, death, life after death, the inevitable consequences of sin and the certain rewards of virtue.

kaṭhina A ceremony among the Buddhists in which robes are given by the believers to the *bhikkhus* or monks. These robes are made of raw cotton and hence designated *kaṭhina*.

kaukilī A variety of Sautrāmaṇi (q.v.) sacrifice. It was performed either for a Brāhmaṇa who desired prosperity, or for a king who was driven from his kingdom, or for one who had no cattle. *Āp.Sr.* XIX.5.2, *Kāt.Sr.* XIX.1.2–4.

kaukkuṭika A group of wandering ascetics mentioned by Pāṇini.

kaulamārga The last of the seven Tantric *ācāras* (q.v.) which is so influential that it is often equated with Tantrism itself. It is the exclusive cult of Śakti as the Female Principle with the rituals of Five Ms or *pañcamakāra* (q.v.), the aim being the realisation of *sāmarasya* (q.v.) of Śiva and Śakti within the self. Śrīvidyā and her forms are the principal objects of this cult. In some texts it is regarded as anti-Vedic and imported from China. The Tantric texts distinguish two categories of Kaulamārga. They also describe in detail the qualification and competence of aspirants, nature of spiritual exercise, physical and mental fitness required in this cult, the *kaula* theory of knowledge, its attitude towards women, its secrecy, warn against its misuse and various kindred topics. See *Saubhāgyabhāskara* on *Lalitāsahasranāma* CXLIV, *Kaulamārgarahasya* 5, *Nirvāṇatantra* XI, *Kulārṇava* II, IX, XI, XVII, *Devībhāgavata* XII.9.96, *Kulacuḍāmani* I.1–2, *Prāṇatoṣaṇi* VII.4, 531–32. *Rudrayāmala* Uttara, XIII, XVII, XXII, *Kaulajñānanirṇaya* XIV, XVI, XXI, *Mahānirvāṇa* I.58–60, IV.38–43, VII.94, X.108, XIV.184 ff., *Kaulāvalinirṇaya* X, XXI. 189–90, *Gandharvatantra* XXXIV–XXXVI, *Niruttara* XII, Rameśvara on *Paraśurāmakalpasūtra* III.31, VII.1 *Śaktisaṅgama*, Ṭārā, XII.43–47, etc.

kaulika Followers of the Kula or Kaula school. For their characteristics see *Nirvāṇatantra* XI, *Kulārṇava* II, XVII.

kaulikī-śakti Same as Kula-nāyikā, the Śakti within the heart which is stainless and independent. It is also known by the names *anuttara, parā, pratibhā, khecarī*, etc. *Tantrāloka* III.67, *Parātriṃśikā* 61.

kaulikī-siddhi Name of mokṣa or liberation according to the Kula-mata of Kāśmīra Śaivism. The experience of Kula or the ultimate reality through body and soul brings this form of liberation. *Parātriṃśikā* 36.

kaulini See Kula-Yoṣit.

kaumudī See Dipāvalī.

kavaca That which saves the body from the weapons of the enemy. In Tantra the term is used to denote a special *mantra* which protects the body and soul of the aspirant. This *mantra* is to be recited during worship and its written version is to be carried on the body as a talisman. Kavacas are connected with the names of different Tantric deities and they are supposed to be more efficacious than worship, meditation, etc. *Śyāmārahasya* IV.

kāya The body; it is regarded in Tantrism as the microcosm of the universe. See Tri-Kāya.

kāyasādhana Disciplining of the body. See Kulakuṇḍalinī, Saṭcakrabheda, Mantra-Yoga, Haṭhayoga, Laya-yoga, Rājayoga, Raseśvara-darśana.

kāyasakkhī A state in Buddhist *arhat*-hood. In the post-Sotāpanna (q.v.) career a Saddhānusārī (who depends more on faith in the *triratna*, his spiritual teacher and meditational practices than the scriptures) is designated as Saddhāvimutta or Kāyasakkhī because while practising the higher meditations he realises both mentally and physically inward calmness.

kāyatattva See Rasa, Raseśvara-darśana, Māheśvara-Siddha, Siddha-cikitsā.

kāyotsarga The posture adopted by standing Tīrthaṃkaras. Same as Khaḍgāsana.

kerala-sampradāya Name of a Tantric sect the followers of which are scattered in nineteen countries from Āryāvarta to the sea. *Śaktisaṅgama*, Kālī, IV.3.6. Their theories and practices are described in the *Siddhāntasaṃgraha*. See *Puraścaryārṇava* IX. 867.

keśānta The rite of shaving the hairs on the head and on the other parts of the body. Same as *godāna*. It follows the procedure for *cuḍākaraṇa* (q.v.), but it is performed in the sixteenth year from conception or birth, or immediately before marriage. The ceremony may also be performed for girls. This sacrament is no longer in vogue. *Śat.Br.* III.1.2.4, *Baudh.Dh.S.* I.2.7, *Āśv.Gr.* I.18–22, *Śān Gr.* I.28, *Manu* II.65, *Yāj* I.36, etc.

keśavapanīya A rite in the Rājasuya which followed the procedure for the *Atirātra* sacrifice and in which hair grown over the period of a year was cut. *Lāt.Sr.* IX.3.1, *Āśv.Sr.* IX.3.24 ff.

kevala The form of knowledge which according to the Jain conception is unobstructed, unconditional and absolute and which is to be attained through Yoga or concentration. It belongs to the *pratyakṣa* or direct category because it is not acquired through the medium of the senses. *TTDS* I, 9, 12, 21–29.

kevala-bhakti Bhakti or devotion of unmixed type. In this stage love flows towards god spontaneously and uninterruptedly like the flow of a river into the ocean or the movement of a piece of iron towards a magnet.

kevala-kumbhaka See Haṃsa. *Gheraṇḍa* V.84, *Haṭhayogapradīpikā* II.72–74.

kevala-mūrti A class of Śiva images belonging to the graceful type. Gopinatha Rao holds that the Candraśekhara-mūrtis (the god with the crescent moon on his matted locks) belong to this type when the god is shown alone.

kevala-narasiṃha A type of Narasiṃha image showing the god in tranquillity and Yogic meditation.

kevaliā Popularly known as Keuliā, it is a liberal Vaiṣṇava religious community of Assam. The followers live within the *satra* (q.v.) precincts and lead a celibate life. They are also called Udāsīn-bhaktas.

khaḍga Sword. The sword in the hand of the Buddhist god Mañjuśrī is called Prajñākhaḍga or the sword of wisdom, which is believed to destroy the darkness of ignorance by the luminous rays issuing out of it.

khanda Sanskrit Skandha. The combination of five aggregates of existence according to Buddhism. In other words the *khandas* are the constituents of a being belonging to Rūpadhātu and Kāmadhātu (qq.v.). The constituted elements are put under two heads, *nāma* and *rūpa*, the former denoting the non-material or mental constituents of a being, while the latter only the material. All inanimate objects are, therefore, included in the term *rūpa*. Nāma is analysed into four mental states: *vedanā* (feeling), *saññā* (perception), *saṅkhārā* (resultant impressions produced through *karma*) and *viññāna* (knowledge derived through the organs of sense). The four subdivisions of *nāma* along with the fifth, *rūpa*, are termed Pañcakkhandha.

kha-puṣpa Menstrual blood required in Tantric worship. The blood of a virgin is known as *sayambhūkusuma* or *raktacandana*, that of a married woman is known as *kuṇḍodbhava* and that of a widow is known as *golodbhava*.

khaṭvāṅga Magic wand. The stick is generally surmounted either by Vajra (q.v.), the Kapāla (q.v.), the Triśūla (q.v.) a banner, or all of them.

khayañānā The Buddhist concept of knowledge of the cessation of rebirth. *AKV* II.11.

khecarī-mudrā A Yogic posture which bestows spiritual attainment and enables one to overcome disease and death. *Gheraṇḍa* III.1–3, *Haṭhayogapradīpikā* III.67. It is required for the meditation of Tripurasundarī. *Mudrānighaṇṭu* 14–16.

khecarī-śakti Same as Kaulikī-Śakti (q.v.). *Kha* denotes brahman and *cara* that power which moves. The kinetic energy of *brahman* is known as khecarī. Though one and undifferentiated it is manifested in numerous forms.

khecari-samatā Identity with Khecari-Sakti which is the cause of Jīvanmukti (q.v.).

khuśī-viśvāsī A religious community of North India which professes liberal social views. It believes in informal devotion to a personal god and was greatly influenced by the Sahajiyās, Nairañjanī and Nātha cults and to a certain extent by Islam.

khyāti Non-apprehension of an object. It is of various types like *asat* (mistaking a non-existent object as existent), *anirvacanīya* (mistaking an undefinable entity as a real thing), *ātma* (projecting a mental state into the external world), *alaukika* (mistaking a superempirical for a real percept), *sat* (objective error), *sadasat* (apprehension which is partly real and partly unreal, *anyathā* (mistaking the reprersented element for the presented due to common traits between the two) and so forth.

kīlaka A Tantric *nyāsa* (q.v.).

kiṃpuruṣa A class of supernatural beings worshipped as Vyantara-devatās (q.v.).

kinnara A class of worshipful beings belonging to the category of Vyantara-devatās (q.v.). They are the denizens of the *antarīkṣa* or atmospheric region.

kiriyam An incentive mental state and effects transpiring from it, according to Buddhist belief.

kīrtana Ordinarily the laudatory recital, verbal and literary of the name and qualities of a person.

Its technical meaning consists in the repeated utterance of the name and description of the qualities of God or the devotional object. Of the nine modes of *bhakti* or devotion, Kīrtana is the second. In a still more technical sense it means a variety of devotional music used in singing the name or the praise of the Lord.

kīrttimukha Lion-like head constituting an art design of symbolical significance.

kleśa Buddhist term for impurities. In Yoga Kleśa means hindrances of difficulties which are five in number and the cause of misery: *avidyā* (ignorance), *asmitā* (mediocrity), *rāga* (attachment), *dveṣa* (hatred) and *abhiniveśa* (self-satisfaction). *Yogasūtra* II.3.

kleśa-bīja Germ of impurities. The Mahāsaṅghikas state that Kleśa-bīja is a *dharma* distinct from Kleśa. *Abhidharmakośa* (Poussin) V.7.

kleśāvaraṇa The veil of impurities which, according to Buddhist ideas, is constituted by *rāga, doṣa, moha, silabbataparāmāsa* and *vicikicchā* (qq.v.).

kojāgara-pūrṇimā The night of the full-moon in Āśvina (Oct-Nov). It is sacred to Lakṣmī, the goddess of wealth. The householders worship the goddess and keep their doors open and keep a vigil at night so that the goddess may enter the house and bestow prosperity. It is also known as Kaumudī-jāgara.

kolaṃkola One who will pass from one family of beings to another; in Sanskrit Kulaṃkula. It is a sub-stage between Sotāpanna and Sakadāgāmi according to Buddhism. A Kolaṃkola acquires the pure faculties (*anāsrava-indriyas*) and thereby counteracts the impurities caused by other faculties (*indriyas*). If reborn twice or thrice among gods he is designated as Devakulaṅkula, if among men he is called Manuṣyakulaṅkula. The Nikāyas do not differentiate between a Sotapānna (q.v.) and a Kolaṃkola. *Abhidharmakośa* (Poussin) II.34, *Visuddhimagga* 709, *Aṅguttara* I.233, IV.380–81, *Saṃyutta* V. 205.

koṣa Sheaths. The relative position of the individual soul and the pure blissful soul is explained in the Upaniṣads by the concept of five sheaths or Koṣas. The grossest Koṣa is called *annamaya*, i.e., body with its sense organs nourished by food (*anna*). The next in ascending order is *prāṇamaya* or that guided by the vital force (*prāṇa*). The third is *manomaya* guided by mind (*manas*). The fourth is *vijñānamaya* nourished by intellect (*vijñāna*) while the fifth is *ānandamaya* nourished by pure bliss-consciousness.

koṭihoma A form of *navagraha-śānti* (propitiation of the nine planets). It is usually performed by the kings and begins either in Caitra (March-April) or in Kārtika (Oct-Nov) and lasts for a year. *Matsya Pu*. CCXXXIX.20–21.

krama A mode of reciting Veda. In Mīmāṃsā tradition it is the order in which several component parts or acts of a sacrifice should be performed. The *PMS* V. deals with six means for determining the sequence of component parts in a sacrifice with examples from five Vedas.

krama-dīkṣā A form of Śākta dīkṣā (q.v.) in the *mantras* of Kālī, Tārā and Tripurasundarī. It is not for all. *Prāṇatoṣaṇi* II.5, 143.

kramamata A Kāśmīra Tantric system, the texts of which are mentioned in *Tantrāloka, Mahārthamañjarī*, etc. Abhinavagupta's *Kramakeli* and *Kramastotra* expound on this system. There are two streams of this system—one Śaiva oriented and the other Śākta; Kālī is regarded as the ultimate reality. *Tantrāloka* IV.157 ff.

krama-mukti Gradual emancipation. Those that lead pure lives devoted to meditation and truthfulness travel the path of the gods (*devayāna*) after death and thereafter through successive stages they ultimately merge in *brahman*, transcending all worlds. *Ch.Up*. IV.15, V.10, *Bṛhadāraṇyaka* VI.2, *Kauṣītaki Up*. I. 2–4, etc.

krāntā Tantric division of Bhāratavarṣa according to the zone of influence of the cult. There are three divisions, viz., Viṣṇu-Krāntā, Ratha-Krāntā and Aśva-Krāntā.

kratavārtha A term introduced by the Mīmāṃsakas and frequently used by the writers of the Dharmaśāstras which indicates generally those injunctions which have an invisible, spiritual and other worldly result or reward. Those that have a visible worldly result are known as Puruṣārtha.

kṛcchra A penance. As many as sixty types of Kṛcchras are mentioned in the Dharmaśāstras.

kriyā Action. In all forms of Indian religion there are three paths of salvation. They are *bhakti* (devotion), *jñāna* (knowledge) and *karma* (action) corresponding to *icchā, jñāna* and *kriyā*, i.e. the affective, congnitive and conative aspects of personality. Kriyā denotes all forms of human actions and endeavours. In the field of religion it is the performance of certain rituals. See under Karmamārga. In Vedic conception there are five forms of Krīya, namely *agnihotra, darśa-paurṇamāsa, paśuyāga, cāturmāsya* and *soma-yāga* (qq.v.).

kriyā-śakti Three forms of occult power—*man-*

ojavītva (doing any act at any time), *kāmarūpītva* (assuming any form at will) and *vikaraṇadharmītva* (infinite mental power to consume and transmit). *Sarvadarśanasaṃgraha* VI.56–57.

kriyāvāda The doctrine according to which the soul acts and is acted upon. The term Kiriyam or Kriyāvāda, with some reservation, also applies to the Jain doctrine. According to the *Suyagaḍa* (I.12.11–12) the followers of this doctrine maintain that misery is caused by oneself and not by any external agent. Liberation may be attained by knowledge and good conduct. Fools are unable to stop the influx of evil actions, but the wise can do so by abstaining from wrongdoing. The Buddha was not, however, ready to accept the view of the Kriyāvādins in general and of the Jains in particular that human suffering is not conditioned by or dependent upon external factors (*Aṅguttara*, III.440). The Jain texts mention 180 forms of Kriyāvāda.

kriyāvatī-dīkṣā One of the forms of Tantric dīkṣā (q.v.) in which the Guru (q.v.) purifies the six *adhvas* (see under *adhvaśodhana*) of the disciple's body, infuses him with his own consciousness and anoints him with different rites. *Prāṇatoṣaṇī* II.5, 140–42.

kriyāyoga A form of Yogic exercise prescribed for those who have attained the status of Puṣpacakra-vīra, a special status in the Tantric cult. *Śaktisaṅgama*, Sundarī, I. 197–200.

kriyopāya Same as Āṇava-Upāya (q.v.).

krodha-bhairava One of the eight forms of Bhairava (q.v.).

kṛṣṇa-janmāṣṭamī A Vrata observed on the birthday of Kṛṣṇa which is the eighth day of the dark half of Śrāvaṇa (July-Aug) or Bhādrapada (Aug-Sept). The celebration requiring a fast, worship of Kṛṣṇa, *jāgara* (waking at night), listening to and repeating hymns and stories of the exploits of Kṛṣṇa, and *pāraṇa* (feeding the Brāhmaṇas on the following day).

kṛtayuga The earliest of the four traditional ages. See Yuga.

kṣaṇikatva, kṣaṇikavāda The doctrine of momentary existence which is the essence of Buddhism. The Buddhists qualify impermanence or *anityatā* (q.v.) with momentariness (*kṣaṇikatva*); phenomenal objects are subject to change every moment, and within each moment takes place their origin (*utpatti*), duration (*sthiti*) and decay (*vināśa*).

kṣara One of the three fundamental categories of existence according to the *Bhagavadgītā*. It is the order of evolutes—the changing principles of the Universe.

kṣatradhṛti A rite for achieving stability of martial power. It formed part of Rājasūya (q.v.) which followed the procedure for *agniṣṭoma* (q.v.). *Āśv.Sr.* IX.3.27, *Lāt.Sr.* IX.3.13, *Śāṅ.Sr.* XV.16.10–11.

kṣaya-jñāna The eradication of *āsravas* or impurities in the Buddhist concept.

kṣayānutpāda The realisation of the truth that decay and non-origin of all living beings is on account of the complete suppression of all sufferings achieved by a potential Bodhisattva when he reaches the *bhūmi* (q.v.) called Sudurjayā (q.v.).

kṣepaṇa The *mudrā* (q.v.) of sprinkling exhibited by the Buddhist Nāmasaṅgiti. The two hands are joined, palm to palm, with fingers extended and pointed downwards to enter a vessel containing nectar.

kṣetra Holy resorts of the deities belonging to different creeds. There are eight Vaiṣṇava Kṣetras: Vadarikā, Śālagrāma, Puruṣottama, Dvārakā, Vilvācala, Ananta, Siṃha and Śrīraṅga. The eight Śaiva Kṣetras are Avimukta, Gaṅgādvāra, Śivakṣetra, Rāmayamunā, Śiva-sarasvatī, Madhya, Śārdula and Gaja. The eight Śākta Kṣetras are Ouḍḍīna, Jāla, Pūrṇa, Kolla, Śrīśaila, Kāñchī and Mahendra. *Bārhaspatyasūtra* III.119–125.

kṣetrajña Term for Self or Knower. Basically Kṣetra denotes ground. In a religious sense it means place or holy resort of a deity. In a more subtle sense it means the human body which is considered as the abode of the Supreme Being residing in the form of the inner self, the soul or pure consciousness. Kṣetrajña is one who is aware of this.

kṣiti-tattva The conception of earth as one of the five traditional material elements. This element is said to reside in the *mūlādhāra* (q.v.) within the human body according to the Tantric ideas. *Ṣaṭcakranirūpaṇa* XL.

kūdu An arched opening projecting from the flexed cornice (*kapota*); same as Caitya window.

kukkuṭika A branch of the Mahāsaṅghikas, often identified with the Gokulikas of the *Kathāvatthu*. According to their views *kleśas* (corruptions) and *mārgas* (paths) exist side by side; so also the *karmas* and *vipākas* (fruits). Mind can permeate the whole body and it is capable of contracting and expanding according to the smallness or largeness of the objects within its purview. There are sixteen different modes of comprehension corresponding to the sixteen different aspects of the four noble truths.

kula Clan or family. In the *Saubhāgyabhāskara* com. on the *Lalitāsahasranāma* I the term is used in the sense of a spiritual lineage from Paramaśiva to one's own Guru (q.v.). This lineage is equated with *gotra* in *Kulārṇava* XVII. Kaulamārga (q.v.) or Kaulācāra is thus a way of *sādhanā* restricted within the spiritual lineage of a particular group of Tantric teachers.

kulācāra See Kaula-mārga. In Buddhism the process of worshipping the Dhyānī Buddhas is also known as Kulācāra.

kuladravya Same as Kulatattva (q.v.) or Pañcatattva (q.v.) *Kaulāvalinirṇaya* VIII.

kulajñāna The knowledge of Kaulamārga, admission to which is highly restricted. Rāmeśvara on *Paraśurāmakalpasūtra* III.31.

kulakaulayoginī Presiding deities of Cakras (q.v.) belonging to the *bahirdaśāra* (q.v.) class. *Gandharvatantra* V. 102.

kulakuṇḍalinī See Kuṇḍalinī.

kulamārga See Kaulamārga. The word Kaula is a derivative of Kula with *ṣna* suffix.

kulamata See Kaulamārga. In Kashmir Śaivism it is regarded as a left handed way in which the rituals of Five Ms are excluded.

kulāmṛta The nectar which flows from the cerebral *candramaṇḍala* (lunar orb) down the inner body of the aspirant when the Kuṇḍalinī (q.v.) pierces the *ṣaṭcakra* (q.v.).

kulanāyikā The Śakti within the heart conceived in the form of the heroine of the clan. *Parātriṃśikā* 61.

kulapatha The way through which Kuṇḍalinī (q.v.) pierces the *ṣaṭcakra*. See *Saundaryalaharī* X.

kulapadma A six petalled lotus within the *sahasrāra* (q.v.).

kula-saṅketa Technical mysteries of Kaulamārga (q.v.). These relate to the practices in connection with *karma* (initiation), *pūjā* (worship), *mantra* (spell), *tantra* (way), *mantrayantralikhana* (drawing of diagrams), and so on. Without initiation into all these the practice of Kaulamārga is regarded as dangerous. *Niruttara* XII, *Kulārṇava* II, Rāmeśvara on *Parasurāmakalpasūtra* VII.1.

kulatattva Another name for Pañcatattva (q.v.) or Pañcamakāra. *Yoginītantra*, Pūrva VI.

kulāvadhūta See Avadhūta.

kulayoṣit The Kuṇḍalinī-śakti (q.v.) situated in the *mūlādhāra* (q.v.); also known as Kaulinī (q.v.). Lakṣmīdhara on *Saundaryalaharī* VIII.XLI.

kumārīpūjā Worship of a virgin as representative of the great goddess.

kumbhaka Breath-control. *Tantrasāra* 85ff. Eight types of Kumbhaka are mentioned in the *Gherandasamhitā* V.46. These are *sahita, sūryabheda, śitalī, bhastrikā, bhrāmarī, murcchā* and *kevalī*. The *Haṭhayogapradīpikā* II. 44 adds two more types, *sitkārī* and *plāvinī*.

kumbhavivāha A ceremony for girls to avoid widowhood. The day before the marriage several gods are invoked in a jar of water. The water is then sprinkled over the girl.

kumbhīpaṭia A community of medieval mystics of Orissa founded by Mukundadeva. This sect does not believe in the efficacy of temples and images or in the superiority of the Brāhmaṇas.

kuṇḍa Pits in the ground for holding fire required in making gifts, sacrifices and various rituals.

kuṇḍa-golodbhava Menstrual blood sacred to any Tantric goddess. *Kuṇḍodbhava* is the menstrual blood of a married woman and *golodbhava* that of a widow.

kuṇḍalinī Śakti which as serpent power remains latent in the *mūlādhāra-cakra* (q.v.); as the source of all energy it reveals itself when roused by yogic exercises. Through different nerve channels it takes an upward motion and eventually reaches the *sahasrāra* (the highest cerebral region) and then comes down to its original place. The rousing and stirring up of Kuṇḍalinī is a form of merger of the individual with the universal consciousness. The whole process is very complex and depends entirely on the mental and intellectual faculties of the aspirant. *Ṣaṭcakra-nirūpaṇa* XI, *Śāradātilaka* XXV.27. It has two forms, dynamic or kinetic and static or potential. For various interpretations of Kuṇḍalinī, its awakening and functions, see Lakṣmīdhara on *Saundaryalaharī* X, *Rudrayāmala*, Uttara, XXI, *Siddhasiddhāntasaṅgraha* IV.20ff, *Prāṇatoṣaṇī* I.6. 41ff, *Tantrarāja* XXX, *Mātṛkābheda* XIV, etc.

kurmāsana A Yogic *āsana* (q.v.) in which the heels are placed crosswise under the gluteals.

kurukullaka A branch of the Sāmmitiyas (q.v.).

kuśa A kind of grass which is required for sprinkling water or clarified butter and for various purposes connected with worship and rituals

kuśala-karmapatha Ten good ways leading to spiritual merits according to Buddhism.

kuśala-mūla The merits of Buddha which are

supposed to be transcendental. *Kathāvatthu* XVIII.4. Subsequently the term came to denote merit-roots, some of which one should acquire before accepting spiritual life.

kusuma Flower of menstrual blood. See Khapuṣpa.

kūṭa Collection or a collective entity. The term is applied as a suffix to denote utterances of *mantras* and letters in Tantrism.

kutuhalaśālā Place where wandering ascetics and also teachers and philosophers congregated for religious, philosophical and other discussions. *Dīgha* I. 179, *Majjhima* II.2, *Papañcasūdanī* III.235.

laghimā One of the ten *siddhis* or miraculous attainments. *Nityaṣoḍaśikārṇava* I. 166–68.

laghu-kṛcchra A form of penance which lasts for four days. It involves eating only once during the day, eating only once at night, eating food obtained without asking for it only once on the third day and a complete fast on the fourth day. Same as Bāla-Kṛcchra and Śiśu-Kṛechra. *Baudh Dh.S.*II.1.92, *Yāj* III. 318.

laghurudra Recital of *ekādaśinī* (Rudra-mantras, *Taitt.Saṃ* IV.5.1.11). It is prescribed for averting evil and for obtaining peace.

lāka-homa Offering of fried grain into and around the fire in marriage rituals and other auspicious events.

lākinī The presiding goddess of the *maṇipura-cakra* (q.v.).

lakṣa-homa The rite for the propitiation of the nine planets. *Matsyapurāṇa* XCIII. 92 deals with the matter of oblations, fees, and rewards and the procedure for invoking and bidding goodbye to the planets, the presiding deities, the *mantras* for *homa*, the ritual bath and gifts in connection with this ceremony.

lakṣaṇa Auspicious marks. Thirty-two special marks of the Buddha are enumerated in the *Dharmasaṃgraha*. Another class of minor marks, eight in numbers, is called Anuvyañjanas.

lakṣaṇā Implication. The term is also used to indicate *gauṇa-vṛtti*, i.e., indirect or secondary and derivative meanings. It is to be resorted to only when the *mukhya* or primary meaning is not admissible. *Alaṅkārakaustubha* II.12. Lakṣaṇā admits of two fold division: *jahat-svārtha* or the secondary meaning sacrificing the original meaning, and *ajahat-svārtha* or the secondary meaning which reinforces the original meaning.

lākula The Pāśupata docrine founded by Lakulīśa. The *Kūrma-purāṇa*, *Purva* XVI uses the word Nākula.

lalanā-cakra See Kālacakra, Lambikāgra.

lambikāgra A minor nerve-cycle situated above the *viśuddha* (q.v.) and below the *ājñā* (q.v.). It is also known as *lalanā* and *kālacakra*.

lāmāvarga A group of Tantric aspirants mentioned in the *Jayadratha Yāmala*. It constitutes twenty-four varieties of Lāmās—Yoginī, Rūpinī, Lāmā, Śākinī, Nalinī, Khāgī, Culī, Bilā, Trikhagagā, Pesinī, Dehinī, Jalā, Klevati, Bedhani, Luki, Padabhī, Raktinī, Hisā, Karoṭhi, Kaluśī, Bhadrā, Dundubhi, Mukharā and Āturā.

latā The female partner of the Tantric aspirant. Also known as Dūtī.

latā sādhanā Pañcamakāra (q.v.) rituals with female partners. *Mahānirvāṇa* I.52.

laukika Folk and popular divinities, cults and beliefs. While commenting on Vārttika 2 on Pāṇini VI.3.26 (*devatādvandve ca*) Patañjali appears to distinguish between two types of divinities—Vaidika and Laukika.

laukika-pratyakṣa Ordinary perception. According to the Nyāya it is of six kinds: visual (*cākṣusa*), auditory (*śrautra*), tactual (*spārśana*), gustatory (*rāsana*), olfactory (*ghrāṇaja*) and mental (*mānasa*).

laukika-pudgala Sarvāstivādin Buddhist concept of such permanent entities (*pudgalas*) which transmigrate; it applies only to the *saṃskāras* or impressions during one's lifetime.

laukika-samyag-dṛṣṭi Buddhist term for worldly right view. It is possible according to the Mahīśāsakas but the Śaila schools do not subscribe to its validity.

laukika-śraddhendriya Buddhist term for the worldly faculty of faith. *Kathāvatthu* XIX.8.

laya A practical demonstration of how the outwardly-directed evolving process is reversed until the whole *prapañca* or universe is resolved into unitary consciousness and perfect bliss. Also known as Kuṇḍalinī-yoga (q.v.) in Tantric tradition.

layabhogāṅgavidhāna The method of separating three fetters—*ānava* (caused by material ingredients), *karma* (caused by the effects of deeds) and *māyīya* (caused by false knowledge)—from the body of an individual. It is part of Smārtī-Dīkṣā. Rāghava on *Śāradātilaka* V.127–40, *Puraścaryārṇava* V. 395.

layasiddhiyogasamādhi The state of absolute bliss according to the Tantras. The aspirant through Yoni-mudrā acquires spiritual power and experiences sexual pleasure leading to realisation of a sense of non-duality with the supreme being. *Gheraṇḍa* VII.12–13.

layayoga The higher form of Haṭhayoga which destroys all forms of mundane desire. It is an experience of eternal bliss in which the mind totally merges in the supreme being. *Yogaśikhopaniṣat* I. 134–36, *Haṭhayogapradīpikā*—IV.31–34.

leśyā Different conditions produced in Jiva (q.v.) by the influence of *karma* (q.v.) according to Jain conception. An individual is always swayed by any of the three good or three bad Leśyās. Kṛṣṇa or black Lesyā is the worst of all which creates bad temper, cruelty and violence. Nīla or blue Leśyā makes one envious of others, lazy, gluttonous and wanting in modesty. Kapota or grey Leśyā makes one a thief, liar, a person who schemes and delights in exposing the bad qualities of others. Of the good Leśyās Tejaḥ or red removes all evil thoughts, Padma or yellow controls anger, pride, deceit and avarice, and Śukla or white makes one completely pure. The Siddhas are free from the influence of all Leśyās. The word appears to have been derived from Kleśa. See under Abhijāti.

līlā Sport; charm; the attributes and pastimes of God when he is viewed by his devotees as the eternal lover. In Vaiṣṇavism, especially in the Caitanya form, the *līlā* of Kṛṣṇa at Vṛndāvana has two aspects—manifest and unmanifest. Usually his *līlā* is not, and cannot be, visible to the worldly-minded, and as such it is known as unmanifest *līlā*. But if he pleases he and his associates come down among human beings and appear to pass through almost all the stages of human life. In such cases the *līlā* is said to be manifest. According to the *Caitanyacaritāmṛta*, the reason behind his *līlā* is God's own desire to relish the sweetness of the love of his associates for him and to make them relish his own sweetness.

līlākīrtana A form of Kīrtana (q.v.) in which songs describing the various sports, dalliances and deeds of Kṛṣṇa are sung. These songs mainly deal with *purvarāga* (dawn of yearning), *anurāga* (love or attachment), *kalahāntaritā* (estrangement), *rasa* (merry group dance) and *viraha* (the inevitable separation).

liṅga In the Mīmāṃsā tradition *liṅga* means the suggestive or indicative power of a word or words.

liṅga The phallic symbol of Śiva. It has been a popular object of worship in India from prehistoric to modern period. Details of the construction of *liṅga*, the names and philosophical significance of its different parts, the materials to be used in making it as well as the various types have been given in the *Viṣṇudharmottara* and the *Śilparatna*. The *Kūrmapurāṇa*, pūrva XXIV describes the origin of *liṅga* and its worship and the *Vāmanapurāṇa* XLVI lauds several holy places where ancient liṅgas are established.

liṅga-dhāraṇa See Liṅga-sāyatta-dīkṣā.

liṅga-puṣpa The Raktakaravī flower. It is used as a substitute for *maithuna* (q.v.), the other item being Yonipuṣpa which is blue Aparajitā flower. Com. on *Paraśurāmakalpasūtra* X.63.

linga-sāyatta-dīkṣā Initiation or Upanayana in the Vīra-śaiva system; it is marked by carrying a small *śivaliṅga* (q.v.) on the body, irrespective of sex.

liṅgatraya Three types of Śiva-liṅgas or Śiva-phallus. They are Itara (q.v.), Svayambhū (q.v.) and Bāṇa (q.v.). They are symbolically connected in Tantrism with the nerve plexuses within the human body.

liṅgāyata An influential and powerful Śaiva sect, also known as Vīraśaiva, which flourished in Karnataka under the leadership of Vasava. The members of this sect worship Śiva in his phallic form, reject the authority of the Vedas, deny the doctrine of rebirth, object to child-marriage, and approve of the remarriage of widows; they have an intense aversion to the Brāhmaṇas.

liṅgodbhava-mūrti A type of Śiva image which is a combination of the god's human as well as columnar form.

lipinyāsa See Mātṛkānyāsa.

lohābhisārika A rite about horses performed from the first to the ninth lunar day of Āśvina (Oct-Nov).

loka Jain conception of the cosmos similar to that of Prakṛti (q.v.), constituted by the Ajīva (q.v.) categories—*pudgala* (matter), *dharma* (motion), *adharma* (rest), *ākàsa* (space) and *kāla* (time), the first one falling in the group of *rūpa* (those with form), and the last four in the group of *arūpa* (those without any form). In other system *loka* stands for regions—celestial, atmospheric or worldly. The Vyāsabhāṣya on *Yogasūtra* III.25 mentions seven *lokas*: *bhur, bhuvaḥ, svaḥ, mahaḥ jana, tapas* and *satya*.

lokadhātu The worlds and their spheres of existence. According to the Buddhist cosmology the universe is composed of millions of ever expanding worlds, of which the Earth is one. It is referred to in the texts as Sahā-lokadhātu. Each *lokadhātu* is believed to be unique.

lokajñatā The Buddhist term for mastering the Śāstras and becoming able to judge what is good and what is evil for beings. This attainment takes place in the *pramuditā* (q.v.) stage of a potential Bodhisattva. *Bodhisattvabhūmi* 9.

lokākāśa See Ākāśa.

lokapāla In the Vedic tradition the four deities—Kubera, Varuṇa, Indra and Yama—who are supposed to be the guardians of the world. Certain texts have references to eight lokapālas and include, in addition to the four mentioned above, Vāyu, Agni, Sūrya, and Soma. Some substitute Nirṛti for Sūrya, vide *Manu* V.96.

lokāyata Literally 'that which belongs to the masses'. The term includes religious customs based on folklore and popular beliefs. It has been equated with the Cārvākas (q.v.) or materialists in Indian philosophical tradition. The term has a broad significance. In Indian literature from the earliest period to the end of the medieval age, there exists a set of ideas, and corresponding practices, different from the officially acknowledged norms, which have found expression in the beliefs and rituals of the Auls, Bauls, Sahajiyās, Kāpālikas, Nāthas and various other sects. All these come within the purview of Tantra (q.v.) which was also basically a Lokāyata system.

lokottaravāda A branch of the Mahāsaṅghikas which believed in the supramundane (*lokottara*) character of Buddha. The followers of this sect upheld certain conceptions which were later accepted and elaborated upon by the Mahāyānists.

lokuttara-dhātu A supramundane state of existence, according to Buddhist cosmological speculations. The beings of this *dhātu* are classified separately on account of their spiritual attainments. Also known as Apariyāpañña-dhātu (i.e. not included in the three *dhātus* namely, Kāma, Rūpa and Arūpa).

lopāmudrā The *mantras* or Śrīvīdyā consisting of fifteen symbolic letters. *Tantrasāra* 242–43.

mada Pride, egoism and the like. It is regarded as one of the six internal enemies (*ripu*) of man.

mādana The highest aspect of *mahābhāva* or supreme love according to the followers of Caitanya. It is maddening ecstasy felt by Rādhā and nobody else, not even by Kṛṣṇa himself. It is the experience of embrace, kiss and union simultaneously in an instant caused by a single touch or sight of Kṛṣṇa. At the same time it is tempered with an acute feeling of separation from Kṛṣṇa despite his proximity. *Ujjvalanīlamaṇi*, sthāyībhāva, 155, 160.

madantī Water heated on *gārhapatya* (q.v.) and used for making dough from pounded grains in connection with *darśapūrṇamāsa* (q.v.). *Āp.Sr.* I.21.8–9.

madhumati Hymn of *RV* (I.90.5–7) which shows succinctly the yearnings of the devotee for an equipoise between the elemental forces and material comforts. The former is concerned with the ingredients of matter and the latter with material objects produced for meeting human needs.

madhuparka A mixture of honey and curds or clarified butter which is offered to honouring distinguished guests: *ṛtvik, ācārya*, bridegroom, king, *snātaka* and a person who is dear to one. *Mānava Gr* I.9.1, *Khādira Gr.* IV.2.21, *Yāj* I.110, *Baudh.Gr.* I.2.65 etc. The procedure for *madhuparka* is set out in *Āśv.Gr.* I.24.5–26.

madhura One of the five kinds of personal loving relationships which the devotee should establish with the object of his worship; the others are *śānta, dāsya, sakhya* and *vātsalya* (qq.v.). It is that of a consort, in which the devotee views God as a personal lover. The attitude is called *madhura-bhāva*, the corresponding emotion is called *madhura-rasa* and the application is called *madhura-rati*.

mādhurya One of the five kinds of personal relationship with God in which the latter is conceived as the loving consort of the devotee. See *madhura*. *Caitanyacaritāmṛta* II.8. The term is also used to denote the sweetness of God, a feature greatly emphasised by the later Vaisṇavas. They say that the *aiśvarya* (majesty) of the Lord begets awe, but his *mādhurya* (the fascinating element of sweetness in him) is what engenders confidence and endears him to his devotees.

madhuvidyā Esoteric knowledge which the Aśvins received from the sage Dadhyac. *RV* IV.39.6, IV.40.5. The *Chāndogya* III.11.5 defines it as knowledge of highest excellence which should be imparted by the father only to his son or to a worthy pupil.

madhya-bandha Band with a relief or frieze in the middle of a member such as *jaṅghā* or pillar in temple architecture.

madhyamā A special type of sound; it lies between *paśyantī* (q.v.) and *Vaikhari* (q.v.) and forms the third stage of its development. It is within and connected with the intellect. Com. on *Prapañca-sāra* II.43. It is also called as state of equilibrium of *parā* (q.v.) and *paśyantī* (q.v.). *Cidvallī* on *Kāmakalāvilāsa* XXVI. According to Bhāskara Rāya, *brahman* having manifested itself as sound as *paśyantī* becomes specially articulated with the help of wind in the heart region as *nāda* (q.v.). This state is known as *madhyamā*. *Saubhāgyabhāskara* on *Lalitāsahasranāma* 99.

madhyamasrota-tantra Tantric works belonging to the middle current of the tradition. These are *Vijaya, Niśvāsa, Svāyambhūva, Vātula, Vīra-bhadra, Raurava, Makuṭa* and *Vīreśa*.

mādhyamika Also known as Śūnyavāda. It is one of the two principal philosophical schools of Mahāyāna (q.v.). It was founded by Nāgārjuna who held that the discourses of the Buddha were dependent on two kinds of truth, the conventional truth which is concerned with the recipient and the received—subject and object—and the absolute truth in which such distinction was meaningless. All phenomenal objects are really non-existent, mental impressions are false and illusory, and what seems to be existing is only apparent existence which is accepted by the ignorant, since they are enveloped in the darkness of ignorance (*avidyā*). The only non-illusory truth is *nirvāṇa* which is the comprehension of Śūnyatā (the vacuity of the world of experience which is an appearance, a mere network of unintelligible relations). The composite substances or *samṣkṛtas* which come into existence, continue, and cease to exist are not real since origination, continuance and extinction cannot happen jointly and simultaneously. It is the nature of *dharmaṣ* (ultimate factors of existence) to be produced by concurrent causes, and what is so produced is not produced in itself and hence does not exist by itself. Those who are ignorant are bewildered by the diversity of beings and objects of the world which is really non-existent, and their suffering is caused because they establish relation between an individual and the objects around it, both of which are unreal being mere figments of the imagination. *Mādhyamika Kārikā* (Bid-Bud) XIII.1–2, XXIV.6, XXV.3.19, 24, XXVI.11, *Mādhyamikavṛtti* 41, 237, 448, *Aṣṭasāhasrikā Prajñāpāramitā* 405, *Sarvadarśanasaṃgraha* II, *Sarvasiddhāntasārasaṃgraha* II.

madya The first of the five Ms; it is wine of various types. *Paraśurāmakalpasūtra* X.62. Paiṣṭī, Gauḍī and Mādhvī are the three best types. *Kulārṇava* V. *Mahānirvāṇa* VI.2–3. Thirteen types of wine were used by the Gauḍa-sampradāya. *Śaktisaṅgama*, Kālī, IX.46. Any type of wine, purified by *mantra*, is fit for *sādhanā* (q.v.). *Mahānirvāṇa* IV.4. Milk, honey and sugar syrup are regarded as substitutes for wine. *Ibid.*VIII.170–171. Symbolically *madya* is described as the nectar-essence of the union of Śiva-Śakti flowing from the highest cerebral region. *Kulārṇava* V.

magaṇḍika A religious community mentioned in *Aṅguttara* III. 276–77.

magga The real path for the ending of all sufferings; it is the third of the four truths preached by the Buddha. It is divided into three sections, namely Sila (q.v.), Citta (q.v.) and Paññā (q.v.). See Aṭṭhaṅgika-magga. In another sense *magga* means four stages of sanctification, viz. Sotapatti, Sakadāgāmi, Anāgāmi and Arahatta (qq.v.).

magga-phala The Buddhist concept of the realisation of four truths through spiritual progress in the four stages of sanctification. See Magga.

māghyāvarṣa A rite in memory of dead ancestors which may be regarded as the precursor of *mahālayā* (q.v.). *Āśv.Gr.* II.5.9.

mahābharaṇī A *śrāddha* (q.v.) performed in *bhādrapda* (Sept-Oct) in the dark half when the moon is influenced by the *bharaṇi* star. It is regarded as equal to Gayāśrāddha in efficacy.

mahābhāva Divine love which is developed to its fullest degree, like the love of Rādhā or the Gopīs to Kṛṣṇa. It is a culmination of several stages: *prema* (attachment), *sneha* (affection), *māna* (jealousy), *praṇaya* (feeling of respect), *rāga* (excessive eagerness), *anurāga* (feeling the attractiveness every moment) and finally *mahābhāva* (supreme love in which the distinction between the subject and the object disappears). *Ujjalanīlamaṇi*, sthāyībhāva 57ff, *Caitanyacaritāmṛta* II.19ff.

mahābhūta The five gross elements emanating from the Tanmātras (q.v.), according to the Sāṅkhya. These are *ākāśa* or ether, the essence of sound (*śabda*); *vāyu* or air, the essence of touch (*sparśa*) plus that of sound; *tejas* or fire, the essence of colour (*rūpa*) plus that of sound and touch; *āp* or water, the essence of taste (*rasa*) plus that of sound, touch and colour; and *kṣiti* or earth, the essence of smell (*gandha*) plus that of sound, colour, touch and taste.

mahābhūtaghaṭa A *mahādāna* (great gift) in which a golden jar filled with milk or clarified butter is to be offered to the donee with certain rituals. *Matsya* CCLXXXIX.

mahācakra One of the five Tantric cakra rituals; the others are *rāja, devī, vīra* and *paśu.* In *mahācakra* mother, sister, daughter, daughter-in-law and wife of the aspirant are to be worshipped as *pañca-śakti* or Śakti in her five forms. *Niruttara* X. See *cakra* and *bhairavī-cakra*.

mahācīnācāra See Cīnācāra and Cīnakrama.

mahādāna Great gifts of certain kinds mentioned in the Purāṇas such as *Agni* CCX, *Linga* II. 28ff. *Matsya* CCLXXIV—CCLXXXIX, etc. These are Hiraṇyagarbha, Brahmāṇḍa, Kalpapādāpa, Gosahasra, Kāmadhenu, Hiraṇyāśva, Hiraṇyāśvaratha, Hemahastiratha, Pañcalāṅgalaka, Dharādāna, Viśvacakra, Mahākalpalatā, Saptasāgaraka, Ratnadhenu and Mahābhūtaghaṭa (qq.v.).

mahākalpalatā A *mahādāna* (great gift) in which ten Kalpalatās with figures of various flowers and fruits are to be offered. *Matsya* CCLXXXVI.

mahākāraṇa-deha, śarīra The subtle body an individual acquires by means of Tantric Sādhanā (q.v.). Also known as Mahākāraṇa-śarīra.

mahākaruṇā Buddhist term for great compassion. It is an essential requirement for a Bodhisattva (q.v.). The thought or intention to work for the deliverance of all sentient beings, fallen into the unfathomable and unbounded ocean of *saṃsāra* (worldly existence) is called compassion or Karuṇā (q.v.). And that Karuṇā with which a Bodhisattva desires bodhi or enlightenment, not for himself but for others, is *mahākaruṇā*.

mahālayā The last day of the dark fortnight of *bhādra* (Sept-Oct) which is dedicated to the forefathers as the All Soul's Day and is marked by offering water to the departed ancestors.

mahāliṅga Vīraśaiva idea of great (*mahā*) Liṅga which represents symbolically the ultimate modification of the Sthala (q.v.) concept. Śiva as the supreme bifurcates himself into *liṅga* and *aṅga*. The former has several names, each representing a stage of conceptual development. For example *ācāra-liṅga*, the practical; *guru-liṅga*, the preceptive; *cara-liṅga*, the dynamic; *prasāda-liṅga*, the gracious and *mahā-liṅga*, the great.

mahāmaitrī Buddhist term for great love. Maitrī is that love for all beings (*sarva sattva*) which a mother feels towards her only and very dear son. The *maitrī* that prompts a Bodhisattva (q.v.) to offer his body and life and all sources of good (*kusalamūla*) to all living beings without any expectation or return is *mahāmaitrī*.

mahā-māṃsa The flesh of eight animals—cow, man, ram, horse, buffalo, boar, goat and deer—regarded as sacred to the deity. *Śyāmārahasya* III, *Tantrasāra* 630.

mahā-maṇḍapa Central pillared hall of a medieval temple which is open on two lateral sides.

mahā-māyā The body of glory and power; it is the transfiguration of the ordinary body caused by purging all the impurities by the several ways and means prescribed in the Siddha tradition. Mahāmāyā is also an epithet for the Female Principle conceived as the supreme being owing to her impersonation of the forces of Prakṛti or Māyā.

mahāmudrā A form of bodily posture intended to maintain physical fitness and mental alertness. In this the fingers of both hands are specially utilised in forming different shapes. *Gheraṇḍa* III.1–3. Mahāmudrā also stands for women and female organ.

mahān, mahat The first product of the evolution of Prakṛti. See Buddhi.

mahānāda Same as *śabda-brahman* (*brahman* in the form of sound) and its constituent *anāhata-nāda* (so called because this sound has a spontaneous origin and is not produced by friction or percussion.) Mahānāda is also different from that form of *nāda* (q.v.) which is produced from the union of *kāraṇa-vindu* and *vīja* (qq.v.).

mahānāmnī One of the four Veda-vratas (q.v.); it consists of studying selected verses to be performed by the student after initiation. *Gaut.* VIII.15, *Śāṅ.Gr.* II.11. 10–12.

mahānubhava-panthā A reformist religious community of Maharashtra founded by the great mystic Govinda Prabhu. Basically the Mahānubhavas follow the Bhāgavata cult. They also worship Dattātreya. They do not believe in the caste system, disregard the authority of the Vedas and disclaim the *āsrama* (q.v.) system. They regarded the *Gītā*, the *Bhāgavata* and the *Sūtrapāṭha* (a collection of aphorism of Cakradhara) as scriptures.

mahāpāriṣada Animal faced *gaṇas* (attendants) of Rudra-Śiva.

mahāpaśu The uninitiated individual. *Niruttara* XII.

mahāpātaka Major mortal sins; the minor sins are called Upapātaka. These are killing a brāhmaṇa, drinking wine, stealing, and adultery with Guru's wife. See under Pātaka, Prāyaścitta, Krcchṛa, Pāpa.

mahāpitṛyajña Rite for propitiating ancestors; it is performed during Cāturmāsya (q.v.) and is also called *śākamedha* (q.v.). *Taitt.Sam.* I.8.5. 1–2.

mahāpralaya The Puranic concept of the great dissolution of the universe which takes place after each *kalpa* (q.v.). During the period of dissolution *śakti* or creative force is supposed to return o its source and stay there until it manifests again in new creation.

mahāpraṇidhāna Buddhist term for resolutions. In a specific sense it denotes the ten resolutions which the potential Bodhisattva adopts in the *pramuditā* stage.

mahāprasthāna Starting on a great journey with inevitable death before the end is reached. The term is used in particular for the Pāṇḍavas after their renunciation of worldly life.

mahāpuruṣa-lakṣaṇa The characteristic signs of a god or Buddha or Jina when represented in images.

mahāpuruṣīya dharma Religion preached by Śaṅkaradeva in Assam. It is a reformed version of the *Bhāgavata* religion based on liberal social views and the doctrine of *bhakti*.

mahārāja A salutation used to address the Gurus, venerable saints, and ascetics since they are considered to be great kings of the spiritual world.

mahārājalīlā See Ardhaparyaṅka.

mahārasa Nātha concept of great juice, which—as *soma* or moon-power—resides below the *sahasrāra* (central cerebral region). The Yogī, by the culture of the body (*kāya-sādhana*) consumes it through the *vakra nālā*, the curved duct or nerve channel connecting the spinal cord with the brain and thus receives an immutable divine body.

mahāsadāśivamūrti A form of Śiva image having fifty arms and twentyfive faces. Each of the five aspects of Śiva—(Vāmadeva, Sadyojāta, Aghora, Tatpuruṣa and Īśāna)—are represented by five faces.

mahāsāmrājya-dīkṣā A form of initiation which is

a precondition of Kaula-sādhanā (q.v.).

mahāsaṅghika The big group which was formed from the original order of the Buddhists after the second Buddhist council. Eventually they split up into various sects like Ekavyavahārika, Lokottaravāda, Kukkuṭika, Bahuśrutīya, Prajñaptivāda, Caityaśaila, Aparaśaila, Uttaraśaila and others (qq.v.). The Mahāsaṅghikas believed in the transcendent nature of the Buddhas and attached greater importance to the Bodhisattvas than to the Arhats. They deified the Buddha, introduced the Bodhisattva conception and changed the ideal from Arhathood to Buddhahood and were the forerunners of Mahāyāna (q.v.). They had their principal centre in the Guntur district.

mahāsāntapana A penance in which the sinner has to subsist on cow's urine, dung, milk, curds, *ghee* and *kuśa* water on the first day and fast on the second day. *Baudh.Dh.S.* IV.5.11, *Manu* XI. 212, *Yāj* III.314.

mahāśānti Rite for averting calamities of various kinds. *Śāṅ.Gr.* V.11. The *Bhaviṣyottara* CXLIII.2–46 describes a *mahāśānti* which should be performed at a king's coronation; when he marches out to war; when a person has bad dreams or inauspicious omens (*nimittas*); when the planets are unfavourable, or when there is lightning and the fall of meteors.

mahāsetu The name of a *mantra*.

mahāsiddha The honorific title given to certain Buddhist saints like Saraha, Nagārjuna, Śabarīpā Anaṅgavajra, Indrabhūti, etc.

mahāsukha Literally the highest pleasure (*nirvāṇa*). The *summum bonum* and the real manifestation of Bodhicitta (q.v.), according to Tantric Buddhism. In order to have this experience woman and man should first realise that they embody Prajñā (q.v.) and Upāya (q.v.) respectively and that only their physical, mental and intellectual union can bring the experience of the highest truth (see Samarasa and Yuganaddha). The union of man and woman, of Upāya and Prajñā, brings the maximum pleasure in which all mental action is abdicated and the world around forgotten. A pleasing experience of non-duality prevails.

mahāsukhasthāna The place of great bliss. According to the Buddhist Siddhācāryas it is the top most station, or the central cerebral region, as the storehouse of psychic energy carried through 32 nerve channels; the female generative organ in certain Hindu and Buddhist Tantric texts.

mahāśūnya Kāśmīra Śaiva concept of the *bījabhūmi* (seed-ground) of all ideas or *bhāvas* in the consciousness of Śiva. It is described as void (*śūnya*) or great void (*mahāśūnya*) because nothing has manifested itself at this stage. *Paramārthasāra* 14.

mahāśūnyatāvādin A Buddhist sect; same as Vetulyakas. They are credited with manitaining that the Buddha never lived as a man on this earth and that the Order (Saṅgha) is also an abstract idea. Their views seem to presuppose Vajrayāna specially when they maintain that sex-relations might be carried on by a human pair, including recluses, who lead a worldly life. *Kathāvatthu* XXIII.1.

mahāśvetā A *mantra*, the recital of which in sunday with fast deem to yield all desires.

mahat The Sāṅkhya category of intelligence as an evolute of Prakṛti; also known as Buddhi (q.v.) or Mahān. In the Tantras it is traced to *śabdabrahma* (*brahman* in the form of sound). *Prapañcasāra* I. 45, Rāghava on *Śāradātilaka* I. 17.

mahātaptakṛcchra See Taptakṛcchra.

mahat-ātman A principle beyond intellect (*buddhi*) in the gradation of existences. *Kaṭha* III. 10–11.

mahāvaikuṇṭha The abode (*dhāma*) of Nārāyaṇa.

mahāvākya Great sayings, especially in relation to the doctrines of Vedānta. Most of the post-Śaṅkara Advaitavādins, except Vācaspati, have given prominence to these sayings as the means to the realisation of *brahman* by holding that not only the senses but words also have the capacity to produce perception in certain cases.

mahāvidyā See Daśa-mahāvidyā.

mahāvidyā-anumāna A mode of logical syllogism propounded by Kulārka Paṇḍita.

mahāvihāra Buddhist monastic establishments. Some of them, in course of time, assumed the character of universities.

mahāvihāravāsin A Buddhist sect in Sri Lanka.

mahāvīja See Vīja.

mahāvindu See Vindu.

mahāvīra Sacrificial vessel used in *pravargya* (q.v.) rite.

mahāvrata Functions on the second day in a *sattra* (q.v.). ritual in which certain features of primitive collective life can be clearly observed. A *mahāvrata* cup of *soma* is offered and *mahāvratasāman* is chanted while the priests sway in tune with the rhythmic chanting during the ritual. An

Ārya and a Śūdra should engage themselves in a mock fight while a harlot and a *brahmacārī* should abuse each other. Sexual intercourse between a selected man and woman should take place in a screened shed after which there is drum-beating, singing and dancing. *Jaimini* X.4.8, *Śat.Br.* XXVI 6.21ff., *Kāt.Sr.* XIII.3.9, *Śāṅ.Sr.* XVII.15, *Āp.Sr.* XXI.10–20, *Ait.Ār.* I,V., *Tāṇḍya Br.* V.5. 14–17.

mahāvrata The 'five great vows' to be observed by the monks belonging to Lord Mahāvīra's creed who resolve to give up worldly pleasures for the cause of uplifting humanity. The vows are non-violence (*ahiṃsā*), non-stealing (*asteya*), truth (*satya*), celibacy (*brahmacarya*) and non-possession (*aparigraha*). These great vows are simplified for laymen who are required to abstain from gross offences against living beings (fettering, beating, wounding, overloading and cruelty, especially with reference to domestic animals used in agriculture and trade); from gross untruthfulness (falsely accusing a person, passing wrong judgement, forgery etc.); from gross appropriation (receiving or dealing in stolen goods, theft and illegal economic transaction, false weights and measures, adulteration, etc.); from gross sensuality (offences against matrimonial faith, adultery, harlotism, incest, etc.); and from gross greed (attachment to gold, cattle, estate, cart, carriages, jewellery, etc.). *Āyāra*, II.15.1–5; *Uvāsaga* 13ff., 45ff., *Ṭhāṇa*. 290, *Samavāya* 10.

mahāvratadhara A designation for the Kāpālikas (q.v.).

mahayajña The five daily observances or performances. They are Brahmayajña, Devayajña, Pitṛyajña, Bhūtayajña and Manuṣyayajña (qq.v.). These differ from the Śrauta sacrifices in two respects. Firstly, the chief agent is the householder himself who does not need the help of a professional priest. Secondly, the central point of the five Yajñas is the discharge of duty to the creator, to the ancient sages, to the Manes and to the whole universe with it myriads of creatures of various grades and intelligence. In the Śrauta sacrifices the main spring of action is the desire to secure some specific ends. *Śat.Br.* XI.5.6.1, *Taitt.Ār.* I.10, *Āśv.Gr.* III.1. 1–4, *Āp.Dh.S.* I. 4.12–13, *Baudh.Dh.S.* II.6.1–8, etc.

mahāyāna One of the two broad divisions of Buddhism. The object of Mahāyāna is not salvation or enlightenment of individual. It stresses the Buddha's anxiety for the salvation of fellow beings. Mahāyānism insists on the ideal of Bodhisattvahood, that is, the attainment of perfect wisdom with a view to being able to lead all beings out of misery; the deification of Buddha in which he is identified with transcendental reality possessed of the power of incarnation; and the doctrine of vacuity or *śūnyatā* (q.v.) as the reality behind all phenomena. See also Mahāsaṅghika, Mādhyamika, Yogācāra.

mahāyantra See Yantra.

mahayogī An attribute of Śiva.

mahāyoni Female sex organ. It is the supposed triangle of the *Sahasrāra-cakra* (q.v.) *Kaulamārgarahasya* 256.

maheśa-sthala A tenet of the *sthala* (q.v.) conception of the Vīraśaivas.

māheśvara-siddha See under Sittar, Siddhacikitsā, Rasa, Raseśvara darśana, Kāyatattva.

māheśvarī-kṛcchra An expiation in which the sinner has to beg at some houses, donate a cow, and drink *pañcagavya*.

mahimāpantha A liberal mystic religious sect which flourished in medieval Orissa. The members of this sect do not believe in the efficacy of temples and images or in the superiority of the Brāhmaṇas.

mahimāsiddhi A kind of miraculous attainment acquired through the rituals of *aṣṭadala-padma*. *Nityaṣoḍaśikārṇava* VIII.143.

mahīśāsaka Two Buddhist sects. The earlier Mahīśāsakas, described in the Pali sources as branching off from the Sthaviravādins, believe that the past and future have no existence while the present along with nine *asaṃskṛta* (unconstituted) *dhātus* or elements has. The Srotāpannas are subject to retrogression but the *arhats* are not. There is no *antarābhava* (intermediate existence) between the present life and the life to come. No deva can lead a holy life and no heretic can gain supernatural power. The Saṅgha includes the Buddha; therefore a gift given to the former is greatly meritorious while that given to the Buddha is not. According to the *Kathāvatthu* XIX.8, XX.5 they believe that there cannot be controlling faculties like faith, etc., and that the eight-fold path really consists of five. The later Mahīśāsakas have more in common with Sarvāstivādins. They believe in the existence of the past and the future and of *antarābhava*. They hold that the *skandhas*, *dhātus* and *āyatanas* (qq.v.) also exist in form of seeds, that *vitarka* and *vicāra* (initial application and reflection) combine with each other and so on.

mahoraga A class of Nāgas regarded as *vyantara devatās* (q.v.).

maithuna Sexual intercourse which is regarded as one of the *pañcamakāras* or Five Ms. For its procedure and reasons see *Mahānirvāṇa* VI. 10ff, *Prāṇatoṣaṇī* VII.4, 548. For its substitutes see com. on *Paraśurāmakalpasūtra* X.63, *Mahānirvāṇa* VIII.172–73. For spiritual interpretation see *Kaulamārgarahasya* 255–56. *Yoginītantra*, pūrva, VI, *Kulārṇava* V. See under *Yuganaddha*.

maitrakṛcchra A form of penance in which cow urine, cow dung, milk, curd and clarified butter etc. are taken by the sinner after a fast of two days.

maitrī See Mahāmaitrī.

majjha 'Middle'; in Sanskrit *madhya*. According to Buddhism, the real solution of any problem arising from the conflict of thought and action lies in the capacity to find the middle path, to fulfil the *majjha*. Majjha is the keyword of the entire system of early Buddhism. See Majjhimā-paṭipadā.

majjhimā-paṭipadā The Middle Path which is explained as the essence of the Buddhist way of life in the *Dhammacakkapavattana-sutta*. Ethically the Middle Path connotes the moderate life of recluse, i.e., the monastic system prescribed in the Vinaya Piṭaka. Philosophically the Middle Path is explained as the doctrine which keeps clear of the two extreme views about the world—*śāśvata* (eternalism) and *uccheda* (nihilism). The Buddha's teaching opens with the statement that one should avoid the two 'extremes'—one being the life of a worldly man immersed in pleasure and the other the life of a recluse absorbed in self-mortification. He should choose a Middle path which will open his eyes to knowledge and lead him ultimately to *nirvāṇa*.

makāra See Pañcamakāra.

makarasaṅkrānti The last day of the month of *pauṣa* (middle of January) which is celebrated by bathing and other religious observances.

mala Fetters which cover knowledge and actions of the individual; it is a term used by different Śaiva schools. It is same as Pāśa, the cause of worldly existence and suffering. It is of three types—*āṇava*, *karma*, and *māyā*. Āṇavamala is the impurity of the bound self which is responsible for non-intuition. Karmamala is responsible for continuing the fetters of embodiment, and Māyāmala covers the individual soul entirely.

mālā See Akṣamālā.

malamāsa The intercalary month in which Kāmya (q.v.) rites connot be performed.

māṃsa Flesh; it is one of the pañcamakāras or Five Ms. See Mahāmāṃsa. It is supposed to be the body of Śiva. Ginger, garlic, etc. can be used as its substitute.

manaḥparyāya A form of knowledge which according to the Jain conception, belongs to the category of *pratyakṣa* (direct knowledge) to be derived from reading the thoughts of others. *TTDS*, I.9ff.

manana One of the three stages of Jñānayoga (q.v.) which consists in reflection on what the texts teach.

manas Mind. It is the central organ of perception according to the Sāṅkhya. Together with Buddhi (q.v.) and Ahaṃkāra (q.v.) it constitutes the internal group (*antaḥkaraṇa*) while the senses of sight, hearing, etc., and the organs of action are the external (*bāhyakaraṇa*). It interprets the indeterminate sense-data supplied by the external organs into determinate perception. The Sāṅkhya view of Manas differs from those of other systems. According to the Nyāya-Vaiśeṣika, Manas is an enternal atomic substance, but the Sāṅkhya holds it to be a composite product of Prakṛti (q.v.) and so subject to origin and decay. While the former admits only Manas and the five external senses as *indriyas* and holds that the external senses are derived from the physical elements, the latter enumerates eleven *indriyas* and derives all of them from the principle of egoity (Ahaṃkāra) which, however, is not recognised as a separate principle by other systems. In Jainism the body, the senses and the mind (*manas*) are all treated as being constituted by *karma* (q.v.), which as external stimuli shape and control all mental actions.

mānasa-dīkṣā See *manodīkṣā*.

mānasa-snāna Reflecting on god Viṣṇu; it is regarded as having the same purificatory effect of bathing in a holy river.

māna-stambha A free standing pillar-standard crowned by Jina images.

mañca A variety of *adhiṣṭhāna* (q.v.) in South Indian temples.

maṇḍala Ājīvika (q.v.) term for persons who have achieved liberation. In the Tantric tradition, *maṇḍala* means a gathering of aspirants who will perform collectively the rituals of the five Ms. They sit in a circle (*cakra*) along with their female partners, with the *nāyaka* or *adhīśvara*, the central figure of the ritual and his consort in the middle. *Kaulāvalīnirṇaya* VIII, *Mahānirvāṇa* VIII. 154–59. Maṇḍala also denotes Tantric diagrams of which there are many varieties such as Sarvatobhadra, etc.

maṇḍapa Platform erected for a variety of religious purposes.

mandiramārgī Term for Jain idol-worshippers.

maṇḍovara Architectural term current in western India for the *pīṭha*, *vedibandha* and *jaṅghā* of temple architecture.

maṅgala Eight objects which are regarded as auspicious.

maṅgalasūtra A string of golden and other beads which is worn round the neck by brides.

maṇi-kūṭa The building in which the holy book is placed on a pedestal, or where the image is installed, for the purpose of worship. Such buildings were erected by the Vaiṣṇava followers of Śaṅkaradeva in Assam.

maṇipura A Tantric *cakra* or nerve plexus located near the navel region. It is also called *nābhicakra*. It looks like a ten-petalled blue lotus, each petal containing a letter. Within the lotus there is a triangle of colour of the rising sun. On the three outer sides of the triangle are represented three *svastika* symbols. The goddess Lākinī presides over by this *cakra*. *Ṣaṭcakranirūpaṇa* XIX–XXI.

maṅkha A class of religious mendicants to which the father of Gośāla Maṅkhaliputta probably belonged. Maṅkha also means painter and bard.

manodīkṣā Also known as *mānasa* or *vedhamayīdīkṣā*, it is a form of initiation performed only by the Guru's thought and mental action. *Kulārṇava* XIV.

manonmanī A state of transcendental bliss which comes about as a result of *bhaktiyoga-samādhi*, i.e., loss of identity through deep meditation in a spirit of absolute devotion. *Gheraṇḍa* VII.14–15. Manonmanī is also the name of the Śakti of Sadāśiva in South Indian Śaivism.

mantra The words rising from the depths (*ninyā vacāṃsi*, *RV* IV.3.16). Mantras are products of spiritual mentation, says Yāska (*Nirukta* VII.12). In the Brāhmaṇa texts and also in the Mīmāṃsā tradition, the sole import of the *mantras* lies in the urge to perform ritualistic action alone. Mantra is also an inspired utterance with an esoteric meaning (*rahasya*) which has been clearly stated in the *Gopatha Br.* I. 2.20. The *RV*.I.164.39, IV.3.16, VIII.100.10, X.71.3–5, X.114.8, X.125.7 etc. draws attention to the esoteric meaning of the Mantras. In commenting on *RV* X.71.5 Yāska says that esoterically the knowledge of the gods and of the self is the flower and fruit of the word, i.e. *mantra*. *Nirukta* I.20. In the Tantric tradition *mantra* is the *śakti* (power) in the form of sound, words and letters. It is the culture (*man*, *manana*) of true knowledge necessary to get rid of worldly fetters. Rāghava on *Śāradātilaka* VIII.1. Mantra is *brahman* or ultimate reality in the form of sound. Letters, words and sentences are its different forms through which *Śakti* appears in the individual. *Gandharvatantra* XL.10. com. on *Tantrarājatantra* XXVI.36–43, *Śāradātilaka* I.55, II 57. The *mantras* constitute the backbone of Vajrayāna worship. The Vajrayanists maintain that the *mantras* are endowed with great powers, and can even confer Buddhahood or omniscience. The *mantra* is powerful when it comes from a preceptor who is pure, and has repeated it continuously, so as to visualize the *mantra*-person or the deity sacred to the *mantra*. When the *mantra* becomes powerful, the vibrations let loose by the worshipper react on the universal *śūnya*.

mantra-adhva Blood, to be purified for Tantric *sādhanā*. Adhva means constituents of the body; these are of six types—*bhuvana* (cerebral organs), *mantra* (blood and flesh), *pada* (muscles), *varṇa* (veins), *dhatu* (bones) and *rita* (fluid substance). Rāghava on *Śāradātilaka* V.95–96.

mantra-caitanya Consciousness latent in the *mantra* which must be roused by efforts. *Prāṇatoṣaṇī* IV, 1,222, *Puraścaryārṇava* VI, 528, *Gandharvatantra* XXIX. 24–25.

mantra-naya Also known as *mantrayāna* it is one of the two subdivisions of the Mahāyāna in which great importance is attached to *mantras* or spells. Naropā and Advayavajra were inclined to use the term *mantranaya* to designate Tantric Buddhism. *Śekoddeśaṭīkā* 2–5, *Advayavajrasaṃgraha* 14. According to this school, if the mantras are applied in a proper way anything can be performed. Their power and efficacy are beyond dispute; they offer the possibility of attaining Buddhahood to the aspirant. *Sādhanamālā* I.87,270,334, II 575, 606, *Guhyasamāja* 27ff, *Hevajra* I.50ff. This *mantra-naya* or *mantrayāna* is the precursor of Vajrayāna (q.v.) and its offshoots *Kālacakrayāna* (q.v.) and *Sahajayāna* (q.v.).

mantrapuruṣa A term for deity in Tantric Buddhist tradition. The deity is supposed to be the embodiment of a cluster of letters which are dynamized by intense concentration and repetition. The second set of letters set up strong vibrations and ultimately condense themselves in the form of deities. This is called the *mantrapuruṣa* or *mantra*-person.

mantrārtha Understanding the significance of *mantra*; it is the sense of identity of the preceptor, deity and *mantra*. The understanding is threefold—the simple meaning of the *mantra*, the belief that every letter of it is the manifestation of the real nature of Śakti, and the merger of the aspirant in the essence of the object of his exercise. *Puraścaryārṇava* VI. 526, *Tantrarāja* XXXV. 64–66.

mantra-śakti The power of *mantra*; it is beyond thinking and reasoning. *Paraśurāmakalpasūtra* I.8. It is neither good nor bad. It is determined only by the purpose of its application.

mantrasaṃskāra Ten ways of purifying *mantras*. They are *janana, jīvana, tāḍana, bodhana, abhiṣeka, vimalīkaraṇa, āpyāyana, tarpaṇa, dīpana* and *gupti* (qq.v.). *Tantrasāra* 52.

mantraśikhā A purificatory flame aroused in the body during the march of Kuṇḍalinī (q.v.). *Puraścaryārṇava* VI, 527–28, *Haṭhayogapradīpikā* IV.10.

mantrasiddhi Spiritual attainment through *mantras*. Those who have attained it acquire a special brightness of body and an ever-peaceful state of mind. *Puraścaryārṇava*, VI. 557–58.

mantra-snāna Sprinkling water on the body with the verses beginning *āpo hi ṣṭhā* from *RV* X.9.1–3.

mantraśodhana Purification of *mantra* with *prāṇāyāma* (breath control) according to the Yonimudrā process (q.v.) and reciting it one thousand and eight times. Rāghava on *Śāradātilaka* II. 111.

mantraśuddhi Purification of *mantra* by reciting the letters from left to right and right to left. *Kulārṇava* VI.

mantra-tanu Transformed state of the body achieved either by Yogic exercise or by the use of drugs. The body of God is also called *mantra-tanu*.

mantrayāna A form of Tantric Buddhism. See *mantra-naya*.

māntrayoga The *haṃsa* (q.v.) practice of Yoga by inhaling (*haṃ*) and exhaling (*saḥ*) of breath. *Yogaśikhopaniṣat* I. 130–32.

māntrī-dīkṣa Initiation in which the Guru by *mantra* and rituals makes himself renovated in spiritual strength and then consecrates the disciple Rāghava on *Śāradātilaka* V. 127–40. It requires *kumbha*, *maṇḍala* and other objects. *Prāṇatoṣaṇī* II.4, 11.

mānuṣa-liṅga Largest group of the Sthira-liṅgas (q.v.). These are made of three parts—*rudrabhāga* or *pūjābhāga*, *visṇubhāga* and *brahmabhāga*. Brahmasūtra design (carving of certain lines) should be present on *mānuṣaliṅgas* which are grouped under various heads on the basis of different criteria. See *mukha-liṅga*.

manuṣyakulaṃkula The Kolaṃkola (Kulāṃkula, a sub-stage between Sotāpanna and Sakadāgami), denoting an individual who has acquired *anāsrava indriyas* (pure faculties) who is reborn among men in the Buddhist scheme of spiritual evolution. *Abhidharmakośa* (Poussin) II.34, *Visuddhimagga* 709.

manuṣyaprakṛti-deva Deities originally human by nature, i.e., deified human beings.

manuṣya-yajña One of the five *mahāyajñas* for householders; it is performed for honouring guests. Also known as Nṛyajña. *Āp.Dh.S.* II. 4.9.2–4, *Baudh.Gr.* II.9.1–2, *Manu* III.70, etc.

manvantara A period in the vast span of time. Each *manvantara* has a separate set of sages, gods, kings, *smṛtis*, etc. fourteen *manvantaras* constitute a Kalpa (q.v.). See Yuga.

māraṇa The black act of killing through rites and spells.

mārga Way of spiritual attainment. There are three *mārgas*: *jñāna* or way of knowledge, *karma* or way of work, and *bhakti* or way of devotion. The Buddhists believe in eight *mārgas*. See magga.

mārgajñātavatara True knowledge of the path, in Buddhist terminology.

mārjanā Part of Saṃdhyā (q.v.) ritual; it is performed by means of *kuśa* grass dipped in water and with chanting of *mantras* from *RV* X.9.

mārjāra-mārga Way of devotion in which the devotee should exert no effort of his own but surrender to God's will just as a kitten remains quite passive in its mother's mouth when she carries it from one place to another.

markaṭa-mārga Way of devotion in which the devotee should cling to God just as a monkey-child clings to its mother.

mārtaṇḍa-bhairava Syncretic image combining the aspects of the sun and Śiva.

maskarin A class of Parivrājakas (wandering ascetics) who used to carry *maskara* or bamboo staff. (*Pāṇini* VI.1.154). Probably Gośāla Maṅkhaliputta, teacher of the Ājīvika sect, belonged to this group.

maṭha Religious establishments.

mati Form of knowledge which according to the Jain conception belongs to the category of *parokṣa* (indirect knowledge of existing things acquired through the senses and mind). *TTDS*, I. 13–14.

mātikā Architectonics of Buddhist thought. As abstract schemes, these are fixed once and for all, while the processions are left to be envisaged through individual experience. In other words, all the words of Buddha contained in the Pali canon can be reduced to certain *mātikās* or abstract schemes of thought, developed and applied variously at different occasions and to suit certain purposes.

mātrā A means of *prāṇāyāma* (q.v.). *Puraścaryārṇava* III, 161.

mātṛkā Divine Mothers. It is also the name of mystic letters.

mātṛkānyāsa Feeling the Mātṛkās or *śakti* manifested in the form of letters in different parts of the body. It is of two kinds, *antarmātṛkānyāsa* and *bahirmātṛkānyāsa*. *Tantrasāra* 88ff.

mātṛkāvarṇa The letters from A to Kṣa, each symbolising an aspect of Śakti or the Great Mother.

mātsarya Jealousy; it is regarded as one of the six enemies (*ripu*) of man.

matsya Fish; it is one of the Five Ms. Three types of fish—*uttama, madhyama* and *adhama*—are described in *Śyāmārahasya* III, *Mahānirvāṇa* VI.8. Substitutes for *matsya* are cakes made of pulses and other articles. Com. on *Paraśurāmakalpasūtra* X.63. Symbolically *matsya* is described as that which destroys the fetters and leads to the way of salvation. *Prāṇatoṣaṇī* VII.2, 508. *Matsya* (fish) is the first incarnation of Viṣṇu.

mattamayūra A Śaiva sect which had its centre in the Haihaya kingdom of Tripuri. The followers of this sect laid emphasis on *atimārga* or out-of-the-way practices. The teachers used *śiva* or *śambhu* as suffixes to their names.

mauli Various types of headgear found in icons. These have been described in the *Mānasāra* as *jaṭā-makuṭa, kīriṭa-makuṭa, karaṇḍa-makuṭa, śirastraka, kuntala, keśabandha, dhammilla* and *alaka-cūḍaka*.

māyā Also known as *avidyā* (q.v.) and *prakṛti* (q.v.) the term is used in many senses. In the Advaita Vedānta it is regarded as the energy of Īśvara (q.v.) which becomes transformed into *upādhi* (q.v.) (limitation), the unmanifested matter (*avyākṛtaprakṛti*) from which all existence issues. Śaṅkara's com. on *Ved.Sūt* I.4.3, II.1.14, II.2.2., The world is also called māyā by Śaṅkara because of its unreality. Kumārila in his *Slokavārtika*, Jha's tr. 355ff, has criticised this view saying that *māyā* cannot be at the root of creation since there was no entity other than the *brahman* on the eve of creation. Thus it cannot be said that *brahman*, the only reality, induced the unreal dreamlike *māyā* to create. The conception of Saguṇa or changing *brahman* who, as Īśvara, combines within himself the nature of both the unattached *brahman* and the unconscious *prakṛti* or *māyā* is not, therefore, tenable. The later Advaitavādins have different views. Padmapāda and his followers hold that the world is a mixture of *brahman* and *māyā*, the former as the existent appears to undergo change and the latter as non-intelligent is subject to change. Sarvajña, on the other hand, holds that *māyā* is the product of *brahman* and a process of its activity, not any substance, and so cannot be regarded as the material cause. There is another group which holds that *māyā* is the only cause of the world, feeling strongly against subjecting *brahman* to any kind of relation. According to the *Padārthatattvanirṇaya*, *brahman* is the *vivarta* cause of the world, i.e., where the cause does not change in quality and substance in the effect just as gold remains gold in the form of a bangle, while *māyā* is the *pariṇāma* cause of the world, i.e., where the cause qualitatively changes in effect just as milk changes when it becomes curd. Vācaspati holds that while *brahman* is the cause, *māyā* is auxiliary (*sahakārī*). In theistic interpretations of Vedānta *māyā* is regarded as the *Śakti* or energy of *brahman* like heat in fire. For the Acintya-bhedābheda concept of *māyā* see *māyāśakti*. Also see Aśuddhamāyā and Śuddhamāyā.

māyāmala One of the three impurities (*malas*) according to the Śaiva schools. It covers or conceals the individual soul as a result of which it begins to experience objects as distinct from the self.

māyāmoha A name of Viṣṇu's Buddha incarnation.

māyā-śakti The material principle which is variously viewed by different schools of thought. (See Māyā). According to the Acintyabhedābheda school, it is that aspect of the power of Kṛṣṇa which is insentient, is constituted of three *guṇas* (*sattva, rajas* and *tamas*) and has two aspects, *pradhāna* and *prakṛti*. As *pradhāna*, it is transformed through the creative energy of God into the inanimate material substance of the created universe and becomes its secondary material cause. As *prakṛti* it makes worldly-minded souls assume material bodies in the created universe by suppressing the knowledge of their true nature and thus becomes the secondary efficient cause of the universe.

māyīamala See under *māyāmala*. According to Kaśmīra Śaivism it represents the whole series of categories of existence, beginning from the covers or Kañcukas. These Kañcukas, like *māyā* of the Vedāntic tradition, are somehow associated with *brahman* or Śiva as creative energy with the potentiality of yielding the material principles. As such they are the cause of the physical organism on the subjective side. Functionally these evolve into the physical world down to earth constituted by the gross elements or the *mahābhūtas* (q.v.), which is a reflection on the objective side.

medhāyajña A sacrament for a child which consists in muttering in its right ear the word *vāk* thrice. *Śān.Gr.* I.24.9, *Baudh.Gr.* II.1.7, *Taitt.Br.* II.5.1, *Manu* II.29. Again on the fourth day after *upanayana* (q.v.) a rite is performed called *medhāyajña* which is supposed to make the student capable of mastering the Vedas. cf. *Āśv.Gr.* I.22.18–19.

mekhalā A girdle; it is given to the initiate at the time of Upanayana (q.v.).

mettābhāvanā Amity towards all beings. See Maitrī, Mahāmaitrī, *Majjhima* I.17, 124.

micchādiṭṭhi False perception in Buddhist terminology.

micchattaniyāma Wrong path or guide in Buddhist terminology.

miśramata One of the approaches of the aspirants belonging to the Śrīvidyā cult. *Saubhāgyabhāskara* on *Lalitāsahasranāma* 144.

miśravindu The Vindu (q.v.) produced from the equilibrium of *prakāśa* (static) and *vimarśa* (kinetic) aspects of Śakti. *Cidvallī* on *Kāmakalāvilāsa* 6–7.

mitavāda Extensionism. *Ṭhāna* IV.4. See Antānantika and Akriyāvāda.

mithyātva Falsity. The word *mithyā* in Śaṅkara's commentary means *anirvacanīyatā* (indefinable ignorance) and not *apahnava* (negation). According to Padmapāda, anything that is neither existent (*sat*) nor non-existent (*asat*) is false. Prakāśātman adds to this definition two others: (1) whatever is destroyed by true knowledge is false; and (2) whatever can be negated for all time on its own ground or where it was known to exist is false.

According to Jainism it is delusion, a constituent of *bhāvāsrava* (q.v.). It is of five kinds: *ekānta* (false belief unknowingly accepted and uncritically followed); *viparīta* (uncertainty in the nature of truth); *vinaya* (retention of a belief knowing it to be false); *saṃsaya* (doubt); and *ajñāna* (ignorance).

moha Delusion; it is regarded as one of the six enemies of man. In Buddhism it is regarded as belonging to the category of four universal bad properties. According to Jainism it is an *āvaraṇa* (cover) which generates worldly attachments and passions.

mokṣa Liberation; salvation; emancipation; the highest good, absolute bliss. According to Jain ideas when a Jiva is freed from the bondage of Karma and has passed for ever beyond the possibility of rebirth, it is said to have attained *mokṣa* or liberation. It is a state of pure happiness (*anantasukha*), pure and infinite knowledge (*anantajñāna*) and infinite perception (*anantadarśana*). Every Jīva (q.v.) has the potential for liberation, which is achieved by faith, knowledge and conduct. *PTSMS*, 28, *DS*, 39–40.

In Buddhism, the term Nirvāṇa (q.v.) is used instead of Mokṣa or Mukti which is cessation of suffering. It is not extinction of existence, but the extinction of misery and of the causes of rebirth. Buddha's silence about the condition of the liberated after death may or may not mean his denial of the existence of such a person after death. The real nature of Nirvāṇa can only be realised, it cannot be described in terms of ordinary experience.

The Nyāya-Vaiśeṣikas hold that liberation is freedom from all pain and suffering. Apavarga (liberation) is absolute freedom from pain which implies that it is a state in which the soul is released from its connection with the body and the senses. It is just that unfettered condition of the soul which had been variously described as freedom from fear (*abhayam*), freedom from decay and change (*ajaram*), freedom from death (*amṛtyupadam*) and so forth. *Nyāyabhāṣya* I.1.22. To attain liberation one should listen to scriptural instructions (*śravaṇa*), understand them by means of reason (*manana*) and meditate on the self in conformity with the principles of Yoga (*nididhyāsana*).

According to the Sāṅkhya, the attainment of liberation means just the clear recognition of the self as a reality which is beyond time and space and also body and mind. It is essentially free, eternal and immortal. The term which the Sāṅkhya uses for liberation is Mukti; it means complete destruction of the threefold misery (*duḥkhatraya-bhighāta*, q.v.). There are two kinds of liberation, viz. Jivanmukti (q.v.) and Videhamukti (q.v.). The former is liberation within the span of life and the latter after the death. *Sāṅ.Sūt.* I.56; 3.66, 75; 5.74–63; 6.20; *Sāṅ.Kārikā* 59–68. According to the *Yogasūtra* I.5–11, II.3–9 liberation consists in restraining the activities of the body, the senses and the mind (*manas*) and in finally suppressing all the mental modifications (*cittavṛtti*).

In the Mīmāṃsā tradition the highest good is the attainment of heaven or a state in which there is absolute bliss. Later Mimāṁsakas conceived of something like liberation in line with other philosophical systems. They hold that since consciousness and other mental states are not inherent in the soul, the liberated soul, being dissociated from the body and sense organs, cannot have any consciousness and therefore cannot enjoy bliss. It is only a condition of unconscious state, free from pleasure and pain.

According to the Advaita Vedānta, realisation of the identity between the self and the *brahman* (q.v.) is liberation from bondage which is possible even while the soul is associated with the body. See Jīvanmukti. It is not the attainment of something new. It is only recognition of what already exists like finding a necklace around the neck after forgetting its existence and searches all over. Bondage is due to illusion, and liberation is only the removal of this illusion. It is not merely the absence of all misery that arises from the illusory sense of distinction between the Self and the *brahman*. It is a state of positive bliss. Work fetters a man only when it is performed with attachment. But one who has obtained perfect knowledge is free from attachment and can work without the hope of gain. Śaṅkara's com. on *Brahmasūtra* I.1.4 etc. on *Bhagavadgīta* III.20–26, IV.14. etc. Rāmānuja and most of the theistic interpreters of Vedānta hold that bondage is due to Karma and liberation is to be sought through knowledge, action and devotion. The knowledge of God matures into constant remembrance, or devotion, which turns into immediate knowledge of God whose grace is required for liberation. The liberated soul has pure consciousness and is a perfect being (*brahmaprakāra*) but it can not be absolutely identical with *brahman*. *Śrībhāṣya* I.1.1.ff. Belief in the possibility of liberation which is regarded as the highest good, is thus common to all Indian systems. See also Bandha, Jivanmukti, Nirvāṇa.

mokṣa-mārga The path to realise salvation.

mudgara Hammer; staff; mace; used as weapons by gods.

mūḍha Superstitious ignorance in Jain terminology. It is of three types—*loka-mūḍha* (general belief among people that by performing certain acts one acquires sanctity), *deva-mūḍha* (belief regarding the efficacy of propitiation of gods) and *pāṣaṇḍī-muḍha* (superstitions regarding false ascetics and so called godmen).

muditā Joy, which is one of the four *brahmavihārabhavanā* or positive contemplations of the Buddhists. The *Yogasūtra* I.33 also uses this term in the sense of taking delight in the virtuous deeds of fellowmen.

mudrā Posture of the body, especially of hands, needed for yogic exercise and spiritual attainment. *Gheraṇḍasaṃhitā* III.1–3 records such *mudrās* as Mahā, Nabho, Uḍḍīyāna, Jālandhara, Mūlabandha, Mahābodha, Khecarī, Viparītakarī, Yoni, Vajroli, Śakticālanī, Tadagī, Maṇḍukī, Śāmbhavī, Pañcadhāriṇī, Aśvinī, Pāśinī, Kākī, Mataṅgī and Bhujaṅginī. See also *Haṭhayogapradīpikā*, III.128. *Mudrās* like Varada, Abhaya, Namaskāra, Añjali, Dharmacakra (qq.v.) etc. are commonly found in iconic representation symbolising the quality associated with the deity.

mudrāpīṭhas One of the four symbolic *pīṭhas* (seats) of Tantric *sādhanā*. The others are *vidyā*, *mantra* and *maṇḍala*.

mudrika General term for pen-names of Tamil devotional writers.

mukhaliṅga A class of *mānuṣa-liṅga*; they are conventional in character. They denote those emblems which show on their *rudra* or *pūjābhāgas* one or more human faces. The *Rupamaṇḍana* mentions three, one and four-faced *mukhaliṅgas*.

mukha-maṇḍapa Frontal *maṇḍapa* or entrance-porch of a temple.

mukhaśodhana Purification of the tongue by

mantras. *Prāṇatoṣuṇi* VI.1, 215.

mukti Salvation. See *mokṣa*.

mukuta See Mauli.

mūlādhāra The first of the six nerve plexuses. It is situated in the lowest extremity of the spinal cord where the Kuṇḍalinī (q.v.) is coiled. *Ṣaṭcakra-nirūpaṇa* V.

mūlaguṇa Fundamental qualities of a Jain ascetic. These are twenty-eight in number.

mūlakṛcchra An expiation in which the sinner has to subsist on lotus stalks or roots. *Viṣṇu Dh.S.* XLVI.15, *Mit* on *Yāj* III.316.

mūla-nāyaka The principal enshrined deity in a temple.

mūla-prāsāda Sanctum proper in a temple.

mūlasarvāstivāda See under Sarvāstivāda. This sect had a Vinaya of its own which was translated into Chinese by I-tsing in 710 A.D.; it is somewhat different from the Sarvāstivādin version.

mūlasūtta Four texts forming part of the Jain canon. They are *Uttarājjhāyā* (Uttarādhyayana Sūtra), *Dasaveyāliya, Āvassaya-nijjutti* and *Piṇḍanijjutti*.

mūlaveda A term for Pāñcarātra Āgamas.

mumukṣutva Yearning for liberation. It is the driving force in the spiritual path according to *Muṇḍaka Up*. I.2.12.

muṇḍana Shaving the hair on the head as well as the moustache and beard.

munitraya-sampradāya A subsect of the Śrī-vaiṣṇavas of South India. It is named after three sages or teachers; Śrīnivāsa, Raṅganātha and Vedānta Rāmānuja.

mūrti Term for an image and incarnation (*avatāra*).

mūrtipūjaka One of the three Śvetāmbara sub-sects of the Jains; also known as Pujera and Derāvāsī.

mūrtisthāna Material used for making images of deities which can be of seven kinds.

muttācāra Lack of social manners.

nābhipadma Another name of *maṇipura-cakra* (q.v.). *Ṣaṭcakranirūpaṇa* XIX.

nāda Sound. In Tantrism, the supreme being (Para Śiva or Parā Śakti) is soundless without any vibration. When this Parā Śakti begins to express itself in creation, its first vibration is known as *nāda*. It is the manifestation of the consciousness of the supreme being revealed as sound. This manifestation is thought of in terms of the union of Śiva and Śakti (the static and kinetic aspects, also known as *prakāśa* and *vimarśa*, of the same ultimate reality). The thrill of the pleasure of this union (*maithuna*) is also known as *nāda*. The condensed form of *nāda* is *vindu*. *Śāradātilaka* I.6ff, Kālīcaraṇa on *Ṣaṭcakranirūpaṇa* XXXIX, *Prapañcasāra* I.41. For other aspects and interpretation see under *vindu* and *vīja*.

nādabrahma Nāda conceived as *brahman* in the form of primordial sound expressed in *parā, paśyantī, madhyamā* and *vaikharī* (qq.v.). Cidvallī on *Kāmakalāvilāsa* IX, Lakṣmīdhara on *Saundaryalaharī* XLI.

nādanta Śiva's dance.

nāda-udbhūta Sixteen *kalās* or *śaktis* which are said to have been derived from *nāda* (q.v.). These are Nivṛtti, Pratiṣṭhā, Vidyā, Śānti, Indhikā, Dīpikā, Recikā, Mocikā, Parā, Parāparāyanā, Sukṣmā, Amṛtā, Āpyāyinī, Vyāpinī, Vyomarūpā and Anantā. *Prapañcasāra* III.25–27, *Śāradātilaka* II.26.

nāḍī Nerves of the human body. These are supposed to be 72,000 in number; 72 are major nerves and the most important 14 are: *iḍā, piṅgalā, susumnā, gāndhārī, hastijihvā, yaśasvinī, alambuṣā, kuhū, śaṅkhinī, sarasvatī, vāruṇī, puṣā, viśvodarā* and *payasvinī*. *Prāṇatoṣaṇī*, 1.4, 32–33.

nāḍiśuddhi Purification of the nerves. When done by *mantras* it is known as *samāna* and when by physical exercises like *dhauti* etc., it is known as *nirvāṇa*. *Gheraṇḍa* V.36.

nāgapañcami A *vrata* or observance either on the fifth day of the bright or dark half of Śrāvaṇa (Aug-Sept) in which *nāga* or snake images or symbols are worshipped in different parts of India. In some places, specially in Bengal, Manasā or the presiding deity of the serpents, is worshipped. The *nāga* cult is of primitive heritage and its importance has not diminished. Indian mythology is full of *nāga* legends, and eight celebrated *nāgas* are objects of extensive cults. Nāga symbols occur frequently in all forms of Indian religious systems. Snakes as *āsana* (seat), *chatra* (umbrella), *bhūṣaṇa* (ornament) and in other capacities are connected with different gods and depicted in their iconic representations.

nāgavali Offering to propitiate snakes in expiation of the sin of killing a snake, which is believed to be an obstacle to securing progeny. According to *Saṃskārakaustubha* 122 in this rite a figure of a serpent is to be made of rice or wheat, placed in a *sūrpa* (winnowing basket) and worshipped with sixteen articles.

nagna-kṣapaṇaka Naked ascetics. The term was often used for the Digambara Jain monks.

nagna-pracchadana A Śrāddha (q.v.) to be performed on the day of the death of a person. It consists in filling a sack with grains and other articles and giving it to a poor Brāhmaṇa of good family for the benefit of the departed. After this the dead person's relatives shave and bathe and only then return to the village and re-enter the home.

naimittika-pūjā Occasional worship for the attainment of a certain purpose. In the sense of 'occasional' the term *naimittika* is prefixed to other categories of acts. There are two other forms—*nitya* and *kāmya* (qq.v.).

nairātmya The denial of *ātman* (q.v.); literally, the 'state of being devoid of *ātman*' which is one of the basic features of Buddhist thought. Nairātmya is two fold, *pudgala-nairātmya* and *dharma-nairātmya*. By the former it is understood that what is believed to be self or *ātman* has no real independent nature of its own and consequently no existence in fact; therefore it is not a thing in reality, but exists merely in imagination as a name. By the latter is meant that the *dharmas*, or things around, internal or external, do not have their *ātman* or independent nature because they depend for their being on causes and conditions. Hence they have no real existence.

naiṣkarmya Complete inaction; it is upheld by certain schools of thought as the goal of life. It cannot be attained by merely abstaining from physical work while continuing to think of sense-objects for such thinking is also action and capable of binding the soul.

naiṣṭhika Students who dedicate themselves to lifelong studentship.

naivedya Food offering to the gods; it is regarded as the sixth *upacāra* (presentable articles), the others being *pādya, gandha, puṣpa, dhūpa* and *dīpa*.

nakṣatra Stars as objects of propitiation for their

auspicious or inauspicious effect. In the Vedic literature and in the Vedāṅga-Jyotiṣa the *nakṣatras* are enumerated from Kṛttikā to Apabharaṇī, and not from Aśvinī to Revatī as in medieval and modern times. The oldest lists of the stars and their presiding deities are found in *AV* XIX.7.2–5, *Taitt.Saṃ.* IV.4. 10.1–3, *Taitt.Br.* I.5.1, III.1.1., *Sān.Gr.* I.20.

nakṣatra-snāna Ceremonial baths in the worship of *nakṣatras* (stars) from Aśvinī to Revatī and their presiding deities which are supposed to yield various benefits. *Atharvanapariśiṣṭa* I.37–50.

nakulī Mongoose, the characteristic animal of Jambhala. The mongoose is believed to be the receptacle of all gems and when the god of wealth presses the animal, it vomits forth all the riches.

nāma Name of God which is prescribed to be recited or sung as the only mode of worship instead of *mantras* and rituals. This has been taught by most of the medieval religious reformers who introduced liberal devotional systems. The concept of *nāma-māhātmya* (glorification of God's name) had an obvious connection with the mystique of institutional worship. Nāma-śaraṇa (refuge in the name of God) as the only means of *sādhanā* or spiritual aspiration may be linked with the *Gītā* maxim, *māmekaṃ śaraṇam vraja*, signifying implicit resignation to one personal God.

namadheya The fourth class of Vedic texts bearing on *dharma* which lists the proper names of sacrifices.

nāma-ghar Prayer houses established by Śaṅkaradeva of Assam in which Kīrtanas or prayer-songs dedicated to the Lord were sung by the devotees.

nāmakaraṇa The ceremony of naming a child. It should be done only on specific days; the Gṛhyasūtras enumerate detailed rules for naming. *Āp.Gr.* XV.8–11, *Āśv.Gr.* I.15.4–10, *Baudh.Gr.* II.1.23–31, *Bhār.Gr.* I.26, *Gobhila.Gr.* II.8.8–18, *Hir.Gr.* II.4.6–15. *Kāṭhaka Gr.* XXXIV.1–2, *Mānava Gr.* I.18.1; *Śān.Gr.* I. 24.4–6.

nāma-kīrtana See Kīrtana.

nāma-rūpa Name and Form, or Mind and Matter. It is the fourth point in the chain of the Buddhist doctrine of causation. Buddhaghoṣa derives *nāma* from the root *nam*, to bend, and says that among the five *khandas* (*skandha*, q.v.) or constituents *sañña, vedanā, saṅkhārā* and *viññāna* (qq.v.) are subjects which can be bent and can direct the mind to the object. *Rūpa*, the fifth, is the material constituent. See Khanda.

nāma-siddhānta A religious movement launched in the Kāverī delta by Śrīdhara Venkaṭeśa and Bodhendra which popularised the idea that the recital of God's name was the most potent means of salvation.

namaskāra Joining the palms to show respect or for the purpose of salutation. It is also *mudrā* or hand-pose. The distinction between *abhivādana* and *namaskāra* is that in the former, one bows and utters some words while in the latter one only bows with folded hands.

nāmavyatiṣañjanīya Name of two *homas* (q.v.) offered in the Rājasūya (q.v.). First the son is declared to be the father of his father and then the relationship is rightly put. This is followed by a symbolic march for the plunder of cows. *Āp.Sr.* XVII.16. 14–15; *Kāt.Sr.* XV. 6.11.

ñāna Jñāna or knowledge in Buddhist terminology. It is of three kinds—*pubbenivāsānussati-ñāna* (the faculty of recalling all past experiences of oneself acquired in successive births or existences); *sattāṇam-cutūpapāṭa-ñāna*(the faculty of visualising the rise and fall of all beings from one state to another according to their deeds); and *āsavānaṃkhaya-ñāna* (the faculty of perceiving the course of the attenuation of all extraneous impediments to consciousness). *Majjhima* I, Bhayabherava Sutta.

ñānadassana The Buddhist term for introspective knowledge.

nāndīśrāddha A form of *Śrāddha* or rite for the spiritual welfare of departed ancestors which is a necessary preliminary in Upanayana and other *saṃskāras* (q.v.). Also known as *nāndīmukha*.

nandivaktra The west-facing bull-face of Śiva.

nandotsava Celebration on the day following *janmāṣṭamī* (q.v.). It is celebrated as the day of Nanda's great joy at his supreme luck in receiving the babe Kṛṣṇa and thus becoming his foster father. The celebration is marked by taking out a magnificent procession..

naṅgālī-bihu An Assamese celebration; it is the festival of amusements. It is basically a harvest festival marked by the feeling of renovation in nature and individuals. Held in the middle of April on the last day of the Indian year, i.e., on *mahāviṣuva-saṅkrānti*, it marks the close of the festive season which starts with *māgha-bihu* or *bhogāli-bihu* in the middle of January.

napuṃsaka-mantra Mantras which are neither male nor female. The mantras for male deities are known as *puruṣa*-mantra and those intended for female deities are known as *strī-mantra* or *vidyā*. The rest belong to the *napuṃsaka* category. *Śāradātilaka* II.57–58.

napuṃsaka-varṇa Letters which are neither male nor female. To this category belong long *r* and long *l*. Rāghava on *Śāradātilaka* II.5–7.

naraka Hell. The word may be derived in two ways: *ni* and *araka*, as meaning 'going below' (the earth) or *na* and *ra* and *ka*, meaning 'where there is not the slightest place for joy'. Narakaloka is mentioned in *AV* XII.4.36. It is supposed to be a place below the earth. Various forms of hell and the tortures inflicted there on sinners are described in the Purāṇas in details.

naraka-caturdaśī Same as *bhūtacaturdaśī*.

naramedha Human sacrifice.

nārayanạbali Offering of *piṇḍas* (food meant for the dead) in the name of Viṣṇu; it is meant only for those who commit suicide. It is to be offered one year after the death of the person concerned. *Mit* on *Yāj* III.6. It may also be performed on the 12th day after death for ascetics.

nāriṣṭha Name of six homas (q.v.) offered in the *darśapurṇamāsa* (q.v.). The *mantras* for these *homas* are adopted from *Taitt.Br.* III. 7.5ff, and *Taitt.Sam.* I.3.10.1. See also *Āp.Sr.* II.20–21.

na-santi-paralokavāda Doctrine identifying body with soul and seeking the *summum bonum* of life in worldly pleasures *Thāṇa* IV.4. See under Akriyāvāda.

nāsikā In temple architecture, the projected arched opening of a southern *vimāna*. Alpanāsikā or Kṣudranāsikā is small, while Mahānāsikā is large.

nāstika See Āstika. Manu II.11 defines *nāstika* as a person who challenges the authority of Vedas. In this sense the Jains, Buddhists and Cārvākas are regarded as *nāstikas* and are condemned. (*Vas.Dh.S.* XII.41, *Viṣṇu Dh.S.* LXXI.83, *Mbh* XII.37.11, *Yaj* II.288, *Gaut.* XXI.1 etc.). According to Kumārila *nāstika* is one who does not believe in the soul. The *Kāśikā* on Pāṇini IV.4.60 holds that it means one who does not believe in the next world.

naṭarāja The dancing form of Śiva. Images showing this form are known as Nṛtyamūrtis.

nātha-pantha A pan-North Indian non-Brahmanical cult having a complicated texture, heterodox rituals and ingredients from Śaivism, Śāktism, Buddhism and local cults as well as from Islam. The aim of the esoteric practices of this cult is the attainment of the state of 'nativity', i.e. neutrality (*sahaja*) where there is no birth and death as such. Existence and extinction are the resultants of man's desire and cognition. His fetters and his release are of his own creation, according to this system.

nātha-siddha The Nātha Yogis; they are supposed to have attained *siddhi*, i.e., psychic and supernatural power. These Siddhas include the 84 Buddhist Siddhas mentioned in the Tibetan tradition, as well as the Raseśvara and Māheśvara Siddhas (q.v.) well known for their knowledge of alchemy. Specially prominent are those who are traditionally associated with the foundation of Nāthapantha and who are credited with composing the texts expounding the system. They are Matsyendra or Mīnanātha, Gorakṣanātha, Jālandharī or Hāḍi-pā, Kṛṣṇapāda or Kānha, queen Maināmati, Caurangīnātha, etc. See Siddhas.

nāthayoga Yogic practices for the attainment of the state of neutrality as prescribed in Nāthism. A Nātha-Yogī, following the Guru's instruction, has to check the downward flow of the semen, hold his breath and stabilise the mind. These processes are technically known as *bindu-dhāraṇa*, *pavana-niścāñcalya* and *citta-nirodha*.

naṭī Female dancer. The term applies to Śakti when the goddess dances out of delight at the performance of her rituals. *Niruttara* XV.

natthikadiṭṭhi Buddhist characterisation of the materialistic schools like the Ucchedavādins (q.v.) etc.

navacakra The nine *cakras* or circles (actually these are triangular) of which Śrīyantra is constituted. According to the *Bhairavayāmala* five of these belong to Śakti and the remaining four to Śiva; thus the Śrīyantra consisting of nine *cakras* is the combined body of Śiva and Śakti. The five Śakti triangles are pointed upwards and the four Śiva triangles downwards. Lakṣmīdhara on *Saundaryalaharī* IX. Navacakra has three parts which deal symbolically with creation, sustention and destruction. *Setubandha* com. on *Nityaṣoḍaśikārṇava* I. 47. It is also known as Āvaraṇacakra and is said also to exist even in the human body. *Ibid.* on VI. 25–27.

navagraha The planetary bodies for the propitiation (*śānti*) for which extensive rituals are prescribed in the Purāṇas and Dharmaśāstras. Each of the nine *grahas* is supposed to have a separate *gotra* or clan and country of birth. The images should be made of copper (Sun), crystal (Moon), red-sandalwood (Mars), gold (Jupiter and Mercury), silver (Venus), iron (Saturn), lead (Rāhu) and bronze (Ketu) or they should be drawn on a piece of cloth with powders of the appropriate colour.

navagraha-śānti Propitiation of the nine planets. This rite is the model of all *Śānti-homas* mentioned in the medieval digests. An individual desirous of property, of removing evils or calamities, or rainfall, long life, health or the destruction of enemies should perform a sacrifice to the planets. *Yāj*.I.294. The *Matsyapurāṇa* XCIII.5ff describes at length three kinds of *navagrahamaka—ayuta-homa*, *lakṣahoma* and *koṭihoma* All religious rites should be performed after *navagrahaśānti*.

navamiśra-śrāddha Those funeral rites which are to be performed ten days after death and for the next six years.

navanāda Nine Nādas, or special forms of sound, supposed to denote the nature of Kuṇḍalinī. These are known as *cini ghaṇṭā, śaṅkha, tantrī, karatāla, venu, bherī, mṛdaṅga* and *megha*. *Cidvallī* on *Kāmakalāvilāsa*, XXVII. The letters A, Ka, Ca, Ṭa, Ta, Pa, Ya, Sa and Kṣa are also known as Navanāda. Lakṣmīdhara on *Saundaryalaharī* XXXIX.

navānna The ceremony of first fruits; literally it means new rice; it is performed in the month of *mārgaśīrṣa* (Nov-Dec) after the harvest has been gathered.

navarasa Nine rasas or mental feelings. They are *śṛṅgāra* (erotic), *bhayānaka* (dreadful), *raudra* (violent), *Vībhetsa* (loathsome), *hāsya* (humour), *vīra* (heroism), *karuṇa* (pity), *adbhuta* (wonder), and *śānta* (tranquillity).

navarātra The worship for nine-nights in autumn with the consecrated pitcher and holy water, and nine kinds of herbs and roots called *navapatrikā—rambhā, kaccvī, haridrā, jayantī, bilva, dāḍima, aśoka, mānaka* and *dhānya*. In many places it is a part of Durgā worship which indicates the connection of the goddess with vegetation and fertility.

navaśrāddha Those funeral rites performed up to ten days after death. The *Garuḍapurāṇa* II.5.67ff holds that these are to be performed at the place where the man died.

navatattva The nine fundamentals of Jainism. These are Jīva, Ajīva, Puṇya, Pāpa, Āsrava, Saṃvara, Bandha, Nirjarā and Mokṣa (qq.v.).

navavarga Nine groups of letters beginning with A, Ka, Ca, Ṭa, Ta, Pa, Ya, Sa and La. *Cidvallī* on *Kāmakalāvilāsa* XXVII.

navayonicakra Cakra or diagram consisting of nine triangles or Yonis. It is also known as *navatrikoṇa*.

naya The Jain logical method of comprehension of things from different view-points. The term is also interpreted as partial knowledge about any of the innumerable aspects of an object of judgement. It is divided into seven kinds: *naigama* (non-analytical method by which an object is regarded as possessing both general and specific properties), *saṃgraha* (collective method which takes into consideration generic properties only), *vyavahāra* (which takes into account the specific properties only), *ṛju-sūtra* (method which considers only the momentary entity without any reference to time and space), *śabda* (method of correct nomenclature), *samabhirūdha* (subtle); and *evambhūta* (such-like). *SDSC* 55, *NVT*.29, *TTDS*.32ff.

nāyanār Devotional Śaiva poets whose works are divided into eleven collections which, together with the Tamil Purāṇa called *Periya Purāṇam*, constitute the sacred literature of the saints and form the foundation of Tamil Śaivism. Foremost among them were Sambandar, Appar, Sundarar, Māṇikkavacagar etc. Also known as Samayācāryas and Nāyanmārs.

nekkahamma See Pāramitā.

neti-neti 'Not this, not this'. It is a negative method of philosophical discussion.

nevasaññanāsaññayātana The highest place of existence where one acquires five transcendental powers (*abhiññā* q.v.) according to the Buddhist concept.

nevasaññināsaññivāda The view that neither conscious nor unconscious soul exists after death. Eight such groups are mentioned in the Buddhist texts and their views were based upon the combination of those upheld by the Saññivāda (q.v.) and Asaññivāda (q.v.).

nibandha Digests of conduct written by Hemādri, Raghunandana and others as supplements to the Dharmaśāstras. They were devoted to the regulation and conservation of social order. Glosses of important legal texts, comprehensive digests, manuals on special topics of law and various other works also pass under the name of Nibandha. These texts are divided into the Banaras or mid-Indian school, Bengal-school, Kāmarūpa school, Mithila school and the South Indian school.

nibbāna See Nirvāṇa.

nibbedabhāgīya A kind of *samādhi* or concentration which belong to the category of *nirvāṇa*, according to the *Visuddhimagga* 84ff.

nidāna Cause. See Paṭiccasamuppāda.

nidhana The finale of a Sāman (q.v.); the earlier stages are *udgītha, pratihāra* and *upadrava*. It is to be chanted by the Udgatṛ (q.v.) priest.

nididhyāsana Roughly translated as meditation. Actually the term means meditation of a higher order in which there is no sense of exertion of will, no conscious employment of the thinking process, in fact, no intellection whatsoever. According to Sureśvara it is a form of *aparokṣānubhūti* or the direct realisation of the Self. It is one of the three ways of *jñāna-yoga*.

nigadha One of the four categories of *mantra* required in sacrifices. These are regarded as *praisas*, i.e., words addressed to another calling upon him to do a certain thing. *Kāt.Sr.* II.6.34. The other three are *ṛk* (metrical), *yajus* (non-metrical) and *sāman* (musical). The *nigadhas* are uttered loudly while a *yajus* is recited in a low voice. *Jaimini* II.1.35 ff.

nigama Pure Vedic tradition. The second part of the *Nirukta* (IV-VI) is called Naigama-Kāṇḍa which includes the etymologies of a large number of *nigama* words, i.e., words extracted from Vedic passages. The Vedānta is known as *nigamānta-vidyā*. The Smṛtis or Dharmaśāstras also belong to the category of *nigama*.

nigamana A conclusion drawn from valid premises.

nigganṭha See *nirgrantha*.

Nigoda A microcosmic group of entities mentioned in Jain doctrinal literature.

nigrahasthāna Sustaining defeat in philosophical disputation. According to Akṣapāda, it consists in contrary comprehension and non-comprehension. It is one of the sixteen topics of the Nyāya.

niḥśreyasa Supreme spiritual beatitude; highest good; the *summum bonum*. The *Nyāyasūtra* I.1.1 and the *Vaiśeṣika-sūtra* I.1.2–4 postulate that *niḥśreyasa* follows from the correct knowledge of the categories of the two *darśanas* obviously in the sense of perfection of knowledge. In the sense of *mokṣa* or liberation *niḥśreyasa* occurs in *Kauṣ.Up.* II.14, III.2, *Gītā* V.2. The word also occurs in Pāṇini V.4.77 which has been explained in the *Mahābhāṣya* as *niścitam śreyaḥ*.

nikācita-karma The *karma* (q.v.) which has already been stored up according to Jain conception.

nikāya One of the principal constituents of the Buddhist Tripiṭaka. It consists of Dīgha, Majjhima, Saṃyutta, Aṅguttara and Khuddaka Nikāyas. In the Chinese versions these are called Āgamas.

nimantraṇa See under Āmantraṇa.

nimeṣa The time required to pronounce a short syllable.

nimeṣa śakti The power of will by which the concept of Sadāśiva is characterised in Kashmir Śaivism. *Īśvarapratyabhijñā*, III.1.3. Nimeṣa technically means the latent condition of 'itness' within 'I-ness'.

nimitta Happenings. According to *Amarakoṣa, nimittaṃ hetulakṣaṇah*, means 'cause or prognostic sign'. Nimitta may be either auspicious or inauspicious. This is one distinction between *utpāta* (which generally denotes an unlucky portent) and *nimitta*. *Manu* VI.50, *Mbh.* VI.2.16–17, *Rām* II.4.17–19, *Gītā* I.31, *Matsya* CCXLI, *Atharva-pariśiṣṭa* LXIV. 10.9–10.

nimitta-kāraṇa Efficient cause, as the potter is who makes the jar.

nimmitavāda Cosmological doctrine. *Ṭhāṇa* IV.4. See under Antānantika and Akriyāvāda.

nirandhāra-prāsāda Shrine without an ambulatory passage.

nirañjana A *śānti* rite for the welfare of the king and his war-requirements. It involves the waving of lights before men and horses and is performed to the accompaniment of the sound of drums.

nirañjana-panthā Cult of the speckless one (*nirañjana*). The term *nirañjana* was originally an epithet of Buddha in the form of Śūnya. It also came later to denote Dharma-ṭhākur of Bengal. The term was attributed to the supreme divinity by Śaṅkaradeva of Assam and also by the Nātha-panthīs. Niranjaña-panthā was popular in Orissa as well.

Nirbīja Seedless; a term qualifying the deeper aspect of *asamprajñāta-samādhi* (q.v.). *Yogasūtra* I.50–51.

nirgrantha-dharma A name of Jainism, because it lays supreme stress on non-possession and on renunciation of the house (*āgāra* or *gṛha*) which is considered as a knot (*grantha*).

nirjarā Purging of the Karmas (q.v.), according to the Jain concept. It is of two kinds, *bhāva* and *dravya*; the former means the change in the soul by virtue of which the Karma particles are destroyed; and the latter, the actual destruction of the Karma particles either by reaping their effects or by performing penances before the time of fruition. These are called *savipāka* and *avipāka* Nirjarās respectively. *TTDS*, IX.47.

nirlepa Non-attachment.

nirmāṇa-cakra One of the four nerve cycles in Buddhist conception. It is situated near the region of the navel and is connected with the *nirmāṇa* or *rūpa-kāya* (q.v.) of Buddha. Like the *kūṇḍalinī śakti* (q.v.) of the Śākta-Tantras, the Buddhist Tantras speak of a female energy having the force of fire, known as Caṇḍālī (q.v.) which resides in this *cakra*.

nirmāṇa-kāya The material or created body of the Buddha; also known as *rūpa-kāya*. See Trikāya.

nirṇaya Ascertainment of truth about something by means of any of the recognised methods or sources of knowledge. It is one of the sixteen philosophical topics of the Nyāya.

nirṇayaṇa See Niṣkramaṇa.

nirnimittavāda The viewpoint according to which things are produced without any cause. *Nyāyasūtra* IV.1.22.

nirodha Inhibition of all desires. In Buddhist terminology it denotes extinction of all sufferings and is regarded as one of the four noble truths.

nirodhinī One of the five aspects of Śakti. *Śāradātilaka*, V.79.

nirudhapaśubandha See Paśubandha.

nirvāṇa The *summum bonum* of Buddhism. The term is also used in Brahmanical and Jain tradition in the sense of liberation (see Mokṣa). It is described as the free state of consciousness, the tranquil state of one's internal nature and the highest emotional state of spirituality and blessedness. It means the annihilation of passion, hatred and delusion. *Majjhima* I.160ff, *Khuddakapāṭha*, Ratna 12, *Dhammapada* 21. It is like a matchless island which possessed nothing, grasps at nothing and which is the destroyer of decay and death. *Suttanipāta* 215. It is the extinction of the five *skandhas* (q.v.). *Visuddhimagga* II.611. Its other names are *nirodha, nirmokṣa, nivṛtti* and *nirveda*. *Saundarānanda* V.15, VIII.62, XVI.19,44. It is uncaused, uncompounded but realisable. From the ethical point of view, to realise *nirvāṇa* involves the process of perfect self-examination, self-purification, self-restraint and self-culture. In spite of the inconceivability of *nirvāṇa*, there are passage in the *nikāyas* which give it a mixture of positive and negative attributes. *Saṃyutta* II.124–26, III.143, IV.372 *Itivuttaka* 37, *Majjhima* I.509. The ethical positive in *nirvāṇa* is perfection in *śīla, samādhi* and *prajñā*, in four *smṛtyūpasṭhāna* (mindfulness) practices leading to a state of perfect bliss. The ethical negative is the eradication of attachment (*rāga*), ill-will (*dveṣa*) and delusion (*moha*), removal of all impurities (*kleśas, āsravas*) and ignorance (*avidyā*). Both the positive and the negative attribute lead to the end of desire for worldly objects or existences. Metaphysically, *nirvāṇa* is eternal and fixed, homogeneous, beyond the scope of discussive and discriminatory thoughts, having neither origin nor decay, without past, present and future, unlimited and unsurpassable, unfathomable and immeasurable, unconditional and unconstituted (*asaṃskṛta*). According to Nāgārjuna, *saṃsāra* and *nirvāṇa* are two relative ideas. The *partītya-samutpāda* (q.v.) viewed and interpreted as a law of sequence of causal antecedents and consequents, explains the essential nature of *saṃsāra* or worldly existence. The same, viewed and interpreted as 'mere origination' (*uppādamatta*) without any idea of temporal relation associated with it, expresses the essential nature of *nirvāṇa*. In other words, the *pratītyasamutpāda* in its *samutpāda* aspect is *saṃsāra* and the same in its *nirodha* aspect is *nirvāṇa*.

nirvāṇa-dhātu Nirvāṇa (q.v.) which is sometimes conceived of in terms of the merger of the individual completely with the process of the functioning and changing of the eternal and immaculate elements (*dhātus*). This fusion has been characterised by Poussin as a perfectly blissful state, while Stcherbatsky thinks that it is eternal death, a return to non-differentiated matter.

nirvāṇa-dīkṣā The highest form of initiation in Āgamānta Śaivism. It is meant for those who are entitled to depend on the way of *jñāna* or knowledge and who aspire to belong to the *sāyujya* (q.v.) stage of spiritual progress in which they feel themselves to be identical with God.

nirvāṇa kalā An aspect of Śakti. It is said to be the essence of Amākalā; is conceived of as the seventeenth Kalā and also as a goddess. *Ṣaṭcakranirūpaṇa* XLVII; *Kaṅkalamālinī*, II.

nirvikalpa Free from *vikalpa* (determination) consisting of conceptual unification of the 'many' into 'one'.

nirvikalpa-pratyakṣa Indeterminate perception which, according to the Nyāya, is the primary cognition of an object and its diverse characters without any judgement to interrelate them.

nirvikalpa samādhi That blissful state of mind

(*samādhi*) in which the distinction between the knower, knowledge and what is to be known vanishes absolutely.

nirvirodhavāda A term for any 'accommodating' doctrine.

niṣedha Prohibitions. See Pratiniṣedha.

nisedhikā Jain memorial pillar or slab.

niṣeka A sacrament or *saṃskāra*, same as Garbhādhāna (q.v.). The term has been used in *Manu* II.16, II.26, *Yāj* I.10–11 and *Viṣṇu.Dh.S.* II.3, XXVII.1.

niṣkāma-karma The practice of duty for duty's sake without looking either for subjective pleasure or objective utility.

niṣkramaṇa The minor rite of taking the child out of the house into the open for the first time. According to most authorities it should be performed in the fourth month after birth. *Pār.Gr.* I.17, *Gobhila Gr.* II.8.1–7, *Khadira Gr.* II.3.1–5, *Baudh.Gr.* II.2, *Mānava Gr.* I.19. It is also known as Ādityadarśana, Nirṇayaṇa and Upaniṣkramaṇa.

nissaya The four minimum requisites for a Buddhist monk. They are *piṇḍiālopa-bhojanam* (to eat only that food received as alms by begging); *paṃsukulacīvaram* (to use robes made only out of rags collected from dust-heaps); *rukkhamūlasenāsanam* (to sit or lie at the root of a tree); and *putimuttabhesajjam* (to use only excrement and urine as medicine).

niṣyanda-kāya The resultant body of Buddha. This conception is an addition to the *trikāya* theory. Some commentators hold that it is the same as *sambhogakāya*. (See *trikāya*. Its Chinese equivalent is *pao-sheng*).

nitārtha 'Definite or direct meaning' in Buddhist terminology, as opposed to *neyārtha*, i.e., 'indirect or implied meaning'.

nitya Obligatory acts such as *agnihotra*, *darśapūrṇamāsa*, daily worship, daily gifts etc. These should be performed regularly even though it may not be possible to perform the subsidiary parts of the complete ritual.

nityā Śakti which is non-different from Śiva.

nityalīlā Sport, in which God, remaining subordinate to the devotee gives him the pleasure of his company. It is generally known as *bhajanānanda* (the bless of devotion) or *svarūpānanda* (the bliss of the lord himself).

nityānuvāda Where the Vedic texts apparently prohibit something when there is no likelihood of its happening. *Jaimini* II.4.26, IV.1.5, VI.7.30, VII.4.5, VIII.1.6, IX.4.36, X.2.38.

nivāraṇa The five hindrances to religious life which should be avoided according to Buddhism. These are *kāmacchanda* (strong desire), *vyāpāda* (hatred), *thinamiddha* (idleness), *uddhaccakukkuccha* (arrogance) and *vicikicchā* (doubt).

nivṛtti A return current; it seeks to reverse the process of creating and maintaining the bonds of propensities and conventions.

nivṛttikalā One of the five Kalās or aspects of Śakti. *Śaradātilaka*, V. 79.

nivṛttimārga The sādhanā or spiritual exercise which insists on abstinence from all worldly pleasures.

niyama Cultivation of good habits; it is the second discipline of Yoga. It consists of *śauca* (purification of body and mind); *santoṣa* (contentment); *tapas* (observation of austere vows); *svādhyāya* (habit of study) and *īśvarapraṇidhāna* (resignation to God).

niyāmaka-niyamya Controller (*brahman*) and the controlled (*jīva*). According to Nimbārka, *niyamya* is secondary to the *niyāmaka*, as the *Śakti* is secondary in the *śakti-śaktimat* relation. So the *jīva* by its *niyamyatva* has only a dependent reality.

niyamavidhi Restrictive injunctions. According to the Pūrvamīmāṃsā tradition they are of three classes: those concerned with *pratinidhis* (substitutes), those about *pratipatti* (the concluding act or final disposal of certain materials employed in a sacrifice); and those that are concerned with matters other than the preceding two.

niyantṛ The controller of the universe. Also known as *vidhātṛ*.

niyati Destiny, conceived as the First Principle in the *Śvetāśvatara Upaniṣad* (I.2). This doctrine was given a religious basis in Ājīvikism by Gośāla Maṅkhaliputta. Details of the doctrine of Niyati are found in a Prakrit work called *Gommatasāra*. Kāla and Niyati are described as evolutes of *asuddha-māyā* in the Śaiva Āgamas. The term is also used to denote a category of vidyātattva.

niyavāda Doctrine of eternalism. *Ṭhāna* IV.4. See Sassatavāda and Akriyāvāda.

nṛtyamūrti See Naṭarāja.

nṛyajña See Manuṣyayajña.

nūpura Anklet, serving as an ornament in icons.

nyāsa Feeling of the deity in different parts of the body. *Saubhāgyabhāskara* on *Lalitāsahasranāma* I, 4. It is an exercise for the aspirant to become god. *Gandharva* IX.2. It also serves as a protection against evil. *Tantrasāra*, p. 93. Without proper Nyāsa worship is meaningless. *Tārātantra*, II.3. There are many types of Nyāsas like Mātrkānyāsa, Soḍanyāsa, Tārakanyāsa, Rsyadinyāsa, Saḍaṅganyāsa, Karaṅganyāsa, Vidyānyāsa, Tattvanyāsa etc., each of which produces a special result. *Sāradātilaka* VII. In Mātṛkānyāsa, which is divided into Antaḥ and Vahiḥ, the Śakti of letters (Mātṛkās) is to be felt consecutively on the head (*ṛsi*), face (*chandas*), rectum (*vīja*), legs (*śakti*) and the whole body (*kīlaka*). *Tārābhaktisudhārṇava*, V. p. 169. In Soḍanyāsa six kinds of Nyāsas are used to experience the Vidyās like Kālī, Tārā, etc. *Puraścaryārṇava*, XII, p. 1165. There are other types of Nyāsas besides those found in the classified lists. For example, in Pīṭhanyāsa, Pīṭhas or holy resorts of Śakti are to be felt in different parts of the body like Kāmarūpa in heart, Jālandhara on the forehead, and so on. *Tantrasāra* 339.

nyāya The system of logic which became the basis of one of the six traditional systems of Indian philosophy. For its necessity in the interpretation of the Veda, Kumārila relies on *Manu* XII. 105–106. According to *Yāj* I.3 it is a source of *dharma*. It also means the *adhikaraṇas* of the *PMS* of Jaimini expounding the points of *dharma*.

odana Grain mashed and cooked with milk, porridge, boiled rice, or any pap or pulpy substance used as sacrificial oblations. Odanapacana is the name of the fire on the southern altar. Odanapāṇinīya means one who studies Pāṇini for the sake of getting boiled rice. *Kāśikā* on Pāṇini VI.2.29, Patañjali on Pāṇini I.1.73. Odanavat is a particular oblation. Com.on *Taitt.Br.* II.7.7.

oduvār A special class of temple singers of south India. They sing devotional songs every evening in the hall of the temple. During festivals they accompany the deity in procession while singing *devāram*.

ojas Strength, vigour, energy, power, ability, etc. The principle of vital warmth, manifestation, etc., which are regarded as qualities. *RV*. VIII. 76.5, *AV*, VIII.5.4. The derivative form is Ojiṣṭha.

om A sacred syllable which is identified with *brahman* in *Taitt.Up.* I.8. "Om is the bow, the soul is the arrow and *brahman* is the target." *Praśna Up* V.5. Om is the most prominent among the symbol (*pratīkas*) under which the *upāsanā* of the supra-sensible *brahman* is possible. *Ch.Up.* I.1.1. According to the *Yogasūtra* I.23ff this mystic syllable is expressive of God, the *japa* of which leads to the one-pointedness of mind. It may be called a *bīja* (q.v.) in Tantric language and it is called Tārā in Tantric works (see *praṇava*). As the mystic syllable par excellence it proved attractive because repetition of it had the effect of inducting concentration. Thus it was made the subject of meditation while it was also regarded as the most natural expression for God. The Buddhists place *om* at the beginning of their mystical formulary.

oṃkāra Same as *om*. It also means a prosperous and auspicious beginning. In feminine form Oṃkāra denotes a Buddhist Śakti or the female personification of divine energy.

oṣadhi Herb, plant, etc. conceived of in terms of divinity. *Nirukta* IX.27, *Śat.Br.* II.2.4.5, *Manu* I.46. Oṣadhigarbha means producer of herbs which is thought to represent the moon and the sun. cf. *RV* I.164.52, *AV*. X.4.23.

ovā A particular exclamation at sacrifices. *Lāt.Sr.* VII.

paccaya The twenty-four ways (*pratyaya*) according to Buddhism which indicate that any two links in the law of causation are related to each other. These twenty-four ways are mentioned in the *Paṭṭhāna*. The Sarvāstivādins admit four *pratyayas* and six *hetus*.

pada Words which are regarded as one of the six paths (*adhvans*) leading to the realisation of the Supreme Being according to the Tantras. In Vaiṣṇavism the word stands for the steps of Viṣṇu. The Besnagar inscription of the second-first century B.C. interprets the *padas* of Visnu as denoting self-control, renunciation and vigilance. In Tantra *pada* or *padādhva* refers to words which are regarded as the body of *mantra*. *Sāradātilaka* V.91.

pādakṛcchra A form of penance which lasts for four days. The sinner eats food only once the first day, ony once at night the second day, once only either by day or night the third day and on the fourth day he observes a total fast. *Yāj* III. 318.

pādanokṛcchra A nine-day penance in which the sinner eats by day only for three days, eats once only for three days without asking for it and observes a complete fast for three days.

padārtha Objects of knowledge or realities which according to the Vaiśeṣika are of seven categories: Dravya or substance, Guṇa or quality, Karma or action, Sāmānya or generality, Viśeṣa or particularity, Samavāya or inherence and Abhāva or non-existence (q.v.).

padāvalī Devotional songs dealing mostly with the love of Kṛṣṇa and Rādhā. Jayadeva was perhaps the first poet to call his lyrics *padāvalī*. Many of the later poets wrote *padāvalīs* in an artificial language called Brajabuli which lends itself easily to musical renderings. Apart from Bengal, a vast *padāvalī* literature has been composed in other parts of northern India. Though the *padāvalīs* mostly belong to Vaiṣṇavism dealing with the divine love of Rādhā and Kṛṣṇa or the events of the life of Caitanya, Śākta *padāvalīs* are common, especially in Bengal, in which the relation between the Great Goddess and her devotee—in terms of mother and son—has been well expressed.

padma Lotus; it serves as an emblem of deities belonging to different creeds The blue lotus is designated by the word Utpala or Nīlotpala. In Tantric terminology Padma is the day lotus while Utpala stands for the night lotus. When the lotus show petals growing upwards as well as downwards it is called Viśvapadma or the double lotus. Viṣṇu's lotus emblem when represented in personified form is called Padmapuruṣa. Padma also denotes lotus-seat of deities, lotus-shaped moulding, capital chamber shaped like a lotus for supporting South Indian *phalakas*, etc. Padmabandha is a decorative band while Padma-śila is the elaborately curved lotus-shaped pendant of a ceiling.

padmāsana A sitting posture for Yogic practices in which the right foot should be placed on the left thigh and the left foot on the right thigh.

pādodaka Literally the water from the feet of the Guru or Jaṅgama which is regarded as sacred by the Vīraśaivas. The custom of touching or drinking the water touched by the Guru with his feet is not confined to the Vīraśaivas alone.

paiṇṇa, prakīrṇa Ten texts forming part of the Jain canon, though their present versions are not approved by the Digambaras. These are Causaraṇa, Bhattapariṇṇā, Saṃthāra, Āurapaccakkhāna, Mahāpaccakkhāna, Caṅdāvijjhaya, Gaṇivijjā, Taṅdulaveyāliya, Devindatthaya and Vīratthaya. Two other texts—Titthogali and Ārāhṇāpaḍāgā—are also said to belong to this group.

pajjusana See also Paryūṣaṇa. On the third day of this festival the Śvetāmbaras make a procession with the manuscript of *Kalpasūtra* and have various other celebrations. According to the Digambaras the fourth day is the birthday or Lord Mahāvīra which they observe in a solemn way. The Śvetāmbaras take out in procession a cradle covered with brocade though according to them the birthday of Mahāvīra is on the bright half of the thirteenth day of Caitra (March-April).

pakativādin Prakṛtivādins. The followers of the Sāṇkhya were so called by the Buddhists.

pākayajña Offering of cooked food at sacrifices. There are seven types of Pākayajñas: *aṣṭakā, pārvaṇasthālīpāka, śrāddha, śrāvaṇī, agrahāyaṇī, caitrī* and *āśvayuji* (*Gautama DS*, VIII. 14–22). The *Baudh. Gr.* I.1 gives the seven Pākayajñas as *huta, prahuta, śūlagava, baliharaṇa, pratyavarohaṇa* and *aṣṭakā-homa*. According to some other sources, these are *aupasāna-homa, vaiśvadeva, pārvana* (*sthālīpāka*), *aṣṭakā, śrāddha, sarpabali* and *īśāṇabali* (*Sm.C.* I.13).

pakṣa See Anumāna. The minor term; the term with which one is concerned in any inference.

pakṣa Fortnight; specially in relation to the moon.

Rites for gods and for prosperity must be performed in the bright *pakṣa* and for *pitṛs* (q.v.) and magic in the dark *pakṣa*.

palāśa-karma A rite performed on the fourth day of the Upanayana (q.v.) ceremonial. The boy goes out with his teacher either to the east or north towards a *palāśa* tree and recites a few *mantras* addressed to the goddesses Śraddhā and Medhā.

palibodha Ten hindrances according to Buddhism; *āvāsa* (dwelling place), *kula* (family), *lābha* (gain), *gaṇa* (community), *kamma* (action), *addhāna* (wayfaring), *ñati* (relatives), *ābādha* (sickness), *grantha* (scriptures) and *iddhi* (miraculous power). *Milinda* 365–99, *Visuddhimagga* 122.

pallava Twigs and leaves considered to be auspicious; *āmra, aśvattha, vaṭa, plakṣa* and *udumbara*. These are also called *pañcabhaṅga*.

pañcabandhana Five fetters resulting from *avidyā* or false knowledge.

pañcabheda Doctrine of the Dāsakūṭa saints of Karṇāṭaka; inspired by the philosophy of Madhva it emphasises the reality of five-fold difference in the universe. See Bheda, Dvaita.

pañcabhūta The five material elements. See Mahābhūta, Bhūtavāda. Bhūta means the state of existence, the word being derived from the root *bhū*, to be. Pañcabhūta, or the five states of existence are *pṛthivī* (earth), *ap* (water), *tejas* (fire), *vāyu* (air) and *ākāśa* (space) and they stand for solidity, liquidity, radiation, gaseousness and ethereality respectively. In iconography *prthivī* is represented by a square or cube; *ap* by a circle, water by aquatic plants or animals; *tejas* by radiation of light or stellate figures; *vāyu* by smoke, a globe, flying bodies, etc; and *ākāśa* by heavenly bodies such as the sun, moon, etc.

pañcabrahmā The five divine forms or aspects of Śiva known as Vāmadeva, Tatpuruṣa, Aghora, Sadyojāta and Īśāna. These forms are also collectively known as Īśānādayah.

pañcācāra Five codes of conduct which dictate the rules of behaviour for the individual members of the Vīraśaivas. They are *liṅgācāra* (worshipping linga as the supreme being); *sadācāra* (moral and virtuous life and profession); *śivācāra* (equality among the members of the community); *bhṛtyācāra* (devotee's attitude of complete humility towards Śiva) and *gaṇācāra* (spirit of benevolence).

pañcadaśākṣarī Mantra in fifteen letters; it is supposed to be the subtle form of Lalitā according to the Tantric tradition.

pañcadevatā Five major deities each heading a monotheistic sect. They are Śiva, Śakti, Viṣṇu, Sūrya and Gaṇeśa.

pañcagavya A mixture of cow milk, curds, clarified butter, cow urine and cow dung which is to be eaten by a sinner for his purification. *Yāj* III.314. *Parāśara* XI.28–34.

pañcāgnividyā Knowledge of *brahman* which Śvetaketu Āruṇeya learnt from Pravāhana Jaivalī. According to the latter this knowledge belonged exclusively to the Kṣatriyas and the Brāhmaṇas learnt it afterwards from them. It is concerned only with one aspect of transmigration, viz., the path of those who practise a life of sacrifices, do works of public utility and alms-giving and follow the *pitṛyāna* (q.v.) path. *Bṛhadāraṇyaka* VI.2.2ff, *Chāndogya* V.3.2 ff.

pañca-kalā Five aspects of Śakti. They are Nivṛtti, Pratiṣṭhā, Vidyā, Śānti and Śāntyatītā. *Śāradātilaka* V.79.

pañca-kalyāṇa Five kinds of Jain rememberence. They are *svargāvataraṇa* (descent of a *deva* to become a *tīrthaṃkara*); *mandarābhiṣeka* or *janmābhiṣeka* (rejoicing at the birth of the *tīrthaṃkara* by performing an *abhiṣeka* or ablution at the summit of Mandaragiri); *dīkṣā* (when the *tīrthaṃkara* renounces the kingdom and worldly pleasures in order to become a Yogin); *kevalotpatti* (which represents the appearance of omniscient knowledge); and *parinirvāṇa* (destruction of all Karmas and the attainment of salvation).

pañca-kañcuka Five evolutes of Aśuddha-māyā (q.v.) (impure material elements)—*kalā, niyati, vidyā, kāla* and *rāga* (qq.v.)—which cause different types of human bondage.

pañcakāraṇī Five-step method of observation of the Buddhist logicians: (1) cause is not perceived, effect is also not perceived, (2) cause is perceived, (3) effect also is perceived, (4) cause disappears, (5) effect also disappears.

pañca-kleśa Five fetters in the form of *avidyā* (false knowledge): *asmitā* (self-conceit), *rāga* (attachment), *dveṣa* (hatred), and *abhiniveśa* (adherence).

pañca-kriyā Five active expressions of Śakti—Sṛṣṭi (creation), Sthiti (maintenance), Saṃhāra (destruction), Tirodhāna (disappearance) and Anugraha (favour). *Tantrāloka* I.121.

pañcalāṅgalaka A *mahādāna* (great gift) of five

ploughshares and ten bulls and their miniatures in gold, and a village or a plot of land. *Matsya* CCLXXXIII.

pañcama-kāla The fifth cosmic period in Jain conception.

pañca-makāra See Pañca-tattva.

pañca-mātukā Irregular form of Pañca-mātṛkā (mātikā); it refers to five Abhidhamma texts.

pañcāmnāya Five āmnāyas (zones) celebrated in Tantric culture.

pañcamatattva Same as *maithuna* (q.v.).

pañcamudrā See Pañcatattva.

pañcamukha-liṅga Five faced Śivaliṅga. For the names of the five faces see Pañca-Brahmā.

pañcamuṇḍī Seat for Tantric *sādhanā* prepared from the severed heads of two Caṇḍālas, a jackal, a monkey and a snake.

pañcāṅga Calendar which deals with five important topics: *tithi*, weekday, *nakṣatra*, *yoga* and *karaṇa*.

pañcāṅga-nyāsa Feeling the deity in the heart, head, central cerebral region, protective symbol (*kavaca*) and intestine.

pañcāṅga-puraścaraṇa *Japa, homa, tarpana, abhiṣeka* (qq.v.) and *viprabhojana* (feeding the Brāhmaṇas). *Tantrasāra* 48.

pañcapreta The collective name of Brahmā, Viṣṇu, Rudra, Īśā and Sadāśiva, who form the seat of the Devī.

pañcaratha. A temple with five projections.

pañcaratna Five jewels which are considered to be auspicious. These are gold, diamond, sapphire, ruby and pearl. According to another view these are gold, silver, pearl, coral and *rājavarta*. Pañcaratna also denotes a kind of temple.

pāñcarātra A form of ritualistic Vaiṣṇavism. It appears that once this term, like Bhāgavata, had a wider denotation since the Pāñcarātra works were associated with the names of deities like Śiva, Devī, Gaṇeśa Brahmā and others. The *Puruṣottamasaṃhitā* I.3ff. says that any system which lays supreme emphasis on *bhakti* or devotion may be called Pāñcarātra which is also known as Ekāyanavāda, Mūlaveda, Sātvata, Tantra and Āgama. It is a *rahasya-āmnāya* or mystrious area of knowledge taught by Viṣṇu to Brahmā who had learnt it in five nights. The *Nāradapāñcaratra* I.1.44 interprets it as a Sāstra which expounds five types of knowledge. The Īśvarasaṃhitā I.62 holds that it is *sāttvika* (q.v.) in nature and superior to Vaikhānasa (q.v.).

pañca-śakti Mother, sister, daughter, daughter-in-law and preceptor's wife are collectively known and worshipped as five great Śaktis. *Niruttara* X.

pañcasaṃskāra Knowledge of the mysteries of the creed (especially of Vaiṣṇavism) which is imparted to the novice by the teacher. The rites include *tapas* (initiation with sacred fire), *puṇḍra* (initiation into wearing a sectarian mark), *nāma* (giving a spriritual name to the novice), *mantratraya*(teaching the mantras like *aṣṭākṣara, davya* and *caramaśloka*) and *śālagrāma* (handing over a *nārāyaṇa*-stone as an object of worship).

pañca-skandha Five elements or constituents in the Buddhist conception. These are material form (*rūpa*), sensation (*vedanā*), conformations (*saṃskāra*) perception (*saṃjñā*) and consciousness (*vijñāna*). See under *Khandas*.

pañca-śuddhi Purification of the self, place, *mantra* articles of worship and deity. *Kulārṇava* VI.

pañcasūtaka Five pollutions according to the Vīraśaiva faith. These are *jāti* (pedigree pollution), *janma* (birth pollution), *maraṇa* (death pollution) *rajas* (menstrual pollution) and *ucchiṣṭa* (leavings, such as the left-overs of a meal eaten, etc. pollution).

pañca-tanmātra Five subtle elements—the essence of sound, touch, colour, taste and smell—conceived of as the physical principles corresponding to the five sense organs.

pāñcatattva Tantric esoteric ritualism which consists in the use of *pañcamakāras* or the five Ms. They are *madya* (wine), *māṃsa* (flesh), *maithuna* (sexual intercourse), mudrā (cereals) and *matsya* (fish). Also known as Pañcamakāra, Pañcamudrā, Kuladravya, Kulatattva, etc.

pañcatīrthika Image with five Jina figures.

pañcavaṭīya A rite in Rājasūya which consists in making five fires, one in each of the four directions and one in the middle. *Āp.Sr.* XVIII.9.10–11, *Kāt.Sr.* XV.I.20–21.

pañcavīra Five Vṛṣṇi heroes.

pañcāyatana A kind of worship in which all the principal deities of the five approved Brahmanical Hindu cults (of Viṣṇu, Śiva, Śakti, Sūrya and Gaṇapati) are the objects of worship. The principal deity, to whose sectarian cult the devotee belongs (which may be any one of the aforesaid five deities), should be placed in the middle while the remaining four deities are placed on the four corners of a square. This form of worship has been popularised by the Smṛti writers to bring the different sects on a common platform. This is also known as Pañcopāsanā. Pañcāyatana is also the name of a temple as surrounded by four minor shrines.

pañcāyatanī-dīkṣā Initiation to the cults of Śiva, Śakti, Viṣṇu, Sūrya and Gaṇeśa. *Tantrasāra* 70–72.

pañcikaraṇa The mixing of the five subtle elements—*ākāśa* (ether), *vāyu* (air), *agni* (fire), *ap* (water) and *kṣiti* (earth) in different ways to produce the gross elements.

pañcopacāra Five Upacāras (materials), which are offered in worship. These are *pādya* (water as the symbol of the element *ap*), *gandha* (sandal, etc. as the symbol of the element *pṛthivī*), *puṣpa* (flower as the symbol of the element *ākāśa*), *dhūpa* (incense as the symbol of the element *vāyu*) and *dīpa* (light as the symbol of the element *tejas*). The seed-*mantras* of these Upacāras, connected with the five elements, are *vam, lam, ham, yam* and *ram* respectively. This *pañcopacāra* was later elaborated into ten (*daśopacāra*), sixteen (*ṣoḍaśopacāra*) and at times even to sixty-four. *Puraścaryārṇava* III.224.

pañcopāsaka, pañcopāsanā See Pañcāyatana.

pañjara Miniature apsidal shrine. Same as *nīḍa*.

paṅkti A row of diners. Elaborate rules are given in the Dharmaśāstras in regard to the manners to be observed. For example, a person in *paṅkti* should not take *ācamana* before others or get up before others; he should not sit in the same row as undeserving persons or with persons belonging to a different caste; persons in a row should not touch one another and so on.

paṅktipāvana Those who sanctify by their presence a company of diners. According to Hārīta they must be from a good family, be endowed with Vedic learning, and have good character and decent conduct.

paññā That which comprehends the whole of man's rational sphere of existence and intellection; in Sanskrit *prajñā*. Also known as Vipassanā it is one of the three main pillars of Buddhist discipline. Pañña means knowledge which is of three kinds; *sutamayī* (the knowledge which develops from an acquaintance with the words and views of others); *cintamayī* (the knowledge which develops from self-induced reason); and *bhāvanāmayī* (the knowledge which develops from the formulation of one's own system in relation to the current thoughts and ideas). *Dīgha* III. 219, *Nettipakaraṇa* 8.

paññā-vimutti One of the two kinds of Buddhist *vimutti* (emancipation), the other being *ceto-vimutti*. It is emancipation through the development of reason and knowledge (*paññā*).

pantha Group or sect based on a common religious bond or on certain ideals. In medieval reformistic religious movements this term acquired a wider significance. For example, when the Sikhs came under a centralised authority, the whole body began to be known collectively as *panth* and came to be regarded as an embodiment of the Guru. Also, the sect of Kabir was split into twelve different schools, each of which was known as a *panth*.

pāpa A sinful act; also see Pātaka, Mahāpātaka, Anupātaka, Upapātaka, Kṛcchra, and Prāyaścitta. In Jainism Pāpa is one of the nine fundamentals. There are eighteen kinds of Pāpa which result in eighty-four consequences. It has evil effects on knowledge, intellect, sight, slumber and so on. It effects the beings to be born in the next incarnation in many ways. It results in personal ugliness of many kinds, in the loss of bodily strength and in various deformities of the human body. The committance of certain sins condemns the soul to be born in the next life in the class of an inferior species. Other sins prevent the soul from acquiring the full powers and senses which are the right of the class in which it is born.

parā Form of sound or speech which corresponds the logos of the Bible. It is *śabda-brahman*, i.e., *brahman* in the form of sound, unmanifest (*avyakta*), the spread of pure *nāda* (q.v.), and can be experienced in deep sleep. According to the Tantric tradition the Kriyā-śakti or the power of action of Śiva remains dominant in it. The *parā* rises from the *mūlādhāra* and is produced by air (*prāṇa*). See also under Paśyantī, Madhyamā, Vaikharī, Parā-śabda, Parā-Vāc.

parā-bhakti Supreme love for God which is an end in itself.

parabrahma The supreme being; the absolute; the ultimate reality in the form of pure consciousness.

parabrahma-sampradāya The sect founded by Dādu, a follower of Kabīr; he wanted to unite all the divergent faiths in one bond of love and comradeship. The followers of this sect did not believe in the autority of the scriptures but in the value of self-realisation.

paracittajñāna The power of reading the thoughts of others; it is mentioned as one of the *abhijñās* in the Buddhist texts.

pārada Mercury. It is regarded as the essence of Śiva's body and is conducive to *mokṣa* or liberation. *Sarvadarśanasaṃgraha* IX.5–9.

parāka A penance which consists of observing a twelve-days fast. *Manu* XI.215, *Yāj* III. 320, *Baudh.Dh.S.* IV.5.16.

parakīyā A female partner of the spiritual aspirant other than his own wife.

paraliṅga Imaginary phallus in terms of which the *vindu* or vacuity within the *sahasrāra* (q.v.) triangle is conceived.

paralokavilopavāda One of the five basic principles of Cārvaka (q.v.) philosophy; it holds that there can be no such thing as the other world.

parama-devatā The 'liberated ones' in Jainism who are supposed to be above the gods. Often the Jinas are also called Parama-devatās.

parama-dharma Parā-bhakti (supreme love for god) when conceived of in terms of will and viewed not as a fruit of any Karma but as the only perfect manifestation and expression in life of the natural bliss of the soul.

parama-haṃsa The Tāntric aspirant who has attained success in Haṃ-sa (q.v.). Parama-haṃsas are of two kinds, viz. *vidvat* (those who have already realised *brahman*) and *vividiṣu* (those who are eager seekers after realisation). The *Jābālopaniṣad* 6, and *Sūtasaṃhitā* II.6 describe the state of Parama-haṃsa at length.

paramaiśvarya Supreme lordliness of *brahman* in the form of Viṣṇu, a concept upheld by Madhva; it is characterised by his *svatantrecchā* (independent will).

paramāṇu Atoms. The Indian conception of atomism was enriched by different schools of philosophical thought. The Nyāya-Vaiśeṣikas hold that all composite objects of the world are formed by the combination of atoms. Among the nine kinds of substances, each of the *pañcabhūtas* (q.v.) or five physical elements possesses a specific quality which can be experienced by an external sense. Earth, water, fire and air can be reduced to material atoms. These are eternal but the compounds made of them are non-eternal. According to the Jain doctrine of atomism, the matter or Pudgala (q.v.) has certain inalienable features but, in spite of this, the transmutation of the elements such as earth, water, fire and air is quite possible. Each of these elements has a structure, and they are divisible into atoms. The atoms are all of the same kind, but they can give rise to an infinite variety of things. The atoms are arranged in two or in three dimensional order in the circular, oblong, triangular and square formations. In the case of linear formation they are arranged in a one dimensional order. The formation of aggregates results in the substance of a second order, i.e., the material mass called *dravya*. There are eight kinds of combinations which shape the substances. The difference between the Nyāya-Vaiśeṣika and Jain viewpoint is that while the former holds that the atoms are different in kind and that all composite objects of the world, formed by the combination of atoms, must have an intelligent maker, the later holds that all atoms are of the same kind and that no intelligent maker is required since sound, light, heat, shadow, darkness, union, disunion, fineness, grossness, shape, etc., are produced by accidental modifications. According to the Ājīvikas (q.v.), the atoms move and combine and may come together densely or loosely to form objects of different kinds. The combination of atoms occurs in fixed ratios. It is only in the Sarvāstivadā school of Buddhism that we come across the doctrine of atomism. Since Buddhism dogmatically asserts the impermanence of all things, the atoms in Buddhist conception cannot be eternal. According to the Buddhists, the atoms have only a functional role which may be compared with a focus of energy. The atoms of the four elements, and also their molecules, are related to the five senses. The four elements have distinctive attributes and functions, e.g., solidity and supporting in the case of earth, moisture and cohesion in that of water, heat and ripening in that of fire, and motion and expansion in that of air. The atoms constitute of molecules which must include at least one atom of all four elements and which acquire their characteristics according to the predominant atoms. Such conceptions are basically different from the Jain formulation which are closer to those of the Nyāya-Vaiśeṣikas. Some Mīmāṃsakas believe, like the Vaiśeṣikas, in the atomic theory but they hold that the atoms do not require, for their arrangement in the world, an efficient cause like god.

parama-pada The highest among the three steps of Viṣṇu which is described as being known only to himself and visible only to the sūris 'like an eye fixed in the sky'. *RV* I.22.20. The popularity of Viṣṇu lies in the importance of his *parama-pada* which is said to have been the home of the departed spirits. In later times Viṣṇu-pada became a synonym for the sky and the abode of Viṣṇu became the goal of spiritual aspirations of devotees, and several places, usually on the top of hills, came to be styled as Viṣṇu-pada.

paramapuruṣārtha The goal of all existence; the universal or supreme good.

parāmarśa Synthetic judgement, according to the Nyāya-Vaiśeṣikas, which is the combined product of the conditions of inference.

paramārthika As an adjective of *paramārtha* it means 'ultimate truth' in the religious and philosophical sense. It also denotes something transcendental and is used as a prefix for different terms to impart to them a distinguished significance. Thus *paramārthika-daśā*, a term used by the Vedantins means an 'absolute state' as opposed to *vyavahārika-dasā* or a 'phenomenal state'. The term *paramārthika-pratyakṣa* likewise denotes superconscious experience.

paramaśiva Ultimate reality in Kāśmīra Śaivism: it is also known as Anuttara, Cit, Caitanya, Pūrṇa or Para-Saṃvid, Parameśvara and Ātman. This state can be attained by an individual. It is the realisation of perfect and supreme *śivatva*—the condition of equilibrium of Śiva and Śakti. The attainment of the state of Paramaśiva is also to become the lord of *Śakti-cakra*, the circle of powers. *Spandanirṇaya* I.1.

parama-vihāra The final stage of spiritual attainment in the career of a potential *bodhisattva*. It is same as Dharmamegha-bhūmi (q.v.).

parameṣṭhī The 'supreme ones' revered by the Jains. There are five such beings—Siddha, Arhat, Ācārya, Upādhyāya and Sādhu—collectively called *pañca-parameṣṭhins* who are objects of worship.

parameṣṭhī-guru The fourth spiritual ancestor of the Guru. *Mahānirvāṇa* VI.98.

parameśvarī Goddess conceived as the supreme being.

paramīkaraṇa Anointing of the deity with the help of *mahāmudrā*. *Puraścaryārṇava* V. 346.

pāramitā The six, or ten, virtues of perfections which a *bodhisattva* is supposed to attain. These are *dāna* (gift), *śīla* (moral or religious observances), *kṣānti* (forbearance), *vīrya* (exertion or energy), *dhyāna* (meditation), *prajña* (knowledge), *praṇidhāna* (aspiration), *upāya-kauśalya* (skilfulness in expedients for doing good to others), *bala* (strength and *jñāna* (knowledge).

pāramitā-naya One of the two subdivisions of Mahāyāna according to the *Tattvaratnāvalī* collected in the *Advayavajrasaṃgraha*; also known as Pāramitā-yāna. The followers of this school based their religious practices on the cultivation of the *pāramitās* and derived the main impulses of their doctrine from the *Prajñāpāramitā* texts. The conception of the goddess Prajñāpāramitā as the embodiment of spiritual knowledge may also have something to do with this school.

paramudrā Subtle form of *mudrā*. *Tantrarāja* IV.55.

parāpara guru Third spiritual ancestor of the Guru. *Mahānirvāṇa* VI.98.

parā-pratibhā Same as Kaulikī Śakti. *Parātriṃśikā* 102, *Tantrāloka* III.24.

parā pūjā The highest form of worship which can be performed only by those who have knowledge of the Self.

para-rūpa The original form of deity which is beyond comprehension by the sense organs. Other forms are *sthūla* (gross) and *sukṣma* (subtle).

parā-śabda One of the four constituents of the sound-producing energy conceived as identical with Kuṇḍalinī (q.v.).

parā śakti A term variously used to denote different aspects of Sakti; it is also that power which denotes the Śivaness of Śiva. *Śivārkamaṇidīpikā* on *Brahmasūtra* II.2.38. Parā Śakti is therefore the energy of Śiva, often regarded as the instrumental cause of creation. The term is also used to denote the power of independence of the supreme being. It is that power, undifferentiated from Saṃvit (pure consciousness) by which the supreme being expresses itself. *Pratyabhijñā-hṛdaya*, p. 68. In *Tantrāloka* III, 103–104 it is regarded as Visarga-śakti which is by nature extrovert. *Ibid.*, III. 141–42. In Śaiva and Śākta outlook Parā Śakti is the Vimarśa, that is, the vibrating or kinetic energy of the supreme being. Parā Śakti is conceived in different names and forms. When it goes to manifest itself in creation the vibration caused thereby is called Nāda. Com. on *Śāradā*, I.7. It is revealed in the form of Vāk, etc. *Nityaṣoḍaśikārṇava*, VI.36. All the goddesses are its forms, *Mahānirvāṇa*, V.2. Conceived as Female Principle Parā Śakti is said to be in union with the other part of her self, that is Para Śiva, within the body of the aspirant, and this forms the *mithunatattva* of Tantra. *Kulārṇava*, V. Ḍākinī, Rākinī etc. are special forms of Parā Śakti. It is force behind the formation of Parā-vāk, Paśyantī, Madhyamā and Vaikharī, the ingredients of Śabdabrahma. *Kāmakalāvilāsa*, XXII–XXIII. It is equated with Kuṇḍalinī and its functioning.

Parā-śakti is also a term for the female partner of the aspirant. *Śāradā*, I. 51–54; Kālīcaraṇa on *Saṭcakranirūpaṇa*, LI.

paraśu Battle-axe serving as a weapon for certain Brahmanical and Buddhist deities.

parataḥprāmāṇyavāda Nyāya-Vaiśeṣika theory that knowledge is not valid in itself (*svataḥprāmāṇya*) unless it is verified in accordance with the origin and sources of validity and the ascertainment of the same.

paratantra In Mahāyāna Buddhism it refers to imaginary existence, depending on something of unreal origination. See also Pratibimbavāda.

parā vāk See also Parā Śabda. It is the first stage of sound expressing itself only at Mūlādhāra. It is without any vibration. It is like a flame of light, unmanifested yet indestructible. *Cidvallī* on *Kāmakalāvilāsa*, XX. It is not only connected with Kuṇḍalinī but also serves as the middle point of the triangle representing Kāmakalā. *Ibid*. XXIII.

parā-vidyā Transcendental knowledge; knowledge of *brahman*; anything which is conducive to the ideal of self realisation.

para-vindu See Vindu.

paridhi A wooden stick in the shape of a circle required in a sacrifice. The *paridhis* are about three spans long and made from the pliable branches of such trees as *palāśa, kārśmārya, khdira, udumbara*, etc. *Āp.Sr.*I.5–7–10, *Kāt.Sr.* II. 8.1. Paridhikarma is the name of a *śānti* (q.v.) rite; it is performed after collecting the charred bones of a deceased person. *Aśv.Gr.* IV.6.

parigraha śakti Material cause of creation, it is divided into two categories—pure and impure.

parijñāna Buddhist term for detailed knowledge.

parikalpita Mahāyāna Buddhist conception which refers to non-existence of worldly objects by their characteristics or signs. Asaṅga distinguishes *parikalpita* as being of three kinds: the basis (*nimitta* or *ālambana*) of one's thought-constructions; the unconscious impression (*vāsanā*) left by them on the mind; and denominations (*arthakhyāti*) following the impressions which are taken as real.

parikamma The first attempt which a Buddhist aspirant to spirituality makes at fixing the mind on the object of meditation. The aid for abstraction is called *parikamma-nimitta* and the entire concept is known as *parikamma-bhāvanā*.

parikara Playmates or associates of Kṛṣṇa in his *līlās* (blissful sports or pastimes). Parikara also means subsidiary figures of an image.

pariṇāmavāda A further specification of the Sāṅkhya theory of Satkārya-vāda (q.v.) according to which when an effect is produced, there is a real transformation or *pariṇāma* of the cause into the effect, e.g. the production of curd from milk. *Pariṇāma* is of two kinds; *svarūpa* or change into homogeneous or virupa or heterogeneous. See Sāmyāvasthā.

pariṇāmī-nitya Real as changing; as opposed to Kuṭastha-nitya, i.e., real as unchanging.

pariṇāmopadāna Material for real transformation which applies to Prakṛti according to the Vivaraṇa school. In the *Padārthatattvanirṇaya* of Gaṅgāpurī *brahman* is viewed as the changeless stuff (*apariṇāmī-upādāna*) and *māyā* as the mutable stuff (*pariṇāmi-upādāna*) of the world.

parinirvāṇa Natural end of life of those gifted men who realise *nirvāṇa* in their present conscious existence, according to Buddhism. In Jainism also, *parinirvāṇa* is the last fruit or final consummation of the highest perfection attained by a man or that is attainable in human life.

pariniṣpaṇṇa Mahāyānic term for absolute reality, denoting *dharmatā* or the real nature of things. Otherwise called *paramārtha* (the highest truth) or *tathatā* (thatness).

pāriplava Recurring narratives recited during Rājasuya by the Hotṛ priest. *Āśv.Sr.* X.6.10, *Āp.Sr.* XX.3, XX.6, *Śat.Br.* XII.4.3.

pariṣad Assembly of Brāhmaṇas.

parisahā One of the constituents of the Jain concept of *bhāvasaṃvara* (q.v.). Twenty-two kinds of hardships are enumerated including the endurance of hunger, thirst, heat, cold, lack of garments and so on.

parisaṅkhyā Mīmāṃsaka term for an injunction; when two alternatives are simultaneously possible one is precluded. *PMS* X.7.4,7. cf. Medhātithi on *Manu* III.45, *Mit.*on *Yāj* I. 79.

parispanda Motion by which the atoms are moved leading to a perpetual succession of integration and disintegration resulting in a variety of forms and appearances, according to Jainism.

parivrājaka Wandering ascetics. In the Buddhist *Niddesa* the parivrājakas are mentioned as a religious sect.

parṇakurca,-kṛcchra An expiation in which the leaves of *palāśa, udumbara, padma, aśvattha* and *vilva* and boiled separately on successive days and the decoction is drunk by the sinner. This penance lasts for five days. *Yāj* III.316.

pārśvadevatā A deity serving as an accessory to the principal diety in a temple. The image is placed in a side-niche of the main sanctum.

pārtha A *homa* (q.v.) required in Rājasūya.

pārvana A *homa* (q.v.) required in *darśapūrnamāsa*.

pārvaṇa-śrāddha One of the main divisions of the Śrāddha rites, the other being Ekoddiṣṭa (q.v.). The *pārvaṇa* is performed on the *amāvasyā* (new-moon) of a month, or the dark half of *bhādrapada* (Sept-Oct) or on *saṃkrānti* (last day of the month). In it three paternal ancestors are principally invoked, whereas in Ekoddiṣṭa the rite is for the diseased person alone.

pārvaṇa-sthālīpāka One of the seven *pākayajñas* (q.v.). It is a sacrifice of a mess of cooked food offered to the gods on new and full moon days. *Khadira Gr.* II.2.1–3, *Áśv. Sr.* I.3.8–12, *Āp.Dh.S.*II. 1.1.4–5.

parvata-dāna Gifts of heaps of corn, salt, jaggery, sesame, etc. Such gifts are of ten or twelve kinds and variously known as *merūdāna, acala-dāna, śaila-dāna,* etc. *Matsya* LXXXIII.92. *Agni* CCX. 6–10.

paryagnikaraṇa A rite in *paśubandha* (animal sacrifice) in which a fire-brand is carried three times round the animal to draw a magic circle around it in order to keep off evil spirits.

paryavasthāna A corollary of *anuśaya* (that which lies in the mind in a latent state with the possibility of its coming into appearance, if it receives an effective impulse). Paryavasthāna is the actual appearance in the mind of *anuśaya* (q.v.) without however a corresponding response in the outer world. Pali Pariyuṭṭhāna.

paryāya Term denoting 'changing modes' in Indian religio-philosophical tradition. In Jainism it has a special significance in which the properties, peculiarities and states of a substance originate and perish, and undergo changes. The Jain writers debated on the question as to whether Guṇa (q.v.) and Paryāya on the one hand and Dravya (q.v.) on the other are identical with or different from one another. Systems like Nyāya-Vaiśeṣika, etc. are of the view that the qualities of a substance are different from the substance itself while systems like the Sāṅkhya, Vedānta, etc., are in favour of their identity. The Jains maintain the relation of identity-cum-difference between Dravya, Paryāya and Guṇa.

paryāyārthika-naya Jain term for judgement from the viewpoint of changing modes. See Paryāya. *Pramāṇa-naya-tattvaloka*, VII.5.

paryaṅka Same as Dhyānāsana. See Vajraparyaṅka.

paryaṅka-śauca Purification by being seated on a stool or a seat. It is generally performed by ascetics.

paryudāsa Proviso or exception, when a particular rule is given in negative. To take an example, *Yāj* I. 132 provides that one should not say anything to a man or woman that would be painful. This does not altogether prohibit speaking of what is painful.

paryūṣaṇa An important fast of the Jains. According to the Śvetāmbaras, it takes place from the twelfth day of the dark half of Śrāvaṇa (Jul–Aug) to the fifth day of the bright half of Bhādra (August-September); and according to the Digambaras, from the fifth to the fourteenth day of the bright half of the month of Bhādra. See Pajjusana. Also known as Daśalakṣaṇaparva.

pāśa A noose or lasso. When a Vajra (q.v.) is attached to the end of it, it is called Vajrapāśa (adamantine noose). It is the weapon of Varuṇa. Certain Buddhist deities have also *pāśa* as their attributes. Pāśa also denotes fetters. These are generally considered to be eight in number. *Paraśurāmakalpasūtra* X.70. See *aṣṭapāśa*. A list of sixtytwo fetters is also found in different texts. See *Saubhāgyabhāskara* on *Lalitāsahasranāma* 129.

paścima āmnāya The western Tantric zone.

paśu Fettered individual. To this category belong men, animals and even gods. *Kauṇḍinyabhāṣya* on *Pāśupatasūtra*, I.1; V.7. In Tantra, Paśu is divided into two classes: Sabhāva (when influenced by knowledge) and Vibhāva (when knowledge leaves a mark on it). *Kaulāvalinirṇaya*, XI. 187. It is also divided into *dīkṣita* (initiated) and *adīkṣita* (uninitiated) categories. *Niruttara* XII.

paśubandha Immolation of an animal in a sacrifice; also called *nirudhapaśubanda*. Six priests are required to perform the sacrifice. The procedure is as follows: selecting a tree and making a *yūpa* (sacrificial post) and a *caṣāla* (head piece) for the post; preparing a *vedī* (altar) and a raised platform on it (*utaravedī*) and a square hole thereon called *nābhī*; invocation of Indra, Agni, Sūrya or Prajāpati; employment of eleven *prayāja* (q.v.) offerings and verses from *āpri* hymns; animal is to be bathed and touched with *kuśa* blade and *plakṣa* branch; its right foreleg and right horn is to be bound with a girdle of two strands; Hotṛ's recital or *adhrigupraiṣa*; killing of the victim; limbs are cut off for *puroḍāśa* and cooked in ukhā; its omentum is offered in the *āhavanīya*. Animal sacrifice in Somayāga is called Saumika-paśu. The sacrifice in which immolation of animal is required can be performed independently by an individual every six months or once a year. *Śat.Br.* III.6. 4ff. XI.7.1ff; *Taitt.Saṃ* I.3.5–11, VI.3–4, *Kāt.Sr.* VI, *Āp. Sr.* VII, *Āśv.Sr.* III.1–8, *Baudh.Sr.* IV.

paśu bhāva The ordinary human state. Certain spiritual exercises and cultivation of virtues are prescribed for individuals belonging to this state; through the performance of these they are able to reach the higher level known as Vīra. *Rudrayāmala*, Uttara VI.50–51, XI.28–29.

paśu-cakra One of the five *cakra* (q.v.) rituals, others being Rāja, Mahā, Deva and Vīra. *Niruttara* X.

paśu-karma A term for *homa* (q.v.) meaning 'the ritual with animal'.

paśupāśavimokṣaṇa Pāśupata rites by which an individual is delivered from the fetters of his painful existence.

pāśupata One of the earlier forms of the Śaiva system; the ultimate cause is believed to be Śiva (Pati or Lord) who is omniscient, omnipotent and almighty. The world, or individual (Paśu) fails to recognise him owing to Pāśa (q.v.) or fetters. All the problems and conditions of worldly existence can be solved by a proper comprehension of the five main tenets of this system—Kārya (q.v.), Kāraṇa (q.v.), Yoga (q.v.), Vidhi (q.v.) and Duḥkhānta (q.v.).

pāśupatavrata The Pāśupata custom of besmearing the body with ashes.

paśu śāstra The Tantric texts belonging to the non-Kaula groups. *Kulārṇava* II.

paśvācāra A term by which Vedācāra, Vaiṣṇāvācāra, Śaivācāra and Dakṣiṇācāra are characterised.

paśyantī One of the constituents of sound, regarded as the second stage of its development. This form of sound belong to the region around the navel. It has little vibration and is connected with Nādatattva. Com. on *Prapañcasāra*, II. 43.

paṭa Two dimensional painting or picture of a deity which often serves as a symbol of worship instead of the three-dimensional image.

pātaka Sinner. One who is polluted by vile action. *Yāj* III.219. *Gautama* XIX.2. The word *pātaka* is derived from the causal root *pat* meaning 'downfall'. The enumeration of sinful acts and the classifications of sins into several grades are found even in earlier works like *RV* VII.86.6, X.5.6, *Nirukta* VI.27, *Taitt.Saṃ.* II.5.1.2, V.3.12, 1–2, *Śat.Br.* XIII.3.1.1, *Kath. Saṃ.* XXXI.1, *Āp.Dh.S.* I.7.21, etc.

pātāla Nether regions which are generally understood as being seven. The names differ in the Purāṇas.

pati Term denoting God or supreme soul which is one of the three entities of most forms of Śaivism; the others are *pāśa* (fetters) and *paśu* (*jīva* or soul, i.e. individual). Pati means one who protects or controls *paśu* by a five-fold activity: creation, preservation, destruction, dispensation and emancipation.

patibhāga-nimitta The stage reached by a Buddhist spiritual aspirant which is a transition from *upacāra* to the higher level of *appanā*. The word *patibhāga* means reflex image. *Visuddhimagga* 125.

paṭicca-samuppāda See Pratītya-samutpāda.

pātihārika-pakkha The last fortnight of the three months of monsoon (*vassā, varṣā*), particularly the first half of the robe-month (*cīvaramāsa*) of Buddhists during which the practice of the eight-fold path is inculcated.

pātimokkha The accepted code of moral duties for Buddhist monks and nuns; in Sanskrit Prātimokṣa. The *pātimokkha* containing 227 articles is to be read twice a month in an assembly of at least four Buddhist monks and any breaches in observance confessed to them. There are punishments prescribed in the *pātịmokkha* for the delinquent monks as also certain observances stipulated for expiation.

paṭpadā That part of mental exercise which is necessary for collecting one's thoughts to reach the *upacāra* stage (i.e., withdrawing the mind from the surrounding objects as also from the characteristics of the subject for mental concentration) in the case of Buddhist aspirant. Literally, it means path.

paṭisambhidā The Buddhist conception of fourfold insight with which the four noble truths are to be viewed and interpreted to make them universally applicable to all matters of truth.

paṭisandhi Buddhist term for desire for rebirth. Patisandhi-viññāna is that which causes rebirth according to one's *karma* (q.v.) and Paṭisandhi-citta is that state of mind which craves for existence.

patitasāvitrīka Those whose *upanāyana* (q.v.) or initiation is not performed and who have no instruction in Gāyatrī *mantra*.

patnīsaṃyāja Literally means offering made to the wives; it is made to the wives of the gods along with some other deities. It consists of four offerings of clarified butter made in succession to Soma, Tvaṣṭṛ, Devapatnīs (wives of gods) and Agni. *Śat.Br.* I.9.2.

pātra Begging bowl or bowl generally found in the images of the five Dhyānī Buddhas and of Buddha Śākyasiṃha. Sometimes the Kapāla (q.v.) is used, as is stated in the *Sādhanamālā*, to designate a bowl.

pātrakṛcchra Expiation; same as Parṇakūrca (q.v.) but less severe.

pauṇḍarīka Sacrifice in which the *dakṣiṇā* is a thousand horses.

paurāṇika-pūjā The worship of five sectarian deities (*Pañcāyatana*, *pañcopāsanā*) and certain other deities which has been prescribed by the Smṛtis and Purāṇas; it is supplemented by the Vedic invocations (*saṃdhyāvandanā*) and sacrifices (*yajña*).

pauruṣeya Texts composed by learned persons. Pauruṣeya texts attempt to elucidate and interpret the contents of Śruti or Vedic knowledge which is regarded as *apauruṣeya* (not composed by any mortal being).

pāvamānī Verses from the ninth *maṇḍala* of the *Ṛgveda* (especially IX.67.21–27) the recital of which is supposed to purify a man.

pavana-niścāñcalya Process of holding up the breath which is a feature of Yogic exercise.

pavitra Loop or ring, made of *darbhas*; to be worn on ring finger in religious rites. Pavitra is also the name of a Soma sacrifice at the beginning of Rājasūya (q.v.).

pavitrāṇi Holy texts; reciting them a man can expiate his sins according to the Dharmaśāstras.

pavitrāropaṇa Offering of sacred *upavīta* (thread) to the gods.

pavitreṣṭi Rite prescribed for one desirous of *śuddhi* or purification *Āp.Sr.*II.12.

phala-kṛcchra Penance for minor offences; it consists in subsisting on only fruits for a month.

phalāpūrva See Apūrva.

phānsanā Superstructure of horizontal tiers; same as Orissan Pīḍhā-deul.

piṇḍa A lump of food offered to dead ancestors and kings. The size of the lump varies in accordance with the length of time of the ancestors. It should be made of boiled rice or other kinds of foodstuff mixed with sesamum. The *piṇḍas* are to be placed on *darbhas* spread on the ground or on an altar. Apart from satisfying the dead ancestors, the *piṇḍas* are also efficacious by themselves, e.g., if the middle one of the three *piṇḍas* is eaten by the performer's wife she is supposed to give birth to a son.

piṇḍabrahmāṇḍamārga The route taken in the upward march of Kuṇḍalinī. It is also known as Ṣaṭcakramārga.

piṇḍapitṛyajña See Pitṛyajña. It is so called because balls of rice are offered to the Pitṛs in this rite. According to Jaimini IV.4.19–21 Piṇḍapitṛyajña is an independent rite and not a mere subordinate part of the *darśa* sacrifice. Details of this rite are found in *Śat.Br.* II.4.2, *Taitt.Br.* I.3.10, II.6.16, *Āśv.Sr.* II.6–7, *Ap.Sr.* I.7–10, *Kāt.Sr.* IV.1.1–30. It is to be performed on *umāvasyā* (new moon) of each month by an *ahitāgni* (q.v.).

piṅgalā One of the major nerves. Together with its sister nerve Iḍā, it rises from Mūlādhāra and ends in the right nostril. *Prāṇatoṣaṇī*, I.4, p. 33. It is also known as Sūrya-nāḍī, and has the masculine characteristics of the sun. *Sanmohana* quoted by Kālīcaraṇa in the com. on Ṣaṭcak-*ranirūpaṇa*, I. It symbolizes waking state and leads individuals to violent actions. Rāghava on *Sāradā*, XXV.38.

piśāca Class of *vyantara-devatās (Q.V.)*.

piśācasiddhi A form of *siddhi* (attainment) by which one is supposed to maintain control over departed souls and other subtle-bodied beings through different types of mental practices.

pīṭha Holy resorts of Śakti, traditionally 51 in number. Their origin is associated with the Puranic Dakṣayajña legend. Each Pīṭha is supposed to contain a limb of Satī, the Śakti of Śiva, a presiding goddess and her Bhairava. There are also minor Pīṭhas known as Upapīṭhas.

pīṭha-nyāsa See Nyāsa.

pīṭha śakti Collective name for the goddesses Icchā, Jñāna, Kriyā, Kamadā, Kāmadāyinī, Rati, Ratipriyā, Nandā and Mānonmānī, each representing an aspect of Śakti. *Śyāmārahasya III*.

pitṛ Fathers or ancestors. The fortnight sacred to the fathers is known as *pitṛpakṣa* which is followed by *devīpakṣa* sacred to the goddess Durgā. The Vedic texts distinguish sharply between the way of fathers and the way of gods in regard to attainments after death. The Pitṛs are sometimes identified with the seven sages in the *Ṛgveda*. They are supposed to have the power of doing benefit or harm to the living. Ordinarily the male ancestors of three preceding generations are called Pitṛs and are identified with the Vasus, Rudras and Ādityas. *Piṇḍas* are offered to these three male ancestors while water is offered to Pitṛs like Aṅgiras, Kratu and Kaśyapa who are supposed to have some divine characteristics though they are placed in a class apart from gods. When gratified by *śrāddha* they bestow on their descendants long life, progeny, wealth, learning, happiness, heaven and liberation.

pitṛ-loka Abode of the Fathers; it is a place of happiness ruled by Yama, where a man is supposed to go after death according to *RV*, IX. 113.7–11.

pitṛmedha Method of disposal of the dead body of ancestors which includes the erection of a structure on his remains.

pitṛtarpana Satiating the ancestors with water. *Āśv. Gr.* III.4.5. See also Tarpaṇa.

pitṛtīrtha Part of the hand between the thumb and forefinger.

pitṛ-yajña Śrauta rite in memory of the dead ancestors in which *piṇḍas* (food-lump) are offered to the more distant ancestors, namely, those of the sixth, fifth and fourth generation and not to the first, second and third generation fathers, as is usual. The word *pitṛyajña* occurs in *RV*. X.16.10 and *Taitt.Ār*. II.10. Manu III.70 defines it simply as *tarpaṇa*.

pitṛ-yāna The way of Fathers which the dead are supposed to travel according to the Vedic tradition to reach the various worlds each according to his deserts. The Pitṛyānists are those who live in villages, perform sacrifices, make gifts, practice austerities, engage themselves in works of public utility and pass to the higher realms along the path called *pitṛyāna* though they have to return to this world. In contrast the Devayānists are those who live in the forest, practise faith, truthfulness and austerities and go to *brahmaloka* along the path called *devayāna* never to return to this world. *Bṛhadāraṇyaka* VI.2, *Chāndogya* V.10, cf. *Dīgha* III.239.

poṅgal South Indian festival of new-rice which resembles *navānna* of North India.

poṣaha Temporary ascetic life undertaken by Jain householders on the eighth and fourteenth day of the fortnight during the *pajjusana*.

prabandham Devotional songs of the Āḷvārs, written mostly in Tamil. These are known as the Vaiṣṇava Veda and form an essential part of Srī-Vaiṣṇava's education.

prabhava Buddhist term for truth of origin on account of births.

prabhāvalī The nimbus around an image.

pradakṣiṇa Circumambulation.

pradhāna See Prakṛti.

pradhvaṃsābhāva The absence of an entity following its destruction.

prāgabhāva The absence of an entity preceding its production.

pragātha Ṛgvedic verses employed in sacrifices. According to *Āśv. Sr.* V. 14.7–8, *pratipad* and *anucara* consist of three verses and *pragāthas* consist of two Ṛk-verses. A *pragātha* is called *bārhata* when the two verses are in *bṛhati* and *satobṛhati* metres and *kākubha* when there is a combination of the verses in *kākubh* and *satobṛhati* metres.

prāggrīva A porch-projection in temple architecture; same as *agramaṇḍapa* (q.v.).

prajāpati Cosmic principle mentioned in *RV* X.85.43, X.169,4, X.184.1, *Vāj.Saṃ*. XXXI.19, XXXII.5, *AV*. X.7.7ff, X.8.13, XI.3.52, XI.4.12. Prajāpati is identified with the universe in *Śat.Br.* II.4.2.1, VII.5.2.6, XI.5.8.1. etc. In *Kāṭhaka Saṃ*. XII.5, XXVII.1 and *Pañc.Br.* XX.14.2 it is stated that Vāk was the consort of Prajāpati and out of their sexual union all beings were produced. In the Brāhmaṇa literature we have a variety of creation legends associated with Prajāpati. *Ait.Br.* V.32, *Tāṇḍa Br.* IV.10.1, *Taitt.Br.* II.2.9, *Śat.Br.* VI.1.1.8ff. Subsequently, the impersonal *brahman* took the place of the personal and more or less ritualistic figure of Prajāpati who was relegated to the position of a deity of the mythological type.

prājāpatya A form of marriage which is the gift of daughter, after the father has addressed the couple ('may both of you perform your religious duties together') and after he has honoured the bridegroom (with *madhuparka*, etc.). Prājāpatya is also a general term for *kṛcchras* (expiations or penances). It is also a special term for expiation in regard to such offences as *gurvāṅganagamana* (union with Guru's wife) by mistake or *jātibhraṃśakara* (by which the caste identity is abolished) acts done unintentionally. Varieties of this penance are described in *Manu* XI.211, *Yāj* III.319, *Atri* 119–20, *Baudh.Dh.S.* IV.6.5, etc.

prajñā The Female Principle in Tantric Buddhism, the union of which with Upāya, the Male Principle, produces great bliss (*mahāsukha*) which is the non-dual quintessence of all entities. The Mahayanic conception of *śūnyatā* (q.v.) and *karuṇā* is substituted by Prajñā and Upāya in Tantric Buddhism. In *Hevajratantra* X, Prajñā is conceived of as *mudrā* or woman and Upāya as the Yogin, and their union is supposed to produce *bodhicitta* (q.v.) as the embodiment of *śūnyatā* and *karuṇā*. Cf. *Prajñopāya* 5, *Advayavajrasaṃgraha* 2,26,55. Prajñā is variously designated as a goddess (bhagavatī), a woman to be adopted for sādhanā (*mudrā*, *mahāmudrā*, *vajrakanyā*), a young woman (*yuvati*) and sometimes the female organ. *Advayavajrasaṃgraha* 62, *Sādhanamālā* 321, 329ff, *Guhyasamāja* 19, 153, *Śrīcakrasambhāra* 28, etc. She is also called *jananī* (mother), *bhaginī* (sister), *rajakī* (washer-woman), *nartakī* (dancing girl), *duhitā* (daughter) and *ḍombī* (Ḍoma-girl). Prajñā and Upāya are also called *lalanā* and *rasanā* which are also names of the two nerves *iḍā* and *piṅgalā* said to carry seed and ovum and to have been associated with the moon and the sun respectively. In certain Buddhist Tantras such as the *Nirṇāda* or *Ucchuṣma*, Prajñā and Upāya have been identified respectively with Śakti and Śiva. The common meaning of *prajñā* is wisdom. For the Hīnayānic concept of Prajñā see under Paññā.

prajñābhiṣeka Initiation of the disciple into *prajñā* or *śakti* according to the *Guhyasamāja* 161. The preceptor takes the hand of a beautiful woman, known by the term *vidyā* or *śakti*, and placing it on the hand of the disciple says that as Buddhahood is impossible to attain by any others means this *vidyā* should be accepted and never abandoned in life.

prajñaptivāda A branch of the Mahāsaṅghikas. The followers of this sect held that except in the case of the five *skandhas* (the constituents of a being), the *dharmas* (q.v.) have no real existence. The twelve *āyatanas* and eighteen *dhātus* are temporary or unreal. There is no such thing as untimely death which is the result of the past *karma*. The *ārya-mārga* is to be attained by good *karma*, and not by mere culture. Once it is attained, it can not be lost.

prakāmyasiddhi A type of Siddhi (attainment of miraculous power) which may be obtained through the rites of Antardasāra. *Nityaṣoḍaśikārṇava*, VIII.159.

prakāra Form of a determinate knowledge. The term is also used in the sense of a *viśeṣaṇa* or attribute.

prakaraṇa Understanding of a context or the intention (*tātparya*) of the speaker which is necessary if a *śabda* or verbal statement is to yield knowledge.

prakāśa The static aspect of the ultimate reality. According to the Śaiva and Śākta schools, *śakti* is Prakāśa-Vimarśamaya. In the background is *prakāśa* or illumination and in the foreground is *vimarśa* or vibration of *prakāśa* which is the subjective awareness of the static and latent power. *Prakāśa* is like the manifestation of all the qualities of an individual and *vimarśa* in his awareness of having those qualities. Prior to creation the *prakāśa-śakti* remains latent in the supreme being.

prakīrṇaka A class of unspecified sins, the penance for which should be prescribed by the brāhmaṇas after taking into account the nature of the deed, the ability of the perpetrator and other circumstances of time and place, etc. *Manu* XI. 209, *Yāj* III.294, *Visnu Dh. S.* XLII.2.

prakṛti Ultimate cause of the world of objects which, according to the Sāṅkhya, is an unintelligent and unconscious principle, uncaused, eternal and all-pervading, very fine and always ready to produce the world of objects. It is the primordial matter or substance, often conceived as a Female Principle, and known by different names like Pradhāna, Avyakta, etc. It is constituted by three *guṇas—sattva* (q.v.), *rajas*(q.v.) and *tamas* (q.v.). See Guṇatraya. *Maitrī Up.* III.5.V.2, *Kaṭha* IV.7, *Śvetāśvatara* I.10, VI-10, VI.16. *Sāṅ.Kārikā* XVI, *Sāṅ.Pra.Bh.*I.6, II.41–42, V.62ff. The whole of the cosmos exists in a subtle form in Prakṛti and becomes manifest in creation through the union with the conscious principle, *puruṣa*, conceived as the male element. The evolutes of Prakrti are *mahān* or *buddhi*, *ahaṃkāra*, *manas*, *buddhīndriya*, *karmendriya*, *tanmātras* and *mahābhūtas* (q.v.). In the Vedānta and in the theistic systems associated with it Prakṛti has been equated with Māyā or Avidyā conceived variously as the energy of *brahman*, the *upādhi* or limitation of *brahman*, the unmanifested matter, an unreal and illusory existence and so forth. The Buddhist conception of *loka* is similar to that of Prakṛti. In theistic systems, Prakṛti is subdivided into two parts, the *parā* and the *aparā*, the former denoting the spiritual or life-factor (*jīvabhūtā*) and the latter, the material (*jaḍā*) universe.

pralaya The dissolution or the closing down (*nimeṣa*) of the world at regular intervals. While *sṛṣṭi* or creation is nothing but the self-manifestation of the supreme being and may be described as opening out (*unmeṣa*) like a flower from the bud, *pralaya* is the reverse process. *Spandanirṇaya* I.1. The Purāṇas refer to recurrent absorptions of all beings and elements at the advent of Brahmā's night and give terrible and harrowing descriptions of the occasional *pralayas*. The Viṣṇuite Purāṇas hold that at the end of a *kalpa* the sage Mārkaṇḍeya alone remains, lies by the side of Viṣṇu and comes out of Viṣṇu's mouth.

pralayākala Śaiva Siddhānta concept of a kind of soul. Those for whom *māyā* alone has been resolved by the involution of the world etc. are called *pralayākalas*. To such souls the Supreme Being reveals itself in a divine supernatural form.

pramā Valid presentative knowledge which, according to the Nyāya, is definite or certain (*asandigdha*), faithful or unerring (*yathārtha*) and non-reproductible experience (*anubhava*) of the object.

pramāda Inadvertence; according to Jainism it is one of the constituents of *bhāvāsrava*. It is of five kinds: *vikatha* (bad conversation), *kaṣāya* (passions), *indriya* (sensuality), *nidrā* (sleep) and *rāga* (attachment).

pramāṇa The knowledge of anything truly which includes all the ways of knowing namely, perception (*pratyakṣa*), inference (*anumāna*), comparison (*upamāna*) and testimony (*śabda*).

pramatha Gaṇa or (attendants) of Śiva regarded as Vyantara-devatās (q.v.).

pramātṛ The knowers of, or experiences in, the five higher *tattvas* (*mantra*, *mantreśvara*, *mantramaheśvara*, *śāktya* and *śāmbhava*) in Kāśmīra Śaivism. In Vēdanta *Pramātṛ* is the term for the perceiver.

prameya Reality or the object of the true knowledge. According to the Nyāya philosophy the objects of such knowledge are self (*ātmā*), body (*śarīra*), sense (*indriya*), their objects (*artha*), cognition (*buddhi*), mind (*manas*), activity (*pravṛtti*), mental defects (*doṣa*), rebirth (*pretyabhāva*), experience of pleasure and pain (*phala*), suffering (*duḥkha*), freedom from suffering (*apavarga*), etc. *Nyāyasūtra* I.1.9–22.

pramuditā Name of a *vihāra* or stage of spiritual progress corresponding to the first *bhūmi* (q.v.) meant for the potential bodhisattvas. In his stage the aspirant goes beyond the *pṛthagjana-bhūmi* (plane of an ordinary being) and is regarded as a member of the Tathāgata family. *Bodhisattvabhūmi* 7.

prāṇa Breath, which is described in *AV* XI.4 as a cosmogonic principle and lord of all to whom the universe is subject and who supports all. It is identified with Prajāpati and other deities. In *Kauṣ. Up.* II.1–2 Prāṇa is identified with *brahman*. The *Bṛhadāraṇyaka* I.4.7 speaks of the fromless creator as having entered the body right down to the tips of the nails and of assuming therein the name and function of Prāṇa. The *Ch. Up.* IV.3ff says that breath or *prāṇa* in the individual is the finality and that it is that last quarter of the *brahman*.

prāṇa-liṅga Vīraśaiva concept of one of the three-fold modifications of *sthala* (q.v.). It is the object of worship of one who has attained the status of *bhogāṅgin* (q.v.), i.e., one who has given up carnal pursuits and takes delight only in what is conducive to spiritual growth. Prāṇaliṅga is the universal divine which takes its stand on possibilities, from the balance and opposition of which every action in the world seems to emerge.

prāṇapratiṣṭhā The endowment of life on the object of worship.

praṇava The three letters, *a*, *u* and *m* or *Aum* (*Om*) which represent the three *guṇas*—Sattva, Rajas and Tamas—and are supposed to be embodied in Viṣṇu, Brahmā and Śiva. It is probable that the Agamic *bījākṣaras* were fashioned after the *praṇava*.

praṇava-tanu Also known as *baindava-śarīra* it is the transubstantiated body which a Siddha (q.v.) attains by disciplining his body and various other processes. The followers of Siddha-mārga believe that by using the ceaseless supply of unseen extraphysical nourishment it is possible to revitalise the body. When the transmutation of *aśuddha-māyā* (q.v.) into *śuddhamāyā* (q.v.) is accomplished the body becomes incorruptible and freed from the thraldom of impure matter. It becomes known as *praṇava-tanu*. The man with *praṇava-tanu* is known as *jīvanmukta* (q.v.).

prāṇayāma Regulation of breath which is the fourth discipline of Yoga. It consists in *recaka* (exhalation), *puraka* (inhalation) and *kumbhaka* (retention) during the breathing process. *Prāṇatoṣaṇī* VI.1, 408. There are also other processes of prāṇāyāma.

praṇītā Water which is required in the principal sacrificial purpose of *darśapūrnamāsa* (q.v.), especially for making dough from the ground grains for *puroḍāśa*. *Jaimini* IV.2.14–15.

prapanna See Prapatti.

prapañca Term for phenomenal order and also for the universe and its constituents.

prapatti That doctrine which insists or complete self-surrender to the Supreme Being. *Śvetāśvatara* VI.23. Complete self-surrender, which is due to the feeling of utter helplessness and absolute belief is god's grace, is called *prapatti* or *śaraṇāgati*, and the devotee who achieves it is known as *prapanna*.

prārabdha Karma (q.v.) that has started functioning. An individual has to wait for the fruition of his *prārabdha* which remains with *avidyāleśa* (trace of ignorance). This trace of ignorance remains with the *prārabdha* which holds the body till final emancipation (*videhamukti*) is attained.

prasāda God's grace to the faithful. The term also means consecrated food.

prasāda-liṅga Modification of the Vīraśaiva conception of *bhāvaliṅga*. When the aspirant attains the *bhogāṅgin* (q.v.) state, i.e., when he is completely fit to take up a purely spiritual life, he becomes a *prasādin*, characterised by a state of undivided attention (*avadhāna-bhakti*) in communion with *prasādī-sthala*—one of the six stages of the Divine. The *liṅga*, i.e., the form of god to be worshipped by the aspirant is called prasāda-liṅga.

prasādī-sthala See under Prasāda-liṅga.

prasaṅga A Mīmāṃsaka term denoting that which occurs when something done in one place becomes of help in another place.

prāsaṅgika One of the two groups of the followers of Nāgārjuna headed by Buddhapālita (fifth century A.D.). They resorted to the *prāsaṅgika* (reductio ad absurdum) method and negated all that was phenomenal.

prastara The first handful of *darbha* grass cut for religious purposes.

pratibhajñāna Telepathy. *Yogasūtra* III. 32–33.

prātibhāsika Concept of illusory creation; just as a shell is mistaken for silver. The term is specially used to suggest that everything other than *brahman* is perceptual, having no existence outside perception (*ajñātasattva*).

pratibimbavāda The view of the Madhva school that *brahman* is independent and maker of all, the *bimba* or source, and that which it makes is *pratibimba* or a reflection. The latter is not independent of the former, nor an illusion. The world is real, essentially *paratantra* (dependent) having derived reality from *brahman*. If it is unreal there is no occasion to find out and conceive *brahman* as the source of all that exists. Therefore to understand the world as *pratibimba* or *paratantra* is the only way to understand its principle which is *brahman*.

pratijñā A proposition which is to be proved. It is one of the five steps of Indian syllogism.

pratīka A symbol, such as *liṅga* in the case of Śiva or *śālgrāma* in the case of Viṣṇu or *yantra* in the case of Śakti, or *stūpa* in the case of Buddha. Sound also serves as a symbol, e.g., *om* representing the undifferential *brahman*. The deity is worshipped not as the symbol, but through the symbol. The aim is to recognise in the limited the presence of the all-pervading spirit which transcends all limitations of time and space. The *pratīka* may be internal like the mind, intellect or soul of the worshipper or it may be external—it may be any token object which serves as a substitute or suggestion for the real object of worship or meditation.

pratimā Image of a deity. In Jainism Pratimā means the eleven stages of right conduct of a householder. These are right faith (*darśana*), vows (*vratas*), self-contemplation (*sāmāyika*), weekly fasts (*paṣadhopavāsa*), renouncing green vegetables (*sacitta-tyāga*), renouncing meals at night (*rātribhojana-tyāga*), celibacy (*brahmacarya*), giving up occupation (*ārambha-tyāga*), foresaking property (*parigraha-tyāga*), giving up interest in public affairs (*anumati-tyāga*) and giving up special food (*uddiṣṭa-tyāga*).

pratinidhi Substitute or representative, especially in the case of sacrificial articles.

pratipad See under *pragātha*. There is also a Pratipadvrata or religious observance in each *pratipad* (day after the new-moon or full-moon). Among such observances the most important is that which is held in the month of Caitra (March-April).

pratipakṣa-bhāvanā Thinking of the opposite view which the *Yogasūtra* II.33–34 advocates as a method of weeding out one kind of disposition by cultivating mentally the converse disposition.

pratipatti Final disposal of sacrifical materials,

like casting into water all utensils and things smeared with Soma at the time of final purification bath, etc.

pratisaṃkhyā-nirodha Buddhist concept of the destruction of *anuśayas* (latent desires) and the existence already produced as well as the non-origination of further *anuśayas*. It is achieved by means of knowledge (*pratisaṃkhyā*).

pratisāṃvatsarika Śrāddha (q.v.) to be performed every year on the days of death of the parents. It belongs to the *ekoddiṣṭa* (q.v.) type.

pratisaṃvid Buddhist term for the branches of logical analysis which are four: *dharma* (nature of condition), *artha* (analysis), *nirukti* (etymology) and *pratibhāṇa* (context). Pratisaṃvid-vihāra is the ninth *bhūmi* of a potential Boddhisattva in which stage he knows truly whether the *dharmas* are good, bad or indifferent, pure or impure, worldly or transcendental, conceivable or inconceivable, definite (*niyata*) or indefinite (*aniyata*), constituted or unconstituted.

pratiṣedha Also known as niṣedha, it is the term for proscription or abstinence.

pratiṣṭhā To instal. In particular the foundation of temple or dedication of wells, tanks, parks, etc., for the benefit of the public. Śabara on *Jaimini* I.3.2, *Sān.Gr.* V.2, *Āśv.Gr. Pariśiṣṭa* IV.9. etc., mention the time and stages of such donations. Reconsecration of images is known as *punaḥpratiṣṭhā*.

pratiṣṭhā-vigraha The fixed idol in a temple.

pratītya-samutpāda Buddhist law of Dependent Origination which explains how the three successive births (past, present and future) of an individual are related to one another. It is based on a twelve-point law of causation. Avidyā (ignorance) in a past life creates *saṃskāras* (impressions) which lead a man to *vijñāna* or birth-consciousness of the present life. From this originates *nāma-rūpa* or mental and physical faculties developing *ṣaḍāyatana*, or internal organs of sense and mind leading to *sparsá* or contact with the corresponding objects. Contact further leads to *vedanā* (sensation) which results in *tṛṣṇā* or desire to be reborn. From the latter arises *upādāna* (grasping) leading to *bhava* (becoming), the basis of *jāti* or birth in the next life. And when birth takes place it is sure to lead to *jarāmaraṇa* or tribulations, old age and death.

pratyabhijñā Method of perception which, according to the Nyāya, is the cognition of an object as what was cognised before. While the Naiyāyikas treat *pratyabhijñā* as a signle act of cognition, the Buddhists treat it as a combination of perception and memory. Pratyabhijñā is also the name of Kásḿīra Śaivism. Since the term means recognition it refers to the way of realising the soul's identity with Śiva.

pratyābhivādana Returning a salutation.

pratyāhāra Withdrawal of the senses from their respective external objects and keeping them under the control of the mind. It is the fifth discipline of yoga.

pratyakṣa Perception, which is the direct knowledge of objects produced by their relation to our senses. It may be external (*bāhya*) or internal (*antara*), according to whether the sense concerned is external like the eye and the ear, or internal like the mind (*mánas*).

pratyakṣaprāmāṇyavāda One of the five basic principles of the Cārvāka (q.v.) philosophy which holds that of all the sources of valid knowledge, perception alone is acceptable.

pratyālīḍha A posture of sitting in which the left leg is outstretched while the right is slightly bent and placed under it. It is the opposite of Ālīḍha (q.v.).

pratyāvarohaṇa A rite performed to mark the giving up of the use of cot for sleeping.

pratyavasita An ascetic who reverts to the life of a householder.

pratyeka-buddha Those Buddhist ascetics who live a life of solitude and attain the knowledge possessed by a buddha, but do not preach it to help other beings. The Hīnayāna branch of Buddhism is therefore called Pratyekabuddhayāna because it is concerned only with the salvation of the individual.

pratyutthāna To honouring by rising from one's seat. One need not rise to receive a brāhmaṇa who has not studied the Veda unless he is old.

pravāraṇā A gathering of Buddhist monks after the rainy season retreat for three months at which they declare their purity or confess their sins, just like the fortnightly *uposatha* ceremony observed regularly in the Buddhist monasteries. For the laity, it is the day of acquiring merits by offering food and robes to the monks. Pali Pavāraṇā.

pravargya A rite which was supposed to provide the sacrificer with a new celestial body. *Ait.Br.* IV.5. Though done during *agniṣṭoma* it was an independent rite by itself. *Āp.Sr.* XV.5. 72, *Kāt.Sr.* XXVI, *Baudh.Sr.* IX.6ff. It was performed for at least three days, twice daily, in the

Somayāga (q.v.). It required an earthenware vessel called mahāvīra and heated milk and water. Women and Śūdras had no right to witness it.

pravrajyā Pali Pabbajjā, meaning 'going out' from one stage of life to another. It is a process of initiation through which admission is gained in the Buddhist Order. The lowest age for initiates is eight years. The initiated one begins his life as a *pravrajita* (a homeless one), and is called *śrāmaṇera* or novice. The period of novitiate generally lasts for twelve years. The higher initiation, known as *upasampadā*, may be conferred on all those who have been admitted to *pravrajyā*. The cirmumstances disqualifying a person for admission and ordination are expounded in minute detail in *Mahāvagga* I. 29–76.

pravṛtti-mārga Spiritual exercise following the course of human nature. Literally *pravṛtti* means one's mental inclination. According to the Nyāya-Vaiśeṣikas, *pravṛtti* means striving for a thing which belongs to the category of *yatna*. *Siddhānta-muktāvalī* 150. In *Pūrvamīmāṃsā* it is the term for volition. In Madhva's system *pravṛtti* is the function of a thing. In Buddhism the group of kinetic forces is called *pravṛttivijñāna*.

prayāja The five offerings in *darśapūrṇamāsa* (q.v.) which are regarded as preliminary to the principal offerings.

prāyaścitta Measures for the expiation of sins. In *Taitt.Saṃ* (II.1.2.4) etc., the word *prāyaścitti* occurs in the sense of 'doing something by which one would get rid of some accidental happening'. It has also been used in other texts in the sense of expiation, especially in lapses in sacrificial and religious matters. But prāyaścitta became a more populer term. Śabara on Jaimini XII. 3.16 says that it is of two kinds— (i) meant to make good the defects in the procedure of sacrifice and (ii) undertaken to atone for not doing what is ordained or doing something which is forbidden. Most digests and commentaries derive the word from *prāya* and *citta*. The former means 'sin' and the latter 'purification'.

prayojana An end to achieve for which one acts or avoids acting. It is one of the sixteen philosophical topics of Nyāya.

prema Term for divine love.

preta Ghost; spirit of a departed person.

preya Desirable things for pleasure or enjoyment as opposed to *śreyas* or those desirable for better ends.

pṛthagjana Buddhist term for the ordinary individual; in Pali: Puthujjana. A person who labours under the delusion of I-ness or Mine-ness and thinks that he has *rūpa*, *vedanā*, etc. Not knowing the true law, he develops attachment to things and thereby increases the inflowing impurities (*āsrava*) of worldly desires, desire for re-existence and ignorance (*kāma*, *bhava* and *avijjā tanhā*).

pubbānta-kappika Certain groups of philosophers who used to speculate on the first beginnings of things. They consist of four kinds of Ṣassatavāda (Eternalists q.v.), four kinds of Ekacca-Sassatavāda (Partial Eternalists q.v.), four kinds of Antānantika (Limitists and Unlimitists q.v.), four kinds of Amarāvikkhepika (Evasive Disputants q.v.) and two kinds of Adhiccasamuppanika (Fortuitous Originists (q.v.).

pubba-seliya Same as Pūrvaśaila.

pudgala Matter in Jain cosmic conception. Etymologically Pudgala means 'that which is liable to integration and disintegration'. It possesses colour, smell, taste and form and is perceptible to touch. It can be consumed or destroyed and it may decay or alter its form. It is divided into four classes—*skandha* (whole), *deśa* (part), *pradeśa* (portion) and *paramāṇu* (atom, q.v.). The smallest parts of matter which cannot be further divided are called Paramāṇu or atoms. Two or more such atoms may combine together to form compounds (*saṃghāta*). The bodies and objects of nature are compounds of material atoms. *TTDS*, V.19–24. In early Buddhism Pudgala denotes *attā* or soul. The concept of soul as Pudgala has been accepted by the Vātsīputrīyas as a valid entity. This viewpoint has been vehemently opposed by the Sthaviravadins in the *Kathāvatthu* and by the Sarvāstivādins in the *Abhidharmakośa*. According to the Buddhist viewpoint, a person must completely eradicate from his mind the notion of individuality, the existence of his self which is only possible through the realisation of *anattā* or *pudgala-śūnyatā*.

pudgala-nairātmya A Buddhist term which means that what is believed to be self or *ātman* has no independent nature of its own and consequently no existence in fact; it is not a thing in reality but exists merely in the imagination.

pudgala-śūnyatā Doctrine of the absence of soul which a Buddhist should understand by removing both *kleśāvaraṇa* (cover of impurities) and *jñeyāvaraṇa* (the cover of ignorance) which shields away the truth.

pūjā Worship, the ultimate purpose of which is

unification with the deity. *Mahānirvāṇa*, XIV. 123–24. It is of two kinds, Bāhya (external) and Abhyantara (internal). It may be Sādhāra (with object) or Nirādhāra (without object). It is often classified into Vedic, Tantric and Miśra. *Śrīmad-bahāgavata*, XI.57.7. Among the other classifications we have Nitya, Naimittika and Kāmya; Sāttvika, Rājasika and Tāmasika; and Uttama, Madhyama and Adhama. *Gandharva*, XXII. 10–12; XXIV.22–23; *Mahānirvāṇa* XIV. 122.

pūjābhāga The upper section fo a Śivaliṅga.

pūjā-śilā-prākāra Wall erected around temples or shrines.

puṃsavana A *saṃskāra* (rite) used to ensure that a male child is born. *Āsv. Gr.* I.13.2–7. The *Āp.Gr.* says that it may be performed when pregnancy becomes apparent. This rite requires *homa* as a religious element, drinking curds, eating beans and grains of barley (elements of primitive fertility rites) and inserting a specified substance into the woman's nostrils as the medical element.

punaḥṣṭoma A *śrauta* sacrifice which removes sin.

punarādheya Re-setting the sacrificial fire. The process is more or less similar to that of *agnyādheya* (q.v.).

punarjanma Rebirth.

puṇya Meritorious acts which, according to the Dharmaśāstras, consists in performing the prescribed rituals, the *saṃskāras* (q.v.), *dāna* (q.v.), five daily sacrifices, going on pilgrimages and so forth. The Buddhist term for meritorious acts is *kusala-karma*. In Jainism these are needed for extinguishing the existing *karma* (q.v.) and to stop its further influx. There are nine kinds of *puṇya* and forty-two ways in which the reward of *karma* can be reaped. See also Cāritra, Mahāvrata, Anuvrata. Pañca-mahāyajñā, Mahādāna, Pāramitā, etc.

puraka A form of *prāṇāyāma* (q.v.) or breath control.

purāṇa-śrāddha Śrāddhas (q.v.) which are performed after a year.

puraścaraṇa Repeated recitation of a Mantra without which it cannot be effective. *Śakti-saṅgama*, Sundarī, III. 155–56; XVI. 45–46; *Gandharva*, XXVIII.7–8. It is regarded as the first step of Sādhanā. *Puraścaryārṇava* VI. 413 lists five steps—Japa, Homa, Tarpaṇa, Abhiṣeka and Viprabhojana. *Tantrasāra*, 48. In some texts another five steps are added. There are different degrees of this rite which apply to aspirants according to whether they belong to Paśu, Vīra or Divya categories. In the Kali-age proper Puraścaraṇa is not possible. *Kālivilāsatantra*, IV.6–7. Japa or muttering the Mantra is the main feature. *Kriyāsāra* quoted in *Tantrasāra* 48. There are elaborate rules and taboos regarding food habits, behaviour, time and space. The purpose of *Puraścaraṇa* is to attain Mantrasiddhi.

purṇābhiṣeka The highest form of initiation.

pūrṇa-bhogīā A religious community of Assam which adopted some of the practices from Buddhist Tantric observances in the Vaisnava rites and ceremonies.

pūrṇāhantā Attainment of perfect subjecthood which takes the form of a complete identification of the subject and the object. This concept found its best expression in Kāśmīra Śaivism. *Paramārthasāra* 13–14, *Īśvara-pratyabhijñā-vimarśinī* II, 192–93.

pūrṇatākhyāti Attaining the highest goal in Tantric aspiration.

purohita General term for priests. In a specific sense *purohita* denotes paid-priests employed by kings and wealthy persons for their spiritual welfare and also secular interests. The Vedic priests were variously known as adhvaryu, agnīdh, brahmā, hotṛ, neṣṭṛ, praśāstṛ, sāmga, udgātṛ and upavaktṛ.

puronuvākyā Invitatory prayer recited by the Hotṛ priest.

pūrtadharma Works of public utility such as digging wells and tanks, making parks, erecting temples and hospitals and so on. Such works are conducive to the attainment of *mokṣa* according to the Purāṇas. *Padma* VI. 243–44.

puruṣa Cosmic principle first mentioned in the Puruṣa-sukta of *RV* X.90. In *AV* X.2 it is the male principle of creation. In *Vāj.Saṃ.* XXXI.18, XXXII.2 it is described as a resplendent principle pervading the universe. In *Śat. Br.* XIII.6.1.1. and *Nirukta* II.3. it is equated with the universe. In *Bṛhadāraṇyaka* I.4 Puruṣa is identified with *ātman* (q.v.), in *Kaṭha* III.10–11 it is the highest entity, in *Muṇḍaka* II.1–10 it is the primeval person who is heavenly (*divya*), formless (*amūrta*), breathless (*aprāṇa*), mindless (*amanas*) and pure (*śubhra*). In the *Praśna* VI.1–6 it is compounded with the physical categories and in the *Śvetāśvatara* I.2, III.11–19 it is the First Principle. In the Sāṅkhya Puruṣa is the male principle, the contact of which with Prakṛti (q.v.) causes the evolution of world. The concept and position of Puruṣa in the Sāṅkhya is highly anomalous. It is indifferent, inactive and many, but not devoid of intelligence and as such it is a conscious principle. Just as a blind and lame man cooperate in order to get out of a forest, so also by the cooperation of the material and unintelligent Prakṛti with the inactive, indifferent but intelligent Puruṣa, the evolution of the world takes place. The identification of Purusa with soul was made in later times mainly due to the influence of Vedānta. The transformation of the original doctrine of the plurality of Puruṣa into that of its non-duality occurred due to the efforts of certain Vedāntins who wished to give the Sāṅkhya a Vedāntic colour.

puruṣakāra Personal effort for achieving the desired end. In religious life it takes the form of certain disciplines such as *dhyāna* (q.v.), *uccāra* (utterances), *varṇa* (attempt to be subtle) and *bāhya-siddhi* (external injunctions).

puruṣamedha Human sacrifice. The Taitt.Br. III.4.1ff.gives a list of persons who might be victims of this sacrifice. The *Vāj.Saṃ.* XXX–XXXI also deals with Puruṣamedha. It was probably only a symbolic rite, improvised as a part of sacrificial mysticism, but never actually performed, according to certain authorities. They hold that the rite of an actual slaying is not described in the Brāhmaṇa texts at all. The offering as such is mentioned in the late Sūtra works. For example under the title 'secret doctrine' *Vāj* XXXI gives a version of the Puruṣa-sukta (RV. X.90) to be recited at Puruṣamedha which confirms this view. However, there are actually some instances of human sacrifices and there is reason to believe that in the earliest stage of the Aśvamedha (q.v.) human beings were sacrificed and the custom was later substituted by the sacrifice of a horse.

puruṣārtha The aim of life. It consists of four values, viz. *dharma*, *artha*, *kāma* and *mokṣa* (qq.v.). The first three are collectively known as abhyudaya and the last one as niḥśreyasa.

pūrva A class of fourteen texts, meaning 'the earliest books', in which Lord Mahāvīra's teachings were first compiled. These texts are lost. The Śvetambaras believe that the Pūrvas were incorporated in the *Ditthivāya* or *Dṛṣṭivāda*, the twelfth Aṅga (q.v.) which is no longer extant.

pūrva-kaula A sect of the Kaulas (q.v.) mentioned by Lakṣmīdhara in his commentary on *Saundaryalaharī* XXXIII.

pūrva-pakṣa Views of the opponents. In the Indian method of logical discourse it is the general rule that the views of the opponent will be introduced first in clear undistorted terms and then each point be refuted.

pūrvaśaila A Buddhist sect connected with the Andhrakas in *Kathāvatthu* XVIII.8. This school believed that the bodhisattvas were not free from evil destiny (*durgati*) and that by making offerings to *stūpas* one cannot gain great merit.

puryaṣṭaka The eight subtle and gross elements of which the body of the goddess as represented in the *aṣṭakoṇa-cakra* is composed. *Kāmakalāvilāsa* XL.

puṣpa-karma A term for *pūjā* or offering worship with flowers. "Whoever with devotion offers me a leaf, a flower, a fruit or water, that I accept—the devout gift of the pure-minded" *Bhagavadgītā* IX.26.

puṣpakṛcchra A form of penance which entails that for a month only a decoction of flowers boiled in water be consumed. *Agni* CLXXI.12, *Mit.* on *Yāj* III.316.

pustaka A book in the form of manuscript which represents the Prajñāpāramitā, or the Book of Transcendental Knowledge, carried by several Buddhist deities, notably Prajñāparamitā, Mañjuśrī and Cundā. The Brahmanical Sarasvatī also contains a book in one of her hands. Sacred books are object of worship among the Jains as well.

puṣṭimārga The way of worldly enjoyment which is not considered as a bar to spiritual realisation according to the views of the Rudra-sampradyaya (q.v.) of Vallabha.

puṣyasnāna The ceremonial bath when the moon comes in the zone of Puṣyā star by which all evils are averted. Clay collected from several places are to be rubbed on the body, leaves of fifteen plants are to be cast in jars filled with water, *maṇḍalas* are to be drawn with powders of different colours and Puranic *mantras* are to be uttered in this occasion. It is also known as Puṣyābhiṣeka when performed by a king. *Bṛhatsaṃhitā* XLVII, *Viṣṇudharmottara* II.103 *Yogayātrā* VII.13–21.

putraka Those who have been initiated into *viśeṣa-dīkṣā* of Āgamānta Śaivism. They are so called because they belong to the *sāmīpya* (q.v.) stage of spiritual progress in which they feel them to be the son of God.

rādhākṛṣṇatattva The *rāsa* concept among Vaisnavas in terms of intense emotional attachment between the male and female principles symbolised by Kṛṣṇa and Rādhā, two aspects of the same ultimate reality, and impersonated by the aspirant and his female partner in *rāsalīlā* (lovesports).

rādhā-mahābhāva Also known as *mādana*, it is the highest aspect of maddening delight which is possessed by Rādhā alone. Its unique feature is that even a touch or sight of Kṛṣṇa is attended with the thrilling delight of being simultaneously kissed, embraced, etc. Along with this delight of union is blended an acute feeling of separation in spite of the proximity of her eternal lover. *Ujjalanīlamaṇi*, sthāyī, 155, *Caitanyacaritāmṛta* I.4.109ff.

rādhāṣṭamī The *aṣṭamī* or eighth lunar day of the bright fortnight following Kṛṣna-janmāṣṭamī in the month of *bhādra* (Sept-Oct). It is the birthday of Rādhā, the consort of Kṛṣṇa, which is celebrated especially by the Vaiṣṇavas of Bengal school.

rāga Attachment. In Vīraśaiva ideology, *rāga* or attachment belongs to the second or *cit-acit* category of thirty-six principles of cosmic evolution. In its negative aspect *rāga* is the attachment towards worldly life and pleasure, but in its positive aspect it is conducive to *bhakti* or devotion, often spoken of as *rasa* (q.v.). Rāga develops into *anurāga* in which object of love, even though realised, is relished always and appears to be clothed in fresh charms and attractiveness every moment. *Ujjalanīlamaṇi*, sthāyī, 102.

rāga-mārga The path of spontaneous love, regarded as the only means to achieve the highest spiritual end which is emphasised by the Sahajiyās. This path is in total contrast to *vidhimārga* or the path of injunctions and prohibitions—the path of duty.

rahasya Certain tenets of the Śrīvaiṣṇava faith. They are (i) the *mūlamantra* or *aṣṭākṣarī*, (ii) the *davya* and (iii) *caramaśloka*. The first is *om namo nārāyaṇāya*; the second is prefixed by the term *śrī* in order to indicate the importance of the grace and the effort of the spiritual aspirant. The third is verse 66 of Ch.XVIII of the *Gītā*. This is the base of *śaraṇāgati* (q.v.) theory.

rahasya-āmnāya Mysterious area of Pāñcarātra (q.v.) knowledge comprising letters and formulae, the meditations on them and special modes of worship by means of *mantras* of various kinds. The *Sātvata-saṃhitā* states that this Śāstra is beneficial for all persons irrespective of caste and colour who take recourse to self-surrender.

rahasya-sampradāya The followers of the Trika (q.v.) doctrine of Kāśmīra Śaivism.

rahasyayoginī The eight presiding goddesses of the *aṣṭakoṇa-cakra* (q.v.). *Gandharva* XVII.74.

rājacakra One of the five forms of Cakra worship in which mother, sister, daughter, daughter-in-law and preceptor's wife are regarded as Śaktis, *Niruttara* X.

rājagirika Buddhist sects connected with the Andhakas. The *Kathāvatthu* XV.9 ascribes to the Rājagirikas the view that it is possible for one to die in a state of trance, that there are no such things as mental properties (*caitasikas*), that gift is a mental state, that an *arhat* cannot have an untimely death and that the consequences of wicked action may extend over a whole *kalpa*.

rajakī Woman of the washerman-caste who serves as a female partner of the Tantric aspirant. The term is also used to denote Śakti as Kulanāyikā. Rajakī also denotes any woman in the third day of her menstruation. *Niruttara* XV, *Tantrasāra* 627.

rājarṣi Saintly kings who had mastery over spiritual topics. A few such kings are mentioned in the Upaniṣads.

rajas That constituent of Prakrti (q.v.) which is of the nature of pain and is mobile (*cala*) and stimulating (*upastambhaka*). It gives rise to wrath, greed, egotism, worldly activity and boastfulness.

rājasenaka Lowest moulding of a Kakṣāsana or balconied window of a temple.

rājasūya Yajña meant for royal consecration. It was performed by the king for achieving sovereignty. It was in form a Soma sacrifice, preceded by the usual *dīkṣā* (q.v.) ceremony, the *upasad* (q.v.) days, and other preliminary rites that lasted well over a year. On the day of the *abhiṣeka* (anointing), which was generally the first day of Caitra (March-April), exactly thirteen months after the opening of the preliminaries, the king, draped in regal raiment, took a bow with three arrows from the *adhvaryu* and announced his anointment with an appropriate formula. He then stepped forth in each of the different quarters and sat on a seat made from the wood of the *udumbara* tree covered with a tiger-skin. He was then libated with a fluid—made of butter, honey, different kinds of holy water and other ingredients—poured over him from a cup of *udumbara* wood. Soma libations and offerings followed next, after which he enacted a mimic raid in his chariot on the cattle of his kinsfolk at whom he discharged his arrows. He then sat on a throne covered with a tiger skin and played a mock-game of dice, with a cow as the stake, in which his victory was guaranteed. The final rite was bath. *Taitt.Saṃ*. I.8.1–17, *Taitt.Br*. I.4.9–10, *Śat.Br*. V.2.3–5, *Ait.Br*. VII. 13, VIII, *Tāṇḍya Br*. XVIII.8–11, *Āp.Sr*. XVIII.8–22, *Kāt.Sr*. XV.1–9, *Āśv.Sr*. IX.3–4, *Śāṅ.Sr*. XV.12ff.

rajasvalā-dharmah Duties and impurities of a *rajasvalā* or a woman in her monthly illness which have been laid down in *Taitt.Saṃ*. II.5.1, *Taitt.Br*. III.7.1, *Baudh.Dh.S*. I.5.139, *Mit*. on *Yāj* III.20, etc.

rājayoga A form of Yoga in which the mind automatically merges in *brahman* just as air merges in the sky. *Prāṇatoṣaṇī*, VI.3, p. 433. It is free from all dualism. *Śivasaṃhitā*, V.17. It leads to Nirvikalpa Samādhi in which there is absolute unity of knower, knowledge and the source of knowledge. This *samādhi* is known as Rāja-yogasamādhi and is also possible by a special *kumbhaka* process of breath control known as Manomurcha which connects the mind with the supreme being. *Gheraṇḍa*, VII.16.

rakṣā-bandhana Also known as *rākhī-bandhana*, The custom of tying a knot on the wrist of another denoting solicitation of protection, usually a sister from a brother. It falls on the day of the full moon in *śravaṇa* (Aug-Sept) and is observed both by the Hindus and the Jains.

rākṣasa The Rākṣasas, derived from the root *rakṣa* (protector), were probably the original settlers of India, though they are mentioned deprecatingly as demonical beings for their professed hostility to the sacrificial cults. In Jain and Buddhist canonical works they are regarded as vyantara-devatās (q.v.). Eight Rākṣasas—Mukhya, Mṛga, Aditi, Udita, Vitatha, Antarīkṣa, Bhṛśa and Pūsaṇ—were objects of propitiation. Rākṣasa is also the name of one of the eight forms of marriage which is the forcible abduction of a maiden.

rāmalīlā Festival in honour of the victories of Rāma which is celebrated in different parts of northern India with dramatic performances of Rāma's life and the miming of various episodes from the *Rāmāyaṇa* on the *dasarā* or *vijayā-daśamī*, the last day of the Durgā worship in autumn. In practice *rāmalīlā* is celebrated all over North India on the first ten days of the bright-half of Āśvina (Oct-Nov).

rāmanavamī The bright ninth in the month of Caitra (March-April) observed by the followers of Rāma cult with fasting and rites of worship as the day of Rāma's birth. However it is not mentioned in the *vrata* texts like *Kṛtyakalpataru*.

raṅga-maṇḍapa A pillared hall opened on all sides used for religious purposes.

rasa An emotion comprising attachment (*rāga*) and intense attraction (*anurāga*) to the Lord. Etymologically *rasa* means anything that may be tasted or enjoyed. But technically it means a thing the taste of which causes a delicious surprise on account of its heightened sweetness. There are five principal *rasas*: *śānta*, *dāsya*, *sakhya*, *vātsalya* and *madhura*.

rasa Sap, elixir, sentiment. According to Rase-śvara-darsána, the use of chemical drugs, especially those prepared from mercury, makes possible the renovation of the body and is conducive to Jīvanmukti (liberation within the span of life). *Sarvadarśanasaṃgraha*, IX. 1ff. Besides chemical elixir, Rasa is also conceived in terms of intense emotional attachment between the male and female principles, symbolising two aspects of Śakti, embodied by the aspirant and his partner. See *Lalitāsahasranāma*, 106. This conception is very popular also among the Vaiṣṇava Sahajiyās, the Bauls and others.

rasacitra Decorative designs used in rituals; same as *ālpanā*.

rāsalīlā See under Rādhākṛṣṇatattva. The *rāsalīlā* consists in dancing in a circle in a particular way, accompanied by singing. It is the miming of the legend of Kṛṣṇa's dalliance with the Gopīs at Vṛndāvana on an autumnal full-moon night. It is symbolic of the divine love (see under *rāga* and *rasa*) or *mahābhāva* in which the loving services of the Gopīs (q.v.) for Kṛṣṇa's pleasure know no restrictions whatsoever.

rasānanda-yoga-samādhi A state of Yogic bliss achieved through breath control. *Gheraṇḍa* VII.10–11.

raseśvara-darśana A Tantric outlook, also known as Kāyatattva, based on the idea of rendering, by varied physico-chemical processes, the human body deathless and also the spiritual liberation of man by his monadic transfiguration. It was believed that preservation of the body could be achieved by the use of mercury, medicaments and breathing exercises. Vibrating, cleansing, stimulating and projecting the body with the help of a special *elixir vitate* were considered to be essential preconditions for emancipation within the span of life. See also Rasa, Siddhacikitsā, Jīvanmukti.

ratha Chariot; also projection of a shrine.

rathakrāntā A zone of Tantric culture extending from the Vindhyas to Mahācīna.

rathayātrā The car-festival of Jagannātha, Balarāma and Subhadrā on the second lunar day of the bright fortnight in *āṣāḍha* (June-July) held at Purī and other places. The chariots adorned with floral wreaths, flags and other decorations are pulled by the devotees along with the entire path of the procession. There are also car festivals in honour of Śiva at Bhuvaneswar and Rameswaram, of Mīnākṣī at Madurai, of both Śiva and Viṣṇu at Kanchipuram and of Avalokiteśvara at Nepal.

rati Sexual intercourse. In Vaiṣṇavism, especially in that of Caitanya school, it is called *premāṅkura* or the first stage of divine love. Its outward indications are forbearance, utilisation of every moment in religious practices, freedom from worldly attachment, sense of submission, firm belief, ardent longing for union with god, chanting god's name, narrating god's attributes and a great liking for the places of his līlā. *Caitanya-caritāmṛta* II.23.5–9, *Bhaktirasāmṛtasindhu* I.4.11. Rati ripens successively into *prema* (sense of belonging), *sneha* (idea of mineness), *māna* (love-jealousy), *praṇaya* (confidence in love), *rāga* (excessive largerness for union with god), *anurāga* (fresh charms) and *mahābhāva* (supreme love). *Ujjvalanīlamaṇi*, sthāyī, 102. There are five kinds of Rati: *śānta* (preliminary which develops up to *prema* stage), *dāsya* (love of servants which develops up to *sneha*), *sakhya* (love of friends which develops up to *rāga*), *Vātsalya* (love of parents which develops up to *anurāga*) and *madhura* (love of Gopis which develops up to *mahābhāva*.) *Caitanya-caritāmṛta* II.23. 34ff.

rātrisattra Certain *sattras* (q.v.) or sacrifices extending over more than twelve days. *Jaimini* IV.3.15ff.

raurava A hell supposed to be below the earth. Raurava is also the name of a *sāman* (q.v.).

rāvaṇānugraha-mūrti A class of *anugraha-mūrti* (q.v.) of Śiva bestowing grace on Rāvaṇa. This type is common in South India.

ṛbhu Three divine artisans mentioned in the Vedic texts. Their names are Ṛbhu, Vibhavā and Vāja. They are connected with the third pressing of Soma. They are said to have been mortals but were made immortal by Prajāpati.

recaka A part of *prāṇāyāma* (breath control); it is the exhaling of breath.

riddhi The Buddhist concept of five supernatural powers.

ṛkvan A class of Pitṛs (q.v.) associated with Bṛhaspati, Soma, Viṣṇu and other gods.

ṛṇa Obligations. According to the Brāhmaṇa literature man is born with certain *ṛṇas* or debts which he must discharge in his life. He has a debt to pay to the gods, to the *ṛṣis*, to the manes, to men and to the lower creatures.

rohita A form of fire or sun described as the creator of heaven and earth and the generator of all beings; also identified with Prajāpati and Kāla (q.v.). *AV* IV.11, XIII.1.

roṣa That power bestowed by Śiva on individual souls which helps them to become free from worldly fetters. This term is common to different Śaiva schools.

ṛṣi Sages, seers or saints who acted as spiritual advisors of people and performed rituals for their welfare. They lived in seclusion in the forests. In the fourfold *āśrama* scheme they had reached the *vānaprasthīya* (q.v.) stage. None of the *ṛṣis* mentioned in the Upaniṣads or in the Purāṇas were ascetics or saṃnyāsins. They also acted as teachers and students used to live in their hermitages.

ṛṣi-cāndrāyana A penance which requires the penitent to eat only three mouthfuls of sacrificial food each day for a month.

ṛṣikula Educational institution in the hermitage of the Ṛṣis where *brahmacārīs* used to stay and learn.

ṛṣipañcami-vrata An observance connected with the seven Ṛṣis or mythical sages; it takes place on the fifth day of the bright half of *bhādra* (Sept-Oct). It was meant for all, but now it is practised mostly by women. The object is to remove all sins and physical ailments of a gynaecological nature while keeping away troubles and ridding women of contacts from all social contacts during monthly illness. The performer is forbidden to eat anything produced on land by oxen or watered by the labour of oxen. The seven sages and Arundhatī are worshipped.

ṛṣi-yajña One of the five daily sacrifices, a householder should perform; the others are Pitṛ, Deva, Manuṣya and Bhūta. Also known as Brahma-Yajna it is the study and teaching of the Vedas. It is based on the ethical precept that one should share one's knowledge with others.

ṛta Vedic term for the laws by which the world is governed; it includes natural, social and moral laws as well. It is an expression of the unchanging, regular cyclic rhythm in nature. The Devas are said to be born in *ṛta* and governed by it. It also stands for the concepts of 'truth' or 'right' as also for 'the order'.

ṛtambharā-prajñā Truth-bearing insight which is obtained by *śravaṇa* (q.v.), *manana*(q.v.) and *nididhyāsana* (q.v.).

ṛtusaṃgamana A *saṃskāra* (sacrament). Same as *niṣeka* (q.v.) and *garbhādhāna* or *caturthīkarma* (q.v.). *Vaik* III.9.

ruddha-mantra Defective Tantric *mantra* (q.v.); it contains *lam* in the beginning, middle or end. *Śāradātilaka* II.72.

rudrabhāga See Pūjābhāga.

rudra-granthi A knot in the *ājñācakra* (q.v.) obstructing the upward march of Kuṇḍalinī. Com. on *Yogaśikhopaniṣat* I. 87, *Saubhāgya-bhāskara* on *Lalitāsahasranāma* 89.

rudra-sampradāya Vaiṣṇava sect based on the *śuddhādvaita* (q.v.) theory of Vallabha. According to this sect *brahman* is not other than Kṛṣṇa. He represents the principle of love by which his relation with individual souls is determined. This love is of that type which takes place between a man and a woman. The Female Principle is idealised in Rādhā. Every individual should feel womanly passion for the beloved who is one and only one, the eternal lover Kṛṣṇa.

rudragāyatrī A *mantra* used by the followers of Śiva which closely resembles the famous *gāyatrī* verse. *Taitt.Ār.* X.1, *Kāṭhaka Saṃ.* XVII.11.

rukkha-cetiya See Caitya. A tree within reilings; it was the earliest form of the Caitya concept.

rūpa One of the two broad divisions of the five constituents (*skandhas*), the other being *nāma* in Buddhist belief. It denotes the material elements.

rūpa-dhātu Buddhist concept of one of the three spheres of earth. The beings of this sphere possess all the five constituents (*khandas*), and originate from attachment to *rūpa* (material objects). They are subdivided into seventeen categories.

rūpa-cakra See Nirmāṇa-cakra.

rūpa-kaṇṭha A recessed course carved with figures; a freize in a temple.

rūpa-kāya The material or created body of the Buddha. Also known as Nirmāna-kāya. See under Trikāya.

rūpa-śākhā Jamb of a temple doorway carved with figures.

śābarotsava A ceremony of festive character, consisting of obscene songs and gestures, associated with Durgā worship.

śabda Verbal testimony; knowledge derived from the statements of authoritative persons. It is sometimes regarded as a valid source of knowledge. There are two ways of classifying Śabda: *dṛṣṭārtha* (that relating to perceptible objects) and *adṛṣṭārtha* (that relating to imperceptible objects). There are two subdivisions of testimony: *vaidika* (scriptural) and *laukika* (secular). The latter is not always regarded as valid. In the sense of sound, *śabda* has a different religio-philosophical significance. See under Śabdabrahma.

śabdabrahma Brahman (q.v.) conceived as the substratum of sound. See under Parā, Paśyanti, Madhyamā and Vaikharī. It is the *caitanya* (tendency towards manifestation in all beings) pervading all creation, and is the source of the letters of the alphabet, of words, and of other sounds through which thoughts are exchanged. From *śabda* arises the ethereal region. See under Sabdādvaita and Sphota.

śabdādvaita A monistic interpretation of. the theory of sphoṭa (q.v.) advocated by Bhartṛhari and others. See under Sphoṭa.

sabhya A kind of domestic fire. *Manu* I. 185, *Kāt.Sr.* IV.9.20, *Āp.Sr.* IV.4.7.

saccidānanda-svarūpa Pure-consciousness, bliss and existence in essense—*brahman*'s description by Nimbārka.

sadācāra Usages or practices of the *śiṣṭas* (decent peoples). There are intricate questions about the relative merits of Śruti (the Vedic way) and Smṛti (the way prescribed by the Dharmaśāstras) in regard to Sadācāra. According to Kumārila, those usages are alone authoritative that are not opposed to Vedic texts, that are practised by *śiṣṭas* in the belief that they are part of *dharma* (right path) and for which no obvious motive can be predicated.

ṣaḍādhāra-pratiṣṭhā Fixing of the six *ādhāras* (supports) in the middle of the *garbhagṛha* (sanctum sanctorum) of a temple where the idol is to be installed. *Tantrasamuccaya* I.70ff.

sādākhya-tattva The experience in which 'I' or *aham* (subject) and 'this' or *idam* (object) are held in unity. Also known s Sadāśiva-tattva in Śaiva and Śākta tradition.

ṣaḍaṅganyāsa Nyāsa for feeling the deity in six parts of the body—heart, head, top of the head, protective amulet, eyes and intestines.

sadāśivamūrti Śaiva images, mostly evolved in South India in medieval times, which are intended to illustrate in an esoteric manner some of the principal tenets of Āgamānta Śaivism or Śuddha Śaivism.

sadasya Seventeenth priest whose services are required in the Soma sacrifices, *Baudh.Sr.* II.3.

saddhā Buddhist term for faith or conviction which is the means for developing the highest reverence for the triad or *triratna* of Buddha, Dharma and Saṃgha. The way of simple faith is known as *saddhāmusārī* and that of religious conviction *saddhāvimutta*. *Aṅguttara* I. 118–20.

sādhaka Spiritual aspirant.

sādhana The middle term in Anumāna (q.v.) in the Indian logical system of inference. Also known as Hetu.

sādhanā Procedure of worship for the invocation of Buddhist gods. In general it is the term for spiritual exercise.

sādhanadeha Purified body for sādhanā.

sādhāraṇī Female partner of the aspirant, drawn from public women.

sādhu Holy person whose life is dedicated to the search for God. Sādhus are often compared to cotton. Their lives are as pure as the whiteness of cotton, as dry (i.e., unattached) as the cotton-pad and as useful for protecting common men as cotton-clothes for the body.

sādhumārgī Term for Jain non-idol-worshippers.

sādhya The major term, the object which one wants to know in relation to the Pakṣa (q.v.) or the inferable character of the latter. See under Anumāna.

sad-vidyā Same as Suddha-vidyā (q.v.). See Suddha-māyā.

sādi-vidyā A branch of knowledge designated after the symbolic first letter of the Śakti Vīja.

sadyaḥśauca Impurity caused by the death of a relative. It can be removed by a mere bath.

sadyojāta One of the five faces of Śiva from which a number of Tantras are supposed to have emanated.

sahaja The *mārga* or way of spiritual exercise which is the easiest and most natural. It is also the term for the ultimate reality among the Sahajiyās, i.e. those who believe in this *mārga*.

sahaja-kāya Same as Vajra-Kāya (q.v.). See also Trikāya.

sahaja-mahāsukha The peaceful, blissful, radiant and waveless experience of *sahaja* (q.v.).

sahajayāna Offshoot of Vajrayāna (q.v.) which

holds that truth is something which can never be found through the prescribed codes of study, discipline, conduct, worship and ritual. What is natural (*sahaja*) is the easiest, and hence there is no need for religious formalities, austere practices of discipline, reading, philosophising, fasting, constructing temples and images and so on. The followers of this school lay greater emphasis on the imperative necessity of making the body sufficiently strong and fit before starting yogic processes and believe in the existence of an internal female-force in the *nirmāṇacakra* (q.v.). The Sahajayāna considers the human body itself as the seat of all human experience including that of *sahaja-mahāsukha* (q.v.).

saha-mārga Literally, 'Path of friend'. In Southern Śaivism the term denotes the way of Yoga.

sahasra-kūṭa Pyramidal shrine-model with a thousand (or at least numerous) figures of Jinas.

sahasraliṅga A king of Śiva phallus so called because the *rudra-bhāga* (q.v.) is ornamented with incised parallel horizontal and vertical lines.

sahasrāra The highest cerebral region above all the *cakras* or never-plexuses where Kuṇḍalinī meets its source. For a description of it see *Ṣaṭcakranirūpaṇa* XLI–XLIII.

śaila Buddhist sect; see under Caityaśaila, Aparaśaila, Uttaraśaila. A subsect of the Vetulyakas was also known by the same name and shared the docetic views of the Lokattaravāda. The *śaila* schools held that the Bodhisattvas were average human beings and might be born in the lowest states of existence and that offerings made to a *caitya* did not necessarily earn great merit.

śaivācāra A form of *dakṣiṇācāra* (q.v.) which insists on the cult of Śiva-Śakti, the Vedic way, eight-fold Yogic practices and animal sacrifices. *Prāṇatoṣaṇī* VII.1, 499.

sājātya-bheda One of the three kinds of *bhedas* (q.v.); literally 'difference within the same species'. According to this doctrine both *brahman* and the *jīva* (q.v.) are *cit* (conscious) in essence and hence they belong to the same species. So the difference between *brahman* and *jīva* belongs to the *sājātya* category according to the *Acintyabhedābheda* school.

śākamedha Vedic sacrifice for *pitryajña* (q.v.); it is performed in autumn in which the *dakṣiṇāgni* (southern fire) is prominent. A sacrificial feast is given to the manes. Another important element in this sacrifice is an offering to Rudra Trambyaka for the protection of the flocks. It is followed by an offering to *śunāśirau*, the two deified parts of the plough, which shows the agricultural affiliation of this ritual. *Taitt.Saṃ*. I. 8.4–6, *Taitt.Br*. I.6.10, *Śat.Br*. II.5.3ff, II.6.1.2, *Āśv. Sr*. II.18–19, *Āp.Sr*. VIII.9–19, *Kāt.Sr*. V.6–10, *Baudh.Sr*. V. 10–17.

sakhya That kind of devotion in which God is looked upon as a friend, as between Kṛṣṇa and Subala. Sakhya-bhaktas are comrades who consider themselves equal to God in every respect. Sakhya is one of the five kinds of *rasas* and *ratis* (qq.v.), i.e., devotional instincts and experiences which develops into *anurāga* (intense love). *Caitanyacaritāmṛta* II.23.

śākinī The presiding goddess of *viśuddha-cakra* (q.v.) Kālīcaraṇa on *Ṣaṭcakranirūpaṇa* XXX.

sakkāyadiṭṭhi A false perception, according to early Buddhism, which holds that the constituted things are everlasting (*dhrūva*), happy (*sukha*) and good (*súbha*).

śakti Power of the Supreme Being conceived as the Female Principle through which the manifestation of the universe is effected. The important modes of this power are *cit* (intelligence), *ānanda* (bliss), *icchā* (will), *jñāna* (knowledge) and *kriyā* (action). See also entries prefixed and suffixed by Śakti.

śakti Female partner of the aspirant. She can be of three kinds—*svakīyā* (the aspirant's wife), *parakīyā* (wife of another) and *sādhāraṇī* (common woman). Her qualifications are described in *Kulārṇava* VII. Women of the lower castes and despised professions are regarded as excellent partners. *Niruttara* XIV, *Tantrasāra* 627, *Gandharva* XXIII, *Prāṇatoṣaṇī* VII.4, 548.

śakti One of the six limbs of *mantra*, others being Ṛṣi, Chandas, Devatā, Vīja and Kīlaka. *Dīpikā* on *Śrīvidyāratnasūtra* I. According to a different tradition there are seven limbs in which *nyāsa* and *dhyāna* have been added and *devatā* dropped.

śakti-cakra The five Śakti triangles in Śrīyantra. *Bhairavayāmala* quoted by Lakṣmīdhara on *Saundaryalaharī* IX.

śakticālanī A *mudrā* which bestows great success. *Haṭhayogapradīpikā* III.6–7. *Gheraṇḍa* III. 1–3. The process is as follows. The aspirant has to sit in *siddhāsana* posture. Through both his nostrils he inhales air and sends to the spinal cord. Until it reaches there he contracts his anus and stops exhaling by *kumbhaka* process. The confined wind will then push the *kuṇḍalinī* and send it upwards.

śākti dīksā Initiation which does not require any

external rite. It is connected with pure knowledge. Rāghava on *Śāradātilaka* IV.1, *Prāṇatoṣaṇi* II.4, 118.

śaktikāraṇavāda The conception of Śakti as the material and the efficient cause of the universe. *Nityaṣodaśikārṇava* IV.5, *Kaulamārgarahasya* 196, *Lalitāsahasranāma* 112ff, *Saundaryalaharī*, I, *Śaktisaṅgama*, Tārā VIII. 28, *Devībhāgavata* I.8.39, III.6.19.

śaktikūṭa Technical name of *śakti-vīja* or symbolic letters. Com. on *Śāradātilaka* I.1.

śaktipāta Grace of the Great Goddess with which the novice must be favoured before he can be initiated into the creed of Āgamānta Śaivism.

śakti-trikoṇa Śakti triangles supposed to exist in different parts of the body, they are depicted on diagrams and carved on stone, wooden or other objects for cultic purposes. The three lines symbolise any set of three fold theories and the angles are said to be presided over by different goddesses.

śakti-varṇa The vowels. Com. on *Śāradātilaka* VI.2.

śakti-viśiṣṭādvaitavāda Vīra-śaiva doctrine according to which *brahman* or Śiva is of eternal existence, consciousness and bliss and it is only through his *vimarśa-śakti* that he is aware of these. The real nature of Śiva is like the luminescence of a gem which the gem itself cannot realise. This realisation is attained only by Śakti. That is why the relation between Śiva and Śakti is that of identity, (*tādātmya* or *sāmarasya*) as that between heat and fire, light and sun, in which there is no difference between the quality of the substance and the nature of the substance.

śaktopāya See under Jñānopāya.

śāktyadvayavāda A theory of the Kāśmīra Śaivas according to which Śakti is not different from Śiva and as such the material world is the *pariṇāma* or consequence of Śakti.

śālagrāma Viṣṇu-stone which represents the *saguṇa* form of the Absolute. It is a black, egg-shaped object, the remains of fossilised ammonite. It has a golden streak within its cavity and is obtained from rivers, notably, the Gaṇḍakī.

sālokya The first stage of spiritual progress in which the devotee should feel like a servant of God, according to the Śaiva-Siddhānta and other theistic schools.

samādhi The mind's perfect absorption in the object of contemplation; it is the eighth discipline of Yoga. The mind loses itself in the object and has no awareness of itself. *Vyāsabhāṣya* on *Yoga-sūtra* I.1, *Gheraṇḍa* VII.1ff, *Haṭhayogapradīpikā* IV.5,IV.7, *Gandharva* VI. 66ff, *Kulārṇava* IX.13–14. In Buddhism *samādhi* is the means of developing three kinds of *vijjā* (*vidyā*) or faculty: of recalling all past experiences of oneself, of visualising the rise and fall of beings from one state to another, and the faculty of perceiving the course of attenuation of all extraneous impediments to consciousness. *Majjhima* I, Bhayabherava-sutta.

samādhimudrā A posture of the hands while in meditation; same as Dhyānamudrā. The hands, with palm upwards lie one upon the other on the lap with all fingers extended. It is the characteristic *mudrā* of Amitābha.

sāmāiya, sāmayika Equality; the Prakrit or Māgadhī equivalent of *samya*, *samatā* or *sama*. it is one of the important religious principles of the Jains. When a layman or an ascetic takes the vow of religious conduct, he utters the oath *karami bhante sāmāyiyam* committing himself to the principle of equality. *Āvaśyaka Sūtra* 3. According to the *Viśeṣāvaśyaka-bhāṣya* 2673, faith, knowledge and conduct constitute what is called *sāmāiya*.

sāman A melody that is sung at sacrifices; it is said to have the power to fulfil any desire. Each *sāman* chant is linked with a particular Vedic verses and has its own tune, prescribed handpose and is meant for a specific purpose. Certain *sāmans* are acknowledged for their efficacy. These are *saubhāra*, *abhivartta*, *śapha*, *ākṣāra*, *divākarī*, *kāleya*, *harivarṇa vāmadevya*, *ariṣṭa*, etc. Sāmans are also used to purify sin. *Jaimini* II. 1.36, IX.2.34–38.

samāna One of the five kinds of Prāṇa (q.v.) (breath) responsible for the voluntary and involuntary activities of the body. It has its abode in the navel and is responsible for the heat of the body and for the digestive processes and assimilation.

sāmānya Generality of the universal. According to Buddhism, generality is only a name because the individual (*svalakṣaṇa*) alone is real, and there is no class or universal other than the particular objects of experience. According to the Jains and the Vedāntins, generality is constituted of the essential common attributes of all the individuals, and hence both are related by way of identity. According to the Nyāya-Vaiśeṣikas, Sāmānya of the universal is a real entity, which is eternal (*nitya*) and distinct from, but inherent in, many individuals (*anekānugata*). Universals may be distinguished as *para* or the highest and all-pervading, *apara* or the lowest, and *parāpara* or the intermediate.

samāpatti See under Samprajñāta-yoga. In Buddhism *samāpatti* is called *samādhi*, eight kinds of which are mentioned as making up the range of minds from the lowest at the *kāma* level to the highest of the *arūpa* (q.v.). *Majjhima* I. 165.

samarasa The union of the female (*prajñā*) and male (*upāya*) principles; same as Yuganaddha (q.v.). One who can unite these two principles in oneself can have the highest knowledge and supreme bliss and become free from the fetters of birth and death. In the Hindu tradition it is Sāmarasya and is regarded as the equilibrium of Śiva and Śakti. Very often this equilibrium is conceived in sexual terms. See under *mahāsukha*. Complete understanding of this equilibrium leads to the sense of non-duality.

samāvartana Literally, return; the return of the student to his paternal home. See under snātaka.

samavasaraṇa-maṇḍapa Jain audience hall. There is a traditional belief that Indra constructed an elaborate moving audience hall of this name which served both as a vehicle for carrying the Tīrthaṃkara from one place to another and for accommodating devout *bhaktas* or followers eager to listen the truth propounded by him.

samavāya Inherence which, according to the Nyāya-Vaiśeṣika, is a permanent or eternal relation between two entities, of which one inheres in the other, e.g., the whole in its parts, quality in substance, universal in particular, and so on. It is distinguished from Saṃyoga (conjunction) which is a temporary or non-eternal relation between two things and can even exist in separation from each other, e.g., man and his room.

samayācāra A *mārga* (way) of the Śrīvidyā cult. For details see Lakṣmīdhara's com. on *Saundaryalaharī* 31ff, *Saubhāgya-bhāskara* on *Lalitā-sahasranāma* 144, Rāmeśvara on *Paraśurāmakalpasūtra* VII.1, X.68, X.80.

samayācārya Nāyanar saints like Appar, Sambandhar, Māṇikya-vācakar, Sundarar, etc. of South India, belonging to 7th-8th century A.D., who composed devotional verses in praise on Śiva. The devotional tradition created by them was later developed in the Tamil Śaiva religio-philosophical systems.

samaya-dīkṣā Initiation into Āgamānta Śaivism for ordinary people. Those who take *samaya-dīkṣā* have to worship the preceptor and Śivāgni (fire dedicated to Śiva) and have to consider themselves as the servants of god. This method is known as *dāsa-mārga* (q.v.) in which the candidate has to follow only the *caryā* (q.v.) aspect in the stage of spiritual progress.

śāmbhavī-dīkṣā A higher form of initiation which is conducted by the mere touch, or a glance, or the will of the *guru*. It is connected with the secret cult of Kāmeśvarī. *Nityotsava* 9.

sambhoga-cakra One of the four nerve-cycles in the Buddhist conception. It is situated near the neck and is connected with the *sambhoga-kāya* (q.v.) of Buddha. It is kindled by the female energy having the force of fire known as Caṇḍālī, just as the Kuṇḍalinī-śakti of the Śākta Tantras.

sambhoga-kāya See under Trikāya.

samboịjhaṅga A group of acquisitions leading to full enlightenment; in Sanskrit *sambodhyaṅga*. They are *sati* (*smṛti*, insight), *dhammavicaya* (discrimination), *viriya* (energy), *piti* (serene joy), *passaddhi* (tranquility), *samādhi* (meditation) and *upekkhā* (equanimity).

saṃdhyā Literally 'twilight'. The term indicates the act of prayer at day-break, noon and sunset. Generally, however, the *saṃdhyā* is performed twice. *Āśv.Gr.* III.7, *Āp.Dh.S.* I.11.30.8, *Manu* II.101, *Yāj.*I.24–25. For specific items of *saṃdhyā* see under Ģāyatrī, Japa, Mārjana, Prāṇāyāma.

saṃgha A collective body, or tribe, or assembly, which in Buddhism and Jainism meant the community of brethren; monastic establishment and so on. Buddha enjoined that the monks living within a defined boundry (*sīmā*) should elect their chief who would be the Samghatthera or Samghanāyaka. In every Samgha office bearers were elected to carry on its various functions, e.g., distribution of food and dress, provision of beds, erection of monasteries etc. In later Jainism the term came to denote localised groups. The Siddharavasti pillar inscription of AD 1398 records the tradition that Arhadbali split and Mūlasaṃgha Kundakundānvaya into four branches, namely, Sena, Nandi, Deva and Siṃha. The earliest mention of the Mūlasaṃgha and Kundakundānvaya is met with in the copper plate grants of the fifth century A.D. Subsequent epigraphs record the names of Dramila, Mūla, Namilura or Mayaura, Kiṭṭura, Kollātura, Nirgrantha, Śramaṇa, Svetāpaṭa, Yāpanīya and other Saṃghas. In Buddha's days the term was specially applied to a body of religieux subscribing to particular principles and rules of discipline—diṭṭhi-sīla-sāmañña-saṃghātabhāvena saṅgha. *Vimānavatthu-aṭṭhakathā* 233. In Buddhism, Saṃgha became almost a technical term and was given the same importance as Buddha or Dharma. All the ecclesiastical acts of the Buddhists were known as *saṃghakamma*, any split in the Saṃgha was called *saṃghabheda* and so forth. See also Gaṇa.

saṃhāra Dissolution by which the manifested universe returns to its original unmanifested state. Same as *laya*.

saṃhāracakra One of the constituents of *nava-cakra*. *Nityaṣodaśikārṇava* I.

saṃhārakramanyāsa Feeling of the destructive aspect of the deity in the body. The symbolic letters are to be felt in an inverse direction, from kṣa to a. *Puraścaryārṇava* V.330.

saṃhāra-mūrti Images depicting the destructive and terrible aspects of Śiva.

samidh Fuel-stick.

sāmīpya The second stage of spiritual progress in which the devotee should feel himself like the son of God, according to the Śaiva Siddhānta and other theistic schools.

samiti One of the constituents of the Jain concept of *bhāvasaṃvara* (q.v.) which consists of the avoidance of killing insects (*iryā*), gentle and holy talk (*bhāṣā*) and receiving proper alms (*eṣaṇā*). There are two more virtues belonging to this category: *ādānanikṣepana* (careful use of material objects) and *pratithāpana* (careful disposal of the extras).

saṃjñā The Buddhist term for perception, one of the five constituents of *skandhas* (q.v.); in Pali Saññā. In Jainism, the term means the faculty of discrimination.

saṃkhata Buddhist term meaning constituted; in Sanskrit saṃskṛta. According to the Buddhists five masses of elements (*khandhas*, *skandhas*) constitute the world. The ingredients of these elements are further elaborated in the Vaibhāṣika and Sautrāntika (qq.v.) systems.

sammā Completing a process of thought; it is the Pali form of *samyak*. This process can be carried out by balancing all statements of truth and centralising all thoughts that appear at first sight to be widely divergent. Thus *sammā* is essentially the way of bringing all thoughts into focus, and the point at which all of them are focused or centralised is *majjha* or *madhya*.

sammelana-cakra A combination of Śivacakra and Śricakra required in the Śrīvidyā cult.

sāmmitīya Buddhists who believe in the doctrine of a permanent entity or soul called *pudgala*. According to them, some *saṃskāras* exist for a little while, while others perish every moment. Like the Sarvāstivadins they believe that even heretics attain the five miraculous powers and that the *arhats* can have a fallibility from *arhat*-hood. According to the *Kathāvatthu* they believe that there is *antarābhava* (q.v.), and that acts of intimation (*vijñapti*) are morally effective. Like the Mahīśāsakas they also held that some of the factors of the Noble Eight-fold Path—right speech, right action and right livelihood—are material and not mental states.

sammuti Samvṛti, term for conventional truth.

sampatti The attainment of a divine body after the destruction of the gross or subtle bodies (Vallabha); a state of merging, of inseparability, as in the case of a river entering the ocean (Vijñānabhikṣu); equality in bliss expressible by the term *avinābhāva*, i.e., individual self not existing apart from the universal soul (Rāmānuja, Śrīkaṇṭha and Śrīkara); attainment of the state of God (Bhāskara).

sampradāya Sect, community, group, etc., upholding different religious ideals.

samprajñāta-yoga Trance of meditation in which, according to the Yoga, there is a clear and distinct consciousness of the object of contemplation. It is also known as *samāpatti* and *samprajñāta-samādhi* and is of four kinds—*savitarka* (when the mind is concentrated on any gross object like an image); *savicāra* (when it is concentrated on a subtle object); *sānanda* (when it is on the real nature of the object); and *sāsmita* (when there is sense of identity between the knowing self and the object). The final stage is known as *dharma-megha-samādhi* in which self-realisation is possible. *Yogasūtra* IV.29. See also Savikalpa Samādhi.

saṃsāra Worldly existence. In Buddhism the term also means the process of the rise and intensification of complexity of the mind. *Majjhima* I.167–68. According to Nāgārjuna, *saṃsāra* and *nirvāṇa* are two relative ideas and as such there is no absolute distinction between the two. The *pratītya-samutpāda* (q.v.), viewed and interpreted as a law of sequence, or causal antecedents and consequents, explains the essential nature of *saṃsāra*. Mādhyamaka-kārikā, Bib.-Bud. 535. While the Mādhyamikas declare *sam-*

sāra or the phenomenal world as *bhrānti* or *abhūtaparikalpa*, i.e., false (which is also the Vedāntist view) the Yogācārins do not dismiss it as absurd or non-existent, but attribute a certain amount of reality, holding that it is a mere ideation or extension of *cittamātra* or *vijñānamātra* in the sense of misplaced reality of mental comprehension.

saṃsarga Association with one guilty of *mahāpātaka* (grave sin). Its expiation lies in several observances extending over years.

saṃśaya Doubt, which arises when there is the suggestion of different alternative views about the same thing. It is regarded as a positive state of cognition. *Nyāyasūtra*, I.1.23.

saṃskāra Etymologically the term signifies 'putting together', 'forming well', 'making perfect', 'accomplishment', 'embellishment', 'purification', 'cleansing', 'preparation', 'dressing', 'refining', 'polishing', etc. From religious point of view it denotes sacraments, rituals, purificatory acts, etc. Śabara on *Jaimini* III.1.3. explains Saṃskāra as that which being effected makes a certain thing or person fit for a certain purpose. More precisely in the Hindu tradition it denotes a sacred or sanctifying ceremony, one which purifies from the taint of sin contracted in the womb and which leads to regeneration. Twelve such ceremonies are enjoined on the first three or twice-born classes in *Manu* II.27. They are: Garbhādhāna, Puṃsavana, Sīmantonnayana, Jātakarman, Nāmakaraṇa, Niṣkramaṇa, Annaprāsana, Cuḍākaraṇa, Upanayana, Keśānta, Samāvartana and Vivāha. *Gautam.Dh.S.* speaks of forty Saṃskāras (VIII.14–24).

samuccaya Ideological basis of Pañcopāsanā (q.v.), i.e., the worship of five sectarian deities. The *samuccaya* doctrine lays down that an individual, even when seeking *brahman*, must perform his ordinary duties and should have a knowledge of the Karmamīmāṃsā as well as the Vedānta. The term also means addition, combination, and harmonisation.

samucchedavāda Doctrine of annihilationism. *Ṭhāna* IV.4. See under Ucchedavāda and Akriyāvāda.

saṃvara The way in which the *āsrava* (q.v.) or influx of Karma (q.v.) is stopped. Just as a large tank, when its supply of water has been stopped, gradually dries up because water is used from it and also it evaporates, so the Karma of an individual, which he acquires in millions of birth, is annihilated by austerities, if there is no influx of Karma. In Jain conception there are two kinds of control, namely, *bhāvasaṃvara* (q.v.) and *dravyasaṃvara* (q.v.) *DS*, Vṛtti 35, VP, 67–68. Saṃvara is also the name of a Jain partial fast.

saṃvartaka Terrible fires or clouds at the time of *pralaya* (dissolution of the world).

samvatsarī Closing day of the Jain year. On this day men and women assemble in Upāśrayas or adjoining temples, sit on the floor and listen to expositions of the tenets of their faith and the twelve vows it enjoins.

saṃvit Pure consciousness which is the form of the Absolute. It is one of the three *svarūpaśaktis* (q.v.) according to the Acintyabhedābheda, the others being *sandhinī* and *hlādinī*.

saṃvṛti-satya Buddhist term for conventional truth. The word *saṃvṛti* means non-existence, and *satya* truth.

samyak All-round comprehension. See under Sammā. The Jains prefix the term *samyak* to conduct (*cārita*), faith (*darśana*) and knowledge (*jñāna*). The Buddhist *samyak-dṛṣṭi* denotes right view. A potential Bodhisattva in his tenth *bhūmi* called *dharmamegha* becomes consecrated as *samyak-sambuddha*.

saṃyama Constraint; it is comprised of *dhāraṇā*, *dhyāna* and *samādhi* (qq.v.), according to the *Yogasūtra* III.4.

sāmyāvasthā The state of equilibrium of the three *guṇas* (q.v.)—*sattva*, *rajas*, *tamas*—which in the Sāṅkhya are collectively known as Prakṛti (q.v.). The *guṇas* (constituents) are subject to transformation. During Pralaya (dissolution of the world), the *guṇas* change each within itself, without disturbing the others. Such transformation is called Svarūpa-pariṇāma in which Guṇas exist as a homogeneous mass (Sāmyāvasthā). The other kind of transformation, called Virūpa-pariṇāma, takes place when this equilibrium is disturbed. This is a change into the heterogeneous and causes the production of a particular object and thus becomes the starting point of the world's evolution.

saṃyoga The term Saṃyoga has special significance in the Sāṅkhya as the connective between Prakṛti and Puruṣa (q.q.v.) See under Samavāya.

saṃyogī A medieval religious community of Bengal holding liberal views influenced by the Sahajī, Nirañjanī and Nātha cults and also to a certain extent by Islam.

sanaka-sampradāya Theistic Vaiṣṇava sect.

founded by Nimbārka (12th century) on the *dvaitādvaita* (q.v.) line which implies that *brahman* (q.v.) is both the material and the instrumental cause of creation. Brahman is not the impersonal absolute but a personal God, Kṛṣṇa or Hari, whose Śakti or energy is Rādhā. Creation is due to his sport (*līla*).

sanātana-dharma A title of modern coinage to designate Hinduism as an eternal and ever-existing religion. The word occurs in *Brahmāṇḍa Purāṇa* II.33.37–38, *Mbh* I. 122.18, the Khanpur plates of Mādhavavarman (*EI*, XXVII.312), etc., in a different sense.

sañcayana Collection of the charred bones of a person after cremation. They should be cast into the Ganges or some other holy river or into the sea.

sañcetanikā Buddhist term for the annulment of voluntary deeds. *Aṅguttara* V.292ff.

sāndhara-prāsāda Temple with ambulatory

sandhinī One of the three *svarūpa-śaktis* (q.v.) of *brahman* which is existent (*sat*) as the absolute and all-inclusive unity. By *sandhinī* the supreme being upholds its own existence and that of others, according to the Acintyabhedābheda. *Caitanya-caritāmṛta* II.8, 118, 119.

saṅghata-śrāddha A form of Śrāddha (q.v.) performed when several people die, because of a common mishap, at the same time on the same day. The order in which the Śrāddhas are to be performed is determined by the nearness of the performer.

saṅgīti Term for Buddhist congregation and conclaves.

saṅkalpa One of the essential elements in any gift or dedication to the public. It also means 'to resolve' and is necessary in every religious rite. Sankalpa denotes a formula in *vrata* as well.

śaṇkha Conch-shell. It is especially given to the gods in iconographical representations as a symbol of omnipresence as the sound vibrated through the shell penetrates far and wide. It is one of the emblems of Viṣṇu. Its personified form is known as *śaṅkha-puruṣa*.

saṅkhārā Same as *saṁskāra* or mental impressions, one of the links of the Buddhist concept of *paṭiccasamuppāda* (q.v.) (dependent origination).

śaṅkhinī Name of a cerebral nerve. *Prāṇatoṣaṇī* I.4, 33.

saṅkhyā Number; it is regarded as one of the fourteen qualities of *ātman* by the Nyāya-Vaiśeṣikas.

saṅkīrtana Singing the name of God in chorus to the accompaniment of musical instruments.

saṅkoca-vikāsa Involution and evolution and vice versa which characterise the world-process.

saṅkrānti Day of transition from one month to another which is held to be sacred. Two of them are specially so, one being the day on which the sun passes to the sign of Aries (*mahāviṣuva*), and the other being the day on which the sun enters capricorn (*uttarāyaṇa*).

saṅkrāntivāda A sect which followed the Sarvāstivāda tenets; see also Sautrāntika. The main teaching of this school, from which it got its name, is that the *skandhas*, in their subtle form, transmigrate from one world to another, while the Sāmmitīyas (q.v.) maintain that it is the *pudgala* (q.v.) that transmigrates. There are four *mūlāntika-skandhas*, and one *ekarasa-skandha*, the subtle consciousness, from which the former four originate. This subtle consciousness corresponds to a certain extent to the *ālaya-vijñāna* or store-consciosness of the Yogācārins. On account of such views this school is considered as a bridge between Hīnayāna and Mahāyāna. The Saṅkrāntivādins were also called Tāmraśāṭiyas, probably on account of their copper-coloured clothes.

ṣaṇmudrā The torque, the bracelet, the jewel, the girdle, the ashes and the sacred thread which represent the six *pāramitās* when one of the six is absent they are called Pañcamudrā.

saññā Same as *saṃjñā*.

saṇṇāgrika A subsect of the Vātsiputrīyas (q.v.). It is variously spelt as Chandagārikas, Chandāgarikas and Channāgarikas.

saññāvedayita-nirodha Buddhist concept of the ninth state of *samādhi* which leads to the *lokottara* (supramundane level).

saññivāda The view holding that the conscious soul exists after death. Sixteen such possibilities are mentioned in the Buddhist texts. According to the Saññivādins, (1) the soul is material (*rūpī*), (2) non-material (*arūpī*), (3) both material and non-material, (4) neither material nor non-material, (5) limited, (6) unlimited, (7) both limited and unlimited, (8) neither limited nor unlimited, (9) conscious, (10) unconscious, (11) conscious of one object (*ekatta*), (12) conscious of many objects (*nānātta*), (13) limited in matter (*paritta*), (14) unlimited in matter, (15) limited in consciousness and (16) unlimited in consciousness.

sannidhi Proximity of both place and time.

sannikarṣa Contact of senses with objects.

sannyāsa The order of ascetics; the fourth and the last state in a man's life, according to the *āśrama* system. It is the life of giving up worldly ties, of begging and contemplation. Several classes of ascetics are enumerated in ancient texts. Opinions differ whether *sannyāsa* is allowed only to the Brāhmaṇas or to all. Ascetics are to give up wife and home and are not to revert to a householder's life. Different orders and organisations of Sannyāsins are known. The principal elements in the procedure of *sannyāsa* are *śrāddhas*, *savitrī-praveśa*, *virājahoma*, declaration of leaving home, forsaking all wealth and desires and taking the vow of *ahiṃsā*, giving up top-knot and sacred thread, teaching by *guru* of *pañcikaraṇa* and *mahāvākyas*, giving of a new name by the teacher, *yogapaṭṭa*, *paryaṅka-śauca*, etc. There is no impurity at his death for his relatives and none attaches to him when any of them die. *Gaut.* III.10–24, *Āp.Dh.S.* III.9.21, *Baudh.Dh.S.* II.6.21–22, II.10, *Manu* VI.33–86, *Yāj* III.56–66, etc.

śānta The relationship of quietness with God. It is one of the five *ratis* and *rasas*, i.e., emotions and instincts. At the lowest stage the attachment to God which may enable the realisation of god is *śānta-rati* which further develops into *prema* or love. *Caitanyacaritāmṛta* II.19ff.

sāntapana Expiation for acts of the category of *jātibhraṃśakara* (q.v.)—those which result in loss of caste. It is same as the *brahmakūrca* (q.v.) according to some digests.

śāntā śakti A form of Śakti containing the aspects of will (*icchā*), knowledge (*jñāna*) and action (*kriyā*).

śānti Rites performed to counteract inauspicious effect. These are performed on the 14th tithi of the dark half of a month or on the *amāvasyā* or on Mūlā, Aśleṣā and Jyeṣṭhā *nakṣatras* and certain astrological conjunctions like Vyātipata, Vaidhṛti, Saṃkrānti, etc. There are various *śāntis* like Gomukhaprasava, Navagraha, Prasava, Udaka, Vināyaka, Vāstu, etc.

śānti, śantyātīta Kalās (q.v.) generated from Nāda (q.v.). *Śāradātilaka* I.26.

sapiṇḍikaraṇa A form of *śrāddha* (q.v.) which can secure the admission of a *preta* (the departed one) to the order of the manes. This ceremony takes places on the twelfth day after death, and is performed each year by the descendants of the dead. Four waterpots filled with sesame, scents and water and four *piṇḍas* (q.v.), one for the departed one and three for his father, grandfather and great-grandfather. The contents of the pot and *piṇḍa* of the departed one are distributed on over the other three lumps with *mantra* from *RV* X.191.3–4.

saptabhaṅgī-naya The seven-fold paralogism of Jain logic. See under Anekāntavāda, Naya and Syādvāda.

sapta-bhūmika Seven stages of Tantric perfection; *veda*, *vaiṣṇava*, *śaiva*, *dakṣiṇa*, *vāma*, *siddhānta* and *kaula*.

saptapadī Marriage ritual in which the couple have to go seven steps in a northern or north-eastern direction. It is a symbol for their co-operation in married life.

saptasāgaraka A *mahādāna* (great gift) in which seven golden vessels filled with salt, milk, clarified butter, jaggery, curds, sugar and holy water are donated with a *homa* to Varuṇa. *Matsya* CCLXXXVII.

śaraṇa A stage in Vīraśaiva perfection which is characterised by a mode of pure delight (*ānanda-bhakti*) derived from the contemplation of Prasādaliṅga. Śaraṇa literally means taking refuge. In Buddhism this literal meaning pertains to Buddha, Dharma and Saṅgha. Vaiṣṇavism and other devotional systems distinguish two kinds: *nāma-śaraṇa* (refuge to the name of God), *guru-śaraṇa* (refuge to teacher) and *bhakte-śaraṇa* (refuge to devotee).

śaraṇāgati Complete resignation to God. cf. *Gītā* XVIII.66. This complete self-surrender, which is due to the individual's feeling of utter helplessness and complete belief in the Lord's grace is also called *prapatti* (q.v.).

śaraṇāpatti The attitude of humility.

sarasvatī-sthāpana Establishment of books as the symbol of Sarasvatī, the goddess of learning, on ninth day of the bright half of *āśviṇa* (Sept–Oct).

śarīra-śarīrin Analogical relationship between *brahman* and the world conceived of in terms of body and its holder i.e., the self, by certain Vedāntin schools.

sārṣṭi, sārṣṭya One of the four kinds of *mukti* or liberation. It is the attainment of that *aiśvarya* (awe-inspiring grandeur and mightiness) which is similar to that possessed by God.

sarūpa-vigraha Anthropomorphic cult images.

sārūpya The third stage of spiritual progress in which the devotee should feel himself as an associate of God, according to the Śaiva Siddhānta and other theistic schools.

sarvajñatā Omniscience; it is one of the five-fold expression of God's perfection.

sarva-kartṛtā Supreme sovereignty and omnipotence; it is one of the five expressions of God's perfection.

sarvamedha Vedic sacrifice (*Vāj.Saṃ.* XXXII-XXXIII), so called because at its conclusion the sacrificer gives away all his possessions as *dakṣiṇā* (q.v.) and retires to the forest as a hermit. It belongs to the ahīna category of sacrifices prescribed in the *Yajurveda*, Brāhmaṇas and Śrauta-sūtras.

sarvasattāprada 'The giver of reality to all'. It is Madhva's characterisation of the *sarvakartṛtā* (q.v.) of *brahman*.

sarvāstivāda Buddhist sect; it is an offshoot of the Sthaviravāda. According to this school, the external world and its constituents, the *dharmas*, have a real existence. The greatest authority of this school was Vasubandhu whose *Abhidharma-kośa* was based upon the seven original works on the Abhidharma (q.v.). According to this school the *arhats* may fall away from *arhat*-hood, though the *śrotāpannas* (q.v.) are not subject to such retrogression. They also believe that the bodhisattvas are ordinary people (*pṛthagjana*), that all the *anuśayas* or latent evil tendencies are associated with the mind (*caitasika*), that heretics can have supernatural powers (*riddhis*), and that there are *laukika-pudgalas* which transmigrate and four transcendental meditations (*lokottara-dhyānas*). They believe in *nairātmya* (absence of any permanent substance) of an individual though not of things, and that there are seventy-five elements in the universe divided into two main groups—sevanty-two *saṃskṛta* (compounded) and three *asaṃskṛta* (non-compounded). They are linked together by a system of ten causal relations, six principal (*hetu*) and four subsdiary (*pratyaya*). For philosophical developments of this school of thought see under Vaibhāṣika and Sautrāntika.

sarvasvāra Religious suicide. It is a one day soma-sacrifice in which the sacrificer commits suicide by entering the fire.

sarvatobhadra A shrine with four faces; a shrine-model with images on the four faces. Same as *caturmukha*.

sarvatobhadra-maṇḍala A geometrical diagram on which the *pūrṇakumbha* (vessel filled with water) is placed during Durgā worship.

śāsanadevatā The twenty-four *yakṣiṇīs* who serve as attendants of the twenty-four Jain Tīrthaṃkaras.

sasaṅkhāraparinibbāyi Those who attain *parinirvāṇa* by putting an end to afflictions with great trouble and effort. *Visuddhimagga* 453. In Sanskrit Sābhisaṃskāra-parinirvāyin.

sassatavāda Eternalism; the belief that the soul and the world exist eternally. The attā (ātman) or soul continues for even without any change. It is the speaker, feeler and enjoyer of the fruits of good and evil actions (*kamma*), is permanent (*nicca*), fixed (*dhruva*) and unchangeable (*avipariṇāmadhamma*). This doctrine has some bearing on the Sāṅkhya since the latter also contains the idea of Puruṣa as soul. *Majjhima* I.8; *Papañcasūdanī* I.71. *Dīgha* I.

sat Existent; real, According to the theistic versions. of the Vedānta it is the all-inclusive unity of the Absolute that imparts substantiality to all beings and thus sustains their value. From a purely monistic viewpoint *brahman* is the only *sat* without a second.

ṣaṭcakra-bheda Piercing of the six nerve-cycles. According to the Śākta-Tāntric scheme there are six nerve-cycles (*ṣaṭcakra*) within the human body. These are in the *mūlādhāra* (rectal region), *svādhiṣṭhāna* (the region around the generative organ), *maṇipura* (around the navel), *anāhata* (region around the heart), *viśuddha* (the region connecting the spinal cord and the lower portion of the medulla oblongata) and *ājñā* (region between the brows). The highest cerebral region is known as *sahasrāra*. The Kuṇḍalinī Śakti, i.e., Śakti as serpent power, remains latent in the *mūlādhāra*. By Yogic exercises this Kuṇḍalinī Śakti has to be pushed up through the two main nerves, *iḍā* and *piṅgalā* so that it may reach the *sahasrāra* (the highest cerebral region) where it should meet its source.

satipaṭṭhāna A Buddhist term denoting mindfulness, alertness and awareness of what is happening in one's body (*kāya*), feeling (*vedanā*), mind (*citta*) and also of the acquisitions (*dhamma*). *Majjhima* I. 55. In Sanskrit Smṛtyupasthāna.

satkañcuka Six veils which are the causes of human bondage. *Tantraloka* IX.164, 204.

satkāraṇavāda A theory of causation popular among the Vedāntins. See under Kāraṇa.

ṣaṭkarma Six purificatory practices of Haṭhayoga—*dhauti*, *vasti*, *neti*, *laukīkī*, *trāṭaka* and *kapāla-bhāti*. *Gheraṇḍa* I.13–60, *Haṭhayogapradīpikā*

II. 24–35. The term is also applied to denote the six black acts—*śānti*, *vaśya*, *stambhana*, *vidveṣaṇa*, *uccāṭana* and *māraṇa*. *Yoginitantra* IV, *Śāradātilaka* XXIII.123ff.

satkāryavāda Sāṅkhya theory of causation according to which the effect exists in the material cause even before it is produced. This view is based on the following grounds. (1) If the effect were really non-existent in the material cause, then no amount of effort on the part of any agent could bring it into existence. (2) There is an invariable relation between a material cause and its effect. (3) Certain effects can be produced only from certain causes. (4) Only a potent cause can produce a desired effect. (5) It is absurd that something comes out of nothing. (6) Effect is not different from, but essentially identical with, the material cause. The theory of Satkāryavāda has two modifications: namely, Pariṅāmavāda (q.v.) and Vivartavāda (q.v.).

satkhyātivāda Rāmānuja's theory of non-illusion according to which all objects are made of a mixture of the same basic elements of matter (*bhūta*) in different proportions. Thus, there is something common between the rope and the snake, and it is this common element which appears in so called illusory perception which is, therefore, not illusory.

satra, satrayāga Same as Sattra.

ṣaṭ-sthala See also *sthala*. An hierarchy of the Vīraśaivas where *upāsanā* (worship which represents a spirit of self-surrender) grows step by step, gaining in content till the apparent duality between *aṅga* (the devotee, the worshipper) and *liṅga* (the *upāsya* or the worshipped, i.e. Śiva) vanishes and *sāmarasya* (the state of identity) is attained.

sattā-karma Karma (q.v.) accumulated in the past life according to the Jain conception.

sattra All soma (q.v.) sacrifices which have more than twelve 'pressing' days. The peculiarity of the *sattras* is that all the officiating priests are jointly or individually sacrificers. The model is the *dvādasāha* (q.v.) or *ahina* (q.v.). An important *sattra* is *gavāmayana* which lasts for one year. There is no limit to the maximum duration of a *sattra*. *Taitt.Saṃ*. III.3.6, III.5.10, VII.5.5–7, *Taitt.Br*. I.2.2–5, *Sat.Br*. IV.6.2, *Āp.Sr*. XXI, *Kāt.Sr*. XIII, *Āśv.Sr*. XI.7, *Baudh.Sr*. XVI.13–23, *Śāṅ.Sr*. XIII.19.

sattva That constituent of Prakṛti (q.v.) which is of the nature of pleasure and is light (*laghu*) and illuminating (*prakāśaka*). It gives rise to happiness and love, tranquility and modesty, health and lightness of body, patience and forgiveness, courage, magnanimity, self-restraint and the illumination of knowledge.

satya Truth. It is of two kinds: conventional (*samvṛti*) and ultimate for transcendental (*paramārthika*). There is another kind of truth known as *prātibhāsika* (q.v.). Satya or truthfulness is one of the five yamas in Yoga, one of the ten yamas of Yāj III.312 and one of the five duties enjoined by Manu X.63 on men of all *varṇas*. In later Vedic texts the term Satya came to denote Ṛta (q.v.) meaning order, natural, and moral. Signal and analytical truths are known as *lakṣaṇa* and *vibhāga* respectively.

satyasiddhi Buddhist school founded by Harivarman. This school believed in *nairātmya* (absence of any permanent substance both of persons as well as of things) which distinguishes it from Sarvāstivāda (q.v.). According to this school, the universe contains eighty-four elements which also are void of any abiding reality. It holds that truth is of two kinds, conventional (*saṃvṛti*) and ultimate (*paramārtha*) and further contends that only the present is real while the past and the future have no real existence.

śauca The act of cleansing; it differs in degree according to *āśramas* or stages of life. Cleansing at night requires half the time prescribed for it in the day time. It is of two kinds, internal and external. The former is subdivided into five parts: *mānasa* (mental), *cāksuṣa* (of the eye), *ghrāṇya* (of the nose), *vācya* (of speech) and *svādya* (of the tongue).

saupādisesa One of the two kinds of *nibbānadhātu*, the other being *anupādisesa*. Both denote perfect *arhats* but the former is subject to pleasant and unpleasant feelings while the latter is completely free from them.

sautrāmaṇi Vedic sacrifice belonging to the *havir-yajña* group. It is not a Soma-sacrifice, *surā* being used instead. The other offerings are a bull, a sheep and a goat dedicated to Indra, Śarasvatī and the Aśvins respectively. *Vāj.Saṃ*. XIX–XXI, *Taitt.Saṃ*. I.8.2, *Taitt.Br*. I.4.2, I.8.5–6, II.6–7, *Śat.Br*. V.5.4–5, *Āśv.Sr*.III.9. *Śāṅ.Sr*. XV.15, *Āp.Sr*.. XIX.1–10.

sautrāntika See under Saṅkrāntivāda. The Sautrāntikas based themselves upon the Sarvāstivada tenets and were considered as opponents of the Vaibhāṣikas (q.v.) as they relied solely on the

Sūtras denying the authority of the Commentaries (*vibhāṣā*) on the Abhidharma. The Sautrāntikas admit the reality of the outer world and the atomic theory. While insisting on the ideality of phenomenal objects, they accept the independence of the thing in itself. They admit the extramental existence of the world, but according to them there is no direct perception of external objects. They are known by inference and not by evidence. The evolution of the world has no beginning. If god was the sole cause, the world would have been created in its totality at once and at the same time, but it is seen that creatures come to existence not simultaneously but successively, some from wombs, some from buds, and so on. The Sautrāntikas also cut down the list of seventy-five *dharmas* (elements) to forty-three under five principal heads.

savana Pressing of Soma-juice which used to take place in the morning, at midday and in the evening. The three metres—*gāyatrī*, *triṣṭubh* and *jāgatī*—are assigned to the three *savanas*. The juice was extracted by pounding the *soma* plant with the pressing stones (*adri*), mixed with water in a vat (*koṣa*) poured into two bowls (*camu*), mixed with milk, and finally transferred to the special vessel (*kalasa*).

śavasādhanā Tantric ritual with a corpse. For details see *Kaulāvalinirṇaya* XIV, *Śyāmārahasya* XIV, *Tārābhaktisudhārṇava* IX, *Puraścaryārṇava* IX.

savikalpa-pratyakṣa Determinate perception which, according to the Nyāya, is the cognition of an object as possessed of some character.

savikalpa-samādhi A state of bliss in which a sense of difference between the knower and his object of knowledge survives.

sāyavāda Doctrine of sensualism. *Ṭhāna* IV.4. See uner Ditthadhammanibbānavāda and Akriyāvāda.

sāyujya The fourth stage of spiritual progress in which the devotee should feel himself as identical with God, according to the Śaiva Siddhānta and other theistic devotional school.

śeṣa-śeṣin Relation between the servant and the Lord, a Viśiṣṭādvaitavāda concept.

setu Bridge made of knowledge to cross the ocean of suffering. Crystallised as a form of *mantra* it should be muttered. The higher form is known as Mahāsetu. *Puraścaryārṇava* VI.532–33.

siddha A being who attains *mokṣa* (q.v.) (liberation) according to the Jains. They are of five kinds: (1) The Tīrthaṃkaras or the liberated ones who preached the Nirgrantha religion in embodied form; (2) the Arhats or the perfect souls who await the attainments of *mokṣa* after shedding the Kārmaṇaśarīra (q.v.); (3) the Ācāryas or heads of ascetic groups; (4) the Upādhyāyas or teaching saints; and (5) Sādhus, a class which includes the rest. *TTDS* X.8, *DS*, 50–54.

siddha Saints (Siddhapuruṣas) who have attained Siddhi or perfection in Tantric-Sahajiyā-Lokāyata tradition and have acquired super-normal powers. Two groups of Siddhas are generally recognised, the first consists of nine and the other of eighty-four, most of them hailing from the East.

siddha-cikitsā Method of treatment by mercurial drugs practised by the Siddha sect of the South. Also known as Māheśvara Siddhas of the Śuddhamārga. The founder of one of their seven subsects was a Chinese Taoist named Bhoga who possessed wonderful knowledge in alchemy. The Nātha Siddhas were closely associated with the Raseśvara Siddhas. Each of the nine Nātha Siddhas was generally held to stand at the head of a community of expert alchemists who were masters in the preparation of antidotes against old age, disease and poisons. See also Rasa, Raseśvaradarsana, Sittar.

siddha-mantra The *mantra* which becomes effective at once. Very few possess such *mantras*. If the occasion arises, such *mantras* may be accepted even by disregarding scriptural rules. *Rudrayāmala*, Uttara III, *Tantrasāra* 6.

siddhānta A view that a certain thing is such-and-such and accepted as true in a system. It is one of the sixteen philosophical topics of the Nyāya.

siddhāntācāra One of the seven Tantric *ācāras* or *mārgas* (ways). In particular it is described as a form of *vāmācāra* and is meant for aspirants of the *vīra* (q.v.) state. It insists more on *antaryāga* (internal worship) than on external. One of the interesting characteristics of Siddhāntācāra is that its followers worship Viṣṇu in the day-time, while at night they practise the rites of pañcamakāra (q.v.). *Puraścaryārṇava* I.22, *Kaulamārgarahasya* 10.

siddhārthika An offshoot of the Mahāsaṅghikas (q.v.) mentioned in *Kathāvatthu* XV.9. They believed that there were no such things as mental properties (*caitasikas*), that gift was a mental satisfaction, that an *arhat* cannot have an untimely death and that the fruit of a wicked action may extend over a whole *kalpa*.

siddhāsana Same as *dhyānāsana*, the yogic posture adopted by seated Tīrthaṃkaras.

siddhi Eight miraculous powers. They are *animā* (atomisation), *laghimā* (levitation), *mahimā* (magnification), *garimā* (greatness), *prāpti* (power of getting anything), *prākāmya* (non-obstruction of desire), *vaśitva* (power of charming) and *īśitva* (sovereignty over all things). *Āp.Dh.S.* II.9.23.6–7, *Prapañcasāra* XIX. 62–63.

śikhā Top-knot with locks of hair. Religious acts done without it become meaningless. An individual cutting it off through hate or foolishness has to undergo expiation. Elaborate rules about keeping locks of hair according to *gotra* are laid down in the Dharmaśāstras.

śikhara Superstructure or the roof of a temple. A North Indian *śikhara* is normally curvilinear, while a South Indian *śikhara* is either domical, octagonal, or four-sided.

śikṣāvrata Vows to be observed by Jain laymen to attain moral discipline. See also Anuvrata, Kaṣāya, Cāritra.

śīla Buddhist term which covers all aspects of a man's moral sphere of existence and behaviour. *Saṃyutta* I.23, *Milinda* 34, *Visuddhimagga* I.1.

sīlabbata-parāmāsa Buddhist term designating all manner of thinking or speculation and assumption that the whole sphere of conduct or behaviour may be governed by a code of ethics or a code of discipline.

sīmantonnayana The sacrament of parting of the hair which takes place anytime from the fourth to the eighth month of the first pregnancy. The husband attaches to the wife's neck an *udumbara* twig and parts her hair from the front across the crown, first with *darbha* blades, then with a sliver of *vīratara* wood, probably for ensuring fertility. *Āśv. Gr.* I. 14.1–9, *Śāṅ.Gr.* I. 22, *Āp.Gr.* XIV.1–8, *Hir.Gr.* II.1, *Baudh.Gr.* I.10.

siṃhāsana Lion-seat or lion-throne on which images of deities are installed in iconic representations. The lion-throne was a symbol of Buddha before the development of the use of his image for worship.

śiśnadeva Gods worshipped in phallic symbol and phallic worshippers. In *RV* VII.27.5, X.99.3, Indra is depicted as crushing and exterminating the Śiśnadevas or phallic worshippers.

śiṣṭa Those who are free from envy, pride, greed, hypocrisy, arrogance, covetuousness and anger, have studied the Veda along with Itihāsa-purāṇa and are distinguished by decent manners. *Baudh.Dh.S.* I.1.5–6, etc.

śiśu-cāndrāyana A penance which entails eating only four mouthfuls of food in the morning and evening for a period of a month. *Manu* XI.219, *Baudh.Dh.S.* IV.5.19, *Agni* CLXXI.5.

śiśu-kṛcchra Expiation which lasts for four days; eating only once on the first day, only once on the second night, eating that obtained without asking for it on the third day and fasting on the fourth day. Same as *bāla-kṛcchra* or *laughu-kṛcchra*.

śiṣya Disciple. His method of selecting a teacher is described in *Kulārṇava* XI, XIV, *Rudrayāmala*, Uttara II, *Prapañcasāra* XXXVI.50. His test before initiation: *Tantrasāra* 3, *Śāradātilaka* II.153. Characteristics of a good disciple: *Śāradā* II. 145–50, *Tantrarāja* I. 23–24. Of a bad disciple: *Rudrayāmala*, Uttara II. His duties: *Kulārṇava* XII, *Kaulāvalinirṇaya* X, *Parasuramākalpasūtra* X.74.

sītāyajña Sacrifice to ploughed land. *Gobhila Gr.* IV.4.27, *Pār.Gr.* III. 13ff.

sithila-karma That type of Karma (q.v.) the influx of which may be evaded according to the Jain conception.

śītkarma To inhale breath through the mouth and to exhale it through the nose. This Yogic practice prevents diseases. *Gheraṇḍa* I. 60–61.

sittar Tamil term for South Indian Tantric Siddhas who were zealous adepts in alchemy. Their works are written in verse, using easy, colloquial and ungrammatical words and often concealing the names of the herbs or minerals in big phrases and metaphors. Many recipes containing minerals, metal, herbs and salts are mentioned in these works. There are are also certain *nigaṇṭus* or explanatory books on these texts. The Sittars recognised Śiva as their god and rejected everything in the Śaiva cult which was inconsistent with pure theism. See under Rasa, Raseśvara-darśana, Māheśvara-Siddha, Siddha-Cikitsā.

śiva-bhāgavata Devotees of Śiva mentioned by Patañjali on Pāṇini V.2.76.

śivacakra The four Śiva triangles as constituents of Śrīyantra. Vinducakra, Aṣṭadalapadma, Bhūpura (qq.v.) etc., are also known as Śivacakra. Lakṣmīdhara on *Saundaryalaharī* IX.

śivahasta The hand of the preceptor which is purified by *mantras* when it is used to initiate someone in *sparśa-dīkṣā* (q.v.). Rāghava on *Śāradātilaka* V.127–40.

śivānubhava-maṇḍapa An assembly founded by Vasava in A.D. 1160 for the propagation of Vīra-śaiva view of life.

śivarātri An obligatory fast for Saivites which takes place in *phālguṇa* (Feb-March). The worship of Śiva goes on during the four watches of the night in spring with milk, curd, honey and clarified butter. Worshippers gather at the Śiva shrines and pass the night in watchfulness. Also known as Śiva-Caturdaśī.

śiva-vīja Name of *pārada* or mercury.

śiva-yogī A term to denote *jīvanmukta* (q.v.) (liberated person). *Bhāvanopaniṣat* XXXV.

śivayuvatī Name of Śakti-triangle. *Saundarya-laharī* XI.

skambha Principle of 'support' mentioned in *AV* X.7. X.8 as a cosmogonic principle within which both entity and non-entity exist. It is described as a great being, like Puruṣa with whom it is identified, and is equated with the universe. It is regarded as superior to Prajāpati who founds the world upon it. The sky and the earth are said to be supported on it.

skandha Same as *khanda*. The Buddhist term for five elements, namely, *rūpa* (matter), *vedanā* (sensation), *saṃjñā* (perception), *saṃskāra* (impressions) and *vijñāna* (consciousness) which are the five aggregates of existence or the constituents of a being. The term is also used by the Jains to denote the minute aggregates of the *paramāṇus* (q.v.) or atoms.

smārtī-dīkṣā Initiation when the candidate is absent. The teacher by mental recall frees him from the three fetters known as *āṇava*, *karma* and *māyīya* (qq.v.) and by his power elevates the soul of his disciple for union with the supreme being. Rāghava on *Śāradātilaka* V. 127–40.

smṛtyupasthāna Same as Satipaṭṭhāna.

snāna Bath for purification. Elaborate rules have been laid down in the Dharmaśāstras governing the procedure for bathing, the nature of water to be used, the method to be used for one who is ill or for a woman in her menstrual period, the accompanying ingredients, consequences, restrictions, etc. Bathing once every day is obligatory on all. It is not allowed at night, except during eclipses, *aśauca*, *vrata*, etc.

snātaka Literally, 'one who has taken the bath'. The return of a student to his paternal home from the teacher's house, after the successful completion of his period of studentship, was signalised or formalised by the rite of *samāvartana* (lit. return) which look place just before his actual re-entry into his paternal abode. Its main feature was a ceremonial bath after which he was known as *snātaka*.

snāna-yātrā Bath-festival of Jagannātha which takes place on the full-moon night of *jyaiṣṭha* (May-June).

ṣoḍaśadala-padma Tantric concept of sixteen-petalled lotus; each petal has a vowel symbolising a Mātṛkā. *Kāmakalāvilāsa* XXXIII. It is also conceived as existing in the *cakra*.

ṣoḍasādhāra Sixteen containers of the human body. They are Mūlādhāra, Svādhiṣṭhāna, Maṇipura, Anāhata, Viśuddha, Ājñā, Vindu, Kalā, Pāda, Nivodhikā, Ardhendu, Nāda, Nādānta, Unmanī, Viṣṇuvaktra and Dhruvamaṇḍalikā (qq.v.) *Prāṇatoṣaṇi* II.2,93.

ṣoḍasopacāra Sixteen articles required for worship. They are *āsana*, *svāgata*, *pādya*, *arghya*, *ācamanīya*, *madhuparka*, *punarācamanīya*, *snānīya*, *bhuṣana*, *gandha*, *puṣpa*, *dhūpa*, *dīpa*, *naivedya* and *vandanā*. *Mahānirvāṇa* XIII.203–04.

ṣoḍaśin A form of Soma sacrifice.

śodhana Purification. In Tantric language it is the establishment of a thing in its real form. It is done by *mantras* and rituals.

ṣoḍhānyāsa A form of *nyāsa* in which the deities are singly felt in the body. It has six processes. For details see *Tārābhaktisudhārṇava* V.163, *Śāradātilaka* VII, *Puraścaryārṇava* XII.1165, *Tantrasāra* 272, 309ff.

so'ham Same as Haṃsa.

somacakra A minor nerve-cycle within the body.

soma-siddhānta A branch of Śaivism which served as a bridge between the Pāśupata and Śākta cults. *Prabodhacandrodaya*, Act III.

soma-yāga Most important Vedic sacrifice originally connected with the rites of pressing the *soma* plant to extract wine. See *savana*. There are three basic kinds of Soma sacrifices: *ekāha*, *ahina* and *sattra*. (qq.v.). The *ekāha* has only one *sutyā* day on which the soma juice is extracted and libations made. All one-day sacrifices belong to this category. The *ahīna* has from two to twelve *sutyā* (separate) days. The *sattra* type lasts for more than twelve days, sometimes for a year or longer. There are seven fundamental forms of Soma sacrifices; *agniṣṭoma*, *atyagniṣṭoma*, *ukthya*, *ṣoḍaśin*, *vājapeya*, *atirātra* and *aptoryāma*. They bear the generic title *jyotiṣṭoma*.

somāyana An expiation which entails forgoing all food for a month except milk obtained by sucking the udder of a cow.

sopādhika Concept of 'conditioned' *brahman* when it is said to be the cause of the world. Upadhi means condition which in the case of *brahman* is known as Māyā.

sopādhiśeṣa-nirvāṇa Nirvāṇa with corporeal residues.

sotāpanna Those attaining the preconditions of *arhat*-hood. See Srotāpanna.

spanda One of the three constituents of Kāśmīra Śaivism named after the Spanda-śāstras consisting of Vasugupta's *Spanda-sūtra* or *Spanda-Kārikā*, Kallata's *Spanda-sarvasva*, Kṣemarāja's *Spanda-nirṇaya* and *Spanda-sandoha*, and other works.

sparśa (spārśani)-dīkṣā Initiation by touch. *Kulārṇava* XIV, *Puraścaryârṇava* V.391, Rāghava on *Śāradātilaka* V.127–140.

sphoṭa A capacity (*śakti*) which is manifested through letters and words conveying meaning. The individual letters cannot make known the meaning in case of the word, nor individual words in that of sentence. Over and above these sounds or letters or words, there is sphoṭa, the essence of the sound or letter or word or the sentence as a whole. Brought into consciousness by different sounds of the word (or the words of the sentence), this *sphoṭa* produces the cognition of what is meant by the word or sentence. This essence of sound is viewed in terms of a monistic metaphysical implication by the followers of Śabda-brahma (q.v.) doctrine.

śraddhā Faith in God and the scriptures which is evidently the basis of spiritual aspiration. It is not identical with *bhakti* or devotion.

śrāddha Ritual for the spiritual welfare of departed ones accompanied by desire to keep in constant touch with the dead by means of ceremonials. The *Mit* on *Yāj* I. 217 defines *śrāddha* as the offering with faith of an article of food or some substitute thereof, intending it for the benefit of the departed. The distant ancestors are known as *pitṛs* and those who have lately departed as *pretas*. The first finds expression in the daily *pitṛyajñas*, the monthly *śrāddha* and the *aṣṭakā* and *anvaṣṭakā* (qq.v.) rites in all of which the *pitṛs* are honoured and receive oblation like gods. The second finds expression in the funeral rites following immediately after and in the *ekoddiṣṭa* and *sapiṇḍīkaraṇa śrāddhas*.

śramabhūmi States of action in the process of pure creation according to the Pāñcarātra Āgamas. These are *bala* (strength), *vīrya* (virility) and *tejas* (splendour).

śramaṇa Ascetics belonging the non-orthodox orders. The best term for describing them is *avaidika* (non-Vedic sects). The common features of Śramaṇa tradition are that they challenged the authority of the Vedas; that they admitted into their church all members of the community irrespective of their social rank and religious career; that they observed a set of ethical principles; that they practised a detached life with a view to liberating themselves from the worldly life and that they could take to a life of renunciation any time except as minors.

śrāvaka, śrāvakayāna Śrāvaka means persons of average intellect who are capable of attaining perfection only by listening to and practising the *dharma* (religion) promulgated by beings of extraordinary intellect like a Buddha. The term Śrāvaka is not confined to Buddhism alone. See also Hīnayāna. In Jainism Śrāvaka and Śrāvikā means laymen and laywomen respectively who follow the precepts of the *nirgrantha* religion preached by the Tīrthaṃkaras under the guidance of an organised system.

śravaṇa Listening to scriptures. It is a precondition of valid knowledge and is necessary for firmness and purity of devotion (*bhakti-dārḍhya*, *bhakti-pariśuddhi*).

śrīcakra Same as Śrīyantra.

śrīkaṇṭha Name of Śiva-triangle of the Śrīyanatra (q.v.). *Saundaryalaharī* XI.

śrīkula A major Tantric school. Texts like *Tripurā-rahasya*, *Subhagodayastuti*, *Prapañcasāra*, *Saundaryalaharī*, *Prayogakramadīpikā*, *Śāradā-tilaka*, etc., belong to this school.

śrī-pañcamī Also known as Vasanta-pañcamī it is the fifth day of the waxing moon in *māgha* or early *phālguṇa* (February) on which Sarasvatī, the goddess of arts and letters—white in colour and seated on lotus and carrying a musical instrument and books—is invoked in almost all parts of India.

śrīvaiṣṇava Sect founded by Rāmānuja on the basis of Viśiṣṭādvaitavāda (q.v.). According to this sect *brahman* (q.v.) is no other than Viṣṇu who appears to his devotees in five forms: *para*, *vyuha*, *vibhava*, *antaryāmin* and *arcā* (qq.v.). It is believed that the relation between Viṣṇu and his Śakti (energy) is one of inseparable connection like that of substance and quality. The entire creative process is the self-expression of *brahman* who reveals himself in creation.

śrīvatsa A small hairy mole which appears on the chest of Viṣṇu images. It is one of the *mahāpuruṣa-lakṣaṇas* (sign of greatness). It is also called *romāvarta*.

śrīyantra The most important Tantric diagram connected with the cult of Śrīvidyā. It is also known as Śrīcakra and Tripuracakra. This diagram symbolises the body of the goddess. It consists of nine triangles (Yonis), five in the name of Śakti and four in that of Śiva. The Śakti-triangles are pointed upwards and Śiva triangles downwards. Lakṣmīdhara on *Saundaryalaharī* IX, *Nityaṣoḍaśikārṇava* VI.24, *Kāmakalāvilāsa* XXXVI.

śṛṅgāra Love; one of the nine *rasas*. It has two aspects: *saṃyoga* (union) and *viprayoga* (separation).

śṛṅkhala Chain. Sometimes used as an emblem in representing certain Buddhist deities especially of Vajraśṛmkhalā.

srota Three currents of the Tantric tradition: *dakṣiṇa* (right), *vāma* (left) and *madhyama* (middle). They represent the three *śaktis* of Śiva and also three *guṇas* (q.v.) of Prakṛti.

srotāpanna Those who have attained a definite stage on the Buddhist path towards the ideal of *arhat*-hood. In Pali works, there are many instances of persons becoming *srotāpanṇa* on the basis of their merits (*kusalamūla*). The steps are as follows: *pṛthagjana* (average man); *gotrabhū* (member of the Ariya fold); saddhānusāri (follower of dharma through a teacher); *dhammānusāri* (follower of the *bodhipakṣīya-dharmas*); and *sotāpanna* (those acquiring attainment of the preconditions of *arhat*-hood).

sṛṣṭi The manifestation or opening out (*unmeṣa*) of the unmanifested.

sṛṣṭi-cakra The three triangles of the Śrīyantra (q.v.) representing the creative aspect of Śakti.

sṛṣṭi-dṛṣṭi-vāda The view that the universe of embodied matter was created by the *jaḍa-śakti* (material energy) of Īśvara (q.v.). It is in opposition to the viewpoint called Dṛṣṭi-sṛṣṭi-vāda (q.v.) which posits that the world is a creation of the mind.

sṛṣṭikramanyāsa Nyāsa or feeling the deity in different parts of the body. The deity should be conceived in terms of letters from A to Kṣa and felt in different spots between the forehead and the heart. *Puraścaryārṇava* V. 328–29, *Tantrasāra* 90.

sruc Ladle required in Śrauta sacrifices. It is of three kinds: *juhu* (made of *palāśā*), *upabhṛt* (made of *aśvattha*) and *dhruva* (made of *vikaṅkaṭa*). Ladle to be used in Gṛhya rites is known as Sruva.

srutārthāpatti One of the two kinds of *arthāpatti* (q.v.) or postulation is used to explain the meaning of the words heard. It implies uncovering the figurative meaning, of understanding why words or sentences are omitted, in short the hidden meaning rather than the overt.

śruti Knowledge; etymologically that form of knowledge which is transmitted orally. Kulluka in his commentary on *Manu* II.1 defines Śruti as traditional knowledge and says that it is two-fold—Vedic (Vaidīkī) and Tantric (Tāntrikī). In a specific sense Śruti denotes the Vedic texts and the Vedic tradition. When any school of thought refers to Śruti to prove something it implies that it refers to a form of divine knowledge which cannot be questioned. The law-makers (*smṛtikāras*) like Manu etc., claim to have based their works on Śruti, which has been characterised by them as of divine inspiration, and hold that if there is any conflict in regard to spiritual questions between Śruti and the contents of their own works (Smṛti), the former is to be taken as more authoritative. In Jainism Śruti is a form of knowledge which belongs to the category of *parokṣa* (indirect knowledge of things, of present, past and future) to be acquired through reasoning and study. *TTDS*, I. 20.

stambhana One of the *ṣaṭkarmas* (q.v.) by which the efforts of the opponents can be arrested. *Śāradātilaka* XXIII.124.

sthala Vīra-Śaiva concept of the source and support of all phenomenal existence. *Stha* means *sthiti* (existence) and *la* mean *laya* (dissolution). It represents the absolute and eternal self-consciousness. The potential and material movement of the absolute is called Śiva while its actual and formal movement is called Śakti. Creation is the result of Śiva's vimarśa-śakti that has power to do anything and everything. Śiva as *brahman* through his Śakti is the material cause and in his own nature the efficient cause of the world. The relation is relative and not indicative of a real difference, for there is identity between Śakti and Śaktimat as between attribute and substance.

sthālīpāka Offering to Kṣetrapati, Lord of the

furrow, represented by a bull. The offering is put in leaves and placed on the track used by the cows. No fire is lit.

sthānakavāsī One of the three Śvetāmbara subsects of the Jains. Also known as Dhuṇḍiyā, Bistolā and Sādhumārgī.

sthāna-śuddhi Purification of the place of worship. *Kulārṇava* VI.

sthaṇḍila Sacrificial altar required for Homa (q.v.).

sthāvara Jain term for immobile Jīva (q.v.). They are of five kinds, depending on whether the body is made up of earth, water, fire, air or vegetable substance. The first four are very subtle forms of life while the fifth is gross. This class of being has only one sense, namely, the sense of touch.

sthaviravāda The earliest form of monastic Buddhism, the theories and practices of which are narrated in the Pali canon; also known as Theravāda. It was later subdivided into Haimavata, Sarvāstivāda, Vātsiputrīya, Mahīśāsaka, Dharmaguptaka, Kāśyapīya, Saṃkrāntivāda, Dharmottarīya, Bhadrayānika, Sāmmitiya and Sannāgarika (qq.v.) all of which belong to Hīnayāna Buddhism. The first school to secede from Sthaviravāda was the Mahāsaṅghika which later branched into seven or eight subsects. This group, though counted as Hīnayāna, revealed some Mahāyānic tendencies.

sthitaprajña See under Jivanmukti.

sthiti-cakra One-third of the triangles of Śrīyantra representing the preserving aspect of Śakti. *Setubandha* on *Nityaṣoḍaśikārṇava* I.42.

sthitikalā Power of preservation symbolised by the Tantric letter U, the sign of Viṣṇu. This is represented by ten goddesses. *Prapañcasāra* III. 21–22.

sthitikramanyāsa Nyāsa in which deities are to be conceived in terms of letters from Da to Kṣa and felt in different spots from the heart to the knee. *Puraścaryārṇava*, V. 322.

sthiti-sāmya The *summun bonum* of Kaśmīra Śaivism. It is the perfect harmony of being and becoming which the individual souls should seek and realise.

sthūla-deha, śarīra Gross body.

sthūla dhyāna Meditation on some specified objects like the image of the deity. etc. It is regarded as very much helpful in spiritual quest. *Mahānirvāṇa*, V. 139; *Śaktisaṅgama*, Śundarī, II. 126.

stobha Musical interjections added or introduced in chants such as *hān*, *hāi*, *i*, *u*, *huṃ*. cf. *Chāndogya* I. 13. 1–3.

stotra Chant of hymns required in the performance of sacrifice. These are of two kinds, *pavamāna* and *dhurya*. There are definite rules about place, time, chanting priests and their movements, accents and method of introduction. Each *sāman* in a *stotra* has five parts—*prastāva*, *udgītha*, *pratihāra*, *upadrava* and *nidhana*.

stri-guru Female preceptor. For her characteristics see *Rudrayāmala*, uttara II. The *Yoginītantra* describes the efficacy of getting initiated under a female teacher. *Tantrasāra*, p. 3; see also *Śaktisaṅgama*, Tārā, LVIII. 7–8. The *Mātṛkābheda* VII gives the verses of her worship. The process of the meditation of her form is given in *Prāṇatoṣaṇī*, III. 1, p. 155.

stri-mantra Mantras attributed to female deities. Com.on *Śāradātilaka* II. 57ff.

strī varṇa The long vowels are known by this name. Com.on *Śāradā*, II. 5–7.

stūpa See Caitya.

śubhāgamapañcaka Five tantric texts, each said to be propounded respectively by Vasiṣṭha, Sanaka, Śuka, Sanandana and Sanat Kumara, which were intended for the followers of the Vedic way.

śuddhādvaita Vallabha's interpretation of *brahman* which considers *brahman* as the embodiment of *sat* (existence), *cit* (consciousness), *ānanda* (bliss) and *rasa* (sentiment). For *līlā* (sport) he creates the world out of himself, and is thus both the efficient and material cause of the universe. He does not undergo any change even when he transforms himself into the world. This doctrine is known as *avikṛtapariṇāma* (q.v.). See Rudra-sampradāya.

śuddha-mārga Theoretical viewpoint of the Māheśvara Siddhas who based their doctrine of the processes of overcoming death by revitalizing the body with extra-physical nourishment on the lines laid down in Āgamic Śaivism and Śāktism. It is said that the Chinese Taoist Bhoga taught the Suddha-mārga of the Siddhas to both Śaivagamics and Śāktāgamics of South India. A *reśume* of the Śuddha-mārga doctrine is available in Kumāradeva's *Śuddasādhaka* and Rāvaṇārādhya's *Śivajñānadīpa* and also in *Kāladahana* and *Mṛtyunāsaka* Tantras beloning respectively to *Kāmikāgama* and *Vijayāgama*.

śuddha-māyā The pure aspect of Māyā (q.v.) the material cause of the world, according to different

Śaiva schools, it represents the stages of the progressive unification of the self with the whole universe. From Śuddhamāyā is produced Nāda (cognitive energy), from Nāda Vindu (conative energy), from Vindu Sādākhya (cognitive and conative energies held in equipoise), from Sādākhya Māheśvarī (cognitive energy subordinated to the conative) and from Māheśvarī Śuddhavidyā (conative energy subordinated to the cognitive). *Mṛgendra Āgama* II.3–7, III.1. VII.11, VIII.1–5, IX.2–4, *Pauṣkara Āgama* II.17, III.4, V.9, *Śivajñānabodham* II.5, XII.3.

śuddha-sattva A combination of the three aspects of the *svarūpa-śakti* (q.v.) of the Supreme Being, namely, *sandhinī*, *saṃvit* and *hlādinī*, corresponding respectively to *sat*, *cit* and *ānanda* (qq.v.), according to Bengal Vaiṣṇavism. When received in a purified heart, this *śuddha-sattva* is transformed into *rati* or the first stage of love. Śuddhasattva also means 'pure-matter'.

śuddhaṣṛṣti A Pañcarātra (q.v.) concept which means pure creation from which other forms of creation take place by stages. The eternally existing supreme being, Viṣṇu, has the germs of all creation nascent in him in the time of *pralaya* or dissolution. He does not take any active part in the beginning of creation, but projects his will or *icchā* (efficient cause) to his Śakti, the Female Principle of creation, often personified as Śrī-Lakṣmī, in whom rest the aspects *kriyā* (acting, instrumental cause) and *bhūti* (becoming, material cause) and the combination of these three Śaktis is responsible for pure creation.

śuddha-vidyā See Śuddha-māyā. It is also known as *sad-vidyā*. It is that stage of knowledge in which the difference between subject and object is not completely wiped out.

śuddhi A comprehensive term meaning purification of a person after aśauca (q.v.), after contact with any impure object or certain evil occurrences and purification of food, pots, wells, temples, etc., after they are deemed to be polluted. Śuddhi also denotes reconversion into Hinduism. See Śauca.

sudurjayā The fifth *bhūmi* or stage of a potential Bodhisattva. In this stage he becomes proficient in the understanding of various truths, viz. conventional (*saṃvṛti*), transcendental (*paramārtha*), signal (*lakṣaṇa*), analytical (*vibhāga*), of overcoming (*nistirana*), of things (*vastu*), of origin (*prabhava*), of decay (*kṣayānutpāda*), of knowledge of the path (*mārgajñātāvatāra*) and of the origin of Tathāgata knowledge (*tathagatajñāna-samudaya*).

śukanāsa Antefix attached to the front face of *śikhara* (q.v.) of a north-Indian temple, showing a large *caitya*-window.

sukşma-deha, śarīra Subtle body.

śūlagava Spit-Ox sacrifice. It is so called because an ox is offered to the spit-bearing Rudra. The offering takes place in spring or autumn, under an auspicious star, at about midnight, away from the village. The usual procedure of animal sacrifice is followed, the victim being a fine ox when it has cut its teeth. Also known as Īśānabali. *Āśv.Gr.* IV.9, *Baudh.Gr.* II.7, *Kāṭhaka Gr.* LII.

śūnyatā Mahāyāna-Vajrayāna Buddhist idea of vacuity conceived in terms of the female principle. It is also known as Prajñā and is symbolised in the forms of different goddesses. The male principle is thought of as Karuṇā of Upāya.

śūnyavāda The basiş of the Mādhyamika philosophy, upholding the doctrine of *pudgala* and *dharma-nairātmya*, which teaches that there is nothing real, as everything is devoid of its innate or independent nature. That being the case any appearance is conditional and as such it is in its imposed form (*āropita*) and not in its own form (*svarūpa*). It is *grāhyagrāhakabhāvarahita* or marked by the absence of subject-object relation. The doctrine of *śūnyatā* therefore implies simply the rejection of all sorts of impositions (*sarvāropa-nirākriyā*) and declares anything, external or internal, that appears to be existing, as unreal, like the imaginary town in the sky (*gandharva-nagara*). See Mādhyamika.

surāśodhana Purification of wine. For the procedure see *Prāṇatoṣaṇī* VII. 2, *Kulārṇava*, VI; *Gandharva*, XXXIV. 86–89; *Mātṛkābheda*, III.13; *Tārārahasya*, III; *Mahānirvāṇa*, V; etc.

sūrya-nāḍī Another name for the *piṅgalā* nerve.

suśikṣita-cārvāka A sect of followers of the Cārvaka (q.v.) system. They were found to be inclined to accept *svabhāva* (q.v.) or nature as the cause of the universe. To a certain extent they also believed in the validity of inference.

susumnā The most important nerve, also known as Brahmanāḍī. It is said that the universe itself is contained in this nerve. *Yogaśikhopaniṣat*, VI.13. It extends from Mūlādhāra to Brahmarandhra. It is the route by which Kuṇḍalinī marches upwards. *Ṣaṭcakranirūpaṇa*, I. ff. According to the *Śāṇḍilyopaniṣat* I.4. 10 if the Prāṇa wind is pushed through this nerve by means of Yogic exercise the aspirant will be liberated. That is why it is also called Mokṣamārga.

sūtaka Term for impurity or pollution. Sūta is one that is born or begotten, hence the basic meaning of *sūtaka* is birth or production. As the process of birth is always attended with filth, this eventually comes to be looked upon as 'filthy'. It is suffixed with such concepts as *jāti* (birth), *rajas* (menstruation), *ucchiṣṭa* (remnants of eaten food), *janma* (birth), *maraṇa* (death), etc.

svabhāva Naturalism conceived as the First Principle in the *Śvetāśvatara Upaniṣad* (I.2. Cf. *Suśruta*, Śārīra I.11). By Svabhāva is meant the power invariably belonging to material objects, as for instance, the radiation of heat by fire (Śaṅkara on *SV.Up.* I.2). Guṇaratna in *TRD* 13 says that by Svabhāva is meant the transformation of objects by themselves. It rejects the idea that nature reveals a divine power underlying it. Early evidence of associating the doctrine of Svabhāva with the materialistic outlook is found in *Mbh.* XII. 232.19 which says *svabhāvaṃ bhūtacintakāḥ*. Subsequently this doctrine was attributed to the Lokāyatikas or Cārvākas.

svabhāvakāya A division of the *dharmakāya* (see Trikāya) of Buddha. According to the *Āloka* on the *Abhisamayālaṅkārakārikā*, there are two kinds of *dharmakāya*, one being the *bodhipakṣīya* and other *dharmas*, which are themselves pure and productive of clear knowledge, and the other transferred resort of the same which is called *svabhāvakāya* or *nityakāya*. The former is called *jñānakāya*.

svādhiṣṭhāna The nerve plexus situated above the Mūlādhāra. It is like a six-petalled lotus. This Cakra is presided over by the goddess Rākinī. *Ṣaṭcakranirūpaṇa*, XV–XVII; Lakṣmīdhara on *Saundaryalaharī*, IX.

svādhyāya Study and memorisation of *ṛks*, *yajus* formulae, *sāmans*, *atharvāṅgirasaḥ*, *itihāsa-purāṇa* and *gāthās* which give the merit of *tapas*. *Śat.Br.* XI.5.7.4–8.

svagata-bheda Difference within the self, or internal difference.

sājātya-bheda Difference within the same species.

svakīyā Female partner who is the valid wife of the aspirant.

svakula varṇa Letters belonging to one's own group. There are three other categories of letters—Mitra (friendly), Udāsīna (neutral) and Śatru (enemy). *Prapañcasāra*, III.70–72.

svapuṣpa The first menstrual blood of a newly married woman sacred to Devī.

svar Synonym of sky, conceived as a region.

svarga Heaven. It is a source of unsurpassed joy according to the epics and Purāṇas where an individual can reach after death in consequence of meritorious actions performed in worldly life. It is imagined as a place thousands of Yojanas above the earth. The drawback of heaven is that no new merit is accumulated there and that when the store of merit is exhausted one has to leave heaven to be born again. According to the Mīmāṃsakas Svarga is the reward of all sacrifices for which no reward is expressly provided by the Vedas.

svarūpa Essential nature. *Brahman* as knowledge (*jñāna*) and bliss (*ānanda*) form the *svarūpa* or the principal reality in consciousness (*cetanā*) or *svarūpa-bimba*. Consciousness in itself is called *svarūpa-caitanya*. Knowledge of quality (*dharma-bhūtajñāna*) is regarded as *svarūpa-dharma* or the natural attribute of Īśvara which is also known as *svarūpalakṣaṇa*.

svarūpa-śakti One of the three principal powers of *brahman* according to the Bengal school of Vaiṣṇavism. The *līlās* (q.v.) of Kṛṣṇa are possible only through the agency of *svarūpa-śakti*. It has three aspects: *sandhinī*, *saṃvit* and *hlādinī*, corresponding respectively to *sat*, *cit* and *ānanda* (qq.v.) the three aspects of *brahman* (Kṛṣṇa).

svastyayana Rites for averting evils and for bringing peace. In these rites verses containing the word *svasti* or a benediction are used. cf. *RV* X.178 is a *svastyayana* hymn.

svātantravāda A name of the Trika aspect of Kaśmīra Śaivism.

svātantrika A group of the Mādhyamikas, headed by Bhāvaviveka, who depended on the method of direct reasoning to arrive at the truth.

svayamācārya Household *gurus* (q.v.) of those followers of the Vaḍakalai group of the Śrī-vaiṣṇavas who were affiliated with the Ahobila Maṭha.

svayambhūkusuma Menstrual blood of a maiden.

svayambhūliṅga One of the three forms of Śiva-liṅga, others being Bāṇa and Itara.

śvetāmbara See Digambara-Śvetāmbara.

syādvāda Assertion of possibilities in Jain logic. It begins with the dictum that every judgement expresses one aspect of reality and is therefore relative and subject to some condition. It is set forth as follows: (1) may be (*syād*), it is (*asti*); (2) may be, it is not (*nāsti*); (3) may be, it is and it is not; (4) may be, it is indescribable (*avaktavya*), (5) may be, it is and yet is indescribable; (6) may be, it is not, and it is also indescribable; and (7) may be, it is and it is n ot, and it is also indescribable. To illustrate, the first and second parts (*syād asti* and *syād nāsti*) may be taken into account. The former is in terms of *bhāva* or existence and the latter in that of *abhāva* or non-existence. A lump of clay becomes non-existent as soon as a jar is made out of it. Here the jar is an antecedent non-existence with reference to the lump of clay as the latter is a subsequent non-existence with reference to the former. Hence, if mere existence is taken into account and non-existence denied, or the reverse is done, it becomes impossible to affirm or deny anything. Again if both existence and non-existence are simultaneously ascribed to a thing it becomes indescribable (*avaktavya*). See also Anekāntavāda and Naya.

śyena-yāga Rite or sacrifice to injure others. It is a general term for black acts.

tāḍaṇa Processing of Mantras. Each letter of the Mantra concerned should be recited either ten times or a hundred times. Tāḍaṇa is also done by writing the letters and sprinkling sandalwood water on them. *Tantrasāra*, p. 54.

taijasa ahaṃkāra Egoity arising from heat which is the cause of the ten sense organs and mind. Com. on *Śāradātilaka* I.19.

taijasa varṇa Same as Āgneya-varṇa, i.e. I, Ī, Ai, Kha, Cha, Tha, Tha, Pha, Ra, and Kṣa, said to have sprung from heat or Tejas. *Prapañcasāra*, III. 70–72; Com. on *Śāradā*, II.10–11.

tairthika A class of religious thinkers who advocated asceticism as the ideal of life and *nirvāṇa* final deliverance as the end of all human endeavour.

tala Storey of a shrine, *vimāna* or *gopura*; same as *bhūmi*. The ground-floor is called *ādi-tala* and the intermediate story *madhya-tala*.

talātraya A measure which the worshipper adopts to protect himself from malefic influences. It consists of three 'taps' with the fingers of the right hand on the left palm, in a vertical plane one above the other, as if erecting an imaginary pillar in the front of the worshipper.

tāmraparṇīya Sthaviravādins or Theravādins of Ceylon.

tamas The constituent of Prakṛti (q.v.) which is of the nature of indifference and is heavy (*guru*) and enveloping (*varṇaka*). It gives rise to drowsiness, sloth, stupidity, ignorance and carelessness.

taṇhā Thirst or desire which forms the eighth feature of the Buddhist law of dependent origination (*paṭiccasampuppāda*). There are as many kinds of thirst as there are sources, i.e., the six objects of sense organs. Each *taṇhā* (Sanskrit tṛṣṇā) may be of three kinds: *kāma*, *bhava* and *vibhava*.

tanmātra Five potential elements of sound, touch, colour, taste and smell, giving rise to the *mahābhūtas* (gross elements) according to the Sāṅkhya. From the essence of sound is produced *ākāśa*, from that of touch air, from that of colour light or fire, from that of taste water, and from that of smell earth. See Mahābhūta.

tantra A general term for any system serving as the guiding principle of work. In the religious sense Tantra first came to mean 'the scripture by which knowledge is spread'. In the next stage it was defined as a class of texts which promulgates profound matters concerning *tattva* (theory, which came to mean 'pure knowledge') and *mantra* (practical means, which later came to denote 'mystic sound') and was therefore looked upon as a technical branch of pure knowledge. Thus Tantra came to mean the essentials of any religious system and subsequently, special doctrines and rituals found only in certain forms of various religious systems.

tantrayukti Main canons or principles of exposition of a Śāstra.

tanu Body. See *mantra-tanu*, *praṇava-tanu*. It also means reduced intensity in the Yogic concept of ignorance.

tanumānasa A term used in the *Yogavāsiṣṭha* III.118–2–16 to denote a stage of realisation when, on account of the knowledge of the ultimate unreality of the world revealed by philosophical thought, individuality becomes less and less assertive and is little felt.

tapas Austerities. In *RV* X.129 it is stated that the self-sustained one, existing in void and wrapped in nothingness, breathed calmly and was developed by the power of *tapas*. The term occurs in post-Rgvedic literature in the sense of fervour. cf. *Śat.Br.* X.5.3.1, XI.5.8.1, XIII.7.1.1, *Taitt.Br.* III.12.3.1. In *AV* XVII.1.24 *tapas* means heat. In Dharmaśāstras *tapas* in the sense of austerity has been prescribed as a means for removing the consequences of sins. It also came to mean *niyama*, i.e., restraint or strict observances.

tapta-kṛcchra Expiation for Brāhmanas for selling articles and animals that should not be sold by them.

taptamudrā-dhāraṇa Making marks of conch, discus, etc. (weapons of Viṣṇu) on limbs or other parts of the body with heated copper or the like. It is a custom followed by the Madhvas.

tāraṇapanthī One of the five Digambara subsects of the Jains, also known popularly Samaiyapanthī.

tāratamya Gradation of the entities of the world; degrees of reality.

tāriṇī-mata Same as Kahādimata. *Śaktisaṅgama*, Tārā LVIII.81.

tarjanī-mudrā A hand pose in which the index finger is raised in a menacing attitude while the other fingers are clenched in the fist. If a *pāśa* (noose) appears round the index finger it is called Tarjanīpāśa. This *mudrā* is characteristic of certain Buddhist icons.

tarka Argument justifying a certain conclusion. It is an important aid to the attainment of valid knowledge and is one of the sixteen philosophical topics of the Nyāya.

tarpaṇa Rememberance of deities, sages and fathers after the recital of Gāyatrī hymn during worship. It is an offering of water and a constituent part of *snāna* or bathing which is to be done while standing in the water. *Manu* II.176, *Viṣṇu Dh.S.* LXIV.23–24, *Parāśara* XII.12–13. It is also a constituent of *brahmayajña*. There are differences between Vedic and Tantric systems of Tarpaṇa. *Puraścaryārṇava*, VI. p. 509. Tarpaṇa to Śakti is to be offered thrice. *Tantrasāra*, pp. 81–82; *Mahānirvāṇa*, V. 65. Tarpaṇa is also a term for processing Mantras. *Tantrasāra*, p. 54.

tarunollāsa One of the seven Ullāsa or stages of Tantric Sādhanā. It is next to the beginning stage. *Parasurāmakalpasūtra*, I.68; *Kulārṇava*, VIII, *Tārābhaktisudhārṇava*, VI, p. 255.

taṭastha-lakṣaṇa Accidental quality as opposed to *svarūpalakṣaṇa* or natural attribute.

taṭasthā-śakti 'Marginal' power, same as *jīva-śakti* of *brahman*, which all the living beings, human or otherwise, are in essence, according to the Acintyabhedābheda.

tathāgata The usual expression by which Gautama Buddha is referred to. According to the Buddhist texts, the Tathāgata is fully aware of the nature of the five constituents of a being, is completely free from of all thought-constructions and mental aberrations, is endowed with ten supernatural powers and four kinds of infallibility, is the embodiment, of clear vision, the propounder of truth and lord of *dharmas*. *Majjhima* I. 179.486. According to the *Sumaṅgala-vilāsinī* 66–68, Tathāgatas are those who come (*tathā-āgata*) in the same way as the previous Tathāgatas, i.e., all of them embrace the recluse-life, through a long and arduous process of self-abnegation perfect themselves in highest meditation, and ultimately realise the truth. After rendering benefit to human beings they pass away from the mortal world (*tathā-gata*).

tathāgata-bhūmi The stage when a Boddhisattva becomes a Tathāgata after passing through the tenth *bhūmi* (q.v.) called *dharmamegha* (q.v.), according to the *Laṅkāvatāra* 277.

tathāgata-garbha A qualifying term for the *dharmakāya* of Buddha. Metaphysically it is the real nature of things that can be equated with *tathatā* (q.v.), which is described as *nitya*, *dhruva* and *sāsvata*, i.e. regular, fixed and eternal.

tathāgata-jñāna Attainment of a potential Bodhisattva in the third stage of his spiritual progress called *prabhākarī* or *adhicittavihāra*. It is *anāvaraṇa-vimokṣa-jñāna* or the unscreened knowledge of emancipation. *Bodhisattvabhūmi* 12–13.

tathāgata-kāya Same as the *dharmakāya* of Buddha according to Nāgārjuna. *Mādhyamikavṛtti* XXII.

tathatā Same as Śūnyatā (q.v.), described as 'suchness' or 'thatness' which is immutable, unchangeable, beyond concept and distinction (tathatāvikāra nirvikārāvikalpā nirvikalpā). In the *Aṣṭasāhasrikā-prajñā-pāramitā* 307 it is said: That which is *tathāgata-tathatā* and that which is *tathatā* in itself are non-dual, one and the same. Tathatā is neither anywhere nor arises from anywhere, nor belongs to anything. Hence it is non-dual and one. Tathatā has two aspects, conditioned and unconditioned, the former being manifested in the empirical sphere and the latter in the transcendental.

tathya-saṃvṛti Empirical truth which refers to things originating out of a cause and perceived in the same way by all persons with unimpaired sense organs.

tātparya Intended meaning of a whole sentence; understanding of the context (*prakarṇa*) or the intention of the speaker.

tatpuruṣa One of the five faces of Śiva from which texts such as *Raurava*, etc., are said to have been produced.

tattva The science of the cosmic principles. In Tantra the term denotes critical values and positions one has to pass through successively. To experience a *tattva* is to become it, for each represents a stage of actual realisation. It is also used for substance, principle and essence. For example, *pañca-tattva* (Five Ms, q.v.) means not the ritual with five articles but the offering of the *tattvas* or principles they represent. In regard to the science of cosmic principles *tattvas* mark different stages of evolution. According to the Śaivas there are thirty-six *tattvas*, to the Vaiṣṇavas thirty-two and to the Sāṅkhyas twenty. The *tattvas* or evolutes of Prakṛti are ten in number. Tattva also means transcendental truth (paramārthika-satya).

tattvacakra Also known as Cakrarāja and Divyacakra. The performance of this Cakra is restricted to only those who have attained a certain stage of spiritual development. No external rites are required. The aspirants sit together under the leadership of the Cakresvara and mediate with Haṃsa-mantra. *Mahānirvāṇa*, VIII. 204 ff.

tattamasi 'That thou art'; the concept of the non-difference between *jīva* (q.v.) and *brahman*. According to Śaṅkara, it means the understanding of *brahman* as the only reality; one, indivisible, without a second, having in itself no *bheda* or difference, and of the world as a phenomenal or illusory reality. The theistic interpreters of Vedānta explain the second part *tvam* as a dependent reality. For example, Nimbārka holds that just as *niyama* is secondary to the *niyāmaka*, and *śakti* to *śaktimat*, so also *jīva* is to *brahman*. Others explain this word in the sense that the *jīvas* are reflection of *brahman*.

tattvanyāsa Feeling of the 36 Tattvas, (threefold knowledge: Atmā, Vidyā and Śiva) in different parts of the body. It has a variety of methods. *Tantrasāra*, 271, 310.

tejas Heat or fire, one of the five mahābhūtas (q.v.)

tejodhyāna See under Jyotirdhyāna.

tenkalai A subsect of the Śrīvaiṣṇavas (q.v.) which follows non-Brahmanical and non-Sanskritic traditions. This group does not believe in rituals, external formalities in regard to religious quest, the caste system, subordination of women and social authoritarianism. In the field of devotion this group believes in *mārjara-mārga* (q.v.).

terapanthī One of the five Digambara subsects of the Jains. The Śvetāmbaras also have a subsect of the same name

tilaka Mark on the forehead usually made with sandalwood paste.

tīrtha Holy place; place of pilgrimage; a certain part of the palm; water used in bathing the image of a god; a suffix to the name of members belonging to certain religious creeds.

tīrthaṃkaras "Ford-makers across the stream of existence" who were responsible for the propagation of the Nirgrantha (Jain) ideals down the ages. They are twenty-four: Ṛṣabha, Ajita, Sambhava, Abhinandana, Sumati, Padmaprabha, Supārśva, Chandrprabha, Subidhi, Śītala, Śreyāṃśa, Vasupūjya, Vimala, Ananta, Dharma, Śānti, Kunthu, Ara, Malli, Munisubrata, Nami, Nemi, Pārśva and Mahāvīra.

tithi Time or period required by the moon to gain twelve degrees on the sun to the east. The period may take more than one day. Different tithis are specificed for various religious acts. The word mahā is prefixed to certain *tithis*, for example, when the full-moon is in the nakṣatra which gives the name to the month and is in conjunction with Jupiter. Tithis are variously classified as *pūrṇa* and *sakhaṇḍá*, *śuddhā* and *viddhā* or *kharva*, *darpa* and *hiṃsra*. The Purāṇas and Dharmasastras give long lists of acts and things like food etc. forbidden on certain *tithis*.

titthiya Sanskrit Tīrthakara. It is a term applied by Buddha in the sense of heretic to his contemporaries.

totāpanthī One of the five Digambara subsects of the Jains.

toya-kṛcchra A form of expiation. Also called Varuṇa-Kṛcchra.

traidhātavi An *iṣṭi* in Rājasūya.

traipura A triangle within the quadrangular Pṛthivīmaṇḍala which is situated within the pericarp of the container lotus near the mouth of Vajranāḍī. It is also called Yoni or Kāmarūpa Pīṭha in human body. *Ṣaṭcakranirūpaṇa*, VIII.

trairāśika A variety of Śiva-liṅga distinguished by the modelling of the Rudra-bhāga.

traiyambaka-homa A rite in Śākamedha (q.v.) to be performed on the northern side of the altar; in it *homa* (q.v.) is to be offered to Rudra. The Yajamāna, his wife and children and unmarried daughters should go round the fire patting their thighs and repeating the *mantra* Tryambakam-Yajāmahe.

trasa Moving Jīvas (q.v.) or animated beings classified into those with five-senses, e.g., men; four-senses, e.g., bees; three senses e.g. ants; two-senses, e.g., worms; one-sense, e.g., plants according to Jain conception. Ekendriya (one-sensed) Jīvas possess only the sense of touch; Dvīndriya (two-sensed), taste and touch; Trīndriya (three-sensed), touch, taste and smell; Caturindriya (four-sensed), sight in addition; and Pañcendriya (five-sensed) in addition, hearing. *Uttara* XXXVI. 171 ff.

trasareṇu Subtle things with minimum visible magnitude.

trāṭaka A form of Yogic Ṣaṭkarma. The aspirant has to focus his eyes on a point until they begin to water. It makes possible the attainment of Śāmbhavī Śakti. It is supposed to cure eye-diseases and give divine eyesight. *Gheraṇḍa*, I. 54–55.

trayī The three Vedas.

tridhāma Collective designation of Soma, Sūrya and Agni. *Kāmakalāvilāsa*, XIII, XIV.

trika Form of Kāśmīra Śaivism also known as Trika-śāsana, Rahasya Sampradāya and Tryambaka-Sampradāya. The Trika is so called either because it accepts as most important the triad of Siddha, Nāmaka and Mālinī, out of ninety-two

Āgamas recognised by it, or because the triad consisting of Śiva, Śakti and Anu, or of Parā, Aparā, Parātparā or of Abheda, Bhedābheda and Bheda. The system is both a statement about the nature of reality and also a way of life. The ultimate reality in this system is variously designated as Anuttara. Cit, Caitanya, Pūrṇa or Para-Saṃvid, Śiva, Parameśvara and Ātman. As transcendent the reality is described as Śiva, and as immanent it is described as Śakti. Like fire and its burning power Śiva and Śakti are identical though they are spoken of as distinct. Consciousness is the Śakti aspect of reality and can be compared to a clear mirror in which reality sees itself. This is the original *bimba* (reflection) of which everything in the universe is *pratibimba* or *ābhāsa*, a secondary reflection or shadow. The important modes of Śakti are *cit* (intelligence), *ānanda* (bliss), *icchā* (will), *jñāna* (knowledge) and *kriyā* (action). The supreme being (Śiva) is at the same time static (container of Śakti in Prākaśa aspect) and dynamic (container of Śakti in Vimarśa aspect), changeless and changing. The realisation of identity with Śiva is to become free from worldly fetters. According to this school *mokṣa* (liberation) is the return to the original state, that is, to the Absolute. *Paramārthasāra* 12ff, 51–52, *Śivadṛṣṭi* III.7, *Īśvarapratyabhajñā* I.5.14, *Sarvadarśanasaṃgraha* 90.

trikālajña Knowers of past, present and future events.

trika-mandapa Maṇḍapa with three *catuṣkīs* (bays) in a medieval temple, normally of the Jain faith.

trikaprasava-śānti Śānti-rite on the birth of a son after three successive daughters or vice-versa.

trikāya Mahāyāna conception of the three bodies (*kāya*) of Buddha, viz. *dharma*, *sambhoga*, and *nirmāṇa* or *rūpa*. The *dharma-kāya* is the real body of Buddha which is all pervading, formless and eternal. This body cannot be seen, but for the sake of the devotees of exceptional merit, Buddha sometimes appears in the form of a god which is his *sambhoga-kāya*. For the welfare of mankind Buddha sometimes assumes human form which is subject to birth and death. This is his material body (*rūpakāya*) or created body (*nirmāṇa-kāya*). Gautama Buddha was thus the human form of the original Buddha and was born in the world (*sahā-lokadhātu*) where we live. See also Sahaja-kāya and Vajra-kāya.

trikoṇa Triangle, also known as Yoni. It is said to be due to the elevation of Vindu. *Kāmakalāvilāsa* XXII. In the drawn triangle, which is required for Tantric worship, Parā Śakti or Parā Vāk serves as the middle point while the three arms forming the three angles smybolise the three other forms of sound (Paśyantī, Mahayamā, Vaikharī). The three Vījas (Vāgbhava, Kāmāraja, Śakti), the three Śaktis (Vāma-Jyeṣṭha-Raudrī or Icchā-Jñāna-Kriyā), the three goddesses Kameśvarī, Vajreśvarī and Bhagamālinī), the three *tattvas* (Prakṛti, Mahat, Ahaṃkāra), three Pīṭhas (Kāmarūpa, Jālandhara, Pūrṇagiri) and all other threefold concepts. *Ibid.*, XXIII; Setubandha on *Nityaṣoḍaśikārṇava*, VI. 26–40; Rāmeśvara on *Parasurāmakalpasūtra*, V. 11; *Gandharvatantra* V. 112–13; *Tantrarājatantra*, XXXV. 12–13.

trikūṭa Three *Vimānas* erected on a common basement or placed around a common *maṇḍapa*.

triliṅga Bāṇa, Itara and Para, three types of phallus. *Kāmakalāvilāsa*, XIII, XIV.

trilokyamohana-cakra A form of Śrīcakra or Śrīyantra.

trimūrti Manifestation of the supreme being in three forms Brahmā (the creator), Viṣṇu (the preserver) and Śiva (the destroyer).

tripiṭaka Buddhist canon comprising Sutta, Vinaya and Abhidhamma.

tripīṭha Collective name of Kāmarūpa, Pūrṇagiri and Jālandhara Pīṭhas. *Kāmakalāvilāsa* XII, XIV.

tripuṇḍra Triple-mark of ashes which the Yogīs wear on their foreheads. It is highly extolled by the Pāśupatas.

tripuracakra Same as Śrīcakra or Śrīyantra.

tripurasundarī-mata Name of Hāḍimata. *Śaktisaṅgama* Kālī, VI. 125.

triratha Temple with three projections.

triratna Knowledge, faith and conduct, which in Buddhism are Buddha, Dharma and Saṃgha.

triśakti Jñāna (knowledge), Icchā (will) and Kriyā (action). *Kāmakalāvilāsa*, XIII, XIV.

tristhalī Three holy places—Prayāga, Kāśī and Gayā.

triśūla Trident, the weapon of Śiva.

tritattva Three realities—*brahman*, *cit* and *acit*—which are the basis of Nimbārka's *Dāśaślokī*.

tri-tīrthika An image with three Jina figures.

trivārga Artha (economic values), Kāma (Psychological values) and Dharma (moral values), which represent ends that are consciously purused by men.

trivīja The seeds of the Mantras of Tripurasundarī which are known as Vāgbhava, Kāmarāja and

Śakti. *Cidvallī* on *Kāmakalāvilāsa*, XXIII.

tulāpuruṣa One of the *mahādānas* (great gifts) in which gold equivalent to the weight of the donor should be donated. There are epigraphic references to *tulāpuruṣa* gifts in the historical period.

tulasī Basil, sacred to the Vaiṣṇava cults. Clay taken from the root of the plant is used to make the mark on the forehead after bath.

turīya A very high state. The *sahasrāra-cakra* is supposed to contain a field to knowledge which is also known as Turīya.

turyagā The seventh stage of realisation, according to the *Yogavāsiṣṭha* III. 118. 2–16, when the mystic experience of being one with the Reality is consciously realised in consciousness.

turīyātīta A class of ascetics; those who are beyond the fourth stage of *paramahaṃsa* are so called. They eat only uncooked fruits in the way cows take food. If they eat cooked food then in must come only from three stipulated houses and deal with their bodies as if they were dead bodies.

tyāgāṅga Vīra-śaiva concept of a category of worshippers (*aṅga*). The worshipper in this stage gives up attachment to worldly objects and becomes the means through which he realises his divine nature. Iṣṭaliṅga is the object of his worship.

ubhatobhāgavimutta One of the two categories of *arhats*, the other being *paññāvimutta*. Those who have attained emancipation by perfecting themselves in the eight releases (*vimokkhas*) from thought constructions and by acquisition of the highest knowledge are included in the Ubhatobhāgavimutta category.

uccāṭana One of the Ṣaṭkarmas (six black acts) by which one can drive away one's rival from the land. *Śāradā*, XXIII. 125.

ucchedavāda Nihilism. Seven groups of the nihilists are mentioned in the Buddhist texts according to which the soul has no separate existence. It is same as the body itself and becomes extinct along with the body.

udāharaṇa Illustration. A concrete instance guaranteeing the material validity of any argument.

udāna One of the five kinds of *prāṇa* (q.v.) or breath. It is in the throat; speech and other activities beloning to the upper part of the body are attributed to it.

udavasānīyā An *iṣṭi* at the end of *agniṣṭoma* (q.v.) in which a cake baked on eight or five potsherds is offered to Agni. A bull, or its value, is the stipulated fee. Sometimes it is done only by offering clarified butter to the fire. *Āp.Śr.* XIII.25.5–8, *Āśv.Śr.* VI.14.24.

udaya-karma The *karma* (q.v.) which will be accumulated in the future life according to the Jain conception.

udayanīya Concluding *iṣṭi* in *agniṣṭoma* (q.v.) which is to be performed in the *prāgvaṃsa* and not on the specially prepared *uttaravedī*. The procedure is like that for the *prāyaṇiya* or the opening *iṣṭi* in which *caru* (rice cooked in milk) and *ājya* (clarified butter) are offered to different deities. *Āp.Śr.* III.23, *Āśv.Śr.* VI.14.

udbhuta-rūpa Manifest forms which are the indispensable conditions for perception.

uddālaka-vrata An expiation for *vrātyatā*, i.e. failure to have *upanayana* at the right time which consists in practising restrictions in food habits for a period of two months. *Vas.Dh.S.* XI.77.

uddhāta A term for yogic breath-control; it has been variously explained by different writers.

udgama The pediment of Caitya-arches. Usually it is employed as the crowning decoration of a niche.

udyāpana Last rite in a *vrata* (observance) when undertaken only once. The concluding rite for observances which are to be continued for life is called *pāraṇa*.

ugra A Śaiva sect mentioned in Ānandagiri's *Śaṅkaravijaya*.

ūha Substituting another word or words in part of a *mantra*. Certain alterations and adaptations are necessary in the matter of *mantras*, *sāmans* and *saṃskāras*, according to the Mīmāṃsakas. The word ordinarily means *tarka* or reasoning.

ukthamukha Name of the principal part of certain *śāstras*.

ukthya A form of Soma sacrifice. *Āśv.Śr.* VI.1.1–3, *Āp.Śr.* XIV.1.2, *Ait.Br.* XIV.3.

ullāsa Stages of Tantric Sādhanā—Ārambha, Taruṇa, Yauvana, Prauḍha, Prauḍhānta, Unmanā and Anavasthā. *Paraśurāmakalpasūtra*, X.68.

umāsahita-mūrti Śiva image with his consort Umā.

unmanā, unmanī The sixth stage in spiritual exercise. The aspirant in this stage has a feeling of great joy and his sense organs apparently cease to function. *Kulārṇava*, VIII; *Tārābhaktisudhārṇava*, VI. 255.

upacāra Articles for worship. They can consist of five, seven, ten, twelve, sixteen, eighteen, thirty-six and even sixty-four items. *Puraścārṇava*, III, 224–25; Rāghava on *Śāradā* IV.92; *Tantrasāra*, 551–52; *Mahānirvāṇa*, VI.78–79; XIII. 203 ff.

upādāna Strong attachment resulting from *tanhā* (desire) which forms the ninth point in the chain of the Buddhist *paṭiccasamuppāda* (q.v.). There are four kinds of *upādāna*: *kāma* (firm grasping of the object), *diṭṭhi* (adherence to wrong views) *śīlabbata* (belief in the efficacy of rituals) and *attāvāda* (belief in the existence of a soul).

upādana-kāraṇa Material cause, like clay in the case of a jar. It is of two kinds: *vivartopādāna* (material of apparent or illusory transformation) and *pariṇāmopādāna* (material of real transformation). The followers of the advaita system believe in the concept of *apariṇāmī-upādāna* or changeless-stuff like *brahman* as opposed to *pariṇāmī-upādana* (e.g. *māyā* or the mutable stuff of the world). The former is called *avikārī* and the latter *vikārī upādāna*.

upadeśa Advice; sermon; gospel; discourse; teaching; training. According to the *Dharmasindhu* in the Kali age there is no *dīkṣā* (q.v.) but only Upadeśa.

upādhi Limiting adjunct in the form of body and senses or material conditions. In Advaita Vedānta Upādhi is said to be a transformation of *māyā* (q.v.) which limits the true nature of *brahman*. Śaṅkara on *Vedāntasūtra* I.4.3, II.1.14, II.2.2. Like the infinite space enclosed in the pot (*ghaṭākāśa*) the unconditioned *brahman* becomes limited by the Upādhis. Those who want to explain the relation between the *brahman* and the world in terms identity-in-difference admit the reality of the Upādhis and hold that the world is naturally one with *brahman* while its difference from the latter is due to the Upādhis.

upākarman A ceremony performed to restart the reading of the Vedas after the break during the rainy reason. It is called *Vārṣika* in some places. *Mit.* on *Yāj* I. 142. *Āśv.Gr.* III.5.2–3, *Khadira Gr.* III.2.14–15, etc.

upalabdhi Experience, realisation. In special sense the term denotes *dharmabhūtajñāna* (knowledge as quality) and is often described as synonymous to *jñāna*, *saṃvit* and *buddhi* (qq.v.).

upamāna Comparison; it is the knowledge of the relation between a name and things so named on the basis of a given description of their similarity to some familiar object. It is sometimes regarded as a valid source of knowledge. The Cārvākas (q.v.) contend that *upamāna* is not *pramāṇa* (q.v.) at all. The Buddhists admit its validity but do not recognise it is a separate source of knowledge while the Jains reduce it to *pratyabhijñā* (q.v.) or recognition. The Mīmāṃsakas and Vedāntins explain it in a different way. The Nyāya view of Upamāna as a form of inference is admitted by the Vaiśeṣika and Sāṅkhya school.

upāna Lowermost part of the footing of the South Indian *adhiṣṭhāna* (q.v.).

upanayana Initiation into studenthood; it is regarded as the second birth. It takes place in the eighth, eleventh or twelfth year of the boy according to his caste. Shaved, bathed and dressed in new garments (made from the skin of a deer, goat or cow), wearing the sacrificial cord over the left shoulder and carrying a staff in hand the candidate has to appear before the domestic fire where the preceptor touches him on the left shoulder with his left hand and draws the student's right hand towards himself with the *vyāhṛtis* reciting the *sāvitrī* and an appropriate formula signifying the initiation. He next touches the pupil's heart region with a formula that proclaims the union of their hearts and recites a prayer imploring the different deities to endow the initiate with intelligence. The boy is first taught the famous stanza from *RV* III.62.10 sacred to Savitṛ. During the period of studentship, the training of the boy consists of a study of the Veda and observance of certain obligatory vows and duties. The custom of the *upanayana* of girls prevailed down to the Sūtra period.

upaniṣkramaṇa A *saṃskāra*, same as *ādityadarśana* (q.v.); it is taking the child out of the house into the open. It is also called *niṣkramaṇa* and *nirṇayaṇa*. *Baudh.Gr.*II.2.

upapāduka Self-born in Buddhist conception.

upapātaka Minor sins, the number of which has varied greatly from time to time, from five to fifty-one. *Vas.Dh.S.*I. 23, *Baudh.Dh.S.* II.1.60–61. *Gaut.Dh.S.* XV.18, *Manu* XI.59–66, *Yāj.* III. 234–42. Expiation for all Upapātakas is the same as for killing a cow; or it is *cāndrāyana*, *parāka* and *gosava* (qq.v.) or subsisting on milk for a month.

upapīṭha The sub-base below the South Indian *adhiṣṭhāna* (q.v.).

upasad Three special days in Soma sacrifices. On each *upasad* day the *pravargya* or hot-milk rite is performed twice. On the second day a great altar is constructed on which the Soma carts are placed. On the last *upasad* day an offering of a goat is made to Agni and Soma. *Jaimini* X.7.43–46.

upasampadā Higher form of Buddhist initiation.

upāsanā Worship, the act by which one can stay near god. *Kaulamārgarahasya*, pp. 113–14. It is the surrendering of one's own self to the supreme being. Rāmeśvara on *Paraśurāmakalpasūtra*, I.1. It may be internal or external; see Antaryāga and Bahiryāga. It is of many types. For the mood of the worshipper see under Grāhyālambana, Grahaṇālambana and Grahītrālambana.

upasaṃgrahaṇa Clasping the feet and bowing.

upavāsa Fasting; it is regarded as a means of purifying body and soul, of removing sins and of mental concentration.

upāya See Prajñā. Originally *upāya* was called *karuṇā* (the principle of compassion); subsequently it came to denote the Male Principle. At a still later stage the original meaning of the term *upāya* (the way or means) became more popular. The ultimate reality of Tantric Buddhism came to be regarded as the unity of *prajñā* (wisdom) and *upāya* (means). In the *Guhyasamāja*, *upāya* is described as *vajrayoga* or the way of obtaining *bodhi* or enlightenment.

upekṣā Indifference; it is one of the four *brahmavihārabhavanās* of Buddhism. In Yoga, the term has the same meaning: 'to practise indifference towards the vicious'. *Yogasūtra* I. 33.

uposatha Days of fasting for the Buddhists. Four days in the month are called so, two at quarter-moon and at the new moon and full moon. In practice, only the new and full moon days are observed as *upasatha*. The monks assemble on these days and declare their activities and even lapses. The recital of *Pātimokkha Sutta* takes place.

ūrdhavapuṇḍra Mark on forehead made with different articles for sectarian identification.

uṣṇīṣakamala One of the four nerve-cycles of the Buddhist conception which is analogous to that of Sahasrāra (q.v.) of the Śākta Tantras. It is in the central cerebral region and is connected with the *vajra* or *sahaja-kāya* (q.v.) of Buddha. It is the place where the female energy having the force of fire and known as *caṇḍālī* (q.v.), meets its source through the nerves known as *upāya* and *prajñā*.

utsarga Dedication to the public. It is different from *dāna* or gift, because the latter is bestowed on an individual or a specific person. But when a man makes an *utsarga* he gives up the thing for the benefit of all (*sarvabhūtebhyaḥ*).

utsarjana Cessation of annual Veda study. *Baudh. Gr.* I. 5. 163, *Āśv. Gr.* III.5.14, *Gobhila Gr.* III. 3.14.

utsarpini Jain cosmic period which is an age of evolution of growth. The age of dissolution and decay is called *avasarpiṇī*. The two together constitute the complete cosmic cycle of time.

utsava Festival. Though festivals may be secular, in many cases, especially in India, they are inevitably observed with religious rites, ceremonies and observances.

utsava-mūrti Also called Yātrā-mūrti. At certain places during the car-festival, or religious procession, the image of the god taken out in the car is not the same as that installed in the shrine. Such substitutes are called *utsava-mūrtis*.

uttarakaula A sect of Kaula worshippers mentioned by Lakṣmīdhara in his com. on *Saundaryalaharī*, XXXIII according to which there is no Śiva-tattva apart from Śakti-tattva. *Ibid.*, on XXIII.

uttarāmnāya The northern zone of Tantric culture.

uttarāpathaka Buddhist sect mentioned in the *Kathāvatthu* XVIII–XIX. It seems to be a general name given to the monks of the north and north-west region. The Uttarāpathakas are credited with the doctrine of 'suchness' (*tathatā*). They believe in the transcendental nature of the Buddhas and in one path instead of the four as claimed by the Sthaviravādins. They agree with the Sarvāstivādins that householders can become *arhats*.

uttaraśaila Buddhist sect, a branch of the Mahāsaṅghikas. They believe that the Bodhisattvas are not free from evil destiny and that by making offerings to a Stūpa one cannot gain great merit.

uttarasādhaka Partner of the Tantric aspirant whose qualifications are mentioned in *Kaulāvalinirṇaya*.

uttarāyana The day from which the sun begins to go to the northern direction, i.e., when the apparent motion of the sun towards the north begins after *makara-saṃkrānti*, that is the last day of the month of *pauṣa* (middle of January). It is regarded as a very auspicious day.

utthāna-dvādaśī Twelfth lunar day in the month of Kārttika (Oct–Nov) on which the recumbent (*śayāna*) images are made seated (*āsīna*) symbolically.

uvaṅga Twelve texts forming part of the Jain canon, though their present versions are not approved by the Digambaras. These are Uvavāiyiya, Rāyapaseṇaijja, Jīvājīvābhigama, Pannavaṇā, Surapannatti, Jambuddīvapannatti, Candapannatti, Nirayāvaliyāo, Kappāvaḍaṃsiyāo, Pupphiyāo, Pupphaculiāo and Vanhidasāo.

vāc A word which expresses something. Its substratum is *śabda* or sound which indicates a slight stir, throb or vibration in reality, the self-expression of which is called *parā-vāc* or the supreme word. The other aspect is *artha* or meaning. Vāc has four forms—*parā*, *paśyantī*, *madhyamā* and *vaikhari* (qq.v.). The stages preceding *parā* (q.v.) are *śūnyā*, *saṃvit* and *sūkṣma*. The first is the vibrational stage, the next is that when the sound is about to form and the third is that when it is forming.

vācaka, vācya Śakti or power of Mantra. The former is the denoting or signifying aspect, while the latter is the basic. Vācya is contained in the Vācaka and formally there is no distinction between them: Janyajanakayorbhedābhāvād vācyasya vācakenāpi. *Varivasyārahasya*, II. 81.

vāciki, vāk dīkṣā The common form of initiation with Mantras. Rāghava on *Śāradā*, V. 127–40; *Puraścaryārṇava*, V. 391.

vāda Discussions and controversies through which the exponent and opponent parties each try to establish their own position. It is one of the sixteen philosophical topics of the Nyāya.

vaḍakalai A subsect of the Śrīvaiṣṇavas (q.v.) which depends on Brahmanical tradition, the Brahmanical social and legal system and uses the Sanskrit language. In the field of devotion this group believes in the *markaṭa-mārga* (q.v.).

vāhana Vehicle or mount of gods. The mount may be any animal, or sometimes men, demons and corpses. Occasionally, even gods of an alien faith serve as *vāhanas*.

vaibhāṣika Philosophical development of Sarvāstivāda (q.v.). This school accepted the seven Abhidharma books as revealed scriptures and the commentaries on them called Vibhāṣā as the most authoritative treatises. The Vaibhāṣikas appeal to experience by which they mean knowledge produced by direct contact with the object. The external world is open to perception. The substance of things has a permanent existence. Permanent substances are not transitory phenomena but the elements which underline them. According to them, objects are distinguished in *bāhya* (external) and *abhyantara* (internal). The former consisting of *bhūta* (elements) and *bhautika* (objects belonging to experience) and the latter of *citta* (intelligence) and *caitya* (those belonging to intelligence). The Vaibhāṣikas believe in the four elements, accept the atomic theory and distinguish the universe into the abode of things (*bhājanaloka*) and the world of living beings (*sattvaloka*)

vaidika The Vedic tradition.

vaikhānasa A kind of ritualistic Vaiṣṇavism. The Vaikhānasa Āgamas are pro-Vedic. According to the *Śāṇḍilyasaṃhitā*, (Bhaktikhaṇḍa I.10.33–36), Tantric method is twofold, Vaikhānasa and Pāñcarātra. The former was created by Brahmā and the latter by Nārada. The prose recension of the original Vaikhanasāgama belongs to the older category of Viṣṇuite Āgamas.

vaikharī One of the four ingredients of sound, others being *parā*, *paśyantī* and *madhyamā*. It is said that sound is carried by the wind inside the body and becomes articulated in the throat. It is the gross sound. According to Rāghava, (on *Śāradātilaka* I.1) *parā* is unmanifested sound, *paśyantī* (q.v.) reveals letters, *madhyamā* (q.v.) words and *vaikharī* (q.v.) sentences. *Setubandha* on *Nityaṣoḍaśikārṇava* VI. 10–11.

vaikṛta One of the three kinds of *ahaṃkāra* (q.v.), connected with the *sāttvika* (q.v.) quality, out of which the eleven organs issue forth according to the Sāṅkhya account of mind.

vaimānika A class of gods in the Jain pantheon beloning to the heavenly group

vaipulyaka Buddhist sect, same as the Vetulyakas or Vetullyavādins (q.v.) who are also called Mahāśūnyavādins and Hetuvādins.

vairāgya Cultivation of dispassion or detachment which is the indispensable condition for all spiritual advancement. *Yogasūtra* I.12–14, *Bhagavadgītā* VI. 35. Vairāgya is of two kinds: *aparā* or lower and *parā* or higher.

vaiśvadeva First 'four-month' (*caturmāsya*) sacrifice in which the five common libations are followed by a cake to the Maruts, a milk preparation to All-gods (Viśvedevas), and a cake to Heaven and Earth. It took place in spring. *Āśv. Gr.* I. 2.21, *Vas.Dh.S.* XI.3, *Manu* III.121, *Gobhila* II.34, *Taitt.Saṃ.* I.8, *Śat.Br.* II.5. 1–3, *Āp.Sr.* VIII. *Āśv. Sr.* II.15–20, *Kāt.Sr.* V.

vaiśvānara The sun in the sky, according to the view of the ancient Yājñikas, and terrestrial Agni or fire, according to Śākapuni. *Nirukta* V.11, VII, 4, VII.21–23.

vājapeya Primitive sacrifice for food (*vāja*) and drink (*peya*) which was later transformed into the consecration for overlordship. It may be regarded as an independent sacrifice to be performed by a Brāhmaṇa or a Kṣatriya desiring super-eminence. The number 17 predominates in it. It requires 17 cups of *soma*, 17 cups of *surā*, 17 chariots and 17 drums. A mock chariot race is held in which the sacrificer is declared victorious. A ladder is raised against the *yupa* on which the sacrificer climbs and holds a ritual dialogue with his wife. Animals for Prajāpati are offered at the time of midday Soma-pressing. The *adhvaryu* decalres the Yajamāna to be *samrāt* (universal monarch). The fees distributed are 1700 cows, 17 chariots with four horses yoked to each, 17 maid-servants, etc. After Vājapeya a king should perform Rājasūya (q.v.) and a Brāhmaṇa Bṛhaspatịsava. For details see *Taitt.Saṃ* I. 7.7–12, *Taitt.Br.* I. 3. 2–9, *Tāṇḍya* XVIII.6–7, *Śat.Br.* V.1–2, *Āśv. Sr.* IX.9, *Āp.Sr.* XVIII, *Kāt.Sr.* XIV.1–5.

vajjiputtaka See Vātsiputrīya.

vajra Thunderbolt shaped in the form of a weapon; it serves as an emblem of certain Buddhist deities. When such weapons are crossed it is called Viśvavajra or double-*vajra*. In Buddhist Tantra the word Vajra generally designates Śūnya or Void, which can not be cut or destroyed but which destroys all evils. In Tantric Buddhism the Mahayanic idea of *śūnyatā* (q.v.) has been transformed into that of *vajra* meaning the real nature of things. This principle has been crystallised in the form of a supreme being, Lord Vajrasattva or Vajradhara, regarded as the essence of Śūnyatā. The same idea underlies the conception of the Vajra-kāya (q.v.) of Buddha. *Advayavajrasaṃgraha* 24, 37, *Prajñapāya* III.9, V. 45.

vajra A penance in which barley grains fried in clarified butter and mixed with cow's urine are required to be partaken. *Atri.* 164.

vajra Name of a nerve situated within the *susumnā* (q.v.).

vajrahuṅkāra An iconic *mudrā* (q.v.). The wrists are crossed at the chest with the two hands holding the *vajra* (q.v.) and the bell, both of which are turned inwards. If the two symbols and the hands are turned outward the *mudrā* is called *Trailokyavijaya-mudrā*.

vajra-kāya The fourth body or *kāya* of Buddha as conceived in Tantric Buddhism; also known as Sahaja-kāya. See under Trikāya. Vajra denotes the real nature of things, otherwise known as Sahaja, which is *śūnyatā* or vacuity, the essence of Mahāyānic teachings.

vajraparyaṅka Also known as Dhyānāsana, it is the meditative pose. Two legs are firmly locked in a seated posture with both the soles apparent, the characteristic sitting attitude of the Dhyānī Buddhas. Sometimes a small thunderbolt is shown on the seat of the god; it indicates the meditative attitude. Dhyānāsana should be distinguished from the *paryaṅka* attitude in which case the legs are also crossed but the feet are tucked under and both the soles are invisible.

vajrayāna A form of Tantric Buddhism which has not been clearly defined. In *Guhyasamāja* 154 it is described as the cult of five Kulas or families of the Bodhisattvas (q.v.), each representing a distinct mental state of the aspirant. In *Sādhanamālā* I. 225, II. 421 it is described as the path of transcendental perfect enlightenment, to be achieved through different rites and ceremonies, *mantras* and meditations. In *Jñānasiddhi* 31 it is compared to a raft on which one can cross the ocean of existence. Vajrayāna considers *śūnya* or *vajra*, i.e., vacuity, as the ultimate reality and the innumerable gods and goddesses as its manifestations. The gods have no real existence; they are born of the mind and issue from the *vījamantras* (q.v.) uttered by the worshippers. In practice, Vajrayāna introduces the theory of the five Dhyānī Buddhas as the embodiments of the five *skandhas* or cosmic elements. It also introduces the cult of Prajñā or Śakti.

vajroli-mudrā A method for prolonging the duration in sexual intercourse for Tantric purposes. It is supposed to confer a long life on Yogin even after indulgence in sexual orgies. *Haṭhayogapradīpikā* II. 82–96.

vākya Sentence; it is the basis of all expression. Three elements are required for constituting words into a sentence, viz. expectancy (*ākaṅkṣā*), compatibility (*yogyatā*) and proximity (*sannidhi*).

vallī-kalyāṇasundara-mūrti Image of Kārtikeya with his South Indian consort Vallī or Mahāvallī.

vāmācāra, vāmamārga See Ācāra. Different forms of Vāmācāra are described in *Puraścaryārṇava* I. 20ff, *Śaktisaṅgama*, Tārā, I. 90ff.

vānaprastha The third stage of life according to the Varṇāśrama system. It is the life of a hermit prescribed for those who have completed the *gārhastha* or householder stage.

vandana Obeisance to God. It is generally held that there is nothing higher than one's chosen deity and no better prescription for the ills and mishaps of life than the practice of obeisance (*vandana*).

varada An iconic *mudrā* (q.v.), depicting the hands of gods while conferring boons. The hand showing this gesture is pendant with its palm outward and fingers all stretched. Sometimes a jewel is seen stamped on the hand showing the *mudrā*; in this case it is known as the *ratnasaṃyukta-varada*, that is, the gift bestowing attitude together with a jewel.

varaṇḍika The set of mouldings separating the *jaṅghā* (middle portion) from the *śikhara* (roof) of a temple.

vardhāpana-vidhi Procedure for the anniversary of the birth of a child or king.

varṇa Letters, also called Mātṛkās, symbolising different manifestations of Śakti.

varṇamayī-dikṣā Initiation by infusing the spirit of letters in different parts of the candidate's body. *Śāradātilaka* V. 116–21.

varṇāśrama The scheme of a society based on four *varṇas* (vocational classes) and four *āśramas* (stages of life). The first is based on the four natural psycho-physical types of human beings: the man of knowledge (*brāhmaṇa*), the man of valour (*kṣatriya*), the man of enterprise (*vaiśya*) and the man of labour (*śūdra*). The second is based on the four natural stages in each individual life: adolescence (*brahmacarya*), youth (*gārhastha*), prime of life (*vanaprastha*) and old age (*sannyāsa*). But the fourth stage has a different implication. See Āśrama.

varṣavardhana A sacrament. See *abdapūrti*.

varuṇa-praghāsa The second 'four-month' sacrifice at the beginning of the rains in which two figures of dough covered with wool, representing the ram and the ewe, are sacrificed to Varuṇa and Maruts respectively in milk-preparations to promote the increase of flocks. Karira fruits are offered to secure rain and plenty. The wife of the sacrificer confesses to Varuṇa name of her lovers, if any. *Taitt.Saṃ*. I. 8.3, *Vāj.Saṃ*. III.44–47, *Taitt.Br*. I. 6.4, *Śat.Br*. II.5.2, *Āśv. Sr*. II.17. *Baudh.Sr*. V.5–9, *Kāt.Sr*. V. 3–5, *Āp.Sr*. VIII.5–9.

vāsanā Desire. According to *Yogasūtra* IV.9 the mind is differently equipped with instinctive cravings in different kinds of beings in accordance with the types of their embodiment. In Jainism *vāsanā* is predisposition which repeatedly originates in human life from ignorance, passions of attachment and hatred.

vasanta-pañcamī See Śrī-Pañcamī.

vaśikāra State of control; it is the highest form of lower detachment (*apara-vairāgya*). *Yogasūtra* I.15. See Vairāgya.

vaśīkaraṇa One of the six black acts; it is to hypnotise someone. *Śāradātilaka* XXIII.123.

vāstuśānti Rite of the appeasement of the *vāstu* (site or house). A mess of sacrificial food is cooked and offered to Vāstoṣpati, the presiding deity of the house. Some Gṛhyasūtras prescribe animal sacrifice for the Vāstuśānti ceremony. The feeding of Brāhmaṇas and relatives concludes the ceremony. *Āśv. Gr*. II. 7–9, *Śāṅ.Gr*. III.2–4, *Pār.Gr*. III.4, *Āp.Gr*. XVII.1–13.

vāsudevaka Follower of the cult of Vāsudeva mentioned in Buddhist *Niddesa* commentaries.

vaṭasāvitrīvrata Fertility rite held on the day of the full moon in *jyeṣṭha* (May–June).

vātsalya One of the five kinds of personal relationships with God—that of paternal or maternal affection. It may be illustrated with reference to Nandagopa and Yaśodā's love for Kṛṣṇa. The instinct which prompts it is called *vātsalya-rasa* and the emotion is called *vātsalya-rati*.

vātsiputrīya A branch of the Sthaviravādins (q.v.) with whom the Sāmmitiyas (q.v.) are identified. They were singled out among the Buddhists for their belief in the doctrine of a permanent entity called *pudgala*. They believe that no transmigration is possible from one life to another without such a *pudgala*, that some *saṃskāras* (q.v.) exist for sometime while others perish every moment, that even heretics may attain five miraculous power and that an *arhat* may have a fall.

vāyavya-kṛcchra An expiation consisting in subsisting for a month on food once a day that will just fill the extended palm. *Agni* CLXXI. 14.

vedabāhya Systems which are outside the pale of the Vedas. These do not recognise the authority of the Vedas and are not approved by the Vedic tradition.

vedācāra One of the seven fold Tantric Ācāras (q.v.). Its followers insist on the Vedic way. *Prāṇatoṣaṇī* II.1.149.

vedanā Feeling or sensation; it is one of the five *skandhas* (q.v.) or constituents of a being.

vedānusārī Systems which recognise the Vedas as authority of *prāmāṇya* or one approved by the Vedic tradition.

vedhamayī-dīkṣā A form of initiation in which the mental faculties of the candidate are determined by the contemplation of the Guru. See Manodīkṣā and Mānasadīkṣā. *Kulārṇava* XIV.

veda-vratas Four observances mentioned in *Gaut. Dh.S*. VIII.15. These four are also included in the list of 16 *saṃskāras* by several Smṛtis. Their names and procedure differ considerably. In *Śāṅ.Gr.* II.11–12 these observances are called *sukriya*, *śākvara*, *vrātika* and *aupaniṣadika*. Elsewhere these are described as *mahānāmni*, *mahāvrata*, *upaniṣad* and *godāna*.

vedī Sacrificial altar. Its different parts have special names, for example, the eastern corners are called *aṃśa* and the western *śroṇi*. See under Yāgaśālā Vedī is also a term for Tīrtha or holy place.

vetāla-siddha Kinds of psycho-physical attainment through which the adepts are supposed to be able to maintain a certain amount of control over departed souls and other subtle-bodied beings using different types of mental practices.

vetullavādin Buddhist sect, also known as Vaipulyaka, Velutyaka, Mahāśūnyatāvādin and Hetuvādin. This sect also has a stronghold in Ceylon. According to the *Kathāvatthu* XXIII.1 they are credited with maintaining that the Buddha never lived as a man on this earth and that the Sangha is also an abstract idea. As such they cannot accept any gifts.

vibhajyavāda Buddhist sect with affiliation unsettled. Members of this sect maintain according to the Abhidharma sources, the existence of the present elements and those in the past which have not yet borne fruit. They deny the existence of the future elements and of those in the past that have borne fruit.

vibhava A term, as opposed to Sabhāva, used as an attribute of the aspirants belonging to Paśu and Vīra grades. The Vibhavas belong to the Rajas level, i.e., to the second grade of spiritual attainment. In the Pāñcarātra system Vibhava is one of the five forms in which the supreme being is conceived. It means the incarnation of God in a special form (*avatāra*) to rescue the world when it is in distress.

vibhutva Ubiquity of the *jīva* (q.v.). According to *Yogasūtra*, the *kāraṇa-citta* (the potential mind) is essentially ubiquitous, and yogic practices can recover this potential ubiquity (*vibhu*) in any individual case.

vibhuti Miraculous power which is acquired by a Yogin in the course of his progress towards concentration. While to the novice these powers prove intoxicating, the adept is advised to treat them as mere signs of spiritual progress and not as the real attainment. *Yogasūtra* III.46, *Haṭhayogapradīpikā* II.78.

vicāra Discussion or enquiry to get rid of ignorance. Vicāra is also called controversy—(Kathā)—(which is of three kinds: *vāda*, *jalpa* and *vitaṇḍā*) and tadvidyasaṃbhāṣā (discussion with people versed in the relevant science).

vicāraṇā Reflection on the nature of Self and the world. *Yogavāsiṣṭha* III.118.2–16.

vicikitsā A mental state according to the *Bṛhadāraṇyaka* I.5.3. In *Kaṭha Up.* I. 20 the word has been used in the sense of philosophic doubt as to man's existence after death.

videhalīna A higher form of existence like that of gods or disembodied beings. *Yogasūtra* I.19, III.51.

videhamukti Liberation of the spirit from all bodies, gross and subtle, which is attained after the death of the body. Vijñānabhikṣu in the *Sāṅkhyapravacana-bhāṣya* III.76–84, V. 116 holds that it is the real kind of liberation since the self cannot be completely free from the influence of bodily and mental changes so long as it is embodied. cf. *Sāṅ. Kārikā* 67–68, *Sāṅ.Sūt.* III.78–84. The term Videhakaivalya was used by the Vedāntins in a more or less similar sense.

vidhi The fourth category of the Pāśupata system which means the ways to achieve the end. The important *vidhis* are known as *caryās* which are again subdivided into *vratas* (vows) and *dvāra* (door). Vidhi is also the term for injunction. Vidhimārga means the way of injunctions and prohibitions or the path of duties. Vidhi is an exhortation that is meaningful on account of enjoining a matter that has a useful purpose and that prescribes something which does not follow from any other authority. Vidhis are variously classified as *apūrva, niyama* and *parisaṅkhyā* or into *puruṣārtha* and *kratvartha*.

vidveṣaṇa Rite for creating bad blood. *Śāradātilaka* XXIII.124.

vidyā See also Prajñābhiṣeka. It denotes knowledge; female deities and their mantras; the female partner of the aspirant; certain forms of *tattvas* and *kalās*; *vimarśa* Sakti expressed in the idea of I-ness; the name of school and sects, and so on. As knowledge, *vidyā* is of two kinds, viz., *parāvidyā* or spiritual knowledge and *aparāvidyā* or material knowledge. The Buddhist concept of *vijjā* (*vidyā*) denotes faculty. See Vijjā.

vidyādevī Jain goddesses of learning, 16 in number, headed by Sarasvatī. They are also known as Śruta-devīs.

vidyādhara A class of worshipful beings of the

antarīkṣa or space region in which figures are generally depicted as flying objects on the top section of the *prabhāvalī*.

vidyārambha A rite at the commencement of learning the alphabet in the fifth year of the child. In is not mentioned in the Gṛhyasūtras and Smṛtis.

vighnāpasāraṇa The clearance of all evil elements with the help of *mantras*. *Puraścaryārṇava* III. 154, Rāghava on *Śāradātilaka* IV.10. Also known as Bhūtāpasārana.

vigraha Idol; image of god. The word is constituted by *vi* and *gṛh* which means 'to grasp firmly'. Hence *vigraha* is a representation which helps the mind to grasp an abstract idea. Vigrahas used for worship may be *arūpa-vigrahas* (formless ones) or *sarūpa-vigrahas* (those with anthropomorphic forms).

vihāra Buddhist monasteries and establishments, examples of corporate living of the monks under the discipline of the Vinaya rules.

vīja Seed. It is the microcosm of the universe, deity, doctrine and mantra. For its formation and Śakti orientation see under Nāda and Vindu. It is one of the seven limbs of *mantra*, the others being Ṛsi, Chandas, Kīlaka, Śakti, Nyāsa and Dhyāna. *Dīpikā* on *Śrīvidyāsūtra* I. As *mantra* it is single-lettered in which the deity is revealed in subtle form. See *Śāradā* I. 57, *Tantrasāra* 182ff.

vijātīya-bheda Bheda or difference between alien species, like *brahman* and the material world, according to certain Vedāntic schools.

vijayā-daśamī The tenth day of the bright fortnight in *āśvina* (Sept–Oct) which concludes the Durgā Pūjā festival. It is regarded as the day of Victory because on this day Rāvaṇa was killed by Rāma. In North India this day is celebrated as *dasarā*.

vijjā Faculty; it is of three kinds according to Buddhism: *pubbanivāsānussati-ñāṇa* (the faculty of reading all past experiences of oneself acquired by successive births or existences); *sattānaṃ-cutūpapāta-ñāṇa* (the faculty of visualising the rise and fall of all beings from one state or position to another according to their deeds) and *āsavānaṃ-khaya-ñāṇa* (the faculty of perceiving the course of attenuation of all extraneous impediments to consciousness). *Majjhima* I.

vijñāna Consciousness which is one of the five *skandhas* (constituents) of a being according to Buddhism.

vijñānākala Those souls for which *māyā* and *karma* (qq.v.) has been resolved, but the *āṇava* (conative impurity) has not, according to the Śaiva schools.

vijñānavāda A philosophical stream of Mahāyāna Buddhism which believes in the reality of thought-waves and denies the objective existence of all perceived through the gross sense organs. For details see Yogācāra.

vijñapti-matratā Pure consciousness or pure wisdom, according to Buddhism.

vikalpa Determination; it consists of conceptual unification of the 'many' into 'one', distinguishing between one object of cognition and another, between 'this' and 'not-this' and accepting one among the many stimuli received from outside. It is the opposite of *nirvikalpa* (apprehension devoid of determination) and discrimination in which the limited 'I' of the individual is united with the unlimited 'I' of its own higher self and in which the difference between 'this' and 'not-this' does not arise. In Mīmāṃsā tradition *vikalpa* means option especially where the contents of two texts are irreconcilable.

vikāsá Unfolding; manifestation; development. In a cosmogonical sense the term denotes evolution as is opposed to *saṅkoca* or involution.

vikṣepa Power of projection or transformation.

vilāsa One of the four principal Tantric schools. The others are Kerala, Kāśmīra and Gauḍa.

vimalīkaraṇa Processing of *mantra*. *Tantrasāra* 54.

vimāna The main shrine in which the deity is installed.

vimarśa The vibrating, dynamic or kinetic aspect of the power (Śakti) of the Absolute, the static being known as Prakāśa. *Tantrāloka*, III, 2ff.

vimokkha That which removes the veil which covers the higher meditations, according to Buddhism. These are eight in number. *Dīgha* II.70–71, *Majjhima* II.12–13.

vimukti, vimutti Free state of consciousness which is the central inspiration of early Buddhism. There are two aspects of *vimutti*: *ceto* (*citta*) and *paññā* (*prajñā*). The former is emancipation through the attainment of the free state of consciousness and the latter by the development of reason or knowledge.

vinaya Branch of the Buddhist Tripiṭaka dealing with laws and regulations of the Buddhist monastic system.

vināyaka-śānti Also called Gaṇapatipūjā; it is the propitiation of Gaṇeśa performed at the beginning of all *saṃskāras* such as Upanayana, marriage, etc. and those for averting or mitigating the effects of portents, or on a Sapiṇḍa's (near kin) death. It may also be performed on thursdays or any auspicious day.

vinayavāda A school of thought the followers of which believed in the practice of certain moral codes probably without knowing their real impact. The likely aim of the Vinayavādins was to gain a better future existence. It was not their aim to exterminate all *karma* (q.v.) or to stop the influx of new *karma* which Jainism taught. Corresponding to the Vinayavāda of the Jain texts we have the Buddhist expression Silabbata-parāmāsa. *Sūyagaḍa*, I.12.3–4; I.3.14.

vindu A term used in a variety of senses. As a dot it denotes Siva and as a double dot (Visarga), Śakti, both being alphabetical signs. In *Śāradā*, II.6. the former stands for solar power, the latter for lunar. In Śaiva conception, Vindu is an evolute of Nāda which is produced owing to the Kriyāsākti of Śiva. *Śivapurāṇa*, Vāyavīya, Uttara, V. 18ff. In Kashmir Śaivism Vindu is one of the ten Vidyāṭattvas. *Tantrāloka*, I. 216. It is Anuttara Śakti as also the Nāda-oriented sound in every being. *Ibid.*, III, 116 ff. It is regarded as the condensed form of Nāda but according to the *Prapañcasāra* I. 41 Vindu is not preceded by Nāda. According to the *Śāradātilaka* I.7ff Vindu, by which Parāśakti is characterised, becomes divided into three parts as Vindu, Nāda and Vīja. Vindu is Śiva-oriented, Vīja Śakti-oriented and Nāda is the combination of both. Nāda and Vindu of this second category are known as Apara-nāda and Apara-Vindu, while their primal forms are prefixed by the term Para. Vindu has three forms—Prakāśa (static), Vimarśa (kinetic) and Prakāśa-Vimarśa (combination of both). *Cidvallī* on *Kāmakālāvilāsa*, V–VII. It is the cause of the origin of letters and elements. Com. on *Śāradā*, II.9: VII.9. The four Kalās—Pīta, Śveta, Aruṇa and Asita—are emanated from it. *Prapañcasāra*, III. 20–21. It also stands for male organ while its complementary principle Visarga, stands for the female.

vindu-cakra Tantric diagrams with *vindu* as the central point. The elevation of *vindu* is said to form a triangle or *trikoṇa*, *Kamakalāvilāsa* XXII. In these diagrams *vindu* represents the equilibrium of Kāmeśvara and Kāmeśvarī. The *vindu* diagrams are also known as Uḍḍīyāna-pīṭha and Brahmacakra. *Gandharva* V. 123. Attainment in the exercise of *vindu-cakra* is known as *Prāptisiddhi*. *Nityaṣoḍaśikārṇava* VIII.173.

viniyoga-vidhi That which conveys the relation between the principal act and its subsidiaries (*aṅgin-aṅga* or *śaṣin-śeṣa*) in religious rites. Viniyoga means application.

viparyaya False knowledge.

vipassanā Same as *paññā* which comprehends the whole of man's rational sphere of existence and intellection. The follower of the path of knowledge is called Vipassanāyānī in early Buddhism.

viprayoga Separation; it is one of the two aspects of *śṛṅgāra* or love, the other being *saṃyoga* or union.

vīra, vīrācāra Tantric aspirant of the second grade whose mental faculties are advanced. For the interpretation of the word *vīra* see *Kulārṇava* XVII, *Rudrayāmala*, uttara I.136. Characteristics are mentioned in com. on *Paraśurāmakalpasūtra* VI.39, *Nirvāṇatantra* XIV, *Kāmākhyātantra* IV, *Niruttara* XI, *Rudrayāmala*, Uttara LI. 20–21. Classifications: *Śaktisaṅgama* Sundarī I. 197–200, Tārā. XLIII. 204, *Puraścaryārṇava* IX.863, *Prāṇatoṣaṇi* VIII.1.495 ff. The spiritual exercises of a *vīra* are known as *vīrācāra*.

vīracakra One of the five *cakra* (q.v.) rituals mentioned in *Niruttaratantra* X. In this *cakra* five *śaktis* are to be worshipped in the form of mother (Bhūmīndrakanyā), daughter (Rajakīsutā), sister (Svapacī), daughter-in-law (Kāpālī) and wife (Yoginī).

viraja-homa Offering of forty oblations in fire by one who has resolved to take *sannyāsa* (life of a recluse).

vīrāsana Yogic *āsana*. It is a posture of *kṛcchra* and *aghamarṣaṇa* observances.

vīrāṣṭamī A *vrata* observed by women desiring heroic sons.

visarga Alphabetical sign of the double dot which is symbolically regarded as the complementary Śakti of Vindu (q.v.). It signifies both the *parā* and *aparā* (qq.v.) aspects of Śakti. *Tantrāloka* III.120 ff. It is also known as Kaulikī-Śakti. *Ibid* III.143. It is the Female Principle (*saḥ*) as complementary to the Male Principle (*haṃ*) *Prapañcasāra* quoted by Kālicaraṇa in his com. on *Ṣaṭcakranirūpaṇa* XLIII. See also Vindu.

viṣaya Object; that which is perceived by the perceiver. Viṣayī is subject. Viṣayī-Viṣaya-bhāva is subject-object-relation. Viṣayatā is a term used by the Nyāya-Vaiśeṣikas which means a distinct external relation.

viśeṣa Particularity; according to the *Nyāya-Vaiśeṣika*, it is the unique individuality of the eternal substances.

viśeṣa-dīkṣā Special initiation into Āgamānta Saivism in which the candidate is entitled to follow the way of *kriyā* (rites) and *yoga* (concentration) so as to reach the *sāmīpya* (q.v.) and *sārūpya* (stages).

viśiṣṭādvaitavāda Rāmānuja's interpretation of the Vedānta Sūtra according to which the universe of *cit* (q.v.), *jīva* (q.v.) and *acit* (q.v.) has its ultimate source in *brahman* which is real (*satya*), conscious (*jñāna*) and infinite (*ananta*). It derives its essential nature and functions from *brahman*, which is known as the indwelling self (*antaryāmin*) of all beings. The entire creative process is the self-expression of *brahman* who reveals himself in creation. *Brahman* is *sat* (q.v.) without a second and becomes the manifold of the sentient and non-sentient, the purpose of which is to give an opportunity for finite beings to realise their divine destiny. He assumes three forms—*bhoktā* (the enjoyer manifested in *jīva* individual souls), *bhogya* (the enjoyable manifested in *acit* or the material world) and *prerita* (manifested in Īśvara or Paramātman), (q.v.) the cause of creation, preservation and destruction).

viṣṇubali A ceremony to be performed in the eighth month of pregnancy to remove harm to the foetus. It consists in offering 64 oblations of boiled rice and ghee to Viṣṇu. *Baudh.Gr.* I.10. 13–17, I.11.2.

viṣṇubhāga One of the three sections of a Śivaliṅga.

viṣṇugranthi A knot on the *anahāta-cakra* (q.v.) which the Kuṇḍalinī (q.v.) has to pierce during its upward march.

viṣṇukrāntā A zone of Tantric culture extending from the Vindhyan range to Caṭṭala.

viśrāmabhūmi Stages of rest in the process of pure creation according to the Pāñcarātra Āgamas. These are *jñāna* (knowledge), *aiśvarya* (lordship) and *śakti* (potency). Each of the qualities of one group has an innate propensity to pair with one of the other. See under Śramabhūmi.

viśuddha The nerve plexus above the *anāhata* (q.v.) in the neck region. It looks like a sixteen petalled lotus. Its presiding deity is the goddess Śākinī. *Ṣaṭcakranirūpaṇa* XXVIII–XXX.

viśvajit An *ekāha* (one day) sacrifice in which the sacrificer gives a thousand cows or all his wealth. He has to stay for three days beneath an *udumbara* tree, for three days in a settlement of Niṣādas, for three days among Vaiśyas and for three days with Kṣatriyas. For a year he should not refuse what is offered but should not beg. *Jaimini* IV.3.10–16, VI.7.1–20, VII.3. 6–11, X.6.13, *Kāt.Sr.* XXII.1.9–33, *Lāṭ.Sr.* VIII.2.1–13. The Viśvajit sacrifice has also been recommended as expiation for murdering a Brāhmaṇa.

viśvarūpa Cosmic form of God. *Gitā* XI.

viśvasa Faith; it is the basis of all forms of spiritual aspiration.

vitānāgni Oblation fire of the Vedic tradition with which the idol of Viṣṇu is identified: vitānāgninibhaṃ viṣṇorbimbam.

vitaṇḍā A kind of debate in which the opponent does not establish his own position but only tries to refute that of the exponent. It is one of the sixteen philosophical topics of Nyāya.

vitaṇḍāvādin A section of the followers of the Cārvāka (q.v.) school who used to engage themselves constantly in refuting the views of others.

vitarka An iconic *mudrā* represented by the right arm bent, all fingers erect except either the index or the ring finger which touch the thumb so as to resemble a ring. If the hand is extended forward with the palm outward, it denotes a discussion.

vivartavāda The theory, favoured by the Advaita-Vedāntins, that the effect is a mere transfiguration of a cause, or that it is of the nature of an illusory modification of any substance. It holds that the change of cause into an effect is only apparent.

vivekajñāna Discrimination between the experiencing subject (*draṣṭā*) and the experienced object (*dṛśya*) by which the suffering caused by ignorance (*ajñāna*) is removed. *Śāṅ.Sūt.* III.23–24, *Kārikā* 44. 63.

vividiṣā Desire for realisation.

vrata Religious vows. In most of the religious systems *vrata* (solemn vow) is regarded as one of the five right means of worship. The others are *yāga* (sacrifice), *homa* (oblation in fire), *japa* (repetition of holy word) and *yoga* (spiritual discipline). In Jainism the term suggests code of conduct, both for the monks and for lay persons. See also Mahāvrata, Anuvrata, Guṇavrata and Śikṣāvrata. Vrata also means rituals intended for certain purposes. These are regional and local in character, performed specially by the women-folk for the welfare of agriculture and cattle, for averting diseases and calamities, for progeny and prosperity and for other practical purposes of life. In many *vratas* there are relics of primitive magical beliefs and practices.

vrātyaṣṭoma Sacrifice through which those who

lead the *vrātya* (fallen un-Vedic) life may be restored to superior status. The *Tāṇḍya-Mahābrāhmaṇa* XVII.1–4 describes four *vrātyaṣṭomas*. *Kāt.Sr.* XXII.4.1–28, *Āp.Sr.* XXII.5.4–14, *Pār.Gr.* II.5.

vṛddha-kṛcchra An expiation lasting for eight days which consists in observing dietary restrictions. Also known as *vṛddhi-kṛcchra*.

vṛddhi-śrāddha A *śrāddha* (q.v.) in which one must offer worship to the seven Mātṛkās, then to one's mother, paternal grandmother, and paternal great-grandmother, then to the Nāndīmukha pitṛs and then to the Mātāmahas (maternal grandfathers) together with their wives.

vṛṣavāhana Image of Śiva on his bull vehicle.

vṛṣotsarga The ceremony of letting loose bull on the day of the full moon in Kārttika (Oct–Nov) to ensure the good breeding of the cattle. It is also a part of the Śrāddha (q.v.) rituals in which the gift of bull is made for the spiritual benefit of the departed one.

vṛtti Occupation or means of livelihood (five and ten kinds are referred to respectively by Manu and Baudhāyana); explanatory or commentarial texts; bodily functions and cognitive modifications of mind.

vyāhṛti Three or seven mystic syllables such as *bhūḥ*, *bhuvaḥ*, etc.

vyāna One of the five kinds of *prāṇa* (breath) which pervades the whole body, coordinates its various parts and their functions.

vyantara-devatās A class of gods in the Jain pantheon belonging to the peripatetic group. These are primitive gods or goddesses, relegated to the position of inferior or secondary deities, most of them becoming accessories and attendants of the chosen divinities or the founders of various sects. The Jain texts refer to Piśācas, Bhūtas, Yakṣas, Rākṣasas, Kinnaras, Kiṃpuruṣas, Mahogras (Nāgas) and Gandharvas as Vyantara-devatās. The Buddhist texts also mention similar orders of divinities such as Devas, Yakṣas, Nāgas, Rākṣasas, Kinnaras, Asuras and Mahogras. The Brahmanical texts, besides the aforesaid names, add many more names of mythical beings such as Kumbhāṇḍas, Kabandhas, Daityas, Dānavas, Apsarasas, Siddhas, Sādhyas, Vidyādharas, Pramathas, Gaṇas, etc.

vyāpakanyāsa A form of Tantric Ṣoḍhanyāsa (q.v.) in which the deity is to be felt over the entire body.

vyāsa-kṛcchra Also known as *maitra-kṛcchra* it is an expiation in which the sinner has to partake of the five products coming out of a cow, namely, dung, urine, milk, curd and clarified butter.

vyāpti See Anumāna. It implies a correlation between what is pervaded (*vyāpya*) and what pervades (*vyāpaka*). The Buddhists base the knowledge of *vyāpti* on the principles of causality and essential identity while the Vedantists hold that *vyāpti* is the result of an induction by simple enumeration. The Nyāya school tries to establish *vyāpti* or a universal proposition on the particular ground of the observation of particular facts, the methods being known as *anvaya* (agreement in presence), *vyatireka* (agreement in absence) *vyabhicārāgraha* (absence of contrary instance), *upādhinirāsa* (elimination of conditions), *tarka* (q.v.) and *sāmānya-lakṣaṇa* (q.v.).

vyāsakūṭa Subdivision of Brahma-sect founded by Madhva. It corresponded to the Vaḍakalai (q.v.) group of the Śrī-Vaiṣṇavas.

vyavahārika Empirical. The term is prefixed to many concepts.

vyūhavāda A development of the localised tribal cult of the four Vṛṣṇi heroes. According to the Pāñcarātra Saṃhitās, the Bhagavat Vāsudeva in the act of creation produces from himself, not only *prakṛti* (q.v.), the indiscreet primal matter of the Sāṅkhyas, but also a *vyūha* or the phase of conditioned spirit called Saṅkarṣaṇa. From the combination of Saṅkarṣaṇa and *prakṛti* spring *manas* corresponding to the Sāṇkhya *buddhi* (q.v.) or intelligence, and also a secondary phase of conditioned spirit called Pradyumna. From the association of Pradyumna and *manas* springs the Sāṅkhya *ahaṃkāra* (the principle of egoity) and also a tertiary phase of conditioned spirit known as Aniruddha. From the association of Aniruddha with *ahaṃkāra* spring the Sāṅkhya mahābhūtas (elements) with their qualities. The four principal characters have been multiplied by the six *guṇas* or qualities as a result of which we have twenty-four emanatory forms. The association of the *vyūha* emanations with the Sāṅkhya categories, the evolutes of *prakṛti*, probably refers to the non-Vedic origin of the *vyūha* doctrine. It also appears that once the Śāmba element was a constituent of this doctrine and it has withdrawn because the cult-character upheld by the Śāmba element was basically different. It is also interesting to observe that subsequent Vaiṣṇavism gave up its original Sāṅkhya association and resorted to a Vedāntic orientation.

yab-yum Goddess-in-union-with-god; it is a characteristic feature of Tibetan Buddhist iconography. Yab means father and yum mother; hence the combined word means the father in the embrace of the mother. For the spiritual significance of the conception of Yab-yum see Yuganaddha.

yadṛcchā First Principle according to certain cosmogonical speculations as recorded in *Śvetāśvatara Up*. I.1–2 and *Suśruta*. Śārīra I.11. Yadṛcchā is pure accidentalism as opposed to *svabhāva* (q.v.) or naturalism. While the former maintains that the world is chaos and ascribes whatever order is seen in it to mere chance, the latter recognises that things are as nature makes them. *Tarkarahasyadīpikā* 15 defines Yadṛcchā as a denial of causation altogether according to which various pleasures and pains of people appear suddenly, just as the flying of a crow has no connection with the falling of a palm fruit (*kākatālīya*).

yāga See Yajña. A Yāga is constituted by *dravya* (materials), *devatā* (gods) and *tyāga* (sacrifice). It is different from *homa* (q.v.) and *dāna* (q.v.).

yāgaśālā Hall for Vedic sacrifice which consists of *yupa*, *uttaravedī daśapada*, *havirdhāna*, *sadas*, *agnihotraśālā*, main *vedī* and *patnīśālā*.

yajamāna Sacrificer, the person paying the cost of sacrifice (Yajña, q.v.), the institutor of a sacrifice (to perform which he employs a priest or priests), any patron, rich man, head of a family or tribe, and so on. In *RV* I.27.12, I.51.8, I.82.2, IV.17.15 etc. there are references to Yajamānas performing the function of the priests in their own sacrifices. In later times Yajamāna is the enjoyer of the fruit of sacrifice, but he does not perform it personally. The priests perform the act against remuneration.

yajña Generally translated as Sacrifice in the sense of offering dear objects to gods, just as Abraham went to sacrifice his own son in order to please god. Modern scholars held that at the root of Yajña is a kind of reciprocal arrangement—to offer something to please god and to expect a favour in return. Such an idea also prevailed in the past. The Mīmāṃsakas hold that their opponents utterly misunderstand the significance of Yajña, in believing that Yajña is a means to please the gods, because in reality there are no gods. According to the Mīmāṃsakas Yajña is for the sake of Yajña only, and not for that of the gods. Ritual is the first and last word, the performance of which yields *apūrva*—'that which was not before'. It means that what did not exist before can be produced by ritual as an effect of performing it. Śabara on *Jaimini* II.1.15, VI.1.2, VII.1.34, X.4.23 says that, according to the Vedas, the cause of producing effect is sacrifice and not the gods, because the effect is *puruṣārtha* (ultimate aim) which is achieved through human efforts and not through the agency of god. If it be said that sacrifice is to be offered to the gods, then the gods must necessarily possess a shape and eat the food offered to them at the sacrifice, but neither is possible. If it is hoped that, being satisfied, god will grant the desired object, this cannot be an argument because god's ownership of worldly objects is not proved. Therefore, Yajña is not prayer or propitiation. It simply consists of some definite rituals for the fulfilment of worldly desires, and these rituals are effective in themselves. These rituals are illusory techniques to control nature. They complement the deficiencies of real techniques. This explanation recalls the primitive magical beliefs and practices. The significance of Yajña can be understood only against the background of primitive, undifferentiated collective life as is proved by rites pertaining to the *satra-yāgas* (q.v.). It is a fact that the original and sophisticated forms of the Vedic Yajñas are not the same and that in the post-Ṛgvedic age the Yajñas became extremely complicated. Their purpose also changed. The *Ait.Br*. VIII.1.4 says that when performing Yajña in company, the members of the company become Brāhmaṇas and there is no distinction of castes. Its class-orientation is indicated in a legend in the same text VII.19 according to which once Yajña deserted the gods and the Kṣatriyas and Brāhmaṇas followed him to bring him back. The Kṣatriyas, who symbolised ruling power, could not get hold of him through their weapons. But the Brāhmaṇas could, because Yajña, being confronted by them, saw in them his own power. So he agreed to return to the Brāhmaṇas and said that he was ready to oblige the Kṣatriyas provided that they would depend on the Brāhmaṇas. Very significantly this story throws light on the entente between the ruling and priestly classes and the subsequent sophistication of the Yajñas in which the ruling and priestly classes were involved. For details of the great Yajñas performed by the kings see under Aśvamedha, Rājasūya and Vājapeya. For Yajñas of the commoners see under

Pākayajña, Ekāha, Ahīna, Soma-Yāgas, Agniṣṭoma, Jyotiṣṭoma, Iṣṭi, Vrātyaṣṭoma etc.

yajña-kṛcchra A one day penance which consists in bathing three times and taking cow-products as food.

yajñatanū Offerings on the last day of *agniṣṭoma* (q.v.).

yajña-vastu A ceremony, performed at the end of a domestic rite, in which a handful of Kuśa grass, dipped in the *ājya* and besprinkled with water, is thrown into the fire with an invocation to Rudra.

yajñayajanīya A *sāman* or chant which is the last item of *agniṣṭoma* (q.v.). During the recital of this the sacrificer's wife is to be brought near the *udgātṛ* priest who will give her the final blessing.

yajñāyudha Implements of sacrifice; they are ten in number according to *Taitt.Saṃ*. I. 6.8.2–3 and *Śat.Br*. I. 1.1.22.

yajñopavīta Sacred thread worn by the brahmacārin during his Upanayana or initiation into student life. It is a symbol of *dvijatva* or rebirth (being consecrated) which is to be used throughout life. Consisting of nine strands in a set of three, its size varies according to the caste status. Each strand is a symbol of a deity. Religious acts done without wearing Yajñopavīta are futile. Taking meal without wearing it makes one liable to expiation.

yajus Formulae relating to sacrifice; they are uttered by special priests.

yakṣa A class of supernatural beings having some element of divinity. In *AV*. VIII.10.28 they are indicated as folk deities, low in status (*itarajana*) but sacred. In the Pali commentaries the word Yakkha means 'a being to whom a sacrifice (of expiation or propitiation) is given. The association of the Yakṣas and their king Kubera with riches, and one of their principal appellations, *guhyakas*, mainly indicative of 'concealment', may also be traced in the *Atharvaveda*. Patañjali's evidence regarding the existence of Yakṣa images and shrines is corroborated by early Buddhist and Jain texts. The Yakṣas were in reality indigenous deities, evidently pre-Vedic and non-Vedic and their cult survived as the suppressed religion of the masses during the Vedic period. Subsequently with the emergence of anti-Vedic systems like Buddhism and Jainism the popular cult of the Yakṣas had a revival. Yakṣas and Yakṣiṇīs found an honourable place in Buddhist and Jain mythologies. Their images formed an essential feature of Buddhist art. The Śāsanadevatās of the Jinas were also conceived of as Yakṣiṇīs. As Vyantara devatās the Yakṣas and Yakṣiṇīs formed the most important and interesting groups. In the epico-puranic literature also one can come across numerous Yakṣa characterisations.

yakṣa-gāna Operatic plays on mythological or religious themes which are popular in South India.

yakṣakardama Unguent with five fragrant substances.

yama Restraint; it is the first discipline of Yoga. It consists of *ahiṃsā* (abstention from all kinds of injury to any life), *satya* (truthfulness), *asteya* (non-stealing), *brahmacarya* (celibacy) and *aparigraha* (non-possession).

yāmala A class of Tantric literature subdivided into eight groups, viz. Rudra, Skanda, Brahma, Viṣṇu, Yama, Vāyu, Kubera and Indra. The Yāmalas not only define various Tantric traditions but also introduce a variety of cults of new gods and goddesses. They assimilate a large number of local cults as well and open up the field of Tantric culture to people belonging to the lower castes.

yāmya Expiation consisting in subsisting for a month on Śaktu grains found in cowdung.

yāna Vehicle, or the way which carries an adept to the highest goal. Two general divisions of Buddhism are known as *hīna-yāna* and *mahā-yāna*. In a special sense *yāna* is of two kinds, viz. *samatha* (psycho-physical, mystical or intuitional) and *vipassanā* (ratiocinative, reflective or philosophical).

yantra Symbol of deity. It is generally in the form of a diagram or geometrical pattern serving as chart for revealing the characteristics of the deity. For the efficacy of Yantra in Tantric worship see *Gandharva* V.1, *Mātṛkābheda* XII.6ff. Yantra is variously interpreted as instrument, the body and abode of deity, amulet, mental faculties, pure consciousness, doctrinal intricacies, microcosm of the human body and so on. *Kulārṇava* VI.XVII, *Gandharva* V.39–40, *Saundaryalaharī* XI, *Śaktisaṅgama*, Tārā, XII.203, LI.2, *Puraścaryārṇava* VI.518ff. *Tantrasāra* 312ff. Yantras are drawn or engraved on cloths, paper, leaves, stones and metals.

yati An ascetic. The term is derived from the root *yat*, to strive, to exert oneself, and is also connected with the root *yam*, to restrain, to subdue, to control. As applied to the priest, etymologically *yati* can only mean a person engaged in religious exercise such as *tapas*, austerities and Yoga. The Yatis were probably not favoured by the Vedic Indians because in the *Kauṣītaki Upaniṣad* III.1 Indra is described as throwing the Yatis to the wolves.

yati-cāndrāyana An expiation in which the sinner eats eight mouthfuls of sacrificial food, only once a day at noon, for a month and exercises control over himself. *Manu* XI.218, *Baudh Dh.S.* IV.5.20.

yati-śāntapana Expiation by partaking of *pañcagavya* (q.v.) Mit. on *Yāj* III.314.

yatna Striving. It is of three kinds: *pravṛtti* (striving for a thing), *nivṛtti* (withdrawing from a thing) and *jīvanakāraṇa* (life-process).

yātrā Literally it means setting out or going from one place to another cf. *Kāmasūtra* I.4) and as such it also means a procession. Derivatively, it has come to mean a festival, as in *snāna-yātrā* (ablution-festival), *hindola-yātrā* (swing festival), *rāsa-yātrā* (festival of circular dance), *ratha-yātrā* (car-festival), *dola-yātrā* (holi festival) etc. Subsequently the term came to mean theatrical performance on mythological and religious themes, such as Kṛṣṇayātrā, Rāmayātrā, etc. Bhavabhuti refers to the Yātrā of Kalāpriyanātha in which his *Uttararāmacarita* was going to be presented. Yātrā in the sense of an open air performance of *nāṭakas* was used commonly as a means of mass contact by the Vaiṣṇavas.

yātudhāna One who employs black magic.

yaugī-dīkṣā Initiation in which the guru enters the body of his disciple in subtle form and impresses his own self on that of the latter. Rāghava on *Śāradātilaka* V. 127–40.

yauvanollāsa The third stage of spiritual exercise in which the Tantric aspirant becomes well-versed in the scriptures. Rāghava's com. on *Paraśurāmakalpasūtra* X. 68.

yāvaka Expiation consisting in partaking of boiled *yavas* for a month. *Śaṅkha* XVIII. 10–11.

yoga The connecting link between the Jiva (q.v.) and *āsrava* (q.v.) causing the *karma*-particles enter into the soul, according to Jainism. It is the employment of body, mind and speech for material and sensual objectives and as such is regarded as one of the four sources of *karma* (q.v.), others being *avirati* (q.v.), *kaṣāya* (q.v.) and *mithyātva* (q.v.). Hence the word is taken in its etymological sense of connection. Subsequently, owing to the influence of the Yoga school of philosophy, and the theories and practices propounded by the latter, the term came to be used in Jainism in the sense of *gutti* or control of mind, speech and body. The ten-fold monastic morality and the twelve passimistic reflections, conceived by Umāsvāti, have a close bearing on the Jain precepts. *TTDS* IX.6–7; cf. *Uttara* XXIV.19ff. Yoga is the third category of the Pāśupata system.

yogācāra See Vijñānavāda. It contends that thought is self-creative and all-producing, the ultimate principle and the ultimate type and form of reality. It denies the real existence of everything except *vijñāna* or consciousness which constitutes the whole universe. The phenomenal existence of the world with its distinction of subject and object is accepted by the Yogācāra. The external objects are unreal since it cannot be said whether they arise from existence or not, whether they are simple atoms or complex bodies. All things have their beings through consciousness; no other medium is known than consciousness through which alone things can exist. The Yogācārins also divide all things into *saṃskṛta* (constituted) and *asaṃskṛta* (unconstituted) giving *citta* or mind the first place instead of *rūpa* (matter).

yogadakṣiṇāmūrti Śiva image showing him as a great teacher of Yoga.

yoganāḍī A nerve which carries the vital air.

yogāsana-mūrti Seated Viṣṇu image in Yogāsana pose on a lotus with drooping petals.

yogasthānaka Type of four-armed Viṣṇu image in which the god is generally shown as standing on a *navaratha* pedestal, the back hands resting on the *gadādevī* and *cakrapuruṣa*, front hands holding lotus and conch shell.

yogavidhi Rules of Yoga as leading to correct knowledge of reality. *Kaṭhopaniṣad* VI.18, *Raghu* VIII.22.

yogāṅga Eight means of Yoga. They are *yama* (q.v.), *niyama* (q.v.), *āsana* (q.v.), *prāṇayāma* (q.v.), *pratyāhāra* (q.v.), *dhāraṇa* (q.v.), *dhyāna* (q.v.) and *samādhi* (q.v.).

yogin A person who is physically, mentally and spiritually disciplined. According to the *Gītā* VI.46 a Yogin is superior to *tapasvin, jñānin* and *karmin* (those engaged respectively in austerity, knowledge and action). A Yogin may develop certain supernormal powers, but he is advised to ignore them as they are hindrances in the way of his goal. *Yogasūtra* III.36.

yoginī A class of goddess, generally sixty-four in number, supposed to be the multiples of the eight Mātṛkās. The term is also used to denote the female partner of the aspirant, the goddesses presiding over the nerve plexuses from *mūlādhāra* to *sahasrāra*, different manifestations of Śakti, a Tantric school, a class of female ascetics imparting Tantric knowledge to the masses, medicine-women, women possessed by goddess, and so on.

yoginī-kaula A school founded by Matsyendranātha which was popular in the Kāmarūpa region. The doctrine of this school, as may be gathered from the *Kaulajñānanirṇaya* has something in common with Buddhist Tantras of the Sahaja class.

yogi-pratyakṣa Ecstatic vision.

yoni First Principle according to certain cosmogonical speculations as recorded in *Śvetāśvatara Up*. I.1–2 along with Bhūta and Puruṣa. In *Suśruta*, śārīra, I. 11 Puruṣa has been excluded and Bhūta and Yoni have been substituted by Prakṛti (q.v.) which implies that Yoni or the Female Principle formed the most primitive substratum of the Sāṅkhya. Yoni also means female organ of generation. There are archaeological evidences of the cult of generative organs and numerous references to sex rites which include actual sexual union. The magical rites designed to secure the fertility of the fields seemed to belong to the special competence of women who were the first cultivators of the soil and whose power of child-bearing had, in primitive thought, a sympathetic effect on the vegetative forces of the earth. The woman was not only the symbol of generation, but the actual producer of life. Her organs and attributes were thought to be endowed with generative power, and so they were the life giving symbols. In the earliest phases of social evolution, it was this maternity that held the field, the life producing mother being the central figure of religion. This primitive empirical and analogical belief in the equation of earth and woman, of natural and human fertility has connected the mystery of nature with that of the human body in Tantrism which holds that the birth of the universe is the result of the same, or a similar process as the birth of the human beings.

yoni-mudrā A seated posture of body in which the aspirant should fix his anus on the left heel, tongue on the palate and eyes on the tip of nose. This posture helps to awaken the Kuṇḍalinī. *Prāṇatoṣaṇī* I.10.70ff. Bhūtāśuddhitantravacana quoted in *Śāradātilaka* IX.

yonipuṣpa Black *aparajitā* flower serving as *maithuna* (sexual intercourse) symbol. *Paraśurāmakalpasūtra* X. 63.

yuga Four ages in Indian mythological tradition. In the first Yuga, called Kṛta or Satya, the duration of which is computed to be 4,800 years of gods (each year of gods being 360 years of men), there is perfect righteousness and the *dharma* is said to be on all its four feet. In next three Yugas, viz. Tretā, Dvāpara and Kali, consisting respectively of 3,600, 2,400 and 1,200 years of gods, *dharma* gradually decreases by one-fourth and so does righteousness. These four Yugas together make a *mahāyuga* or a *manvantara*, and 2000 such *manvantaras* make a *kalpa*. However there are divergent views in the texts in counting the Yugas. In astronomical texts a Yuga denotes a very limited span of time.

yuga-dharma Concept of *dharma* caused by time and age which introduces the element of adaptation and adjustment with the changing demands of time and space. *Manu* X. 98ff. *Mbh*. XII. 35. 266ff.

yuganaddha Iconic representation of god Heruka-in-union-with the goddess Nairātmā, symbolising the union of Karuṇā and Śūnyatā or Upāya and Prajñā, in Tantric Buddhism. It is conceived in terms of the male and female principles respectively. The Yuganaddha symbolises unique harmony and interpretation of masculinity and feminity. For a man, woman is the material object of concentration, a goddess for meditation and a symbolic truth for comprehension. See under Prajñā, Upāya, Śūnyata and Karuṇā.

yukti Justification of reason or critical intelligence.

yūpa Sacrificial post which is an essential feature of animal sacrifice. *RV* III.8 is meant for anointing of the Yūpa. It has various names like *pātnivata*, *upāśaya*. etc. The head piece is called *caṣāla*. The Yūpas are made of *palāśa*, *khadira*, *vilva* or *rauhitaka* wood and in the case of Somayāga of only *khadira*.

Abbreviations

Ait, Ar.	*Aitareya Āraṇyaka.*
Ait, Br.	*Aitareya Brāhmaṇa.*
AKV	*Abhidharmakoṣavyākhyā.*
Aṅguttara	*Aṅguttara Nikāya.*
Āp. Dh.S.	*Āpastamba Dharmasūtra.*
Āp. Gr.	*Āpastamba Gṛhyasūtra*
Āp. Sr.	*Āpastamba Srautasūtra.*
Ār	*Āraṇyaka*, added after the first name of the text.
A S S	Anandasrama Sanskrit Series, Poona.
Āśv. Gr.	*Āśvalāyana Gṛhyasūtra.*
Āśv. Sr.	*Āśvalāyana Śrautasūtra.*
AV	*Atharvaveda.*
Baudh. Dh.S.	*Baudhāyana Dharmasūtra.*
Baudh. Gr.	*Baudhāyana Gṛhyasūtra.*
Baudh. Sr.	*Baudhāyana Śrautasūtra.*
Bib. Bud.	Bibliotheca Buddhica, St. Petersburg.
Bib. Ind.	Bibliotheca Indica series published by the Asiatic Society of Bengal.
Br.	*Brāhmaṇa*, added after the first name of the text.
Br. Up.	*Bṛhadāraṇyaka Upaniṣad.*
Br. S.	*Bṛhatsaṃhitā.*
B S T	Buddhist Sanskrit Texts, Mithila Institute, Darbhanga.
Ch. Up.	*Chāndogya Upaniṣad.*
Dakṣa	*Dakṣasaṃhitā* (*Smṛti*)
Dasav	*Dasaveyāliya.*
Devī Bh.	*Devībhāgavata.*
Dh.S.	*Dharmasūtra*, added after the first name of the text.
Dīgha	*Dīgha Nikāya.*
DS	*Dravyasaṃgraha* of Nemicandra.
EI	*Epigraphia Indica*
Gaut. Dh.S.	*Gautama Dharmasūtra.*
Gītā	*Bhagavadgītā*
GNB	*Gods of Northern Buddhism*, by A. Getty, Oxford 1928.
GOS	Gaekwad Oriental Series, Baroda.
Gr.	*Gṛhyasūtra*, added after the first name of the text.
Hir. Sr.	*Hiranyakeśī Gṛhyasūtra.*
HOS	Harvard Oriental Series, Cambridge Mass.
IA	*Indian Antiquary.*
ISPP	*Indian Studies Past and Present*, Calcutta.
Jaimini	*Pūrvamīmāṃsā Sūtra*
JAOS	*Journal of the American Oriental Society.*
JBBRAS	*Journal of the Bombay Branch of the Royal Asiatic Society.*
JPTS	*Journal of the Pali Text Society.*
JRAS	*Journal of the Royal Asiatic Society.*
Jāt	*Jātaka.*
Kat. Sr.	*Kātyāyana Śrautasūtra.*
Kaut	*Arthaśāstra* of Kauṭilya.
Lāṭ. Sr.	*Lāṭyāyana Śrautasūtra.*
Majjhima	*Majjhima Nikāya.*
Mbh	*Mahābhārata.*
Milinda	*Milinda pañho.*
Pāṇini	*Aṣṭādhyāyī* of Pāṇini.
Pār.Gr.	*Pāraskara Gṛhya Sūtra.*
Patañjali	*Mahābhāṣya* of Patañjali.
PMS	*Pūrvamīmāṃsāsūtra.*
PP	*Prajñāpāramitā.*
PTS	Pali Text Society.
PTSMS	*Pañcāstikāyasamayasāra.*
Pu	*Purāṇa.*
Rām	*Rāmāyaṇa.*
RV	*Ṛgveda.*
Saṃ.	*Saṃhitā*, added after the first name of the text.
Saṃyutta	*Saṃyutta Nikāya.*
Śāṅ. Gr.	*Śāṅkhyāyana Gṛhyasūtra.*
Sāṅ. Kārikā	*Sāṅkhyakārikā.*
Sān. Pra. Bhā	*Sāṅkhyapravacanabhāṣya.*
Sāṅ. Sū.	*Sāṅkhya Sūtras.*
Śat. Br.	*Śatapatha Brāhmaṇa*
SBB	Sacred Books of the Buddhists, London.
SBE	Sacred Books of the East, Oxford.
SBH	Sacred Books of the Hindus, Allahabad.
SBJ	Sacred Books of the Jains, Arrah.

SDS	*Sarvadarśanasaṃgraha.*
SDSC	*Ṣaḍdarśanasamuccaya.*
SDVM	*Syādvādamañjarī.*
TAPA	Transactions of the American Philological Association.
TSS	Trivandrum Sanskrit Series.
TT	*Tantric Texts*, ed. by A. Avalon.
TTDS	*Tattvārthādhigama Sūtra.*
UDS	*Uttarādhyayana Sūtra.*
Vāj.Saṃ	*Vājasaneyī Saṃhitā.*
VP	*Vardhamāna Purāṇa.*
ZDMG	*Zeitschrift der Deutschen Morgenlandischen Gesellschaft.*

Bibliography

Abhidhammatthasaṅgaha: ed. by C.A.F. Rhys Davids in *JPTS*, 1884; Eng. trans. by T.W. Rhys Davids and S.Z. Aung, *Compendium of Philosophy*, PTS, London 1910.

Abhidhānacintāmaṇi of Hemacandra: ed. by Hargovindas, Becharadas and Muni Jinavijaya, 2 vols. Bhavanagar 1914–19.

Abhidhānaratnamālā of Halāyudha: ed. by Th. Aufrecht, London 1861.

Abhidharmakośa: ed. by La Vallee Poussin, London 1918; French trans. with Yaśomitra's *Kośavyākhyā* by the same in 6 Vols. Louvain, 1923–31; by U. Wogihara, Tokyo.

Ācāramayukha of Nīlakaṇṭha: ed. by J.R. Gharpure, Bombay 1921.

Ācārāṅga Sūtra: ed. by H. Jacobi, London 1882; Eng. trans. in *SBE*, XXII, Oxford 1884; first part re-ed. by W. Schübring, Leipzig 1910.

Advaitabrahmasiddhi of Sadānanda Yati: ed. by Vāmana Śāstrī Upādhyāya, Bib. Ind., Calcutta 1888–90.

Advaitacintakaustubha of Mahādeva Śastrī; ed. by G.N. Datta and A.K. Sastri, Bib. Ind., Calcutta 1901–22.

Advayasiddhi of Lakṣmīnkarādevī: ed. by M.J. Shendge, M.S. University Oriental Series, No. 8. Baroda 1964.

Advayavajrasaṃgraha: ed. by M.M. Haraprasad Sastri, GOS, XL, Baroda 1927.

Agni Purāṇa: ed. by R.L. Mitra, Bib. Ind., Calcutta 1873–79; also Anandasrama Press ed., Poona 1957; Eng. trans. by M.N. Dutt, Calcutta 1901.

Ahirbudhyna Saṃhitā: by R. Krishnamacharya, Adyar Library, Madras 1966.

Āhnikaprakāśa, part of *Vīramitrodaya* of Mitramiśra; pub. in Chowkhamba Sanskrit Series, Varanasi.

Aitareya Āraṇyaka: ed..by R.L. Mitra, Bib. Ind., Calcutta 1876; ed. with Eng. trans. by A.B. Keith, Oxford 1909.

Aitareya Brāhmaṇa: ed. with com. of Sāyaṇa by Satyavrata Samasrami, Bib. Ind., Calcutta 1894–1906; Eng. trans by A.B. Keith, HOS, Cambridge Mass, XXV, 1920.

Aitareya Upaniṣad with com. of Śaṅkara and gloss of Ānandagiri; ed. by E. Roer, Bib. Ind., Calcutta 1849–50; Eng. trans. by the same, 1852. See under Upaniṣads.

Amarakoṣa: ed. with marginal notes by H.T. Colebrooke, Serampore 1808; ed. by Satis Chandra Vidyābhusana, Bib. Ind., Calcutta 1911–12.

Amitayurdhyāna: Eng. trans. in *SBE*, XLIX, Oxford 1894.

Ānandalaharī: ed. and trans. by A. Avalon, 5th ed. Madras 1961.

Anekārthatilaka of Malipa: ed. by M.M. Patikar, Poona 1947.

Āṅgirasa Smṛti: pub. by Anandasrama Press, Poona 1905; ed. Jivananda, Calcutta 1876; also pub. in *Ārya-śāstra* sries, Calcutta.

Aṅguttara Nikāya: ed. by R. Morris and E. Hardy, 6 Vols. with Index by M. Hunt, London 1885–1900, PTS; re. ed. by A.K. Warder 1961; Eng. trans. 1961; Eng. trans. by F.L. Woodward and E.M. Hare, *The Book of Gradual Sayings*, PTS, London 1935–36.

Anubhāṣya of Vallabha on *Brahmasūtra*: ed. by Hem Chandra Vidyaratna, Bib. Ind., Calcutta 1888–97.

Apadāna: ed. by M.E. Lilley, 2 Vols. PTS, London 1925–27.

Aparājitapṛcchā: Pub. in GOS, CXV, Baroda, 1950.

Āpastamba Dharmasūtra: ed. by G. Bühler, Bombay Sanskrit Series, 1892, 1894; ed. with Haradatta's *Ujjvala*; com. by Mahādeva Sastri and K. Rangacharya, Mysore 1898; Eng. trans. by G. Bühler in *SBE*, II, Oxford 1897.

Āpastamba Gṛhyasūtra: ed. by M. Winternitz, Vienna 1887; Eng. trans. by H. Olderberg in *SBE*, XXX.

Āpastamba Smṛti: Pub. by. Anandasrama Press, Poona 1905; ed. by Jivananda, Calcutta 1876.

Āpastamba Śrautasūtra: ed. with Rudradatta's com. by R. Garbe, Bib. Ind., Calcutta 1881–1903; books I–VII translated into German by W. Caland, Gottingen 1921.

Arthaśāstra of Kauṭilya: ed. by R. Shamasastry, Mysore University Oriental Library Publications 1919; ed. by J. Jolly and R. Schmidt, 2 Vols. Lahore 1923–24; Eng. trans. R. Shamasastry, Mysore 1929.

Āryamañjuśrīmūlakalpa: ed. by Ganapati Sastri in 3 Vols, TSS, Trivandrum 1920–25.

Āryāsaptaśatī of Govardhana: ed. by S.N. Sarma, Dacca, 1864.

Aṣṭādhyāyī of Pāṇini with *Siddhakaumudī* of Bhaṭṭoji Dīkṣita: Nirnaya Sagara Press, Bombay 1929; Eng. trans. by S.C. Vasu, Allahabad 1891–98.

Aṣṭāṅgasaṃgraha of Vāgbhaṭa: Pub. by Nirnaya Sagara Press, Bombay.

Aṣṭasāhasrikā Prajñāpāramitā: ed. by R.L. Mitra, Bib. Ind., Calcutta 1888; Eng. trans. by E. Conze, Bib. Ind., Calcutta, 1970.

Aṣṭaviṃśatitattva of Raghunandana: ed. by S.K. Vidyabhusan, Calcutta 1377 B.S.

Āśvalāyana Gṛhyasūtra: ed. with com. of Gārgya Nārāyaṇa by R.N. Vidyāratna and A.C. Vedantavāgīśa, Bib. Ind., Calcutta 1866–69; with com. of Haradatta by Ganapati Sastri, TSS, No. 78, Trivandrum 1923; Eng. trans. by H. Oldenberg, *SBE*, XXIX.

Āśvalāyana Śrautasūtra: ed. with Gārgya Nārāyaṇa's com. by R.N. Vidyaratna, Bib. Ind., Calcutta 1864–74.

Ātharvaṇa Upaniṣad with com. of Nārāyana: ed. by R.M. Tarkaratna, Bib. Ind., Calcutta 1872–74; see under Upaniṣads.

Atharvāsiras Upaniṣad ed. by G.S. Murti and Eng. trans by T.R.S. Ayyangar in *Śaiva Upaniṣads*, Adyar Library, Madras 1958; see under Upaniṣads.

Atharvaveda: Eng. trans. in part by M. Bloomfield in *SBE*, XLII. Oxford 1897; by W.D. Whitney, Cambridge Mass, 1905.

Atri Saṃhitā: Anandasrama Press Poona, 1905; ed. by Jivananda, Calcutta 1876; also pub. in *Ārya-śāstra* series, Calcutta.

Atthasālini: ed. by F.W.K. Muller, PTS, 1897, Eng. trans. by P.M. Tin, *The Expositor*, 2 Vols. PTS 1920–21.

Aupapātika: ed. with Vṛtti of Abhayadeva, Agamodaya Samiti, Bombay 1916.

Āvaśyaka Sūtra: ed. with *niryukti* of Bhadrabāhu, along with the Com. of Malayagiri, Agamodaya Samiti 56, Bombay 1928.

Bālambhaṭṭi of Bālambhaṭṭa, a com. on *Mitākṣarā*: ed. by G. Das, Bib. Ind., Calcutta 1904; also by J.R. Gharpure Bombay 1923.

Bārhaspatyasūtra: ed. by F.W. Thomas, Lahore 1921.

Basava Purāṇa: trans. by G. Würth in *JBBRAS*, VIII, 1864–64, 65–97.

Baudhāyana Dharmasūtra: Eng. trans. by G. Bühler in *SBE*, XIV, Oxford 1882.

Baudhāyana Gṛhyasūtra: ed. R. Shamasastry, Mysore 1920.

Baudhāyana Śrautasūtra: ed. W. Caland, Bib. Ind., Calcutta 1904–23.

Bhagavad Gītā: Eng. trans. by K.T. Telang in *SBE*, VIII, Oxford 1882.

Bhāgavata Purāṇa: ed. Swami Dhananjaya Das and Nrisimhadas Vasu, Nimbārkāśrama, Sibpur 1930–40; Eng. trans. by J.M. Sanyal in 5 vols. Calcutta.

Bhagavatīsūtra: pub. by Agamodaya Samit in 3 vols. Bombay 1918–21.

Bhaktisūtra: of Śāṇḍilya, with com. of Svapneśvara; ed. by J.R. Ballantyne, Bib. Ind., Calcutta 1861; Eng. trans. by E.B. Cowell, Bib. Ind., Calcutta 1878.

Bhāmatī of Vācaspati Miśra: ed. by P.B. Sastri, Bib. Ind., Calcutta 1876–80; ed. and Eng. trans. by S.S. Suryanarayana Sastri and C. Kunhan Raja, Madras 1933.

Bhāradvāja Gṛhyasūtra: ed. Solomon, Leiden 1913.

Bhāradvaja Saṃhitā: ed. K.S. Sresthi, Bombay, Śaka 1827.

Bhāṭṭadīpikā of Khaṇḍadeva: ed. by Chandrakanta Tarkālankara and Pramathanath Tarkabhusana, Bib. Ind., Calcutta 1889–1912.

Bhavanopaniṣad: pub. in Tantric Texts, XI, ed. A. Avalon, London 1912.

Bhaviṣya Purāṇa: Venkatesvara Press, Bombay 1904.

Bodhicaryāvatāra of Śāntideva: Buddhist Text Society, Calcutta 1894; *Pañjikā* with com. of Prajñākaramati ed. by Louis de la Vallee Poussin, Bib. Ind., Calcutta 1901–14; by Vidhusekhara Bhattacharya, Bib. Ind., Calcutta 1960; Bengali trans. by S.K. Mukhopadhyaya, Calcutta 1947

Bodhisattvabhūmi: portion pub. by Rahder as an Appendix to *Daśabhūmika* (Sanskrit ed.) Louvain 1926.

Brahmāṇḍa Purāṇa: Venkatesvara Press, Bombay 1913.

Brahma Purāṇa: Anandasrama Press, Poona 1896.

Brahmasaṃhitā: Eng. trans. by Bhaktisiddhānta Sarasvati, Gauḍıya Math. Madras 1931.

Brahmasiddhi of Maṇḍanamiśra: ed. with com. of Śaṅkhapāṇi, by S. Kuppuswami Sastri, Madras 1937.

Brahmasūtra of Bādarāyana: ed. by R.N. Vidyaratna, Bib. Ind., Calcutta 1854–63; Eng. trans. Rev. K.M. Banerjee, Bib. Ind., Calcutta 1870; ed. with *bhāṣya* of Śaṅkara along with Vācaspati Miśra's *Bhāmati* and other coms. by B. Sastri, Nirnaya Sagara Press, Bombay 1938; with com. of Śaṅkara by N.S. Eksambekar, Anandasrama Sanskrit Series, Poona 1900–1903; with Rāmānuja's com. by Ramanatha Tarkaratna, Bib.Ind., Calcutta 1888–91; by V.S. Abhayankar, Bombay 1914–16; by J.J. Johnson, Benares 1916; Eng. trans. with coms. of Śaṅkara and Rāmānuja by G. Thibaut in *SBE*, 1890–1904, Rāmānuja's *Śrībhāṣya* on *BS*: Eng. trans. by M. Rangacharya and M.B. Varadaraja Aiyangar, Madras 1899, ed. and tr. by R.D. Karmakar, 2 vols. Poona University, 1959–62; *Brahmasūtrabhāṣya* of Bhāskarācārya, ed. by V.P. Dvivedin, Chowkhamba S.S. Nos. 70, 185, 209, Benaras 1915; Madhva's *Sūtrabhāṣya*, on *BS*, ed. by Raghavendracarya, 4 Vols. Mysore 1911–22, Eng. trans. by S. Subha Rau, Madras 1904: Nimbārka's *Vedāntapārijātasaurva* on *BS*, ed. by V. Dvivedin, Chowkhamba, Benaras 1910, Eng. trans of the same and Srinivasa's *Vedāntakaustubha* by Roma Bose, Bib. Ind., Calcutta 1940–42; Vallabha's *Anubhāṣya* on *BS*, ed. by H.C. Vidyaratna, Bib. Ind., Calcutta 1888–97; by S.T. Pathak, Bombay 1921–26; Śrīkaṇṭha's *Śaivabhāṣya* ed. in *The Pandit*, Vols. VI–VII.

Brahmavaivarta Purāṇa: pub. by Vangavasi Press Calcutta, Śaka 1827.

Bṛhadāraṇyaka Upaniṣad: Eng. trans. R.A. Hume, *Thirteen Principal Upanisads*, Oxford 1921; also Max Müller's trans. in *SBE*, I; ed. and trans. O. Böhtlingk, Leipzig 1889, see under *Upaniṣads*.

Bṛhaddevatā: ed. and Eng. trans. by A.A. Macdonell, HOS, Cambridge, Mass., V–VI, 1904; ed. R.L. Mitra, Bib. Ind., Calcutta 1889–92.

Bṛhaddharma Purāṇa: ed. M.M. Haraprasad Sastri, Bib. Ind., Calcutta 1886–97.

Bṛhannāradīya Purāṇa: ed. Hrisikesh Sastri, Bib. Ind., Calcutta 1886–91.

Bṛhaspati Smṛti: Eng. trans. by J. Jolly in *SBE*, XXXIII, Oxford 1889.

Bṛhaspatisūtra: ed. and Eng. trans. by F.W. Thomas, Lahore 1921.

Bṛhatī of Prabhākara: pub. in Madras University Sanskrit Series 1936.

Bṛhatsaṃhitā: ed. by H. Kern, Bib. Ind., Calcutta 1865; trans. by the same in *JRAS*, IV–VII; ed. and trans. by V. Subrahmanya Sastri, Bangalore 1947.

Buddhacarita: ed. and Eng. trans by E.H. Johnston, Punjab University Oriented Publication 1935–36; ed. trans. by E.B. Cowell in *SBE*, XLIX, 1894.

Caitanya Caritāmṛta: of Kṛṣṇadāsa Kavirāja; ed. by Nripendra Krishna Chattopadhyaya, Calcutta 1368 B.S.

Canna-Basava Purāṇa: Eng. trans by G. Würth in *JBBRAS*, VIII, 1864–66, 98–221.

Caraka Saṃhitā: ed. by N.N. Sengupta, Calcutta, Śaka 1849.

Caturvarga cintāmaṇi of Hemādri: Vol. I ed. by B.C. Siromani, Vol. II (Part 1–2) by Yogesvara Bhattacharya, Vol. III (part 1–2) by K.N. Tarkaratna and Vol. IV by P.N. Tarkabhusana, Bib. Ind., Calcutta 1871–1911.

Caturviṃśatimatasaṃgraha: pub. in Benaras Sanskrit Series.

Chāndogya Upaniṣad: ed. M.C. Pal, Calcutta 1885; Eng. trans. R.L. Mitra, 1854–62; R.A. Hume, *Thirteen Principal Upaniṣads*, Oxford 1921; ed. and trans. by O. Bhötlingk, Leipzig 1889. See under *Upaniṣads*.

Cidgagana candrikā: ed. by Trivikrama Tīrtha in *Tantric Texts*, XX.

Cullaniddesa: ed. by W. Stede, PTS, 1918.

Cullavagga of the *Vinaya Pitaka*: Eng. trans. T.W. Rhys Davids and H. Olderberg, *SBE*, XIII, XVII, XX; I.B. Horner, PTS, 1938–52.

Dakṣusaṃhitā: pub. Anandasrama, Poona, *Āryaśāstra* Series, Calcutta.

Dakṣiṇāmūrtisaṃhitā: pub. in Sarasvati Bhavana Series, Benaras.

Dānakriyākaumudī of Govindānanda: ed. by K.K. Smṛtibhusana, Bib. Ind., Calcutta 1904–05.

Dānamayukha of Nīlakaṇṭha: pub. in Chowkhamba Sanskrit Series, Varanasi 1909.

Daśarūpa of Dhanañjaya: ed. with com. of Dhanika by F.E. Hall, Bib. Ind., Calcutta 1861–65; Eng. trans. by G. Hass, New York 1912.

Daśaślokī: ed. with com. of Puruṣottama by R.G. Bhatta, Chowkhamba Sanskrit Series No. 103, Varanasi 1907.

Dasaveyāliya: ed. and trans. by E. Leumann in *ZDMG*, XLVI, 1892, 581–663.

Devībhāgavata: Ed. P. Tarkaratna, Vangavasi Press, Calcutta, Śaka 1832.

Devīpurāṇa: Ed. P. Tarkaratna, Vangavasi Press, Calcutta, 1302 B.S.

Dhammapada: ed. by S.S. Thera, PTS, London 1914; Eng. trans. by F. Max Müller in *SBE*, Oxford 1898.

Dhammasangaṇi: ed. by E. Muller, PTS, London 1885, Eng. trans. by C.A.F. Rhys Davids, second ed. London 1923.

Dharmabindu of Haribhadra: ed. with com. of Minicandra by L. Suali, Bib. Ind., Calcutta, 1940.

Dharmasindhu: pub. Nirnaya Sagara Press, Bombay 1926.

Dīgha Nikāya: ed. by T.W. Rhys Davids and J.E. Carpenter, 3 Vols. PTS, London 1890, 1903, 1911; Eng. trans *Dialogues of the Buddha* by T.W. Rhys Davids, 3 Vols. *SBB*, London 1899, 1910, 1921.

Dravyasaṃgraha of Nemicandra: ed. with intro. Eng. trans., notes and *Vṛtti* by S.C. Ghosal, Central Jain Publishing House, Arrah 1917.

Gadhādharapaddhati: ed. Sadasiva Misra, Bib. Ind., Calcutta, Part I, 1904; Part II, 1908.

Gandharvatantra: ed. R.C. Kak and H.B. Sastri, Srinagar 1934.

Garuḍa Purāṇa: pub. in Chowkhamba Sanskrit Series, Varanasi; ed. P. Tarkaratna, Vangavasi Press, Calcutta 1314 B.S.; Eng. trans. by M.N. Dutt, Calcutta 1908.

Gautama Dharmasūtra: Eng. trans. by G. Bühler, *SBE*, II, 1879.

Gautama Saṃhitā: ed. Jivananda, Calcutta 1876; pub. in *Āryaśāstra* Series, Calcutta.

Gautamīya Tantra: pub. by R.M. Chatterjee, Calcutta 1283 B.S.

Gayatrī Tantra: pub. by R.M. Chatterjee, Calcutta 1283 B.S.

Gheraṇḍa Saṃhitā: pub. by Pāṇini Office, Allaha bad 1914; Eng. trans. by S.C. Vasu, Adyar Library, Madras 1895.

Gobhila Gṛhyasūtra: ed. by C. Tarkalankara, Bib. Ind. Calcutta 1907–08; Eng. trans. by H. Olderberg in *SBE*, XXX.

Gobhila Pariśiṣṭa: ed. by C. Tarkalankara, Bib. Ind., Calcutta 1909.

Gobhila Smṛti, also called *Chāndogyapariśiṣṭa*, *Karmapradīpa* and *Kātyāyana Smṛti*: pub. by Anandasrama Press. Poona 1905.

Gommaṭasāra: ed. with intro., Eng. and Sanskrit trans., with com. in English by J.L. Jaini, in *SBJ*, Vols. V and VI, Lucknow 1927.

Gopālatāpanīya Upaniṣad with com. of Visveśvara: ed. by H.C. Vidyabhusana and V.N. Sastri, Bib. Ind., Calcutta 1870; See under Upaniṣads.

Gopatha Brāhmaṇa: ed. by R. Mitra and H.C. Vidyabhusana, Bib. Ind., Calcutta 1870–72.

Gorakṣasiddhāntasaṃgraha: ed. by M.M. Gopinath Kaviraj, Sarasvati Bhavana Text Series No. 18, Varanasi 1925.

Gṛhastharatnākara of Caṇḍeśvara: ed. by K.K. Smrtitirtha, Bib. Ind., Calcutta 1928.

Gṛhyasaṃgraha of Gobhilaputra: ed. by C. Tarkalankara, Bib. Ind., Calcutta 1910; ed. by M. Bloomfield in *ZDMG*, XXXV, 53 ff.

Guhyasamāja Tantra: ed. by B.T. Bhattacharyya, GOS, LIII, Baroda 1931.

Haṃsavilāsa: pub. in GOS, Baroda 1937.

Hāralatā of Aniruddha Bhatta: ed. by K.K. Smrtitirtha, Bib. Ind., Calcutta 1909.

Harivaṃśa with com. of Nīlakaṇṭha: pub. by Gopal Narayan, Bombay 1895; ed. and Eng. trans. by M.N. Dutta, Calcutta 1897.

Haṭhayogapradīpikā: Eng. trans by P. Singh, Allahabad 1915; by T.R.S. Ayyangar, Adyar Library, Madras 1933.

Hevajra Tantra: ed. and Eng. trans. by D. Snellgrove, 2 Vols., London 1959.

Hiranyakeśī Gṛhyasūtra: ed. by J. Kirste, Vienna 1899; Eng. trans. by H. Olderberg in *SBE*, XXX.

Īśānaśivagurudevapaddhati: pub. in Trivandrum Sanskrit Series.

Īśā Upaniṣad: Eng. trans. by R.A. Hume, *Thirteen Principal Upaniṣads*, Oxford 1921; see under *Upaniṣads*.

Īśvarapratyabhijñāvimarśinī: pub. in Kashmir Series of Texts and Studies, XXII, 1928; XXXIII, 1922.

Itivuttaka: Eng. trans. by J.H. Moore, *Sayings of Buddha*, New York 1908.

Jābalopaniṣad: F.O. Schrader, *Minor Upaniṣads*, Madras 1912, see under *Upaniṣads*.

Jaiminīya Brāhmaṇa: Portion ed. with German trans. by W. Caland 1919; ed. by Raghu Vira and L. Chandra, 1954.

Jaiminīya Upaniṣad Brāhmana: text, trans. and notes by Hanus Oertel in *JAOS*, XVI, 1896.

Jātaka: ed. by V. Fausböll, 7 Vols. Index by D. Anderson, PTS, London 1877–97; rep. 1962–64; Eng. trans. ed. by E.B. Cowell, 7 Vols., Cambridge 1895–1913.

Jātakamālā of Āryasura: ed. by H. Kern, Boston 1891; Eng. trans. by J. Speyer, SBB, London 1895.

Jayākhya Saṃhitā: ed. by E. Krishnamacharya, GOS, LIV, Baroda 1931.

Jñānārnava Tantra: pub. by Anandasrama Press, Poona.

Jñānasiddhi: B.T. Bhattacharyya, *Two Vajrayāna Texts*, GOS, XLIV, Baroda 1929.

Kālanirṇaya of Madhavāçārya: ed. by C. Tarkalankara, Bib. Ind., Calcutta 1885.

Kālavivaka of Jīmutavāhana: ed. by M.S. Smrtiratna and P.N. Tarkabhusana, Bib. Ind., Calcutta 1905.

Kālikā Purāṇa: ed. by P. Tarkaratna, Vangavasi Press, Calcutta.

Kāli Tantra: pub. in Sanskrit Sahitya Parisat Series, No. 2, Calcutta 1329 B.S.

Kālīvilāsa Tantra: ed. by A. Avalon in *Tantric Texts*, VI, Madras 1917.

Kalpadrukośa of Keśava: ed. R.V. Sharma, GOS, 2 Vols, Baroda 1928, 1932.

Kalpsūtra of Bhadrabāhu: ed. H. Jacobi (1879) and Eng. trans. by the same in *SBE*, XXII.

Kāmakalāvilāsa: pub. with com. *Cidvallī* in Kash mir Series of Texts and Studies; ed. with trans. and notes by A. Avalon in *Tantric Texts* X, Madras, rep. 1953.

Kāmakhyātantra: pub. by R.M. Chatterjee, Calcutta 1283 B.S.

Karmapradīpa: ed. by C. Tarkalankara and A.K. Sastri, Bib. Ind, Calcutta 1923.

Kāśyapa Saṃhitā: Tirupati 1860.

Kāṭhaka Gṛhyasūtra with coms. of Ādityadarśana, Devapāla and Brāhmaṇabala: ed. by W. Caland, Lahore 1925.

Kāṭhaka Saṃhitā: ed. by L. Von Schroeder, Leipzig, 1900–10; A.B. Keith in *JRAS*, 1910, 517 ff; 1912, 1095 ff.

Kaṭha-(Kāṭhaka) Upaniṣad: ed. with Sankara's com. by S.S. Pathaka, Poona 1919; Eng. trans. by W.D. Whitney in *TAPA*, XXI, also Hume, *op.cit.*, see under *Upaniṣads*.

Kathāvatthu: ed. by A.C. Taylor, PTS, London 1894; Eng. trans. *Points of Controversy or Subjects of Discourse* by S.J. Aung and C.A.F. Rhys Davids, PTS, London 1915.

Kātyāyana Smṛti: ed. and trans. by P.V. Kane, Bombay 1933.

Kātyāyaṇa Śrautasūtra: ed. with com. of Karka and Yājñavalkya by A. Weber 1859; by Vidya dhara Sharma, Banares 1933–37.

Kaulajñānanirṇaya: ed. by P.C. Bagchi, Calcutta Sanskrit Series, 1934.

Kaulamārgarahasya: ed. by S.C. Vidyabhusana, Sahitya Parisat Series No. LXXVI, Calcutta.

Kaula Upaniṣad: pub. in *Tantric Texts*, XL, London 1922.

Kaulāvalinirṇaya: ed. by A Avalon, *Tantric Texts*, XIV, Madras 1915.

Kaulāvalitantra: pub. by R.M. Chatterjee, Calcutta 1283 B.S.

Kauśika Sūtra: ed. by M. Bloomfield, New Haven 1890.

Kauṣītakī Brāhmaṇa: ed. by E.B. Cowell, Calcutta 1861; Eng. trans. by A.B. Keith, *HOS*, XXV, Cambridge Mass. 1920; ed. by B. Lind ner, Jena 1887.

Kauṣītaki Gṛhyasūtra: pub. in Madras University Sanskrit Series.

Kauṣītaki Upaniṣad: see under Upaniṣads.

Khādira Gṛhyasūtra: ed. by A. Mahadeva Sastri and L. Srinivasacarya, Mysore 1913; Eng. trans. by H. Olderberg in *SBE*, XXIX.

Khaṇḍanakhaṇḍakhādya: ed. by G.N. Jha, Chowkhamba Sanskrit Series, Varanasi 1904–14.

Khuddakapāṭha: ed. and trans. by R.C. Childers in *JRAS*, 1870, 309–39; ed. with *Paramatthajotikā* com. by H. Smith and M. Hunt, PTS, London 1915; Eng. trans. *Minor Anthologies of the Pali Canon*, Part I by C.A.F. Rhys Davids, *SBB*, London 1931.

Kiraṇāvalī of Udayana: ed. with com. by S.C. Sarvabhauma, Bib. Ind., Calcutta 1911–12.

Kramadīpikā: ed. by G. Bhattacharya, Chowkhamba Sanskrit Series No. 233.

Kṛtyakalpataru of Lakṣmīdhara: pub. in GOS, Baroda 1941–50.

Kṛtyaratnākara of Caṇḍeśvara: ed. by K.K. Smriti tirtha, Bib. Ind., Calcutta 1925.

Kulacuḍāmaṇi Tantra: ed. G.C. Vedantatirtha in *Tantric Texts*, IV, Calcutta 1915.

Kulārṇava Tantra: ed. by A. Avalon in *Tantric Texts*, V, London 1917; by Taranath Vidyaratna, Madras 1965 (rep.).

Kūrma Purāṇa: ed. by Nilmani Mukhopadhyaya, Bib. Ind., Calcutta 1890; by P. Tarkaratna, Vangavasi Press, Calcutta 1321 B.S.

Laghu Atri Smṛti: ed. Jivananda, Calcutta 1876.

Laghu Hārīta Smṛti: pub. Anandasrama Press, Poona 1905; ed. Jivananda, Calcutta 1876.

Lakṣmī Tantra: ed. by V. Krishnamacharya, Adayar Library Series No. 87, Madras 1959; Eng. trans. with notes by Sanjukta Gupta, Leiden 1972.

Lalitāsahasranāma of *Brahmāṇḍa Purāṇa* with com. *Saubhāgyabhāskara* of Bhāskara Rāya: Nirnaya Sagara Press, Bombay 1935.

Lalitavistara: ed. and Eng. trans. by R.L. Mitra, Bib. Ind., Calcutta 1877, 1886; ed. by Lefmann, Halle 1902–08; rep. by P.L. Vaidya in BST series, Darbhanga 1958.

Laṅkāvatārasūtra: Sans. ed. by B. Nanjio, Kyoto 1923; Eng. trans. by D.T. Suzuki, London 1932.

Lāṭyāyana Śrautasūtra: ed. with com. of Āgniśvāmin by A.C. Vedantavagisa, Bib. Ind., Calcutta 1872.

Laugaṣi Gṛhyasūtra (Same as *Kāṭhaka Gr)*: pub. with com. of Devapāla, 2 Vols. in Kashmir Series of Texts and Studies, 1928.

Liṅga Purāṇa: ed. by Jivananda Vidyasagara, Bib. Ind., Calcutta 1885.

Madanapārijata of Madanapāla: ed. by Madhusudan Smrtiratna Bib. Ind., Calcutta 1893.

Madhyamakāvatāra: ed. by La Vallee Poussin, in Bibliotheca Buddhica, Leningrad 1907–12; trans. by the same in *Le Museon*, Louvain 1907, 1910, 1911.

Madhyamakavṛtti: Sanskrit ed. La Vallee Poussin, Bibliotheca Buddhica, 1903–13; trans. by Th.Stcherbatsky et al. along with Nāgārjuna's *Kārikās*, Leningrad 1927.

Madhyāntavibhaṅga: Sans. ed. by Yamaguchi, 2 Vols., Nagoya 1934, trans. by Stcherbatsky with com. of Vasubandhu and Sthiramati in Bib. Bud., Leningrad 1936; rev. ed. 1899, Calcutta 1971.

Mahābhārata: Critical edition Poona 1927 ff., Eng. trans. by K.M. Ganguly, pub. by P.C. Roy, Calcutta 1884–96; rep. Calcutta 1926.

Mahābhāṣya of Patañjali: ed. by Kielhorn in 3 Vols., Bombay Sanskrit Series 1880–85.

Mahakāla Saṃhitā: pub. by G.N. Jha, Kendriya Samskṛta Vidyapītha, Allahabad, 1971.

Mahānārāyaṇopaniṣad: Ed. by G.A. Jacob, Bombay 1888; see under *Upaniṣads*.

Mahāniddesa: ed. by Poussin and Thomas, PTS, London 1916–17.

Mahanirvāṇa Tantra: pub. in Chowkhamba Sans krit Series, Varanasi; ed. by A. Avalon in *Tantric Texts*, XIII, Eng. trans. *The Great Liberation*, Calcutta 1929.

Mahāniśītha Sūtra: ed. by W. Schubring, Berlin 1918.

Mahāvagga: See under Cullavagga and Vinaya Piṭaka.

Mahāvaṃsa: Eng. trans., *The Great Chronicle of Ceylon*, by W. Geiger, London 1912.

Mahāvastu: ed. by E. Senart, Paris 1892–97; Eng. trans. by J. Jones in 3 Vols. PTS, London 1949–56, Bengali trans. by R.G. Basak, Calcutta.

Mahāvyutpatti: ed. by I.P. Minayev. Bib. Bud., No. XIII, Leningrad 1911; by Ogiwara, Tokyo 1915; by Sakaki, Kyoto 1916–25.

Mahāyānasaṃgraha: ed. and trans. of the Tibetan version by E. Lamotte, Louvain 1938–39.

Mahāyānasutrālaṅkāra: ed. and trans. of the Sanskrit version by S. Levi, Paris 1907, 1911.

Maitrī, Maitrāyanīya Upaniṣad: ed. and Eng. trans. by E.B. Cowell, Bib. Ind., Calcutta 1863; revised ed. by S.C. Vidyabhusana, Bib. Ind., Calcutta 1913; ed. and trans. by J.A.B. Van Buitemen, The Hague 1962; see under *Upaniṣads*.

Majjhima Nikāya: ed. by V. Trenckner and R. Chalmers, in 3 Vols., PTS, London 1888–99, rep. 1948–51; Eng. trans. by I.B. Horner, *Middle Length Sayings*, PTS, 1954–59.

Mānasāra: ed. and trans. by P.K. Acharya, Oxford 1933.

Mānasollāsa of Someśvara: pub. in GOS, 3 Vols., Baroda 1925–61.

Mānava Gṛhyasūtra: ed. by F. Knauer, St. Petersburg 1897; pub. with com. of Aṣṭāvakra in GOS, Baroda 1926; trans. by Dresden, Groningen 1941.

Māṇḍukyopaniṣad with Gauḍapāda's *Kārikā*: Text with trans. of Śaṅkara's com., Ramakrishna Asrama, Mysore.

Maṅkhakoṣa of Maṅkha: ed. by Th. Zachariae, Vienna 1897.

Mantramahodadhi: pub. by Venkatesvara Press, Bombay 1908.

Manu Smṛti: ed. with com. by N.N. Mandlik, Bombay 1886; Eng. trans. by William Jones, Calcutta 1794; by G. Buhler in *SBE*, XXV, Oxford 1886; trans. by A.C. Burnell and E.W. Hopkins, London 1884; trans. with notes in 5 Vols. by G.N. Jha, Bib. Ind., Calcutta 1922–29.

Manuṭīkāsaṃgraha: ed. by J. Jolly, Bib. Ind., Calcutta 1889.

Mārkaṇḍeya Purāṇa: ed. K.M. Banerjee, Bib. Ind., Calcutta 1862; Eng. trans. by F.E. Pargiter, Calcutta 1904; ed. by P. Tarkaratna, Vangavasi Press, Calcutta 1910.

Mātṛkācakraviveka of Svatantrānandanātha: pub. in Sarasvati Bhavana Series, Varanasi 1934.

Matṛkābheda Tantra: ed. by C. Bhattacharyya, Calcutta Sanskrit Series VII.

Matsya Purāṇa: pub. by Anandasrama Press, Poona 1907; Eng. trans. by a Taluqdar of Oudh in *SBH* series, 2 Vols., Allahabad 1916–17.

Mayamatam: ed. by T. Ganapati Sastri, Trivandrum 1919.

Medinīkoṣa of Medinīkara: pub. in Kasi Sanskrit Series, Varanasi 1916.

Merutantra: pub. by Venkatesvara Press, Bombay 1908.

Milindapanho: ed. by V. Trenckner, London 1880; Eng. trans. by T.W. Rhys Davids in *SBE*, Oxford 1890–94.

Mimāṃsāsūtras of Jaimini with *Śabarabhāṣya*: ed. by M. Vidyaratna, Bib. Ind., Calcutta 1873; also pub. by Anandasrama Press, Poona, 1929–34; Eng. trans. by G.N. Jha in SBH, Allahabad 1910; separate trans. of *Śabarabhasya* by G.N. Jha in GOS, Baroda, 1933–36.

Muṇḍakopaniṣad: see under *Upaniṣads*.

Nāmamālā of Dhanañjaya: ed. by S.N. Tripathi, Benares 1950.

Nāmamālikā of Bhoja: ed. by E.D. Kulkarni and V.D. Gokhale, Poona 1955.

Nānārthārṇavasaṃkṣepa of Keśavasvāmin: ed. by T. Ganapati Sastri, Trivandrum Sanskrit Series, 1913.

Nārada Bhaktisūtra: text, trans. and notes by Swami Tyagisananda, Sri Ramakrishna Math, Madras 1952.

Nāradapāñcarātra: ed. by K.M. Banerjee, Bib. Ind., Calcutta 1865; trans. in *SBH*, XXIII, Allahabad 1921.

Nārada Smṛti: ed. with extracts from the com. of Asahāya and others by J. Jolly, Bib. Ind., Calcutta 1885; trans. by the same in *SBE*, XXXIII, 1889; trans. of a shorter text by Jolly, London 1876.

Nāradīya Purāṇa: pub. by Venkatesvara Press, Bombay.

Naradīya Śikṣā: pub. in Benares Sanskrit Series.

Nāṭyaśāstra of Bharata: ed. with com. of Abhinavagupta in GOS, 2 Vols., Baroda 1926, 1934; Eng. trans. with intro. and notes by M.M. Ghosh, Bib. Ind., Calcutta 1950, 1961.

Nirṇayasindhu: pub. by Nirnaya Sagara Press, Bombay 1935.

Nirukta of Yāska: ed. by S.V. Samasrami, Bib. Ind., Calcutta 1891; rev. ed. H.V. Samasrami 1912; ed. with Eng. trans. by Lakshman Sarup, 2 Vols., Lahore 1922.

Niruttara Tantra: pub. by R.M. Chatterjee, Calcutta 1283 B.S.

Niṣpannayogāvalī of Abhayākaragupta: ed. by B.T. Bhattacharyya, GOS, No. 109, Baroda 1949.

Nirvāṇatantra: pub. by R.M. Chatterjee, Calcutta 1283 B.S.

Nityācārapaddhati of Vidyākara and *Pradīpa* of Narasimha: ed. B.B. Bhattacharyya, Bib. Ind., Calcutta 1903, 1928.

Nityaṣoḍaśikārṇava: pub. with *Setubandha* com. of Bhāskara Rāya in Anandasrama Sanskrit Series, LVI, Poona 1944.

Nityotsava of Umānandanātha: pub. in GOS, XXII, Baroda 1923.

Nṛsiṃha Purāṇa: pub. by Gopal Narayan, Bombay 1911.

Nrsiṃhatāpanīya Upaniṣad: ed. by R. Tarkaratna, Bib. Ind., Calcutta 1871.

Nyāyabindu of Dharmakīrti: ed. with com. of Vinītadeva by L. de la Vallee Poussin, Bib. Ind., Calcutta 1913; *Tīkā* of Dharmottara, ed. by P. Paterson, Bib. Ind., Calcutta 1890; *Ṭīkā* of Vinītadeva reconstructed from the extant Tibetan version with Eng. trans. and notes by M.K. Gangopadhyaya, *ISPP*, Calcutta 1971.

Nyāyakandalī of Śrīdharabhaṭta: trans. by G.N. Jha, Benares 1916.

Nyāyakusumāñjali of Udayana: ed. by C.K. Tarkalankara, Bib. Ind., Calcutta 1895; Eng. trans. by Ravi Tirtha, Madras 1946.

Nyāya Sūtra: ed. with Eng. trans. by S.C. Vidyabhusana in *SBH* series, Allahabad 1911.

Nyāyavārttika of Uddotakara: ed. by V.P. Dvivedi, Bib. Ind., Calcutta 1914.

Nyāyāvatāra: ed. with Eng. trans. by S.C. Vidyabhusana, Bib. Ind., Calcutta; Eng. trans., Indian Research Society, Calcutta.

Padma Purāṇa: ed. by V.N. Mandlik, Anandasrama Press, Poona, 4 Vols., 1893–94.

Pādma Tantra: Sadvidya Press, Mysore 1888.

Padārthadharmasaṃgraha with *Nyāyakandalī* of Śrīdhara: trans. by G.N. Jha in *The Pandit*, Benares.

Pādukapañcaka: ed. Taranath Vidyaratna in *Tantric Texts*, II, 1913.

Pañcadaśī of Vidyāraṇya: trans. by N. Dhole, Calcutta.

Pañcāstikāyasāra of Kundakunda: ed. and trans. by Appaswamy Chakrabarti, *SBJ*, Arrah 1920; *Samayāsara*: pub. in Sanatana Jaina Granthamata Series, Benares 1914.

Pañcaviṃśa Brāhmaṇa: ed. by A. Vedantavagisa, Calcutta 1874; Eng. trans. W. Caland, Bib. Ind., Calcutta 1931.

Papañcasūdanī: ed. by J.H. Woods, D. Kosambi and I.B. Horner, PTS, London 1922–38.

Paramārthasāra of Abhinavagupta: ed. with Yogirāja's com. in Kashmir Series of Texts and Studies, Srinagar 1916; Eng. trans. by L.D. Barnett, *JRAS*, 1910, 707–47.

Parama Saṃhitā: ed. and trans. by S. Krishnasvami Aiyangar, GOS 86, Baroda, 1940.

Parameśvara Saṃhitā: ed. by Sri Govindacharya, Srirangam 1953.

Pārānanda Sūtra: pub. in GOS, Baroda 1931.

Parāśara-Mādhāviyā of Mādhavācarya: ed. by V.S. Islampurkar in Bombay Sanskrit Series.

Parāśara Smṛti: pub. in Bombay Sanskrit Series; Eng. trans. by K.K. Bhattacharya, Bib. Ind., Calcutta 1887.

Pāraskara Gṛhyasutra: ed. by Gopal Sastri Nene, Benares 1926; Eng. trans. by H. Olderberg in *SBE*, XXIX.

Paraśurāmakalpasūtra: pub. in GOS, XXII–XXIII, Baroda 1923.

Parātriṃśikā: pub. in Kashmir Sanskrit Series, No. XVIII, Srinagar 1918.

Paribhāṣaprakāśa: pub. in Chowkhamba Sanskrit Series, Varanasi.

Parikṣāmukhasūtra of Māṇikya Nandi, ed. by S.C. Vidyabhusana, Bib. Ind., Calcutta 1909.

Pāśupata Sūtras: ed. with Kauṇḍinya's *Pañcārthabhāṣya* by R. Ananthakrishna Sastri, Trivandrum Sanskrit Series No. 143, Trivandrum 1940.

Patisaṃbhidāmagga: ed. by A.C. Taylor, PTS, London 1905–07.

Pauṣkara Saṃhitā: ed. by Y.S. Sampathkumara Ramanuja Muni, Melkota 1934.

Prabodhacandrodaya: ed. with com. by V.L. Pansikar, Bombay 1924.

Prajñāpāramitā Vajracchedikā: ed. by Max Müller, Oxford 1881, and Eng. trans. by the same in *SBE*, XLIX, 1894.

Prajñāpradīpa: of Bhāvaviveka, ed. by M. Walleser, Bib. Ind., Calcutta 1914.

Prajñopāyaviniścayasiddhi of Anaṅgavajra: ed. by B.T. Bhattacharyya, GOS, XLIV, Baroda 1929.

Pramāṇamañjarī: ed. by Priyabala Shah, Oriental Institute, Baroda, 1958.

Pramāṇamīmaṃsā of Hemacandra: Eng. trans. *Critique of Organ of Knowledge*, by S. Mookherjee and N. Tatia, Jain Culture and Research Society, Bombay.

Prāṇatoṣaṇi: Compiled by Ramatoshana Bhattacharya, pub. by Vasumati Sahitya Mandir, Calcutta.

Prapañcasāra with com. *Vivaraṇa* by Padmapāda: pub. in *Tantric Texts* III and new ed. in *ibid.*, XVIII–XIX, 1939.

Praśna Upanışad: see under *Upaniṣads*.
Pratiṣṭhamayukha of Nilakaṇṭha: ed. by J.R. Gharpure, Bombay.
Pratyabhijñāhṛdaya: pub. in Kashmir-Series of Texts and Studies III, 1911; Eng. trans. *Secret of Recognition* with notes by K.F. Leidecker, Adyar Library, Madras 1938.
Pravaramañjarī of Puruṣottama: ed. by C. Rao, Mysore 1900.
Prāyaścittasāra: pub. in Sarasvati Bhavana Series, Varanasi.
Puggalapaññatti: ed. by R. Morris, PTS, London 1883; Eng. trans. *Designation of Human Types*, by B.C. Law, London 1923.
Pūjāpaddhati: pub. in Chowkhamba Sanskrit Series, Varanasi.
Puraścaryārṇava: pub. by Pratapasimha Shah Bahadur Verma in 3 Vols., Calcutta 1901, 1902, 1904.
Pūrvamīmāṃsāsūtra: see under Mīmaṃsā Sūtra.
Rājadharmakaustubha of Anantadeva: pub. in GOS, Baroda 1935.
Rājamārtaṇḍa of Bhoja: ed. and Eng. trans. by R. Mitra, Bib. Ind., Calcutta 1883.
Rājataraṅginī of Kalhaṇa: ed. by M.A. Stein, Bombay 1892; Eng. trans. by the same, London 1900.
Rāmāyaṇa: Eng. trans. by N.M. Dutt, Calcutta 1893–94; by R.T.H. Griffith, Benares 1915.
Rasārṇava: ed. by P.C. Ray and H.C. Kaviratna, Bib. Ind., Calcutta 1910.
Ṛgveda: cr. ed. by Vaidika Saṃśodhana Maṇḍala, 4 Vols., Poona 1933 ff.; Eng. trans. by F. Max Müller in *SBE*, XXXII, 1891; by H. Oldenberg in *SBE*, XLVI, Oxford 1897; by R.T.H. Griffith, Benares 1896–97.
Ṛgveda-Pratiśākhya: ed. by M.D. Sastri, Punjab Oriental Series, 1937.
Ṛgvidhāna: ed. by Rudolt Meyer, Berolini 1878.
Rudrayāmala: ed. Jivananda Vidyasagara, Calcutta 1892.
Rūpamaṇḍana: pub. in Calcutta Sanskrit Series, No. XII.
Sabdaratnāvalī of Mathureṣa: ed. by M.M. Chaudhuri, Bib. Ind., Calcutta 1970.
Ṣaḍdarśanasamuccaya of Haribhadra: ed. with Guṇaratna's *Tarkarahasyadīpikā* by L. Suali, Bib. Ind., Calcutta 1914.
Saddharmapuṇḍarīka: Sanskrit ed. by H. Kern and B. Nanjio, Bib. Bud., Leningrad 1908–12; Eng. trans. by H. Kern in *SBE*, 1909.
Sādhanamālā: ed. by B.T. Bhattacharyya, 2 Vols., GOS, Baroda 1925–28.
Sahyādrikhaṇḍa: ed. by G.D. Kunha, Bombay 1887.
Śaivabhāṣya on *Brahmasūtra* of Śrīkaṇṭha: ed. in *The Pandit*, VI–VII, Varanasi.
Śaktisaṅgama Tantra: ed. by B.T. Bhattacharyya, 3 Vols. GOS, Nos. 61, 91, 104, Baroda 1932–47.
Śakti Sūtra: pub. in Sarasvati Bhavana Series X, Varanasi.
Samavāya: ed. with Abhayadeva Suri's com., Agamodaya Samiti, Bombay 1918.
Sāmaveda: ed. with trans. by Th. Benfy, Leipzig 1848; ed. by S. Samasrami, Bib. Ind., Calcutta 1878.
Samayapradīpa of Śrīdatta, ed. by A. Chatterjee Sastri, Bib. Ind., Calcutta 1971.
Sāmrājyalakṣmīpīṭhikā: pub. in Tanjore Sarasvati Mahal Series.
Saṃskārakaustubha: pub. by Venkatacarya Upadhya, Baroda.
Saṃskāraprakāśa: pub. in Chowkhamba Sanskrit Series, Varanasi.
Saṃskāraratnamālā of Gopīnātha: pub. by Anandasrama Press, Poona.
Saṃyukta Nikāya: ed. by L. Feer, 5 Vols., PTS, London 1884–91; Eng. trans. *Book of the Kindred Sayings*, by C.A.F. Rhys Davids and F.L. Woodward, PTS, London 1917–30.
Sanatkumara Saṃhitā: ed. by V. Krishnamarchya, Adyar Library, No. 95, Madras 1969.
Sanatkumāra Tantra: pub. in GOS, 2 Vols., Baroda; pub. by R.M. Chatterjee, Calcutta 1283 B.S.
Śāṇḍilya Sūtras: Eng. trans. with text and com. by E.B. Cowell, Bib. Ind., Calcutta 1878.
Śaṅkaravijaya of Ānandagiri: ed. by J. Tarkapanchanana, Bib. Ind., Calcutta 1868.
Saṅkha Smṛti: pub. by Anandasrama Press, Poona 1905.
Sāṅkhya Kārikā of Īśvarakṛṣṇa: Eng. and Beng. trans. by H.T. Colebrooke and H.H. Wilson, Calcutta 1837; text and trans. with *Tattvakaumudī* of Vācaspati Miśra, by G.N. Jha, Bombay; Eng. trans. from the French with *Māṭharavṛtti* studied in the light of its Chinese verson, by S.S. Suryanarayana Sastri, Madras University.
Sāṅkhya Pravacana Bhāṣya: ed. by R. Garbe, HOS, Cambridge Mass 1895.
Sāṅkhyasāra of Vijñānabhikṣu: ed. by F. Edward Hall, Bib. Ind., Calcutta 1865.

Sāṅkhya Sūtra: ed. with extracts from Vijñānabhikṣu's com. and trans. by J.R. Ballantyne, Bib. Ind., Calcutta 1862–65; ed. with Aniruddha's com. and trans. by R. Garbe, Calcutta 1892.

Śāṅkhyāyana Āraṇyaka: pub. in Anandasrama Sanskrit Series No. 70, Poona 1922.

Śāṅkhyayana Gṛhyasūtra: Eng. trans. by H. Olderberg in *SBE*, XXIX.

Śāṅkhyāyana Śrautasūtra: ed. by A. Hillebrandt, Bib. Ind., Calcutta 1889; Eng. trans. by W. Caland, Nagpur 1953 (rep.).

Saptapadārthī of Śivāditya: ed. with notes by V.S. Ghate, Bombay 1909.

Śāradātilaka: pub. in Kasi Sanskrit Series with Rāghavabhaṭṭa's com., also in *Tantric Texts*, XVI–XVII, 1933.

Sarasvatīvilāsa: pub. in Oriental Library Publications of Mysore University, 1927.

Śārīrakabhāṣya: see under Brahmasūtra.

Sarvadarśanasaṃgraha of Mādhavācārya: ed. by Iśvara Chandra Vidyāsagara, Bib. Ind., Calcutta 1858; ed. by K.V. Abhayankar, Poona 1950; trans. E.B. Cowell and A.E. Gough, London 1899.

Śataduṣanī of Veṅkatanātha: ed. P. Ananda Charlu, Bib. Ind., Calcutta 1904.

Śatapatha Brāhmaṇa: ed. S. Samasrami, Bib. Ind., Calcutta 1906; Eng. trans. by J. Eggeling in *SBE*, XII, XXVI, XLI, XLIII, XLIV, Oxford 1882–1900.

Śataśāhasrikā Prajñāpāramitā: ed. by P.C. Ghosh, Bib. Ind., Calcutta 1914.

Ṣaṭcakranirūpaṇa: ed. with Kālicaraṇa's com. and Eng. trans. by J. Woodroffe as *The Serpent Power*, 7th ed, Madras 1964.

Sātvata Saṃhitā: ed. by P.B. Ananthachariar, Kanchipuram 1902.

Saubhāgyabhāskara: com. on *Lalitāsahasranāma* by Bhāskara Raya, Nirnaya Sagara Press, Bombay 1935.

Saunakīya Caraṇavyūha Sūtra: ed. by A.R. Sastri, Varanasi 1938.

Saundarānanda: ed. and Eng. trans. by H. Johnston, Punjab University Oriental Publications, 1928, 1932.

Saundaryalaharī: ed. by J. Woodroffe, Adyar 1937; ed. with 3 coms. and Eng. trans., Ganesh and Co. Madras 1957; ed. with text and Eng. trans. by W. Norman Brown, Harvard 1958.

Saura Purāṇa: pub. by Venkatesvara Press, Bombay.

Sekoddesaṭīkā: ed. with intro. and notes by Marlo. E. Carelli in GOS, Baroda 1941.

Siddhasiddhāntasaṃgraha: ed. by M.M. Gopinath Kaviraj, Sarasvati Bhavana Series No. XIII, Varanasi 1925.

Śilparatna: ed. by Ganapati Sastri in Trivandrum Sanskrit Series 1922.

Śivadṛṣṭi: pub. in Kashmir Series of Texts and Studies, No. LIV. Srinagar 1934.

Śivādvaitanirṇaya of Appaya Dīkṣita: ed. with intro., trans. and notes by S.S. Suryanarayana Sastri, Madras.

Śivajñānabodham: Eng. trans. with intro. and com. by J.M. Nallasvami Pillai, Dharmapuram Adhinam 1945.

Śivajñānasiddhiyār: Eng. trans. with intro. and com. by J.M. Nallasvami Pillai, Dharmapuram Adhinam 1948.

Śivaprakāsam of Umāpati: Eng. trans. by H.R. Hoisington in *JAOS*, IV, 1854, 125–244.

Śiva Purāṇa: pub. by Venkatesvara Press, Bombay; ed. by P. Tarkaratna Vangavasi Press, Calcutta 1314 B.S.; *Vāyavīya Saṃhitā*, ed. by M. Sastri, Sholapur 1905–06.

Śivasaṃhitā: pub. in *SBH* series, XIV, part I, Allahabad 1942.

Śivasūtravārtikam: pub. in Kashmir Series of Texts and Studies No. IV–V, Srinagar 1897.

Skanda Purāṇa: ed. by G.P. Raverkar, Venkatesvara Press, Bombay 1909–11.

Ślokavārtika: Eng. trans. by G.N. Jha, Bib. Ind., Calcutta 1900.

Smṛticandrikā of Devanna Bhaṭṭa: ed. by L. Srinivasacharya in 6 Vols. Mysore 1914–21, Eng. trans. by J.R. Gharapure, Bombay 1940–46.

Smṛtimukaphala of Vaidyanātha: ed. by J.R. Gharpure, Bombay.

Smṛtiratnākara of Caṇḍeśvara: ed. by K.K. Smrtitirtha, Bib. Ind., Calcutta 1925.

Smṛtyarthasāra of Śrīdhara: pub. by Anandasrama Press, Poona 1912.

Sphutārtha Abhidharmakoṣavyākhyā of Yaśomitra: ed. by V. Wogihara, Tokyo.

Śrāddhakriyākaumudī of Govindananda: ed. by K.K. Smrtibhusana, Bib. Ind., Calcutta 1904.
Sragdharāstotra of Sarvajña: ed. by S.C. Vidyabhusana, Bib. Ind., Calcutta 1908.
Śrībhāṣya: see under Brahmasūtra.
Śricakrasambhāra Tantra: Tibetan text and Eng. trans. by Kazi Dawa Sandup and ed. in *Tantric Texts*, VII, 1919.
Śrividyāratnasūtra: ed. by M.M. Gopinath Kaviraj, Sarasvati Bhavana Texts series No. XI, Varanasi 1919.
Suddhikaumudī of Govindānanda: ed. by K.K. Smṛtibhusana, Bib. Ind., Calcutta 1905.
Sukhāvativyūha: Eng. trans. in *SBE*, XLIX, 1894.
Sumangalavilāsinī: ed. by T.W. Rhys Davids et al. PTS, London 1931.
Suśrutasaṃhitā: Eng. trans. by V.C. Dutt and A.C. Chattopadhyaya, Bib. Ind., Calcutta 1891; by Y.N. Sarkar, Calcutta 1318 B.S.
Sūtasamhitā: ed. with Mahādeva's com. by V.S. Pansikar, 3 Vols., Poona 1893.
Sūtrabhāṣya of Madhva: ed. by Raghavendracharya in 4 Vols., Mysore 1911–22; Eng. trans. by S. Subba Rau, Madras 1904.
Suttanipāta: ed. by V. Fausböil, PTS, London 1885, 1893; Eng. trans. in *SBE*, X (2) Oxford 1881; *Woven Cadences of the Early Buddhists*, E.M. Hare, *SBB*, London 1944.
Suyagaḍa: Eng. trans. by H. Jacobi in *SBE*, XLV; pub with Śīlāṅka's com. Agamodaya Samiti, Bombay 1917.
Śvetāśvatara Upaniṣad: see under *Upaniṣads*.
Syādvādamañjarī:ed. in Chowkhamba Sanskrit Series, No. IX, Varanasi 1900; and also in Yasovijaya Jain Granthamala.
Śyāmārahasya: ed. by Jivananda, Bib. Ind., Calcutta; pub by R.M. Chatterjee, Calcutta 1283 B.S.
Taittirīya Āraṇyaka: ed. by R.L. Mitra, Bib. Ind., Calcutta 1872.
Taittirīya Brāhmana: ed. by R.L. Mitra, Bib. Ind., Calcutta 1890.
Taittirīya Saṃhitā: ed. by A. Weber 1871–72; with com. of Mādhava, by E.B. Cowell, Bib. Ind., Calcutta 1899; Eng. trans. by A.B. Keith, Cambridge 1914.
Taittirīya Pratiśākhya: ed. with *Trībhāṣyaratna* com. by R. Mitra, Bib., Ind., Calcutta 1872.
Taittirīya Upaniṣad: ed. with Śaṅkara's com. in Anandasrama Sanskrit Series, Poona 1929.
Tāṇḍyamahābrāhmaṇa: ed. by A.C. Vedantavagisa, Bib. Ind., Calcutta 1874; Kasi Sanskrit Series, 1935.
Tantrābhidhāna: pub. in *Tantric Texts*, VIII, XII; rep. Ganesh and Co., Madras 1954.
Tantrāloka: pub. in Kashmir Series of Texts and Studies, No. XXII, 1913, XXVIII–XXX, 1921, LII, 1933, LVII, 1936.
Tantrasāra of Abhinavagupta: pub. in Kashmir Series of Texts and Studies, No. 17. Srinagar 1918.
Tantrasāra of Kṛṣṇānanda: ed. P.K. Sastri, Vasumati Sahitya Mandir, Calcutta 1341 B.S.
Tantravārtika of Kumārila: Eng. trans. by G.N. Jha, Bib. Ind., Calcutta 1903 ff.
Tārābhaktisudhārṇava: ed. by A. Avalon, *Tantric Texts*, XXI, 1940.
Tārārahasya: pub. by R.M. Chatterjee, Calcutta 1283 B.S.; ed. by Jivananda, Calcutta 1896.
Tārātantra: ed. by G.S. Vedantatirtha, Varendra Research Society Gauḍa Series No. 1, Rajshahi 1913.
Tarkabhāṣā of Keśava Miśra: ed. by N.N. Kulkarni and Eng. trans. by G.N. Jha, Poona 1924.
Tattvacintāmaṇi of Gaṅgeśa Upādhyāya: ed. by K.N. Tarkavagisa, 5 Vols., Bib. Ind., Calcutta 1884–1901.
Tattvasaṃgraha of Śāntarakṣita with com. of Kamalaśīla; Eng. trans. by G.N. Jha in GOS, Baroda 1937–39.
Tattvavaiśāradī of Vācaspati: Eng. trans. by J.H. Woods, HOS, Cambridge Mass, 1914.
Tattvārthādhigama Sūtra of Umāsvāti: ed. by M.K. Premchand, Bib. Ind., Calcutta 1903–05, with intro., trans., notes and com. in English by J.L. Jaini in *SBJ* series, II, Arrah.
Ṭhāṇa: ed. in Agama Saṃgraha III, Benares 1880, with a Sanskrit and a Prakrit com.; with Abhayadeva's com., Bombay 1918–20.
Thera-Therīgātha: ed. by H. Oldenberg and R. Pischel, PTS, London 1883; Eng. trans. by C.A.F. Rhys Davids, PTS. 1909, 1913.
Tīrthacintāmaṇi of Vācaspati Miśra: ed. by K.K. Smrtitirtha. Bib. Ind., Calcutta 1912.

Tīrthakalpa of Jinaprabha Śuri: ed. by D.R. Bhandarkar, Bib. Ind., Calcutta 1943.
Tithitattva: ed. by N.K. Vidyanidhi, Calcutta 1304 B.S.
Trikāṇḍamaṇḍalam of Bhāskara Miśra: ed. by C. Tarkalankara, Bib. Ind., Calcutta 1883.
Trikāṇḍaśeṣa of Puruṣottama: ed. by C.A. Silakkhanda, Bombay 1916.
Tripuramahopaniṣad: pub. in *Tantric Texts*, XI, London 1922.
Tripurārahasya of Haritāyana: pub. with com of Śrīnivāsa in Sarasvati Bhavana Series, XV, Varanasi 1925.
Tripurasārasamuccaya: ed. by Jivananda, Calcutta 1897.
Triṣaṣṭiśalākāpuruṣacarita of Hemacandra: Eng. trans. by Helen M. Johnson, 6 Vols. Oriental Institute, Baroda 1931–62.
Udāna: ed. by P. Steinthal, PTS, London 1885; Eng. Trans. *Minor Anthologies of Pali Canon* by F.L. Woodward, *SBB* 1935.
Ujjvalanīlmaṇi of Rūpa Gosvamin: ed. with com. of Vāsudeva Gosvamin, Navadvıpa: ed. P. Das with com. of Jīva Gosvāmin, 1954.
Upaniṣads: Acharya Narayana Rama (ed.) *Īśādivimśottara-śatopaniṣadāh*, text of 120 Upanisads, Nirnaya Sagara Press, Bombay 1948; K. Narayanaswami Aiyar, *Thirty Minor Upanisads*, Madras 1914; Svami Gambirananda, *Upaniṣads*, with Śaṅkara's com. 2 Vols. Eng. trans., Advaita Asrama, Calcutta 1957–58; R.E. Hume, *Thirteen Principal Upaniṣads*, Oxford 1921; G.N. Jha and S. Sitarama Sastri, *The Upaniṣads*, with Śaṅkara's com., 5 Vols. Eng. trans., Madras 1898–1901; F. Max Müller, *The Upaniṣads*, 2 Vols. trans. in *SBE*, Oxford 1879, 1884; Swami Nikhilananda, *The Upaniṣads*, 3 Vols. Harpar and Bros., New York; S. Radhakrishnan, *Principal Upaniṣads*, ed. with intro., text, trans. and notes, George Allen and Unwin, London 1953.
Uttarādhyana Sutra: ed. with intro., notes and com. by Jarl Charpentier, Upsala 1922; Eng. trans. by H. Jacobi in *SBE*, XLV.
Uvāsagadasāo: ed. with Sanskrit com. of Abhayadeva and Eng. trans. with notes by A.F.R. Hoernle, Bib. Ind., Calcutta 1888; pub. with com. of Abhayadeva by Agamodaya Samiti, Bombay 1920.
Uvavāiya: pub. by Agamodaya Samiti 1921.
Vaijayantī of Yādavaprakāśa: ed. by G. Oppert, Madras 1893.
Vaikhānasa Smārta Sūtra: Eng. tr. by W. Caland, Bib. Ind., Calcutta 1929;—*Śrautasūtra*: ed. by W. Caland, Bib. Ind., Calcutta 1941.
Vaiśeṣika Sūtra: ed. with *Upaskāra* com. by J. Tarkapanchanana, Bib. Ind., Calcutta 1861; Eng. trans. A.E. Gough, Benares 1873.
Vājasaneyi Saṃhitā: ed. with Mahīdhara's com. by A. Weber, London 1852.
Vajracchedidikā: Eng. trans. in *SBE*, XLIX, Oxford 1894.
Vāmana Purāṇa: pub. by Venkatesvara Press, Bombay 1908; ed. P. Tarkaratna, Vangavasi Press, Calcutta 1908.
Vaṃśa Brāhmaṇa: ed. A.C. Burnell, Mangalore 1873.
Varāha Purāṇa: ed. H.P. Sastri, Bib. Ind., Calcutta 1887.
Varivasyārahasya of Bhāskara Rāya: ed. by S. Sastri, Adyar Library, Madras 1941.
Vasiṣṭha Dharmasūtra: ed. by A. Füher, Bhandarkar Oriental Research Institute, Poona 1934; Eng. trans. by G. Bühler in *SBE*, XIV, Oxford 1882.
Vāyu Purāṇa: pub. by Anandasrama Press, Poona 1905; ed. by P. Tarkaratna, Vangavasi Press, Calcutta 1921; pub. by Venkatesvara Press, Bombay 1895.
Vedāntakalpataru of Amalānanda: pub. in Vizianagram Sanskrit Series, XI, part I, 1895; ed. by Bhargava Sastri, Bombay 1938.
Vedāntakaustubha of Śrīnivāsa: Eng. trans. with notes by Roma Bose, Bib. Ind., Calcutta 1940.
Vedāntapārijātasaurabha of Nimbārka: ed. by V. Dvivedin, Chowkhamba Sanskrit Series, Benares 1910; Eng. trans. by Roma Bose, Bib. Ind., Calcutta 1940 ff.
Vedāntasāra: ed. by S. Yogindra, Nirnaya Sagar Press, Bombay 1916.
Vedānta Sūtra: see under Brahmasūtra.
Vimalaprabhā: com. on *Kālacakra* ed. by B.N. Banerjee, Bib. Ind., Calcutta.
Vimānavatthu: ed. by E.R. Goonaratne, PTS, London 1886.

Vinaya Piṭaka: ed. by H. Olderberg, 5 Vols. PTS, London 1879–18; Eng. trans. by T.W. Rhys Davids and H. Olderberg in *SBE*, 1881–85; Eng. trans. by I.B. Horner in 6 vols. PTS 1938–52.

Vīramitrodaya: Eng. trans. by G.C. Sarkar, Calcutta 1879.

Viṣṇu Dharmaśāstra (*Smṛti*): ed. by J. Jolly, Bib.Ind., Calcutta 1881; Eng. trans. by the same in *SBE*, VII, Oxford 1880; M.N. Dutt, Calcutta 1909.

Viṣṇudharmottara: pub. by Venkatesvara Press, Bombay; ed. by Priyabala Shah, Oriental Institute, Baroda 1961; trans (part) by S. Kramrisch, Calcutta 1924.

Viṣṇu Purāṇa: ed. B.L. Sarkar, Vangavasi Press, Calcutta 1294 B.S.; Eng. trans. By H.H. Wilson, London 1840, rep. Calcutta 1961.

Viṣṇu Saṃhitā: ed. by T. Ganapati Sastri, Trivandrum Sanskrit Series No. 85, Trivandrum 1925.

Visuddhimagga: ed. by C.A.F. Rhys Davids, PTS, London 1920–21; by Warren and D. Kosambi, HOS, 1950; Eng. trans. as *Path of Purity* by P. Mungtin, PTS, 1922–31; by Ñānamoli as *The Path of Purification*, Colombo Semage 1950.

Viśvāmitra Saṃhitā: ed. by U.S. Bhatta, Kendriya Sanskrit Vidyapith Series No. 13, Tirupati 1971.

Viśvaprakāśa of Maheśvara: ed. by R.G. Bhatta, Chowkhamba Sanskrit Series, Varanasi, 1911.

Vyavahāramayukha: ed. and trans. by V.N. Mandlik, Bombay 1880.

Yājñavalkya Smṛti: ed. by A.F. Stenzler, Berlin 1849; ed. with com. of Aparāditya, Anandasrama Sanskrit Series, Poona 1903–04; ed. with com. *Mitākṣarā*, Bombay 1909; by N.R. Acharya, Nirnaya Sagara Press, Bombay 1949; ed. with com. of Viśvarupa, Trivandrum 1922–24; Eng. trans. by S.C. Basu and S.N. Naraharayya in *SBH*, Allahabad 1913, 1918; Eng. trans. with coms. of Vijñāneśvara (*Mitākṣarā*), Mitramiśra (*Vīramitrodaya*) and Śūlapani (*Dīpakalika*) by J.R. Gharpure, Bombay 1936–42.

Yamaka: ed. by C.A.F. Rhys Davids, PTS, London, 1911–13.

Yoga Pradīpa: pub. in Kasi Sanskrit Series No. 85, Varanasi 1931.

Yoga Sūtra of Patañjali: ed. with com. of Vyāsa and gloss of Vācaspati by R. Bodas, Bombay Sanskrit Series 1982; Eng. trans. by Rama Prasada in *SBH*, Allahabad 1910; by J. Woods, HOS, Cambridge Mass 1914; by J. Ballantyne, fourth rep. Calcutta 1963.

Yoga Upaniṣads: ed. by A. Mahadeva Sastri, Adyar Library, Madras 1925.

Yogāvacara: F.L. Woodward and C.A.F. Rhys Davids, *Manual of a Mystic*, London 1916.

Yogavāsiṣṭha: ed. by V.L. Sastri Pansikar, Nirnaya Sagara Press, Bombay 1918.

Yoginīhṛdayadīpikā: ed. by M.M. Gopinath Kaviraj, Sarasvati Bhavana Series No. 7, Varanasi 1924.

Yoginītantra: pub. by R.M. Chatterjee, Calcutta 1283 B.S.

Index

INDEX